ENTREPRENEURSHIP
Perspectives and Cases

Edited by

Paul Westhead
Durham University Business School, UK and
Bodø Graduate School of Business, Norway

Mike Wright
Nottingham University Business School, UK,
University of Ghent, Belgium and EMLyon, France

and

Gerard McElwee
Nottingham University Business School, UK

Financial Times
Prentice Hall
is an imprint of

Harlow, England • London • New York • Boston • San Francisco • Toronto
Sydney • Tokyo • Singapore • Hong Kong • Seoul • Taipei • New Delhi
Cape Town • Madrid • Mexico City • Amsterdam • Munich • Paris • Milan

Pearson Education Limited
Edinburgh Gate
Harlow
Essex CM20 2JE
England

and Associated Companies throughout the world

Visit us on the World Wide Web at:
www.pearsoned.co.uk

First published 2011

ISBN: 978-0-273-72613-5

British Library Cataloguing-in-Publication Data
A catalogue record for this book is available from the British Library

Library of Congress Cataloging-in-Publication Data
A catalog record for this book is available from the Library of Congress

10 9 8 7 6 5 4 3 2 1
15 14 13 12 11

Typeset in 10/12.5 pt Minion by 73
Printed by Ashford Colour Press Ltd., Gosport

£42.99

ENTREPRENEURSHIP
Perspectives and Cases

To Benjamin, Andrew and Anthony,
Creative Dealers, as well as Paul, John,
Kevin and David, Family Entrepreneurs.

Brief contents

Note: All chapters written by Paul Westhead and Mike Wright with the exception of Chapter 10, written by Peter Somerville and Gerard McElwee.

Contents

List of figures and tables

List of Entrepreneurship in action boxes

List of case studies

List of contributors

Zafar U. Ahmed is Professor of Marketing and International Business at the Department of Marketing, Management College of Business and Technology, Texas A&M University-Commerce, USA.

Gerard M. Campbell is an Associate Professor of Information Systems and Operations Management at the Charles F. Dolan School of Business, Fairfield University, Fairfield, USA.

Andy Corcoran is a Principal Lecturer at Lincoln Business School, University of Lincoln, Lincoln, England.

Carol Craig is the Chief Executive, The Centre for Confidence and Well-Being, Glasgow, Scotland.

Leo Paul Dana is Professor of International Business at the Department of Management, University of Canterbury, Christchurch, New Zealand.

Donald M. DePamphilis is at the College of Business Administration, Loyola Marymount University, USA.

Truls Erikson is an Associate Professor at the Department of Industrial Economics and Technology Management, Norwegian University of Science and Technology, Trondheim, Norway.

Louis J. Filion is Professor of Entrepreneurship at the HEC, Montreal, Canada.

Mark Freel is an Associate Professor in Innovation and Entrepreneurship at the Telfer School of Management, University of Ottawa, Ottawa, Canada.

Kirk Frith is a Post-Doctoral scholar at Lincoln Business School, University of Lincoln, Lincoln, England.

Suzanne Hetzel Campbell is an Assistant Professor of Nursing at the School of Nursing, Fairfield University, Fairfield, USA.

Christopher L. Huntley is an Assistant Professor of Information Systems and Operations Management at the Charles F. Dolan School of Business, Fairfield University, Fairfield, USA.

Ulla Hytti is a Research Manager at the Small Business Institute, Turku School of Economics and Business Administration, Turku, Finland.

Eva Jarošová is an Assistant Professor at the University of Economics, Prague, Czech Republic.

Povl Larsen is a Senior Research Officer at the The National Centre for Product Design and Development Research (PDR), University of Wales Institute, Cardiff, Wales.

Alan Lewis is at the The National Centre for Product Design and Development Research (PDR), University of Wales Institute, Cardiff, Wales.

Angela Loihl is a Licensing Officer at the Center for Commercialization, University of Washington, Washington, USA.

Danielle Luc is a Graduate Student at the HEC, Montreal, Canada.

Gerard McElwee is Professor of Entrepreneurship at Nottingham University Business School, Nottingham, UK.

Ed McMullan is Professor of Entrepreneurship at the Faculty of Management, University of Calgary, Calgary, Canada.

Frank Martin is a Senior Teaching Fellow, The Management School, University of Stirling, Stirling, Scotland.

Marlene Mints Reed is Professor of Entrepreneurship at the Samford School of Business, Samford University, Birmingham, USA.

Caroline Mireault is with the Department of Foreign Affairs and International Trade, Canada.

Kirsi Peura is a Project Manager at the Small Business Institute, Turku School of Economics and Business Administration, Turku, Finland.

Joëlle Piffault is a Lecturer at the HEC, Montreal, Canada.

Peter Robinson is an Associate Professor at the Calgary Business School, University of Calgary, Calgary, Canada.

Wai-Sum Siu is Professor of Marketing at the Department of Marketing, Hong Kong Baptist University, Hong Kong, China.

Alf Steinar Sætre is an Associate Professor at the Department of Industrial Economics and Technology Management, Norwegian University of Science and Technology, Trondheim, Norway.

Pekka Stenholm is a Researcher at the Small Business Institute, Turku School of Economics and Business Administration, Turku, Finland.

Gloria H. Y. Ting is a Graduate of the Department of Marketing, Hong Kong Baptist University, Hong Kong, China.

Alex S. L. Tsang is an Assistant Professor at the Department of Marketing, Hong Kong Baptist University, Hong Kong, China.

Paul Westhead is Professor of Entrepreneurship at Durham University Business School, Durham, UK and a Visiting Professor at Bodø Graduate School of Business, Bodø, Norway.

Joan Winn is Professor of Management at the Department of Management, Daniels College of Business, University of Denver, Denver, USA.

Mike Wright is Professor of Financial Studies at Nottingham University Business School, Nottingham, UK and a Visiting Professor at the Department of Economics, Finance and Control EMLyon, Lyon, France and the University of Ghent, Belgium.

Preface

'He who is afraid to throw the dice will never throw a six.'

Eric Cantona in *Looking for Eric*

Our motivation in writing this book is to address what we see as a false dichotomy between theory and practice in entrepreneurship studies. After all there is 'nothing so practical as a good theory'. The distinctive feature of the book is to integrate rigorous academic research with short insightful vignettes and practical and relevant cases.

In so doing, we aim to meet the need for an accessible resource that will stimulate critical thinking and reflective learning that will provide undergraduate and postgraduate students, as well as academics, policy-makers and practitioners, with deeper insights into the processes relating to entrepreneurship and small business development, particularly entrepreneur and enterprise diversity.

The text, vignettes and cases presented in this book have been developed and refined over a number of years amongst numerous entrepreneurship students covering a range of levels including undergraduate business and science and engineering students, MBA students and specialist Masters in Entrepreneurship. Insightful comments from guinea pigs in Bodø, Durham, Imperial College, INSEAD, Lincoln, Nottingham, Siena, Stirling and Warwick are appreciated.

We extend thanks to our case study contributors who have provided us with a range of thought-provoking and insightful examples of issues facing real entrepreneurs, businesses and practitioners. The generous support of John Edmondson (IP Publishing Ltd) who allowed us to publish revised versions of cases published in the International Journal of Entreprenurship and Innovation is appreciated. Thanks to Riya Chopraa for help with the vignettes. A number of colleagues at Pearson helped move this project from an idea to a published reality, to whom we owe many thanks: Matthew Walker, Rufus Curnow, Jennifer Mair, Tim Parker and Rob Sykes. Insightful comments from the five book reviewer commentators are warmly acknowledged.

Paul Westhead
Durham University and Bodø Graduate School of Business

Mike Wright
Universities of Nottingham, Ghent and EMLyon

Gerald McElwee
Nottingham Trent University

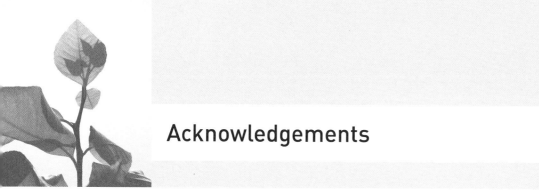

Acknowledgements

We are grateful to the following for permission to reproduce copyright material:

Figures

Figure 6.1 from "Critical Junctures in the Growth in University High-Tech Spinout Companies", *Research Policy*, Vol 33 (1), pp. 147–175 (Vohara, A., Wright, M., and Lockett, A., 2004), copyright © 2004, Elsevier; Figure 6.2 from "Spinning out new ventures: a typology of incubation strategies from European research institutions", *Journal of Business Venturing*, Vol 20 (2), pp. 183–216 (Clarysse, B., Wright, M., Lockett, A., Van de Elde, E., and Vohara, A., 2005), copyright © 2005, Elsevier; Figure 7.1 from "'Types' of Family Firms: An Exploratory Conceptual and Empirical Analysis", *Entrepreneurship and Regional Development* Vol 19 (5), pp. 405–431 (Westhead, P., and Howarth, C., 2007), copyright © 2007 Routledge; Figure 8.1 from "Toward a Reconciliation of the Definitional Issues in the Field of Corporate Entrepreneurship", *Entrepreneurship Theory and Practice*, Vol 23 (3), pp. 11–27 (Sharma, P., and Chrisman, J.J., 1999) (Figure 1, p. 20). Reproduced with permission of Blackwell Publishing Ltd; Figure in case study 18 from "Fleet Sheet's final word: Strong unions needed", *The Fleet Sheet*, 24/04/2007, No. 1593, copyright © The Fleet Sheet; and Figure in case study 20 from *Angel Investing: Matching Start-up Funds with Start-up Companies – a Guide for Entrepreneurs and Individual Investors*, Jossey-Bass Business & Management (M. Van Osnabrugge, R.J. Robinson 2000) p. 37. Reproduced with permission from John Wiley & Sons Inc.

Tables

Table 5.1 from "Habitual Entrepreneurs", *Foundations and Trends in Entrepreneurship, Now Publishers*, Vol 4 (4), pp. 309–449 (Ucbasaran, D., Alsos, G.A., Westhead, P., and Wright, M., 2008), reproduced with permission of the authors; Table 7.1 from "Family Firm Research: The Need for a Methodological Rethink", *Entrepreneurship Theory and Practice*, 23 (1), pp. 31–56 (Westhead and Cowling, 1998), reproduced with permission of Blackwell Publishing Ltd; Table 7.2 from "Ambitions, 'External' Environment and Strategic Factor Differences between Family and Non-Family Companies", *Entrepreneurship and Regional Development*, Vol 9 (2), pp. 127–157 (Westhead, P., 1997), copyright © 1997 Routledge; Table 8.1 from "Toward a Reconciliation of the Definitional Issues in the Field of Corporate Entrepreneurship", *Entrepreneurship Theory and Practice*, Vol 23 (2), pp. 11–27 (Sharma, P., and Chrisman, J.J., 1999) (Table 3, p. 21). Reproduced with permission of Blackwell Publishing Ltd; Table 8.2 from "Corporate Entrepreneurship and the Pursuit of Competitive Advantage", *Entrepreneurship Theory and Practice*, Vol 23 (3), pp. 47–63 (Covin, J., and Miles, M., 1999) (Table 1. p. 57). Reproduced with permission of Blackwell Publishing Ltd; Tables 9.1, 9.12. Reproduced with permission of McGraw Hill Companies (UK) Ltd; Table 11.1

from "Cross-National Comparisons of the Variation in New Firm Formation Rates", *Regional Studies*, Vol 28 (4), pp. 443–456 (Reynolds, P., Storey, D.J., and Westhead, P., 1994), copyright © 1994 Routledge; Table 13.1 from "Internationalization of Small and Medium-Sized Enterprises (SMEs) and International Entrepreneurship: A Critique and Policy Implications", *Regional Studies*, Vol 41 (7), pp. 1013–1030 (Wright, M., Westhead, P., and Ucbasaran, D., 2007), copyright © 2007 Routledge; Table 14.1 from *The State of British Enterprise: Growth, Innovation and Competitive Advantage in Small and Medium-Sized Firms.*, CBR (Cambridge Small Business Research Centre, 1992) Tables 3.1 and 3.2. Reproduced with permission of Professor Alan Hughes; Tables 14.2 and 14.3 adapted from *Entrepreneurial and Growth Firms in Entrepreneurship and Small Firms 2nd edition*, McGraw Hill (Deakins, D., and Freel, M., 1999) pp. 205, 207; Table 14.4 from "Five stages of growth in small business", *Long Range Planning*, Vol 20 (3), pp. 45–62 (Scott, M., and Bruce, R., 1987), copyright © 1987 Elsevier, and Table 14.5 from *Understanding the Small Business Sector*, Cengage Learning EMEA (Storey, D.J., 1994) Table 5.6, p. 123, copyright © Cengage Learning EMEA Ltd.

Text

Extract on page 3 from *Fostering Entrepreneurship*, The OECD Jobs Strategy, OECD Publishing (http://dx.doi.org/10.1787/9789264163713-en, 1998) copyright © OECD; Extract on page 15 from Incumbent businesses, DTI, 2004: 17. © Crown copyright 2010; Entrepreneurship in action 2.2 from "Critical Junctures in the Growth in University High-Tech Spinout Companies", *Research Policy*, Vol 33 (1), pp. 147–175 (Vohora, A., Wright, M., and Lockett, A., 2004), copyright © 2004, Elsevier; Entrepreneurship in action 2.3 from "Bank Deal Boost for Development Plans", *Yorkshire Post*, 28/06/2007 (Parkin, D.) copyright © Yorkshire Post; Entrepreneurship in action 2.5 from "Scotland's Birth Rate (SBRS): Entrepreneurship Policy Delivery", www.scottish-enterprise.com, copyright © Scottish Enterprise; Entrepreneurship in action 3.1 from "James Dyson spent Years Fighting Hoover. Now he intends to clean up", *The Independent*, 04/10/2000 (Buncombe, A., and Arthur, C.) copyright © The Independent 2000; Entrepreneurship in action 4.3 from "The Diva Storyline: An Alternative Social Construction of Female Entrepreneurship", *International Journal of Gender and Entrepreneurship*, Vol 1 (2), pp. 148–163 (Smith, R., 2009), copyright © 2009, Emerald Group Publishing Limited; Entrepreneurship in action 4.7 from "John Mackey's Yahoo Rants are The Dark Side of Entrepreneurship", *Fast Company*, 24/07/2007 (Hanft. A.) www.fastcompany.com. Used with permission of Fast Company copyright © 2011. All rights reserved; Entrepreneurship in action 4.8 from The Toilet Paper Entrepreneur Blog by Mike Michalowicz, www.toiletpaperentrepreneur.com, copyright © Mike Michalowicz; Entrepreneurship in action 5.1 adapted from "George Parker: Serial Entrepreneur at Large . . . Batten down the hatches!" 19/03/2009, www.psfk.com, copyright © George Parker, author of "The Ubiquitous Persuaders"; and the blog www.adscam.typepad. Reproduced with kind permission; Entrepreneurship in action 5.2, 5.3 and 5.4 from "Habitual Entrepreneurs in Scotland, Characteristics, Search Processes, Learning and Performance – Summary Report" by Westhead et al. 2003, www.scottish-enterprise.com. Copyright © Scottish Enterprise; Entrepreneurship in action 7.1 from "Passing the Baton at Family Firms", *Eastern Daily Press*, 03/03/2010 (Aiken), copyright © Eastern Daily Press; Entrepreneurship in action 7.3 from "How to Run the Family Firm", *The Mail on Sunday*, 26/03/2007 (Taylor, K.) copyright © Solo Syndication, 2007; Entrepreneurship in action 7.4 from "Family Firms Benefit from Outside Help", *The Times*, 03/09/2006 (Stone), copyright © NI Syndication, 2006; Entrepreneurship in action 8.2 from "Ergo to create 33 jobs as spin-off goes global", *Siliconrepublic*, 24/06/2010 (Kennedy, J.), www.siliconrepublic.com, copyright © Silicon Republic.com; Entrepreneurship in action 10.1 from "The Big Issue – a handup, not a hand out", www.bigissue.com, copyright © The Big Issue; Extract 10.2 adapted from Ummah Foods, www.ummahfoods.com, copyright © Ummah Foods; Entrepreneurship in action 10.3 from Cafédirect, www.cafedirect.co.uk, copyright © Cafédirect Plc; Entrepreneurship in action 12.1 from "No Plan Survives First Contact with Customers – Business Plans versus Business Models", 08/04/2010 (Steve Blank), reproduced by permission. Steve Blank is an educator, author and blogger who developed the Customer Development process for startups. Read more at www.steveblank.com; Entrepreneurship in action 13.1 from "Small firms put off overseas trade by "perceived" barriers", *The Marketing Donut*, 08/06/2010, www.marketingdonut.co.uk, reproduced with permission; Entrepreneurship in action 13.3 from "Growth, Value Creation and Resources in Young High Growth Technology Based Firms: the Impact of Environmental Contingencies" Working paper, *Strategic Entrepreneurship Journal* (Clarysse, B., Bruneel, J., and Wright, M., 2010). Reproduced with permission of the authors; Entrepreneurship in action 13.4 from "The internationalization process of Born Globals: a network view", *International Business Review*, Vol 12 (6), pp. 739–753 (Sharma, D.D., and Blomstermo, A., 2003), copyright © 2003, Elsevier; Entrepreneurship in action 14.1 from "Critical Junctures in the Growth in University High-Tech Spinout Companies", *Research Policy*, Vol 33 (1), pp. 147–175 (Vohora, A., Wright, M., and Lockett, A., 2004), copyright © 2004, Elsevier; Entrepreneurship in action 14.2 and 14.3 from *Habitual Entrepreneurs in Scotland*, Scottish Enterprise, Glasgow (Westhead, P., Ucbasaran, D., Wright, M., and Martin, F., 2003) copyright © Scottish Enterprise; Entrepreneurship in action 14.5 from "Why I Quit Entrepreneurship and Got a Real Job", *Business Pundit*, 04/01/2006 (May, R.), www.businesspundit.com, copyright © Business Pundit; Case Study 9 adapted from "Arran Aromatics in Bid for Cash to fight Off the Taxman", *The Scotsman*, 31/01/2009 (Ranscombe, P.), copyright © The Scotsman;

We would like to thank IP Publishing Ltd for permission to reprint the following material:

'Fickle Rooster Productions: Turning a Hobby into a Profitable Business' (Kirk Frith). Frith, K. (2007). Fickle Rooster Productions: Making a Business from a Hobby. *International Journal of Entrepreneurship and Innovation*, 8 (2): 149-153. Copyright © 2007 IP Publishing Ltd. Used by permission; 'The Recording Room: Ben Wallace's Musical Ventures' (Ed McMullan). McMullan, E. (2000). Case Study: 'Ben Wallace'. *International Journal of Entrepreneurship and Innovation*, 1 (1): 57-57. Copyright © 2000 IP Publishing Ltd. Used by permission; 'Portable Patient Lifts, LLC: Patent and Start-Up Issues' (Gerard M. Campbell). Campbell, G. M. (2004). Portable Patient Lifts, LLC – US Patent and Start-Up. *International Journal of Entrepreneurship and Innovation*, 5 (3): 203-210. Copyright © 2004 IP Publishing Ltd. Used by permission; 'Original Voddy Company Limited' (Andy Corcoran). Corcoran, A. (2006). Original Voddy Company Limited. *International Journal of Entrepreneurship and Innovation*, 7 (4): 261-266. Copyright © 2006 IP Publishing Ltd. Used by permission; 'Alba Adventures: An Entrepreneur Pushed into Entrepreneurship' (Marlene Mints Reed). Mints Reed, M., and Reed Brunson, R. (2000). CASE STUDY: Alba Adventures. *International Journal of Entrepreneurship and Innovation*, 1 (3): 183-191. Copyright © 2000 IP Publishing Ltd. Used by permission; 'The OffQuip Saga: Partnerships for Growth' (Louis J. Filion). Filion, L. J. (2000). CASE STUDY: The OffQuip Saga. *International Journal of Entrepreneurship and Innovation*, 1 (3): 192-197. Copyright © 2000 IP Publishing Ltd. Used by permission; 'Marine Products Limited: Confronting Barriers to

Innovation' (Povl Larsen and Alan Lewis). Larsen, P., and Lewis, A. (2006). Confronting Barriers to Innovation. *International Journal of Entrepreneurship and Innovation*, 7 (2): 121-126. Copyright © 2006 IP Publishing Ltd. Used by permission; 'Deep Sea Fishing Inc: Acquiring the 'Right' Capital for a New Technology-Based Firm' (Alf Steinar Sætre and Truls Erikson). Saetre, A. S., and Erikson, T. (2003). Dealcrafting the Right Capital for a Venture: The Case of Deep Sea Fishing Inc. International Journal of Entrepreneurship and Innovation, 4 (3): 197-203. Copyright © 2003 IP Publishing Ltd. Used by permission; 'Painatolo Ltd and Rakennusalevet Ltd: Family Business Transfer Issues' (Ulla Hytti, Kirsi Peura and Pekka Stenholm). Hytti, U., Peura, K., and Stenholm, P. (2005). Managing Business Transfer: Comap Ltd and FirmX Ltd. *International Journal of Entrepreneurship and Innovation*, 6 (1): 61-66. Copyright © 2005 IP Publishing Ltd. Used by permission; 'Wemas Limited: Purchase and Turnaround of an Existing Business by Brent Lybbert' (Ed McMullan). McMullan, E. (2001). CASE STUDY – Brent Lybbert: A Turn-Around Opportunity. *International Journal of Entrepreneurship and Innovation*, 2 (2): 119-127. Copyright © 2001 IP Publishing Ltd. Used by permission; 'Rad-Amer Intourist: American Entrepreneur Opportunity Recognition and Exploitation in Moscow' (Zafar U. Ahmed, Peter Robinson and Leo Paul Dana). Ahmed Z. U., Robinson P., and Dana L. P. (2001). A US Entrepreneur in Moscow. *International Journal of Entrepreneurship and Innovation*, 2 (1): 51-58. Copyright © 2001 IP Publishing Ltd. Used by permission; 'AAC Limited: Entrepreneurial Team Dynamics' (Eva Jaroová and Joan Winn). Jarošová, E., and Winn, J. (2005). Unique Glass Beads from the Bohemian Paradise. *International Journal of Entrepreneurship and Innovation*, 6 (3): 201-209. Copyright © 2005 IP Publishing Ltd. Used by permission; 'Model Kit World: Firm Growth through Geographic Expansion' (Alex S. L. Tsang, Wai-Sum Siu and Gloria H. Y. Ting). Tsang, A. S. L., Siu, W-S., and Ting, G. H.Y. (2007). Model Kit World. *International Journal of Entrepreneurship and Innovation*, 8 (3): 231-234. Copyright © 2007 IP Publishing Ltd. Used by permission; 'Upstart Graphics: Merger and Acquisition Issues' (Donald M. DePamphilis). DePamphilis, D. M. (2001). Case Study: Managing Growth Through Acquistion: Time-Tested Techniques for the Entrepreneur. *International Journal of Entrepreneurship and Innovation*, 2 (3): 195-205. Copyright © 2001 IP Publishing Ltd. Used by permission; 'Private Health Practice: Limits to Growth' (Suzanne Hetzel Campbell and Christopher L. Huntley). Campbell, S. H., and Huntley, C. L. (2003). Limits to Growth: A Private Family Health Practice. *International Journal of Entrepreneurship and Innovation*, 4 (2): 133-137. Copyright © 2003 IP Publishing Ltd. Used by permission.

In some instances we have been unable to trace the owners of copyright material, and we would appreciate any information that would enable us to do so.

Chapter 1

Introduction: Context, issues and case study selection

Contents

Learning objectives

- To explain why entrepreneurship is an important ('hot') topic.
- To identify the main themes in studying entrepreneurship and how these are used to structure this book.
- To identify the main learning issues that the book will focus upon.

Entrepreneurship in action 1.1
Sir Stelios Haji-Ioannou and easyJet

EasyJet Airline Company Limited (referred to as easyJet) is a British airline headquartered in London Luton Airport. At 6.50 on 10 November 1995 easyJet's first flight took off from Luton in England to Glasgow in Scotland. Incorporated earlier during the same year by Stelios Haji-Ioannou, easyJet began operations by taking customer bookings through its telephone reservation centre at easyLand (i.e., home of easyJet at London Luton airport), prior to the business going virtual in 1998. Stelios wanted to provide low-cost scheduled air travel on short haul routes within Europe. He supported his venture with the advertisement that stated, 'making flying as affordable as a pair of jeans – £29 one way'. Stelios encouraged airline passengers to 'cut out the travel agent'. On 5 November 2000 easyJet was floated on the London Stock Exchange. Today his dream has materialised into a pan-European airline with links to 100 airports in a network which flew 50 million seats in 2008, reporting £2,363 million and £123 million in sales revenue and pre-tax profit, respectively. EasyJet has 20 bases throughout Europe and the hub is London Gatwick. In 2009, easyJet carried 45.2 million passengers and behind Ryanair the company is the second-largest low-cost carrier in Europe.

Born on 14 February 1967 to Greek Cypriot shipping tycoon Loucas Haji-Ioannou and Nedi Haji-Ioannou, Stelios was the second of three children. He grew up amongst the privately-owned fleet of ships witnessing his entrepreneurial father dominate the global shipping industry for the latter half of the twentieth century. After finishing his secondary education at Doukas High School in Athens, Greece, Stelios moved to London in 1984 to continue his undergraduate education at the London School of Economics. In London, he then pursued an MSc in Shipping, Trade and Finance from Cass Business School. Due to his entrepreneurial success Stelios has subsequently been awarded a total of four honorary doctorates from Liverpool John Moores University, Cass Business School, Newcastle Business School and Cranfield University, and he was awarded a knighthood.

After a short stint working in his father's shipping company, Troodos Shipping Co. Ltd, Stelios successfully negotiated a $30 million payout from his father to fund his own shipping company called Stelmar Shipping. Contrary to popular belief, this was his maiden entrepreneurial expedition. In 2001, he floated Stelmar on the New York Stock Exchange. Stelios sold the company in 2005 to the rival OSG shipping group for $1.3 billion, which generated tremendous personal wealth for Stelios.

Stelios admired his father's success but was determined to be independent. Modestly apologetic about his wealthy upbringing Stelios asserted: 'I always respect self-made people more than rich boys like me. I cheated because I got money from my father. Then again, when you're 28 and you want to start an airline; and your last name's unpronounceable venture capitalists aren't going to give you any money!'

Although Stelios went on to create a number of other businesses, many of them linked to travel, easyJet is his most successful endeavour. While Stelmar proved the credibility of Stelios as an entrepreneur, easyJet has confirmed his ability as a habitual entrepreneur (i.e., creating multiple businesses).

Source: http://en.wikipedia.org/wiki/Stelios_Haji-Ioannou; www.easy.com; and various.

1.1   Entrepreneurship is a hot topic

The experience of Sir Stelios Haji-Ioannou and easyJet in Entrepreneurship in action 1.1 provides a graphic illustration of the impact that entrepreneurs can make in creating a new venture that helped change fundamentally the rules of the game in the airline market. But entrepreneurship takes a variety of forms and appears in both small and large firms, in new firms and established family firms, in the formal and informal economy, in legal and illegal activities, in innovative and more conventional concerns and in all regions and economic sub-sectors (Organisation for Economic Co-Operation and Development (OECD), 1998: 35). Entrepreneurial events, such as the formation and development of businesses to pursue an opportunity, attract interest from policy-makers and practitioners (Department of Trade and Industry (DTI), 2004). The entrepreneurial function is widely viewed as a vital component in the process of economic growth (Baumol, 1968). The OECD (1998: 12) asserted:

> Entrepreneurship is central to the functioning of market economies. Entrepreneurs are agents of change and growth in a market economy and they can act to accelerate the generation, dissemination and application of innovative ideas. In doing so, they not only ensure that efficient use is made of resources, but also expand the boundaries of economic activity. Entrepreneurs not only seek out and identify potentially profitable economic opportunities but are also willing to take risks to see if their hunches are right. While not all entrepreneurs succeed, a country with a lot of entrepreneurial activity is likely to be constantly generating new or improved products and services.

Policy-makers and practitioners are seeking to promote the supply of entrepreneurs in order to encourage economic benefits such as wealth creation, job generation and competition as well as social benefits (i.e., choice and opportunity for under-represented groups in enterprise societies such as women, young people, ethnic minorities, etc.). Promoting entrepreneurship is part of a formula aimed at reconciling economic success with social cohesion (OECD, 1998).

Small and medium-sized enterprises (SMEs) account for the vast majority of businesses in most countries. Yet only a small proportion of new firms enter a high growth trajectory like easyJet, providing a substantial contribution to jobs and sales (Storey, 1994). Entrepreneurs establish new and smaller firms for a variety of reasons, and not solely to satisfy the goals of policy-makers (see Case 1, IPS Communication – Distribution: Claude Guinet's career in entrepreneurship). Notably, entrepreneurs may want to maintain independence and control (Birley and Westhead, 1994). Some entrepreneurs may focus on lifestyle objectives rather than profit making, professional management and job generation (Westhead and Howorth, 2007).

Attention should, therefore, be directed towards a greater appreciation of the attitudinal, resource, operational and strategic barriers to business formation and development, as well as the resources and strategies selected by different types of entrepreneurs to grow their ventures (Westhead, 1995). The economic outputs (e.g., prices, competition, innovation, job generation, wealth creation, balance of payments, etc.) made by different types of entrepreneurs and organisations need to be understood.

1.2 Entrepreneurship as a field of study

The entrepreneurial process involving all the functions, activities, and actions associated with the perception of opportunities, and the creation of organisations to pursue them (Bygrave and Hofer, 1991) has generated considerable academic interest. There is no agreed definition of entrepreneurship. Further, there is concern over what entrepreneurship constitutes as a field of study (Gartner, 2001; Busenitz et al., 2003). In order to promote the study of entrepreneurship, academics have utilised a wide variety of definitions. It is, however, widely recognised that entrepreneurship involves the creation of new businesses and the development of new and established firms.

To encourage the advancement and propagation of knowledge in the field of entrepreneurship (Low and MacMillan, 1988), Ucbasaran et al. (2001) have emphasised the need to consider the contextual and process issues associated with entrepreneurship. The context of the entrepreneurial phenomenon can be discussed not only in terms of the creation of new independent firms, but also in terms of corporate ventures, management buyouts and buyins, social enterprises, and the inheritance and development of family firms. Studies have revealed that entrepreneurs are not a homogeneous entity and different types of entrepreneurs exist (Woo et al., 1991; Chapters 5 and 6 of this book). Sir Stelios Haji-Ioannou represents a good example of a habitual entrepreneur who has created many businesses (see Chapter 5). The processes associated with the entrepreneurial phenomenon can be discussed with regard to opportunity recognition and exploitation by entrepreneurs; ability based on skills, competencies and knowledge; and ability to obtain resources and co-ordinate scarce resources (Shane and Venkataraman, 2000).

There has been concern that entrepreneurship is a fragmented field (Ucbasaran et al., 2001; Schildt et al., 2006), and this fragmentation may hinder scholarly development and legitimisation of the field. However, there is evidence of maturity and convergence in entrepreneurship as a set of codified theories, models, methods, and measures that direct the research agenda emerge (Grégoire et al., 2006). With reference to the citation patterns of entrepreneurship articles published in the years 2000 to 2004, Schildt et al. (2006) detected that the ten most frequently cited themes relate to:

- societal consequences of entrepreneurship (see Chapter 2);
- conceptualisation of the entrepreneurial process (see Chapter 3);
- alertness, opportunity creation and creative destruction (see Chapter 3);
- psychological characteristics of entrepreneurs (see Chapter 4);
- entrepreneurial networks and resource accumulation (see Chapters 3, 5, 6 and 10);
- corporate entrepreneurship and venturing (see Chapter 8);
- born-global firms (see Chapter 13); and
- entrepreneurial firm survival and growth (see Chapters 13 and 14).

The following themes have also attracted considerable attention:

- risk-taking among entrepreneurs (see Chapter 3);
- organisational (entrepreneur) learning and problem-solving (see Chapter 5);
- trust and relational capital (see Chapter 5);
- leadership and management teams (see Chapters 6, 7, 8 and 9);

- organisational decision-making (see Chapter 6, 7, 8, 9 and 14);
- knowledge-based view of the firm (see Chapter 6);
- high-technology entrepreneurship (see Chapter 6);
- environmental determinants of entrepreneurial success (see Chapter 11);
- institutions and institutional entrepreneurship (see Chapters 6, 11 and 12).

Chapters in this text key into established and emerging dominant themes within the field of entrepreneurship, which are being explored using a variety of theoretical and methodological lenses (Busenitz et al., 2003; Gartner et al., 2006). Markedly different lists of key articles and scholars in the field of entrepreneurship have, however, recently been presented (Cornelius et al., 2006; Reader and Watkins, 2006).

1.3 Growth in enterprise education and the need for a text and case study collection

Recognition that entrepreneurship is the oxygen that ensures national, local and economic development as well as facilitating social cohesion linked to personal choice and empowerment for disadvantaged members of society (OECD, 1998; DTI, 2004), has led to a massive growth in entrepreneurship teaching (Gormon et al., 1997). In the United Kingdom, for example, this has been aided by funding through the Department of Trade and Industry's Science Enterprise Challenge Fund Centres, which has encouraged more engineering and science students to consider business ownership as a career option. The Lambert Review (2003) has further emphasised that science and technology students need to accumulate entrepreneurial skills. Arts students in the United Kingdom are also being encouraged to accumulate entrepreneurial skills to enter creative industries (Department for Culture, Media and Sport (DCMS), 2006) (see the example of Kylie Minogue the diva and entrepreneur in Entrepreneurship in action 1.2). Throughout Europe, the European Commission is seeking to facilitate the 'fostering of entrepreneurial mindsets' throughout society (European Union, 2000; Hannon, 2007).

Why entrepreneurship should be seen as different from other subjects is quite baffling. Yet, there is debate on whether students can be taught how to become entrepreneurs (Fiet, 2000). Evaluation is difficult because there is a lack of clarity about what is meant by an enterprise culture (Della-Giusta and King, 2006), and the definition of the skills required for enterprise. Jack and Anderson (2001) suggest that teaching entrepreneurship is difficult because the entrepreneurial process (i.e., imagination, creativity, innovativeness, creating and/or identifying resources, assembling and managing resources, etc.) involves both an 'art' (i.e., the creative and innovative attributes) and a 'science' (i.e., functional skills of business and management). Numerous business and management schools worldwide (Solomon, 2007) now deliver an array of entrepreneurship and small business modules at various levels. There is growing appreciation that even more institutions should provide entrepreneurship and small business modules. Programmes are now being designed for non-business students (i.e., arts, media, design, science and engineering students). Evidence from the United States suggests that

Entrepreneurship in action 1.2
So Lucky: Kylie Minogue the diva and entrepreneur

It's rare to get a glimpse inside the world of a celebrity's actual business empire, which is what makes a story from British newspaper *Mail on Sunday* about the financial world of Kylie Minogue so interesting.

The paper obtained the financial accounts of Kylie's company Darenote Limited from Britain's financial reporting regular, Companies House. They show the business empire of the pop princess made a profit of $6.8 million in the 12 months to April 2009, up sharply from the $2.1 million it made the previous corresponding period.

According to the report, the accounts (signed off by Kylie's accountant father Ron Minogue) show a dividend of almost $2 million was paid from Darenote to Kylie herself. For someone who had her first hit more than 20 years ago, the Darenote profit really highlights the singer's impressive longevity and remarkable earnings power.

But look closely at the way Kylie has structured her business affairs and you can see some lessons that all entrepreneurs can use:

- *Concentrate on high margin jobs.* It's worth noting that as with most performers, Minogue's earnings are drawn mostly from the old-fashioned source of long, hard tours – mainly due to the fact that she gets to keep so much more of the revenue generated by ticket sales as opposed to album sales. Indeed, albums increasingly act as loss-leaders for many artists, particularly those who can draw huge crowds like Kylie.

- *Premium pays.* In late 2009 (during the period covered by the Darenote accounts) Kylie appeared at a special concert to open a hotel in Dubai. VIP or private appearances attract huge dollars for artists – all of which shows that exclusivity does have a real value.

- *Diversify.* The problem for many celebrities is that earnings can be so up and down. To smooth this out, artists such as Kylie extend their brands into other areas. Minogue's endorsements include homewares, perfume (for women and men), books and clothing.

- *Tap into new markets.* Minogue has been brilliant at constantly finding new markets – just look at the way she still attracts customers who loved her as an actor, 1980s music star, pop diva, gay icon and fashion icon. She's also continued to look to expand geographically. The Dubai hotel show was her first in the Middle East, while she launched her first major US tour in late 2009.

Source: J. Thomson, SmartCompany, Entrepreneur Watch, 15 March 2010.

there is still a demand for 'business plan'/'new venture plan' modules that require evidence to guide:

> teaching the nuts and bolts of entrepreneurship and small business management (Solomon, 2007: 179).

There is, however, a growing need to craft courses and programmes that meet the rigours of academia, while keeping a reality-based focus and entrepreneurial climate in the learning experience environment.

A common element of most entrepreneurship and small business management modules is the exploration of case studies to illustrate how problems and opportunities are addressed by *real* entrepreneurs. Case studies can illustrate the 'art' (i.e., the creativity, imagination, innovativeness and problem-solving skills) (Lumsdaine and Binks, 2003) and 'science' (i.e., strategy, planning, marketing, financial, project management, time management, leadership, motivation, delegation, communication and negotiation skills) (Westhead and Matlay, 2006; Wickham, 2006) skills and capabilities that have to be accumulated and leveraged by entrepreneurs.

Numerous practical, theoretical and policy books are available relating to entrepreneurship and small business developmental issues (Storey, 1994; President and Fellows of Harvard College, 1999; Bolton and Thompson, 2000; Bridge et al., 2003; Kirby, 2003; Lumsdaine and Binks, 2003; Kuratko and Hodgetts, 2004; Carter and Jones-Evans, 2006; Deakins and Freel, 2006; Wickham, 2006; Burns, 2007; Storey and Greene, 2010). Most books generally focus on small business issues, or solely discuss how to establish a new business. A distinction can be made between practically orientated books as opposed to theoretical and policy orientated books. Both streams of textbooks seek to illustrate key issues with regard to very brief case study examples. In many instances, the case studies appear as an afterthought to illustrate how theoretical or practical issues are actually exhibited by *real* entrepreneurs and businesses.

This text and case study collection is designed to meet the need for an accessible resource that will stimulate critical thinking and reflective learning relating to issues generally abstractly (and briefly) discussed in lectures. In addition, it will be useful in seminars focusing on key issues that need to be considered with regard to an idea and/or a business plan module, as well as theory or policy orientated entrepreneurship and small business modules. Our aim is to provide undergraduate and postgraduate students, as well as academics, policy-makers and practitioners, with deeper insights into the entrepreneurial and wealth-creating processes, as well as the processes relating to small business development. Case studies are linked to clear learning outcomes that are stated prior to the presentation of each case study. A separate teaching note solely available to module convenors and tutors will guide students through the issues that need to be considered. Students are encouraged to read one or more of the longer cases for each chapter, presented at the end of the book. Some cases relate to more than one theme. The 25 longer cases are listed in Table 1.1.

We do not provide an exhaustive review of all themes in the field of entrepreneurship and small business development, or a detailed discussion of all tools that can be used to generate and exploit business opportunities. This textbook provides contextual evidence relating to the actual behaviour of *real* entrepreneurs and organisations, like Sir Stelios Haji-Ioannou and easyJet, and it complements materials available elsewhere. Articles included within the Carter and Jones-Evans (2006) edited edition, for example, cover many important themes and illustrate patterns and behaviour with regard to entrepreneurs and their organisations. Several edited volumes of general readings also focus upon entrepreneurship and small business development (Casson, 1990; Acs, 1996; Birley, 1998; Storey, 2000; Westhead and Wright, 2000; Hitt and Ireland, 2005; Casson et al., 2006; Cuervo et al., 2008; Storey and Greene, 2010), as do readings relating to new firm formation (Davidsson, 2006a), technological entrepreneurship (Siegel, 2006), management buyouts (Wright and Bruining, 2008), family firms (Poutziouris et al., 2006), female entrepreneurship (Brush et al., 2006) and international entrepreneurship (Dana, 2004).

Table 1.1 Case studies and linkage to chapters

Case title	Author(s)	Chapter link	Secondary chapter links
1 IPS Communication – Distribution: Claude Guinet's career in entrepreneurship	Joëlle Piffault and Louis J. Filion	1	3, 4, 5, 7
2 Fickle Rooster Productions: Turning a hobby into a profitable business	Kirk Frith	2	3
3 The Recording Room: Ben Wallace's musical ventures	Ed McMullan	3	2
4 Portable Patient Lifts, LLC: Patent and start-up issues	Gerard M. Campbell	3	2, 6, 12
5 Original Voddy Company Limited	Andy Corcoran	3	12, 13
6 Alba Adventures: An entrepreneur pushed into entrepreneurship	Marlene Mints Reed	4	10, 11, 12
7 Ace Cleaning (UK) Limited: Development of a purchased firm by a novice entrepreneur	Mark Freel	4	2, 9, 11, 12, 14
8 The OffQuip saga: Partner entry and exit dynamics	Louis J. Filion	5	14
9 Iain Russell and Arran Aromatics Limited: Portfolio and serial entrepreneurship	Carol Craig and Frank Martin	5	3, 4, 11, 13, 14
10 Marine Products Limited: Confronting barriers to innovation	Povl Larsen and Alan Lewis	6	2, 12
11 Deep Sea Fishing Inc: Acquiring the 'right' capital for a new technology-based firm	Alf Steinar Saetre and Truls Erikson	6	12
12 Painatolo Ltd and Rakennuspalvelu Ltd: Family business transfer issues	Ulla Hytti, Kirsi Lamminpää and Pekka Stenholm	7	2
13 Spin-offs at Tremcar: Partnerships for growth	Caroline Mireault, Danielle Luc and Louis J. Filion	8	14
14 Wemas International Limited: Purchase and turnaround of an existing business by Brent Lybbert	Ed McMullan	9	3, 12
15 Seagate Technology	Mike Wright and Angela Loihl	9	12, 14
16 Hill Holt Wood: Community-owned social enterprise	Kirk Frith and Gerard McElwee	10	11, 14
17 Rad-Amer Intourist: American entrepreneur opportunity recognition and exploitation in Moscow	Zafar U. Ahmed, Peter Robinson and Leo Paul Dana	11	3
18 *The Fleet Sheet*: New firm creation in a transition economy	Marlene Mints Reed	11	2
19 BCH TeleCommunications	Marlene Mints Reed	11	2, 3
20 UFO Pictures: The challenges of film production	Marlene Mints Reed	12	2, 11
21 New Covent Garden Soup Company: Contributions made by venture capitalists	Mike Wright	12	14
22 AAC Limited: Entrepreneurial team dynamics	Eva Jarošová and Joan Winn	13	3, 11
23 *Model Kit World*: Firm growth through geographic expansion	Alex S. L. Tsang, Wai-Sum Siu and Gloria H. Y. Ting	13	3, 11
24 Upstart Graphics: Merger and acquisition issues	Donald M. DePamphilis	14	12
25 Private family health practice: Limits to growth	Suzanne Hetzel Campbell and Christopher L. Huntley	14	2

1.4 The organising framework

Themes explored in this book illustrate developments in the field of entrepreneurship. A broad view of entrepreneurship is operationalised. Gartner (1985) presented a conceptual framework for describing the phenomenon of new venture creation that integrated four major perspectives in entrepreneurship: the characteristics of the individual(s) starting the new venture; the organisation they create; the environment surrounding the new venture; and the process by which the new venture is created. Guided by these insights, the six themes within the emerging stream entrepreneurship studies highlighted by Ucbasaran et al. (2001) are drawn upon in the chapters presented here. Short entrepreneurship in action vignettes and longer cases are linked to one or more of the six themes highlighted in Figure 1.1. The themes are as follows:

- **Theme 1: Theory.** Cases can be linked to economic, psychological, cognitive, sociological, and opportunity identification and exploitation theories exploring the entrepreneurial process and the behaviour and performance of entrepreneurs and their organisations. Entrepreneur and/or organisation resources and behaviour are illustrated in contrasting industrial, locational, national and cultural contexts.
- **Theme 2: Types of entrepreneur** are examined in terms of academic, novice, serial, portfolio and social entrepreneurs.
- **Theme 3: The process of entrepreneurship** is examined in terms of opportunity creation, recognition, information search and learning, and resource acquisition and leverage as well as the competitive strategies selected by entrepreneurs. Methods of best entrepreneur and business practice are illustrated.

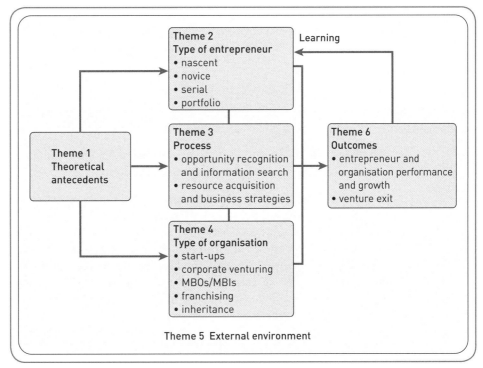

Figure 1.1 The focus of entrepreneurship research
Source: Ucbasaran et al. (2001, Figure 1:59).

- **Theme 4: Organisational types**. Organisational modes selected by entrepreneurs are examined, including family firms, corporate entrepreneurship, management buyouts and social enterprises.
- **Theme 5: The external environment for entrepreneurship**. Governments in developed and developing economies have introduced policies to address attitudinal, resource, operational and strategic barriers to business formation and development. The merits and disadvantages of targeted and customised support to entrepreneurs and firms are being considered by practitioners. Case studies from the United Kingdom and United States are presented as well as other institutional contexts such as emerging economies.
- **Theme 6: Outcomes of entrepreneurial endeavours**. The economic and non-economic outcomes of entrepreneurial endeavours are illustrated with reference to the entrepreneur and firm units of analysis. The issue of entrepreneurial learning is discussed throughout the book.

Text, short entrepreneurship in action vignettes and longer cases illustrate the dynamics of entrepreneurs and the organisations they own. Evidence relating to the actual resources and behaviour of different types of entrepreneurs and organisations are illustrated. We highlight that the 'entrepreneur' and the 'organisation' should be the unit of academic and policy analysis. We explore the behaviour of entrepreneurs and illustrate how entrepreneurs acquire information, how they learn from their entrepreneurial experiences, and how they utilise acquired knowledge to develop their organisations. A distinction between different 'types' of entrepreneurs and organisations is highlighted in several national contexts. Methods of best entrepreneur (and organisation) practice in relation to imagination, creativity and innovation as well as methods to address barriers to enterprise and business development are raised. Several cases highlight that the entrepreneurial process can be moderated by external environmental conditions. Outcomes associated with contrasting enterprise and competitive strategies are illustrated.

1.5   Learning issues

This book seeks to develop an understanding of entrepreneurs and the organisations they create, own, manage, develop and exit. It is designed to:

- provide an understanding of the nature, role and functions of different types of entrepreneurs and organisations owned by entrepreneurs;
- examine the characteristics, attributes and resources of different types of entrepreneurs;
- demonstrate the variety of forms of entrepreneurial processes relating to new firm creation, enterprise within larger firms, business development and exit route selection;
- critically consider the array of factors associated with enterprise development;
- demonstrate the influence of external environmental conditions, including public policy, on the entrepreneurial process;
- highlight the barriers faced by entrepreneurs and discuss methods selected by entrepreneurs to address identified barriers; and
- highlight practical issues that need to be considered to create, identify, evaluate, pursue and exploit a business opportunity.

In the following chapters, text, short case study entrepreneurship in action vignettes and longer cases are presented to highlight key issues relating to entrepreneur and organisation behaviour. The broad purpose of each chapter and its associated cases is to enable the reader to:

- acquire an understanding of practical and policy debates in developed and emerging economies (i.e., Europe, North America, Scandinavia, China and Russia);
- think critically about the concepts presented in each case;
- think critically about the practical options available; and
- use the case studies to formulate and guide their individual studies for a dissertation and/or assignments.

Each chapter will review the literature relating to the selected theme. Key issues will be highlighted and they will be illustrated in the cases, which will 'talk' and exhibit people, pattern and process issues.

Short entrepreneurship in action vignettes and longer cases illustrate issues that students have to consider with regard to both the 'art' (i.e., the creative and innovative attributes) and the 'science' (i.e., business and management functional skills) of entrepreneurship and small business development. Cases illustrate 'how' and 'why' entrepreneurs and their organisations behave as they do in relation to the creation, pursuit and exploitation of opportunities. Several cases highlight key practical and/or policy issues. Longer case study authors make linkages to the current body of knowledge to emphasise issues the reader should critically reflect upon. Specific questions are presented at the end of each case to guide students' critical reflection and learning.

Case study authors are drawn from several disciplines. Consequently, alternative practical lenses are exhibited in the cases to explore and critically reflect upon the actual behaviour of entrepreneurs and their organisations. Cases relate to a variety of industrial, locational, national and cultural contexts. Several cases highlight that the institutional context and the profiles of entrepreneurs shape the entrepreneurial process and business development.

Education institutions throughout the world are encouraging Science, Engineering, Media, Art and Design students to participate in entrepreneurship and small business management modules. Selected cases will interest students drawn from a variety of disciplines. The cases explore and illustrate business formation and development issues relating to traditional industries as well as the increasingly important creative, knowledge and technology-based industries. Notably, the cases illustrate the judgements and behaviour of actual entrepreneurs. Further, the cases illustrate the dynamics of entrepreneurs and the organisations they own. Cases illustrate how entrepreneurs acquire information, how they learn from their entrepreneurial experiences, and how they utilise acquired knowledge to develop their organisations. The following important and novel themes are raised in the cases:

- The ways in which entrepreneurs' attitudes and human capital resources (i.e., specific human capital relating to industry know-how, management know-how, and entrepreneurial capabilities, etc.) can shape the business start-up process and subsequent firm development. Issues relating to the supply of entrepreneurs are, therefore, discussed.

- The cases illustrate several dimensions of the entrepreneurial process relating to imagination, creativity and innovation as well as issues relating to information search, opportunity identification, evaluation and pursuit. The increasing importance of international business is also highlighted in several cases.
- Obstacles faced by particular types of entrepreneurs (i.e., young and inexperienced entrepreneurs, owners of knowledge-based firms and family firms, social entrepreneurs, as well as female entrepreneurs and experienced portfolio and serial entrepreneurs) are illustrated.
- Resource assemblage and leverage issues to exploit an opportunity are explored. The need for teams of entrepreneurs with diverse human capital profiles is highlighted. In addition, the methods used by entrepreneurs to circumvent attitudinal, resource, operational and strategic barriers to firm formation and development are shown. The assets and liabilities associated with solo entrepreneurship as well as team entrepreneurship are highlighted. Further, the accumulation and leverage of social capital (i.e., networking) to address barriers to innovation and firm formation and development is illustrated.
- Issues relating to corporate entrepreneurship within existing larger organisations are raised. The academic entrepreneurship context is discussed.
- The emerging theme of social entrepreneurship is illustrated.
- The external environment for entrepreneurship is considered throughout the book as a moderator that can impact on the behaviour of entrepreneurs and organisations. Cases relate to several national and industrial contexts (i.e., traditional, knowledge and technology-based, creative industries, etc.). The role played by public policy (i.e., provision of grants and advice, education and training) shaping the entrepreneurial process is described.
- Outcomes associated with entrepreneurial endeavours are highlighted. Financial and non-financial issues are explored. As entrepreneurship is not a single action event, with some entrepreneurs having careers in entrepreneurship, the habitual entrepreneur phenomenon is illustrated. Several exit routes are open to entrepreneurs. Business transfer issues are highlighted.

After reading the entrepreneurship in action vignettes and the cases the reader should be able to:

- demonstrate a knowledge of issues pertaining to the role, nature and function of the entrepreneur;
- apply various concepts to understanding the needs and contributions made by different 'types' of entrepreneurs and organisations;
- demonstrate a knowledge of the stimuli and obstacles (i.e., resource needs) to business formation, purchase and development;
- demonstrate a knowledge of the tools used by entrepreneurs to generate, create, evaluate, pursue and exploit business opportunities;
- demonstrate a knowledge that the external environment (i.e., institutional context) can shape entrepreneurial processes and business development;
- demonstrate knowledge of the tools that can be applied to ensure a firm's competitive advantage and to address constantly emerging barriers to business development; and
- demonstrate how entrepreneurs learn from their successes as well as their mistakes.

1.6 Looking forward

This chapter has highlighted that encouraging entrepreneurship (i.e., innovation, opportunity identification and exploitation, new firm creation, and firm grow in domestic and international markets) in new and established organisations can encourage economic and non-economic benefits to society. Established and emerging themes relating to the entrepreneurial process have been summarised. Key elements of the entrepreneurial process were briefly discussed. A distinction between the 'art' and 'science' of entrepreneurship was made. The content and structure of the book as well as key learning issues were also discussed. Chapter 2 explores in more detail the economic and non-economic contributions of entrepreneurial firms. Barriers to new private firm formation and business development are summarised. The case for intervention to address barriers (i.e., market failures) to business formation and development is presented. The need to focus on the entrepreneur (as well as the firm) as the unit of analysis in academic and policy studies is raised.

Discussion questions

1 What is entrepreneurship? Discuss the elements of the entrepreneurial process.
2 What are the key elements of the 'art' and 'science' of entrepreneurship?
3 Why is entrepreneurship important for society?
4 Why do governments in both developed and developing countries attach an importance to promoting enterprise?

Recommended further reading

Gartner, W. B. (2001). Is There an Elephant in Entrepreneurship? Blind Assumptions in Theory Development. *Entrepreneurship Theory and Practice*, 25 (4): 27–39.

Gartner, W. B., Davidsson, P. and Zahra, S. A. (2006). Are You Talking to Me? The Nature of Community in Entrepreneurship Scholarship. *Entrepreneurship Theory and Practice*, 30 (3): 321–331.

Grégoire, D. A., Noël, M. X., Déry, R. and Béchard, J-P. (2006). Is There Conceptual Convergence in Entrepreneurship Research?: A Co-Citation Analysis of Frontiers of Entrepreneurship Research, 1981–2004. *Entrepreneurship Theory and Practice*, 30 (3): 333–373.

Schildt, H. A., Zahra, S. A. and Sillanpää, A. (2006). Scholarly Communities in Entrepreneurship Research: A Co-Citation Analysis. *Entrepreneurship Theory and Practice*, 30 (3): 399–415.

Ucbasaran, D., Westhead, P. and Wright, M. (2001). The Focus of Entrepreneurial Research: Contextual and Process Issues. *Entrepreneurship Theory and Practice*, 25 (4): 57–80.

Chapter 2

Contributions of entrepreneurial firms

Contents

Learning objectives

- Highlight differences between smaller and larger enterprises and barriers to enterprise.
- Discuss diverse economic and social contributions made by entrepreneurs, new firms and growing firms.
- Analyse issues relating to job generation, wealth creation, job generation, competitiveness and innovation, as well as reduction of social and regional inequality.
- Consider the case for intervention to support enterprise.
- Analyse the case made for the entrepreneur and the firm to be units of academic and policy attention.
- Discuss the case for 'targeted' support.

2.1 The positive contributions of entrepreneurial firms

Debate surrounds the economic and non-economic contributions made by entrepreneurs, new firms and a growing stock of entrepreneurial firms (Acs and Storey, 2004; Johnson, 2007). These contributions are summarised in Table 2.1. Entrepreneurial firms are important because they can make several economic and non-economic contributions. They play a role in encouraging economic development (Baumol, 1968; Carree et al., 2007). Entrepreneurial firms have a role in reducing unemployment and poverty (Storey, 1982). They are major creators of new jobs when large firms are downsizing (Birch, 1979), irrespective of the economic cycle (DTI, 2004). Entrepreneurial firms generate wealth creation and the firm, entrepreneur(s) and employees can be taxed. Government can reinvest this taxation into economic development projects (i.e., enterprise and small firms policy and/or other social projects). Entrepreneurial firms are seen as the seeds from which large successful organisations grow (i.e., Microsoft, Cisco Systems, Body Shop, etc.).

Entrepreneurial firms stimulate competition, which limits the ability of dominant firms to raise prices. Competition can lead to a reduction in prices, more consumer choice, encourage the creation and dissemination of new innovative products/services and/or better quality products and services. Moreover, competition encourages more efficient use of resources and the displacement of non-viable inefficient businesses:

> If incumbent businesses are unable to match the productivity of new or fast growing small businesses, then they are either forced to exit the market or their market share is reduced, so increasing the productivity of the market as a whole (DTI, 2004: 17).

Viable businesses that are more efficient users of resources will be associated with superior levels of productivity, which can enable them to sustain competitive advantage in local and international markets. Efficient entrepreneurial firms that can internationalise can create jobs and wealth. Internationalising firms are also less likely to displace new and established firms in local markets. Efficient firms can reduce the flow of imports, and they can play a role in reducing balance of payments deficits.

Table 2.1 Entrepreneurial firms: Positive economic and non-economic contributions and negative barriers to enterprise

Positive contributions	Negative barriers
Economic	*Macro-economic*
• Economic development	Business and personal taxation, interest rates, exchange rates, public spending, inflation policy, regulatory framework
• Reduction of unemployment and poverty	
• Job generation when large firms are downsizing, irrespective of economic cycle	*Cultural barriers and narrow education base*
• Wealth creation	*Advantages of large firms*
• Taxes (firm, entrepreneur and employees) and this tax income can support the economic, social and political agendas of government	*Attitudinal barriers*
	Reluctance to select a career in enterprise; establish a firm for independence, and/or lifestyle reasons, reluctance to move outside the 'management comfort zone'; desire for a 'born small stay small firm', reluctance to sell equity to 'outsiders' and to use 'external' professional advice, etc.
• Entrepreneurial 'seed' firms can grow into large 'oaks' firms	
• Competitiveness (i.e., reduction of power of large firms, lower prices, better quality products/services, consumer choice, better utilisation of scarce resources, displacement of inefficient firms, etc.)	
• Productivity	
• Large firm competitiveness enhanced by entrepreneurial firms involved in the supply-chain	*Resource barriers*
	Information, finance, premises, skilled labour, machinery, equipment, etc.
• Internationalisation, reduction of flow of imports and balance of payments deficits	*Operational barriers*
• Radical and incremental innovation, technology; creation of new industries and markets; competitive advantage not solely related to 'sweating low cost labour'	Imagination, creativity, innovation (radical or incremental), legitimacy, appropriate administrative, management and production systems, inability to protect the product/service/brand, skills and capabilities deficiencies, etc.
• Service role – provision of essential consumer services for 'quality of life'	
• Harmonious working environment with fewer industrial disputes and lower absenteeism	*Strategic barriers*
• Seedbed role promoting the next generation of entrepreneurs	Focus on low price strategy rather than a premium price strategy, inability to introduce market and/or technological differentiation, inability due to attitudinal and resource deficiencies to create new source(s) of competitive advantage, and/or to proactively adapt to constantly changing market, technological and regulatory conditions, etc.
• Protection and promotion of local communities	
• Local economic development in inner cities, former coal, fishing, mining and steel communities and peripheral rural communities	
• Multipliers – direct and indirect job generation and wealth creation generated by new clusters of entrepreneurial firms	*Government failure*
	Government supports firms that do not require assistance and this assistance does not generate positive externalities
Non-economic	
• Reduction of social and regional inequality with regard to access to wealth creation	
• Under-represented groups (i.e., disabled, ethnic minorities, graduates, women, young people, etc.) to select careers in enterprise	
• Empowerment (i.e., independence, control, satisfaction, fulfil family and household responsibilities, etc.)	
• Votes – policy-makers supporting enterprise are re-elected	

Entrepreneurial firms have a key role in introducing new product and process innovations. Some firms play a niche role providing something marginally different. Entrepreneurs with unique scientific or technological knowledge create radical innovations that can lead to the creation of new industries, which can promote economic development associated with the 'creative destruction' of some old industries (Schumpeter, 1934). 'Born global' innovative firms can play a role in reducing balance of payments deficits (see Chapter 13). However, only a small proportion of firms are engaged in truly innovative activities (Storey, 1994). Many new and small firms are imitative, and they generally introduce incremental innovations to sustain their competitive advantage.

Most entrepreneurial firms, especially smaller firms, are engaged in the service sector, either servicing private consumers (i.e., catering, retail or repair) or other enterprises (i.e., business services). They provide an essential service role (i.e., personal and community services) to the way of life of many people. The servicing relationship between an entrepreneurial firm and its customers (i.e., subcontracting) can range from co-operation to dependency and exploitation. Entrepreneurial firms support the infrastructural needs of larger firms. Many large firms would not be able to remain profitable without the service provided by new and small firms in their supply-chain (i.e., Nissan in the north-east of England is supplied by small firms who may solely exist to service the needs of Nissan). Entrepreneurial firms indirectly ensure the competitiveness, profitability and contribution to economic development made by major 'corporate prime movers'.

Entrepreneurial firms, especially small firms, can provide a harmonious working environment that is often reflected in fewer industrial disputes and lower absenteeism. They can provide a nurturing role model and learning environment for potential entrepreneurs (i.e., management, industry and finance know-how, diverse business networks, etc.). An environment that supports individualism and reduces a dependency culture on the state and larger firms can also reduce the power of the trade union movement.

Entrepreneurial firms are developers of the local economy. They make a contribution to the regeneration of deprived rural as well urban communities. New and small entrepreneurial firms frequently service local markets. The entrepreneur(s) may live locally and feel an allegiance to the area where the business is located. They generally employ local people and they use local services and suppliers. This activity can generate local multiplier effects that promote the demand for other potential new firms, which can promote a local spiral of wealth creation and job generation to reduce local unemployment and poverty.

2.2 Challenges of entrepreneurial firms

2.2.1 Reluctance or inability of most new and small firms to grow

There are numerous barriers to enterprise (Bridge et al., 2003; DTI, 2004). Broad types of negative barriers to enterprise are summarised in Table 2.1. The attitudes of individuals are a major barrier to new firm creation and development. There are different types of firms and entrepreneurs with most new firms not desiring or reporting significant growth. Most new firms are 'born to die young' as most cease to trade within three years of inception (Storey, 1994). The majority of firms that survive are 'born small and stay small'. Many small firms are more interested in maintaining their current level of profit than in expansion. One reason for firms wishing to stay small is that the ownership and management reside in the same person, or persons; so future firm goals are determined not only by commercial considerations but by personal lifestyles and family factors relating to the individuals or teams of individuals who own and manage them (see Chapter 14). However, it seems that the proportion of small businesses that want to grow is greater than the numbers that actually do grow (DTI, 2004).

A distinction can be made between *'failures'* (i.e., the high proportion of small firms that have a short life), *'trundlers'* (i.e., a large group of surviving small firms that remain small), and *'flyers'* (i.e., the small proportion of firms that have rapid growth in employment) (Storey, 1994). Firm development may be restricted by entrepreneurs who want to maintain ownership and control of their firms and who may only grow their ventures to an internal *'management comfort zone'*, which allows owners to maintain control and ownership. Storey et al. (1987) noted that 4 per cent of firms generated 50 per cent of job generation by the firms in the sample over a decade. Similarly, Gallagher and Miller (1991) detected that the high flyers in their sample (18 per cent of firms) accounted for 68 per cent of all jobs created. Policy-makers concerned with job generation, wealth creation, competition, efficient markets, technology diffusion and votes (i.e., re-election) (Storey, 1994) may seek to increase the supply of entrepreneurs and entrepreneurial firms in society because each new firm can play a valuable economic and/or social role, but they particularly want to increase the number of high-growth ventures.

2.2.2 Differences between smaller and larger enterprises

Entrepreneurial firms can be both large and small. Many large enterprises have become so by having been entrepreneurial and growing rapidly, and may continue to be entrepreneurial through continuously investing in innovation, as well as seeking and exploiting new opportunities (see Chapter 8). Not all smaller enterprises are entrepreneurial. Smaller private enterprises cannot therefore be regarded as a homogeneous entity. Further, smaller private enterprises cannot be viewed as scaled down versions of larger enterprises. Smaller private enterprises differ in many respects from larger enterprises. Smaller private enterprises are associated with *advantages as well as disadvantages*. There are broad differences between smaller and larger enterprises with regard to:

- firm structure,
- management and control,
- operations/production,
- resources,
- strategic planning,
- the market, and
- the business environment,

each of which are briefly discussed in turn, below.

Some smaller entrepreneurial firms are highly flexible because they have *loose firm structures*. Many smaller enterprises do have an organisational hierarchy, and there is a focus on informal communication within the organisation. A loose structure can generate the following advantages for some smaller private enterprises:

- focus on imagination, creativity, flexibility and/or the ability to make quick decisions to seize opportunities;
- no agency problems because ownership and management are aligned;
- easy access to the owner can generate speed and flexibility in decision-making;
- everyone involved and motivated in the organisation;
- 'family' unit and people are not numbers;

- structure easy to change in response to changing external environmental conditions;
- no need for memos and time-consuming meetings; and
- accessible and friendly to outsiders, customers, suppliers, etc.

On the downside, a loose structure can generate the following disadvantages for some private smaller enterprises:

- owners may dominate and pursue 'family' rather than 'business' interests;
- owners may exhibit diminished motivation, blind spots, denial, and/or a focus on lifestyle issues that may retard enterprising behaviour (see Chapter 3) and firm development (see Chapter 14);
- some owners exhibit favouritism with key positions held by 'family' members, and this allocation of managerial positions based on kinship ties rather than ability can retard firm performance;
- owners resistant to change may be reluctant to sell equity to 'outsiders' and to deal with banks and financial institutions;
- owners seeking to maintain ownership and control may retard venture performance by being resistant to external monitoring, which could improve firm performance;
- some owners have only one good business idea and they may repeat the recipe that worked in the past in changed circumstances;
- some owners are not receptive to technological change and emerging market opportunities; and
- some owners are reluctant to consider and/or apply for external expertise required to ensure enterprising behaviour and venture development.

The *management and control* of private smaller enterprises can also be associated with the following disadvantages, which can retard continued enterprising behaviour and venture development:

- Some smaller enterprises have a small management team (if they have one at all), and due to the limited expertise and knowledge of management, the firm may be unable to key into emerging profitable opportunities because there is insufficient attention given to imagination, creativity, innovation, spotting gaps in the market, market research, feasibility analysis, reluctance and/or inability to use the latest technologies, and the reluctance or the inability to use 'external' professional support.
- In many smaller enterprises, staff have multifunctional roles and firm development can be retarded if there are no clear lines of responsibility.
- In many smaller enterprises, the management focus on day-to-day fire fighting (production) issues, and they do not allocate sufficient time to management thinking that focuses on the long-term and strategic competitive advantage issues.
- Due to cost constraints and/or limited technical knowledge, some smaller enterprises use informal systems and procedures, and there can be a reluctance and/or inability to use more technologically sophisticated formal control tools relating to production, cashflow, quality, etc., which can retard firm survival and development.

With regard to *operations and productions issues*, some smaller enterprises can seize business opportunities that require low price product or service delivery, flexible service provision, quick speed of service or product delivery, and a focus on service or product design and quality (see the example of Coffee#1 in Entrepreneurship in action 2.1). Flexible entrepreneurial smaller enterprises can provide short production runs for the customers

Entrepreneurship in action 2.1
Welsh-based company Coffee#1 beats big boys to award

It was the growing coffee shop culture in shows like *Friends* and *Frasier* that convinced him to quit investment banking for cappuccinos and muffins. Now, a coffee chain founded 10 years ago by a Welsh entrepreneur, has been named the best in Britain, beating global competitors like Costa at the Café Society Awards in London. The chain, which was founded in Cardiff [in Wales] by James Shapland in 2000, now has 12 branches across South Wales and South-West England. And Mr Shapland said last night the key to the firm's success is limiting itself to one new shop a year. 'As a chain, we try not to grow too quickly or people become anonymous,' said Mr Shapland, who set up the business with chairman, David Jones, a former Microsoft director from Bargoed [in Wales] who now lives in Seattle, a city at the forefront of the global coffee movement. 'This can happen with bigger companies. Some global chains open a new store every six to seven days, which means they do extremely well in terms of their profits . . . But we try to make things a little more intimate and we try to open a shop once a year. It's growing but we are people who believe that our chains, although small and local, will be recognised with our name out there . . . The likes of Costa and Starbucks are so powerful with their positions on the high street and their marketing resources, that to be able to be recognised on a simple local level is great. What we are trying to do is offer great coffee and produce and great service. It's brilliant that an independent judge has come in and recognised our standards.'

Coffee#1 beat the likes of Costa Coffee, Caffé Gusto, Boston Tea Party and Soho Coffee Company to the award, which recognises its innovation, standards and customer satisfaction. It follows success at the Beverage Service Association awards, where it also picked up top prize.

Mr Shapland said his staff play a key role in making the chain a success. 'We are very lucky that we have a sound mix of great people whom we try to look after,' he said. Further, 'I think obviously the core product needs to stand up. We spend an awful lot of time developing a good cup of coffee and we make sure you can taste the coffee, whereas some competitors offer oversized cups which mean you cannot taste the coffee . . . We want people to feel like they have got the value out of their £2 they might spend on coffee.' He added: 'We offer warm and friendly customer service and we have an appreciation of customers and we don't take them for granted . . . We recognise the need to appreciate them and try to make people feel special when they come in – it's easy to become too manufactured and sterile . . . Customer loyalty is important to us. We like to offer a nice, warm cosy environment where you can sit on comfy sofas and read a good book or have a chat with your friends . . . It's easy to have a cold feel in some of the competitors' shops and they can have a dirtiness to them . . . We have clean tables and toilets. I think these factors make for a good experience.'

The company has been growing since 2000 and has featured in the Wales Fast Growth 50 project, an annual search for the 50 fastest growing companies, for three of the past four years.

Source: J. McWatt, *The Western Mail*, 6 March 2010.

'ignored' by larger enterprises. However, smaller enterprise performance can be retarded if the enterprise is associated with one or more of the following production and operations characteristics:

- smaller enterprises may be associated with few, if any, economies of scale;
- labour intensive rather than a focus on using modern mechanised equipment that can generate efficiency and productivity benefits;

- limited focus on quality control mechanisms;
- inability to take advantage of bulk buying; and
- inability to carry stocks.

Many smaller enterprises are established and managed by a 'solo' entrepreneur. Team ownership of a venture is usually associated with business activities that require more substantial *human and financial resources*, for example, knowledge and technology-based activities. The *human capital* (i.e., management and industry know-how, technical and entrepreneurial capabilities, ability to secure resources, prior business ownership experience, etc.) of the founding entrepreneur (see Section 4.2.2), or the entrepreneurial ownership team, can shape enterprising behaviour as well as business survival and development (Matlay and Westhead, 2005). Smaller private enterprises associated with 'solo' entrepreneurs generally have more limited pools of *skills, capabilities and knowledge* to draw upon to create, spot and seize profitable business opportunities. Many smaller enterprises are disadvantaged because they have small management teams with few or no specialists. Many cash-strapped smaller enterprises have no or limited capacity to develop staff using job-related formal training due to 'ignorance' and/or 'market' forces reasons (Storey and Westhead, 1997). The inability of entrepreneurs to invest in training people in the smaller enterprises can retard imagination, creativity and innovative behaviour as well as firm development (Cosh et al., 1998).

New firms are generally financed by entrepreneurs who utilise their own (limited) personal savings. Smaller private enterprise survival and development can be retarded by a lack of *finance and/or poor cashflow control*. Entrepreneurs with no proven track record in business (i.e., they lack credibility) find it difficult to obtain external finance, particularly if the entrepreneur fails to provide complete information in a business plan relating to the risk (i.e., current and future size of the market size, current and future competitive and legislative threats, etc.) and return issues that need to be considered by financiers. Entrepreneurs with limited collateral (i.e., a house) may be denied finance and/or charged very high interest rates with regard to any bank finance provided. Very few smaller enterprises are able to attract venture capital from formal venture capital firms, or even 'business angels', because they have limited growth prospects. Mistakes relating to financial management (i.e., high gearing, cashflow problems, over-trading, inability to reduce the problem of trade bill late payment, etc.) in smaller enterprises can be expensive, and can lead to business closure.

Strategic planning to achieve long-term competitive advantage is usually exhibited by larger enterprises, but this is often absent in smaller enterprises. Many smaller enterprises solely focus on low price competition alone to satisfy immediate customer demand. Smaller enterprises are generally associated with the following features, which can retard enterprising behaviour, firm survival and development:

- limited knowledge of the business environment;
- no specialist staff;
- no time for planning;
- short, if any, planning horizon;
- survival/lifestyle perspective rather than a growth perspective;

● reactive rather than a proactive stance to the external environment; and

● short-term opportunistic stance rather than a long-term strategic competitive advantage stance.

External environmental conditions shape enterprise behaviour as well as firm survival and development (see Chapter 11). Smaller enterprises generally have a limited *market share*. They also typically have the following features, which can retard firm development:

● small product range;

● limited number and range of customers (especially at business start-up);

● dependence on a single customer or small number of customers;

● limited influence on their market; and

● a tendency to resist change.

With regard to the *business environment*, smaller enterprises generally perceive the following constraints on business development:

● a business environment hostile to smaller enterprises;

● have no influence on credit/discounts with suppliers;

● have no or little credibility with financial institutions;

● believe they are overwhelmed by government regulation, legislation and paperwork;

● are unaware of most direct (and indirect) government assistance to support smaller enterprises; and

● reluctant to use (and pay) for professional external private and/or public sector advice and support.

Smaller enterprise owners typically blame mistakes on events in the external environment (i.e., attribution theory) rather than mistakes made by themselves. Some owners of smaller enterprises are reluctant to admit mistakes and to learn from their mistakes. To minimise their exposure to risk in the external environmental, many owners of smaller enterprises focus on business survival, independence and/or lifestyle issues rather than the pursuit of rapid business growth, which can involve higher risk exposure as well as more resources and knowledge to be invested by the entrepreneur. Consequently, many surviving small enterprises remain small. Whilst smaller enterprises are associated with numerous advantages, which can be leveraged to ensure competitive advantage, they are also generally associated with several disadvantages relating to firm structure, management and control, operations/production, resources, strategic planning, the market, and the business environment. Practitioners may intervene to reduce the problems faced by smaller enterprises to facilitate the wider benefits associated with creative, innovative, flexible and dynamic and opportunity seeking smaller private enterprises.

2.2.3   Barriers to new and small firm growth

Some new and small firms want to grow but they may be blocked by *attitudinal, resource, operational and strategic barriers* to business development (see the example of Human

Human Genome: Barriers to firm growth

Human Genome [a fictitious name] emerged from work done by a biomedical scientist who designed new protein molecules based on an industry sponsored research project. The scientist realised that he had created a set of new protein molecules that could combat a particular viral infection in humans. Patents were filed for the new invention. The scientist, however, did not know how to exploit the innovation. This novice entrepreneur with no prior business ownership experience to leverage needed to recruit a team of advisors from industry to guide his new firm formation and development decisions. Due to his reluctance to let go of some of the equity in the business idea as well his limited social capital, the scientist found it was difficult to assemble a team with the skills, capabilities and knowledge to exploit the new technology. In part, due to resource constraints, the scientist began working in his company on a part-time basis. Funding was needed for a clinical trial. The inexperienced novice entrepreneur who did not have a successful track record in business

was unable on his own to secure external finance from private venture capital firms. A business plan was subsequently written with the team of advisors from industry, and it was used to secure public funding for early stage clinical trials. The new ownership team continued to develop the technology and they discovered new and more lucrative market applications. A new chairman and chief executive officer (CEO) joined the board to help commercialise the technology. The team learned how to professionally present the potential rewards (and reduce the risks) associated with the opportunity to potential investors. Notably, they conducted additional market research, attracted high quality human capital, and acquired a valuable portfolio of patents. The earlier inability of the founding scientist entrepreneur to develop the firm's human and technological resources, therefore, had a knock-on effect in reducing the firm's ability to obtain venture capital.

Source: Vohora et al., 2004.

Genome in Entrepreneurship in action 2.2). Practitioners, therefore, focus on business development issues facing new and smaller firms.

Firms may face market resource barriers to business development (i.e., access to information, finance, premises, training, skills, compliance costs associated with statutory and regulatory administration, etc.) (Bridge et al., 2003; DTI, 2004) (see Case 2, Fickle Rooster Productions: Turning a hobby into a profitable business). Barriers that prevent a level playing field can be termed '*market failures*'. Some entrepreneurs face market failures that can impede business formation and development (Johnson, 2007). The concept of market failure is the notion that markets cannot always be relied upon to deliver outcomes that are optimal from society's perspective. Where this is the case, there may be a role for government intervention. Intervention will seek to foster the government's enterprise policy objectives (i.e., wealth creation and job generation and reduction in social inequality). It can also be viewed as a vote-enhancing strategy to maximise a government's chances of re-election. Many governments encourage private sector organisations to address the barriers faced by new, small and growing firms. For example, property developers are encouraged to provide premises and these sponsored environments can increase the flows of resources to new and growing firms (see Chapter 11) (see the example of Evans Easyspace in Entrepreneurship in action 2.3).

Evans Easyspace: Provision of flexible premises to encourage new firm formation and growth

Evans Easyspace, the Leeds-based provider of flexible workspace for the SME market, has entered into a new deal with European bank Eurohypo AG. The agreement sees an increased facility of up to £150m, more than double that previously available, to support the plans Evans Easyspace has in place for growth over the next five years. This growth will be achieved through new build, refurbishment and acquisition of existing sites and with more than 50 business centres open or under construction across the UK, Evans Easyspace is aiming to achieve a £500m portfolio by 2012. Easyspace is 75 per cent owned by the Evans Family Trust and 25 per cent is held by the Kodak Pension Plan. Michael Evans, the Monaco-based chairman of Leeds-based Evans

Property Group, established the company. Bradley Cooper, finance director of Evans Easyspace, said, 'The Evans Easyspace winning concept of easy-in, easy-out terms has been proven across Scotland, the North and Midlands, demonstrating the continued demand for flexible accommodation tailor-made to suit small and growing businesses.' Further, he commented, 'Evans Easyspace has a clear programme in place for development over the next five years, with wide scope for nationwide expansion including the South and Ireland, which reflects our confidence in the Evans Easyspace brand.'

Source: D. Parkin, Bank Deal Boost for Development Plans, *Yorkshire Post*, 28 June 2007.

2.3 Policy to support enterprise

2.3.1 Context

In the light of the gap between the importance of entrepreneurial firms and the challenges to their ability to realise their potential, various policy initiatives have been introduced. The objectives of enterprise policy may relate to growth in employment, wealth creation, improved innovation and technology diffusion and/or competitiveness as well as reducing social exclusion and regional inequality (Storey, 1994; DTI, 2004) (see the example of A big help for small businesses: Borough businesses benefit from grant scheme in Entrepreneurship in action 2.4). Debate surrounds the pros and cons (Mole et al., 2008) associated with publicly supported intervention to alleviate market failures faced by some entrepreneurs and firms. Most governments in OECD countries provide advisory services to enable entrepreneurs to circumvent attitudinal, resource, operational and strategic barriers. For example, support for enterprise in the United Kingdom has evolved through marked phases (Bennett, 2008). Business Link Operator franchises have encouraged Regional Development Authorities (RDAs) in England and Wales to provide consultancy support. Decentralised local business support (Bennett and Robson, 2003) has been provided by local enterprise companies (LECs) in Scotland. Local support agencies are encouraged to increase market penetration (i.e., contact more entrepreneurs and smaller firms) and to report high customer (i.e., entrepreneur) satisfaction (DTI, 2004) with the impartial diagnostic advice provided to local people and local businesses (Chancellor of the Exchequer, 2004). The

Entrepreneurship in action 2.4
A big help for small businesses: Borough businesses benefit from grant scheme

Small and medium sized enterprises (i.e., firms with 250 or less employees and an annual turnover of less than 40m Euros (£27.9m as at January 2005)) in Knowsley, Merseyside [in England] can apply to the council for an Industrial Improvement Grant (IIG) for projects creating or protecting jobs. Recently there have been several examples of how this cash has been used to create jobs in the borough. These include:

Mainsway Limited
This skip hire and building waste recycling business has been operating from a site in St Helens for over 30 years. After acquiring 5.5 acres of a former land-fill site in the centre of Huyton Business Park, the company will be investing heavily to construct a purpose built facility. The council has approved an IIG to assist the company in their project and the creation of 14 new jobs.

WG Wholesale/Distribution Ltd
A new start business that has successfully applied for an IIG to help make improvements to the car park and hard-standing area of a 30,000 square feet unit in Yardley Road, Kirkby. With this assistance the company intends to create 18 new jobs.

Alphasonics Ltd
An industrial cleaning equipment manufacturer based in Caddick Road, Knowsley. The company has been awarded an IIG to help with the costs of an extension to their 6,000 square feet premises. Six new jobs will be created.

Source: Knowsley Economic Forum, *Business Know How, Jobs for Knowsley*, Spring 2005.

British government has realised the need for a balanced policy agenda (DTI, 2004), and is encouraging business formation by novice entrepreneurs with no prior business ownership experience, as well as supporting some existing entrepreneurs and the growth of some 'types' of existing firms. Although local enterprise agencies are seeking firms with employment and wealth generation potential (Mole et al., 2008), support is potentially available to all types of entrepreneurs and firms, irrespective of their growth ambitions. Government also recognises the need to provide targeted assistance for 'special groups' of entrepreneurs, such as women and people from ethnic minorities (DTI, 2004).

2.3.2 Intervention to address barriers (and market failures) to new and small firm growth

To encourage new firm formation and business development, government may provide 'hard' (i.e., financial assistance and premises) (see Chapters 6 and 12) and/or 'soft' assistance (i.e., education and training) to enable entrepreneurs and firms to address barriers (or 'market failures') (see the example of Scotland's Birth Rate Strategy to encourage new firm creation in Entrepreneurship in action 2.5). Intervention is associated with *costs* and the *benefits* of the intervention should not solely accrue to the recipients (i.e., supported entrepreneurs and firms). There is no guarantee that intervention will address a '*market failure*' and generate positive externalisers (i.e., the benefits of the intervention should outweigh the

Entrepreneurship in action 2.5
Scotland's Birth Rate Strategy (SBRS): Entrepreneurship policy delivery

Description of the approach

In 1993, Scotland Enterprise (SEn) – the government's economic development agency for lowland Scotland – launched the Scottish Business Birthrate Strategy (SBRS). It set an ambitious target to close the gap in the business birth rate between Scotland and the rest of the United Kingdom by the year 2000.

Six priorities of the SBRS

- *Unlocking the potential*: persuading more people in Scotland to set up businesses – including building enterprise into the education system, at both school and university levels.
- *Improving the environment*: making Scotland a more encouraging place for entrepreneurs by improving formal and informal support networks.
- *Improving access to finance*: helping potential entrepreneurs gain access to appropriate funding to develop their businesses – including venture capital, business angel capital, and bank finance.
- *Widening the entrepreneurial base*: unlocking the untapped potential among women, the under-35s and non-home owners – all under-represented among Scotland's entrepreneurs.
- *Increasing start-ups in key sectors*: generating more new firm start-ups in key industries, such as manufacturing, high-technology and business services.
- *Increase the number of fast-growing new starts*: increase the number of new firm start-ups that achieve substantial growth, across all sectors.

Implementation of the strategy

SEn and their partners implemented the SBRS through a variety of initiatives. These included: Personal Enterprise Shows to encourage more people to consider starting businesses; new materials to support enterprise education in schools; the Prince's Scottish Youth Business Trust; the Higher Education Entrepreneurship Programme; new business network groups; and easier access to improved advisory services and finance. SEn expenditure on the strategy was in the order of £20 million per year.

Policy re-focus after an evaluation of the SBRS

The SBRS had the following goal:

> The objective is for Scotland to at least equal the UK average of the annual number of new businesses created per head of population by the end of the 1990s. This currently implies that Scotland would achieve a 50% increase in the number of new businesses started every year by the end of this decade. This would involve the creation of an additional 25,000 businesses by the year 2000.

The SBRS failed to achieve this over-optimistic target. After a major review of the strategy, the SEn adopted a more focused approach to entrepreneurship in February 2002. The new approach had the following three main priorities:

- Encourage innovative high-growth new starts-ups, increase the number and value of high-growth start-ups, including start-ups in technology-based sectors; this involved the establishment of a new, specialist unit to support 'high growth' start-ups.
- Encourage more people to start businesses, by providing quality 'volume' business support services, mainly through the Business Gateway (including specific support and targets for more start-ups by women, the young and individuals from socially excluded groups).
- Increase the contribution of education to the development of entrepreneurship: develop enterprise among young people, school and university students, and socially excluded groups. The establishment of a High Growth Start-Up Unit (HGU) was at the core of the focus on those start-ups with the greatest potential. It focused on technology-based starts with potential to reach a £5m valuation after three years. It offered intense, high-value support, with a focus on intellectual property (IP), fundraising, leadership, routes to market. It was closely linked to external networks.

Over recent years, Scottish Enterprise has developed a suite of investment programmes (and an investment readiness programme) in conjunction with private sector providers. In addition to the high growth focus, there has been a continued effort to encourage more people to start businesses. This is a major component of the work of the revamped Business Gateway, which provides an easy point of access for existing and potential businesses.

Source: Scotland's Birth Strategy: Entrepreneurial Culture and Attitudes, Entrepreneurship Policy Delivery, Charlie Woods, www.oecd.org/dataoecd/10/54/40352714.pdf.

Website: http://www.scottish-enterprise.com/sedotcom_home/about_se/research-andpublications/business_birthrate_strategy.htm.

costs of intervention and the recipients of the intervention should not solely benefit). Intervention may lead to the problem of *'government failure'* (i.e., government funding supports entrepreneurs and firms that do not require assistance and whose behaviour is not positively affected by the assistance) (Johnson, 2007). Rather, intervention should address areas of *'market failure'* where public initiatives contribute to additionality by encouraging actions that would not otherwise have been undertaken (i.e., input additionality), contributing to better results than would otherwise have been achieved (i.e., output additionality), or changing behaviour in a desired direction (i.e., behavioural additionality) (OECD, 2006; Clarysse et al., 2009). The array of *macro and micro-level* of types of intervention are discussed elsewhere (Storey, 1994; Bridge et al., 2003; DTI, 2004; Johnson, 2007).

2.3.3 Scepticism surrounding policy towards new and small firms

There is scepticism surrounding the value of 'external assistance' to new and small firms (Bridge et al., 2003). Flynn (1993) has warned that schemes supporting new firm formation may encourage *negative selection* (i.e., non-survival attributes being transferred to the next generation of firms), and the survival of competitively weak organisations. Subsidies may bring about a major bias in the process of market selection that hampers post-entry scale adjustment of new firms. Holtz-Eakin (2000) has questioned whether smaller firms need special policy help. He asserts that public policies should be devoted to developing an environment favourable to innovation, employment and growth in the economy as a whole, rather than support to particular types of smaller firms.

2.3.4 Need to monitor intervention and issues with blanket support

Nevertheless, governments are seeking to directly and indirectly support an enterprise culture (OECD, 1998). Numerous agencies on the ground are seeking to assist the formation and development of different types of smaller firms. British government policy, for example, has moved from encouraging new firm formation and self-employment, toward supporting growing firms, and more recently to a more balanced policy agenda (DTI, 2004). An intervention needs to be monitored with regard to the following issues (Storey, 1994, 2006):

- *effectiveness* (i.e., extent to which an intervention achieved its aim);
- *efficiency* (i.e., the amount of direct output that the inputs achieved);
- *additionality* (i.e., the net benefit that accrued due to the intervention, whether intended or not, which would not otherwise have accrued);
- *deadweight* (i.e., 'what would have happened anyway without the measure' because some people would have started their own businesses even if the intervention had not been available);

- *displacement* (i.e., how much of the gain in one area is offset by losses elsewhere – a supported firm (i.e., job gain) may take the market share of a firm that has not been supported (i.e., job loss);
- *multiplier effects* (i.e., additional benefits from the indirect side-effects of intervention).

'*Blanket support*' allocated to anyone, irrespective of need, ability or previous propensity to use external publicly supported support can be questioned. To maximise returns on public policy investments, attempts have been made to '*target*' external support to '*winning firms*', that is, businesses with significant wealth creation potential (Storey, 1994; Westhead, 1995). This has been linked, for example, to a focus on policies targeted at stimulating sectors with the capacity to be world leaders to fulfil their potential, and ensuring that emerging technologies become future growth sectors (Mustar and Wright, 2009). Surprisingly, the characteristics and behaviour of '*winning entrepreneurs*' have been relatively neglected (Westhead et al., 2005a) (see Chapter 5).

2.3.5 The entrepreneur as the unit of academic and policy analysis

External support is primarily provided at the level of the individual entrepreneur during the firm start-up process. After the firm initiation hurdles have been addressed and the firm has commenced trading, external support for enterprise becomes more focused on the needs of different types of firms (i.e., high-technology, family, exporting firms, etc.) (see Chapters 6, 7 and 13). There may be a need to *focus upon the entrepreneur, rather than the firm alone*, throughout all stages of the entrepreneurial process. Certain types of entrepreneur may require *specific (and customised)* types of assistance (see Chapters 5 and 6). Analysis of the heterogeneity of entrepreneurs may contribute toward the development of *policies tailored to* different types of entrepreneur, rather than the provision of broad 'blanket' policies to all types of entrepreneur, irrespective of need or ability (Westhead et al., 2005a).

In considering the *entrepreneur as a unit of policy analysis*, it is necessary to appreciate that entrepreneurs are not a homogeneous entity with regard to their human capital profiles, motivations, resources, behaviour and performance. An increase in the number (stock) of businesses in an economy may not necessarily be a reliable indicator of the development of entrepreneurship (Westhead and Wright, 1999). This is because different types of entrepreneur own both new and established businesses. Practitioners monitoring the growth in the supply of new firms need to be aware that habitual (i.e., serial and portfolio) entrepreneurs with business ownership experience own a sizeable proportion of new firms. Studies that judge the scale of entrepreneurship in terms of the number of new firms, but ignore the scale of serial and portfolio entrepreneur activity may overestimate the gross number of entrepreneurs, and underestimate the contribution made by particular 'types' of entrepreneur (Westhead and Wright, 1998a) (see Chapter 5).

2.4 Looking forward

This chapter has highlighted the economic and non-economic contributions associated with encouraging new firm formation and business development. Barriers to business formation and development were summarised, and a case for practitioner intervention to address barriers (i.e., market failures) to new private firm formation and business development were summarised. The need to focus on the entrepreneur and the firm as units of analysis in academic and policy studies was raised. In Chapter 3, we discuss 'what entrepreneurs do' with regard to the entrepreneurial process. With reference to economic approaches we discuss entrepreneurial inputs, processes and events. The following five themes are highlighted with regard to the views of leading economists: imagination and creativity: new ideas, products and businesses (Theme 1), new combinations, radical innovation, new industries and economic development (Theme 2); opportunity identification, evaluation and pursuit: demand, supply and arbitrage (Theme 3); functions and judgements of entrepreneurs (Theme 4); and entrepreneurial business: knowledge management, incremental innovation, and resource assemblage and leverage to exploit an opportunity (Theme 5).

Discussion questions

1 The promotion of entrepreneurship is seen as a means of combating unemployment and poverty (Storey, 1994). Critically evaluate the contributions of new and growing firms.

2 Why should policy-makers and practitioners intervene to support enterprise?

3 Should policy-makers and practitioners solely focus on increasing the supply of entrepreneurs and new firms?

4 What challenges would practitioners be likely to face in implementing policy support toward entrepreneurs rather than firms?

5 Should practitioners provide support to under-represented (and/or special) groups?

6 Should practitioners provide 'blanket support' to all entrepreneurs and firms?

7 Should practitioners 'target' support to 'winners'?

Recommended further reading

Clarysse, B., Wright, M. and Mustar, P. (2009). Behavioural Additionality of R&D Subsidies: A Learning Perspective, *Research Policy*, 38 (10): 1517–1533.

Department of Trade and Industry (DTI). (2004). *A Government Action Plan for Small Business. Making the UK the Best Place in the World to Start and Grow a Business: The Evidence Base.* London: DTI, Small Business Service.

Holtz-Eakin, D. (2000). Public Policy Toward Entrepreneurship. *Small Business Economics*, 15 (4): 283–291.

Johnson, P. (2007). *The Economics of Small Firms.* London: Routledge.

Storey, D. J. (1994). *Understanding the Small Business Sector.* London: Thomson Learning.

Chapter 3

Theoretical insights I: Economic approaches

Contents

Learning objectives

- Highlight that economists have explored the knowledge, judgements, actions and functions of entrepreneurs in relation to their firms with reference to the *economic system*.

- *Understand entrepreneurial processes* with reference to opportunity *creation*, *discovery* and *exploitation*.

- Analyse the following *five themes* with reference to the ideas presented by 'classic' scholars: imagination and creativity: new ideas, products and businesses (Theme 1); new combinations, radical innovation, new industries and economic development (Theme 2); opportunity identification, evaluation and pursuit: demand, supply and arbitrage (Theme 3); functions and judgements of entrepreneurs (Theme 4); and entrepreneurial business relating to knowledge management, incremental innovation, and resource assemblage and leverage to exploit an opportunity (Theme 5).

- Discuss the views of *'classic' scholars* (i.e., Shackle, Schumpeter, Cantillon, Say, Kirzner, Shane and Venkataraman, Knight, Leibenstein, Casson, Marshall, Penrose, and Porter).

- Discuss views relating to Porter's competitive strategy theory, the resource-based view (RBV) of the firm and the emerging strategic entrepreneurship perspective.

3.1 Introduction: Approaches to explore entrepreneurs and the entrepreneurial process

Entrepreneurship has been studied from a variety of disciplines (MacMillan and Katz, 1992). Numerous theories have been developed to explain the activities of entrepreneurs and the organisations they own (Bygrave and Hofer, 1991; Cuevas, 1994; Shane, 2002; Busenitz et al., 2003). The following approaches have been used to explore the behaviour and contributions of entrepreneurs and their firms:

- Economic approaches;
- Personality/traits approaches;
- Psychodynamic approaches;
- Social-psychological approaches;

● Cognitive approaches; and
● Sociological approaches.

Economic approaches are discussed in this chapter, whilst other approaches are discussed in the following chapter. Each approach suggests that several factors are associated with entrepreneurial processes within *de novo*, established, purchased and inherited ventures.

3.2   The relative neglect of entrepreneurship by economists

Baumol (1968: 65–66) suggested that: 'the entrepreneurial function is a vital component in the process of economic growth and by ignoring the entrepreneur we are prevented from accounting fully for a very substantial proportion of our historic growth.' Similarly, Casson (1982: 9) asserted that:

> It may be said quite categorically that at the present there is no established economic theory of the entrepreneur. The subject area has been surrendered by economists to sociologists, psychologists and political scientists. Indeed, almost all the social sciences have a theory of the entrepreneur, except economics.

The main reason for the neglect of entrepreneurship by economists relates to a focus on the 'neo-classical model' (Binks, 2000). Underpinning this approach are the notions of equilibrium and equilibria (Loasby, 1991). This equilibrium can be defined as a condition where provision of a product will remain unchanged unless some external events disturb the supply and/or demand for the product. Unless there is a change in the demand for a product or the conditions for supplying a product, the price and output will remain unchanged and the market for that product will be in equilibrium. When considering firm behaviour it is assumed, under the neo-classical model, that the single overriding objective of firms is profit maximisation. It is assumed that those who own and run firms are fully aware of the cost implications of taking on more staff and producing higher levels of output, as well as being certain of the impact upon their revenues that increased sales will create.

By developing this model and making these assumptions in terms of the awareness and level of information available to the firm, changes in price and output are not a matter of judgement, they are produced automatically in the model (Casson, 1982). This model renders entrepreneurship (i.e., spotting a gap in the market, etc.) irrelevant, because at any one time, and in any situation, there will only be one logical way to proceed, given the assumption that the sole objective is profit maximisation as far as the firm is concerned (Storey, 1982). There is no need to study or explain entrepreneurship in this model because it does not feature in the system.

Economists have made a valuable contribution to the study of the functions and judgements of entrepreneurs in relation to the firms they own and/or manage. Notably, economists focusing upon the role of the firm in the economic system have considered the actions of entrepreneurs. The entrepreneur is viewed as a means of explaining why the economic system functions properly. Entrepreneurial behaviour relates to action. Notably, an entrepreneur's knowledge and sound judgement is exercised to take actions (McMullen and Shepherd, 2006). Within this literature, a distinction between dynamic and static approaches to entrepreneurship has been made (Hébert and Link, 1988, 2006). The dynamic approaches explore the entrepreneurial function in relation to: a decision-maker; an organiser and co-ordinator of economic resources; a risk taker; an arbitrator; an allocator

Table 3.1 Approaches and themes related to entrepreneurship highlighted by economists

Approach/Theme	Author(s)
Manager	Say, Marshall, Keynes and Penrose
Decision-maker	Cantillon, Marshall, and Shackle
Entrepreneur as a possessor of special knowledge	Marshall and Kirzner
Entrepreneur as an outsider	Weber and Kets de Vries
Organiser and co-ordinator of resources	Say and Schumpeter
Assumes risk associated with uncertainty	Cantillon, Knight and Shackle
Arbitrageur	Cantillon and Kirzner
Allocator of resources among alternative uses	Cantillon, Say and Kirzner
Entrepreneur as a destroyer of equilibrium	Schumpeter
Entrepreneur as a restorer of equilibrium	Kirzner
Supplies financial capital	Pigou and Mises
Role of imagination and decision-making is a creative process	Shackle
Entrepreneur as a visionary	Schumpeter
Innovator	Schumpeter
Industrial leader	Say, Marshall and Schumpeter
Owner of an enterprise	Pigou and Hawley
Employer of factors of production	Keynes
Contractor	Bentham

Source: Derived from Hébert and Link (1988).

of economic resources; an innovator; an industrial leader; and a contractor. In contrast, the static conceptualisations relate to: management; supplying financial capital ownership of an enterprise; and employment of factors of production. Approaches and themes related to entrepreneurship highlighted by economists are summarised in Table 3.1.

3.3 Entrepreneurial inputs, processes and events: Themes explored by economists

Economic concepts can be used to explore entrepreneurship (Parker, 2004, 2006) as an *input* added to land, labour and capital to extend the theory of production, and to complete the explanation of four kinds of income (i.e., profit, rent, wages and interest) (Casson, 1982). Entrepreneurial events may relate to the introduction of *novelty* such as new work practices, innovation, new products/services, and new venture creation. Economists have explored the *entrepreneurial processes* to *create an opportunity* (i.e., imagination, creativity, radical or incremental innovation to create disequilibrium), *discover* an opportunity (i.e., 'alertness' and information search to address disequilibrium), and to *exploit* an opportunity in a firm (i.e., entrepreneurs drew upon skills, experience and knowledge to deal with uncertainty; to assume risk and to make (calculated risk-taking) judgements; and to assemble and manage appropriate resources). The following five themes have been explored:

- Imagination and creativity – new ideas, products and businesses (Theme 1).
- New combinations, radical innovation, new industries and economic development (Theme 2).
- Opportunity identification, evaluation and pursuit – demand, supply and arbitrage (Theme 3).

- Functions and judgements of entrepreneurs (Theme 4).
- Entrepreneurial business – knowledge management, incremental innovation, and resource assemblage and leverage to exploit an opportunity (Theme 5).

Each theme is discussed, in turn, in the following sections with reference to views of classic authors.

3.4 Theme 1: Imagination and creativity – New ideas, products and businesses

Shackle (1979) used the term *'the enterpriser'* rather than entrepreneur. The 'enterpriser' deals with uncertainty, makes skilled judgements, assembles and allocates scarce resources, and provides novel products. Shackle (1979) presented a process-based approach that provides insights into the sequential nature of the decision-making process. He stressed that any process of business planning cannot be directed at actual knowledge of what is to come, but merely towards our imagination of how events are likely to unfold (Batstone and Pheby, 1996: 47).

Shackle (1966) regarded the whole of the business person's business as decision-making and risk bearing under conditions of uncertainty. He rejected the equilibrium paradigm and adopted an anti-determinist stance. Shackle asserted that individuals are unique in their experiences. He stressed the importance of *creativity and spontaneity*, which limit the scope of economic rationality, since human actions cannot be completely explained in terms of past events and fixed preferences (see Case 3, The Recording Room: Ben Wallace's musical ventures). Shackle used the term 'unknowledge' to characterise the effect of uncertainties. In the absence of knowledge, which might be relevant to the decision-making process, decision-making should be understood as 'the focal, creative, psychic event where knowledge, thought, feeling and imagination are fused into action' (Shackle, 1962: 105).

3.5 Theme 2: New combinations, radical innovation, new industries and economic development

3.5.1 Radical innovation

The German-Austrian tradition associated with the work of Schumpeter (1934, 1943) is concerned with instability and economic development (Cheah, 1990). Schumpeter suggests that entrepreneurs are the creators and catalysts of dynamic change. An entrepreneur is viewed as a special person who has the ability to bring about extraordinary events. Within this tradition, an entrepreneur is an innovator and brings about change through the introduction of a new technological process or product. Entrepreneurs are associated with a dream and a vision. They exhibit the impulse to fight; to prove oneself superior to others; to succeed not for the fruits of success, but for the sake of success itself. Further, they exhibit a joy in creating and getting things done. Schumpeterian innovation is distinguished from routine management involved in running a business, and can be performed by both salaried managers and business owners (Johnson, 1986). The same people may exercise both innovative and non-innovative functions. They are, however, only entrepreneurs while undertaking the former. Risk-taking is the function not of the entrepreneur but of those who give credit. Schumpeter explicitly suggests that innovation or novelty is a prerequisite for genuine entrepreneurship (see Case 4, Portable Patient Lifts, LLC: Patent and start-up issues). He made a distinction between gradual and discrete innovation:

- Gradual change involves merely a set of small adjustments that lead to improvements in design, and does not constitute economic development.
- Discrete changes occur when individuals innovate new combinations of productive resources to an end that is discretely different from any preceding activities.

Schumpeterian innovations are discrete and substantial. They are linked to the following five sources of significant change (i.e., *new combinations*):

1 the introduction of a new good (or an improvement in the quality of an existing good);
2 the opening of a new market, in particular, an export market in a new territory;
3 the conquest of a new source of supply of raw materials or half-manufactured goods;
4 new method of production as yet unproven; and
5 the creation of a new type of industrial organisation, particularly, the formation of a trust or some other type of monopoly.

The overriding motive for entrepreneurial activity is the profit that may result from being the first to innovate a particular process or product. Schumpeter sees these profits as being temporary. He argues, in the absence of monopoly protection, others will see the profits available in the new innovation and will emulate the original innovation, providing competition, and a gradual erosion of the monopoly profits available. Schumpeter suggested that the entrepreneur was a temporary phenomenon. He predicted the demise of the function of the entrepreneur. Teams of workers and scientists operating in large organisations would carry out technological advance and change. The latter teams have the resources and pool of skills to translate the vision into a feasible plan of action.

3.5.2 'Creative destruction'

Schumpeter raised the issue of *'creative destruction'*. In a stable economic environment, the entrepreneur estimates the advantage (i.e., profit) of a new combination (i.e., a new product/process). Notably, the original new venture's products associated with radical innovation will create new wealth and jobs. Other individuals cannot anticipate a Schumpeter type entrepreneur's vision. The launch of the new venture creates new possibilities which threaten the continued viability of many existing products/processes. Consequently, an innovative new firm's activity may destroy the traditional markets serviced by existing firms. This kind of entrepreneurship destroys as it creates and creates as it destroys (i.e., *a cycle of 'creative destruction'*).

The success of the initial new venture may also encourage imitators, and increased uncertainty and competition may lead to the closure of some established and new entrants. This process of erosion will continue until the level of profitability in the new industry or process is comparable to the rates of return in established activities. At this point, the activity is no longer entrepreneurial but part of the traditional circular flow. The Darwinian flavour of Schumpeter's work (Casson, 1990) has been linked to an evolutionary approach to the study of invention and innovation. 'Lesser entrepreneurs' (i.e., Kirzner type opportunist entrepreneurs),

Entrepreneurship in action 3.1
James Dyson: Schumpeterian entrepreneur

James Dyson created a new type of vacuum cleaner after realising that the suction in his traditional vacuum cleaner fell substantially when its cloth bag became filled up with particles. When James Dyson first came up with the idea of the bagless vacuum cleaner no one was interested. Using his Georgian house near Bath in England as security, he took out a loan and hawked his idea around manufacturers such as Black and Decker, Electrolux, Hoover and Phillips. Dyson reflected, 'Hoover would only see me if I signed an unfair confidentiality agreement.' Further, Dyson commented, 'Electrolux turned it down twice after two good looks at it. They must make millions a year selling bags.' In the end, Dyson borrowed £600,000 to set up his own company. After producing 5,000 prototypes he started producing the revolutionary cleaners himself. Although he patented the idea in June 1980, the product was not launched until 1993. Dyson reflected, 'I struggled over many years to develop this idea . . . It was not

something that happened in a flash.' James Dyson's invention, however, turned the industry on its head. By 2000, the Dyson empire was worth around £530m and workers were assembling about 10,000 cleaners every day. By 2010, 40 per cent of the British vacuum cleaner market sales were provided by Dyson, and this success turned James Dyson into a billionaire. In response, Hoover developed its own bagless cleaner which operates using centrifugal force. Hoover were taken to court by Dyson who claimed that the Hoover Triple Vortex 'clearly' used the same cyclonic technology he had patented. The court sided with Dyson.

Source: This is an edited version of A. Buncombe and C. Arthur. James Dyson Spent Years Fighting Hoover. Now he Intends to Clean Up. *The Independent*. 4 October 2000.

Two years later, Dyson accepted damages of £4m from Hoover. Dyson has become a habitual entrepreneur, generating further technological advances and entry into additional new markets (for discussion of habitual entrepreneurs see Chapter 5).

however, may introduce a range of new activities, complementary to the original venture. Utilising the radical technology in new markets and adapting the radical technology, 'lesser entrepreneurs' may generate additional wealth creation and job generation not originally envisaged by the Schumpeterian type entrepreneurs that generated the radical innovation (see the example of James Dyson in Entrepreneurship in action 3.1).

3.5.3 Rapid environmental change

The key to Schumpeter's system is that entrepreneurs are able to formulate their actions with confidence only when there is a stable, well-co-ordinated pattern of economic activities to generate the data needed to evaluate their vision and calculate profit. The problem arises when the entrepreneur's own innovation destroys that pattern. The latter action removes the basis for the entrepreneurs' calculations (Loasby, 1991). Schumpeter's theory thus serves as a warning that zero predictability is as destructive of enterprise as total predictability.

Conditions have changed dramatically since Schumpeter proposed his theory. The significant changes to which he refers now seem to occur in an almost continuous flow, rather than in waves as he described. Global markets and highly sophisticated communications systems now provide a richer environment for innovation. Innovations and breakthroughs in one discipline may quickly be incorporated into changes in an entirely unrelated area. Potential for entrepreneurial change is greater because of progress made in the utilisation of Information and Communication Technology (ICT). Despite weaknesses in the theory when examined in the modern context, Schumpeter has provided a useful concept of entrepreneurship as operating as a *catalyst* to create *economic development*.

3.6 Theme 3: Opportunity identification, evaluation and pursuit – Demand, supply and arbitrage

3.6.1 Bearing uncertainty and arbitrage

In early sixteenth century France, men engaged in leading military expeditions were referred to as entrepreneurs. The French government in the early eighteenth century applied the term to road, harbour and fortification contractors (Johnson, 1986).

Cantillon (1755) suggests that entrepreneurs react to *profit opportunities*, *bear uncertainty* and continuously serve to *bring about a (tentative) balance between supplies and demands* in specific markets. Entrepreneurs undertake activities and the entrepreneur is the pivotal figure who operates within a set of economic markets. Cantillon used the term entrepreneur to refer to individuals who pursue the *profits of arbitrage* (i.e., the process whereby the prices of the same product in different markets are equated in the absence of transport costs) under conditions of *uncertainty* (Casson, 1990). He suggests that the entrepreneur is a bearer of uncertainty who might or might not own capital. The actions taken by an entrepreneur are associated with a profit (or loss). The entrepreneur's income is residual, received after all contractual payments have been met. Cantillon argued that the entrepreneur is a *speculative middleman*, who buys in order to resell, but does not know with any certainty the market conditions that will prevail at a later point in time. His analysis identifies those who live on uncertain incomes as the entrepreneurs whilst those who live on fixed incomes are either literally or metaphorically their employees (Casson, 1990). Cantillon presents a broad definition that suggests that anyone who runs a business can be regarded as an entrepreneur. In contrast to Schumpeter, Cantillon's entrepreneur is an 'administrator' rather than an 'innovator'.

3.6.2 Co-ordinating factors of production

Say (1821) claimed that entrepreneurs *combine and co-ordinate the factors of production* to accommodate the unexpected and overcome problems. His law suggests that *supply can create its own demand*. This perspective focuses on *supply-side issues* (i.e., administration and organisation of resources and the characteristics of entrepreneurs).

Say emphasises the multiplicity of roles that the entrepreneur must adopt in order to succeed. Entrepreneurs are not concerned simply with the production process or the product market. They are required to confront markets for raw materials, premises, labour, plant, equipment, and finance. In addition, they must be versed in the relevant legislation and the tax regime. From this viewpoint, the calculation of arbitrage potential is now more complicated and the entrepreneur needs to rely upon *judgement*. A high degree of skill and competence is a prerequisite for successful entrepreneurship. Say, therefore, suggests the entrepreneur has to deal with risk and exhibits the essential *co-ordination function* (Johnson, 1986).

3.6.3 'Alertness' to opportunity identification

Hayek (1949) asserted that the absence of entrepreneurs in neo-classical economic theory was associated with the assumption of market equilibrium. Whilst acknowledging the

Entrepreneurship in action 3.2
Sir Stelios Haji-Ioannou: A Kirznerian entrepreneur

Commercial aviation was once solely the preserve of the wealthy but various attempts have been made to make it accessible to the masses. Inspired by the no frills business model of the United States carrier Southwest Airlines, Stelios Haji-Ioannou [introduced in Chapter 1] identified an opportunity to serve the business and leisure travel needs in Europe by developing a great value, low-cost airline. EasyJet seeks to keep operating costs down. A cost-cutting strategy has been followed by easyJet associated with using a young fleet of aircraft, high aircraft utilisation, quick turnaround times, extra charges for food, baggage and priority booking. In part to attract more business passengers, easyJet generally flies to the primary airports in the cities that it serves.

Source: http://en.wikipedia.org/wiki/Stelios_Haji-Ioannou; http://corporate.easyjet.com/en/about-easyjet.aspx.

importance of the process of adjustment to equilibrium, he recognised that the *conditions* under which this tendency is supposed to exist, and the nature of the *process* by which individual knowledge is changed, were poorly understood.

The modern Austrian tradition in economics, however, regards static market equilibrium models as being irrelevant in explaining behaviour because there are constant shifts in, and movements along, the demand and supply functions. Entrepreneurs are viewed as those individuals who are most *'alert'* to messages from the economy which signal some failure of co-ordination, and which therefore indicate potential gains from trade. The entrepreneur attempts to secure these gains by simple arbitrage, which can generate further messages that can be *'noticed'* by entrepreneurs (Loasby, 1991) (see Case 5, Original Voddy Company Limited).

Kirzner's (1973) entrepreneur is very different from Schumpeter's. According to Kirzner, the prospect of monopoly profits motivates individuals to search for information, which can be used to *'spot'* business opportunities (Casson, 1990). By exploiting a gap in the market, an entrepreneur's firm can move an industry towards equilibrium. However, Kirzner does not explain where change comes from in an economy (i.e., disequilibrium – the gap in the market) (see the example of Sir Stelios Haji-Ioannou in Entrepreneurship in action 3.2).

3.6.4 Experience and knowledge

Kirzner noted that some entrepreneurs accumulate *experience and knowledge*. The possession of additional knowledge by individuals provides opportunities for creative discovery. Entrepreneurs can collect and join information together, which can lead to the *'developmental approach'* to opportunity identification. An entrepreneur recognises an (obvious) opportunity for profitable trade, and has the ability based on their knowledge to exploit the opportunity. Further, an entrepreneur is able to identify suppliers and customers and acts as an *intermediary* (i.e., middleman/market trader) taking advantage of opportunities to trade. The identification and pursuit of an opportunity can also lead to the collection and analysis of additional data and business opportunities (i.e., *shadow options*) (McGrath, 1999). Individuals who have the ability to collect and process information may record a spiral of opportunity identification and exploitation.

In contrast to Schumpeter, Kirzner's theory suggests anyone can be an entrepreneur if there are no barriers to perception. A competitive threat can emerge from anywhere and outsiders may be quicker to recognise an opportunity. Opportunities occur at every level of the economy and a successfully co-ordinated economy needs many entrepreneurs. Kirzner's *'allocator' entrepreneurs* can be seen as individuals that are *reactive* rather than proactive to economic development. Kirzner's entrepreneurs enable the process of economic development, but they do not cause it. The views of Kirzner are developed within Shane and Venkataraman's (2000) opportunity identification and exploitation approach discussed in the next section.

3.6.5 Individuals, firms and information processing

The emerging opportunity-based conceptualisations of entrepreneurship have focused on the role of *knowledge* and the *acquisition and processing of information* by the entrepreneur (Fiet, 1996). Shane and Venkataraman (2000: 218) argue that entrepreneurship:

> . . . involves the study of *sources* of opportunities; the *processes* of discovery, evaluation and exploitation of opportunities; and the set of *individuals* who discover, evaluate and exploit them . . . scholars of organizations are fundamentally concerned with three research questions about entrepreneurship; (1) why, when and how opportunities for the creation of goods and services come into existence; (2) why, when and how some people and not others discover and exploit these opportunities; and (3) why, when and how are different modes of action used to exploit entrepreneurial opportunities.

The logic of this approach is drawn from theoretical perspectives in economics (Schumpeter, 1934; Hayek, 1945; Baumol, 1968; Casson, 1982; Kirzner, 1997), and in language taken from ecological views that celebrate the dynamic processes of firm formation. Although Shane and Venkataraman (2000) do not appear to offer a specification of the *level of analysis* (Gartner, 2001), they suggest that entrepreneurship *research should not focus* on:

> the relative performance of individuals or firms in the context of small or new business (217) (for dissenting views see Davidsson and Wiklund (2001) and Gartner (2001: 30)).

Notably, they differ from other frameworks in their focus on the existence, discovery, and exploitation of opportunities; their examination of the influence of individuals and opportunities, rather than environmental antecedents and consequences; and their consideration of a broader framework than firm creation.

Shane and Venkataraman's (2000) definition of entrepreneurship is questioned by Gartner who proposes an alternative definition (Gartner, 2001: 30–31):

> . . . entrepreneurship is about 'organizing', and this phenomenon has a greater likelihood of being understood through the study of firm creation . . . I approach entrepreneurship from a psychological perspective (Weick, 1979, 1995), and I am willing to celebrate studies of firm creation from other disciplinary perspectives (Gartner and Gatewood, 1992), as well. I agree with Shane and Venkataraman (2000) that their focus on individuals and opportunities is complementary to the study of firm creation (p. 219). What seems less complementary to both of these views is the study of new, small, and growing firm.

Low and MacMillan (1988) indicate that entrepreneurship is a process that occurs over time. Previous studies have focused upon the start-up process (Gartner, 1985). Gartner (2001) concluded that there appears to be no direct way to ascertain how Shane and Venkataraman (2000) consider *time frame* in the context of their theoretical framework.

3.7 Theme 4: Functions and judgements of entrepreneurs

3.7.1 Skill in assessing risk and uncertainty

The Chicago tradition is associated with the work of Knight (1921, 1942) who suggests entrepreneurs are responsible for their own actions, and can make judgements. Knight argues that *uncertainty-bearing* is the true entrepreneurial function. Knight (1921: 233) made a distinction between *risk and uncertainty* as follows:

> . . . in the former the distribution of the outcome in a group of instances is known (either through calculation *a priori* or from statistics of past experience), while in the case of uncertainty this is not true, the reason being in general that it is impossible to form a group of instances, because the situation dealt with is in a high degree unique.

According to Knight, entrepreneurs may be prepared to take risks in an uncertain world. Moreover, an entrepreneur should be regarded as a *'calculated risk taker'*. An entrepreneur is prepared to accept the remaining risk that cannot be transferred through insurance. The reward to an entrepreneur for bearing uncertainty is profit. Knight suggests that entrepreneurs have different *skills* from other individuals. Based on these *skills and competencies*, entrepreneurs can make more informed judgements about business opportunities and can more successfully co-ordinate scarce resources. Knight appreciates that entrepreneurs require *command over resources* (see the views of Say (1821) in Section 3.6.2) if they are to back their judgements.

Sarasvathy (2008) has focused upon a further dimension of Knightian uncertainty, which is when some entrepreneurs are dealing with a future that is unknown and unknowable. Her approach, which she terms *effectuation*, relates to entrepreneurs controlling and shaping the future rather than attempting to predict it. Effectuation represents the inverse of causation approaches to the analysis and estimation of the future. Sarasvathy highlights the following six elements (or assumptions) relating to effectuation. First, *effectuators* begin with a set of given means rather than a predetermined goal. Second, effectuators follow the *principle of affordable loss*, and they focus on what they can afford to lose, rather than try to predict an ideal return from each project. Third, effectuators view customers as partners. Effectuators need to quickly sell directly to customers because they can learn from customers. Fourth, effectuators prefer to create the initial target market segment prior to analysing the competitors. Fifth, effectuators develop, shape and define the market themselves rather than find a market. Sixth, effectuators focus on unanticipated ends rather than preselected goals. This enables effectuators to turn the unexpected into valuable opportunities, or to turn 'lemons into lemonade'.

3.7.2 Reducing inefficiency in resource use

Leibenstein (1966, 1978) combines elements of both the Marshallian (see Section 3.8.1) and Schumpeterian views (see Section 3.5) into a wider framework. He distinguished between two broad types of entrepreneurship. The first is routine entrepreneurship, which involves:

> co-ordinating and carrying on a well-established, going concern in which the parts of the production function in use . . . are well known for a firm which operates in well-established and clearly defined markets (1978: 401).

The second is new type (or N type) entrepreneurship, which is closest to the Schumpeterian concept, and occurs where it is necessary to create (or carry on) an enterprise where not all the markets are well established, or clearly defined, and/or in which the relevant parts of the production function are not clearly known. With reference to both types, entrepreneurship is concerned with *reducing inefficiency by improving co-ordination and providing motivation* (Johnson, 1986).

Leibenstein introduced *X-efficiency* theory to illustrate the role of the entrepreneur (Casson, 1982). X-efficiency is the degree of inefficiency in the use of resources within the firm. He measured the extent to which the firm fails to realise its own productive potential. Two causes are identified:

1 *Cause 1:* X-efficiency arises because the firm's resources are used in the wrong way; and/or
2 *Cause 2:* X-efficiency arises because the firm's resources are wasted (i.e., they are not used at all).

Leibenstein recognised that in the 'real world' information is costly and there are 'opportunity costs' in terms of time and effort. He suggested that:

- entrepreneurs exhibit rational behaviour in response to the constraints imposed by incomplete information;
- individuals identify optimal decision rules and these optimal decision rules *vary* according to the circumstances;
- X-efficiency theory assumes that there are *psychological costs* of being fully rational, and decisions made by individuals are moderated by *psychological costs*;
- Leibenstein asserted that his psychologism is incompatible with the neo-classical view of rational economic man; and
- psychological costs *limit* the extent to which individuals plan to exploit all opportunities available, and the extent to which individuals can satisfy all the constraints to which they are subject.

There are several differences between X-efficiency and neo-classical theory. If *ex ante* plans only approximate to actual constraints then *ex post* the plans will turn out differently from what was expected (i.e., disequilibrium) (Casson, 1982). The anticipation of disequilibrium leads to internally felt pressure. Different individuals have contrasting attitudes, and hence exhibit different degrees of concern and different degrees of neo-classical 'irrationality'. X-efficiency *assumes* that:

- contracts are incomplete (i.e., employment contracts do not specify jobs precisely);
- individual effort is discretionary (i.e., employee decides how hard they will work);
- the employee will make decisions in pursuit of their own interests and not those of the employer;
- effort is required in order to change the allocation of resources (i.e., change old habits) and address psychological inertia; and
- objectives of firm owners (i.e., *profit maximisation*) are not the same as the decision-makers (i.e., agents such as professional managers do not seek to maximise their own efforts).

X-efficiency theory makes the following contributions to the study of entrepreneurs and the entrepreneurial process (Casson, 1982):

- entrepreneurship is viewed as a creative response to X-efficiency;
- other people's lack of effort and consequent inefficiency of the organisations that employ them create opportunities for entrepreneurs;
- entrepreneurial activities pose a competitive threat to an inefficient organisation;
- entrepreneurial activities can put 'pressure' on agents (i.e., managers); and
- agents are encouraged to maintain an adequate degree of constraint concern.

The theory highlights the following two key entrepreneurial roles (Casson, 1982):

1 'input completion', making available inputs that improve the efficiency of existing production methods: improve the flow of information; improve the flow of venture capital; and improve the flow of management skills and professional expert assistance; and
2 'gap-filling', closely akin to the arbitrage function emphasised by Kirzner.

This perspective also considers alertness to disequilibrium. Alertness enables some individuals to intervene to link 'nodes' down 'pathways'. Intervention will be in the markets that are poorly defined and poorly marked from the viewpoint of other actors.

X-efficiency theory is associated with several drawbacks (Casson, 1982). This broad framework can accommodate nearly anything. Without further assumptions it can say very little about *entrepreneur behaviour*. It also fails to present specific hypotheses relating to the behaviour of different *'types' of entrepreneurs*. Nevertheless, the concept of X-efficiency as a motive for entrepreneurship is a useful one despite considerable criticism from neo-classical economists. Leibenstein's identification of two types of entrepreneurs is useful because it highlights that there may be *more than one category of entrepreneurial event.*

3.7.3 Specialist judgements about resource co-ordination

Casson (1982) made the following distinction between *inductive* and *functional* approaches towards the *functions* of the entrepreneur:

- The *inductive approach* provides a description of the entrepreneur in terms of their societal position, contractual relations, etc.
- The *functional approach* specifies certain functions and classifies anyone who performs those functions as an entrepreneur.

Casson highlighted that entrepreneurs have different skills from other people. He suggested that entrepreneurs exhibited the following *functions and judgements*:

- Entrepreneurs take decisions about uncertainty.
- An entrepreneur is someone who specialises in taking *judgmental decisions about the co-ordination of scarce resources.*
- An entrepreneur is a dynamic agent of change concerned with *improving the allocation of resources.*
- An entrepreneur requires *command over resources* if they are to back their judgements.
- An entrepreneur operates within a set of technological conditions.
- External environmental conditions can facilitate (or retard) the judgements and contributions made by entrepreneurs. Participation in entrepreneurship is shaped by factors such as access to resources and facilities in the local environment.
- By making difficult judgemental decisions entrepreneurs are able to enjoy the reward of profit (for bearing uninsurable risk).

These insights, however, have been questioned as follows:

- Casson's entrepreneur is a *'specialist'* (i.e., judgemental decisions relating to the co-ordination of scarce resources) rather than a *'generalist'*.
- Does not isolate the particular economic contribution of the entrepreneur.
- Does not make a linkage with innovative activity or discrete changes from the status quo (i.e., Schumpeter).
- Fails to discuss how social context (see Section 4.2.1) can shape an individual's propensity to become an entrepreneur, or a successful entrepreneur.
- Different 'types' of entrepreneurs (see Section 4.2.3) are not discussed.

3.8 Theme 5: Entrepreneurial business – Knowledge management, incremental innovation, and resource assemblage and leverage to exploit an opportunity

3.8.1 Knowledge and management

For Marshall (1890, 1920), the principal requirement of any method of *co-ordinating activities* was that it should *promote economic development* (Loasby, 1991). After appreciating the contribution of land, labour and capital, Marshall illustrated *how firms should be organised and how 'businessmen' should accumulate and manage (knowledge) resources*. The functions of entrepreneurs in relation to their 'entrepreneurial businesses' are as follows:

- The entrepreneur is central to the *promotion of economic progress*.
- *Knowledge* accumulation, co-ordination and leverage by an entrepreneur within an 'entrepreneurial business' leads to novelty and discontinuity, and knowledge is the *'most powerful engine of production'*.
- Knowledge can be leveraged to introduce *'incremental innovation'* (i.e., less resistance to incremental change such as application or extensions of established routines) rather than radical innovation.
- 'Entrepreneurial businesses' leverage knowledge to ensure that a *cycle of incremental change and innovation* will be associated with positive outcomes relating to increased response to customer needs; broader product/service range; firms that are more efficient and productive; firms will be able to offer reduced priced products/services; and firms will report sales growth and/or enhanced firm survival because knowledge-based and 'learning' firms constantly invest in knowledge and people to proactively or reactively *adapt* to changing technological, market and regulatory external environmental conditions.
- The entrepreneur is a natural leader.
- The *managerial (or management) function* is an essential feature of the 'entrepreneurial business'.
- *Management is a resource and a source of competitive advantage* for the firm.
- Firms have to *'learn'* and apply new knowledge to ensure a competitive advantage.

Marshall suggested a *connection between knowledge and organisational forms*, with three forms being distinguishable (Casson, 1982). First, Marshall's 'businessmen' are expected to use their knowledge to experiment with both processes and products, both in response to demand and in anticipation of it. They are expected to build up an organisation – which takes time – that will combine specialisation and integration, and to encourage initiative in their 'subordinates'. Also they make use of their own abilities and experience in their own particular circumstances, thus generating an appropriate equivalent of Darwinian variation (i.e., adapting firms are more likely to survive). Second, where similar businesses are collected together in an industrial district, this district serves as an *invisible college, in which ideas are exchanged and developed* (see Section 6.2). Third, firms are linked to suppliers and customers in a network of information and ideas.

Marshall focused upon the managerial (or management) function as the essential feature of entrepreneurial activity (Johnson, 1986). He highlighted that the *'vigour of management'* can raise firm efficiency. However, older 'businessmen' with declining vigour may be associated with firms reporting declining competitiveness.

Marshall highlighted that firm efficiency can change over time. Older firms may become less efficient if they allow their costs to drift upward. Two forces can offset the ageing process (Johnson, 1986). First, older management has more experience, and business people that have learnt from their experiences may compensate for declining vigour of management. Learning effects, however, only provide temporary compensatory benefits. Second, the ownership of a firm may be transferred into the hands of new owners who were not the original founders. With regard to the advent of joint stock companies, Marshall (1920) acknowledged that these companies often stagnate, but do not readily die.

Marshall's attempt to integrate his analysis into a static theory of income distribution has been questioned (Loasby, 1991), particularly the reduction of entrepreneurship to a fourth factor of production (Casson, 1982). The distinguishing characteristics of entrepreneurship might be neglected by viewing entrepreneurship as a homogeneous factor service traded in a competitive market. Marshall's viewpoint fails to appreciate that the 'entrepreneurial business' may not solely involve a single owner-manager. The skills, experience and knowledge of all entrepreneurial ownership team members may be leveraged to ensure firm development. Notably, for the business to grow the original founder of the firm may have to go and be replaced with new entrepreneurial ownership team members.

3.8.2 Power of external environmental conditions

3.8.2.1 *Demand and supply factors*

Bain's (1956) industrial organisation theory suggests that the owners and managers of firms are unable to influence industry conditions (i.e., *demand-side factors*), or the performance of their firms. Population ecology theorists assert the *deterministic power of external environmental conditions* on firm survival (Hannan and Carroll, 1992). This macro-level perspective suggests that the processes of carrying capacity (i.e., availability of resources), density (i.e., number of firms competing for scarce resources), legitimation (i.e., legitimacy and status of the entrepreneur(s) and firm), and competition play a determining role in the size of organisational populations. Two conflicting theoretical traditions have, however, questioned the assumed dominant power of external environmental conditions. Both the resource-based view (RBV) of the firm (Penrose, 1959; Barney, 1991, 2001) and Porter's framework of competitive advantage (1991) suggest that *actions* made by a firm (i.e., *supply-side factors*) can be a source of sustainable competitive advantage (see Section 3.8.3).

3.8.2.2 *Resources*

The RBV of the firm proposed by Penrose (1959) is now increasingly used to explore the behaviour of entrepreneurs, and their firms. She identified several *resources that need to be accumulated and leveraged* by entrepreneurs that can ensure firm survival and profitability. Resources relate to an entrepreneur's human capital resources as well as firm resources relating to tacit knowledge, technological resources (i.e., imagination, creativity, innovativeness, etc.), finance, reputation and goodwill, organisational routines and skills. Penrose presented a *dynamic theory* of the firm, which explains how the *creation and use of information* governs the growth of the firm through a feedback mechanism (Casson, 1982).

Penrose focuses upon the '*firm*' rather than the '*entrepreneur*' as the unit of analysis (Kor and Mahoney, 2000). The *firm is viewed as a pool of resources*, the utilisation of which is organised in an administrative framework (Penrose, 1959). The content of the pool changes over time due to the firm's activities (i.e., external search, internal search, and people within the firm learning by doing). The firm's productive opportunity relates to all the opportunities that the firm's 'managers' see and take advantage of (Penrose, 1959). Perception of opportunities is shaped by the firm's administrative framework. Each firm's opportunities depend on a combination of:

- firm-specific advantages; and/or
- perception of ways in which they can be profitably used.

Penrose suggested that entrepreneurs need to accumulate appropriate resources, and they need to utilise them efficiently, to ensure firm development. She viewed the firm as a '*knowledge community*'. Notably, all competitive advantage depends on the development and use of knowledge. The '*filter of knowledge*' shapes how the firm's resources and capabilities can be best employed to enhance the firm's competitive advantage.

A major influence on the firm's capacity to grow is the volume of managerial resources, which are uncommitted to current projects (Casson, 1982). These managerial resources are available for investigating new avenues of growth. Undertaking new projects expands the demand or routine managerial services and leads to an expansion of the management team. Expansion is 'lumpy', so unused managerial resources may persist, leading to further growth in the future. The limit on the rate of expansion is determined by the ability of the entrepreneur and the existing management team to accommodate changes in the organisation.

Penrose (1959) recognised that entrepreneurs are *not a homogeneous entity*. She highlighted the following qualities of entrepreneurs (Casson, 1982):

- entrepreneurs exhibit versatility, wider business horizons, the desire to experiment, the ability to acquire resources, and the ability to obtain external finance;
- informed judgement by an entrepreneur allows imagination to be exercised;
- entrepreneurs exhibit the ambition of the 'product-minded' or 'workmanship-minded', and they may be satisfied to maintain the firm at a stable size; and
- conversely, entrepreneurs may only be satisfied if the firm achieves dominance (i.e., rapid growth through a variety of methods such as acquisition or merger) in its particular industry.

Following Penrose, RBV of the firm theorists (Kor and Mahoney, 2000; Barney, 2001; Barney et al., 2001) focus upon the importance of the individual firm as opposed to industry/external environmental conditions. RBV theorists suggest that:

- firms *accumulate tangible and intangible resources (or assets)*;
- firms *accumulate and leverage resources from the internal and external environment* of the firm to secure a competitive advantage;
- firms are heterogeneous with regard to the resources they control, and these resources may not be mobile between firms;
- *idiosyncratic firm resources* (i.e., tangible and intangible assets including efficient procedures, brand name, knowledge of technology, trade contacts, etc.) are accumulated that are *valuable, rare, non-imitable and non-substitutable* (Barney, 1991);
- strategy selection is based on careful evaluation of available resources;
- strategies followed by a firm are shaped by both the opportunities imposed by the external market environment, and the constraints that result from the firm's accumulated resource base (Barney, 1991); and
- changing environmental conditions enable owners and managers of firms to make strategic decisions, but the *existing pool of resources might limit the options open*.

Alvarez and Busenitz (2001) specifically bring an entrepreneurship perspective to the RBV by highlighting how entrepreneurship involves the founder's unique awareness of opportunities, their ability to acquire resources to exploit an opportunity, and their organisational ability to recombine homogeneous inputs into heterogeneous outputs.

3.8.2.3 *Capabilities*

A distinction has been made between *resources* and *capabilities* (Amit and Schoemaker, 1993). *Resources* are assets that are either owned or controlled by a firm. *Capabilities* refer to a firm's ability to exploit and combine resources through organisational routines. Organisational development can be shaped by the leverage of a firm's existing firm-specific assets. Firms need to develop new capabilities. Consistent with the RBV, this *dynamic capabilities approach* analyses the sources and methods of wealth creation and capture by firms operating in rapidly changing environments (Madsen, 2007). Eisenhardt and Martin (2000) classify dynamic capabilities into three groups. These include those capabilities that integrate resources, those that reconfigure resources, and those that gain and release resources.

3.8.2.4 *Resources leveraged to ensure competitive advantage*

Whilst Porter views firm strategy as being industry/external environment driven, RBV theorists assert that resources are valuable and a firm's unique resources and capabilities can drive the choice of strategy pursued by a firm (Spanos and Lioukas, 2001). In contrast to Porter's perspective, and Bain's industrial organisation theory, RBV theorists believe firms obtain returns from acquiring and deploying valuable idiosyncratic resources/assets/capabilities rather than from industry structure/external environmental conditions. However, in line with Porter's view, RBV theorists appreciate the value-creating potential of strategy. RBV theorists appreciate that persistent differences in firm performance require that either the firm's product/service be differentiated, or the firm has a low cost position relative to its rivals.

Debate rages surrounding the applicability of the RBV (Kor and Mahoney, 2000; Barney, 2001). Nevertheless, the RBV has been applied to the internationalisation process undertaken by firms (McDougall et al., 1994) and entrepreneurs (Westhead et al., 2001a).

An important challenge that is receiving increasing attention is how entrepreneurs evolve their resources and capabilities over time. Important recent insights into entrepreneurial resource assemblage have drawn upon the concept of 'bricolage', which relates to making do with what is at hand. Baker and Reed (2005) studied 29 resource-constrained firms that varied considerably in their responses to similar environmental contexts. Firms that were able to create something from nothing exploited physical, social, or institutional inputs. These resources were rejected or ignored by other firms. The former firms engaging in bricolage in sparse resource environments were able to render unique services by recombining elements at hand for new purposes. We return to the issues surrounding resource and capability development over time in the context of spin-out firms from universities in Chapter 6.

3.8.3 Competitive strategy behaviour

3.8.3.1 *Competitive strategy*

Porter (1980, 1985, 1991) does not present a theory of entrepreneurship but like Penrose (1959), highlighted several crucial skills exhibited by entrepreneurs that own growing firms. Porter's (1980, 1985, 1990) competitive strategy perspective focuses on the following:

- firm rather than industry performance;
- industry is viewed as neither wholly exogenous or stable;
- the external market environment is viewed as partly exogenous, and partly subject to influences by firms' actions (Porter, 1991); and
- the role of the firm's conduct (i.e., firm activities and market positioning) in influencing performance, together with industry structure, is explicitly recognised (Spanos and Lioukas, 2001).

Porter asserted that industry structure affects the sustainability of firm performance, whereas market positioning reflects the firm's ability to establish competitive advantage over its rivals. A firm can obtain rents from its ability either to defend itself against competitive forces (i.e., *defensive effects*), or to influence them in its favour (i.e., *offensive effects*) (Porter, 1980, 1985, 1991). Porter (1991) views strategy as a configuration of activities with the firm creating a competitive advantage relative to its competitors by following a *differentiation or low cost strategy*. Strategy choice is the product of (and response to) a sophisticated understanding of industry structure. In contrast to the RBV, Porter does not view a firm's resources alone as being valuable. Porter (1991) views a *firm's assets* as being built from performing activities (i.e., strategy) over time, or acquiring them from the external environment, or both (Spanos and Lioukas, 2001). A firm's stock of resources reflects prior entrepreneurial and managerial choices, the latter related to the *choice of strategy*.

Porter (1990) has asserted that a firm can derive a competitive advantage from its local competitive conditions. He assumed that an individual firm is constrained by, or responds to, the local domestic market conditions it faces. Porter (1990, 1998) suggested that a *'competitive diamond'* of the following four mutually reinforcing factors shape competitive advantage:

1 factor conditions such as availability of finance, premises, technology, information and innovation;
2 demand conditions such as market size, agglomeration economies and industry structure;
3 related and supporting industries such as the presence of suppliers and customers as well as business service firms; and

4 business strategy, structure and competition relating to how firms are created, managed and organised.

Firms can enhance their strategic position and gain access to additional resources such as customers by exploiting their relative power position. For example, a firm may develop a capacity to innovate and adapt within and beyond the local market context.

3.8.3.2 *Resource-based view (RBV) of the firm and competitive strategy approaches exhibit complementarity*

The RBV of the firm and Porter's competitive strategy perspective can be viewed as constituting two sides of the same coin. Both perspectives suggest that a firm can achieve persistent above-normal returns, and an attractive strategic position is essential to reap these rents (Amit and Schoemaker, 1993). By drawing insights from the RBV and the competitive strategy perspective, Spanos and Lioukas (2001) assert that a balanced view of the sources of competitive advantage can be obtained (i.e., the internal and external determinants of competitive advantages). The RBV highlights that firm-specific efforts are important in developing and combining resources to achieve competitive advantage. Porter's competitive strategy perspective appreciates that industry/external environmental conditions are crucial.

The ability of entrepreneurs to establish and develop their firms is, therefore, shaped by their ability to deal with uncertainty, and to assemble, command and leverage resources from both the internal and external environments. To exploit 'created' or 'discovered' opportunities, entrepreneurs need to draw upon their skills, experience and knowledge to make judgemental decisions about how to undertake actions that promote new firm creation to exploit identified opportunities. To ensure firm survival and to generate profits for their firms, entrepreneurs guided by their skills, experience and knowledge (and existing resources within their firms) have to acquire new resources and/or develop new competencies. Entrepreneurs have to proactively or reactively make informed judgements surrounding the ownership, management and strategic orientation of their ventures.

3.8.3.3 *Strategic entrepreneurship*

Recently, a strategic entrepreneurship perspective has been presented, which focuses on the *integration of entrepreneurial (i.e., opportunity-seeking behaviour) and strategic (i.e., advantage-seeking) perspectives* in developing and taking *entrepreneurial actions* designed to create wealth (Hitt et al., 2001). Strategic entrepreneurship, grounded in the RBV of the firm, recognises the importance of accessing the resources and capabilities required to support opportunity-seeking behaviour aimed at achieving competitive advantage (Ireland et al., 2003). *Entrepreneurial actions* can entail creating resources or combining existing resources in new ways to develop and commercialise new products/services, and to service new customers/markets (Hitt et al., 2001). Entrepreneurs have the ability to choose between competing identified business opportunities. The strategic entrepreneurship perspective suggests that entrepreneurs have to make *strategic management choices*. For example, the ability of firms to exploit new opportunities in domestic and/or international markets by leveraging their current resources and capabilities is regarded as an entrepreneurial strategy. Given the emergent nature of the concept of strategic entrepreneurship (Kuratko and Audretsch, 2009), the sources of these resources and capabilities are still relatively under-explored.

3.9　Looking forward

This chapter has highlighted 'what entrepreneurs do' with reference to economic approaches that have focused on the following five themes: imagination and creativity – new ideas, products and businesses (Theme 1), new combinations, radical innovation, new industries and economic development (Theme 2); opportunity identification, evaluation and pursuit – demand, supply and arbitrage (Theme 3); functions and judgements of entrepreneurs (Theme 4); and entrepreneurial business – knowledge management, incremental innovation, and resource assemblage and leverage to exploit an opportunity (Theme 5). In Chapter 4, we discuss insights relating to the backgrounds, motivations, resources and behaviour of entrepreneurs from a non-economic lens. We discuss the resource 'assets' and 'liabilities' accumulated by entrepreneurs that can shape the entrepreneurial process. Notably, the issue of 'types' of entrepreneurs is raised. Chapter 4 highlights issues relating to sociological, personality/traits, psychodynamic, social-psychological and cognitive approaches. The strengths and weaknesses of each non-economic approach are critically discussed.

Discussion questions

1　The entrepreneurial function is a vital component in the process of economic growth (Baumol, 1968). Discuss the functions of entrepreneurs from an economic lens.

2　The entrepreneur of economic theory is a function not a personality (McMullen and Shepherd, 2003). Discuss the functions, actions, and judgements of entrepreneurs.

3　'The crucial factor in entrepreneurial success is the effective use of the entrepreneur's special knowledge.' What skills, expertise and knowledge do entrepreneurs accumulate and leverage to create, discover and/or exploit opportunities?

4　Schumpeter (1934) suggests that the entrepreneur is an agent of change. What new combinations and contributions do Schumpeter 'type' entrepreneurs make?

5　Do practitioners need to increase the supply of more Schumpeter (1934) rather than Kirzner (1973) 'type' entrepreneurs?

6　Knowledge is the 'most powerful engine of production' (Marshall, 1920). Critically discuss this statement with regard to views surrounding how an entrepreneurial enterprise is organised.

7　The sole role of the entrepreneur is to reduce the degree of inefficiency in the use of resources within the firm. Discuss.

8　Identify the key differences between an entrepreneur and a manager. To what extent do you think their roles overlap?

9　'It is important not only to gather resources for entrepreneurship but to know what to do with those resources.' Discuss.

10　How might entrepreneurs choose between competing opportunities?

Recommended further reading

Casson, M. (1982). *The Entrepreneur: An Economic Theory.* Oxford: Martin Robertson.

Cuevas, J. G. (1994). Towards a Taxonomy of Entrepreneurial Theories. *International Small Business Journal*, 12 (4): 77–88.

Hébert, R. and Link, A. A. (2006). Historical Perspectives on the Entrepreneur. *Foundations and Trends® in Entrepreneurship*, 2 (4): 261–408.

Johnson, P. (1986). *New Firms: An Economic Perspective.* London: Allen & Unwin.

McMullen, J. S. and Shepherd, D. A. (2006). Entrepreneurial Action and the Role of Uncertainty in the Theory of the Entrepreneur. *Academy of Management Review*, 31 (1): 132–152.

Chapter 4

Theoretical insights II:
Sociological and psychological approaches

Contents

Learning objectives

- Consider that entrepreneurship takes place in a social context and social contexts can shape expectations and access to resources required to enter entrepreneurship.
- Appreciate that an individual's demographic characteristics and human capital profile can shape the propensity to enter entrepreneurship.
- Illustrate that different 'types' of entrepreneurs and firms can be identified.
- Consider Smith's (1967) craftsman and opportunist typology as well as alternative classifications of entrepreneurs and firms.
- Illustrate the strengths and weaknesses of the personality, psychodynamic and social-psychological approaches to explore entrepreneur behaviour.
- Appreciate the emerging cognitive approaches to explore entrepreneur behaviour.

4.1 Introduction

The *motivations, resources and behaviour* of entrepreneurs can be explored from a *non-economic* lens. Insights from non-economic approaches can be used to ascertain the *'assets'* and *'liabilities'* associated with entrepreneurs. These approaches can be utilised to explore why entrepreneurs in particular contexts and points in time made decisions and judgements relating to the entrepreneurial process. In this chapter, the personality/traits, psychodynamic, social-psychological, and cognitive approaches are discussed, in turn.

4.2 Sociological approaches

4.2.1 Social context: Expectations and access to resources

Entrepreneurship exists in a social context (Licht and Siegel, 2006). Sociologists suggest that social contexts shape an individual's propensity to become an entrepreneur, and propensity to be a 'successful' entrepreneur. The sociological approach recognises the importance of *internal and external* factors in shaping an individuals motivation and access to resources. *Social contexts* can shape the 'supply' and 'demand' for entrepreneurial behaviour (Keeble and Walker, 1994). An individual can be constrained in making *career choices* due to their social context (Kets de Vries, 1977). Choices can be limited by the *expectations* and *experience* people face in the social world. Individuals are *socialised* to behave in ways that meet with the approval of their role set. Dominant values of close associates may translate into *expectations that shape individual behaviour.* Social context can shape individual's expectations, access to higher quality education, ability to obtain a job, and ability to obtain an employment position, which promote the accumulation of financial resources and managerial, technical and entrepreneurial capabilities. Notably, *social context shapes access to resources* that can either promote or retard an individual's career in entrepreneurship (see the example of American-style wealth creation the way forward in Entrepreneurship in action 4.1). Isaksen (2006) noted the entrepreneurs reporting subjective norms (i.e., influence of family and friends and significant others) were significantly more likely to report an intention to grow their new firms. Individual's social surroundings can be linked to the desire and ability to pursue a career in entrepreneurship.

Entrepreneurship in action 4.1
American-style wealth creation the way forward

Entrepreneurship in Wales has received little attention over recent years: the emphasis has been on using resources to attract inward investors – large companies with the capability of employing a vast amount of people. But small businesses create the majority of new jobs – 64 per cent of the 2.5 million new jobs created in the United States in 1996 were in small firms. Since 1980, America's top 500 companies have shed more than five million jobs while the United States as a whole has added 34 million new jobs. Most of these have come, of course, in small businesses.

These statistics are very impressive but when compared with such statistics for Wales we can see that small businesses are even more important for jobs. For instance, 97 per cent of all businesses in Wales employ fewer than 20 people and 94 per cent employ fewer than 10. And small businesses account for nearly 50 per cent of employment outside the public sector. Also, it has been estimated that as much as one-third of the differences in national economic growth are due to differences in entrepreneurial activity. It follows logically from this that small businesses and their ability to create such wealth and employment should be given more importance. But in Wales, business risk-taking has been ranked alongside gambling. If it succeeds, fine; but failures are not the subject of polite conversation.

As many as nine out of every 100 United States adults are trying to start businesses. This is because of a culture that strongly encourages and supports self-enterprise. Americans generally favour self-

starters and the independent spirit that underpins their success. Business failures are not considered a personal failure and many consider 'not to have tried' as a personal weakness. Successful entrepreneurs are not only accepted but are considered 'champions of industry' and presented as role models for others. Americans accept and respect entrepreneurs; some business failures are expected and they are considered a normal part of the process. It is also interesting to note that United States women are responsible for more than a third of all start-up efforts.

More fundamentally, the American population generally does not expect the government to provide for its well-being. Also, it is likely to accept differences in standards of living. Within that fundamental cultural tradition, Americans are more likely than people in other countries to recognise opportunities for start-ups and to be motivated to pursue those opportunities through the creation of a new venture.

The Americans realise that while not every high school graduate has the capacity or desire for higher education, almost everybody has the potential to start a new business. The average high school graduate may not start a fast-growth, high-technology company but he or she can start a landscaping business, a retail business or some other venture that will employ other people. As such, they realise that it is critical to provide at least the basic instruction to ensure that these future entrepreneurs have the understanding of, and a certain level of proficiency in, the skills necessary to implement and manage a business.

This means that ideas that already operate across the pond can be implemented here, such as the Mini-Society, a highly-successful idea that is in full swing in America where entrepreneurial leadership is taught to elementary and secondary school children. The programme is an experienced-based approach directed at children aged eight to 12. Through Mini-Society, children design and develop their own society and identify tasks for which they can earn money. Ultimately, the children identify opportunities and establish their own businesses to provide goods and services to their fellow citizens. Other schemes are run in the States such as programmes by the National Foundation for Teaching Entrepreneurship (NFTE) which teach low-income teenagers how to start their own businesses. Babson College in Massachusetts runs a programme where teams of students are given $3,000 in seed capital to set up new ventures.

In Wales we need to begin respecting wealth creators in the same way as the United States and this may be happening in some institutions. For example, bankers have discovered that what appears in statistics as a business closure is not necessarily a humiliating failure. It is encouraging that bankers are at last beginning to admit that we overestimate the true failure rate of new businesses. Evidence now shows that 20 per cent of start-ups are false starts. Research by NatWest's Small Business Services found that of the 81 per cent of start-ups that had 'failed' and were on their books, only 27 per cent did so for financial reasons. The rest sought better prospects elsewhere, got bored or wanted to try a new idea.

Source: R. Lawson, *The Western Mail*, 23 August 2002.

Sociology provides a perspective that can contribute to the understanding of entrepreneurship in three broad areas (Reynolds, 1991):

1 At the societal level, the sociological approach challenges the inevitable dominance of large productive organisations with reference to a focus on flexible specialisation and the dual nature of advanced economies in which entrepreneurship plays a role.
2 The sociological approach enables understanding of the specific societal characteristics that affect entrepreneurship.
3 The sociological approach directs attention towards patterns of entrepreneurial behaviour, both within and between populations. Sociologists have explored the effects of entrepreneur profiles on entrepreneurship and have linked the effect of societal and cultural context, such as ethnicity, social networks and embeddedness, and work experiences on the decisions of individuals to pursue entrepreneurial activities.

Socio-economic factors considered relate to social class, family composition, and parental background. The latter factors can impact on *opportunity structures and entrepreneurial decision-making.* For example, parental role models can raise expectations and encourage family members to become business owners (i.e., children drawn from families associated with business ownership are more likely to pursue careers as business owners) (see the example of Christopher George Jewellers in Entrepreneurship in action 4.2).

The sociological approach also recognises that an individual's age, education and employment history can shape expectations and access to resources, which can be leveraged to create, identify and exploit business opportunities. Entrepreneurial skills are acquired over time and an individual's age can impact on the decision to own a business (i.e., less than 30 years, no resources; 45 or more years, no energy) (see the example of Heidi Klum in

Entrepreneurship in action 4.2
Christopher George Jewellers

www.christophergeorgejewellers.co.uk

Independent jeweller; growth (2003–2005) = 253 per cent.

Description: As an independent family retailer, Christopher George prides itself on its quality of service. It employs watchmakers and goldsmiths, as well as a qualified gemmologist and diamond grader. This provides a complete service not found in any other jeweller in Cardiff [in Wales]. Its wholesale business supplies independent jewellers with loose diamonds and coloured stones, as well as a custom-made range of 18ct gold diamond set jewellery.

Origins: George Dagley has been repairing watches for more than 50 years, and his son Christopher has worked in his family's jewellers shop since his teens. When they relocated to Cardiff in the 1970s, they started by offering a clock and watch repair facility in a small unit in the Alders Arcade. After noticing a gap in the market for quality jewellery, they extended their offering. A major challenge has been three compulsory purchases of premises, resulting in moving the business while retaining customers. This was achieved as client loyalty had been gained through outstanding customer service.

Success factors: The business has succeeded by offering an exceptional service, listening to customers and exceeding expectations, and by employing experts in each area of the business. If the firm does not have what they are looking for, it will source it or make it for them. As an independent business, Christopher George is free to carry a more unusual range of products than other jewellers, and monitors current trends to gain inspiration, stocking lesser known gemstones and interesting designer pieces. Finally, marketing focuses on different means to regular advertising, such as donating prizes to charity, gaining newspaper editorials, and wedding fairs. It is also looking into sponsorship opportunities and provides jewellery for fashion shows and photo shoots.

The future: The aim of the business is to continue to grow in terms of turnover, profitability and staff, increasing its wholesale coverage to cover the South East and the Midlands [of England]. It will also stock larger and higher quality diamonds as standard, increase the amount of handmade pieces it sells, and improve quality and standards within the business. It aims to update and utilise its website, start e-trading and produce a trade-only transactional website for our business customers. Given its success in this area, it will extend the workshop and employ additional craftspeople to take on further trade repair accounts.

Source: icWales, WalesOnline, 24 October, 2006.

Entrepreneurship in action 4.3). Length of work experience and relevance of that experience (i.e., management know-how and industry specific knowledge) (Cooper et al., 1994) can have an impact on the decision to become an entrepreneur. Entrepreneurial decisions can be shaped by the type and size of incubator organisation (i.e., previous employer prior to business ownership), and the extent to which it allows individuals to develop problem-solving skills (Reynolds et al., 1994). Some locations/social contexts have *institutions* that seek to address attitudinal, resource, operational and strategic barriers to business formation and development (see Chapters 6 and 11). Unfortunately, sociological approaches do not conclusively inform us about the entrepreneurial process(es). Insights from sociological approaches can be used to describe entrepreneurs, and to explore entrepreneur heterogeneity. Social context variables can be used to identify individuals who are more likely to become self-employed, business owners and successful entrepreneurs.

Entrepreneurship in action 4.3
Heidi Klum's years of learning

To date, the life story of supermodel Heidi Klum reads very much like a traditional fairy-tale. We are told that as a child she grew up with parents in the fashion industry. Her father worked in the cosmetic industry and her mother was a hair stylist. We are asked to believe that the young Heidi had no plans on a career in the fashion industry yet (as if by miracle), she became one of the most famous supermodels of the past decade. By chance, when perusing a magazine in 1991, she stumbled across an advertisement for a modelling competition. Encouraged by her friends, she sent off a few photographs. Eighteen-year-old Heidi won the competition and was soon engaging in modelling assignments in Paris, Milan and then the States. She signed with the Elite Modelling Agency in New York, eventually becoming famous as the face of Victoria's Secret. Other prime contracts followed as she adorned the front pages of fashion magazines. Television appearances and a part in the hit movies *The Devil Wears Prada*, *Ella Enchanted* and *Perfect Strangers* followed. This platform of legitimacy allowed her to launch her own successful fashion project, *Project Runway*, which is a television programme. We are told of a busy Heidi launching her own jewellery and shoe collections. In the process, the model became successful in business and has turned to designing. The philanthropic married mother of three has turned to charity work with fundraisers for organisations such as the For All Kids Foundation, the American Red Cross and the Pediatric AIDS Foundation.

Source: Smith, R. The Diva Storyline: An Alternative Social Construction of Female Entrepreneurship, *International Journal of Gender and Entrepreneurship*, 1(2), 2009, 148–163.

4.2.2 Demographic characteristics of entrepreneurs: Human capital profiles

Social context variables are considered in studies seeking to identify (and predict) individuals who are more likely to become entrepreneurs, and those who are more likely to become successful entrepreneurs. Drawing upon an economics lens, Becker (1975) suggested that an individual's human capital profile could shape productivity. An entrepreneur's demographic characteristics, achieved attributes, and accumulated work experience are assumed to have a positive (or negative) impact on productivity (Becker, 1993). A distinction is made between *'general'* (i.e., age, gender, ethnic background, social class, education, etc.) and *'specific' human capital* (i.e., management and industry know-how, technical and entrepreneurial capabilities, ability to acquire resources, prior business ownership experience, etc.). Many of the latter human capital variables are shaped by an individual's social context before and during the entrepreneurial process (see Case 6, Alba Adventures: An entrepreneur pushed into entrepreneurship). Human capital theorists have explored *'inputs'* accumulated by entrepreneurs in relation to *'outputs'*. Studies have explored the linkage between social context variables focusing upon general and specific human capital *'inputs'* relating to the following *entrepreneurial processes and events*:

- engage in information search and identify business opportunities (Ucbasaran et al., 2008);
- identify innovative opportunities (Ucbasaran et al., 2009);
- become self-employed (Parker, 2004; Kolvereid and Isaksen, 2006) or a business owner (Reynolds et al., 1994; Isaksen, 2006);
- business survival (Cressy and Storey, 1994); and
- superior business performance (Cooper et al., 1994; Gimeno et al., 1997; Isaksen, 2006).

4.2.3 'Types' of entrepreneurs and firms: Firm survival and performance differences

Entrepreneur typologies have been developed on the presumption that different types of entrepreneurs exist and entrepreneurs are not a homogeneous entity. *Conceptual typologies* and *empirical taxonomies* of firms (Birley and Westhead, 1990a) and entrepreneurs (Miner et al., 2000) have been presented. Social context variables relating to an individual's *general and specific capital* have been considered in typologies and taxonomies of entrepreneurs (Smith, 1967; Woo et al., 1991) and firms (Westhead, 2005; Westhead and Howorth, 2007). Studies identify a small number of distinct entrepreneur (and firm) types. Typologies (or taxonomies) are used to illustrate contrasting entrepreneur motivations, assets and liabilities, behaviour, resource needs, performance, and best entrepreneur practice.

Smith (1967) presented an insightful classic typology of 'types' of entrepreneurs. He conceptually divided entrepreneurs into *'craftsman'* and *'opportunist' entrepreneurs*. Smith suggested that the two types of entrepreneurs had contrasting potential for job generation and wealth creation. Table 4.1 summarises the profiles of the two 'types' of entrepreneurs. *Craftsman entrepreneurs* have a blue-collar background, with limited educational and managerial experience, with a preference for technical work, and they are generally motivated by needs for personal autonomy. Conversely, *opportunist entrepreneurs* typically have higher levels of education and broader experience, with a motivation to build a successful organisation and achieve financial gains.

Woo et al. (1991) challenged the usefulness of Smith's dichotomy. There are major differences in the criteria used by researchers to classify entrepreneurs. Entrepreneurial typologies are sensitive to the selection of elements (i.e., themes) relating to entrepreneurs. Woo et al. warned that the predictive power of the craftsman-opportunist dichotomy might have been exaggerated. They recognised the need to identify and discuss other finer subtypes of entrepreneurs.

So what, if there are different 'types' of entrepreneurs and firms? Studies have detected links between 'types' of entrepreneurs and firms (with regard to entrepreneur social context as well as general and specific human capital profiles) and superior firm survival and performance (Birley and Westhead, 1990a). Focusing upon the *entrepreneur as the unit of analysis*, several studies have compared the performance of venture owners with reference to the nature of their *prior business ownership (i.e., entrepreneurial) experience*. The latter is regarded as a key dimension of entrepreneurship-specific human capital

Table 4.1 Profiles of craftsman and opportunist entrepreneurs

Craftsmen	Opportunist
• Narrow education	• Broader education
• Blue-collar background	• Middle class
• Successful worker	• Variety of work experience
• Identified with a 'task' rather than management	• Identified with management
• Paternalistic	• Delegate more
• Utilised personal relationship in marketing	• Market orientated
• Finance from savings and family only	• Many sources of finance
• Rigid strategies followed	• Diverse and innovative competitive strategies

Source: Smith (1967)

(Ucbasaran et al., 2008). Studies have explored whether owners with prior business owner-ship experience (i.e., *habitual (serial and portfolio) entrepreneurs*) own superior performing businesses relative to *inexperienced (novice) entrepreneurs* (see Chapter 5). A number of studies have failed to detect any significant link between prior business ownership experi-ence and superior firm performance (Ucbasaran et al., 2008). However, studies in several national and industrial contexts have detected firm performance differences when an entrepreneur's specific human capital relating to prior business ownership experience is considered. There is some support for the view that the performance of the newest firms owned by habitual entrepreneurs, particularly those owned by portfolio entrepreneurs, are associated with superior levels of firm survival and performance compared to new firms owned by novice entrepreneurs (Dahlqvist and Davidsson, 2000; Westhead et al., 2005a), as well as the propensity to identify additional opportunities for wealth creation (Ucbasaran et al., 2009).

Westhead et al. (2005a) detected several size and performance differences between novice, serial and portfolio entrepreneurs in Scotland. Reflecting a common weakness of studies focusing upon portfolio entrepreneurs, the survey instrument utilised failed to gather information on the characteristics and the performance of the other business(es) in which portfolio entrepreneurs have ownership stake(s). Consequently, the full eco-nomic contribution of portfolio entrepreneurs in Scotland was not assessed. The uni-variate analysis conducted by Westhead et al. (2005a) revealed that the average sales revenues of businesses in 1999 owned by *portfolio entrepreneurs* were larger than those owned by *novice and serial entrepreneurs*. On average, businesses owned by portfolio en-trepreneurs reported larger absolute sales growth over the 1996 to 1999 period than those owned by novice entrepreneurs. A larger proportion of portfolio rather than novice entrepreneurs reported that their current operating profit performance was above average relative to competitors. Further, a larger proportion of serial rather than novice entrepreneurs reported that their current profit performance was above average relative to competitors. Supporting the finding relating to sales, portfolio entrepreneur firms were larger than those owned by other entrepreneurs in terms of total employment size in 2001. Portfolio entrepreneur firms, on average, reported higher absolute and percent-age total employment growth over the 1996 to 2001 period than firms owned by novice and serial entrepreneurs. Additional analysis revealed that the top 4 per cent of fastest growing businesses owned by portfolio entrepreneurs in Scotland generated 55 per cent of gross new jobs created, while the comparable subsample of firms owned by novice and serial entrepreneurs generated 44 per cent and 38 per cent of gross new jobs, respectively. With reference to the surveyed firms alone, portfolio entrepreneurs accounted for more absolute employment growth than other entrepreneurs. Westhead et al. (2005a) sug-gested that to maximise returns from investments, practitioners should consider allocat-ing resources to portfolio entrepreneurs who are actively seeking to maximise wealth creation, as well as job generation. Ucbasaran et al. (2008) have asserted that there might be a need to focus upon the entrepreneur, rather than the firm alone, throughout all stages of the entrepreneurial process. Certain 'types' of entrepreneur may require *specific (and customised)* types of assistance.

Westhead's (1995) taxonomy of high-technology firms confirmed that firms should not be viewed as a homogeneous entity with equal ability to report rapid business develop-ment. He found that some founders (and firms) had no enthusiasm or ability to grow. This study confirmed that only a *few firms reported rapid employment growth and were 'growers'* (Storey, 1994). *Assuming an interventionist stance* to support enterprise, broad and unfocused policies to encourage all firms to survive risk being ineffective if the aim of public policy is to encourage firm growth. *Blanket policies* risk being ineffective if the objective of public policy is to foster the maximum level of economic development with the minimum amount of public support. A case for *targeting support to 'winning firms'* (Storey, 1994) has been made to maximise the economic returns from publicly subsidised investments (i.e., 'soft' and 'hard' support) to remove *'market failures'* faced by entrepreneurs seeking rapid firm growth. Practitioners may adopt a *'policy of avoiding losers'* rather than *'picking winners'* because the 'losers' are easier to identify (Westhead, 1995). Conceptual typologies and empirical taxonomies provide practitioners with the entrepreneur and firm 'profiles' to pursue *'targeted'* or *'customised'* policy.

4.3 Personality/traits approaches

4.3.1 Overview

Psychologists have explored issues relating to person, process and choice. The unit of analysis in personality studies is the individual entrepreneur. Studies have explored the personality profiles of people who *intend (i.e., nascent entrepreneurs)* to become entrepreneurs (Korunka et al., 2003), as well as those who *enter self-employment and business ownership* (Gartner, 1989; Brandstätter, 1997; Hansemark, 2003; Frank et al., 2007). The personality profiles of entrepreneurs who *run successful ventures* (Miner et al., 1992; Mueller and Thomas, 2000; Lee and Tsang, 2001; Baum and Locke, 2004) have also been monitored. *Personality* is often loosely defined in terms of the *regularities in action, feeling and thoughts* that are characteristic of the individual (Snyder and Cantor, 1998). It is assumed that the personality of individuals explains their *actions*. Notably, the possession of a *personality trait (or traits)* predisposes an individual towards enterprising behaviour. Entrepreneurship in action 4.4 provides some examples of entrepreneurs with their supposed personality traits.

More formally, several detailed academic studies have highlighted the following traits (Korunka et al., 2003): risk-taking propensity, strong need for achievement (or Nach), locus of control, need for autonomy, determination, initiative, creativity, and self-confidence and trust (see the example of South Wales Caravan Centre Limited in Entrepreneurship in action 4.5).

A longstanding debate has focused upon whether entrepreneurs are *'born'* or *'made'* relating to their personality profiles. Some personality traits (i.e., need for achievement, locus of control and the ability to take responsibility for actions/decisions) can be acquired by individuals. Practitioners seeking to increase the supply of entrepreneurs may provide schemes that encourage more people to adopt a simplistic *'ideal personality profile'* of an entrepreneur (Gartner, 1989) associated with moderate risk-taking, a high need for achievement, higher tolerance of ambiguity, and a high internal locus of control. However, it is believed that some *attributes* (i.e., high energy, emotional stability, etc.) are innate and cannot be acquired by individuals, and they mark out 'born' entrepreneurs. In the following sections, several personality traits are highlighted.

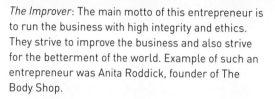

Entrepreneurship in action 4.4
Examples of successful entrepreneurs and their supposed personality traits

The Improver: The main motto of this entrepreneur is to run the business with high integrity and ethics. They strive to improve the business and also strive for the betterment of the world. Example of such an entrepreneur was Anita Roddick, founder of The Body Shop.

The Advisor: These entrepreneurs focus on customer needs and they will do anything to please customers. Customer requirements become business objectives. They will tend to forget their own objectives. An example of such an entrepreneur is the founder of Nordstrom, John W. Nordstrom.

The Super Star: Business success revolves around the chief executive officer (CEO). The CEO becomes the brand for the company. Further, the CEO can be too competitive and a workaholic. An example of this kind of entrepreneur is Donald Trump, CEO of Trump Hotels and Casino Resorts.

The Artist: This entrepreneur is creative and often shows their creativity in promoting the business through creative means such as designing websites, advertisements. Such an entrepreneur is very sensitive to the customer feedback even though they are positive. An example of such a person is Scott Adams, creator of 'Dilbert'.

The Visionary: Their business plans depict future vision and thoughts of the entrepreneur. Plans focus on their dreams rather than on reality. Bill Gates of Microsoft Inc. is an example for this kind of personality trait.

The Analyst: These kinds of businesses include scientific firms, engineering and technical firms. Entrepreneurs will analyse problems in a systematic way and fix them. They are very good at problem-solving and they trust others easily. An example is Gordon Moore of Intel.

The Fireball: Entrepreneurs balance impulsiveness and their attitude describes their company goals and company strategy. Entrepreneurs are full of energy and fun loving. An example for this kind of entrepreneur is Malcolm Forbes, Publisher, and Forbes Magazine.

The Hero: They are the leaders and they use full tactics to face challenges and achieve success in their strategy. They are the heroes of the company and possess strong leadership. An example for this kind of entrepreneur is Jack Welch, CEO GE.

Source: http://www.bizoppjunction.com/business-forums/leadership-management/183-traits-business-entrepreneurs.html

4.3.2   Risk-taking propensity

In Section 3.7.1, it was highlighted that economic theory suggests that entrepreneurs are *risk-takers (or risk-bearers)*. Yet some studies have found that entrepreneurs are not attracted to risk-taking any more than non-entrepreneurs. Risk-taking is dependent on the perception of the situation and/or the decision-maker's perception of being an expert. Kahneman and Tversky's (1979) 'prospect theory' suggests that a person's willingness to take risks is dependent on their perception of the situation. Individuals will be *risk-averse* if they perceive themselves to be in a *loss situation*. Conversely, individuals will be *risk-seeking* if they perceive themselves to be in a *win situation*. Heath and Tversky (1991) also suggest that people who feel competent will take more risks.

Risk-taking is related to an entrepreneur's age, education, motivation, business experience, and number of years in business. Evidence relating to risk-taking by entrepreneurs is mixed. The *perceived context* (i.e., knowledge and situational characteristics) has been

Entrepreneurship in action 4.5
South Wales Caravan Centre Limited

www.southwalescaravancentre.co.uk

Caravan dealership; growth (2003–2005) = 302 per cent

Description: South Wales Caravan Centre Limited is a caravan dealership, mainly for new Adria and Fleetwood caravans. It has a large range of used touring caravans and a fully stocked awning and accessory shop with mail order facilities. The business also has full workshop facilities for warranty, repair and insurance work.

Origins: South Wales Caravan Centre was established in Treorchy [in Wales] in 2002 by three brothers – Simon, Andrew and Jonathan Bound. Simon had wanted to establish a vehicle-related business for some time whilst brothers Andrew (a corporate lawyer) and Jonathan (an accountant) provided some of the initial funding requirements, professional expertise and moral support. The company faced the challenge of being established with limited funds and initially a small amount of stock. All three wanted the business to be based in the Rhondda, although finding suitable premises was difficult. They eventually acquired a former Austin Rover dealership and had to renovate the derelict site. Another challenge faced was persuading suppliers that it was viable to operate a caravan business based in the Rhondda.

Success factors: Without Simon's drive and ambition, the business would not have been established nor have grown to its present size. He had the vision of what the business could become and his persuasion skills with suppliers and incredible hard work have

paid dividends. He worked in the business during the days and at weekends, whilst continuing employment with his nightshift job. Once the business was safely established after nine months, he gave up his well-paid, secure job to drive Caravan Centre forward. Also, through Simon's vision and drive, two new caravan dealerships were secured against the odds and, in 2004, South Wales Caravan Centre Limited was appointed the sole South Wales dealer for new Adria Caravans, one of Europe's leading caravan manufacturers. In 2005, the company won a national award from Adria as the best new caravan dealer in the UK for 2005. Finally, the founders have invested heavily in advertising and marketing the business and building up its reputation. They have taken a stand at a number of caravan shows and won the award for best stand at the Welsh Caravan and Camping Show in 2005.

The future: The plans are to consolidate the business. For example, workshop facilities have just been redeveloped and the firm has taken on more trained staff to handle the repair and insurance side of the caravan business. The business is continuing to expand very rapidly and as main dealers for Adria and Fleetwood, it can supply caravans that are both high quality and at a price the customer wants to buy. However, one of the major challenges remains the handling of the volume of caravans that need to go through the site to meet demand and so the business is actively seeking a second site to expand its workshop and storage facilities.

Source: icWales, WalesOnline, 24 October 2006.

found to be a more important determinant of risk-bearing than personality traits (Delmar, 2000). Many entrepreneurs are moderate risk-takers and/or *'calculated risk-takers'*.

4.3.3 Strong need for achievement (or Nach)

Need for achievement (or Nach) is closely related to risk-taking. It takes into account the perceived risk of the situation as well as the perceived level of competence. According to McClelland (1965), entrepreneurs have a high need for achievement. People with a strong need for achievement are distinguished from others as *'high achievers'*. 'High achievers' prefer striving to achieve targets that are challenging but not beyond their capabilities. Some 'high achievers' will establish new ventures. McClelland identified the *situations preferred* by individuals who are associated with a high need for achievement. His theory identified situations that arouse the *achievement motivation*. High achievers will choose situations associated with (Delmar, 2000):

- individual responsibility;
- moderate risk-taking as a function of skill;
- knowledge of results of decisions;
- novel instrumental activity; and
- anticipation of future possibilities.

The entrepreneur may be driven by the prospect of *achievement satisfaction* rather than financial gain per se. Studies, generally conducted in the United States, empirically support the link between the achievement motivation and entrepreneurial actions (Johnson, 1990). However, studies have questioned whether it is possible to predict behaviour or performance on the basis of a single value (i.e., Nach). Miner et al. (1992) suggest that an overall '*index of task motivation*' should consider self-achievement, risk-taking, feedback of results, personal innovation, and planning for the future. Studies in the United States have detected a significant relationship between Miner et al.'s index and superior business performance.

4.3.4   Tolerance of ambiguity

Tolerance of ambiguity is a concept relating to risk-taking. It is an *emotional reaction* to ambiguity and uncertainty. Entrepreneurs reporting a high tolerance of ambiguity are assumed to be associated with (Scheré, 1982):

- an open mind;
- responding quickly to change;
- needing to know only the key facts; and
- having a flexible attitude.

An individual with a lower propensity to become an entrepreneur will exhibit a low tolerance of ambiguity because they will report stress and unpleasantness in a complex situation. Conversely, an individual with a higher propensity to become an entrepreneur will exhibit a high tolerance of ambiguity because they find complex situations desirable and challenging. People reporting high tolerance for ambiguity will expose themselves to higher risks than people reporting low tolerance for ambiguity. The latter individuals generally prefer well-understood situations. Scheré (1982) found that entrepreneurs reported higher tolerance of ambiguity scores than managers. Few studies have, however, found a linkage between an individual's propensity to report a high tolerance of ambiguity and an increased likelihood to become an entrepreneur (Gartner, 1989).

4.3.5   Locus of control

The concept of '*locus of control*' can be traced back to Rotter's (1966) 'social learning theory' of how a person's *perception of control* affects their behaviour (i.e., propensity to innovate) (Ajzen, 2002). People can categorise events and situations based on their underlying shared properties. Locus of control is conceived as one determinant of the *expectancy of success.* The following distinction between *internal and external control* has been made:

- Internal control where a person believes that the achievement of a goal is dependent on their own behaviour or individual characteristics. An individual with high internal locus of control believes that they can personally change events in given situations. They are reactive rather than proactive. A person's ability, hard work, determination and planning in achieving outcomes is appreciated (Rotter, 1966). Frustration may encourage an individual to establish a new venture.
- External control is where a person believes that the achievement of a goal is the result of luck or external factors.

Studies have detected a low to moderate significant link between people reporting internal control and an increased likelihood to become entrepreneurs (Delmar, 2000). A few studies have detected a weak tendency for people reporting internal control to own superior performing firms. Studies comparing entrepreneurs and managers have failed to detect any differences in reported internal locus of control (Gartner, 1989). The concept of locus of control has been abandoned in psychology but some management and entrepreneurship scholars still consider it.

4.3.6 Desire for autonomy

Some entrepreneurs have a high *need for autonomy* (Birley and Westhead, 1994), and a fear of external control (Smith, 1967). Further, some entrepreneurs value *individualism and freedom* (i.e., the possibility to make a difference for themselves) more than non-entrepreneurs (see Case 7, Ace Cleaning (UK) Limited: Development of a purchased firm by a novice entrepreneur). They frequently report the desire to manage their own firm. Desire for autonomy can encourage an individual to establish a new business, but this desire may be expressed as a result of having established a new firm.

4.3.7 Critics of personality/traits approaches

Personality theories do not adequately explain why some individuals engage in entrepreneurial behaviour and others do not (Delmar, 2000). Studies focusing on entrepreneurs' personality/traits have been widely criticised with regard to the following issues:

- Most entrepreneurs do not possess all of the *'ideal' personality traits.*
- People who are not entrepreneurs can possess several 'ideal' personality traits.
- Biased studies of surviving and successful entrepreneurs can overestimate the importance of some personality traits.
- Methods used to measure personality traits are diverse, and doubts surround the validity and reliability of some presented personality scales.
- There is inconsistency within the empirical evidence base. 'With the exception of the need for achievement, the results have been poor and it has been difficult to link any specific traits to entrepreneurial behaviour' (Delmar, 2000: 145).
- 'Traits are supposedly stable over time' (Delmar, 2000: 153) but some traits can be acquired through learning or experience.
- No single personality trait has been found within multivariate statistical studies to be the determinant explaining why some people are more likely to enter business ownership.

- Ajzen's (2002) *'theory of planned behaviour'* suggests that an individual's attitudes and personality traits have only an *indirect impact* on specific behaviour. *Attitudes and subjective norms* (i.e., perceived behavioural control) rather than personality promote the intention of individuals to become self-employed (Tkachev and Kolvereid, 1999), and to own high-growth firms (Isaksen, 2006).
- Multivariate statistical studies have failed to detect a *consistently strong causal* link between the personality of entrepreneurs (i.e., single trait) and the subsequent propensity to establish a new venture (Shook et al., 2003), and to own superior performing firms.
- Social context variables and general and specific human capital variables relating to the entrepreneur are more consistently found to 'explain' the propensity of some people to establish new ventures, and the ability to own superior performing firms (Storey, 1994).
- Personality/traits theories depict general tendencies and they neglect the importance of situational factors (i.e., need to consider psychodynamic approaches (Kets de Vries, 1977) (see Section 4.4).
- Some personality traits that mark out 'born' entrepreneurs are *innate* and cannot be acquired.
- Personality/traits theories relate to a static approach that focuses on *'who the entrepreneur is'* and *'not what the entrepreneur does'* (Gartner, 1989).
- Cognitive perspectives (see Section 4.6) are a counterpoint to the personality/traits approach. It may be easier to change an individual's mental processing abilities rather than an individual's personality.

4.4   Psychodynamic approaches

4.4.1   Socialisation process

Building upon Freud's psychoanalytic theory of personality, psychodynamic approaches have been utilised to explore entrepreneur behaviour. This approach suggests that the *socialisation process* in childhood determines *personal attributes* (i.e., instinctive drives), and some people seek instant gratification for their desires. Negative characteristics and drives can promote entrepreneurial behaviour. A disturbed childhood with an absent father, and conflicts with a parent and other authority figures during early childhood can shape an individual's personality. If instinctive behaviour is severely constrained it can lead to frustration, which can be a source of *entrepreneurial motivation*. Individuals can be classified as *'deviant'* or *'marginal' people*, and they may frequently change jobs and potentially gain entrepreneurial experiences in a variety of settings.

4.4.2   Dark-side of entrepreneurship: The 'deviant' perspective

Kets de Vries (1977) focused upon the motivations of entrepreneurs, and presented a conceptualisation of the entrepreneur as a highly complex individual. Entrepreneurial behaviour can be due to *negative drives*. Financial benefits do not always lead to personal satisfaction and happiness. Personal crises and even poverty often follow success. Kets de Vries, focusing upon the dark side of entrepreneurship, believes some entrepreneurs are drawn from *'marginal groups'* and exhibit *'deviant'* behaviour. For Kets de Vries,

Sir John Madejski: The 'dark knight'

Sir John Madejski has 'no regrets' about baring his soul in front of the TV cameras for a documentary on his life. The Royals chairman has allowed himself to be filmed over three years which have seen a turn in the tide of the multi-millionaire's fortunes as the credit crunch began to bite. At first cash was flowing freely, according to the publicity material for the film, and 'Madejski was building big, here a City Academy, there an office block'. While carrying out work in his 'beloved home town' of Reading, he was also funding big projects for the nation including a wing for the Royal Academy and a piazza and garden at the Victoria and Albert Museum. At the same time Reading FC were in the Premier League. But when the financial tide began to turn, the film-makers found Sir John beginning 'to question the meaning of his life and determined to discover more about his origins'.

He was born with a different name in wartime under circumstances which had 'given him issues about his identity and relationships'. The documentary-makers say their film shows Sir John realising he has 'been made the success he is by emotional privations'. And when he is about to be knighted, they describe him as a 'dark knight-to-be'.

Source: L. Fort, *Reading Post*, 14 August 2009.

frustrations and perceived deprivations experienced in the early stages of life can have an impact on an individual's personality. Behaviour is explained by experiences related to a troublesome and very disturbed childhood where the father is absent (see the example of Sir John Madejski in Entrepreneurship in action 4.6 who is a successful portfolio entrepreneur with ownership stakes in Benham Goodhead Print, Reading Football Club and Sackville Properties). The latter entrepreneurs are propelled by feelings of poor self-esteem, insecurity, lack of self-confidence and an inability to fit into an organisation. Consequently, some people search for independence and control over their destiny. Distrust and suspicion of those in positions of authority makes it very difficult for such individuals to pursue careers in large, structured organisations. Some people may choose high-risk situations and prefer working for themselves.

Kets de Vries argues that the careers of many entrepreneurs are associated with a succession of *successes and failures* (see Chapter 5). This is because some entrepreneurs at an unconscious level fear *'success'* (i.e., success is not seen to be deserved) and *'failure'*. Due to their frustrations, some entrepreneurs are more likely to exhibit impulsive behaviour and make decisions without careful deliberation. While an entrepreneur's complete immersion in the enterprise may be crucial for initial success, it is appreciated that this focus may be exhibited in an autocratic leadership style. This latter leadership style associated with a reluctance to delegate, introduce formal systems and a propensity to focus on short-term horizons may put at risk the survival and transition of firms owned by this type of entrepreneur. The entrepreneur is seen by Kets de Vries as a *personality at the crossroads*. An entrepreneur can be highly creative and imaginative but also highly rigid and unwilling to change. This perspective questions the view that entrepreneurs are 'special people' (i.e., Schumpeter) (see Section 3.5). Moreover, this perspective stresses the need to explore entrepreneurial behaviour in crisis and *'failure'* as well as *'success'* situations (see the example of John Mackey in Entrepreneurship in action 4.7).

Entrepreneurship in action 4.7
John Mackey: The dark side of entrepreneurship

When it was revealed that John Mackey, the celebrated founder of Whole Foods Market, had posted hundreds of messages, using an alias, over an eight-year period on Yahoo finance message boards – some blasting competitors, others lavishing praise on himself (even his own haircut) – most were shocked. How could the subject of such business hagiography, an entrepreneur who transformed the face (and the aisles) of supermarket retailing, a vegan who made the organic lifestyle the New American Badge, a passionate advocate of small producers who introduced us to more kinds of honey than we thought there were bees, behave in well, such an inorganic fashion. After all, Whole Foods Market is all about transparency. You know in sometimes excruciating detail about where your persimmons and your pork chops come from, but in the case of John Mackey's opaque postings, you were completely in the dark about where they were manufacturing them. I view this turn of events as the dark side of passionate entrepreneurship. Mackey lived and breathed his business so profoundly, and he is such a competitive animal, that he simply could not resist the temptations dangled by the Internet's fortress of anonymity. And once having been seduced by being able to hide in plain sight under the user name 'Rahodeb' – a scrambling of his wife's name – Mackey just kept going and going and going . . . According to the *Wall Street Journal*, Mackey said 'his anonymous comments didn't reflect his or his company's policies or beliefs'. Some of the views Rahodeb expressed, Mr. Mackey said, 'didn't match his own beliefs' . . . That's pretty amazing, when you think about it. Mackey moved beyond using Rahodeb as a mouthpiece for himself, as a vehicle for bashing Wild Oats and its then CEO Perry Oldak, and onto a meta level of performance art where he used his alias to try on different viewpoints and test different arguments. There was something irresistibly seductive in the sheer thrill of pretending. That such a successful entrepreneur – one for whom a culture of ethical behavior has long been a business imperative – could be driven to these levels of clearly inappropriate behavior is a cautionary tale.

Source: Used with permission of Fast Company copyright © 2011.

4.4.3   Critics of psychodynamic approaches

The psychodynamic approaches (i.e., the '*deviant perspective*') to the study of entrepreneurship have been criticised in the following ways:

- Lack of empirical support to universally support this view.
- Its subjective nature does not cover all situations.
- Lacks validity in a number of contexts (i.e., many business start-ups are not prompted by rejection or frustration).
- Other social pressures to enter self-employment or business ownership need to be considered.
- 'Deviants' are found throughout society and there is no reason to believe that proportionally more are found in self-employment or business ownership.
- Many entrepreneurs are no more troubled than non-entrepreneurs, and numerous entrepreneurs come from emotionally and financially stable families.
- Some parents can act as role models, particularly those owning a family business (see Chapter 7).

- The approach fails to consider life-long development, and the ability of some people to 'reinvent' themselves.
- Dealing with 'failure' is an important attribute of entrepreneurs. A distinction between 'failure' and 'intelligent failure' (Sitkin, 1992) can be made (i.e., it is assumed that entrepreneurs learn more from *'intelligent failure'*).

4.5 Social-psychological approaches

Bygrave and Hofer (1991) suggest that there has been an overemphasis on the entrepreneur to the detriment of the entrepreneurial process. They assert it is necessary to move away from the focus upon the *'characteristics and functions of the entrepreneur'* towards an emphasis upon the *'nature and characteristics of the entrepreneurial process'*. Methodologies used in studies may have failed to explore the realities of the entrepreneurial setting. Bygrave and Hofer suggest future studies need to focus upon the *functions, activities and actions associated with the perception of opportunities and the creation of organisations to pursue them.*

The social-psychological approach (Carsrud and Johnson, 1989) takes into account the context in which the individual is operating, and the individuals' personal characteristics. Some social contexts are more likely to promote entrepreneurial behaviour. Shaver (2003: 331) asserted that social-psychology concentrates on the socially meaningful actions of people who establish and grow new ventures. The social-psychological approach highlights that variations in social context can lead to variations in entrepreneur 'type', and differences in firm performance.

4.6 Cognitive approaches

4.6.1 Overview

Personal traits may be difficult to change. To increase both the 'quantity' and 'quality' of entrepreneurs, intervention schemes may focus on improving the *mental processing* (i.e., patterns of thought) of individuals to identify and exploit 'quality' business opportunities (i.e., innovative opportunities with wealth creation potential) (Shepherd and DeTienne, 2005). Following disappointment with early psychological approaches, scholars have drawn upon *cognitive psychology* to provide the psychological foundations for understanding the behaviour of entrepreneurs. *Cognitive processes in decision-making* reported by entrepreneurs have attracted attention (Manimala, 1992). Cognitive approaches have become a significant subfield within entrepreneurship (Baron, 2004; Mitchell et al., 2007). *Entrepreneurial cognition* studies provide insights into *'the way in which entrepreneurs think and behave'* (Baron, 1998). Mitchell et al. (2002: 97) suggest that entrepreneurial cognition refers to:

> . . . the knowledge structures that people use to make assessments, judgments, or decisions involving opportunity evaluation, venture creation and growth.

An entrepreneur's *'dominant logic'* is a key component of specific human capital. Reuber and Fischer (1999) describe dominant logic as an information funnel through which the entrepreneur's attention is filtered. This information funnel is akin to the entrepreneur's cognition (Baron, 1998). *Cognitive theory* is concerned with *how incoming sensory stimulation (i.e., information) is transformed, reduced, elaborated, recovered, and used.* Differences in cognitive processes may explain why people report variations in behaviour and performance. Cognitive theories aid understanding relating to how people make sense of their experiences.

4.6.2   Cognitive differences reported by entrepreneurs and non-entrepreneurs

Cognitive theory has been used to examine the difference between the risk-taking propensities of entrepreneurs and non-entrepreneurs (Wadeson, 2006). Baron (1998) proposed that entrepreneurs are more likely than non-entrepreneurs to experience regret over previously missed opportunities. Entrepreneurs are more likely to *search for, identify and act upon perceived opportunities.* They are more likely to engage in careful, constructive thought. Entrepreneurs are more likely to experience stronger levels of emotion in relation to their work. Also, they are more prone to their decisions being influenced by affective states unrelated to these decisions. Entrepreneurs are more likely to be more *susceptible to self-serving biases* regarding the outcomes of decisions. Baron suggested that more successful entrepreneurs may be less prone to such biases. Successful entrepreneurs are, however, more likely to be more susceptible to *overly confident predictions* about future outcomes, and to be more susceptible to *escalation of commitment effects* in their decision-making.

Busenitz and Barney (1997) found that entrepreneurs used *heuristics* (see below) more extensively than non-entrepreneurs, particularly *overconfidence and representativeness heuristics* in complex environments where comprehensive assessment of information is not possible. Simplifying heuristics may enable entrepreneurs to make decisions that exploit brief windows of opportunity (Tversky and Kahneman, 1974). In decision-making environments characterised by uncertainty and complexity, heuristics can be a rational approach to ensure appropriate decisions are made.

4.6.3   Links between an entrepreneur's cognition and behaviour

4.6.3.1 *Overview*

The following themes have been use by cognition theorists to explain entrepreneur behaviour (Delmar, 2000):

- *heuristics* (i.e., simplifying strategies (such as short-cuts and rules of thumb) that entrepreneurs and non-entrepreneurs use to make strategic decisions, especially in complex situations where less complete or uncertain information is available);
- *intrinsic motivation* (i.e., interest and enjoyment rather than a focus on external reward); and
- *perceived self-efficacy* (i.e., individual beliefs about their own capabilities to achieve a goal).

These themes are discussed, in turn, below.

4.6.3.2 *Heuristics and biases: Representativeness and overconfidence*

Heuristics refer to *simplifying and time-saving strategies* that individuals use to make decisions. Entrepreneurs operating in complex and changing environments may make use of heuristics and biases (Baron, 1998). Three types of heuristics and biases have been considered:

● *representativeness* (i.e., a willingness to generalise from a small number of observations (Busenitz and Barney, 1997);
● *overconfidence* (i.e., an unwarranted belief in an individual's abilities to bring about a particular outcome) (Forbes, 2005); and
● *overoptimism or what we henceforth call comparative optimism* (i.e., the tendency of people to report that they are less likely than others to experience negative events, and more likely than others to experience positive events) (Helweg-Larsen and Shepperd, 2001).

The *representativeness* heuristic (Tversky and Kahneman, 1974) manifests itself when decision-makers generalise on the basis of small, non-random samples usually based on personal experience. People who report *overconfidence* are more likely to enter business ownership (Koellinger et al., 2007). Overconfidence exists when decision-makers are *overoptimistic* in their initial assessment of a situation. Due to initial overconfidence, decision-makers may be too slow to incorporate additional information about a situation into their assessment (Busenitz and Barney, 1997). Some heuristics can lead to poor decisions. *Overconfidence and comparative optimism* may encourage an individual to exploit an opportunity, but they may establish under-capitalised firms (Hayward et al., 2006). Under-capitalised firms that over-stretch entrepreneurs' actual rather than perceived resources may be more susceptible to higher business closure rates. High new firm failure rates have been attributed to the indiscriminate use of heuristics, such as *overoptimism* by entrepreneurs (de Meza and Southey, 1996). As yet, it is not clear whether entrepreneurs who exhibit representativeness and overconfidence are markedly more likely to own 'failing' new firms, or surviving firms that report poorer economic contributions. Studies exploring the consequences of an entrepreneur's comparative optimism reveal that comparative optimism, for example, can be advantageous under certain circumstances, but it can also be disadvantageous (Alvarez and Busenitz, 2001; Hmieleski and Baron, 2009).

4.6.3.3 *Intrinsic motivation*

Intrinsic motivation is both an antecedent and a consequence of *high self-efficacy* (Bandura, 1995). Studies focusing on intrinsic motivation explore an individual's representation of what they find enjoyable (and self-fulfilling). Individual behaviour is viewed as an action, which can be related to personal interest and enjoyment. Intrinsically motivated behaviour may have no apparent (financial) reward (Delmar, 2000). Intrinsic motivation may shape emotions, attitudes and goals. It may subsequently shape an individual's ability to be creative, attraction to challenges, and their ability to search for information to identify and exploit an opportunity. Also, it is assumed that entrepreneurs reporting a high level of interest in their commercial activities will report a higher feeling of enjoyment, and superior decision-making. Conversely, *extrinsic motivation* relates to individual behaviour that is influenced by external motivators such as financial reward, rather than interest in the task itself (Amabile et al., 1994).

4.6.3.4 *Perceived self-efficacy*

Linked to the concept of *locus of control* is the concept of *perceived self-efficacy*, which is part of a social cognition theory of self-regulation (Boyd and Vozikis, 1994). Locus of control can be viewed as generalised self-efficacy. An individual's self-efficacy is closely related to a situation. People reporting high levels of perceived self-efficacy suggest an assurance in their own capabilities to report subsequent attainments (Bandura, 1997). They are motivated individuals seeking to control events in their lives. Delmar (2000: 149–150) claimed that:

> People with a high level of self-efficacy (i.e. with high assurance in their capabilities) approach difficult tasks as challenges to be mastered rather than issues to be avoided. They set themselves challenging goals and maintain strong commitment to them. They are persistent even in the face of failure, and they maintain an analytical distance that guides effective performance. They also tend to attribute failure to insufficient effort and poor knowledge. On the other hand, people with a low self-efficacy shy away from difficult tasks, which are perceived as personal threats. They have a low level of aspiration and commitment to the goals they have chosen to pursue, do not maintain any analytical focus, and they give up easily. Failure is attributed to external obstacles and personal deficiencies. As a consequence they rapidly lose faith in their own capabilities. A person's level of self-efficacy is often the result of previous successful or unsuccessful experiences (either personal experiences or those of role models). Therefore, self-efficacy has the tendency to form the pattern of positive or negative circles – success breeds success and failure breeds failure.

The latter viewpoints have, however, been questioned by Ucbasaran et al. (2008) focusing upon the behaviour of *habitual entrepreneurs*. Some habitual entrepreneurs may have accumulated several *liabilities* during their business ownership careers. These liabilities may impact on subsequent firm performance. The performance of a subsequent venture owned by a habitual entrepreneur may be below that of their first venture (or may be simply not higher than the first if assets offset liabilities). Some habitual entrepreneurs may subsequently exhibit *diminished motivation*. In the case of a previously successful habitual entrepreneur, the same amount of effort may not be put into running the subsequent firm. Some habitual entrepreneurs, who have not accumulated sufficient resources, may not have the ability and/or the flexibility to choose appropriate opportunities a second time. Previous success may result in the *success syndrome, illusion of control, blind spots and overconfidence* (Simon et al., 2000). As a result of previous business failure, some habitual entrepreneurs may experience *hubris and denial*. A *liability of 'sameness'* may also be reported. Some habitual entrepreneurs may continue to focus upon interpersonal interactions that hinder their ability to change, or adapt to changing external environmental conditions.

Links between an individual's reported perceived self-efficacy and their entrepreneurial intentions (Chen et al., 1998; Krueger et al., 2000), and firm performance (Isaksen, 2006) have been explored. People reporting high levels of perceived self-efficacy are more likely to establish new firms and to explore new opportunities (Krueger and Dickson, 1994; Chen et al., 1998). Conversely, Isaksen (2006) noted the entrepreneurs reporting high levels of perceived self-efficacy were not significantly more likely to report an intention to grow their new firms.

4.6.3.5 *Cognition, experience and learning*

Cognitive theories, including prototype theory, expert information processing theory and information processing theory (Baron, 2004) suggest that *experience can shape an individual's cognition.* Habitual entrepreneurs can *learn* from the *feedback from entrepreneurial experience* to adjust their *judgement* (Politis, 2005). By evaluating carefully the 'feedback' from earlier firms owned, habitual entrepreneurs can create a dynamic cycle of learning. Experience can influence an individual's *capacity to acquire and organise complex information.* It provides a framework for processing information and can allow experienced entrepreneurs to foresee and take advantage of disequilibrium profit opportunities that they proactively (or reactively) identify (Kaish and Gilad, 1991). Highly experienced decision-makers (i.e., *experts*) can manipulate incoming information into recognisable patterns. Information can be leveraged to make appropriate actions. Experience-based knowledge can create *'cognitive pathways'* which, when followed, can lead to greater *creativity.*

Habitual entrepreneurs who have multiple experiences to draw upon may be more likely to rely on information processing based on heuristics than novice entrepreneurs. Novice entrepreneurs may have fewer experience-related benchmarks (or *mental short-cuts*) to draw upon. Inexperienced individuals are more likely to adopt more analytical or systematic information processing styles (Gustafsson, 2006). *Heuristic-based information processing* has the advantage of speed. It also enables individuals to make decisions that allow them to exploit successfully brief windows of opportunity. Without heuristic-based logic, the identification and pursuit of new opportunities may become overwhelming and costly. A reliance on heuristics can reduce the burden of cognitive processing, which can allow the entrepreneur to concentrate on novel or unique material (see the reflections of the toilet paper entrepreneur in Entrepreneurship in action 4.8). Habitual entrepreneurs who rely on heuristic information processing may identify more creative and innovative opportunities (Ucbasaran et al., 2008, 2009).

Heuristic-based information processing is less accurate than systematic and thorough information processing techniques. Habitual entrepreneurs may display an over-reliance on heuristic principles and decision-making processes, which may not necessarily be appropriate in new situations, especially in changing environments. Some habitual entrepreneurs may be prone to some of the *biases* associated with heuristic decision-making discussed above. *Cognitive experience* may be associated with *'liabilities' and 'assets'.* The following *'liabilities'* may be exhibited:

- Some experienced individuals may think that they know enough (Baron, 1998);
- Infer too much from limited information because they want to confirm prior beliefs;
- Become constrained by what is familiar to them (Rabin, 1998); and
- Become overconfident in their judgements (Simon et al., 2000).

When entrepreneurs utilise what they have learnt from their past experiences, it becomes harder for them to recognise industry, technology or market changes, and to modify heuristics that worked in the past (Rerup, 2005). Experienced habitual entrepreneurs may attempt to *repeat the same 'recipes' in changed circumstances* (Wright et al., 1997a). Experience and the feeling of 'knowing how it is done' can be a barrier to new useful perspectives. This *'liability of staleness'* (Starr and Bygrave, 1991) can retard an entrepreneur's ability to identify new business opportunities, and/or to develop strategies to exploit new opportunities. Because of previous business success or failure, some habitual entrepreneurs may experience hubris or denial, respectively (Simon et al.,

Entrepreneurship in action 4.8
Trust your gut

As a toilet paper entrepreneur, I am a big believer in 'less is more'. When you have less money, you are more innovative. When you narrow your niche, you attract more targeted customers. And when you take in less information, you make better decisions.

The saying, 'Go with your gut' is so overused, we sometimes forget that it's 100 per cent true. We are genetically programmed with a lifetime of knowledge that equips us with the ability to make GOOD decisions, quickly. You may call it instinct, or street smarts, or even ESP. Whatever you call it, you must trust it, because your gut will be right most of the time.

In Malcolm Gladwell's book *Blink*, he presents studies and stories confirming that snap decisions are often better than decisions made based on volumes of research. Gladwell refers to rapid cognition, our ability to make decisions in the blink of an eye as 'thin-slicing', and explains how information overload can negatively impact our ability to 'thin-slice' effectively.

The solution to a problem often comes in a flash, almost like a premonition. The key to success is acting on your premonition, trusting that part of you that is able to 'thin slice', to collect a small amount of information – the most important information – and make the best decision.

You have enough experiences from your own life to prove Gladwell's theory. I'm sure you can come up with a bunch of your own stories about going with your gut times you trusted your instincts and totally kicked ass, and other times when you hesitated or ignored your gut feeling, and totally sucked.

You don't need a mountain of evidence to prove you've chosen the right path. Going for more and more research to backup your choices clouds your decision making process. It kills the spark of a good idea or solution – and if you keep doing it, you'll kill the dream. We've all had our own experiences with 'analysis paralysis', the inability to make a decision due to information overload. When we wait to take action until we have all of the facts, very often we end up doing nothing at all.

You already know enough to make a great decision. Don't let yourself get caught up in analytics or mired down in information, or you'll end up with a bad case of 'shoulda coulda woulda'. Less is more, my friend. Less is best.

Source: The Toilet Entrepreneur Blog, http://www. toiletpaperentrepreneur.com/blog/trust-your-gut.

2000). An entrepreneur's *previous investments and repertoire of routines* can constrain future behaviour. Some habitual entrepreneurs may continue to focus upon interpersonal relationships used in the past. They may employ existing resources and knowledge in the new firm, thereby reducing the tendency to acquire context relevant resources. This *'liability of sameness'* may hinder their ability to change (Starr and Bygrave, 1991), or to adapt to changing external environmental conditions. The latter entrepreneurs may not be able to adjust their interaction and learning patterns to the demands of their new firm. Some experienced habitual entrepreneurs, who are overconfident or who have failed in their previous venture(s) *may not have accumulated sufficient resources*, thereby reducing their ability and/or the flexibility to choose appropriate business opportunities a second time.

The *value of experience* depends on the knowledge gained, as well as how this knowledge is subsequently used. Mindful use of prior experience is required (Rerup, 2005).

Entrepreneurs need to appreciate when it is necessary to switch away from heuristic information processing toward more systematic information processing to guide decision-making. Gustaffson (2006) explored the mindsets of *expert entrepreneurs* (i.e., entrepreneurs with no less than seven to ten years of experience since their first start-up). Experts can demonstrate a greater awareness of the nature of a decision task (e.g., level of uncertainty involved in opportunity identification), and are able to match their cognitive processes to the task in hand. Experienced habitual entrepreneurs have the potential to become expert entrepreneurs, but experience is a necessary but not a sufficient condition for becoming an expert.

4.6.3.6 *Critique of cognition approaches*

Few empirical studies have explored the wider applicability of cognitive theories relating to the behaviour of entrepreneurs, outside closed experimental settings. Relatively few studies relate to large and representative samples of 'real' entrepreneurs reporting 'actual' rather than potential behaviour scenarios. Longitudinal studies in a variety of cultural, locational and industrial settings need to be conducted to ascertain whether entrepreneurs reporting high levels of intrinsic motivation/perceived self-efficacy report superior opportunity identification and exploitation (i.e., superior wealth creating firms). Relationships need to be explored with regard to 'types' of entrepreneurs (Ucbasaran et al., 2009). Family, friends and practitioners can also shape the goals reported by entrepreneurs, and the ability to access and leverage appropriate resources to create, discover and exploit an opportunity. Nevertheless, cognitive theorists suggest that cognitive models are better at explaining entrepreneurial behaviour, and they can be used to create instruments to educate and train (i.e., 'make') potential entrepreneurs.

4.7 Looking forward

This chapter has highlighted the backgrounds, motivations, resources and behaviour of entrepreneurs from a non-economic lens. The strengths and weaknesses of the sociological, personality/traits, psychodynamic, social-psychological and cognitive approaches were discussed. Chapter 5 highlights that entrepreneurship is not a single-action event because some entrepreneurs have careers in entrepreneurship. In this chapter, we discuss *habitual entrepreneurs* (also known as experienced or, latterly, repeat entrepreneurs). A conceptual distinction is made between inexperienced novice entrepreneurs with no prior business ownership to leverage, and habitual (i.e., serial and portfolio) entrepreneurs with prior business ownership experience. Notably, a conceptual as well as a policy case is made to focus on 'types' of entrepreneurs relating to prior business ownership experience. The backgrounds, motivations, resources, behaviour and performance of habitual and novice entrepreneurs are highlighted. A case for customised assistance to each type of entrepreneur is made.

Discussion questions

1 Owner typologies have been developed on the presumption that different types of entrepreneurs exist and entrepreneurs are not a homogeneous entity (Woo et al., 1991). Discuss the contribution of sociological and human capital approaches to entrepreneurship.

2 What is meant by entrepreneurial traits?

3 Discuss the strengths and weaknesses with the entrepreneurial personality/traits approach.

4 Critically review the contribution played by cognitive approaches to our understanding of entrepreneurship.

Recommended further reading

Baron, R. A. (2004). The Cognitive Perspective, A Valuable Tool for Answering Entrepreneurship's Basic 'Why' Questions. *Journal of Business Venturing*, 19: 221–239.

Busenitz, L. W. and Barney, J. B. (1997). Differences Between Entrepreneurs and Managers in Large Organizations: Biases and Heuristics in Strategic Decision-Making. *Journal of Business Venturing*, 12: 9–30.

Gartner, W. B. (1989). 'Who is an Entrepreneur?' is the Wrong Question. *Entrepreneurship Theory and Practice*, 13 (4): 47–68.

Gimeno, J., Folta, T. B., Cooper, A. C. and Woo, C. Y. (1997). Survival of the Fittest? Entrepreneurial Human Capital and the Persistence of Underperforming Firms. *Administrative Science Quarterly*, 42: 750–783.

Shaver, K. G. (2003). The Social Psychology of Entrepreneurial Behaviour, in Z. J. Acs and D. B. Audretsch (eds). *Handbook of Entrepreneurship Research. An Interdisciplinary Survey and Introduction*. Dordrecht, The Netherlands: Kluwer Academic Publishers, pp. 331–357.

Chapter 5

'Types' of entrepreneurs I: Habitual entrepreneurs

Contents

Learning objectives

- Appreciate that entrepreneurship is not a single action event because some people having careers in entrepreneurship.
- Illustrate the extent of habitual entrepreneurship (and subgroups of portfolio and serial entrepreneurs).
- Show that prior business ownership experience can be leveraged to circumvent barriers to business development.
- Consider the demographic characteristics and general and specific human capital profiles of entrepreneurs, particularly prior business ownership experience can shape entrepreneur cognition and behaviour as well as firm and entrepreneur performance.
- Appreciate profile and performance differences between novice entrepreneurs with no prior business ownership experience and serial and portfolio entrepreneurs.
- Consider 'picking winners' with reference to portfolio entrepreneurs and/or need for customised support to each 'type' of entrepreneur.

5.1 Introduction

In Section 4.2.3, studies that have identified 'types' of entrepreneur and variations in business performance by 'type' of entrepreneur were highlighted. Purpose, theory and/or data availability shape the selection of themes and variables considered within typologies and taxonomies. Consequently there is no consistent identification and labelling of entrepreneur 'types'. Nevertheless, there is growing academic and practitioner awareness that there is a need for a greater understanding of the processes and strategies selected by different 'types' of entrepreneurs to establish and grow their venture(s). This chapter will discuss 'types' of entrepreneurs with regard to their ability to *leverage prior business entrepreneurial experience* in relation to the entrepreneurial process.

5.2 Entrepreneurial careers

Entrepreneurship is not necessarily a single-action event. One dimension of the heterogeneity of entrepreneurial types relates to the possibility that an entrepreneur can have an equity stake and key decision-making role in more than one venture. Some people have *entrepreneurial careers* (Dyer, 1994). An entrepreneur's decision to exit from an initial firm raises issues about the factors that influence the subsequent decision to exit completely from an entrepreneurial career, or to own a further venture. Firm exit may depend on an entrepreneur's own threshold of performance (Gimeno et al., 1997; Ucbasaran et al., 2011). Wennberg et al. (2009) noted that entrepreneurs exited their firms due to liquidation or sale, irrespective of firm performance (i.e., financial distress and superior firm performance). They noted that an entrepreneur's human capital profile (i.e., age, education and entrepreneurial experience) and failure-avoidance strategies (i.e., outside job, reinvestment) were associated with the form of exit route selected (also see DeTienne and Cardon, 2006). Using a real options perspective, McGrath (1999) suggested that entrepreneurs may *learn* from the experience of owning a business that ceased to trade (or failed) to avoid repeating mistakes in subsequent ventures.

In this chapter, we discuss *habitual entrepreneurs* (also known as experienced or, latterly, repeat entrepreneurs). A conceptual distinction is made between inexperienced novice entrepreneurs with no prior business ownership to leverage, and habitual (i.e., serial and portfolio) entrepreneurs with prior business ownership experience.

5.3 Habitual entrepreneur phenomenon

5.3.1 Context

Information relating to experience accumulated by an entrepreneur is used by practitioners (i.e., financial institutions and enterprise agencies) to screen applications for assistance (Westhead and Wright, 1999; Baum and Silverman, 2004). The *nature* and *extent* of entrepreneurial experience, in particular *business ownership experience*, is attracting research attention (Reuber and Fischer, 1999; Westhead et al., 2004a). Direct entrepreneurial experience from business ownership contributes to entrepreneurship-specific human capital, that is entrepreneurial, managerial and technical skills applicable to entrepreneurial activity (Chandler and Hanks, 1998). Entrepreneurial skills focus upon the perceived ability to create, identify and exploit opportunities. Managerial skills concern the ability to manage and organise people and resources. Technical skills focus upon technical expertise. Repeated business ownership experience contributes to the development of these skills.

An experienced entrepreneur may be able to identify what is required to earn profits in a particular market more clearly than novice entrepreneurs (Starr and Bygrave, 1991). A novice entrepreneur who can only leverage the experience accumulated through their current venture may be unable to move down the experience curve relating to the issues and processes associated with identifying and exploiting entrepreneurial opportunities. Entrepreneurial experience adds to human capital through enhanced reputation and better understanding of financial institutions' requirements (Wright et al., 1997a, b). Enhanced specific human capital from entrepreneurial experience may be interrelated with broader and deeper networks (Shane and Khurana, 2003). Some experienced entrepreneurs benefit from business proposals being presented to them by other entrepreneurs.

An entrepreneur's business ownership experience may differ according to the number of private businesses they have established, inherited and/or purchased. The *nature* of an entrepreneur's business ownership experience may not be homogeneous. The resource needs, behaviour and contributions made by inexperienced novice entrepreneurs with no prior business ownership experience may not be the same as those reported by experienced habitual entrepreneurs with prior business ownership experience. With reference to habitual entrepreneurs, a distinction has been made between serial and portfolio entrepreneurs (Westhead and Wright, 1998a, b; Ucbasaran et al., 2008a). Definitions of serial and portfolio entrepreneurs are presented in Section 5.3.2. Obstacles to subsequent business start-up and purchase as well as barriers to business development (i.e., the *liabilities of newness and small firm size* (Delmar and Shane, 2004)) may be circumvented by habitual entrepreneurs who can attain developmental milestones more quickly.

The wealth creation potential of habitual entrepreneurs is attracting growing attention (Westhead and Wright, 1998a; Westhead et al., 2003a; Rerup, 2005; Baron and Ensley, 2006). This wealth creation relates both to private returns in terms of financial gains at the personal level and for investors, as well as at the societal level through the creation of ventures and development of purchased ventures that generate employment and taxation revenues that may not otherwise have occurred (Rosa, 1998).

5.3.2 Defining novice, habitual, serial and portfolio entrepreneurs

Defining habitual entrepreneurs is a conceptually difficult task (Ucbasaran et al., 2008a). There is no generally accepted habitual entrepreneur definition. It is difficult to compare evidence from studies that have used contrasting definitions. Ucbasaran et al. (2008a) defined entrepreneurs with regard to three well-established dimensions: business ownership, a decision-making role, and an ability to identify and exploit opportunities. Business ownership and a decision-making role within the venture are recognised as important dimensions of entrepreneurship. Further, given the prevalence of team-based entrepreneurship (Ucbasaran et al., 2003), this ownership may involve minority or majority equity stakes. The emerging opportunity-based conceptualisation of entrepreneurship suggests that entrepreneurship involves the identification and exploitation of at least one business opportunity (see Section 3.6.5). A business opportunity can relate to new firm formation or the purchase of an existing private firm. Entrepreneurs can be viewed as having a minority or majority ownership stake in at least one business that they have either created or purchased, within which they are a key decision-maker.

A categorisation of the *nature of entrepreneurship* by type of entrepreneur is summarised in Table 5.1. The entrepreneurs covered by cells 1a, 2a and 3a are involved in the founding of a new independent firm. Novice founders (cell 1a) have only founded one firm, while

Table 5.1 Categorisation of novice and habitual entrepreneurship by type of entrepreneur

Nature of entrepreneurship		*Single* activity	*Multiple* activity	
		Novice entrepreneurs	Habitual entrepreneurs	
			Sequential Serial entrepreneurs	Simultaneous Portfolio entrepreneurs
Involving new business(es)	*De novo business*	Novice founders (1a)	Serial founders (2a)	Portfolio founders (3a)
	Spin-off (including corporate and university spin-offs)	Novice spinout entrepreneurs (1b)	Serial spinout entrepreneurs (2b)	Portfolio spinout entrepreneurs (3b)
Involving existing business(es)	*Purchase (including buyouts/ buyins)*	Novice acquirers (4a)	Serial acquirers (e.g., secondary MBOs/MBIs) (5a)	Portfolio acquirers (e.g., leveraged build-ups) (6a)
	Corporate entrepreneurship	Novice corporate entrepreneurs (4b)	Serial corporate entrepreneurs (5b)	Portfolio corporate entrepreneurs (6b)
Involving no new legal entity	*Self-employment*	Novice self-employed (7)	Serial self-employed (8)	Portfolio self-employed (9)

Source: Adapted from Ucbasaran et al. (2008a, Table 7.1: 111).

serial founders (cell 2a) and portfolio founders (cell 3a) have founded more than one firm sequentially or concurrently/simultaneously, respectively. The entrepreneurs in cells 1b, 2b and 3b are involved in new firms that are spin-offs from other organisations such as universities or large corporations (see Chapters 6 and 8). The entrepreneurs in cells 4a, 5a and 6a have acquired an ownership stake in an established independent firm (see Chapters 7 and 8). The term 'acquirer' is used to reflect ownership if the existing firm is acquired even though this may take a variety of forms. Acquirers include individuals from outside, who undertake a straight purchase or a management buyin (MBI), and individuals from inside the firm who undertake a management buyout (MBO). While novice acquirers (cell 4a) may have only acquired a single firm, serial acquirers (cell 5a) and portfolio acquirers (cell 6a) have purchased more than one firm sequentially or simultaneously, respectively. The entrepreneurs in cells 4b, 5b and 6b are also involved in existing firms but as corporate entrepreneurs rather than purchasers of the firm. Finally, the entrepreneurs in cells 7, 8 and 9 are self-employed individuals who do not form a specific legal entity. Note that some current novice entrepreneurs will become future habitual entrepreneurs. See the example of George Parker relating to serial entrepreneurs in Entrepreneurship in action 5.1.

The following definitions of novice, habitual, serial and portfolio entrepreneurs have been proposed (Westhead et al., 2003a; Ucbasaran et al., 2008a):

- *Novice entrepreneurs*: Individuals with no prior minority or majority firm ownership experience, either as a firm founder or as purchaser of an independent firm, who currently own a minority or majority equity stake in an independent firm that is either new or purchased.
- *Habitual entrepreneurs*: Individuals who hold or have held a minority or majority ownership stake in two or more firms, at least one of which was established or purchased.

Entrepreneurship in action 5.1
Serial entrepreneurs cannot help it: George Parker

My all time favorite was Nolan Bushnell. He's the guy who invented electronic gaming with 'Pong', the foundation of his Atari Empire. Then he sold it for a gazillion dollars and went off and founded Chucky Cheese, purveyors of the world's worst pizza, but with lots of games for kids.

But, as is common with these people, they can't just park their millions under the sidewalks of Zurich and enjoy life, they have to go off and found another company, 'cos they're 'Serial Entrepreneurs'! Up to date, Nolan has founded over twenty companies; problem is, since Atari, most of them have not enjoyed the success of his very first venture, and the reputation he enjoyed in the eighties

has been somewhat diminished. But 'Serial Entrepreneurs' never stop looking for the next 'Killer App'.

Back in the late eighties I was working on 3Com when they bought Bridge Communications, a company founded by Judith Estrin and her husband, Bill Carrico. Over a period of a few years, they had founded three companies and sold them for hundreds of millions of dollars. So they decided to pack it all in and spend a few years travelling the world. They came back after two weeks, 'cos they were bored. She has since founded four more companies.

Source: George Parker: Serial Entrepreneur at Large . . . Batten Down the Hatches! www.psfk.com.

Habitual entrepreneurs are subdivided as follows:

- *Serial entrepreneurs*: Individuals who have sold/closed at least one firm in which they had a minority or majority ownership stake, and currently have a minority or majority ownership stake in a single independent firm; and
- *Portfolio entrepreneurs*: Individuals who currently have minority or majority ownership stakes in two or more independent firms.

5.3.3 The scale of the habitual entrepreneur phenomenon

Habitual entrepreneurs are a widespread phenomenon. The proportion of habitual entrepreneurs identified in United Kingdom studies ranges from 12 per cent (Cross, 1981) to 52 per cent (Ucbasaran et al., 2006a); this may indicate increased prevalence of the phenomenon, but the differences are partly attributable to variations in operationalised definitions, and the industrial activities focused upon between studies. High proportions of habitual entrepreneurs have also been detected in the United States (51 to 64 per cent) (Ronstadt, 1988; Schollhammer, 1991), Finland (50 per cent) (Pasanen, 2003), Australia (49 per cent) (Taylor, 1999), Norway (47 per cent) (Kolvereid and Bullvåg, 1993), Sweden (40 per cent) (Wiklund and Shepherd, 2008), and Malaysia (39 per cent) (Taylor, 1999).

Some scholars focus on business groups relating to the set of businesses under the control of the habitual entrepreneur (Rosa and Scott, 1999a, b). Iacobucci (2002) noted that 25 per cent of Italian manufacturing firms were members of a business group created by a habitual entrepreneur (or their associated entrepreneurial team). Iacobucci and Rosa (2005) found that growth through the formation of business groups in Italy was a strategy to organise geographical extension, product diversification or market differentiation. They noted that business groups were more prevalent among larger rather than smaller firms. Iacobucci and Rosa (2005) found sectoral variations in the prevalence of business groups. Rosa (1998) and Rosa and Scott (1999a) also mapped out business clusters in Scotland, and they noted a complex picture of portfolio entrepreneurship.

This discussion suggests that the 'correct' incidence of habitual entrepreneurs may be difficult to determine. The scale of the phenomenon is shaped by the definition selected, the industrial sector focused upon, and whether team ownership is considered. Nevertheless, its scale suggests increased academic and practitioner interest is warranted to understand the resource profiles and needs, behaviour and contributions made by habitual entrepreneurs and their firm(s).

5.3.4 Conceptual differences: Human capital and cognitive profiles

In Section 4.2.2, a distinction was made between an individual's general and specific human capital. Business ownership experience is a key dimension of *specific/entrepreneurial human capital* (Audretsch and Keilbach, 2004). It may provide habitual entrepreneurs with a *variety of resources* that can be leveraged to identify and exploit subsequent business opportunities such as:

- direct entrepreneurial experience;
- additional managerial experience;
- an enhanced reputation;
- better access to and understanding of the requirements of finance institutions; and
- access to broader social and business networks.

Habitual entrepreneurs are generally more able to accumulate (and utilise) additional human capital, and other types of capital (e.g., social and financial capital). Therefore, habitual entrepreneurs with more diverse human capital profiles and access to a wider set of resources need to be distinguished from novice entrepreneurs.

The *cognitive mindsets* (i.e., in terms of how people think, process information and learn) (see Section 4.6) of experienced habitual entrepreneurs and inexperienced novice entrepreneurs are assumed to differ (Ucbasaran et al., 2008a). Experience can shape an individual's cognition. Guided by insights from *information processing theory and expert information processing theory* (Baron, 2004), it is reasonable to assume that:

- experience can influence an individual's capacity to acquire and organise complex information;
- experience provides a framework for processing information;
- experience can allow experienced entrepreneurs with diverse skills (i.e., networks, knowledge, etc.) to foresee and take advantage of disequilibrium profit opportunities that they proactively or reactively identify; and
- experience-based knowledge can create cognitive pathways which, when followed, can lead to greater creativity.

With reference to *information processing theory*, it is assumed that novice entrepreneurs may have fewer *experience-related benchmarks* (or mental short-cuts) to draw upon. Conversely, habitual entrepreneurs who have multiple experiences to draw upon may be more likely to rely on information processing based on *heuristics* (i.e., simplifying strategies (or mental short-cuts) used to make strategic decisions, especially in complex situations when complete information is not available) than novice entrepreneurs. Heuristic-based logic enables individuals to make quick decisions that allow them to successfully exploit brief windows of opportunity (Tversky and Kahneman, 1974).

With regard to *expert information processing theory*, it is assumed that:

- experience can shape differences between 'novices' and 'experts';
- experts are able to manipulate incoming information into recognisable patterns, and then they are able to match the information to appropriate actions;
- experts can concentrate on novel or unique material; and
- experts can leverage knowledge to avoid cognitive biases (i.e., inappropriate use of a heuristic) in their decision-making.

Habitual entrepreneurs who have learnt from their prior business experience may, therefore, resemble 'experts'.

Studies generally assume that more experience (i.e., extent of experience) will be associated with superior outcomes. For example, McGrath and MacMillan (2000) provocatively asserted that repeat (or habitual) entrepreneurs might have an *'entrepreneurial mindset'* that prompts them to search out opportunities with enormous discipline, and to pursue only the very best opportunities. Currently, there is limited empirical evidence to support these assertions. There is also inconclusive evidence relating to the link between an entrepreneur's prior business ownership experience and the propensity to identify additional opportunities (Ucbasaran et al., 2009, 2010) and superior levels of firm performance (Ucbasaran et al., 2008a). Habitual entrepreneurs can accumulate both *assets and liabilities* associated with their previous business ownership experience (Starr and Bygrave, 1991).

Hence, it may be a myth to suggest that all habitual entrepreneurs are successful and outperform novice entrepreneurs (Ucbasaran et al., 2006a). The current stock of novice entrepreneurs is the *breeding ground* (i.e., pool) for future experienced habitual entrepreneurs. Some highly successful entrepreneurs may have been associated with prior business *'failures'*, which represent potentially valuable opportunities for *learning*, and the revision of expectations (Sitkin, 1992).

5.3.5 Policy case to focus on types of entrepreneurs relating to their entrepreneurial experience

An increase in the number (stock) of businesses in an economy may not necessarily be a reliable indicator of the development of entrepreneurship (Westhead and Wright, 1999), or an enterprise culture. New firm start-up rates can be distorted by *habitual entrepreneurs and 'transient novice entrepreneurs'* (i.e., novice entrepreneurs who subsequently become serial or portfolio entrepreneurs). Studies that ignore the scale of serial and portfolio entrepreneur activity may overestimate the gross number of entrepreneurs and underestimate the contribution made by particular types of entrepreneur.

In Section 4.2.3, it was suggested that to maximise returns on public policy investments, attempts have been made to 'target' external support to *'winning firms'*, that is, firms with significant wealth creation potential. It was, however, asserted that policy should support entrepreneurs throughout all stages of the entrepreneurial process, and not just in relation to business creation. Analysis of the heterogeneity of entrepreneurs may contribute toward the development of policies customised to different types of entrepreneur (Westhead et al., 2003a). To guide the resource allocation decisions of practitioners, an evidence base is required relating to the assets and liabilities associated with prior business ownership experience. Several commentators suggest there is a need to provide customised support to build and increase the pool of 'winning firms and entrepreneurs' (Westhead et al., 2003a, 2004a; Baum and Silverman, 2004).

5.3.6 Evidence base

5.3.6.1 *Context*

Studies have detected statistically significant differences between novice and habitual entrepreneurs, as well as between novice, serial and portfolio entrepreneurs with regard to their profiles and the firms they own (see Ucbasaran et al. (2008a) for a detailed review). Differences have been noted with regard to their personal backgrounds and motivations, their human capital profiles, cognitive mindsets, access to resources, opportunity identification and exploitation processes, as well as firm and entrepreneur performance. These themes are discussed, in turn, below.

5.3.6.2 *Demographic characteristics and general and specific human capital*

Entrepreneurs' human capital can shape their ability to assemble and leverage resources that are required to ensure superior firm performance (Bosma et al., 2004; Colombo and Grilli, 2005). Differences between novice and habitual entrepreneurs, as well as between novice, serial and portfolio entrepreneurs with regard to *demographic characteristics* (i.e., gender, age and parental background), together with their *general* (i.e., education and managerial experience) *and specific human capital profiles* (i.e., entrepreneurial team experience, motivations, perceived skills and cognitive mindsets) have been identified. In general, evidence indicates that habitual entrepreneurs are younger when they start their first business and they are male (Westhead and Wright, 1998b; Westhead et al., 2003b). Portfolio entrepreneurs are generally more likely to have parents who were business owners (Westhead et al., 2003b) (see Case 8, The OffQuip saga: Partner entry and exit dynamics). Habitual entrepreneurs have generally accumulated different resource pools than novice entrepreneurs, which can impact on subsequent behaviour and performance. Regarding general human capital, habitual entrepreneurs tend to be more highly educated and to have higher levels of managerial human capital (Westhead et al., 2003b; Ucbasaran et al., 2006a).

With reference to *specific human capital*, habitual entrepreneurs tend to have worked for more organisations prior to starting a business (Ucbasaran et al., 2006a). Portfolio entrepreneurs proactively seek to reduce any deficiencies by selecting '*team ownership*'. In order to avoid biases resulting from previous experience, and to increase their awareness in decision-making, many portfolio entrepreneurs prefer to be 'team' owners, rather than 'solo' owners of private firms. Habitual entrepreneurs, particularly portfolio entrepreneurs are more likely to compensate for their own personal human capital deficiencies by attracting other individuals with more diverse human capital to join the entrepreneurial ownership team. Ucbasaran et al. (2006a) detected that portfolio entrepreneurs in Great Britain more frequently reported the prevalence of team ownership to start or purchase surveyed businesses (34 per cent, 36 per cent and 41 per cent reported by novice, serial and portfolio entrepreneurs, respectively). Attracting additional equity partners into the entrepreneurial team can enable a solo entrepreneur to accumulate human capital. A partner may be able to offer a wider range of skills and knowledge as well as financial resources. The team aspect of entrepreneurship may be important in providing the resources and skills needed to establish and maintain ownership stakes in multiple businesses. The resources required to develop a portfolio of businesses suggest that portfolio entrepreneurs may require contributions from more partners than do serial or novice entrepreneurs. Portfolio entrepreneurs may be able to establish and own multiple businesses because they use partners, whereas novice and serial entrepreneurs may establish and/or own a business without a partner. Partners can reduce some of the *liabilities associated with firm newness and small size*. They can provide legitimacy to a business principally owned by a serial entrepreneur, whose reputation may have been tarnished due to a prior business ownership failure. Partners can provide successful (and unsuccessful) habitual entrepreneurs with a greater depth of expertise, access to wider networks, and a means of delegating responsibility.

5.3.6.3 *Specific human capital: Motivations*

Gimeno et al. (1997) suggested that the motivations for establishing a new venture can be viewed as a component of venture-specific human capital. The initial reasons leading to the ownership of a business can, in part, influence the development trajectory of a business. Motivations may have an impact on the behaviours and strategies selected by different 'types' of entrepreneurs. Scholars have identified a diverse range of motivations reported by habitual entrepreneurs; a desire for independence and autonomy and the desire for (personal) wealth creation (Wright et al., 1997a), and motivations related to the operation of an existing business (i.e., need for more income and the desire to grow the business activities) (Alsos and Carter, 2006) (see Case 9, Iain Russell and Arran Aromatics Limited: Portfolio and serial entrepreneurship).

Westhead and Wright (1998a) found that the reasons leading to start-up varied both between the type of entrepreneur and the type of locality where the surveyed business was located. Portfolio rural founders were markedly more likely than novice and serial rural founders to have started their businesses for wealth and/or welfare reasons. Further, a smaller proportion of serial rather than portfolio or novice rural founders reported they had established their businesses to obtain tax benefits.

Westhead and Wright (1998c) showed that novice and portfolio urban founders were more likely than serial urban founders to emphasise autonomy reasons for start-up. Habitual urban entrepreneurs, particularly serial founders, were more likely than novice urban founders to have suggested that they started the business in order to develop an idea for a product. Portfolio and novice urban founders were more likely than serial founders to have reported that they were taking advantage of an opportunity that appeared. A larger proportion of portfolio urban founders rather than novice and serial urban founders reported that they were seeking tax benefits. Novice urban founders were more likely than portfolio urban founders to have emphasised that they started a business to achieve something, and to get recognition for it. Habitual urban entrepreneurs, particularly serial founders, were more likely than novice urban founders to have reported starting a business to continue a family tradition. Entrepreneurship in action 5.2 provides examples of the motivations reported by portfolio and serial entrepreneurs.

Motivations reported by habitual entrepreneurs for owning businesses can change over time. While independence is a strong reason for starting a first business, a variety of other more materialistic reasons may come to the fore when an entrepreneur establishes (or purchases) a subsequent business (Donckels et al., 1987). Other evidence suggests that monetary gain may become less important in subsequent ventures (Wright et al., 1997a). This is because owners of second or later ventures generally desire less risky ventures. Wright et al. (1997a) detected that habitual entrepreneurs continually reported the desire/need to work independently, and to build a larger organisation.

Iacobucci (2002) explored the reasons why some entrepreneurs start a group of businesses. The three main reasons were the firm's growth policy, entrepreneurial dynamics, and capital accumulation on the part of the entrepreneur or their family. Rosa (1998) showed that the motivations why portfolio entrepreneurs added new businesses to their

Entrepreneurship in action 5.2
Examples of the motivations reported by portfolio and serial entrepreneurs

Portfolio entrepreneur
Mary Fairburn's motivation for the first two firms was to become more independent and involved in something that would be physically less demanding than her employment at the time. Having learnt how to deal with the problems of running a firm and having acquired assets from previous firm ownership, she developed the confidence and ability to develop a portfolio of related firms.

Serial entrepreneur
For Norman Rough, the main motivation for starting a firm was to make use of the positive name he had developed in the world of weight training and body building to help others in the sport. At the time, there was an absence of gyms that were visually attractive and which would provide a pleasant experience. The motive for subsequent businesses was to build on the client base in the health studio.

Source: Westhead et al., 2003b.

business groups centred on: diversifying into a new market; to spread risk or to overcome potential adversity; business creation as a challenge or a hobby; to protect a new area or brand name; to ringfence a geographical diversification; to ringfence risk; to add value to existing ventures owned by the entrepreneur; to assist a friend or relative; to launder money, profits and/or family assets; to avoid paying taxes; and to cut costs and enhance internal efficiencies. Carter and Ram (2003: 375) concluded that motivations for portfolio entrepreneurship can:

> range from entrepreneurs who invest in several sectors at once and who are thus able to move their capital between various enterprises as the market conditions require; to small scale traders who diversify their economic activities to cover both productive and distributive functions; to the only survival strategy available to marginal businesses.

5.3.6.4 *Specific human capital: Perceived managerial, technical and entrepreneurial capabilities*

Entrepreneurs must demonstrate skills relating to *entrepreneurial, managerial and technical* functional areas (Chandler and Jansen, 1992). Perceived specific human capital skills can correspond with actual skills. Westhead et al. (2003b) found that portfolio entrepreneurs were more likely than novice entrepreneurs to report managerial capabilities relating to professionalised resource accumulation and management skills, as well as entrepreneurial capabilities relating to the alertness and developmental approach to opportunity identification (see Sections 3.6.3 and 3.6.4). Serial entrepreneurs were more likely than novice entrepreneurs to suggest entrepreneurial capabilities relating to customer focus and need, whilst they were more likely than portfolio entrepreneurs to report technical capabilities in a technical or functional area. Ucbasaran et al. (2006b) detected that habitual entrepreneurs were associated with lower levels of perceived technical skill than novice entrepreneurs. Portfolio entrepreneurs were associated with higher levels of managerial skill than serial entrepreneurs. Alsos et al. (2003) found that portfolio farm-based entrepreneurs reported higher entrepreneurial abilities than farmers with no other business activities.

5.3.6.5 *Specific human capital: Cognitive mindsets*

'Dominant logic' is a key component of an entrepreneur's stock of experience (see Section 4.6). Reuber and Fischer (1999) describe a dominant logic as being an information funnel through which the entrepreneur's attention is filtered. This information funnel is akin to the entrepreneur's cognition (Baron, 1998). The cognitive characteristics of entrepreneurs may shape their attitudes and behaviour. Westhead et al. (2005c) identified differences in the attitudes to entrepreneurship reported by novice, serial and portfolio entrepreneurs in Scotland. Drawing upon prior business ownership experience, habitual entrepreneurs were more cautious and realistic about the barriers they would face. Habitual, particularly portfolio, entrepreneurs suggested they were more creative than novice entrepreneurs. Portfolio entrepreneurs intimated that they were more innovative than novice and serial entrepreneurs.

5.3.6.6 *Behaviour: Acquisition of financial resources*

An entrepreneur's previous business ownership experience can have a profound influence on the amounts of initial capital, and types of finance used during the launch period of a subsequent new or acquired business. Successful habitual entrepreneurs may have larger amounts of personal capital, and greater access to external sources of funds than novice entrepreneurs. Serial (and portfolio) entrepreneurs may use funds from private business sales to invest in subsequent ventures. A novice entrepreneur lacking an established track record may have to rely upon internal sources of initial capital, including personal savings and family and friends, to obtain an ownership stake.

Habitual entrepreneurs with successful track records are generally more credible than those who have failed the first time around, and may leverage their prior business ownership experience to obtain external financial resources from banks and venture capitalists for their subsequent ventures. Portfolio entrepreneurs who have not exited from a venture(s) in which they have an ownership stake(s) may be able to leverage the internal financial resources from their existing business(es) (Alsos and Kolvereid, 1998), and may make use of finance from existing customers and suppliers. In contrast, serial entrepreneurs may have accumulated funds from the sale of a previous business. However, a reluctance to be involved in projects that may undermine their standing amongst the financial and business community, and a desire to invest a smaller proportion of their personal wealth the second time around (Wright et al., 1997a) may mean that some habitual entrepreneurs become risk-averse over time. Venture capitalists make their investment decisions with regard to an individual's previous business ownership experience, as well as their motivation and ability to succeed the next time around (Wright et al., 1997b). Prior founding experience, especially financially successful experience, increases the likelihood of venture capital funding via a direct tie, and the level of venture valuation (Hsu, 2007). Evidence from the United States suggests that 'failed' serial entrepreneurs rather than 'successful' serial entrepreneurs were more likely to have obtained funding from the venture capital firm that had funded their first venture (Bengtsson, 2007). In addition, a repeat venture capital relationship was more likely if an entrepreneur's subsequent start-up was similar to the previous start-up, if the venture capital firm was older, and if the subsequent business start-up was located outside California.

Alsos et al. (2006) detected that portfolio and serial founders invested significantly more money in their firms in Norway than novice founders at start-up. Similarly, Westhead et al. (2003a) found that, on average, portfolio entrepreneurs in Scotland invested more total initial capital (and personal capital) to establish or purchase the surveyed businesses than novice entrepreneurs. Portfolio entrepreneurs were able to leverage their prior business experience to acquire more initial capital from external sources (i.e., banks). Serial entrepreneurs invested more total initial (and personal) capital to establish or purchase the surveyed businesses than novice entrepreneurs. A larger proportion of serial entrepreneurs, rather than novice entrepreneurs, had used personal savings and/or a mortgage on their home as part of their initial capital. In terms of the proportion of initial funds contributed by each source, serial entrepreneurs, rather than other entrepreneurs, reported a higher proportion of initial capital had been obtained from personal savings. This evidence may indicate that their first (previous) venture had been a financial success. However, this finding may be consistent with the views of venture capital firms that one of the main reasons for not funding serial entrepreneurs in a subsequent venture relates to the inability of serial entrepreneurs to identify attractive subsequent ventures.

5.3.6.7 *Behaviour: Information*

Information represents a potentially valuable resource for entrepreneurs, particularly with regard to opportunity identification and exploitation (Shane, 2000). Two perspectives relating to information search behaviour have been presented (Kaish and Gilad, 1991). Search by an entrepreneur can be viewed as a *means of optimising performance*. Inexperienced entrepreneurs who are less prepared may be more likely to engage in extensive search (Woo et al., 1992). Conversely, more experienced habitual entrepreneurs may be less likely to engage in proactive search strategies because they can draw upon routines and responses that worked well in the past (see Section 4.6.3.5). Alternatively, information search can be viewed as part of the *process of identifying or 'noticing' opportunities* that are present (see Section 3.6.3). Less experienced novice entrepreneurs may conduct search routines that are narrower in terms of the sources and amount of information. Individuals with no prior business ownership experience have fewer benchmarks to assess whether the information they have collected is appropriate to identify and exploit a business opportunity. This is because they will be less attuned to the variety and implications of signals in their environment. Entrepreneurs with limited experience may use simplified decision-making methods to guide their search, while the opposite may be the case with experienced entrepreneurs.

Information search by novice and habitual entrepreneurs varies. Cooper et al. (1995) suggested that novice entrepreneurs would search for less information, due to their limited understanding of what is needed. Contrary to expectation, they found that novice entrepreneurs, on average, sought more information than habitual entrepreneurs. However, Westhead et al. (2005b) found that, on average, portfolio and serial entrepreneurs had used a wider range of information sources than novice entrepreneurs. Ucbasaran et al.'s (2006a) analysis of entrepreneurs in Great Britain did not find a significant association between an entrepreneur's prior business ownership experience and the number of information sources utilized, or the information search intensity. Entrepreneurship in action 5.3 provides examples of information search reported by portfolio and serial entrepreneurs.

Entrepreneurship in action 5.3
Examples of information search reported by portfolio and serial entrepreneurs

Portfolio entrepreneur

For Mike Kosic the firms he owns have been brought to him by family and friends who had either been involved in the firms, or who had expressed an interest in starting a firm in a particular area. In contrast, from initially searching for a firm that would enable a lifestyle shift and discovering opportunities almost by 'accident',

Mary Fairburn has become more systematic. First, she consciously looked to expand into a related business area in her third firm, although the precise venture was identified by 'accident'. Second, following a deliberate decision to move into the funeral director business, she invested considerable effort into looking at how funerals were managed in the United Kingdom and Europe, as well as attending an exhibition on funeral directing in Paris.

Serial entrepreneur

After working in his father's haulage firm, Wilson Smith decided to move into the licensed trade. Funds from the sale of his father's struggling firm were used to purchase a poorly performing public house. He has subsequently owned several public houses and restaurants as well as a nightclub but currently owns one hotel. Smith only became involved in the search process once he had decided to move on from the business he was in. He always used the same process, that was to look around for an area that should be good but was not. This included looking at the trade press for what was for sale and by developing contacts in the trade.

Source: Westhead et al., 2003b.

5.3.6.8 *Behaviour: Networks*

Entrepreneurs' social networks can provide access to information and facilitate the identification of opportunities. Network contacts can help expand the boundaries of an entrepreneur's thinking by offering access to knowledge and information, and may in this way expose the entrepreneur to new venture ideas and opportunities (Singh et al., 1999). With each business ownership experience, habitual entrepreneurs may develop contacts that provide them with a flow of information relating to business opportunities (Rosa, 1998), implying that they may need to be less proactive in information search relative to novice entrepreneurs. Having earned a reputation as a successful entrepreneur, financiers, advisers, other entrepreneurs, and business contacts may *present business proposals* to some habitual entrepreneurs.

Ronstadt (1988) suggested that the best new venture opportunities could be most often revealed only after an individual is already involved in a venture. This is because once the venture has been initiated, greater information becomes available about relevant contacts, viable markets, product availability, and competitive resources. Similarly, McGrath (1999) has argued that habitual entrepreneurs (particularly, portfolio entrepreneurs) may be more likely to pursue ventures as a means of gaining access to a wider range of *'shadow options'* (i.e., business opportunities that had not been previously recognised) than other entrepreneurs.

Alsos et al. (2003) found that farmers in Norway who identified opportunities based on the daily activities of the farm business, were more likely to engage in the start-up of new business activities. Wiklund and Shepherd (2007) detected that an entrepreneur's business networks and links with support agencies were a significant predictor of habitual entrepreneurship. Consequently, the nature (i.e., quality) and the amount of information (i.e., quantity) should be considered.

Mosey and Wright (2007) have developed theory relating to how differences in the human capital derived from the entrepreneurial experience of academic entrepreneurs can influence their ability to develop social capital to address barriers to venture development. They identified three types of academic entrepreneurs with differing levels of entrepreneurship experience (i.e., nascent, novice and habitual entrepreneurs). Using a longitudinal study of 24 academic entrepreneurs in England, they proposed that habitual entrepreneurs had broader social networks and were more effective in developing network ties to gain equity finance and management knowledge. Conversely, less experienced entrepreneurs were likely to encounter structural holes between their scientific research networks and industry networks, constraining their ability to recognise opportunities and gain credibility for their fledgling ventures.

5.3.6.9 *Behaviour: Opportunity identification*

Information is a necessary but insufficient condition for the identification of business opportunities. Prior business ownership experience may allow habitual entrepreneurs to be more alert to opportunities than inexperienced novice entrepreneurs. Experience-based knowledge can direct an individual's attention, expectations, and interpretations of market stimuli. Habitual entrepreneurs can leverage their experience-based knowledge to generate additional business ideas, as well as spot business opportunities that are ignored, or not recognised by novice entrepreneurs. Westhead et al. (2003b) found that a larger proportion of novice entrepreneurs compared with serial or portfolio entrepreneurs had failed to identify any opportunities for creating or purchasing a business within the last five years.

Entrepreneurship in action 5.4
Examples of opportunity recognition reported by portfolio and serial entrepreneurs

Portfolio entrepreneur

Mary Fairburn's first two business opportunities arose because of lifestyle choices, yet she had no experience in running either of the firms. The first opportunity, to go into antiques retailing, was recognised as a way of enabling a move from an existing location and occupation. The second, the acquisition of a private cemetery firm, arose because of a relocation decision and a search for something different from the first but which would not be seasonal. The third opportunity was the result of a search to expand by doing something connected to the cemetery and materialised when the memorials firm with whom she had traded went into liquidation and the entrepreneur took the view that she could run it better than the previous owner. The fourth opportunity, a funeral service firm was recognised as an opportunity to move into a related business where she felt she could offer a better service.

Serial entrepreneur

Norman Rough identified his first business opportunity of a health and fitness club as a result of being asked by people how they could do body building in an organised way. He decided to make use of this level of interest and his reputation from competing nationally in the sport. The subsequent opportunity for a cosmetic salon presented itself as an extension of the customer base in the health and fitness club. However, the third business emerged from an active decision to start a design consultancy. Having trained in architectural design, Rough identified an opportunity to provide clients with small-scale, specialised design work that met a need for a complete service including both design and architectural work.

Source: Westhead et al., 2003b.

A larger proportion of serial rather than portfolio entrepreneurs had failed to spot any opportunities. As expected, a significantly larger proportion of portfolio entrepreneurs rather than serial or novice entrepreneurs had identified two or more opportunities. Alsos et al. (2006) also found that portfolio and serial entrepreneurs had identified significantly more opportunities than novice entrepreneurs. Further, portfolio entrepreneurs had identified more opportunities than serial entrepreneurs. Entrepreneurship in action 5.4 provides examples of opportunity recognition reported by portfolio and serial entrepreneurs.

Ucbasaran et al. (2008b) found that habitual entrepreneurs identified significantly more opportunities for creating or purchasing a business in a given period than novice entrepreneurs. They noted that the latest business opportunities exploited by habitual entrepreneurs tended to be associated with higher levels of innovation. They, in addition, detected that entrepreneurs' entrepreneurship-specific human capital, in particular business ownership experience, and perceptions of managerial and entrepreneurial skills were associated with the identification and pursuit of more opportunities. Portfolio entrepreneurs identified significantly more opportunities than serial entrepreneurs. Ucbasaran et al. (2008b) also explored the relationship between the number of businesses owned by habitual entrepreneurs and the subsequent number of business opportunities identified. Entrepreneurs with more business ownership experience identified significantly more business opportunities and more innovative opportunities, albeit at a diminishing rate. These findings support the view that experience may be associated with both assets and liabilities. Up to a fairly high level (some 15 firms), prior business ownership experience may be a valuable resource for opportunity identification. Beyond this point, experience may lead to biases. Individuals may believe that they already have sufficient knowledge and they do not have to search for additional information, and if information is sought there is a reliance on familiar domains. For example, habitual entrepreneurs may rely too much on strong ties in the networks in which they are embedded that encourage them to search for opportunities in familiar domains, whereas the development of weak ties may enable them to expand their knowledge into new areas.

Ucbasaran et al. (2006b, 2010) noted that habitual entrepreneurs with higher proportions of prior business failure experience identified significantly more business opportunities. However, habitual entrepreneurs who reported that more than 26 per cent of their businesses had failed identified significantly fewer business opportunities. Thus, a certain amount of business failure can encourage entrepreneurs to learn from their mistakes, and to put into practice what they have learned. In addition, it lends support to the view that business failure can be a traumatic event that can hinder learning, as well as reduce an individual's self-confidence and motivation to re-enter business ownership (Shepherd, 2003). Entrepreneurship in action 5.5 provides an example of 'failure' reported by Kamran Elahian who is a habitual entrepreneur.

Entrepreneurship in action 5.5
Habitual entrepreneurs and 'failure': Kamran Elahian

'My ego was as big as the Titanic. And we all know what happened to that ship,' Kamran Elahian, 47, likes to say. By the age of 30, Kamran Elahian, an Iranian immigrant, had co-founded a company heralded as one of the more important of the 20th century – a semi-conductor company named Cirrus Logic. That's a nice confidence builder, but there were troubles ahead for the young Elahian . . . It's the ugly truth. For every company started, there are hundreds of reasons it can fail. 'What are you going to do, commit suicide?' Elahian says, 'You have to learn to just crack a joke and keep moving forward.'

Elahian, who has a smile that must have rivalled the size of his ego even at its peak, experienced the failure that changed his life in 1992, when he was fired from his job as chairman of Momenta Corp., the pen-based computer company he'd co-founded just a few years before. The company had sprung up on the hype of Elahian's wunderkind status and the industry's high hopes for the portable computer. But after hemorrhaging $40 million, the company collapsed.

In hindsight, it's easy to pick apart what went wrong. The public wasn't ready for the product, too much money was spent on marketing, and there were software problems, among other things. But at the time, Elahian says, he was too sure of his own infallibility to see these problems clearly. 'I had come to believe my own PR.' Elahian says now, 'and that's never good.'

The advantage of already being a multimillionaire when you first experience defeat is that you can travel around the world and study philosophy while you lick your wounds. When Elahian came back from his self-imposed exile, he founded Neo-Magic Corp., a multimedia company that went public in 1997 with a valuation of $400 million. Although he's been on a roll ever since, Elahian never tries to obscure his big flop. In fact, he keeps a reminder around so that he can't forget – and because it amuses him. The license plate of his fire-engine-red Ferrari spells it out: Momenta.

Source: http://www.derbymanagement.com/knowledge/pages/success/serial.html, accessed 15 July 2010.

5.3.6.10 *Behaviour: Organisational strategies*

Entrepreneurs' organisational practices offer insights into how they exploit opportunities. Westhead et al. (2003b) found that habitual entrepreneurs (particularly portfolio entrepreneurs) were significantly more likely to emphasise innovation and growth. They were also more likely to report professionalised management practices to enable the firm to respond (and to be efficient and productive), irrespective of the market, technological and regulatory conditions. The fact that portfolio entrepreneurs own more than one business may explain their greater focus on managerial competence and human capital resources than serial or novice entrepreneurs. In line with case study evidence (Rosa, 1998), this evidence supports the view that portfolio entrepreneurs may develop synergistic relationships between the firms they own to gain competitive advantages for individual ventures. Some portfolio entrepreneurs can utilise this distinct advantage to ensure the survival and development of firms they own.

5.3.6.11 *Firm performance*

Few studies have monitored firm performance differences between novice and habitual entrepreneurs as well as between novice, serial and portfolio entrepreneurs. Cross-sectional survey evidence is usually gathered. Most studies have failed to gather information relating to the array of firms owned by portfolio entrepreneurs. Consequently, the full economic contribution made by portfolio entrepreneurs relative to other types of entrepreneurs has not been adequately assessed. Carter (1999) and Rønning and Kolvereid (2006) have, however, compared performance information from all the firms currently owned by portfolio and novice entrepreneurs.

No consistent pattern of association has been identified between an entrepreneur's prior business ownership experience and superior firm performance. More experienced entrepreneurs tend to own firms which are more likely to survive, and to report *superior firm performance* across several outcomes (Reuber and Fisher, 1994; Dahlqvist et al., 2000; Haynes, 2003; Delamar and Shane, 2004). However, several studies have *failed to detect any significant link* between prior business ownership experience and superior firm performance (Birley and Westhead, 1993a; Kolvereid and Bullvåg, 1993; Westhead and Wright, 1998a, c; Ucbasaran et al., 2006a). There is some support for the view that habitual entrepreneurs, particularly *portfolio entrepreneurs, own superior performing firms* relative to novice entrepreneurs (Dahlqvist and Davidsson, 2000; Westhead et al., 2003a, b; 2005b, d) (see Section 4.2.3). Alsos et al. (2006) found that new firms owned by novice founders reported significantly lower early new business employment growth than those owned by serial and portfolio entrepreneurs. The latter difference was not detected when resource access was considered within a multivariate regression framework (also see Ucbasaran et al., 2006a).

5.3.6.12 *Entrepreneur performance*

Few studies have monitored the performance of habitual entrepreneurs with regard to entrepreneur performance indicators. Entrepreneur performance can be assessed with regard to array of indicators (i.e. incomes, satisfaction, standard of living and desire to own an additional venture). Portfolio entrepreneurs have been found to draw larger incomes than novice entrepreneurs (Westhead et al. 2005b; Rønning and Kolvereid, 2006).

Westhead et al. (2003b) asked habitual entrepreneurs whether they were satisfied with the surveyed business in relation to their first business. Over three-quarters of serial and port-folio entrepreneurs reported that they were satisfied with the surveyed business. No signifi-cant differences were detected between entrepreneurs with regard to their standard of living today compared to when they first established/owned the surveyed business. An additional aspect of satisfaction relates to the willingness to start or purchase a business again in the future. They found that a larger proportion of portfolio rather than novice and serial entre-preneurs indicated that they intended to establish or purchase an additional business. Prior entrepreneurial experience has been linked to the propensity to report the intention to start a business again (Kolvereid and Isaksen, 2006). Flores-Romero and Blackburn (2006) noted that serial entrepreneurs following the closure of a business were markedly more likely to start another business than novice entrepreneurs.

5.4 Policy and practitioner implications

To *maximise returns on their investments* at national and/or local levels, practitioners may seek to encourage the *development of existing entrepreneurs (and firms),* rather than solely to provide additional support to increase the supply of nascent entrepreneurs, novice entrepreneurs and new firms (Global Entrepreneurship Monitor (GEM) 2004; Westhead et al., 2004a, 2005d). Rather than '*blanket support*' given to all entrepreneurs (see Section 2.3.4), irrespective of aspirations, needs and existing resource profiles, a case for *customised sup-port* to each type of entrepreneur linked to their prior entrepreneurial (i.e., business own-ership) experience has been proposed (Westhead et al., 2004a). This strategy may be useful for practitioners concerned with rising business closure rates. There is an emerging view that the retention of habitual entrepreneurs represents an important *enterprise sustainabil-ity issue* (Westhead et al., 2004a, 2005d).

Westhead et al. (2003a, b; 2004a; 2005d) suggested that practitioners should consider allocating resources to *portfolio entrepreneurs* who are actively seeking to maximise wealth creation and job generation. From a policy perspective, there may be a need to reconcile the *private* (i.e., the financial gains at the personal level for entrepreneurs and investors) and *social returns* (i.e., the employment as well as the wealth and taxation revenues generated) from habitual entrepreneurship. Schemes could be introduced to encourage the wider take-up and utilisation of methods of best business practice exhib-ited by portfolio entrepreneurs. The benefits derived from previous business ownership experience were found to be less clear for serial entrepreneurs. Initiatives should be designed to provide customised assistance to serial entrepreneurs. *Serial entrepreneurs* who have owned a previously unsuccessful venture may require special external support to ensure that they can learn from their prior business ownership 'failure'. There may also be a case to provide both serial and portfolio entrepreneurs with 'hard' financial incen-tives through changes in the tax regime to encourage the investment of profits, or funds realised from the sale of a business, into subsequent ventures with growth potential. In addition, there may be scope to develop schemes that encourage *novice entrepreneurs* to take up and exhibit the methods of best business practice displayed by successful portfo-lio entrepreneurs. Schemes could be introduced to establish mechanisms that encourage networking and information exchange between novice entrepreneurs and successful portfolio entrepreneurs.

Looking forward

This chapter has highlighted that entrepreneurs should not be viewed as a homogeneous entity. Several important gaps in the habitual entrepreneur knowledge base need to be addressed relating to the nature of opportunities; information search; leveraging human capital; entrepreneurial teams; measures of habitual entrepreneurship; the role of the external environment; contexts for habitual entrepreneurship; and data and method issues (see Ucbasaran et al., 2008a).

Research is warranted to explore the 'quality' of opportunities identified by each 'type' of entrepreneur. The innovativeness of an opportunity is being used to gauge the wealth creating potential of business opportunities (Ucbasaran et al., 2006b, 2008a), but several measures should be used to assess the 'quality' of business opportunities.

Future studies could explore whether the motivations of entrepreneurs change, and how this impacts the nature of subsequently identified, pursued and exploited opportunities. Attitudes to risk exposure by habitual entrepreneurs who have accumulated significant wealth (Wright et al., 1997a) could be assessed in relation to the value of the opportunities they subsequently identify. Future studies might undertake direct comparisons of initial and subsequent opportunity identification and exploitation behaviour reported by each 'type' of entrepreneur.

Additional studies could explore the links between an entrepreneur's information search behaviour and their subsequent alertness to business opportunities. Differences in the human and social capital profiles of novice and habitual entrepreneurs may be associated with particular approaches to information search. The role of social capital has generally been neglected in habitual entrepreneur studies. Additional research is warranted that engages in a more fine-grained exploration of the social capital of habitual entrepreneurs and how social capital accumulation and leverage changes (or why it does not change) from one venture to the next.

Further studies could explore the interaction effects between business ownership experience and other general and specific human capital variables. Studies have explored the link between human and social capital (Davidsson and Honig, 2003). Additional research is warranted to explore this issue with specific reference to habitual and novice entrepreneurs.

Debate surrounds whether entrepreneurs *learn from business failure*. Future studies need to ascertain whether the *extent and/or nature of business failure experience* is associated with an ability to identify more opportunities, and opportunities associated with superior wealth creation and job generation potential. Entrepreneurs having experienced business failure should not be aggregated into a single crude business failure group that does not differentiate *economic business failure and failure to meet an entrepreneur's expectations* (Ucbasaran et al., 2010). Future studies need to monitor performance with regard to an array of performance indicators for different 'types' of entrepreneur.

Longitudinal studies offer the advantage of being able to establish causal relationships between an entrepreneur's human capital profile, entrepreneurial behaviour and firm (and entrepreneur) performance. Studies monitoring the *'stock' of skills and experience* of each type of entrepreneur, and the *'flows'* across the entrepreneur categories shown in Table 5.1 would provide rich process and contextual evidence. They could explore the characteristics and skills associated with novice entrepreneurs who are able to transform into serial or portfolio entrepreneurs. Studies, in addition, might focus on the initiation processes leading to the ownership of subsequent ventures by experienced entrepreneurs, and 'why' they accept or reject particular types of deals. Similarly, there is a need to understand 'how' serial and portfolio entrepreneurs learn from their previous business ownership experiences. There is also a need for research that analyses the total economic contribution of portfolio, serial and novice entrepreneurs to local and national economies.

Discussion questions

1 Entrepreneurship is not a single action event. Discuss with reference to a typology that illustrates variations in the nature of entrepreneurship.

2 Do habitual entrepreneurs report the same motivations for business ownership as those reported by novice entrepreneurs?

3 With reference to human and cognitive profiles discuss the assets (i.e., strengths) of portfolio, serial and novice entrepreneurs.

4 With reference to human and cognitive profiles discuss the liabilities (i.e., weaknesses) of portfolio, serial and novice entrepreneurs.

5 Should practitioners intervene to support new firm creation by novice entrepreneurs alone?

6 Are portfolio entrepreneurs 'winning entrepreneurs'?

7 Should practitioners seek to maximise returns from public policy investments by 'targeting' assistance to portfolio as well as serial entrepreneurs?

8 Discuss why habitual entrepreneurs may be expected to perform (1) better and (2) worse in their subsequent ventures than in their initial ones.

9 Is there a need for customised support towards novice, serial and portfolio entrepreneurs? If yes, what support does each type of entrepreneur require?

Recommended further reading

Iacobucci, D. and Rosa, P. (2005). Growth, Diversification, and Business Group Formation in Entrepreneurial Firms. *Small Business Economics*, 25 (1): 65–82.

Rosa, P. (1998). Entrepreneurial Processes of Business Cluster Formation and Growth by 'Habitual' Entrepreneurs. *Entrepreneurship Theory and Practice*, 22 (4): 43–61.

Ucbasaran, D., Alsos, G. A., Westhead, P. and Wright, M. (2008a). Habitual Entrepreneurs. *Foundations and Trends® in Entrepreneurship*, 4 (4): 309–449.

Westhead, P., Ucbasaran, D. and Wright, M. (2004a). Policy Toward Novice, Serial and Portfolio Entrepreneurs. *Environment and Planning C*, 22 (6): 779–798.

Chapter 6

'Types' of entrepreneurs II: High technology and academic entrepreneurs

Contents

Learning objectives

- Appreciate that innovation is a key driver of opportunity creation.
- Appreciate that innovation can provide a firm with sustained competitive advantage in local and national makers, and innovation can promote economic development.
- Consider that knowledge generated in universities can be commercialised into new products, services and processes that can be exploited in new firms.
- Illustrate the various ways universities support the commercialisation of knowledge (i.e., spin-offs and licensing), and reduce barriers to the formation of knowledge and technology-based firms.
- Consider the 'types' of spin-offs (i.e., venture capital backed, prospector and life style) owned by academic entrepreneurs.
- Appreciate the various processes and strategies exhibited by academic entrepreneurs and university spin-off firms.
- Consider the strategies (i.e., low selective, incubator and selective models) exhibited by universities to promote the commercialisation of knowledge through new spin-off firms.
- Consider the assets and liabilities of academic entrepreneurs and the methods (i.e., entrepreneurial teams and networking) used to accumulate and leverage resources to exploit knowledge and technology-based opportunities.

6.1 Introduction

Innovation is of central importance in entrepreneurship (Marvel and Lumpkin, 2007). The *innovativeness of an opportunity* is a surrogate measure of potential value (or wealth creating potential) (Shane, 2000). Firms that focus on innovation can accrue competitive advantages, which can promote superior business survival and performance (Cefis and Marsili, 2006) with wider societal and macro-economic benefits. A cornerstone of enterprise policy in developed and developing countries relates to the promotion of innovative new firms (Technology Strategy Board, 2008).

There are a number of conceptual as well as methodological problems in devising an appropriate definition of high technology and technology-based activities (Cosh and Wood, 1998). Most of the research examining *'technological innovation'* has tended to equate the term with *'high technology'*. There has been considerable debate surrounding the industries that can be regarded as technologically innovative. Butchart (1987) presented a *'process'*-based classification of high technology sectors. He suggested high technology industries are associated with above average R&D intensity, and an above average proportion of scientists, professional engineers and technicians.

New technology-based firms (NTBFs) (also called *high-technology firms*) are alleged to play a key role in enhancing entrepreneurship and economic growth (Malecki, 1991;

Storey and Tether, 1998; Siegel et al., 2003a). The success of NTBFs located in the vicinity of Stanford University and Massachusetts Institute of Technology (MIT) inspired the development of *Science Parks* near universities and higher education institutes (HEIs) (Westhead and Storey, 1995; Link and Scott, 2003). Several studies have provided additional justification for such efforts. Acs et al. (1992) and Anselin et al. (1997) have asserted that university research generates *local technological spillovers* to other firms. According to Link and Rees (1990), small firms are more likely to benefit from such spillovers than larger, more established companies. Universities stimulate local innovative activity by attracting clusters of R&D intensive firms (Harris and Trainor, 1995). The clustering of firms (Rocha, 2004), particularly NTBFs, is assumed to generate the following additional benefits:

- Encourage national economic development;
- Technological spillovers will broaden the industrial base of regions;
- Make less favoured areas more competitive and self-reliant;
- Efficient and productive NTBFs will improve the competitive capability of existing (larger) firms;
- NTBFs will be able to expand into international markets; and
- Direct (and indirect) job generation will generate wealth, which can be used to support economic and social agendas.

Governments in developed economies have sought to increase the *'supply'* of *'high quality'* entrepreneurs and firms, which leverage knowledge and technology to create and exploit market opportunities (see Case 10, Marine Products Limited: Confronting barriers to innovation). Siegel et al. (2003b: 1358) asserted that,

> In OECD nations, two policy initiatives are alleged to have accelerated the rate of knowledge transfer from universities to firms: targeted legislation designed to stimulate research joint ventures between universities and firms (e.g., the European Union Framework Programmes) and a major shift in the intellectual property regime in favor of universities (e.g., enactment of the Bayh–Dole Act of 1980 in the USA).

These initiatives foster university technology transfer and the *commercialisation of knowledge* in universities through licensing and the formation of NTBFs by university academics.

With the support of universities, HEIs, local governmental authorities and various financial institutions, governments have sought to stimulate the formation of NTBFs. To increase the stock of growing NTBFs, governments have directly and (indirectly) sought to address the *'market failures'* (i.e., information, skill, financial, networking and property barriers, etc.) impeding the formation and development of NTBFs. Notably, inexperienced academics with no prior business ownership experience working in universities as well as other public and private sector research-focused organisations may face attitudinal, financial, skill and expertise barriers that may impede the successful commercialisation of knowledge (Lambert, 2003) (see Case 11, Deep Sea Fishing Inc.: Acquiring the 'right' capital for a new technology-based firm). Market failures to innovation and the creation of NTBFs are widely recognised, and numerous schemes have been introduced to address these barriers (Massey et al., 1992). A detailed mapping of innovation policies has been presented relating to functional, resource and spatial issues (Bodas Freitas and Tunzelmann, 2008).

6.2 Property-based initiatives to increase the supply of NTBFs

Science Parks represent one mechanism to stimulate technology transfers between academia and industry (i.e., other mechanisms relate to research consortia, joint ventures, licensing, consulting, contract research, etc.) (Wright et al., 2008a) (see Section 11.5). Governments throughout the world have supported property-based initiatives that stimulate NTBF formation and development. Developers who design and manage Science Parks argue that new firm formation and development obstacles can be surmounted by providing NTBFs with proximity to specialised services; flexible premises (to facilitate growth); shared resources and business services; links with local universities or higher education institutes (HEIs); and opportunities for co-operation with other tenants (Siegel et al., 2003a). Indeed, the marketing of Science Parks to potential and practising entrepreneurs highlights factors that typically influence firm location choices (Westhead and Batstone, 1998). These include the cost of transportation, real estate, skilled labour, financial subsidies, site adequacy, the provision of complementary services to overcome an entrepreneur's weaknesses with regard to key business skills, environmental quality, and the presence of a local university. Entrepreneurs owning NTBFs may also value the provision of joint services on Science Parks, which can help them reduce overhead costs.

NTBFs that select *sponsored environments* (Flynn, 1993) such as a Science Park location can transmit signals to other firms, conferring a reputational advantage (or legitimacy) for their organisations. Science Park managers (i.e., gate-keepers) can also help reduce uncertainty (and fixed costs) for entrepreneurs who locate their NTBFs on a Science Park (Johannisson et al., 1994). A gate-keeper could enhance the reputation of fledgling firms with limited social/business networks, which might help them, attract additional financial capital and better employees. Moreover, Science Park managers can foster technology transfer, by promoting linkages between local HEIs and tenant firms.

There is also the issue of the clustering of NTBFs. By reducing uncertainty and transaction costs, as well as enabling entrepreneurs to exploit commercial and technical information, Science Parks may provide access to key *resources* for NTBFs. Further, institutional factors within a Science Park can provide a context for acquiring tacit knowledge and experience.

Studies have monitored the profiles of entrepreneurs and firms that select Science Parks (Westhead and Batstone, 1998). A distinction has been made between *'managed'* (i.e., a park with a generally full-time manager on-site whose principal task is to manage the park) and *'non-managed'* (i.e., a park which does not have a full-time manager on-site) Science Parks (Westhead and Batstone, 1999). Debate surrounds how the effectiveness of Science Parks should be monitored (Johannisson et al., 1994; Westhead and Storey, 1995; Siegel et al., 2003a). The extant literature suggests that Science Parks could influence various dimensions of *firm performance* with regard to firm survival, employment growth, R&D activity and productivity.

Westhead et al. (1995) detected no significant difference in *business survival rates* between independent firms located on Science Parks and similar firms not located on Science Parks in the United Kingdom. They concluded that sponsored Science Park environments did not significantly increase the probability of business survival. Another dimension of performance is *job creation*. Westhead and Cowling (1995) found that the mean absolute employment growth of firms located on Science Parks and those not located on Science Parks was virtually identical. There has also been some analysis of the importance of *links with an HEI*. Westhead and Storey (1995) compared survival rates over the 1986 to 1992 period for NTBFs on Science Parks with and without HEI links reported in 1986. They detected a significantly higher survival rate among firms with an HEI link than firms without such a link. Westhead (1997a), in addition, examined differences in *R&D 'outputs'* and *'inputs'* of NTBFs located on Science Parks and similar NTBFs located off Science Parks. R&D input measures monitored related to the percentage of scientists and engineers in total employment, the level and intensity of R&D expenditure, and information on the thrust and the nature of the research undertaken by the firm. Proxies for R&D outputs monitored related to the counts of patents, copyrights, and new products or services. Westhead (1997a) noted that Science Park firms were not significantly more R&D intensive than off-park firms. He also detected insignificant differences between Science Park and non-Science Park firms with reference to all dimensions of R&D output. The *research productivity* (i.e., a R&D production function relating to three R&D 'outputs' (new products, patents or copyrights) and two R&D 'inputs' (R&D expenditure and number of scientists and engineers)) of independent firms located on and off Science Parks in the United Kingdom was monitored by Siegel et al. (2003b). Econometric analysis confirmed that firms located on Science Parks reported slightly higher research productivity than observationally equivalent firms not located on Science Parks. Studies monitoring the contributions made by Science Parks have also been conducted in other national contexts (Link and Scott, 2003; Löfsten and Lindelöf, 2003).

6.3 Commercialisation of knowledge from universities: Support for academic entrepreneurs

Several reports (Lambert, 2003) have stimulated attention surrounding the growing phenomenon of *'academic entrepreneurship'*. Academics have long been entrepreneurial in the way that they spot opportunities for new research areas, and to raise grants to fund their research. The licensing of innovations, whereby the scientists receives a royalty, has been a traditional means to commercialise academic research (Thursby and Thursby, 2002). Academics also can be entrepreneurial in terms of the consultancy they undertake and the copyrights and patents they take out (Wright et al., 2008a). Today, there is considerable worldwide attention relating to the NTBFs created by academics that are spun-off from the university or research institute (Rasmussen, 2006; Mueller, 2010). This development has been driven by decreases in public funding for research at universities, growing public discussion about the role of universities in society, and legislative changes regarding the ownership and exploitation of *intellectual property* (IP) created in universities.

Universities target the creation of spin-off firms by academics, in which both the university and the academic hold equity stakes, in the belief that these NTBFs will create significant profit streams and capital gains when they are sold. It is assumed that the returns from spin-off firms will exceed the returns from more traditional licensing agreements and contract research. There is some debate about whether this is in fact the case, or whether universities have been successful at creating spin-off firms with significant capital gains potential.

6.4   Definitions of academic entrepreneurship

6.4.1   Types of spin-offs owned by academic entrepreneurs

Narrowly defined, NTBFs that emerge as university spin-offs relate to new ventures dependent upon licensing or assignment of a university's IP for initiation. Where legislation allows, a university may own equity in the spin-off firm in return for the patent rights it has assigned or in lieu of licence fees. In general, these spin-off firms where the university owns an equity stake in the spin-off are the easiest to identify. However, a substantial proportion of NTBFs spun-off from universities do not build upon formal, codified knowledge embodied in patents, and they do not involve equity stakes held by universities. The latter start-ups by university faculty draw on the individual's own IP or knowledge. To some extent academics have for many years created such ventures. Recent developments by university employers have attempted to limit, if not eliminate these informal ventures. The relative importance of both spin-off firms that involve formal IP and those that do not depends upon the research composition at the university, the country context (i.e., in some countries the IP belongs to the scientist not the university), university policy regarding IP rights, and the entrepreneurial activity of the academics themselves.

NTBFs are, in addition, created by graduates after they have left the university, or by outsiders who draw on IP created by universities. Although there are likely to be substantial numbers of these kinds of NTBFs, it is usually unclear whether the start-up can be linked to specific knowledge created and transferred in the university setting, or whether it is based on knowledge that the graduate cumulated outside the university. The latter NTBFs are not generally considered within the emerging literature relating to the academic entrepreneurship phenomenon.

Academics creating spin-off firms have a number of options open to them. They may leave the university to devote themselves completely to the NTBF. Alternatively, they may remain with the university and work with the venture part time. There is some debate about the efficacy of academics as entrepreneurs given their traditionally non-commercial background. Franklin et al. (2001) distinguished between *academic and surrogate (external) entrepreneurs*. Surrogate entrepreneurs are individuals with commercial experience who are brought in to academic spin-offs to provide the entrepreneurial input, which will enable the innovation to be developed from the laboratory to a viable product in the marketplace. Franklin et al. suggested that the best approach for universities that wish to launch successful technology transfer start-ups is a combination of academic and surrogate entrepreneurship. This would enable universities to simultaneously exploit the technical benefits of inventor involvement and the commercial know-how of surrogate entrepreneurs.

Although spin-off firms have been viewed as mechanisms to generate significant capital gains and revenue for universities and academics, by no means all NTBFs have the potential to do this. Indeed, spin-off firms are heterogeneous. Table 6.1 illustrates that the *nature of support provided by universities* to spin-offs can vary, which can shape venture development.

Table 6.1 Three types of academic spin-off firms

		Venture capital backed type	Prospector type	Lifestyle type
Institutional link	*Formal involvement*	Equity relation based upon a complex IP system	Equity relations based upon one patent or none	Licence, contract, informal relations
	Prestige of research group	Wordwide recognition in a broad domain	Wordwide recognition in a focused subdomain or local recognition	Various
Business model	*Investor vs market acceptance*	Investor acceptance	Both	Market acceptance
	Mode of value capturing	Clear IP maximising strategy or value chain acquisition. Strategy to prepare trade sale/initial public offering (IPO)	Optimise time to break even and future trade sale value, no clear exit yet	Optimise profit
Technology resources	*Degree of innovativeness*	Disruptive technology or market	New product based upon non-disruptive technology	New product/service addresses clear, unmet market need
	Stage of product/service development	Early, sometimes not even defined	Early (alpha) prototype	Almost market-ready product/service
	Broadness of the technology concept	Can be broad	Narrow	Not relevant
Financial resources	*VC involvement*	Able to attract €1–5 million in the first 18 months after founding	Lower amount of business angel, baby venture capital or public fund kind of investment	Usually no external equity, some business angel involvement possible
	Financing mix	High amount of external equity, some debt financing, intensive use of subsidies	Mix of external capital, soft loans and subsidies	Internal funding, debt and some soft loans
Human resources	*Balanced team*	Surrogate entrepreneur or hired guns	Technical scientists act as entrepreneurs	Technical scientists
	Sectoral experience	Management experience, research excellence	Little experience	Considerable sector experience
Social resources	*Partnership at start-up*	Form partnerships with stakeholders (venture capital, technology providers)	None	Formal availability of lead user

Source: Wright et al. (2007).

Three 'types' of spin-off NTBFs can be identified with regard to the nature of their link with their parent university institution, their resource base, and their business model. A distinction has been made between (Wright et al., 2008a):

- 'venture capital backed type' (10 per cent of spin-offs);
- 'prospector type' (50 per cent); and
- 'lifestyle type' (40 per cent).

The *'venture capital backed type'* is probably the most attractive from a policy perspective. These firms are believed to have technology that has the potential to create large new markets, and with a capital gain likely to be realised through a stock market flotation (i.e., *Initial Public Offering* (IPO)), or sale to an established multinational corporation. Venture capital (VC) backing is sought in the early stages to enable the technology to be developed into products that will subsequently generate revenue. In many cases, these ventures may not have generated revenue streams from their products (apart from consultancy income) prior to their IPO, because of the extremely long lead times, and high risk in their development through various stages of clinical trials and regulatory approval (see the case of Renovo in Entrepreneurship in action 6.1).

Venture capital backed type spin-offs need to attract significant amounts of venture capital at start-up to be credible. They also must be able to attract most of the researchers that were working on the technology at the university to retain the scientific credibility. Most universities are likely to have very few research groups with world-leading research capable of generating this kind of NTBF.

Many academic spin-offs will have more limited potential and can be labelled *'prospector type'* NTBFs. The technology base underpinning their founding is generally not sufficiently novel to generate radically new growth businesses and markets. These NTBFs typically have a patent protected prototype or maybe a beta version that can be sold to generate revenue. *'Prospector type'* NTBFs attract external funding from public or private equity funds linked to

Entrepreneurship in action 6.1
Renovo

Renovo is a university spin-off firm that has developed novel techniques to heal wounds which does not leave disfiguring scar tissue. The company has four lead product candidates in Phase 2 development each with a different mechanism of action and a clear understanding of the underlying biological pathways. The company achieved an IPO in April 2006 while the products were still going through their clinical trials. Over the previous five years the company had developed its management team through the recruitment of executives with commercial experience, non-executives as well as building up its scientific advisory board. The company went through two rounds of fund raising to finance product development. Following an initial venture capital investment of £8 million, in January 2003 Renovo's second round funding led by HealthCap was over-subscribed and raised £23 Million (US$37.5 Million). In March 2008, almost two years after the IPO, Renovo announced Phase 2 clinical trial results for its lead drug, Juvista (human recombinant TGFß3) in scar revision (RN1001-1009) and breast augmentation (RN1001-1010) surgery. The company lost half its value on the stock market after announcing the failure of the latest trial of Juvista, its scar pre-

vention drug, which had been touted as a breakthrough product with a potential $12 billion (£6 billion) market. In August 2009, the company's shares tumbled by more than 20 per cent after the expected launch of Juvista was delayed by around two years. However, subsequent positive clinical trial results for Juvista mean that the causes of the two failed trials are now clearly understood (wrong dose and dosing frequency).

Juvista is now in Phase 3 in the process for EU drug approval using what is believed to be the optimal dose and dosing frequency, with results expected in the first half of 2011. The company's licence with Shire was revised in 2010 giving it the ability to licence everywhere except USA, Canada and Mexico. Juvista is on track for EU approval in 2014 and USA timing could be similar depending on discussions with the US Federal Drug Administration. The company has two other products with Phase 2 trial data reporting in 2011 and a licensing deal for Juvidex is also expected. Renovo was the sixth highest rising share on the London Stock Exchange in 2010. Market capitalisation is £138m and the company had £51.8m in cash at 30 September 2010.

the university or public research laboratory. These NTBFs begin with a business model that essentially follows a contract research or consulting path, and they attempt to identify a product to commercialise. In the early phases of the start-up, especially when the business model is not clear, pre-seed sources of finance should allow the NTBF to fail, or to be free to adopt a different business model that is not in line with a seed fund investor's expectation.

'*Lifestyle type*' NTBFs generally start small in a market for products or services and optimise the time to break even. Some of these NTBFs might become high growth NTBFs later, but this is often not clear at start-up. Even if they remain as low growth oriented NTBFs, their value added as a population might be significant because 40 per cent of all spin-off firms relate to this type of spin-off. Technology transfer officers (TTOs) usually overlook these initiatives and universities show very little support for researchers or academics that want to create a NTBF that does not involve a formal transfer of technology from the university. '*Lifestyle type*' NTBFs are, however, less demanding in terms of human, financial and technological resources, and they can increase the visibility of the university in the host region. This type of NTBF forms the heart of what is often referred to as the '*entrepreneurial university*'.

6.4.2 Development of spin-offs

The development of spin-off firms involves an iterative process through a number of well-defined phases. In moving between phases, spin-off firms needed to address specific critical junctures (Vohora et al., 2004). Four *critical junctures* are illustrated in Figure 6.1 and are discussed, in turn, below.

- *Opportunity recognition*: requires the spin-off NTBF to acquire the capability to synthesise scientific knowledge with an understanding of the market to which it might apply. There may be a need for networks of market contacts outside the scientific environment of the university.
- *Entrepreneurial commitment*: requires the NTBF to acquire an entrepreneurial champion committed to the development of the venture. Where this is a problem, it appears to arise from universities not providing sufficient resources and network contacts, or not

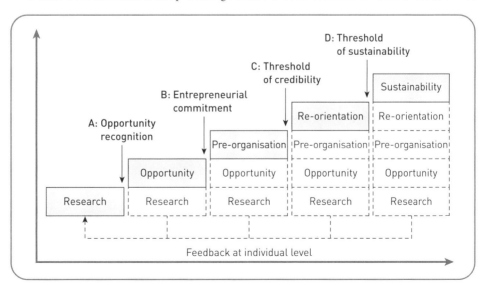

Figure 6.1 Critical junctures in the development of university spin-off firms
Source: Vohora et al. (2004).

developing appropriate incentives and policies. As a result, academic scientists or surrogate entrepreneurs fail to become sufficiently committed to developing the NTBF.

- *Credibility*: requires the NTBF to address the liabilities of newness and smallness. Credibility is particularly problematical because of the lack of commercial track record of the academic entrepreneurs, the often intangible nature of the spin-off firm's resources at this early stage, and the non-commercial environment from which the NTBF has emerged. All these elements create barriers to the attraction of customers and financiers. Building links with surrogate entrepreneurs at earlier phases in the development process may help the NTBF overcome this juncture. Universities need to devise policies to attract the surrogate entrepreneur (i.e., through building network links). The demonstration of proof of concept and the potential for a portfolio of products may also help to establish credibility in relation to financiers. Relocation in commercial premises away from the university can help signal a commercial approach to prospective customers.
- *Sustainable returns*: requires the NTBF to develop entrepreneurial capabilities that enable the spin-off firm to reconfigure deficiencies from earlier phases into resource strengths, capabilities and social capital.

6.4.3 Strategies to grow spin-offs

Despite efforts to stimulate academic entrepreneurship, studies conducted in several countries consistently reveal that the majority of public-research spin-off NTBFs are *'born small and stay small'*. Very few NTBF spin-off firms report significant growth (Heirman and Clarysse, 2007). For example, in France three-quarters of spin-offs are still in business six years after set up, but 80 per cent of the NTBFs employ less than ten people (Mustar, 2000).

Given the different types of spin-off firms we identified above, these ventures may adopt the following contrasting types of growth (Clarysse et al., 2007):

- A *product market strategy* is more likely to aim at achieving growth in terms of sales revenues to create a sustainable growing business.
- A *financial market strategy* places greater emphasis on creating value to enable the business to IPO, or be sold to a strategic partner. In this latter instance, the strategy is to grow value which can be through building up the value of the science and technology in the business, even if no product sales are generated, or through a hybrid strategy of both building the value of the technology and generating sales, perhaps initially from consulting and services. The nature of the venture's sector and appropriability regime, for example biotech versus ICT or engineering, may influence this choice.
- A hybrid strategy involving a combination of the two above.

The choice between these commercialisation strategies can be shaped by accessibility to the necessary complementary assets associated with each growth strategy (Gans and Stern, 2003). *Product market* strategies imply a need to acquire human capital with commercialisation expertise. *Financial market strategies* imply a need to access complementary human capital assets that can help develop the technology.

Developing links with trading partners is an important means to access complementary assets but the latter strategy raises challenges for spin-off firms. While larger corporations may be important trading partners for spin-off firms, the technology from spin-off firms may be a minor part of a larger corporation's portfolio; there is, therefore, likely to be an asymmetry of interdependence between the trading partners. This raises several issues

---

Entrepreneurship in action 6.2
Idmos

Idmos is a university spin-off created in 2001 that listed on the London-based Alternative Investment Market (AIM), but which subsequently entered bankruptcy proceedings in April 2008. Idmos entered into an agreement with Dentsply in 2005 and the latter partner would invest in product development and distribute the product. Dentsply would have exclusive global rights to market and sell current and future dental products based on IDMoS ACIST technology, and to participate in the development of products based on the Company's 3D technical platform, with the products being branded by Dentsply with co-branding as 'powered by IDMoS' technology.

At the time, Dentsply was a NASDAQ-listed $4 billion market capitalisation, world-leading manufacturer and distributor of dental prosthetics, precious metal dental alloys, endodontic instruments and materials, and other dental products that were distributed in over 120 countries. The agreement foundered amid accusations by Dentsply that Idmos had not met milestones or provided products that were commercialisable and counter-accusations by Idmos that Dentsply had unrealistic expectations about what the technology could do.

Source: http://business.scotsman.com/businesstechnology/
Idmos-blames-distribution-deal-for.3990435.jp.

---

concerning the nature of the contractual agreement between the spin-off firm and the corporate partner, such as pricing, length of contract, milestones, expectations about the contribution of each partner, and whether there is an anticipation that the trading relationship will be a precursor to acquisition by the corporate partner. The spin-off firm may need to ensure that it can deliver on the contract it has entered into with the trading partner, which may require the spin-off firm to continue to develop the technology into a commercialisable product. The problems that can arise are illustrated by the example of the spin-off of the dental technology firm Idmos in Entrepreneurship in action 6.2.

6.5 University strategies and spin-offs

6.5.1 General strategies

The existence of an entrepreneurial culture, that is social norms that give at least tacit approval to entrepreneurs, is viewed as a critical determinant of academic entrepreneurship (Roberts, 1991). Universities that generate large numbers of NTBFs generally have clear and well-defined strategies regarding the formation and management of spin-off firms (Degroof and Roberts, 2004). This involves a support policy for generating NTBFs that can exploit ventures with high growth potential. Part of such a policy is the necessity for TTOs to have appropriate commercial expertise and capabilities built up over time (O'Shea et al., 2005). Universities investing in IP protection and the business development capabilities of TTOs, and those with structures that do not favourably distribute royalty income to university faculty members, generally report high NTBF formation rates (Lockett and Wright, 2005). Universities wishing to generate more spin-off firms should devote greater attention to the recruitment and development of TTOs with broad-based commercial skills. This approach should also enable universities to have the expertise to select whether a new innovation that is disclosed to them by their employees (i.e., academics) is developed through a spin-off firm, or through a licensing arrangement (i.e., if the innovation does not appear capable of sustaining an independent NTBF). This choice may be moderated by the role of particular academics. For example, some scientists may be very forceful in wishing to develop the idea as a spin-off firm even though assessments suggest it is unlikely to be a viable business entity. If the individual concerned is a 'star' scientist in an important research department, the university may need to make important trade-offs, or risk losing the academic to another institution.

Incentives for universities and academics are important. Equity ownership provides an incentive for academics, and tends to be more widely distributed among the members of spin-off firms in universities associated with commercialisation success. The ability of the university and inventor(s) to assume equity in a start-up, in place of licensing royalty fees, can impact on business start-up rates (Di Gregorio and Shane, 2003). A royalty distribution formula that is more favourable to faculty members reduces start-up formation, probably due to the higher opportunity cost associated with launching a new firm, relative to licensing the technology to an existing firm (Markman et al., 2005).

A major incentive concerns the link between the creation of spin-off firms and academic career development. Universities need to integrate into promotion and remuneration systems mechanisms that value commercialisation activities as an additional 'academic output'. Standard royalty distribution and equity holding formulae might be adapted to specific case contexts. For example, if there is a need to retain 'star' scientists, universities may seek to provide a more generous deal than the norm. Formalised periods of leave mechanisms might be introduced to enable academics to focus on the development of a spin-off firm with the possibility of a return if the NTBF is not successful, or the academic skills are no longer required.

Universities need to develop strategies to access equity finance to fund the start-up and growth of spin-off firms (see Chapter 12). Venture capital firms find investing in NTBFs from universities can be more challenging than other high-technology ventures given the non-commercial environment from which they emanate; the greater need to build management teams; the newness of the technology; the timescales to development; and the potential conflicts of objectives associated with investing alongside a public sector body (Wright et al., 2006). Also, venture capital firms consider that universities fail to present proposals for the funding of spin-off firms that are investor ready, which emphasises the need for universities to have TTOs with the appropriate expertise and contacts (Wright et al., 2008). Venture capital firms note that universities' decision-making processes are often not conducive to the timescales they require. Few venture capital firms have developed links with universities, and even fewer with more than one university.

6.5.2   Incubator models

Academic entrepreneurs generally lack all the key resources to develop their spin-off firms. The selected incubator regime can provide essential resources. As highlighted with reference to Science Parks, incubators can provide a range of resources and activities to foster NTBF survival and development. Clarysse et al. (2005) have made a distinction between types of incubator models with regard to the goals of universities. Notably, some universities are seeking to promote a small number of NTBFs that are 'born global' (see Chapter 13) and have the potential to generate significant capital gains. However, most universities are seeking to encourage NTBFs that generate substantial revenue streams, and smaller consultancy and service NTBFs that generate local employment opportunities. Clarysse et al. (2005) made a distinction between the following three types of incubator models to

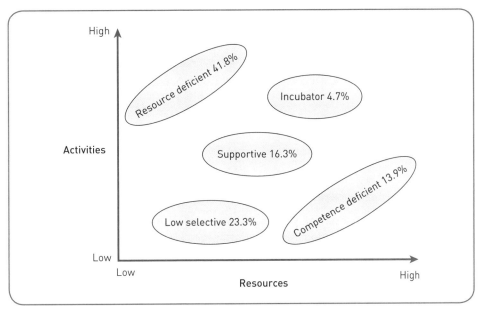

Figure 6.2 Different types of spin-off firm incubators
Source: Clarysse et al. (2005).

support academic entrepreneurs and the development of their spin-off firms. As shown in Figure 6.2, these relate to:

1 *'Low selective model'*. The objective of the university is to stimulate as many NTBFs as possible, typically lifestyle firms that do not rely on technology developed in the university. This model fits very well with the idea of an entrepreneurial university that services social science departments. Researchers or academics will have a tendency to set up an NTBF with a business model that is familiar to their pre-start-up activities and which requires little investment. The spin-off process is facilitated by the university, which provides small amounts of money to potential entrepreneurs, and they provide office space in the university.

2 *'Incubator model'*. The objective of the university is to stimulate growth-oriented venture capital-backed spin-off firms. This model can service a research department which is leading in its field, and which has developed a critical mass in a certain domain. Only a small number of projects involving innovative technology that can be protected are supported. TTOs devote significant time to protect the technology base in the incubation or pre-start-up phase, including the licensing of missing elements. Later on in the process, this model assumes that a well-balanced founding team, preferably with experience in the selected sector. During the incubation phase, the TTO actively searches to compose a *team* that can attract an investor. This model assumes that the spin-off firm can attract a sufficient amount of capital at start-up. The technology transfer office actively looks for private venture capitalists that are willing to invest the capital at start-up. Because of its size at founding, public venture capital firms cannot provide the capital required without the help of private venture capital firms.

3 *'Supportive model'*. This model relates to many universities that provide an in-between type of support. Universities are less selective in terms of the kind of spin-off firms they stimulate. NTBFs with limited growth prospects can be supported. In contrast with the

'*low selective model*', NTBFs receiving support usually embody a formal transfer of technology from the university to the NTBF. They also start with a larger capital basis than '*lifestyle type*' NTBFs, and they might attract surrogate entrepreneurs to complete the founding team. This model generally relates to '*prospector type*' NTBFs. The public money associated with the university allows these NTBFs to start. The development of a structure to support academics that want to create a NTBF within the university is viewed as a key success factor. Academics usually perform contract research or consulting. Without having to leave the university and with a business model very familiar to them, academics can experience whether creating an entrepreneurial venture is attractive to them, or not. The '*supportive model*' is useful for university departments where the critical mass is lower, but the department has developed a specific type of technology that might be a success in the market-place.

A major difficulty at most universities is that TTOs tend to be structured in line with one of the above models. Traditionally very few universities allow more than one model to be exhibited at the same time. A uniform approach may be adopted to a heterogeneous set of spin-off firms, many of which may not be suitable for venture capital firm support. Some universities still select an incubator approach that is not adequately financially as well as skill and capabilities resourced to enable the goal of high growth and high value NTBFs to be fulfilled. This mismatch between objectives, resources, and capabilities gives rise to resource deficient and competence deficient incubator models. There is a need to match universities' objectives for commercialisation, and for spin-off firms in particular, with appropriate resources and capabilities and with a realistic perspective on the types of successful spin-off firms that can be created given a particular university's science and resource base.

6.6   Academic entrepreneurs and start-ups

This section discusses the nature and characteristics of academic entrepreneurs.

6.6.1   Academic entrepreneurs' characteristics

Entrepreneurs at universities are different from other entrepreneurs in certain respects. Academic entrepreneurs tend to be older and more scientifically experienced than other entrepreneurs. Faculty quality in terms of generating world-class research of sufficient novelty is also associated with start-up activity (Di Gregorio and Shane, 2003; O'Shea et al., 2005). Analysis of the propensity of life-science faculty to engage in various aspects of technology transfer, including commercialisation, shows that the most important determinant of involvement in technology commercialisation was local group norms within the schools in which the scientists were located (Louis et al., 1989). While some departments and schools are resistant to the creation of spin-off firms, others have developed a more proactive and supportive approach where more experienced faculty can provide support for junior faculty. This situation seems to be changing with a more favourable approach becoming more evident.

An important issue, which to some extent lies behind the attitude of schools towards spin-off firm creation, concerns the potential for conflicts with high-level research output. There is evidence that faculty members creating NTBFs are more productive researchers than equivalent colleagues before they establish their firms, and that their research productivity does not decline following their entrepreneurial activity (Lowe and Gonzalez-Brambila, 2007).

Engagement in entrepreneurial activity may be associated with an increase in research output (i.e., publications), without affecting the nature of the publications involved (Van Looy et al., 2004). However, Lowe and Gonzalez-Brambila (2007) noted a differential discipline effect with faculty entrepreneurs in engineering experience a more positive effect than their colleagues in chemistry and biomedicine. This finding indicates that academic entrepreneurship in some disciplines requires more time and resources than in others. Assuming an interventionist stance, this justifies the case for 'customised' support linked to the aspirations, resources profiles and needs of academics in each type of faculty (or department).

'Non-star' faculty who are frustrated by lack of academic recognition can develop research contracts with private and public sector organisations that can generate possibilities for joint venture spin-offs. As noted earlier, there may be a need to move beyond standard royalty distribution and equity holding formulae adopted by TTOs to make them negotiable in specific case contexts, such as for 'star' researchers. Formalised periods of leave mechanisms might be introduced to enable 'non-star' academics to focus on the development of a spin-off firm with the possibility of a return if the venture is not successful, or the academic skills are no longer required.

Zucker and Darby (2001) examined the outcomes of collaborations between 'star' university scientists and biotechnology firms in Japan. They found that such interactions substantially enhanced the research productivity of Japanese firms with regard to the rate of firm patenting, product innovation, and market introductions of new products. However, the wider benefits of such collaborations to local regions appear to differ between countries depending on institutional differences. With reference to the United States, academic scientists typically work with firm scientists at the firm's laboratories and the local benefits are strong. Conversely, in Japan, firm scientists typically work in the academic scientist's laboratory and the local benefits are generally absent.

6.6.2 Entrepreneurial experience

An academic entrepreneur's human capital profile linked to specific human capital relating to entrepreneurial experience can shape an academic's propensity to accumulate and leverage *networks and social capital* to address barriers to business formation and development (see Chapter 4). With regard to a longitudinal study of 24 academic entrepreneurs supplemented with interviews with 20 TTOs and heads of schools, Mosey and Wright (2007) examined the development of networks (see Section 11.5.2.5) by three types of academic entrepreneurs with differing levels of entrepreneurial experience. A distinction was made between nascent, novice and habitual entrepreneurs (see Chapter 5 for definitions). They proposed that habitual entrepreneurs (i.e., those with prior business ownership experience) would have broader networks, and they would be more effective in developing network ties to gain equity finance and management knowledge. Conversely, less experienced nascent and novice academic entrepreneurs would be more likely to encounter disconnects (sometimes referred to as *structural holes*) between their scientific research networks and industry networks. This would constrain their ability to recognise opportunities and to gain credibility for their fledgling ventures. While support initiatives, such as technology transfer offices and proof of concept funds, help attract industry partners to selected novice entrepreneurs, there appears to be no obvious substitute for business ownership experience to *learn* how to build relationships with experienced managers and potential equity investors. Development of social capital for nascent and novice entrepreneurs is influenced by the human capital related to the entrepreneurs' discipline-base, with individuals from engineering and material sciences being more likely to build network ties outside their scientific research networks than those in biological sciences and pharmacy.

6.6.3 Entrepreneurial teams

NTBF growth may require different types of skills and investment in human capital. A particularly important issue is the evolution of entrepreneurial teams as the spin-off firm progresses through its phases of development. Some academics, actively involved in the first phase of the spin-off process, exit at subsequent stages and new members enter, especially those with commercial human capital (Vanaelst et al., 2006). Further, some exiting team members make a career choice to stay with the university, preferring to continue their research but often having a part-time role in the NTBF providing the spin-off firm with continuing technological development.

TTOs can play an important role as 'privileged witnesses' in nurturing the emergence of entrepreneurial teams in spin-off firms. They need to recognise the need for different personalities in the team (Vanaelst et al., 2006). More successful NTBF teams tend to have diverse functional backgrounds. Further, they have joint working experience and possibly different views on how the spin-off firms should develop. This *cognitive diversity* stimulates team members to challenge each other about the strategy the spin-off firm should ideally follow. Team dynamics can promote more informed and better decision-making. It is important that these discussions do not result in affective conflict (i.e., the academic entrepreneur equity owners start to dislike each other). Teams who know each other and who have developed non-instrumental relations, such as joint working experience or even social relations, before starting the spin-off firm have much less chance of experiencing affective conflict than those who do not know each other (Wright et al., 2008a).

Team members who combine *flexibility* and *external orientation* tend to be innovative persons that embody a high degree of *creativity and vision* (Wright et al., 2007). Many high-flying academics tend to report a high degree of *creativity and vision* orientation. Conversely, people reporting a high degree of *external orientation* also have a propensity to report a high degree of *focus on control*, and they tend to be goals oriented. A founding team requires a goal-orientated person to ensure that the necessary steps in the development of the NTBF are achieved. A potential problem is that the surrogate entrepreneurs attracted to form a founding team with academics often have the same kind of *creativity and vision* orientation as the academics themselves, producing team homogeneity rather than heterogeneity.

6.6.4 Academic entrepreneurs' networks

An academic's networks can shape the development and performance of a NTBF. Mustar (1997) made a distinction between types of spin-off firms with regard to the nature of co-operation arrangements with other public and/or private bodies. The breadth of an academic entrepreneur's social network (see Section 11.5.2.5), in part, shapes spin-off firm survival and growth. The embeddedness of an academics network ties (i.e., internal and/or external) can be linked to the growth trajectory followed by a NTBF (Nicolaou and Birley, 2003).

There may be a need for universities to recruit and develop individuals who can act as intermediaries (or boundary spanners) between academics in the university and the commercial market-place and providers of finance. Schemes such as the Medici Fellowship Scheme in the

United Kingdom, which involves the use of skills relating to marketing, finance, opportunity identification, etc. to academics that typically are post-doctorates with a science background suggests that these can have a positive impact (Mosey et al., 2006). For schemes to be effective, there is a need to provide sustained support rather than short-term schemes, and to establish defined career paths for supported academic fellows so that the skills developed are retained, rather than quickly lost if the academic fellows leave the university (Wright et al., 2008a).

6.7 Looking forward

Universities have developed and adapted their approaches to the stimulation of academic entrepreneurship as they have begun to *learn* 'what works' and 'what does not work'. Major shifts concern a pulling back from too much emphasis on spin-off firms to a case-by-case assessment of whether an innovation is likely to be a viable business or not. A major challenge relates to the reluctance and/or inability of many NTBFs to report rapid growth and substantial capital gains envisaged by universities. Most of the NTBFs established by academic entrepreneurs are 'born small stay small ventures' (see Chapter 2). Universities have a role in addressing the attitudinal, resource, operational and strategic barriers to rapid NTBF development. There is a need for universities to incentivise academics and resolve conflicts with promotion systems that focus on 'academic output', and reward academics that (successfully) engage in the commercialisation of university knowledge with superior remuneration packages. There is also a need for managers of universities to understand disconnects between universities' espoused strategies for commercialisation at the top, and what actually happens on the ground in the faculties (or departments). To some extent, there remains a need for universities to attract and incentivise both the right calibre of TTOs and surrogate entrepreneurs. Future studies are warranted to provide insights into the nature of barriers to commercialisation, and how they might be resolved.

Discussion questions

1 Should universities promote entrepreneurship? Why do universities promote entrepreneurship? How do universities promote entrepreneurship?

2 Critically consider the strategies selected by universities (i.e., low selective, incubator and selective models) to generate new spin-off firms.

3 What are the distinctive aspects and challenges facing academic entrepreneurs compared with entrepreneurs that establish 'traditional' new firms?

4 How can academic entrepreneurs circumvent barriers to the creation and development of new spin-off firms?

5 Critically consider whether academic scientists have the appropriate skills sets to become entrepreneurs.

6 What processes and strategies do academic entrepreneurs exhibit to create and develop new spin-off firms?

7 Critically discuss the profiles of various 'types' of spin-offs (i.e., venture capital backed, prospector and lifestyle) owned by academic entrepreneurs.

Recommended further reading

Anselin, L, Varga, A. and Acs, Z. (1997). Local Geographic Spillovers between University Research and High Technology Innovations. *Journal of Urban Economics*, 42: 422–448.

Clarysse, B., Wright, M., Lockett, A., van de Elde, E. and Vohora, A. (2005). Spinning Out New Ventures: A Typology of Incubation Strategies from European Research Institutions. *Journal of Business Venturing*, 20 (2): 183–216.

Lambert, R. (2003). *Lambert Review of Business – University Collaboration*. London: HM Treasury.

Vohora, A., Wright, M. and Lockett, A. (2004). Critical Junctures in the Growth in University High-Tech Spinout Companies. *Research Policy*, 33: 147–175.

Wright, M., Clarysse, B., Mustar, P. and Lockett, A. (2008) *Academic Entrepreneurship in Europe*. Cheltenham, UK: Edward Elgar.

Chapter 7

'Types' of organisations I: Family firms

Contents

Learning objectives

- Consider the contributions played by private family firms to economic development.
- Appreciate that promoting private family firms' survival and development is an important enterprise sustainability issue.'
- Illustrate the assets and liabilities associated with private family firms.
- Consider agency and stewardship theory to explore the objectives, ownership, management and performance of family firms relative to non-family firms.
- Consider empirical evidence relating to the profiles of family and non-family firms.
- Appreciate there are 'types' of family firms, and there may be a need for customised support to each 'type' of family firm.

7.1 Introduction

Approximately two-thirds of private firms are family owned. In aggregate, *they make notable contributions to wealth creation, job generation and competitiveness.* Family firms in the United States generate between 12 and 59 per cent of the gross national product depending on the definition of family firm used (Shanker and Astrachan, 1996). They generate between 19 and 78 per cent of new jobs created, and family firms employ between 15 and 59 per cent of the workforce. The development of family firms can have a profound impact on *local economic development and social cohesion.*

Elements of the 'familiness' (Chrisman et al., 2005) of private family firms can have a detrimental (or positive) influence on firm development, notably firm survival in family hands. Concentrated ownership and management by members of the kinship group owning the majority of shares in the business may limit the pool of experience and retard family firm development. While the founding of a family firm fits with conventional definitions of entrepreneurship, the inheritance and development of an existing family firm raises issues about whether the inheritors engage in entrepreneurial behaviour. Family may, however, be the oxygen that feeds the fire of entrepreneurship (Rogoff and Heck, 2003).

Some family firms do not solely focus on '*business agendas*' (i.e., profit maximisation). Rather, some owners of family firms may place more emphasis on '*family agendas' and broader 'social agendas*' (i.e., social cohesion, protection of a local culture and/or a minority language, employment of local people, utilisation of local suppliers, etc.). To protect 'family agendas', the family owners may focus on non-financial objectives (Zahra et al., 2004) to the detriment of firm development. *Familial ties* can, however, provide increased firm stability. Indeed, loyalty and trust between family owners, employees and customers may enhance firm development.

Private family firm development is an important *enterprise sustainability issue* (Westhead, 2003). Johannisson and Huse (2000) suggest that family firm sustainability *calls for continued entrepreneurship, continued family involvement and professional management*. They assert that a viable firm must host all three aspects and deal with the *tensions between entrepreneurialism, paternalism and managerialism*. This chapter provides insights into the diversity of entrepreneurial processes relating to private family firms.

7.2   Unique group of firms: Theoretical and definitional insights

7.2.1   Context

Family firms are a unique group of established firms (Chrisman et al., 2003a; Poutziouris et al., 2006). A business can be linked to a *performance-based system*, whilst a *family can be linked to a relationship-based system* (Ward, 1987). Family members can be involved in the ownership and management of the firm, and there can be the intertwining of family and business objectives. Business objectives can be shaped by the three *interdependent subsystems of family, ownership and management* (Hoy and Verser, 1994).

7.2.2   Family firm assets and liabilities

Family involvement and objectives can be a source of both strengths and weaknesses. Family firms can be associated with the following *assets*:

- experience and knowledge;
- family resources (i.e., employ family members);
- stability and longevity; and
- familial ties provide loyalty and trust between family owners, employees, suppliers and customers (Chrisman et al., 2003b).

To ensure 'independence' of the family and the firm, some family firm owners may seek to protect '*family agendas*', rather than *sustained entrepreneurship and professional management* that focuses on profitability and competitive advantage. Family firms can, therefore, be associated with the following *liabilities*:

- reluctance to sell equity to 'outsiders';
- an aversion to debt that may constrain firm growth;
- reluctance to adopt a performance-related system;
- key managerial positions held by 'kinship relations' rather than most talented and experienced individuals;
- reluctance to use external professional expertise that may question 'family agendas' and 'family management'; and
- firm performance retarded because of the placing of 'family agendas' over business objectives (Birley et al., 1999).

7.2.3　Theoretical insights to explore family firms

7.2.3.1　*Context*

Agency and stewardship theories provide frameworks to explore family firm ownership and management, performance and business transfer issues. They are briefly discussed, in turn, below.

7.2.3.2　*Agency theory*

Agency theory is employed to examine links between ownership and management structures, objectives and performance in listed firms with diffuse ownership (Fama and Jensen, 1983). This perspective:

> . . . assumes self-interested, boundedly rational actors, information asymmetry and goal conflict to motivate principals (i.e. *family firms owners*) to devise mechanisms to monitor and control agents' actions (i.e. *non-family managers*) (Sapienza et al., 2000: 336).

Firm ownership and governance as well as firm objectives can shape family firm strategic behaviour (Sharma et al., 2003).

If individuals are assumed to be self-serving within a *performance-based system*, agency theory suggests that owners may focus on *financial objectives. Ownership and management* are viewed as dimensions of a *performance-based system* where rational economic objectives (i.e., *profit maximisation*) are assumed. *Agency problems* may arise if there is little overlap between the objectives of family, ownership and management. Managers are assumed to be opportunistic agents who focus upon maximising their potential welfare at the expense of shareholders. Where there is separation of ownership and control, agency control mechanisms are put in place by owners. There is, however, debate surrounding the usefulness of agency theory in a private family firm context (Sharma, 2004). Agency theory may not apply to closely held and managed family firms associated with little outside influence or representation, where the firm's objectives are entangled with family objectives.

The stereotypical family firm is assumed to be owned and managed by a concentrated group of family members, where the firm's objectives are closely-linked to family objectives (Zahra et al., 2004). In these circumstances, the agency cost issue may not apply. However, in order to develop, some family firms may no longer have aligned ownership and management in the same 'family' hands, and this raises the potential for agency issues between separated family owners and non-family managers. Family firm owners seeking to minimise risks when focusing on financial objectives may introduce 'outsiders' to monitor and control managers, and to align the goals of managers with those of the owners. To enhance firm performance, owners may introduce agency control mechanisms such as performance-related pay (Schulze et al., 2003) and non-executive directors (NEDs) (Westhead et al., 2001).

7.2.3.3　*Stewardship theory*

The family system in private firms can increase ownership and management complexity. Reported behaviour may not be economically rational because *non-financial (family) objectives or agendas prevail.* Family firm managers may act as stewards over the business's assets and its continuity. These family managers would seek to protect the assets of the family firm, rather than to pursue interests that maximise their own personal gain. In some family firms, stewardship theory (Donaldson, 1990) provides a useful counterpoint to agency theory, and suggests additional insights. Stewardship theory assumes a *relationship-based system with a focus on non-financial objectives*. The family can be viewed as a part of a *relationship-based system*. This theory is applicable when examining a context where the owners', managers' and employees' motives are aligned to those of the organisation (Schulze et al., 2003). A strong psychological ownership of the firm and a high occurrence of altruism are assumed.

7.2.4   Definitional issues

There is no consensus surrounding the definition of a family firm. Broad all-embracing definitions such as those that focus on the degree to which the owners' family dynamics influence managerial behaviour have been questioned on the grounds that they are *too 'inclusive'*. A definition that requires both that majority ownership or control of the business to reside within a single family, and that at least two family members are involved in management of the business are regarded as being *too 'restrictive'*. The following *elements* could appear in a family business definition (Westhead and Cowling, 1998):

- whether the Chief Executive/Managing Director/Chairperson regarded their company as being a family business;
- whether the majority of ordinary voting shares in the company were owned by members of the largest family group related by blood or marriage;
- whether the management team in the company was comprised primarily of members drawn from the single dominant family group who owned the business; and
- whether the company had experienced an intergenerational ownership transition to a second or later generation of family members drawn from a single dominant family group owning the business.

Studies in which the numerical dominance of family firms is greatest have used the broadest definitions, by asking respondents whether their business satisfied *one* specific criterion. Westhead and Cowling (1998) have argued that *two or more* of the above elements in combination need to be considered when identifying family businesses. They selected several family firm definitions to measure the scale of family business activity. The 427 independent unquoted companies they surveyed were subdivided with regard to majority share ownership of ordinary voting shares, perception by the Chief Executive/Managing Director/Chairperson of being a family business, family members involved in the management team and the generation of family business ownership. Table 7.1 shows that the proportion of businesses classified as 'family businesses' is highly sensitive to the definition utilised. Using the widest definition, 81 per cent of companies sampled could be viewed as 'family businesses'. Using the narrowest definition, this fell to only 15 per cent.

Westhead (1997b) suggested that the elements that most closely encapsulate the concepts of a family firm are *perception, share ownership by family members* and *management of the business by family member*. He argued that 'ownership' rather than 'family management' is the crucial family element that distinguishes family companies from non-family companies. Westhead suggested that *Definition (3)* in Table 7.1 should be more widely utilised.

Table 7.1 Numbers of surveyed family and non-family unquoted companies in the United Kingdom

Definition	Family company		Non-family company	
	No.	%	No.	%
(1)	335	78.5	92	21.5
(2)	345	80.8	82	19.2
(3)	272	63.7	155	36.3
(4)	265	62.1	162	37.9
(5)	139	32.6	288	67.4
(6)	122	28.6	305	71.4
(7)	62	15.0	365	85.0

Notes:

(1) The company was perceived by the Chief Executive/Managing Director/Chairman to be a family business.

(2) More than 50% of ordinary voting shares were owned by members of the largest single family group related by blood or marriage.

(3) More than 50% of ordinary voting shares were owned by members of the largest single family group related by blood or marriage and the company was perceived by the Chief Executive/Managing Director/Chairman to be a family business.

(4) More than 50% of ordinary voting shares were owned by members of the largest single family group related by blood or marriage, the company was perceived by the Chief Executive/Managing Director/Chairman to be a family business and one or more of the management team was drawn from the largest family group who owned the company.

(5) More than 50% of ordinary voting shares were owned by members of the largest single family group related by blood or marriage, the company was perceived by the Chief Executive/Managing Director/Chairman to be a family business and 51% or more of the management team were drawn from the largest family group who owned the company.

(6) More than 50% of ordinary voting shares were owned by members of the largest single family group related by blood or marriage, the company was perceived by the Chief Executive/Managing Director/Chairman to be a family business, one or more of the management team were drawn from the largest family group who owned the company and the company was owned by second generation or more family members.

(7) More than 50% of ordinary voting shares were owned by members of the largest single family group related by blood or marriage, the company was perceived by the Chief Executive/Managing Director/Chairman to be a family business, 51% or more of the management team were drawn from the largest family group who owned the company and the company was owned by second generation or more family members.

Source: Westhead and Cowling (1998).

7.3 Evidence base

7.3.1 Firm demographic characteristics

The demographic differences between family and non-family firms are discussed, in turn, with regard to business age and size, principal industrial activity of the business, and the location of the business. Issues relating to firm objectives, management structure, strategy, performance and business transfer are then discussed.

7.3.1.1 *Age*

Only 30 per cent of family firms are transferred to second generation family owners and only 13 per cent of family firms survive to third generation family owners (Ward, 1987). Westhead and Cowling (1998) found independent unquoted family companies in the United Kingdom were more likely to be older than non-family companies.

7.3.1.2 *Size*

Daily and Dollinger (1993) found professionally-managed independent manufacturing firms with fewer than 500 employees in the United States were larger in terms of number of employees than family-owned and managed firms. Outside the United States private family firms have been found to be generally smaller than non-family firms (Donckels and Fröhlich, 1991).

7.3.1.3 *Principal industrial activity*

Reynolds (1995) found that new family firms in the United States were less likely to be engaged in manufacturing and business services associated with higher capital requirements. Evidence from the United Kingdom shows that family firms were more likely to be overrepresented in agriculture, forestry and fishing as well as in the distribution, hotels and catering industrial sectors (Westhead and Cowling, 1998). However, family firms were underrepresented in the banking, financing, insurance and business services sectors.

7.3.1.4 *Location*

Saturated urban areas (at their business stock carrying capacity level) associated with high levels of new firm entry and exit may not be conducive environments for long-term family firm survival. Family firms in the United Kingdom have been found to be overrepresented in rural locations (i.e., in areas with fewer than 10,000 people), and slightly overrepresented in the East Midlands of England (Westhead and Cowling, 1998). They are markedly underrepresented in the south-east of England (associated with the Greater London agglomeration). Reynolds (1995), however, found family firms in the United States were overrepresented in urban areas.

7.3.2 Firm objectives

Managers of family and non-family firms may have many *common objectives*. Smyrnios and Romano (1994) explored the main objectives of family firms in Australia. They found that over 40 per cent of respondents reported the following main objectives: to increase the value of the business, to increase profitability, to accumulate family wealth, to pass the business on to the next generation, to provide family members with business careers, and to employ family members.

Family firm owners may focus on the following priorities:

- More emphasis upon ensuring the survival of the firm as a going concern.
- Seek to ensure continued independent ownership of their firms. Owners that avoid selling all or part of the firm to any 'outsider' could enable ownership transfer of the firm (i.e., succession) to the next generation of family members.
- Only grow the firm to provide employment positions for family members.
- Allocate key managerial positions to family members based on kinship ties rather than expertise and knowledge.

Objectives reported by family and non-family firms, in part, might reflect firm age differences rather than ownership form differences. Westhead and Cowling (1997) compared the company objectives reported by family and non-family companies in the United Kingdom using *Definition (3)* in Table 7.1. *Family and non-family companies were paired/matched on four criteria*: age of the company since receiving its first order; location of the company in a rural (or urban) area; location of the company by standard region type; and the main industrial activity of the company. Family and non-family firms sought to 'ensure the survival of the business'; 'to ensure that our employees have secure jobs in the business'; and to 'ensure independent ownership of the business'. To a lesser extent family and non-family firms sought 'to enhance the reputation and status of the business in the local community'. However, family firms were more likely to have reported the following non-financial objectives 'to maintain/enhance the lifestyle of the owners', and 'to provide employment for family members of the management team'.

7.3.3 Management structure

Given the objectives of family firms' owners may be prioritised differently from those of non-family firms, in many instances, family firms are managed differently than non-family firms. Family firms have been found to exhibit the following characteristics:

- Owners may be prepared to take a long-term view on the length of time they are willing to wait for an economic return on an investment.
- A greater willingness to target long-term investments towards workforce training and/or research and development.
- Long-term investments may ensure that high quality employees are retained in family businesses and a strong relationship develops and/or is maintained between employees and the owners/managers of the family firms.
- Family firm owners whose prime objective is to maximise income to family members may ensure and guarantee employment for family members. Senior managerial positions may be allocated based upon family membership rather than managerial ability or experience.
- Managerial talent could be eroded if able non-family members decided to seek employment positions outside the family firm.
- Non-family managers retained may be less ambitious and have insufficient skills to focus on competitive advantage that ensures firm development.

Using a *'matched paired'* comparison, Westhead et al. (1997) found differences in management practices between family and non-family companies but also noted numerous *similarities*. The key findings of the study were as follows:

- On average, the tenure periods of Chief Executive Officers (CEOs) in their companies before being appointed to the CEO position were very similar for CEOs in family and non-family companies (on average 2.0 and 3.5 years for CEOs in family and non-family companies, respectively). Both groups of companies had managerial stability at the top of their organisations, with CEOs having been employed in this position, on average, for 15 years.
- Directors in family companies held more ordinary shares in their companies than directors in non-family companies (on average, 93 per cent compared with 82 per cent).
- CEOs from the kinship group owning the family company generally served shorter apprenticeships in their respective companies than 'outside' CEOs (on average, 1.8 years for CEOs from the family owning the company compared with 3.9 years for CEOs not from the family owning the business), although the difference between the two groups was not significant.

- CEOs had been in situ in their respective companies for 15 years (on average, 15.0 years for CEOs from family companies compared with 14.6 years for CEOs employed in non-family companies).
- In family firms, CEOs from the kinship group owning the family business had been employed in that senior position for markedly longer than 'outside' CEOs employed in family firms (on average, 16 years compared with 8 years).
- The majority of respondents in family and non-family companies (58 per cent compared with 65 per cent) reported that they did not hold directorships in other companies.
- Family firms were less likely to have utilised the services of 'outsiders'. They were markedly less likely than family firms to have employed a NED (9 per cent of family compared with 19 per cent of non-family firms). Reluctance to use 'outside' expertise may cause some family firms to become introverted, inflexible and uncompetitive (Cromie et al., 1995), and to grow only if family members need employment positions.
- Both groups were reluctant to consider and select a successor for the CEO position.

The influence of family seems to persist and shape decision-making even in contexts where it may be expected that its influence would be very limited. Fiegener (2010) noted that most firms retained at least a little *'familiness'* even after substantial ownership had been transferred to *'outsiders'*.

7.3.4   Strategy

Business development can be ensured if a firm develops an appropriate strategic orientation with its *'internal'* (i.e., human resources of owners, managers and employees and resources and capabilities of the firm) and *'external' environments* (i.e., consumer demand, strength of competition, fiscal policies, sectoral trends and social, legal and political conditions) (see Chapter 11). Westhead (1997b) found that the number of *similarities* between the competitive strategies of family and non-family companies vastly outnumbered the differences between the two groups of firms. *Family and non-family companies had adopted very similar competitive strategies in terms of the following:*

- family firms were more likely to explore new sources of funds but they were no more or less likely to have actually used them;
- few family or non-family firms pursued a premium pricing strategy;
- family and non-family firms operating in well-defined and established market niches had generally focused upon the needs of their customers; and
- both family and non-family firms generally differentiated their products/services from lower quality competitors by offering products/services of superior quality.

Table 7.2 summarises the statistically significant strategic orientation contrasts between family and non-family companies. Non-family firms were less insular and were more willing to use external technology. They were more aware of emerging industry and market opportunities, driven by short-term financial considerations, and had developed technologically sophisticated products (either purchased or developed in-house) to increase their market share. Non-family firms were found to be more aware of the implications of a risky dependency on a single supplier or a single customer. More non-family firms had reduced their dependence on a single supplier or customer. Family firm development, however, may be at risk because of a reluctance to terminate long-established relationships with dominant suppliers and customers.

Table 7.2 Strategic orientation differences between matched-paired family (n = 73) and non-family (n = 73) unquoted companies

Strategic factor	Family companies were more likely to:[a]	Non-family companies were more likely to:
1 *Approach to management*		• Promote managers based on their specific skills, knowledge and competence[b]
2 *External financing*	• Frequently explore for new sources of funds[c]	
3 *Long-term financial orientation*		• Emphasise immediate profitability[d] • Emphasise long-term capital investments[b]
4 *Industry awareness*		• Actively attempt to predict competitors moves[b] • Actively attempt to predict industry trends[b]
5 *Planning-related issues*	• Use formalised management information systems to support decision-making[b]	
6 *Advertising*	• Use frequent advertising[c]	• Use advertising that differentiates our products/services from those of our competitors[d]
7 *Technology concerns*	• Actively further refine a technology developed by others[d]	• Actively use technology developed by others[d] • Actively improve our existing technology[b]
8 *External independence*	• Actively attempt to minimise our dependence on any single supplier[d]	• Actively attempt to minimise our dependence on any single customer[b]
9 *Quality concerns*	• Offer products/services of superior quality[c]	• Emphasise the building of company image and reputation within our industry[d]
10 *Product/service-related issues*	• Use product or process patents and/or copyrights to provide a competitive advantage[d] • Offer a wide range of products/services[c]	

Notes:

(a) More than 50% of the ordinary voting shares were owned by members of the largest family group and the company was perceived by the Chief Executive/Managing Director/Chairman to be a family business.

(b) Statistically significant univariate analysis difference between matched family and non-family companies.

(c) Statistically significant multivariate analysis difference between matched family and non-family companies.

(d) Statistically significant univariate as well as multivariate difference between matched family and non-family companies.

Source: Westhead (1997b).

Respondents in non-family companies were markedly more likely:

- to have been promoted based on their specific skills, knowledge and competence rather than kinship;
- to have placed more emphasis on immediate profitability;
- to have directed resources towards increasing their industry awareness;
- to have attempted to predict industry trends and competitors moves;
- to have used advertising which differentiated their products/services from those provided by competitors;
- to have used technology developed by others and improved internal existing technology;
- to have reduced risk exposure due to dependence on any single customer; and
- to have promoted company image and reputation to increase firm credibility and legitimacy.

Respondents in family companies were markedly more likely:

- to have reported that they frequently explored opportunities for new sources of funds (these sources may not have been used by family firm owners who were reluctant to lose ownership and control to 'outsiders');
- to have used formalised management information systems to support their decision-making;
- to have engaged in frequent advertising campaigns to secure (or increase) their market share;
- to further refine a technology developed by others rather than support in-house creativity and innovation;
- to have reduced risk exposure by reducing dependence on any single supplier;
- to ensure business development, to have generally provided a wide portfolio of products/services;
- to have focused upon product/service-related issues (i.e., taking out product or process patents and/or copyrights); and
- to have perceived that they had provided products/services of superior quality to ensure customer loyalty and satisfaction.

The following two strategic factor differences were unexpected:

1 Despite a greater focus on immediate profitability, non-family companies had focused more upon long-term capital investments.
2 Reflecting a catching up process, non-family companies seem to have invested more resources in building up their company image and reputation within their respective industries.

Family control can strongly influence diversification decisions. Family-controlled firms may engage in riskier strategies in order to preserve *socio-emotional wealth* (SEW) (i.e., family agendas). Gomez-Mejia et al. (2007) found that family-owned firms in Spain were willing to exchange greater financial risks by remaining independent and not joining a co-operative in order to preserve family SEW.

7.3.5 Performance

7.3.5.1 *Context*

Family firms might be expected to *perform better* than non-family firms because of:

- avoidance of strategies focusing only on short-term gains;
- an ethos of mutual trust between workers and family managers; and
- more investment in employee and management training and/or research.

However, family firms might be expected to *underperform* compared with non-family firms because of the following:

- lack of commitment in some family firms to profit maximisation;
- family issues take priority over short-term financial performance objectives;
- to ensure family ownership and control, the owners of family businesses may be unwilling to finance firm growth utilising resources gained by the partial sale of equity in the firm to 'outsiders';
- the allocation of key managerial positions to family members may reduce the quality of the management pool; and
- family firms may be more difficult to manage due to the need to satisfy both business as well as 'family agendas'.

7.3.5.2 *Bivariate and matched-sample studies*

Westhead and Cowling (1997) compared the performance of matched unquoted family and non-family unquoted companies in the United Kingdom with regard to several performance indicators. Over the 1991 to 1994 period, family companies, on average, recorded higher levels of absolute gross sales revenue growth (means of £791,000 and £406,000 for family and non-family companies, respectively). To the layperson, it appears that family companies, on average, recorded faster growth in sales over the 1991 to 1994 period. Absolute gross sales revenue growth was concentrated in a small number of family and non-family firms. The absolute and percentage gross sales growth difference between family and non-family firms were not statistically significant. Family firms over the 1991 to 1994 period, on average, increased their gross sales revenues by only 27 per cent, compared with a 55 per cent growth recorded by non-family firms. However, this latter difference was not statistically significant.

Family companies were not significantly larger than non-family companies in employment size in 1991. Family companies in 1994 were, on average, significantly larger in employment size than non-family companies (means of 23.2 and 22.0 employees for family and non-family companies, respectively). Family companies, on average, recorded significantly lower levels of absolute (means of 2.4 and 3.1 employees for family and non-family companies, respectively) growth over the 1991 to 1994 period. Family companies, on average, recorded significantly smaller percentage employment growth (means of 17 per cent and 19 per cent for family and non-family companies respectively) over the 1991 to 1994 period.

Financial data can be difficult to interpret, particularly for small unquoted companies, where the compensation strategies of owners can have a profound influence on recorded profits. Absolute scores on financial performance criteria can be affected by industry-related factors. A *weighted performance score* was calculated for each company (Naman and Slevin, 1993), based upon the importance respondents attached to six selected performance indicators (i.e., sales revenues level, sales revenue growth rate, cashflow, return on shareholder equity, gross profit margin, and net profits from operations) and the level of satisfaction their business had achieved with regard to each of these indicators. No significant difference was recorded between family and non-family companies in terms of reported weighted performance scores (means of 12.4 and 12.2 for family and non-family companies, respectively).

Westhead and Cowling (1997) did not find any significant differences between family and non-family companies with regard to the propensity to export outside the United Kingdom, and the percentage of gross sales exported. They concluded that *family firms (even with 'family agendas') performed similarly to non-family firms* with regard to several performance indicators.

Westhead and Cowling (1997) noted that family firms were not a homogeneous group exhibiting equal inclination or ability to report employment growth. They identified that the five fastest-growing family firms (7 per cent of the subsample) had generated 72 per cent of gross new jobs compared to 56 per cent of gross new jobs generated by the five fastest-growing non-family firms (7 per cent of the subsample). Both the *family and non-family samples included a small number of 'high-flying' fast growth firms* and a numerical dominant group of 'trundlers' (see Chapter 2).

Westhead and Howorth (2006) concluded that the majority of selected ownership and management structure variables in their study were not individually significantly associated with superior (or weaker) family firm performance. They found that firms associated with *high levels of family ownership and management did not report significantly weaker firm performance.* However, firms with larger teams of directors and managers reported higher levels of absolute growth in sales revenues. Firms with CEOs drawn from the dominant family group owning the firm were less likely to be exporters.

While the presence of a family CEO may promote superior firm performance, the presence of factions of family and non-family managers within the top management team (TMT) can create schisms among the subgroups that can adversely affect firm performance; this is especially a problem in listed family-controlled firms. With reference to Italian family-controlled firms, Minichilli et al. (2009) found that firms with TMTs whose ratio of family to non-family was either high or low performed better than firms that had a strong representation of both factions. Further, Ling and Kellermans (2010) noted that it was the level of information exchange within and among the TMT members and not team diversity that shaped firm performance.

7.3.6   Business transfer

Relatively few family firms are transferred to the next generation of family members that own the majority of shares in the family firm (Sharma et al., 2000). Family firm succession has been defined as the passing of the leadership baton from the founder–owner to the successor who will either be a family member or a non-family member (i.e., a 'professional manager') (Handler, 1994). *Succession is more a process than an event.* Further, succession is not simply a single step of handing over the baton; it is a *multi-staged process* that exists over time, beginning before heirs enter the business (Bjuggren and Sund, 2001) (see Case 12, Painotalo Ltd and Rakennuspalvelu Ltd: Family business transfer issues). The succession process involves the transferral of leadership experience, decision-making power and equity (see the example of D&F McCarthy in Entrepreneurship in action 7.1).

Entrepreneurship in action 7.1
Example of successful family firm succession to the next generation of family members

D&F McCarthy is a sixth generation family business that was founded in 1877 by Irishman Thomas McCarthy in Great Yarmouth, England. This fruit delivery business subsequently moved to Norwich. Recently, the business has relocated to a new warehouse complex on the Broadland Business Park, just outside Norwich. The business has seen a steady increase in sales, rising from less than £5m in 2002 to more than £10m last year. Its 44 employees now deliver fruit and vegetables across the counties of Norfolk and Suffolk. Four brothers – Simon, David and Peter and managing director Martin – own 90 per cent of the business. Their father John, when he was 60, retired from day-to-day involvement in the firm 15 years ago, but he remained as the chairman. Simon's son Daniel, 22, is now employed in the

business working on deliveries. Two years ago, the company completed a share buy back. Until then, John's sister and her children had also been shareholders. John's sister and her family run a holiday homes business at Clippesby Hall, near Great Yarmouth. Her family once grew and stored produce and serviced the vehicles for D&F McCarthy. Martin McCarthy commented, 'With the steady growth of the business over the last few years, we've been able to stand back and take a more strategic view of where the company is going.' He reflected, 'As four brothers, we might not always see eye to eye, but we try to take emotion out the situation and judge what is best for the business.'

Source: Aiken, Passing the Baton at Family Firms, *Eastern Daily Press*, 3 March 2010.

Three intertwined systems (i.e., the family, management and ownership) can influence the succession decision in family firms. In family firms, the succession decision involves both strategic and family issues. The choice of successor affects family relationships and the long-term direction of the business. Succession can also be shaped by the *abilities and commitment of potential successors* (Sharma and Irving, 2005). Some children whose parents own family firms do not want to join the family businesses because they want to establish their own independent firms. This decision may be influenced by many factors including personal choice, capacity of the family firm to support more family members, etc. (Zellweger et al., 2010). But attitudes of the second and subsequent generations to entrepreneurship may be moderated by their experience with their family's firm.

Chapter 1 illustrated that Sir Stelios Haji-Ioannou, the founder of easyJet, admired his father's entrepreneurial success, and he worked in the family business to acquire skills and knowledge. Nevertheless, Stelios wanted to be his own boss and independent from the family business. This desire for independence helped fuel his search for a business opportunity that he could exploit on his own.

Lansberg (1999) highlighted that management and ownership issues can impact on the succession process in family firms. A *correlation between basic business form and family generational stage* is widely assumed. For example, a controlling owner business in the first generation becomes a sibling partnership in the second generation and a cousin consortium in the third generation. Lansberg warned that the business form progression does not always follow a predetermined sequence. He made a conceptual distinction between three types of succession transitions. First, *succession transitions that recycle the business form* (i.e., transitions that involve replacing the senior leadership without changing the fundamental form of the business – the people change but the authority structure remains the same). Second, *evolutionary successions* that involve fundamental changes in the authority and control structure of the system from a simple form to an increasingly complex one (i.e., controlling owner to sibling partnership, sibling partnership to cousin consortium and controlling owner to cousin consortium). Third, *devolutionary successions* that move the system to a simpler form (i.e., cousin consortium to sibling partnership, sibling partnership to controlling owner business and cousin consortium to controlling owner business). Devolutionary successions are relatively rare because a considerable amount of liquidity is required to concentrate the control of voting shares in family firms. In some cases, the succession issue can have a major adverse impact on both the firm and the family. This issue is illustrated in Entrepreneurship in action 7.2.

Despite the importance of succession to the continuity of a family firm, many issues have not been explored in large-scale empirical studies (Westhead, 2003). Succession may be influenced by the objectives pursued by the family owning the business. Somewhat paradoxically, emphasis on the maintenance of a particular lifestyle objective that involves family dominance in management and 'family agendas', can adversely affect a firm's ability to adapt and survive in the long term. Quality of management may suffer, captive boards may not bring the necessary pressure to change, and there may be a reluctance to bring in outsiders who would contribute equity finance and monitoring. Family firm survival has been assisted by the development of *management buyouts* where next-generation family owners are either not available or unwilling to take on the running of the business (see Chapter 9).

Entrepreneurship in action 7.2
Family firm succession problems

When Chris Wanken's father, a branch manager affiliated with Raymond James Financial Services Inc., fired him last March, it ignited a smouldering family dispute that experts say might have been avoided with better planning. In the past year, Chris Wanken and his father, John, have fired arbitration claims and counter claims with each other that centre on their business relationship at Beacon Financial Advisors of Addison, Texas. Making the family dispute more painful, Chris Wanken was sued last month in the Texas state court in Collin County by his father, who is seeking custody of his son's two children. Chris Wanken alleged in his arbitration claim that he was essentially an equal partner in Beacon Financial Advisors. Further, he asserted that his father turned his back on that agreement, and put a black mark on his son's brokerage records because the latter was terminated for 'job performance'. John Wanken, in an arbitration countersuit, claimed that his son was not a partner but 'did what was asked and required of him as an employee', at least in the early years of the business relationship. From 2003 until Chris Wanken was fired in 2008, his father John claimed that he paid his son 50 per cent of the net profits relating to the firms sales, excluding insurance commissions, for which the latter received 30 per cent. Chris Wanken said in an interview last Wednesday that after the death of his mother (who also worked at the firm until 2007), he and his father realised they had failed to make adequate plans for the future of their business. They had operated as a team for seven years, building the firm to about $80 million in client assets. However, they never put their business agreement on paper. Chris Wanken said that, 'Unfortunately, that lack of planning played a significant part in a bitter family rift.' He claimed that this resulted in his father firing him six months after his mother's death. The father and son are now enmeshed in various bitter legal disputes. Chris Wanken stated that, 'I loved my father and trusted him. Working with family, it's awesome.' Further, he asserted that, 'And clients love it. It creates an instant contingency plan.' But Chris Wanken has learned an extremely painful lesson over the past year. In business, Chris Wanken indicated, 'you have to treat family as you would anyone else.' Moreover, he reflected that, 'Families can have arguments. Take the business and money part out of it, and lay the agreement out in black and white.'

Source: B. Kelly, Family Feud Drives Home Need for Succession Plans, *Investment News*, 12 April 2009.

7.4 Family firm heterogeneity

7.4.1 Sharma's (2004) typology of family firms

Family firms cannot be viewed as a homogeneous entity (Chrisman et al., 2005). Studies are now discussing the profiles of 'types' of private family firms. Sharma (2004) discussed the following *four 'types' of family firms with regard to the family and business dimensions: warm hearts-deep pockets, pained hearts-deep pockets, warm hearts-empty pockets, and pained hearts-empty pockets*. Sharma's study suggests that a fruitful avenue for future studies is the exploration of whether variations in firm performance are shaped by family firm 'type'. Further, *private family firm heterogeneity* needs to be considered when business development and sustainability initiatives are designed.

7.4.2 Westhead and Howorth's (2007) conceptual typology of firm types

7.4.2.1 *Introduction*

Westhead and Howorth (2007) presented two classifications of private family firms: a conceptually derived typology and an empirically derived taxonomy. The themes (and variables) of company ownership and management structures as well as company goals (i.e. financial and family objectives) were utilised to illustrate six conceptualised 'types' of private family firms. These three themes are discussed, in turn, below. The conceptual classification is then presented. Further, the validity of the conceptual typology is discussed with regard to an empirical taxonomy.

7.4.2.2 Company ownership structure

As family firms progress from one generation to the next, the structural form of ownership and management may change. Over time, the ownership base of the firm may become more complex if more family members acquire an equity stake. To ensure business development, owners of some family firms may sell ordinary voting shares to 'outsiders' who are not drawn from the dominant family group. The vertical axis in Figure 7.1 illustrates that ownership of the firm may be held by a close family, but ownership can also be diluted within the family, or diluted outside the family when non-family members acquire an equity stake.

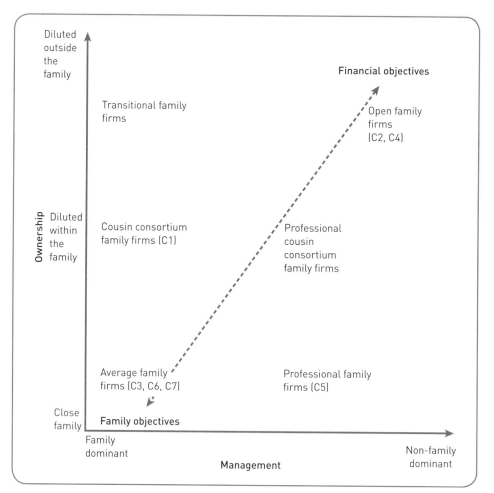

Figure 7.1 Conceptualised 'types' of family firms[a]

Notes: (a) Empirical types of family firms are reported in brackets; C1 = 'cousin consortium family firms';
C2 = 'large open family firms'; C3 = 'entrenched average family firms'; C4 = 'multi-generational open family firms';
C5 = 'professional family firms'; C6 = 'average family firms'; C7 = 'multi-generational average family firms'.

Source: Westhead and Howorth (2007, Table 1).

7.4.2.3 *Management structure*

Owners focusing on 'family agendas' may favour the recruitment of family members to manage the family firm. Directors who are members of the dominant family can exert pressure to ensure that 'family agendas' and the cultural foundations of the business are considered. An important challenge is to clarify the intertwining of ownership and management issues, as the accompanying example of 3 Bear Animations illustrates in Entrepreneurship in action 7.3.

Owners focusing on wealth creation and business development may prefer to recruit non-family professional managers (see the example of Warburtons in Entrepreneurship in action 7.4). The likelihood that a small private firm employs an 'outside' board member can increase with regard to the proportion of ownership held by individuals outside the firm (Fiegener et al., 2000). Family firms may vary with regard to whether management is dominated by family or non-family members. The horizontal axis in Figure 7.1 illustrates that family members may hold management of the family firm alone, but in some family firms management can be allocated to non-family managers.

Entrepreneurship in action 7.3
Resolving ownership and managerial issues

Sisters Linnhe, Bryony and Cadi Cadlow set up their short film production studio 3 Bear Animations nine years ago near Kendal in Cumbria, England. Although the three sisters are close, and they rarely row, [they] decided it would be sensible to have a shareholder agreement. Linnhe, 29, stated: 'Though we all have long-term plans for the company, we know that if we go our separate ways, everything will be split equally.' Assigning the key roles for each sister was straightfor-

ward. Linnhe, who manages the marketing and website operations reflected that, 'When we started out, we were all trying to do a bit of everything, which wasn't terribly productive, so we identified our individual strengths and skills and decided on our individual roles.' Her twin sister Cadi heads the creative side, while Bryony, 25, handles finance and accounting.

Source: K. Taylor, How to Run the Family Firm, *Mail on Sunday*, 26 March 2007.

Entrepreneurship in action 7.4
Warburtons: Role of non-executive directors

The Warburtons bakery established in Lancashire in England has been a family-owned business for five generations. Family members still hold senior management positions. With regard to the last two generations of family ownership, the firm has used senior non-family executives to assist business growth and prosperity. In May 2006, a non-family member took over as the managing director. The firms executive chairman, Jonathan Warburton, sees it as an obvious way to do business. He reflected

that, 'It's very simple; the family's interests are best served by bringing in the best people.' Jonathan Warburton asserted that, 'There are no jobs for the boys here.' Further, he indicated that, 'We are surrounded by people who are better at their jobs than we are. Why wouldn't you use the best people?' It may seem obvious to Warburton, but many family firms still find it hard to bring in outsiders.

Source: Stone, 'Family Firms Benefit from Outside Help', *Sunday Times*, 3 September 2006.

7.4.2.4 *Company objectives*

Family firms differ with regard to the extent that family objectives are emphasised. They can focus on financial and/or organisation serving objectives. Firms associated with increasing numbers of non-family managers may move towards greater self-serving behaviour, and a focus on financial objectives. Conversely, if a family maintains control of the firm, and seeks to provide employment positions for family members, the family firm may be associated with organisation serving objectives. Dilution of ownership outside the family may enable non-family members to shape firm objectives. Non-family shareholders seeking to protect their interests may encourage the adoption of governance issues that may lessen a focus on family objectives towards a focus on financial objectives. Some firms can report a combination of financial and family objectives. Company objectives of family firms are considered within Figure 7.1. Family objectives are expected to be most important for closely family owned and family managed firms. Conversely, financial objectives will have increased importance when ownership of the firm is diluted, and when non-family members dominate management. A spectrum of objectives may be reported between the two extremes (i.e., closely family owned and managed firms compared with firms with diluted ownership outside the family that are managed by non-family members).

7.4.2.5 *Six conceptualised 'types' of family firms*

With reference to the three cross-cutting themes of company ownership and management structures as well as company objectives, Westhead and Howorth (2007) illustrated differences between the *six conceptual 'types'* of family firms highlighted in Figure 7.1. A distinction was made between firms that have close family ownership, those that are diluted within the family, and those diluted outside the family (i.e., the vertical axis). Moreover, a distinction was made between firms that have family dominated management and those that have non-family dominated management (i.e., the horizontal axis). The cross-cutting theme of financial objectives (i.e., agency theory) and family/non-financial objectives (i.e., stewardship theory) is represented by the dotted line within Figure 7.1. The relative importance of financial or family objectives is represented by the distance in a straight line between the ends of the arrow.

'*Average family firms*' emphasise family objectives and have closely-held family ownership and family management. '*Professional family firms*' report a mix of family and non-family objectives, but emphasise family objectives. They have closely-held family ownership and management dominated by non-family members. '*Cousin consortium family firms*' report a mix of family and non-family objectives. They have diluted ownership within the family and management dominated by family members. '*Professional cousin consortium family firms*' have diluted ownership within the family and management dominated by non-family members. Further, '*professional cousin consortium family firms*' place more emphasis on financial objectives than '*cousin consortium family firms*', and they place less emphasis on family objectives. '*Transitional family firms*' report both family and non-family objectives, but they place greater emphasis on financial objectives. They have diluted ownership outside the family but family members dominate management. These firms are transitional because the management is expected to move towards less family dominance. Finally, '*open family firms*' focus on financial objectives. They have diluted ownership outside the family and non-family management is dominant. Due to separated firm ownership and control, the latter firms may report agency issues.

7.4.2.6 *Validity of the conceptual typology of family firm types*

With reference to 17 variables relating to the themes of company objectives, ownership and management, Westhead and Howorth (2007) generated a theoretically grounded empirical taxonomy of family firm 'types'. The seven isolated *empirical 'types'* were as follows:

1 cousin consortium family firms;
2 large open family firms;
3 entrenched average family firms;
4 multi-generation open family firms;
5 professional family firms;
6 average family firms; and
7 multi-generation average family firms.

Firms focusing more upon financial objectives generally reported organisational structures that suggest a self-serving culture (i.e. 'large open family firms', 'multi-generation open family firms' and 'professional family firms'). Moreover, firms predominantly focusing upon non-financial objectives generally reported an organisation-serving culture as expected by stewardship theory (i.e., 'cousin consortium family firms', 'entrenched average family firms', 'average family firms', and 'multi-generation average family firms). *Four out of the six conceptualised 'types'* of family firms shown in Figure 7.1 were empirically validated as follows: *'average family firms', 'professional family firms', 'cousin consortium family firms', and 'open family firms'.* However, two conceptualised 'types' relating to *'transitional family firms'* and *'professional cousin consortium family firms'* were not empirically validated.

The typology presented in Figure 7.1 casts doubt on the wider validity and utility of a proposed *'familiness' continuum scale* (Klein et al., 2005) to explore family firm dynamics. *Typologies* presented by both Sharma, and Westhead and Howorth suggest that practitioners should not regard family firms as a homogeneous entity. Rather than blanket policy support for family firms, there may be a case to provide micro-level *customised support to each 'type' of family firm.*

7.5 Looking forward

The scale of the family firm phenomenon is highly sensitive to the family firm definition used. If researchers decide to use a single family firm definition, there is a case to select the reasonably broad family firm, *Definition (3)* in Table 7.1.

Practitioners are concerned with *enterprise sustainability* and new firm creation. Before introducing *macro* (i.e., reduce capital gains and/or increase inheritance tax thresholds) and/or *micro-level schemes* to assist the survival and development of private family firms, policy-makers need to know whether family firms generally perform better than non-family firms. Family firms are associated with several assets and liabilities. A firm's objectives, management, ownership and strategic orientation can shape firm performance. Family firms protecting 'family agendas' could report weaker levels of performance than non-family firms. Evidence suggests that family firms, like their non-family firm counterparts, make notable contributions to wealth creation and job generation. There is no conclusive evidence to suggest that family firms report consistently significantly superior (or weaker) performance than non-family firms. Additional evidence is warranted to justify fiscal macro-level policies in favour of family firm owners.

Studies should consider *family firm heterogeneity* rather than crude demographic differences between family and non-family firms. Section 7.4 highlighted that there are several 'types' of family and non-family firms. The conceptual typologies presented by both Sharma (2004) and Westhead and Howorth (2007) cast doubt on the wider relevance and generalisability of theories relating to 'average' family firms. Studies that have focused on firm performance differences between a single group of family firms relative to a single group of non-family firms may be flawed. Results from the latter *'average comparison' studies* may have been distorted by the contribution made by the numerically dominant group of '*average family firms*'. Practitioners concerned with enterprise sustainability may need to provide customised support to each 'type' of family firm.

Future studies need to identify the 'types' of family firms associated with superior (and weaker) levels of financial performance. Additional conceptual approaches relating to the emerging entrepreneurial cognition and entrepreneurial experience and knowledge literatures (see Chapters 4 and 5) need to be considered to explore the profiles of different 'types' of family firms. Future research may benefit from exploring the following broad research question. How do the goals, competencies, resources, and ownership and management structures of firms shape the financial (and non-financial) performance of different 'types' of private family firms? Qualitative researchers seeking to build theory could use the presented conceptual typology (Figure 7.1) as a platform for theoretical sampling linked to the agency and stewardship perspectives. Researchers could gather information relating to emerging research themes (i.e., the role of founder(s), next generation family members, women and non-family employees; the value and type of contractual agreements selected; the sources of conflict and the selected management strategies; and the knowledge accumulation and dissemination processes reported within family firms) (Sharma, 2004). Future studies could explore 'why' and 'how' some family firm owners seek to 'professionalise' their firms (Chittoor and Das, 2007). Monitoring family firm movement over time around the conceptual typology 'types' could provide fresh insights into family dynamics and governance issues. The critical incidents and causal issues associated with the movement from '*average family firms*' to '*professional cousin consortium family firms*', for example, could be explained. Evidence from in-depth cases could then be used to revise the conceptual typology, and after the data has 'talked' precise theoretically derived propositions could be reported. The latter propositions could then be subsequently explored in future qualitative and quantitative studies.

Complexities of the succession process in the family firm (i.e., the three intertwined systems of the family, management and ownership) and the overlap between entrepreneurship and family firm need to be explored. To develop more appropriate public policies to support private family firms, additional theoretical and conceptual work needs to be conducted surrounding the role played by owners and managers in each 'type' of family firm.

Discussion questions

1 What are the assets (i.e., strengths) of private family firms?

2 What are the liabilities (i.e., weaknesses) of private family firms?

3 Do private family firms report superior levels of performance relative to private non-family firms?

4 What issues need to be considered when comparing the performance of private family firms?

5 Are firm performance studies focusing on aggregate groups of private family and non-family firms flawed?

6 Do 'types' of private family firms exist? Illustrate with reference to a conceptual typology and/or an empirical taxonomy.

7 Should policy-makers reduce capital gains and/or inheritance tax to encourage private family firm ownership transfers to the next generation of family members?

Recommended further reading

Astrachan, J. H. and Shanker, M. C. (2003). Family Businesses' Contribution to the US Economy: A Closer Look. *Family Business Review,* 16 (3): 211–219.

Chrisman, J. J., Chua, J. H. and Sharma, P. (2005). Trends and Directions in the Development of a Strategic Management Theory of the Family Firm. *Entrepreneurship Theory and Practice,* 29 (3): 555–575.

Poutziouris, P. Z., Smyrnois, K. X. and Klein, S. B. (2006). *Handbook of Research on Family Business.* Cheltenham: Edward Elgar.

Sharma, P. (2004). An Overview of the Field of Family Business Studies: Current Status and Directions for Future Research. *Family Business Review,* 17 (1): 1–36.

Westhead, P. and Howorth, C. (2007). 'Types' of Private Family Firms: An Exploratory Conceptual and Empirical Analysis. *Entrepreneurship and Regional Development,* 19 (5): 405–431.

Chapter 8

'Types' of organisations II: Corporate entrepreneurship

Contents

Learning objectives

● Illustrate that entrepreneurship is conducted in existing organisations, which is termed corporate entrepreneurship.

● Identify various features of corporate entrepreneurship relating to innovation, strategic renewal and the creation of new ventures (i.e. internal and external corporate venturing to the host organisation).

● Consider internal corporate venturing variability with reference to structural autonomy, relatedness to existing business, extent of innovation and nature of sponsorship.

● Illustrate that the form of corporate venturing (i.e., sustained regeneration, organisational regeneration, strategic renewal or domain redefinition) is linked to the form of competitive advantage.

● Explain that external environmental conditions can shape the pursuit of corporate entrepreneurship and firm performance.

8.1 Introduction

The organisational form an entrepreneurial venture takes is a crucial aspect of entrepreneurship research. However, there is considerable heterogeneity among organisational modes selected by entrepreneurs. The new independent venture organisational form associated with the entrepreneur has been discussed in earlier chapters. In this chapter, we discuss corporate entrepreneurship.

8.2 Definitions of corporate entrepreneurship

Numerous definitions of corporate entrepreneurship have been operationalised (Sharma and Chrisman, 1999). The following terms have been used to describe entrepreneurial efforts within an existing organisation: corporate entrepreneurship, corporate venturing, intrapreneurship, internal corporate entrepreneurship, internal entrepreneurship, strategic renewal, and corporate venturing.

A distinction can be made between independent and corporate entrepreneurship (Sharma and Chrisman, 1999). Independent entrepreneurship is the process whereby an individual or a group of individuals, acting independently of any association with an existing organisation, create a new organisation. Corporate entrepreneurship is the process whereby an individual or a group of individuals, in association with an existing organisation, create a new organisation or instigate renewal or innovation within that organisation. Definitional issues relating to corporate entrepreneurship terminology are summarised in Table 8.1.

Table 8.1 Unique features of corporate entrepreneurship terminology

Terms	Unique criteria
Entrepreneurship	Organisational creation, or innovation, within or outside organisations
Independent entrepreneurship	Organisational creation: • by individual(s) not associated with an existing corporate entity
Corporate entrepreneurship	Organisational creation, renewal, or innovation: • instigated by an existing organisational entity
Strategic renewal/strategic entrepreneurship	Organisational renewal involving major strategic and/or structural changes: • instigated by an existing organisational entity • resides within existing organisational domain
Corporate venturing	Organisational creation: • instigated by an existing organisational entity • treated as a new business
Innovation	Introduction of something new to market-place: • potential to transform competitive environment and organisation • usually occurring in concert with corporate venturing or strategic renewal
External corporate venturing	Organisational creation: • instigated by an existing organisational entity • treated as new businesses • resides outside existing organisational domain
Internal corporate venturing	Organisational creation: • instigated by an existing organisational entity • treated as new business • reside within existing organisational domain
Dimensions of internal corporate venturing	1 Structural autonomy 2 Relatedness to existing business(es) 3 Extent of innovation 4 Nature of sponsorship

Source: Adapted from Sharma and Chrisman (1999, Table 3: 21).

Figure 8.1 illustrates the hierarchy of terminology in corporate entrepreneurship, as portrayed by Sharma and Chrisman (1999). Corporate entrepreneurship is associated with the following three distinct but related dimensions (Guth and Ginsberg, 1990; Zahra, 1993a):

1 *Strategic renewal.* Corporate entrepreneurship embodies renewal activities that enhance a corporations' ability to compete and take risks, which may or may not involve the addition of new businesses to a corporation. Sharma and Chrisman (1999: 19) assert that strategic renewal refers to the corporate entrepreneurial efforts that result in significant changes to an organisation's business or corporate level strategy or structure. These changes alter pre-existing relationships within the organisation or between the organisation and its external environment, and in most cases will involve some sort of innovation. Morris et al. (2008) and Kuratko and Audretsch (2009) define this aspect of corporate entrepreneurship as *strategic entrepreneurship*. Strategic entrepreneurship has been defined as involving the identification and exploitation of opportunities, while simultaneously creating and sustaining a competitive advantage (Ireland et al., 2003) (see Section 3.8.3.3). It may involve strategic renewal, sustained regeneration, domain redefinition, organisational rejuvenation, and business model reconstruction (Covin and Miles, 1999), to which we return below.

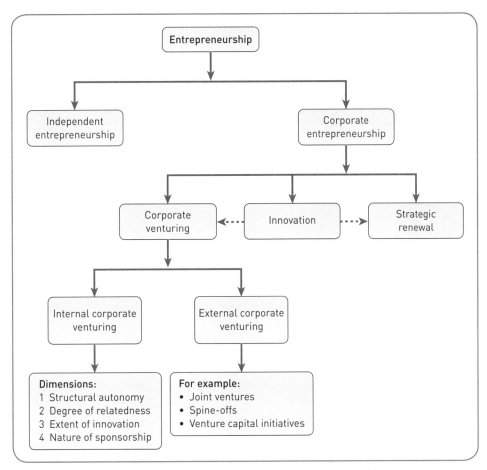

Figure 8.1 Hierarchy of terminology in corporate enterpreneurship

Source: Sharma and Chrisman (1999, Figure 1:20).

2 *Innovation and corporate venturing.* Narayanan et al. (2009) state that corporate venturing focuses on the various steps and processes associated with creating new businesses and integrating them into the firm's overall business portfolio. The new business organisations may follow from or lead to innovations that exploit new markets, or new product offerings, or both. These venturing efforts may or may not lead to the formation of new organisational units that are distinct from existing organisational units in a structural sense (e.g., a new division). Corporate venturing provides corporations with a financial return and the opportunity to assess new technologies and markets at a relatively early stage in their development. The following distinction has been made between *external* and *internal* corporate venturing:

3 (a) *External corporate venturing.* Corporate venturing activities that result in the creation of semi-autonomous or autonomous organisational entities that reside outside the existing organisational domain (Sharma and Chrisman, 1999: 19) (see Case 13, Spin-offs at Tremcar: Partnerships for growth). Some examples of corporate ventures are formed as a result of joint ventures, spin-offs (see Chapter 6), and corporate venture capital initiatives (see the examples of Intel Capital and Google Ventures in Entrepreneurship in action 8.1). Although these may vary in their

Entrepreneurship in action 8.1
Examples of corporate venture capital: Intel Capital and Google Ventures

The venture capital arm of computing giant Intel makes equity investments in companies at any stage working on hardware, software and services targeted across a range of sectors, including enterprise, home, health, consumer Internet, semiconductor manufacturing and green technology. One of the most active corporate venture initiatives, Intel Capital has invested more than $9.5 billion in upwards of 1,050 companies in 46 countries since 1991, including what has been described as a 'long and agonizing foray into communications semiconductor business' during the 'go-go 1990s'. At least 174 companies from the Intel Capital portfolio have gone public, and 231 have merged with another firm or been acquired.

Google's venture capital arm, Google Ventures, has been operating for about a year and has named 10 companies in its portfolio. During an event last month down at Google headquarters, executives from the VC [venture capital] branch said Google Ventures plans to invest at least $100 million per year in startups across various industries. They also emphasized that the venture arm intends to make returns on its investments and doesn't plan to invest just for the sake of acquiring the startups and bringing them into Google.

Part of the overarching goal for Intel's venture capital arm is to 'drive global Internet growth, facilitate new usage models, and advance computing and communications platforms', or in other words, support tech that could eventually – and even indirectly – boost demand for Intel's own products and services. That's why you see Intel investing in the ecosystem of communications and the Internet, and not just in the latest chip technology.

Earlier this year, Intel CEO Paul Otellini announced that Intel Capital had put together a new $200 million investment fund aimed at 'key innovation and growth segments such as clean technology, information technology and biotechnology', and that it had brought in 24 VC firms (including Kleiner Perkins, Menlo Ventures, Mohr Davidow Ventures, New Enterprise Associates, Draper Fisher Jurvetson, Khosla Ventures and North Bridge Venture Partners) to invest a total of $3.5 billion over the next two years . . . one of the best ways to garner a Google Ventures investment is to work with one of the two VC firms that have closely aligned themselves with Google: Kleiner Perkins and August Capital. But as the saga of V-Vehicle (a startup that basically bet it all on a federal loan that has not come through to build a high PG car with a plastic shell) illustrates, following along with Kleiner Perkins' greentech investments isn't always the best move . . . The Google Ventures team also said it will be aiming for better-than-average venture capital returns, meaning they hope more than one out of every 10 investments will make money. But as Katie has explained (in this analysis of Google Ventures' investment in V-Vehicle) going out of its way to operate as a VC fund and investing large sums outside of its core competency (the web) means Google Ventures – like other VCs [venture capitalists] . . . will have to brace itself for those other nine startups that merely break even or lose money.

Source: J. Garthwaite, Lessons for GM from Google, Intel's Venture Capital Arms, 4 June 2010) http://earth2tech.com/2010/06/04/lessons-for-gm-from-google-intels-venture-capital-arms/, accessed 14 July 2010.

degree of separateness from the parent company, their common feature is that they reside outside the domain or boundaries of the existing organisation.

3 (b) *Internal corporate venturing.* The creation of new businesses that generally reside within the corporate structure although they may be located outside the firm as semi-autonomous entities, such as spin-offs (see the examples of spin-off creation relating to Energy Innovations and Ergo in Entrepreneurship in action 8.2). Pre-existing internal organisation structures may accommodate these new ventures or newly created organisational entities may be created within the corporate structure.

Entrepreneurship in action 8.2
Spin-off creations: Energy Innovations and Ergo

Energy Innovations

Energy Innovations has announced that its RayTracker product group has been spun off to form RayTracker Inc. The new company will allow the team to take advantage of the growing demand for its RayTracker GC product line. The GC line was made to be cost-effective while boasting high efficiency and reliability. RayTracker had been included in over 2MW [megawatt] of installations in 2008. The company claims that PV panels mounted on a RayTracker system yield up to 38 per cent more energy than fixed flat PV systems annually and up to 23 per cent more than fixed-tilt systems. Kang Sun, with over two decades in business creation and management, has been named the CEO of RayTracker. He had previously been president and COO of JA Solar Holdings Co. in China. Before his stint at JA Solar, Kang had been managing director, new business development, and chief strategy officer, new business and new products group, for Applied Materials.

Source: J. Haines, Energy Innovations Creates Spin-Off for RayTracker Products, 3 March 2009, http://www.pv-tech.org/news/_a/energy_innovations_creates_spin_off_for_raytracker_products/ (accessed 14 July 2010).

Ergo

Ergo has built up a multi-million euro business in the IT services space and now the established IT firm has raised €3m in venture capital and will create 33 new jobs as its Fenergo financial software business goes global. Fenergo – derived from the Latin 'to lend' – has raised €2m in funding from Enterprise Ireland and the European Investment Bank to internationalise the product that helps financial operators like banks and building societies to reduce their exposure to risk. The Fenergo software, which spun out of an IT implementation Ergo made in recent years in Ireland, manages the end-to-end processing of a bank's exposure to customer in terms of pre-approval, collateral, loan origination, arrears, time line and portfolio.

'The technology spun out of a services engagement we had in Ireland where banks were discovering they didn't always know how much money had been loaned out to an individual or entity,' said John Purdy, managing director, Ergo. 'It is very much a product of now. We've already sold the product in Ireland to a number of key clients. We conducted research with Enterprise Ireland and were satisfied that it is a unique application that fills a significant gap in the global financial marketplace.' Purdy said that the Ergo IT services business has successfully maintained profitability in recent years focusing on alliances with HP and Microsoft to deliver solutions to the business market . . . Purdy explained that 15 of the 33 new jobs have already been filled and that the company has embraced constant change as part of its business model. 'Our internal culture is geared around change. Over the last seven years we have undergone several significant shifts. Change is now part of the planning process. The key is to stay fresh – your chances of survival are greater. We're here for the long haul, trading for 17 years. Our strategies from the service front are aligned with Microsoft and HP. Our move into international exports with Fenergo demonstrates our appetite, passion and hunger for growth or change.'

Source: Ergo to Create 33 Jobs as Spin-Off Goes Global, 24 June 2010; http://www.siliconrepublic.com/careers-centre/item/16718-ergo-to-create-33-jobs-as-s, accessed 14 July 2010.

There are various forms of corporate venturing. *Direct corporate venturing* involves innovations by corporations through direct investment in new ventures that may be subsidiaries of the corporation, spin-offs or independent entities. *Indirect corporate venturing* concerns the investment by corporations in venture capital funds, which in turn are invested in new ventures (McNally, 1994). Indirect and direct corporate venturing serve purposes that may be complementary. The indirect approach provides contacts and access to deal flow, whilst the direct approach may enhance specific business relationships.

An *ideal* corporate venture has high corporate fit, low initial investment, experienced venture champions, experience with product/service, low competitive threat, proprietorial technology, high gross margins, and high rate of return. A corporate venture involves an activity new to the organisation; is initiated or conducted internally; involves significantly higher risk of failure or large losses than the organisation's base business; is characterised by greater uncertainty than the base business; will be managed separately at some time during its life; and is undertaken for the purpose of increasing sales, profit, productivity or quality.

8.3   Internal corporate venturing variability

Although internal corporate venturing activities are located within existing organisations, they are created in different ways, have different relationships with the corporate parent, involve different levels of innovation, and differ in strategic importance (Sharma and Chrisman, 1999: 21). Internal corporate ventures may vary in terms of at least four dimensions that may influence their subsequent development and performance: structural autonomy, relatedness to existing businesses, extent of innovation, and nature of sponsorship. Each of theses dimensions is discussed, in turn:

- *Structural autonomy.* Relates to the crucial decision of where to locate the venture within an organisation. Block and MacMillan (1993) suggested that the ideal place to locate a venture will depend on its needs for managerial attention, resources, learning opportunities, and protection from corporate antagonism. The venture may be totally embedded within the ongoing operations of an existing division, or a separate new-venture division may be created, which is isolated from the rest of the organisation but reports directly to top management (Kanter et al., 1991).
- *Relatedness to the existing businesses.* Considered with regard to product offerings, markets, or core competencies and resources required. Relatedness ranges on a continuum from closely related to the organisation's present activities to completely unrelated to the organisation's present activities. The latter leads to variation and numerous learning challenges for company owners seeking to effectively manage the internal corporate venture (Block and MacMillan, 1993).
- *Extent of innovation.* Refers to the degree of newness of a venture to the market-place. This can range from imitative activity to highly *innovative 'frame-breaking'* activity (Stopford and Baden-Fuller, 1994). Imitative ventures will require considerable learning on the part of an organisation. Some lessons may be learned from experiences of pioneering competitors (i.e., organisations that have created new markets) (Sharma and Chrisman, 1999). Ventures that are new to the market-place and those that create markets (i.e., pioneers) face considerably greater learning challenges than imitative ventures.
- *Nature of sponsorship.* Relates to the degree of formal authorisation for the venture. Formal or induced ventures are sponsored by an organisation (Zahra, 1993a), typically through 'top-down' entrepreneurial processes (Day, 1994). Dess et al. (2003) have emphasised the role of top management leadership in shaping the internal organisation of corporate entrepreneurship. *Informal* or *autonomous* ventures are entrepreneurial efforts based on employees' initiative without formal organisational sponsorship (Zahra, 1993a). In the case of autonomous entrepreneurial efforts, the role of an organisational champion and sponsor is extremely important, whereas it may not be critical in

the case of formally induced efforts. Organisational members from all managerial levels and divisions are likely to be required for innovation-based corporate entrepreneurship to be effective. The extent to which a corporate entrepreneurship programme can draw upon these organisational members will depend on the organisation's culture and attitude towards knowledge sharing, as well as individual project leaders' networks. Overall, both *'bottom up' and 'top down' processes* are important. However, the capabilities for taking advantage of corporate entrepreneurship may vary by managerial level (Hornsby et al., 2009); more senior managers may have greater expertise and wider networks that can help facilitate corporate entrepreneurship. Actors at different levels of the organisation have corporate entrepreneurship roles, and these are not independent of each other. There is a need to understand how these interdependencies are facilitated. The key seems to be how the inevitable collisions between 'skunk works'-type (i.e., informal) processes, and the need for internal controls are resolved without the consequences of suppressed innovation and risk-taking.

A strategic competitive advantage may not be created if the corporate governance system does not *incentivise and monitor management* to undertake the appropriate actions to recognise opportunities, and to gather and utilise resources. The board of directors can play an important role in developing corporate entrepreneurship. Rather than viewing the sole function of the board of directors as protectors of shareholders' interests, directors may serve an entrepreneurial function in assisting and guiding managers in relation to corporate entrepreneurship. Effective boards can enable wealth creation by providing managers with better information and leads about entrepreneurial opportunities; sharing valuable information; suggesting innovative ideas and initiatives; offering and evaluating avenues for exploiting opportunities identified by corporate entrepreneurship programmes; encouraging investment in building the *firm's absorptive capacity*; and ensuring that members of the top management team have the requisite knowledge, skills and abilities to lead the company and engage in value-creating corporate entrepreneurship activities. Similarly, appropriate remuneration for management may have a crucial role to play. The idiosyncratic knowledge possessed by management is key to opportunity recognition, itself central to corporate entrepreneurship. The nature of remuneration for managers with specialist knowledge poses important issues for corporate entrepreneurship because it can influence whether they exploit opportunities for their own ends, or act in the interest of the firm.

8.4　Corporate venturing and competitive advantage

8.4.1　Context

Covin and Miles, 1999: 50) have asserted that:

> Corporate entrepreneurship . . . is the spark and catalyst that is intended to place firms on the path to competitive superiority or keep them in competitively advantageous positions.

Four distinct forms of corporate entrepreneurship can be adopted to achieve competitive advantage: sustained regeneration, organisational regeneration, strategic renewal, and domain redefinition (see Table 8.2). Each theme is discussed, in turn, below:

Table 8.2 Key attributes of the four forms of corporate entrepreneurship

Form of corporate entrepreneurship	Focus of corporate entrepreneurship	Typical basis for competitive advantage	Typical frequency of new entrepreneurial acts	Magnitude of negative impact if entrepreneurial act is unsuccessful
Sustained regeneration	New products or new markets	Differentiation	High frequency	Low
Organisational rejuvenation	The organisation	Cost leadership	Moderate frequency	Low-to-moderate
Strategic renewal	Business strategy	Varies with specific form manifestation	Less frequent	Moderate-to-high
Domain redefinition	Creation and exploitation of product/market arenas	Quick response	Infrequent	Varies with specific form manifestation and contextual consideration

Notes:
New entrepreneurial acts for:
- Sustained regeneration: a new product introduction or the entrance of a new (to the firm) but existing market;
- Organisational rejuvenation: a major, internally focused innovation aimed at improving firm functioning or strategy implementation;
- Strategic renewal: the pursuit of a new strategic direction; and
- Domain redefinition: the creation and exploitation of a new, previously unoccupied product/market arena.

Source: Covin and Miles (1999, Table 1: 57).

8.4.2 Sustained regeneration

A sustained regeneration form of corporate entrepreneurship is exhibited by firms that regularly and continuously introduce new products or services or enter new markets (Covin and Miles, 1999: 51). The latter entrepreneurial firms intend to capitalise on latent or underexploited market opportunities using the firm's valued innovation-producing competencies. These firms have cultures, structures and systems supportive of innovation. Notably, they are learning organisations that embrace change and willingly challenge competitors in battles for market share. They continually cull older products and services from their lines in an effort to improve overall competitiveness through product lifecycle management techniques. Arm & Hammer, for example, selected a sustained regeneration corporate entrepreneurship strategy (Covin and Miles, 1999). The core product of the company was baking soda and the company was a small and narrow-line player within its industry. Arm & Hammer creatively introduced its core product into *new products* with regard to toothpaste and deodorising products. The company identified *new markets* unseen or unappreciated by competitors in its core industry segment. A sustained regeneration strategy is not simply one of product development, or related diversification. The proactive, competence-expanding actions reflect conscious decisions to regularly and strategically expand the business of the company for the purpose of ensuring long-term competitiveness.

8.4.3 Organisational regeneration

Organisational regeneration relates to an organisation that seeks to sustain or improve its competitive standing by altering its internal processes, structures and/or capabilities

(Covin and Miles, 1999: 52). The focus and target of innovation is the organisation per se. This form of corporate entrepreneurship is referred to as organisational renewal, corporate renewal or corporate rejuvenation. It relates to efforts to sustain or increase competitiveness through the improved execution of particular, *pre-existing* business strategies. Improved strategy execution via organisational rejuvenation entails actions that reconfigure a firm's value chain, or otherwise affect the pattern of internal resource allocation. Organisational regeneration relates to the introduction of an innovation or innovations that: redefine how some major aspects of the firm's operation is conducted; create value for the firm's customers; or sustain or improve the firm's ability to effectively implement its chosen strategy. It is a form of corporate entrepreneurship that would be likely to meet with minimal disagreement.

Procter and Gamble, for example, improved its inventory and distribution systems through the adoption of bar-coding technology (Covin and Miles, 1999). The latter technology has revolutionised the entire outbound logistics function. The company sustained its competitive position by setting the customer service standards against which competitors are being judged.

The Chrysler Corporation recognised that the entire process through which automobiles are designed and produced had to be reconfigured (Covin and Miles, 1999). They used a 'platform' team structure to achieve this goal. The structure brought together managers and employees from across the corporation to achieve strong and effective functional integration. Process re-engineering principles adopted had a positive impact on product development cycle time and product quality. This enabled the firm to sustain its competitive position.

8.4.4   Strategic renewal

A firm following a strategic renewal form of corporate entrepreneurship seeks to redefine its relationship with its markets, or industry competitors, by fundamentally altering how it competes. The focal point for strategic renewal is the firm within its environmental context and, in particular, the strategy that mediates the organisation–environment interface (see Section 3.8.3). The phenomenon of strategic renewal necessarily implies the implementation of a new business strategy. New business strategies differ significantly from past practices in ways that better leverage the firm's resources, or more fully exploit available product-market opportunities. Corporate strategy is viewed as both the key to energising the firm and the medium through which long-term competitive advantage is sought. Strategic renewal is associated with deliberate and major repositioning actions.

Harley-Davidson, in response to years of decline within the motorcycle industry, selected a strategic renewal strategy (Covin and Miles, 1999). The company was no longer content to let its reputation as an American company with its classically styled motorcycles be the prime source of competitive advantage. This case illustrates a declining firm facing a turnaround situation. The strategic renewal embraced new product and process technologies that allowed the company to redefine how it competed. Major investments in product and process R&D were reported. The adoption of new marketing orientation allowed the firm to change the bases on which it competed. They followed a niche-differentiation strategy. The company subsequently differentiated on the bases of superior quality, excellent service, and responsiveness to customers' product desires.

IBM selected a strategic renewal strategy, which facilitated the maintenance of competitive superiority among industry leaders (Covin and Miles, 1999). Industry leaders may embrace strategic change to ensure their viability. IBM introduced the 'System 360' line of mainframe computers in the mid-1960s when they held over two-thirds of the market. It was a new product line for the company but it was also a new strategy for competition in the mainframe computer industry. The new strategy emphasised the technological compatibility (not just performance) of IBM products, an increasingly valued basis for advantage that was not immediately matched by IBM's competitors.

8.4.5 Domain redefinition

A domain redefinition form of corporate entrepreneurship relates to an organisation that proactively creates a new product-market arena that others have not recognised, or actively sought to exploit (Covin and Miles, 1999). The firm takes the competition to a new arena where its first or early mover status may create some bases for sustainable competitive advantage. The firm may be able to create the industry standard, or define the benchmark against which later entrants are judged. Firms are entrepreneurial because they exploit market opportunities in a pre-emptive fashion, redefining where and how the competitive game is played in the process. Exploration of a new product-market arena can help to energise and reorient a firm. Products introduced are innovative from the perspective of the firm, the industry, and the market. Proactiveness and some moderate amount of risk are associated with new product introductions.

Bypass strategies are a form of domain redefinition (Covin and Miles, 1999). These strategies are motivated by a desire to decrease overall vulnerability to adverse current competitive conditions. For example, a business-level strategy may be adopted to avoid competitive confrontation in a specific product-market arena. Further, it is a business-level strategy to move the competitive battle to a new arena where current or prospective competitors are likely to suffer from later-entrant status.

A *bypass strategy* has been exhibited by Merrill Lynch (Covin and Miles, 1999). Several years ago, Merrill Lynch faced stiff and increasing competition in the financial services industry. The company introduced the Cash Management Account (CMA), an all-purpose brokerage account. Introduction of the CMA decreased its vulnerability to the hostilities and uncertainties of the financial services industry. Further, introduction of the CMA created a new product-market arena within this industry. It took competitors over a decade to catch up. Merrill Lynch bypassed the competition and enhanced its profitability and competency base through redefining its competitive domain.

A *product-market pioneering strategy* is also a form of domain redefinition. Opportunistic organisations select product-market pioneering domain redefinition strategies in order to exploit the potential competitive conditions (Covin and Miles, 1999: 54). A focus on innovation can redefine a firm's product-market domains or product categories (i.e., a group of products that consumers view as substitutable for one another yet distinct from those in another product category). Established firms that *'pioneer'* (i.e., the first firm to sell in a new product category (Golder and Tellis, 1993)), by definition, redefine their domains.

Sony created and exploited a new product-market arena within the audio portion of the consumer electronics industry (Covin and Miles, 1999). They introduced the Walkman to a receptive public. Numerous competitors later entered this product-market arena. Due to

Sony's accumulated first-mover advantage (in the areas of, for example, patent protection, channel access, and reputation), competitors subsequently sought to catch up with Sony's level of success.

8.5 Role of the external environment

The characteristics of the environment play an important role in executives' pursuit of corporate entrepreneurship and in the resultant performance (Guth and Ginsberg, 1990; Zahra, 1991, 1993b; Covin and Miles, 1999). Executives' perceptions of the environment frame their definitions of the issues facing their company and their actions. Zahra (1993a) suggested that environments within and across industries are heterogeneous (see Chapter 11). These perceived environments arise from the variations in companies' definitions of their industry's boundaries and business domain, and from the differences in senior executives' perceptions of the institutional and competitive forces that shape their industry. Zahra and Covin (1995) concluded that corporate venturing was particularly effective for enterprises operating in hostile environments, and that its effects may only fully emerge in the long term.

The 'parent' incubator environment may also be important. Parent corporations may be unwilling, or unable, to support all entrepreneurial initiatives that emerge from the technology and knowledge they generate. Established firms with abundant but underexploited knowledge are especially fertile grounds for new ventures created by employees who wish to pursue business ideas that are not supported by the parent company (Agarwal et al., 2004). Rather than the parent corporation developing a spin-off firm, employees leave the firm and establish an independent new venture. The development of corporate spin-off firms may be contingent upon the resources inherited from the parent incubator organisation (Sapienza et al., 2004; Klepper and Sleeper, 2005), and the overlap of knowledge between parent and the spin-off firm being especially important. Variations in the nature of the resource dependence and complementarity relationships between corporate parents and spin-off firms are an important source of heterogeneity (Parhankangas and Arenius, 2003). The knowledge overlap between parent organisation and corporate start-up firm (Sapienza et al., 2004) can shape performance. Related technology based upon knowledge held in common between the parent organisation and the spin-off firm can enhance the spin-off's ability to recognise valuable from irrelevant knowledge, and thus increases the company's efficiency to focus on the valuable knowledge. At the same time, knowledge *not* held in common is a differentiating factor between the spin-off firm and the parent organisation. In sum, some degree of overlap is considered to be optimal, while too little or too much is dysfunctional.

Corporations and universities represent distinct environments for corporate venturing and the creation of spin-off ventures (see Chapter 6). University spin-off firms typically develop innovations that are far from commercialisation because their innovations tend to hinge on basic research and raw science (Wright et al., 2008a). In contrast, corporate spin-off firms are driven by the necessity to differentiate themselves from their parent corporation, yet remain useful to customers. Many universities are not involved in commercialisation activities, that is, they do not directly enter the market. University spin-off firms are an ideal means to exploit some of the explorative research conducted in universities.

Corporate spin-off firms can be seen as a way to exploit knowledge that has been developed based upon exploratory activities inside the parent firm. The nature of knowledge endowed to a spin-off by these different environmental contexts may shape the competitive advantage of a spin-off. The nature of knowledge can be considered with regard to the 'tacitness' of the knowledge, the 'pervasiveness' of the technology, the 'novelty' of the technology, and its 'appropriability'. With regard to a sample comprising the whole population of corporate and university spin-offs in Flanders, Clarysse et al. (2010) found that the source of knowledge mattered, especially with regard to knowledge scope and tacitness. University spin-off firms benefit from a broad technology to start from, with multiple application possibilities. This might be because university spin-offs tend to have less market knowledge, and have to experiment in the market to find the best opportunities. They seem to benefit from a broader scope of technology at start-up, allowing them to change from one market application to the other, if the initial application turns out to be a dead end. This is in marked contrast to corporate spin-offs. In part, this is because corporate spin-offs are founded by managers who know the market better. Further, they tend to pursue a specific market opportunity with a given technological solution. Maintaining a narrow scope of technology by focusing on a few products instead of a platform of technologies positively contributes to growth of corporate spin-offs. A narrow scope of technology allows the attention of the founders to be focused on a few products and potential product applications. This facilitates the singling out of a few products and their development into market-ready products, hence facilitating firm growth. These findings are in line with Abetti (2002) who found that the best strategy for a corporate spin-off is to practise technological innovations that attack new market niches where the parent lacks core competencies, or is currently not interested. A specific product focus allows the corporate spin-off to produce goods and services based on the new explorative technology, targeting markets for products. This permits the spin-off to derive revenues primarily from product-related sources.

The newness of technology can retard university spin-off growth. Newness may lead to an inability to process and interpret the increased information generated by excessive exploration, which then poses a challenge to the commercialisation process (Gavetti and Levinthal, 2000). High-technology products based upon novel technologies generally take a long time to reach market. This might explain why the newness of technology does not contribute to the growth of corporate spin-offs.

Knowledge tacitness promotes the growth of corporate spin-offs. Keeping something secret and, relatedly, having a company which is based on knowledge dependent upon being kept secret has a larger impact on performance of a corporate spin-off than having a patentable technological knowledge base. Especially in corporate spin-offs, quick time to market seems to be a key source of competitive advantage. This is not the case in many university spin-off firms, although the fact that technological knowledge can be codified and thus patented does not explain later growth of these companies.

8.6 Looking forward: Corporate entrepreneurship

Different conceptualisations of firm-level entrepreneurship need to be explored. For example, different conceptualisations of the link between entrepreneurial activities and firm performance are warranted. Large sample studies conducted in a wide range of industrial, regional, national and cultural environments are required to explore the interplay between environment, corporate entrepreneurship and financial performance. Studies have focused upon entrepreneurship as either an independent or a dependent variable. Most firm-level studies have not examined the lag effect that might exist between antecedent variables and entrepreneurship (Zahra et al., 1999). Additional research is, therefore, required focusing upon the causal sequences between entrepreneurship and outcomes (e.g., firm-level performance). Corporate venturing has generally been depicted as an antecedent of company performance. Given the problems that may arise where corporations have perspectives that are too short term, and where there is inadequate continuing senior management support for corporate venturing activities, there remains a need for additional studies to address the barriers to corporate venturing.

Corporate entrepreneurship studies have generally neglected the role of corporate governance (Phan et al., 2009). Some corporations may fail to realise the strategic competitive advantages from corporate entrepreneurship if their corporate governance systems fail to incentivise and monitor management to undertake the appropriate actions with regard to opportunity recognition, and the gathering and utilisation of resources required to exploit an opportunity. Boards potentially play a central role in this corporate governance system. Additional research is warranted to explore how boards are developed to promote and enable corporate entrepreneurship. The composition of boards and the role of outside directors warrant particular attention.

Management's idiosyncratic knowledge represents a key resource for firms, especially in relation to opportunity recognition (Castanias and Helfat, 2001). The nature of compensation for management poses important issues for corporate entrepreneurship. There is a need to consider extending ownership rights to corporate entrepreneurs. These rights will permit the entrepreneur to make decisions about the co-ordination of resources to gain entrepreneurial rents, in return for bearing the uncertainty associated with owning those resources. A related issue concerns how far down in large organisations managers and employees at different levels can be expected to be involved in entrepreneurial activities.

There is a need to consider the lifecycle dimension of corporate entrepreneurship. Studies have tended to ignore the possibility that the nature of corporate entrepreneurship activities may change over the lifecycle of the firm. Recently, Zahra et al. (2009) have considered the threshold of professionalisation of new ventures, including spin-offs from corporations. Other thresholds in the management and governance of firms have been identified, notably the initial public offering (IPO) threshold and the threshold between maturity and decline, but they have not been fully explored. Further research is needed on the challenges relating to stimulating corporate entrepreneurship across different stages.

Corporate venture capital may play an important role in facilitating corporate entrepreneurship, but it is distinct from traditional venture capital (see Chapter 12). Corporate venture capital places much greater emphasis upon strategic objectives, rather than the purely financial objectives typical of venture capital firms. Therefore, rather than relying on perspectives developed to understand formal venture capital, new perspectives are necessary to fully understand the role that corporate venture capital plays in the discovery and exploitation of new opportunities.

Discussion questions

1 Is innovation crucial for corporate entrepreneurship?

2 Can strategic renewal be considered a dimension of corporate entrepreneurship?

3 What stimulates and retards corporate entrepreneurship?

4 Which form of corporate entrepreneurship will meet the least internal (and external) resistance?

5 Critically discuss the attributes of alternative forms of corporate entrepreneurship.

6 Discuss the linkage between the form of corporate entrepreneurship and competitive advantage and superior firm performance.

7 What are the benefits and challenges in conducting corporate entrepreneurship through a corporate spin-off?

Recommended further reading

Covin, J. and Miles, M. (1999). Corporate Entrepreneurship and the Pursuit of Competitive Advantage. *Entrepreneurship Theory and Practice*, 23 (3): 47–63.

Dess, G. G., Ireland, R. D., Zahra, S. A., Floyd, S. W., Janney, J. J. and Lane, P. J. (2003). Emerging Issues in Corporate Entrepreneurship. *Journal of Management*, 29 (3): 351–378.

Morris, M., Kuratko, D. and Covin, J. (2008). *Corporate Entrepreneurship and Innovation*. Mason, OH: Thomson/South-Western Publishers.

Narayanan, V., Yang, Y. and Zahra, S. (2009). Corporate Venturing and Value Creation: A Review and Proposed Framework. *Research Policy*, 38 (1): 58–76.

Sharma, P. and Chrisman, J. J. (1999). Toward a Reconciliation of the Definitional Issues in the Field of Corporate Entrepreneurship. *Entrepreneurship Theory and Practice*, 23 (3): 11–27.

Chapter 9

'Types' of organisations III: Management buyouts

Contents

Learning objectives

- Illustrate that entrepreneurial behaviour is exhibited in existing organisations that have been purchased by former 'inside' incumbent managers (i.e., management buyouts), or 'outside' acquiring managers (i.e., management buyins).

- Appreciate that the purchase of an existing firm can lead to the creation of a new independent entity, and entrepreneurial behaviour can be exhibited in various forms in post-buyout contexts.

- Consider that the mindsets of former 'inside' incumbent managers can shape the resultant 'type' of buyout with regard to an efficiency buyout, revitalisation buyout, entrepreneurial buyout and buyout failure.

- Appreciate that private equity investors can shape the buyout process and the governance, behaviour and performance of firms post-buyout.

- Consider the issues involved in the buyout process and the actors involved in the process relating to the buyout of former private family firms and secondary buyouts.

- Appreciate the entrepreneurial effects of buyouts and their lifecycle.

9.1 Introduction

In this chapter, we discuss issues relating to the purchase and development of existing organisations with reference to management buyouts (MBOs) and management buyins (MBIs). MBOs, where incumbent management purchase an existing organisation in which they are employed, and MBIs, where outside managers effect a purchase of an existing organisation with institutional finance. Both MBOs and MBIs are a *form of corporate entrepreneurship* (see Chapter 8). In this chapter, we outline definitions of buyouts, identifying their variety and heterogeneity. We then discuss theoretical perspectives associated with expectations that buyouts may lead to entrepreneurial activities. This is followed by an overview of the empirical evidence surrounding the entrepreneurial effects of buyouts, and of the factors that generate post-buyout changes. Finally, we consider whether buyouts represent a long-term entrepreneurial organisation form.

9.2 Definitions of buyouts

In general, buyouts involve the creation of a new independent entity in which ownership is concentrated in the hands of management and private equity (PE) firms, if present, with substantial funding also provided by banks (see Case 14, Wemas Limited: Purchase and turnaround of an existing business by Brent Lybbert). PE firms become active investors through taking board seats, and specifying contractual restrictions on the behaviour of management that include detailed reporting requirements. Lenders also typically specify and closely monitor detailed loan covenants (Citron et al., 1997). Further examination of the development of buyout markets and detailed mechanics of PE buyouts are beyond the scope of this chapter; for detailed treatments see Wright et al. (2000a, b) and Gilligan and Wright (2010).

Buyouts can take the following forms:

- **Leveraged buyout (LBO)**. Typically a publicly-quoted corporation or a large division of a group is acquired by a *specialist LBO association or PE firm*. In the United States, the resulting private company is typically controlled by a small board of directors representing the LBO association, with the CEO usually the only insider on the board (Jensen, 1989). As the name suggests, these deals are generally highly leveraged with the PE firm acquiring a significant equity stake.

- **Management buyout (MBO)**. Usually involves the acquisition of a divested division or subsidiary of a private family owned firm by a new company in which the *existing* management takes a substantial proportion of the equity. In place of the LBO association, MBOs usually require the support of a PE firm. The former parent may retain an equity stake, perhaps to support a continuing trading relationship. In smaller transactions, management are likely to obtain the majority of the voting equity (Centre for Management Buyout Research (CMBOR), 2008). MBOs typically involve a small group of senior managers as equity-holders, but depending on the circumstances equity-holding may be extended to other management and employees creating a *management-employee buyout* (MEBO). MEBOs may occur, for example, where it is important to tie in the specific human capital of the employees, or where a firm is widely spread geographically making direct management difficult, or on privatisation where there is a need to encourage trade unions to support the transfer of ownership (e.g., in bus services and transportation).

- **Management buyin (MBI)**. Simply an MBO in which the leading members of the management team are *outsiders* (Robbie and Wright, 1995). Although superficially similar to MBOs, MBIs carry *greater risks* as incoming management do not have the benefits of the insiders' knowledge of the operation of the business. Venture capitalists have sought to address this problem by putting together hybrid buyin/management buyouts (so-called *BIMBOs*) to obtain the benefits of the entrepreneurial expertise of the outside managers, and the intimate internal knowledge of the incumbent management.

- **Investor-led buyouts (IBOs)**. They involve the acquisition of a whole company or a division of a larger group in a transaction *led by a PE firm*, and they are also referred to as *bought deals or financial purchases*. The PE firm will typically either retain existing management to run the company or bring in new management to do so, or employ some combination of internal and external management. Incumbent management may or may not receive a direct equity stake, or may receive stock options. IBOs developed in the late 1990s when PE firms were searching for attractive deals in an increasingly competitive market. Here, corporate vendors or large divisions were seeking to sell them through auctions, rather than giving preference to incumbent managers.

- **Leveraged build-ups (LBUs)**. Involve the development of a *corporate group* based on an initial buyout or buyin. It serves as a *platform investment* on top of which a series of acquisitions can be added. LBUs developed as PE firms sought new means of generating returns from buyout type investments. The initial platform deal may need to be of a sufficiently large size for it to attract the management with the skills and experience to grow a large business through acquisition. LBUs may be attractive in fragmented industries associated with strong demand prospects. The potential problems with LBUs relate to the identification, purchase and subsequent integration of suitable acquisition candidates.

● **Other buyout forms**. Although large public to private deals involving the taking private of listed corporations tend to attract considerable media attention and public scrutiny, they account for only about 3 per cent of deal numbers, and around 30 per cent of deal value (CMBOR, 2008). Other important vendor sources of PE deals include buyouts of divisions, secondary buyouts, buyouts of family firms, buyouts of public sector firms and buyouts of firms in receivership.

9.3 Theoretical perspectives

9.3.1 Agency and cognition theory

A distinction can be made between *principals* (i.e., shareholder owners) and *agents* (i.e., managers) (see Section 7.2.3.2). *Agency problems* arise when the interests of principals and agents are not aligned. MBOs and MBIs have often been viewed as a solution to the *agency problem* in large corporations with diffuse ownership. In the latter circumstances, managers with little if any equity ownership may not act in the interests of shareholders. These problems have been argued to be particularly acute in mature businesses. Some firms would tend to engage in unprofitable diversification rather than disgorge their cash in abnormally large dividends (Jensen, 1989). Diversification may benefit managers remunerated on the basis of firm size, but this diversification may not benefit shareholders. A MBO or MBI that introduces significant managerial equity ownership is a mechanism to *realign managerial incentives* with the objectives of owners. As a result, *performance improvements*, especially efficiency gains, may be expected to follow the buyout.

The *cognition perspective* developed by Busenitz and Barney (1997) opens up potentially interesting applications to the analysis of entrepreneurship in buyouts. Although it is possible to extend *agency theory* to apply to the design of incentives to encourage innovation buyouts, this may be limited to the case of more routine innovation where incumbent managers rely on detailed information and systematic analyses in their decision-making. To achieve more radical innovation, there may be a need for individuals with an entrepreneurial cognition orientation to be supported.

9.3.2 Types of buyouts

Wright et al. (2000a, 2001a, b), guided by insights from agency theory and cognition perspectives, have presented a *conceptual typology* of buyout 'types'. Table 9.1 illustrates that four types of buyouts were identified with regard to the *mindset of managers* (e.g., managerial or entrepreneurial) and the *pre-buyout context*. Each 'type' (or quadrant) is discussed, in turn:

9.3.2.1 *Efficiency buyout*

Wright et al. (2000a) argue that the control and incentive mechanisms typically used in buyouts can produce enhancements to efficiency. These firms can be labelled *efficiency buyouts* (Quadrant 1). The incentives enabled by the introduction of significant managerial equity ownership, the pressure to perform in order to service interest payments introduced by the high leverage taken on to acquire the business, and the active monitoring by PE firms all contribute to reducing *agency problems* in mature firms with significant cashflows

Table 9.1 Typology of buyouts

	Individual mindset	
	Managerial mindset	Entrepreneurial mindset
	Quadrant 1: Efficiency buyout	Quadrant 4: Buyout failure
Pre-buyout context and decision mindset	Agency problems; low risk Decisions based primarily on systematic data and financial criteria	Mismatch of mindset, incentives and governance
	Post-buyout: High leverage and financial control	Post-buyout: High leverage and financial control
	Quadrant 2: Revitalisation buyout	Quadrant 3: Entrepreneurial buyout
Pre-buyout context and decision mindset	Bureaucratic procedures stifle innovation and investment needed to be competitive; moderate risk Decisions to renew competitive capabilities via innovations are based on their already proven success among key competitors	Bureaucratic procedures stifle radical innovations associated with uncertainty and limited information; or technology-based businesses headed in the wrong direction; high risk Heuristic-based logic can lead to strategic innovations and efficient decision-making
	Post-buyout: Flexible leverage and financial monitoring by private equity firms	Post-buyout: Flexible leverage; financial monitoring and technical skills of private equity firms

Source: Adapted from Wright et al. (2000a, 2001a).

that would otherwise be dissipated on inefficient diversification. Executives with a managerial mindset are expected to respond positively to enhanced monetary incentives by improving efficiencies.

9.3.2.2 *Revitalisation buyout*

In large, integrated, diverse organisations, bureaucratic measures may be adopted to try to ensure performance. These measures may restrict experimentation and constrain innovative activity. Managers can be pushed into entrepreneurship by these bureaucratic decision-making processes that reject investment proposals because of a lack of the appropriate information to fit this process. Further, managers in the pre-buyout situation may face investment restrictions from headquarters, particularly if their firms are peripheral to the core activities of the parent company (Wright et al., 2001a, b). These problems may be eased after the buyout. Instead of following headquarters' controls designed to optimise the goals of the diversified parent company but which block innovation and investment, the buyout creates discretionary power for the new management team to decide what is best for the business (Wright et al., 2000a, 2001a, b). Limited or incremental innovation will result if the new-owner managers possess only managerial cognition. The latter firms can be labelled *revitalisation buyouts* (Quadrant 2).

9.3.2.3 *Entrepreneurial buyout*

Management with an entrepreneurial cognition or mindset, who adopt heuristic-based decision-making (see Section 4.6), may be able to pursue entrepreneurial opportunities that they have identified, but which could not previously be pursued within a larger group. In some cases, entrepreneurial buyouts may emerge in technology-based industries where the parent did not have the capability to manage, or understand the technology, but where divisional management do. This subset of entrepreneurial buyouts can be labelled *entrepreneurial release buyouts* (Quadrant 3). These entrepreneurial buyouts require management with superior and idiosyncratic skills to process limited and incomplete information on new opportunities, rather than managers who respond well to close monitoring to prevent shirking (Wright et al., 2001a). Studies of management's motivation for buying out show the importance of being able to develop strategic opportunities that could not be carried out under the previous owners (Wright et al., 1991), and to control their own destiny (Baruch and Gebbie, 1998). For example, the management of the clothing retailer Kohl's bought out the company from the large conglomerate BAT, and they introduced numerous innovations including new store design. The new owners transformed the company into a discounter/department store hybrid.

In some cases, entrepreneurial owner-managers may have the skills and incentives to pursue strategic innovations with regard to a new venture. Little control may have been exercised over management even when the firm has grown sufficiently to achieve an initial public offering (IPO). When a firm in such circumstances encounters financial difficulties, a buyout opportunity may arise to introduce necessary governance mechanisms, which will allow the innovative opportunities to continue to be exploited, but in a better controlled way. The latter entrepreneurial buyouts are labelled *busted tech buyouts*. For example, ZiLOG was a listed computer-chip manufacturer that had run into difficulties. The firm was bought out in a deal led by the PE firm Texas Pacific Group with modest leverage and with advice from a venture capital firm, Mayfield Fund. This firm was turned around due to the technical expertise of management, as well as the expertise provided by Texas Pacific Group's technical venture capital advisers.

9.3.2.4 *Buyout failure*

In order to facilitate the development of more entrepreneurial buyouts, firms may require a level of leverage that is below the norm for buyouts in mature sectors, and a PE firm that has more innovative skills than has traditionally been associated with buyouts. This approach allows for the extension of the PE-backed buyout concept to more innovative, growth-oriented sectors. *Buyout failure* can be reported (Quadrant 4).

9.3.3   Strategic entrepreneurship theory

9.3.3.1 *Context*

A strategic entrepreneurship perspective (see Section 3.8.3.3), grounded in the resource-based view (RBV) of the firm (see Sections 3.8.2.2 and 3.8.3.2), provides recognition of the resources required to exploit growth opportunities in order to create and sustain competitive advantage (Ireland et al., 2003). Complementarity between strong governance, in the form of active PE investors, incentives and leverage, and strong resources, in the form of human capital competences, may be especially important in generating superior performance (Castanias and Helfat, 2001). PE firms may provide complementary resources and capabilities that may be missing from the management team. Some PE firms may be more skilled in how they implement otherwise common selection, monitoring and advisory devices. This is because they are more effective at learning from experience to create distinctive organisational capabilities (Barney et al., 2001; De Clercq and Dimov, 2008). The scope for making these improvements may be greater in divisional MBOs than in MBIs involving family and in secondary buyouts (Meuleman et al., 2009).

9.3.3.2 *Family firm buyouts*

For reasons outlined above, divisional MBOs may have been more severely constrained in the pursuit of opportunities. This differs from family firms where the private owners become *risk-averse* in an effort to preserve wealth even though, with a substantial equity stake, they have incentives and control as peak-tier co-ordinators to seek and implement profitable opportunities. Suitable family members may not be willing or able to take on the ownership and management of the business (Wright et al., 1992) (see Section 7.3.6). Second tier (non-family) management may possess *greater information* about the running of the business, and have the skills to introduce needed *professional management*. Non-family managers, however, may not be in a position to take appropriate decisions (Howorth et al., 2004). A management buyout may be a means of ensuring the survival of the firm. All or the majority of the ordinary voting shares in the former private family firm can be bought by former managers who had no family ties with the former dominant family or kinship group owning the firm. A buyout can preserve the identity and culture of the (former) family firm, and the psychic income (i.e., the benefits or enjoyment that cannot be measured in financial terms) of the former family owners can be maintained if they secure continuing involvement in the family firm buyout (i.e., networking links with established suppliers, customers, etc.). New buyout owners who were former second tier management will have the ability to identify and exploit growth opportunities, which may have been resisted by former family firm owners who may have been more interested in *'family agendas'* (i.e., lifestyle rather than profit-maximisation, reluctance to use external financial support to maintain ownership and control of the business within the family, only grow the firm to provide employment opportunities for family members, etc.), rather than *'business agendas'* (i.e., efficiency, productivity, innovation, diversification and profit-maximisation) (Wright et al., 2001a, b) (see Section 7.3). Supporting these arguments, Scholes et al. (2010) noted significant gains in efficiency and growth following buyout in former private family firms where non-family managers were not equity holders prior to the change in ownership. In some cases, dominant family founders (and successors) may not have developed strong second tier management. Consequently, a pool of managerial talent located outside the family firm may be required to purchase and transform the family firm (Robbie and Wright, 1995). Owners of some family firms may seek a MBI. Whether management are able to *negotiate a fair price* with the vendor may depend largely on whether the family owners seek to maintain a continued interest in the business. A fair price may be sought by family firm owners who have an altruistic desire to reward (loyal) managers who may have ensured the survival and development of the family firm (i.e., the family store of wealth). Not all family buyout deals are perceived to be *mutually beneficial* (Scholes et al., 2007) with regard to the vendors (i.e., former family owners) and purchasers

Entrepreneurship in action 9.1
Messer Griesheim

Messer Griesheim was acquired in April 2001 by Allianz Capital Partners and Goldman Sachs from pharmaceutical firm Hoechst, which later became Aventis. The private equity firm acquired a 66 per cent stake and the remaining minority stake was owned by the Messer family. At € 2.1 billion, the buyout represented the largest private equity deal closed in Germany and the largest industrial buyout in Europe at that time. The Messer Griesheim transaction epitomized a deal where a family regained control of some of its traditional, industrial-based company's entities. An overall restructuring plan enabled the company to divest non-core entities and focus on its core activities. Despite reductions in employment, employee development remained a critical issue for management throughout the deal, as the team provided incentives to encourage key employees to stay with the core businesses.

Source: Achleitner, A-K, Herman, K., Lerner, J. and Lutz, E. (2010). Family Business and Private Equity: Conflict or Collaboration? The Case of Messer Griesheim. *The Journal of Private Equity*, 13 (3): available at SSRN: http://ssrn.com/abstract=1120222.

(i.e., MBO/I teams). In some cases, a buyout can enable the family to regain control of a business and improve its focus and performance (see the example of Messer Griesheim in Entrepreneurship in action 9.1). However, where a PE firm takes a majority stake, family members will need to recognise that when they complete the buyout they are effectively transferring control of the business. They, therefore, need to be prepared to be removed if the PE firm deems it necessary to introduce new management to implement the strategy.

9.3.3.3 *Secondary buyouts*

Secondary buyouts provide a means to continue the buyout organisational form, albeit with a different set of investors. In contrast to managers in divisions of larger corporations, increased managerial equity stakes and loosened controls by PE firms, or the introduction of more skilled PE firms, may facilitate *improved performance* through *pursuit of growth opportunities*. The first buyout will have introduced *governance mechanisms and incentives* for improved performance and growth. Consequently, the scope for further entrepreneurial improvements in secondary buyouts is less likely than for divisional buyouts. If performance changes in the first buyout are step changes to resolve agency problems, or to take advantage of opportunities that could not previously be pursued, secondary buyouts should generally underperform relative to primary buyouts. However, if secondary buyouts involve increased incentives for management and new PE investors with the expertise to continue to create value through exploiting entrepreneurial growth opportunities, higher performance may result. As yet, there is limited analysis of the performance of secondary buyouts. Evidence from first buyouts that exit as a secondary buyout show that they generate significantly lower returns than do exits through IPOs, and strategic sales to other corporations (Nikoskelainen and Wright, 2007).

Entrepreneurship in action 9.2
Quantum Specials

Quantum Specials, which was founded in 2004, is one of the UK's largest suppliers of tailor-made medicines to the pharmaceutical industry. The company, based in the North East, produces bespoke drug formulations not readily available from drug manufacturers. It supplies wholesalers, pharmacies, chemists, dispensing doctors, hospitals and veterinary surgeries across the UK. The company has developed a strong reputation for quality of service and customer relationships involving a 24 hour turnaround from pharmacist' order through manufacture to delivery to the patient.

At the time of the £32m buyout in early 2009, Quantum Specials employed 145 people. Two of the company's founders bought out the other two founders as well as Phoenix Medical Supplies, which bought a 30 per cent stake in the company in 2005. The four founders previously worked for Eldon Laboratories, which was owned by UniChem, and set up the firm when that company was acquired and moved away from the region. The deal arose as one of the founders was looking to retire, and following

the buyout the remaining team were joined by a new finance director. The management team pledged to maintain employment in the region. The managers invested their own money, alongside Lloyds TSB Development Capital (LDC) investing £14m, and Yorkshire Bank Corporate and Structured Finance, which provided an £18.5m package of senior debt and working capital facilities. In addition, a level of vendor consideration was reinvested.

The company experienced five years of rapid growth before the buyout, with the number of employees doubling in the year prior to the buyout. Further growth in sales and employees was forecast in the following year. The buyout was viewed as providing the opportunity to bring on board the expertise and financial backing needed to develop the business further. The management had sought a private equity investor, with experience of their sector, with whom they could work closely to develop new products. The management of the company envisaged a long term future for the business.

9.4 Entrepreneurial effects of buyouts

Evidence from the first wave of buyouts in the 1980s relating to European and United States buyouts generally show significant improvements in profitability and cashflow for up to five years post-ownership change (Thompson and Wright, 1995; Cumming et al., 2007; Wright et al., 2007). The evidence relating to profitability improvements for the second buyout wave of the 1990s/2000s is less convincing with regard to *public to private buyouts* (Guo et al., 2007; Weir et al., 2008), and other sources of buyout (Kaplan and Strömberg, 2009). However, there is evidence from *public to private buyouts* that *liquidity* improves (Weir et al., 2008), and from *divisional buyouts* of significantly greater growth than in family or secondary buyouts (Meuleman et al., 2009).

Efficiency improvements in terms of factor productivity also occur, measured at both the firm (Amess, 2003) and the establishment level (Lichtenberg and Siegel, 1990; Harris et al., 2005; Davis et al., 2009). In contrast to research in the United States, plant-level evidence relating to the United Kingdom shows that MBO establishments were less productive than comparable plants before the transfer of ownership, but substantially increased productivity afterwards (Harris et al., 2005). Studies generally show an initial reduction in employment followed by subsequent increases in employment, although the impact on employment has been more positive with regard to MBOs rather than MBIs (Amess and Wright, 2007). Davis et al. (2008) have presented evidence that PE backed buyouts in the United States reported lower employment growth both pre- and post-buyout, but that PE backed firms engaged in more greenfield job creation than other firms. Conversely, Amess and Wright (2010) and Amess et al. (2008) noted that PE backed buyouts did not have significantly different levels of employment compared to control firms.

Buyouts are associated with *refocusing the strategic activities* of the firm, especially for deals involving listed corporations and firms in distress (Easterwood, 1998; Liebeskind et al., 1992; Smart and Waldfogel, 1994; Wiersema and Liebeskind, 1995). *Divestment activity* by buyouts appears to be greater than for comparable non-buyouts.

The transfer of ownership in a buyout is typically accompanied by *entrepreneurial actions*, which reconfigure the way in which the firm operates (Bull, 1989; Malone, 1989), although buyouts may not perform as well as owner-started businesses (Chaganti and Schneer, 1994). Wright et al. (1992) showed that although there has been a dominant agency cost perspective concerning buyouts (Jensen, 1989), there is significant evidence of their *entrepreneurial effects* in the form of new product development and capital investment that would not otherwise have occurred (see the example of Travelodge in Entrepreneurship in action 9.3). Zahra (1995) has also provided evidence of the entrepreneurial impact of management buyouts in terms of technological alliances, R&D staff size and capabilities. Wright et al. (1996) found over a period of ten years following management buyouts, new markets and product development were reported to be the most important influences on sales and profitability growth. Divisional buyouts reduced their trading dependence on the former parent by introducing new products that they had previously been prevented from developing (Wright, 1986; Wright et al., 1990). See Case 15, Seagate Technology, which raises potential issues relating to the balance between restructuring, efficiency and entrepreneurial actions following potential buyout.

PE funders have been found to contribute to keeping added-value strategies on track. They have assisted new ventures to broaden their market focus and to assess the merits of investment in product development (Bruining and Wright, 2002). Also, PE firms contribute positively to the development of management control systems that facilitate *strategic change* (Jones, 1992; Bruining et al., 2004). The case of Seagate Technology introduces issues relating to the nature of the skills required of PE investors in a buyout context. In particular, to what extent expertise relating to the technology and associated markets is important.

Entrepreneurship in action 9.3
Travelodge

Travelodge is a budget hotel chain that was a buyout in a deal led by Permira as a divestment from Compass. The company was sold in 2006 after three years of PE ownership. Although under PE ownership the company engaged in sale and leasebacks, divestment of unwanted divisions and efficiencies in room cleaning times, it also embarked on a major expansion programme involving building the brand and opening more hotel rooms than any other operator over this period in the United Kingdom.

Source: Centre for Management Buyout Research, Nottingham University Business School (CMBOR).

Evidence from the United States relating to the 1980s strongly supports the view that *capital investment* falls immediately following a LBO. This is due to increased leverage (Long and Ravenscraft, 1993). Further, this is consistent with two competing views:

1 post-buyout firms are cash-constrained and underinvest; and
2 buyout governance structure induces managers to reduce capital expenditures that are non-value-maximising.

Evidence from the United Kingdom relating to the 1980s indicates that MBO asset sales were offset by new capital investment, particularly in plant and equipment (Wright et al., 1992).

The effect of buyouts on *R&D* has not been extensively researched due to data limitations. Studies that have been conducted do not provide clear evidence because they do not support each other on all aspects of R&D expenditures. Lichtenberg and Siegel (1990) did not find any evidence to suggest that R&D intensity (measured by R&D expenditure/sales) significantly declined post-buyout. Conversely, Long and Ravenscraft (1993) reported that post-buyout R&D intensity dropped by up to 40 per cent compared to pre-buyout levels. Both studies confirmed, however, that pre-buyout firms reported about 50 per cent lower R&D intensity than non-buyouts. Long and Ravenscraft (1993) found that R&D intensive LBO firms outperformed their non-LBO peers, and LBOs that did not have any R&D expenditures. This evidence suggests that LBO firms are effective users of R&D expenditure (Zahra, 1995). More recent worldwide evidence from PE backed buyouts shows that buyouts increase patent citations after PE investment, but the quantity of patenting remains unchanged, while patent portfolios become more focused after PE investment (Lerner et al., 2008).

9.5 Drivers of performance improvements

Studies have shown that the most significant contribution to performance improvements following buyouts emanate from managerial equity stakes, rather than the commitment to servicing the debt, typically used to finance the purchase of a business (Phan and Hill, 1995). This finding supports the argument that entrepreneurial activities are taking place in new organisational forms.

Active monitoring and involvement by PE firms who invest in MBOs is an important contributor to improved performance (Guo et al., 2007; Cornelli and Karakas, 2008). The industry specialisation of the PE firm adds significantly to increases in the operating profitability of PE backed MBOs over the first three post-buyout years in the United Kingdom (Cressy et al., 2007). With reference to data from the United Kingdom, Meuleman et al. (2009) found that the *extent* of PE firm experience was not related to higher levels of profitability, or efficiency. They found it was, however, associated with higher levels of growth in buyout firms. The *intensity* of follow-up activity by PE firms has been found to significantly improve profitability and growth following the buyout, especially for divisional buyouts. Acharya and Kehoe (2008) noted important operating changes in a sample of investments by mature PE firms. They highlighted the importance of high levels of PE firm interaction with executives during the initial 100-day value creation plan, creating an active board, significant replacement of chief executive officers (CEOs) and chief financial officers (CFOs), either at the time of the deal, or afterwards, and leveraging of external support. The last two actions were especially related to *investee out-performance*.

9.6   Longevity of buyouts

There is considerable debate surrounding the longevity of buyouts as *entrepreneurial structures*. Evidence from the first wave of buyouts in the 1980s, in both the United Kingdom and United States, has suggested a heterogeneous lifecycle. Some buyouts exit over a relatively short period of time, while others remain with the buyout structure for periods in excess of five years. On average, larger deals exit significantly sooner than small deals. Few deals are short-lived, involving what have been described as *'flipping'*, whereby PE firms buy and sell firms within a short period for quick financial gain (Kaplan, 1991; Wright et al., 1994, 1995; Strömberg, 2008). Indeed, evidence suggests that the time to exit in PE deals has been increasing.

Some deals fail quickly, while others may receive unsolicited bids by trade buyers within a short time after the buyout. However, it is important to consider the time of *exit* of a particular cohort (i.e., deals completed in a particular year), as a whole. The average period to exit in recent years is quite low, reflecting the small number of buyouts that exit in a short period of time. The very long average exit periods for deals completed in the first half of the 1980s reflect the lower emphasis on exit at that time. These extremities apart, the most common timing of exit for those deals that had exited to mid-2007 is in the range of four to five years.

Economic recessions are typically associated with growing numbers of corporate failures. High levels of PE backed management buyout failure were noted with regard to the recession relating to the early 1990s, and the 2008 to 2009 recession (CMBOR, 2010). A key issue is whether such enterprises are more or less likely to fail than enterprises that have not gone through a buyout. A study relating to the population of firms in the United Kingdom which distinguished between PE backed buyouts and buyins and enterprises that had not gone through this form of restructuring found that PE backed deals completed post-2003 were not significantly more likely to fail than other firms (Wilson et al., 2010a). Formal insolvency was avoided in many cases where PE buyouts became 'distressed' (i.e., they breached their debt covenants or were unable to service their debt commitments). Timely restructuring through debt for equity swaps with banks enabled these enterprises to continue, if the underlying trading business was sound. However, debt-equity restructurings often leave PE firms with a 'signature stake', but with little if any continuing involvement in the business. While a debt-equity swap helps avoid the formal bankruptcy process, it can have a negative impact on growth strategies and future development (Wilson et al., 2010b). Banks are typically ill-equipped to provide added value in this respect even when finance becomes available again. PE firms with a track record of deal making can adopt a positive proactive approach to working with the banks, so that over time the business can recover value. Further, PE firms can retain a board seat and be the first point of contact with management.

9.7   Looking forward

The first wave of buyouts and PE occurred during the 1980s. They generated significant increases in portfolio firm profitability, productivity, liquidity and employment as the review in this chapter has shown. When the first wave ended in a recession in the early 1990s, high leverage, interest payments and capital repayments contributed to sharply increased rates of default on covenants, and difficulties in paying interest on debt. However, the governance mechanisms present in PE buyouts enabled high recovery rates for secured creditors (Andrade and Kaplan, 1998; Citron et al., 2003). The second wave of the buyout and PE market reached record highs in 2007. These conditions produced an 'overshoot' marked by PE firms raising substantial amounts of debt for deals, and entry by 'tourist' PE firms with little experience in the sector (Kaplan, 2009). During the 2008 to 2009 recession, the value of PE backed buyouts completed plummeted to a fifteen year low, while restructurings rose sharply. These dramatic changes marked the end of a 'golden age' for PE, and gave rise to concerns about how the buyouts and PE model can be recalibrated to generate the returns in the future that have occurred in previous waves.

In conditions of severe credit constraints, the availability of debt to fund PE buyouts became limited, and they seem unlikely to regain the levels seen in previous boom conditions. This makes it more difficult to generate returns on PE buyouts from the effects of leverage. Increased emphasis is likely to be placed in future on the roles of management and PE executives to create value through gains in efficiency, and the exploitation of entrepreneurial opportunities. While many PE firms have often claimed particularly close involvement in their portfolio companies, and a focus on selected industries where they have specialist expertise, it is debatable how far this was indeed the case. In the future, the capability to develop leading insightful active board participation will be important. Further, the ability to be able to contribute positively to the development and subsequent overseeing of portfolio companies' strategy will be an even more important differentiator of successful PE funds in the future. Many PE firms investing in buyouts and buyins are likely to need to recruit more executives who have the specialist industry and operational and technical skills to create value in their portfolio companies. This represents a significant departure for many PE firms, which historically have focused on deal completion, deal management and financial structuring. There will be an increased need for PE firms to devote more attention to recruiting more seasoned management teams, some of which will have exited from earlier investments and still have the appetite to create significant value. While buyouts of divisions may offer high growth opportunities, they are also more likely to need expertise to help them develop. There will be a need to pay careful attention to the selection of portfolio management with business skills who can identify and deliver development strategies.

Following buyout, PE firms have generally engaged in an intensive 100-day period of detailed appraisal. Notably, they set the portfolio company's strategy to create value. The need for strategies that include the development of new products, technologies and markets implies that in the future, PE firms will need to become more closely involved in their portfolio companies post the initial 100-day period, even when they are not in distress. The need for greater understanding of the business models of portfolio companies emphasises that in future pre-deal due diligence will assume greater importance for PE firms.

Consequently, in an environment where it is expected that more value will need to be created through business performance, investments are likely to be held in portfolios for considerably longer than historically. This will negatively impact expected internal rates of return (see Chapter 12), and it will focus management efforts towards sustained value enhancing strategies.

In the future, finding good deals is unlikely to become any easier. Consequently, holding on to and continuing to develop existing deals with growth potential has its attractions. This means a likely resurgence in build-up deals based on an initial buyout platform company. These companies will likely provide a strong base around which can be built larger groups through consolidating acquisitions in fragmented sectors.

Discussion questions

1 Does entrepreneurship take place in management buyins and management buyouts?

2 What are the major differences between a management buyin and a management buyout?

3 What are the alternative forms of buyouts?

4 Critically discuss the profiles of the four 'types' of buyouts (i.e., efficiency buyout, revitalisation buyout, entrepreneurial buyout and buyout failure).

5 What are the strengths and weaknesses of the former 'inside' incumbent managers (i.e., management buyouts), 'outside' acquiring managers (i.e., management buyins) and private equity investors?

6 What are the entrepreneurial effects of buyouts?

7 Are all buyouts subsequently associated with superior business performance post-buyout?

8 Why may some firms remain with the buyout form for short periods while others retain this form into the longer term?

9 To what extent do secondary buyouts provide a means to maintain the buyout form into the longer term?

10 To what extent is it important to change the ownership of all or part of an established organisation in order to be able to engage in entrepreneurship?

Recommended further reading

Centre for Management Buyout Research (CMBOR). (2008). *Trends in Management Buy-outs. Management Buy-outs: Quarterly Review from the Centre for Management Buy-out Research.* Nottingham: Nottingham University Business, Centre for Management Buyout Research, Autumn.

Wright, M., Hoskisson, R. and Busenitz, L. (2000a). Entrepreneurial Growth through Privatization: The Upside of Management Buy-outs. *Academy of Management Review*, 25 (3), 591–601.

Wright, M., Thompson, S., Chiplin B. and Robbie, K. (1991). *Management Buy-ins and Buy-outs: New Strategies in Corporate Management.* London: Graham & Trotman.

Chapter 10

'Types' of organisations IV: Social entrepreneurship

by Peter Somerville and Gerard McElwee

Contents

Learning objectives

- Illustrate how entrepreneurship can occur in contexts not involving commercial gain.
- Understand the different conditions under which social and commercial enterprises are appropriate.
- Appreciate that there is a debate about the nature of social entrepreneurship and the nature of social value.
- Recognise that social enterprises and social entrepreneurs are heterogeneous.
- Appreciate how local social value can be created.

10.1 Introduction

Entrepreneurship is frequently portrayed as the driving force through which individual firms, and by extension the economies within which they are situated become more competitive (Harper, 2003). Consequently, entrepreneurship has been commonly perceived as an individualistic pursuit in which the goals, qualities, and competencies of the founder are the critical components in determining whether or not a venture is successful (Shane, 2003). This perception of the entrepreneur as hero goes back to Schumpeter (1934: 93), who suggested that the entrepreneur has 'the dream and the will to found a private kingdom . . . the will to conquer, the impulse to fight, to prove oneself superior to others, to succeed for the sake, not of the fruits of success, but of success itself'.

Following this perception, studies have focused on the behaviour of individual entrepreneurs, and specifically on their ability to be proactive and innovative, and to manage risk (Covin and Slevin, 1991). Recent studies have shown that some new ventures are founded by teams of entrepreneurs rather than solo entrepreneurs (Ucbasaran et al., 2003). Interest has grown in the *social embeddedness of entrepreneurship*, that is, the ways in which entrepreneurship relates to the *social context* in which it figures (Johannisson et al., 2002; Sarasvathy, 2004). Entrepreneurship is a social process (Zafirovski, 1999; Jones and Spicer, 2005), involving complex networking (Birley, 1985; Aldrich and Zimmer, 1986), 'co-opetition' and collective construction of local contexts (Putnam, 1993; Johannisson et al., 2002), and experimenting with different resource combinations (Sarasvathy, 2001). This 'social' perspective views entrepreneurs as being networked in a variety of ways that are crucial for the formation and development of an enterprise (Haugh, 2007). In contrast to traditional *commercial entrepreneurship*, which is associated with the creation of personal and shareholder wealth (Schumpeter, 1934; Kirzner, 1973), 'the underlying drive for social entrepreneurship is to create social value' (Austin et al., 2006: 2). In this chapter, we consider how social entrepreneurship differs from traditional commercial entrepreneurship as commonly understood. We discuss typologies of social enterprise and consider the meaning of social embeddedness and social value.

Characterising social entrepreneurship, social entrepreneurs and social enterprise

A naïve way of understanding social entrepreneurship is to think of it as the form of entrepreneurship that occurs in social enterprises. Enterprises as organised activities or businesses have been commonly thought of as either being *privately* owned (i.e., aiming to produce surpluses that can be reinvested in the business or distributed among its (private) owners), or *publicly* owned by the state (i.e., aiming to produce whatever the state decides, according to publicly agreed priorities). A social enterprise could then be characterised as one that is neither private nor public, but is part of a distinct sector commonly known as the *'third sector'* (Nyssens, 2006). For Nyssens, third sector enterprises are not private because they place limits on the distribution of their surpluses, for the purpose of a social or public benefit, and they are not public because they are governed entirely by their own members and not by politicians or public officials.

There are problems with this characterisation of social enterprises. It is possible to identify enterprises that limit the distribution of their surpluses, yet are clearly part of the private sector. Many family firms are a notable example (see Chapter 7). It is also possible to identify organisations, variously described as arm's-length organisations, non-departmental public bodies or quangos, which have their own independent governing bodies but are clearly part of the public sector.

An alternative way of analysing enterprises is in terms of *who owns the assets*. If they are owned entirely by government, it could be concluded that the enterprise is a public sector body. If the assets are all held in private hands, the enterprise could be said to belong to the private sector. This distinction appears to correspond closely with everyday conceptions of the public and private sector. Unfortunately, it appears to allow no room for a third sector except as a hybrid of public and private sectors. That is, these are enterprises whose assets are partly owned by governments, and partly by private individuals and corporations. A possible exception is trusts, in so far as trusts are owned by anyone; rather, their assets are held in trust for others, the beneficiaries of the enterprise. It is difficult, however, to think of a reason for restricting social enterprise to the form of a trust. The distinctiveness of social enterprise, therefore, appears to have nothing to do with whether the assets of the business are state-owned or privately-owned, or whether the enterprises themselves are controlled or managed publicly or privately. Social enterprises do not have an organisational or institutional form that is inherently different from that of a private or public enterprise.

For these and other reasons, scholarly attention has shifted away from attempts to specify the nature of social enterprise as a social form towards improving understanding of *social entrepreneurship* (see the example of *The Big Issue* in Entrepreneurship in action 10.1). It is now widely accepted that social entrepreneurship can be found in all sectors. Austin et al. (2006: 1 and 2) defined social entrepreneurship as 'entrepreneurial activity with an embedded social purpose' or 'innovative, social value creating activity'.

It is argued in this book that social purpose and social value creation distinguish social from commercial entrepreneurship (see Case 16, Hill Holt Wood: Community-owned social enterprise). Further, Austin et al. (2006) have suggested that social entrepreneurship differs from commercial entrepreneurship with regard to its purpose or mission, the type of opportunities it identifies, the type of resources it mobilises, and the ways in which its performance is measured. These themes are discussed, in turn below.

Example of a social enterprise: *The Big Issue*

The Big Issue was launched in 1991 by Gordon Roddick and A. John Bird in response to the growing number of rough sleepers on the streets of London. Roddick, who also co-founded The Body Shop, was inspired by a newspaper called *Street News*, which was sold on the streets of New York. Returning from America he enlisted the help of Bird, who had experience in the print trade and who had himself slept rough. They both believed that the key to solving the problem of homelessness lay in helping people to help themselves, and were therefore determined to offer a legitimate alternative to begging.

This they did when *The Big Issue* magazine hit the streets in September 1991. It was initially a monthly publication sold by ten vendors in London. In June 1993 the title went weekly, and regional editions soon followed. There are currently five editions of the magazine which collectively cover the whole of the UK – *Big Issue Scotland*, *Big Issue Wales*, *Big Issue in the North*, *Big Issue South West* and the original *Big Issue*.

In November 1995 The Big Issue Foundation (a registered charity) was created with the aim of tackling the underlying issues which cause homelessness, and supporting vendors in their journey away from the streets. Since its creation the Foundation has provided services and referrals to address issues around housing, health, finances, education and employment. It also exists to support vendors in fulfilling their personal aspirations.

The Big Issue is one of the UK's leading social businesses, which 20 years since its inception continues to offer homeless and vulnerably housed people the opportunity to earn a legitimate income.

The organisation comprises two parts; a limited company which produces and distributes a magazine to a network of street vendors, and a registered charity which exists to help those vendors gain control of their lives by addressing the issues which have contributed to their homelessness.

The Big Issue Company publishes a weekly entertainment and current affairs magazine, which *Big Issue* sellers (or vendors) buy for 85p and sell for £1.70, thereby earning 85p per copy. Any post-investment profit generated through the sale of the magazine or the sale of advertising is passed on to the charity, The Big Issue Foundation. The Foundation is also reliant upon donations from the public to fund its crucial work with vendors. The organisation currently supports over 2,900 homeless and vulnerably housed people across the country. The magazine is read by over 670,000 people every week throughout the UK. The Big Issue Foundation is a registered charity which exists to link vendors with the vital support which will help them find routes out of homelessness.

Source: *The Big Issue* – a hand up, not a hand out; http://www.bigissue.com/.

- *Purpose or mission.* Entrepreneurs and enterprises commonly have a variety of purposes. Commercial entrepreneurship aims to create profitable operations resulting in private gain, whereas social entrepreneurship is more concerned with creating social value for the public good. This social purpose is the 'integrating driver' of social entrepreneurship.
- *Type of opportunities identified.* Austin et al. (2006: 3) have asserted that 'A problem for the commercial entrepreneur is an opportunity for the social entrepreneur'. Thus, where private enterprise has failed to meet a need, social enterprise may be able to respond more effectively. This does not work the other way round; the inability of social entrepreneurship to meet a need due to lack of resources does *not necessarily* present an opportunity for a commercial entrepreneur.

Social entrepreneurship differs from commercial entrepreneurship in its way of responding to context. Contexts that are difficult for commercial entrepreneurship can be precisely those that stimulate social entrepreneurship. 'In fact, social entrepreneurs may choose to pursue opportunities to address social change not despite of, but because of, an inhospitable context . . . Indeed, an adverse context may often lead the social entrepreneur to seek to change the context itself, as often the social problem is deeply embedded in contextual factors' (Austin et al., 2006: 9). Opportunities arise in a different way for social entrepreneurship because its purpose is different. 'Commercial entrepreneurship tends to focus on breakthroughs and new needs, whereas social entrepreneurship often focuses on serving basic, long-standing needs more effectively through innovative approaches' (Austin et al., 2006: 6).

- *Resource mobilisation.* In a sense, there are too many opportunities for social entrepreneurship because resources are insufficient to meet all the needs that are identified or expressed. 'The demand for social entrepreneurial programs and services usually far exceed [sic] the capacity of the social enterprises to serve these needs' (Austin et al., 2006: 7). Social entrepreneurship involves creating ways of mobilising and managing these scarce resources, for example by resisting the temptation to grow an organisation beyond its capacity, aligning the organisation with its context and its different stakeholders, looking more to the longer term, working with and through other organisations with greater resources, and so on. Social entrepreneurship is radically different from commercial entrepreneurship in not being so much concerned with the fortunes of one particular enterprise. It more broadly relates to the achievement of a social purpose that may be shared by a number of organisations, some of which may not even be regarded as social enterprises. Social entrepreneurship involves the mobilisation of different kinds of resource, which have to be managed in a different way. Typically, this involves building a large network of strong supporters, going beyond the boundaries of an individual social enterprise, and a capacity to manage a wide diversity of relationships with funders, managers, and staff from a range of backgrounds, volunteers, board members and other partners.

- *Performance measurement.* Social entrepreneurs aim to have a social impact, which has to be measured differently from commercial performance measures such as profit, market share and customer satisfaction (see Chapter 14). 'The value transactions [or deals] in social entrepreneurship differ from commercial entrepreneurship in kind, consumers, timing, flexibility and measurability' (Austin et al., 2006: 14). Social entrepreneurs have to provide different kinds of value to their different stakeholders (i.e., staff, volunteers, members and funders). Their consumers often lack economic power. Further, they often have to rely on short-term grants and contracts, causing them to give top priority to fund-raising activities. Measurement of their social impact is complicated, for a variety of reasons, which include lack of clarity about the nature of social value itself. Thus, 'It is critical for social entrepreneurs to have a clear understanding of their enterprise's theory of change, or the process by which the social innovation is going to have a social impact, and moreover, to be able to make a compelling case to participants and contributors so that the enterprise's social-value production chain can generate superior social returns' (Austin et al., 2006: 15). This seems to imply that social value is whatever is recognised as such by those who have a stake in the enterprise. This, in turn, suggests that the set of stakeholders for social enterprise are characteristically different from stakeholders in commercial enterprises.

Entrepreneurship in action 10.2
Involving the community: Ummah Food

Ummah is a food production company with a social conscience, combining the creation of Halal chocolate products with philanthropy. By 2012, the worldwide halal food market will be worth £500 bn. Mainstream food manufacturers have failed to respond to this huge opportunity – leaving the way clear for young entrepreneurs to satisfy demand.

Khalid Sharif launched Ummah Foods in 2004 and since then has persuaded retailers including Tesco and Asda to stock his halal chocolate products. Ummah food is bought by more non-Muslims than Muslims, and vegetarians in particular are loyal customers. Khalid understands that sometimes the only way to market a new idea is to open up a new market.

Ummah also uses its business processes to give something back to the community, whether it is through challenging young artists to come up with wrapper designs, using marketing material to support helplines, or creating commercials which address the misrepresentation of Muslims in the media.

Source: http://www.ummahfoods.com/index.html.

There is a difficulty with Austin et al.'s (2006) analysis. It tends to shift from a discussion of (social) entrepreneurship towards a discussion of (social) enterprises. Yet we have already seen that social enterprises do not have any distinctive organisational form. What makes them different from commercial enterprises is just that they involve stakeholders of a different kind, for example volunteers and donors, as well as customers and lenders (and possibly investors) (see the example of Ummah Food in Entrepreneurship in action 10.2).

Townsend and Hart (2008) considered this issue. They start from the position of the social entrepreneur, as someone who aims to create both *economic and social value* and argue that this dual focus leads to difficulties in deciding which organisational form is appropriate for the nascent social enterprise. This suggests yet another difference between commercial and social entrepreneurship. For commercial entrepreneurship, institutionalisation is usually seen as reducing uncertainty about the future by securing regularity of positive and supportive action. For social entrepreneurship, however, institutionalisation processes may actually increase such uncertainty in so far as they serve to highlight conflicts in values, thus creating ambiguity about what counts as the appropriate course of action for the entrepreneur. Further, 'Perceived institutional ambiguity stemming from the lack of normative agreement over the appropriateness of trying to concurrently create social and economic value accounts for a significant portion of the variance in the choice of organisational form in SE [social entrepreneurship] ventures' (Townsend and Hart, 2008: 687).

This perspective suggests conditions under which an entrepreneur would choose whether to form a commercial (for profit) or social (non-profit) enterprise. First, if an entrepreneur is more concerned with creating economic value than social value, they will tend to form a for-profit firm. Second, if they are centrally concerned to maximise social value, they will tend to form a non-profit venture. Third, if they aim to create economic and social value more or less equally (as appears to be the case with most social enterprises;

Dorado, 2006; Thompson and Doherty, 2006), the choice of organisational form will depend on the nature of the institutional environment and specifically, on the preferences of stakeholders, the sources of resources (for example, from charitable donations, government grants and contracts, loans, private investors, etc.), and whether it is the entrepreneur's economic or social goals that are perceived as more legitimate by the general public and by government.

The convergence of profit-maximisation with social value maximisation in the functional double bottom-line of social enterprises may create conflict regarding appropriate courses of action. This conflict concerns the normative uncertainty as to whether individuals should personally profit from solving social problems (Townsend and Hart, 2008). In the long run, institutional ambiguity surrounding social enterprises may dissolve as societal norms coalesce around a specific functional mission for the firm (e.g., dual social and economic value creation). However, the creation of an organisational form with an accepted 'double bottom-line' of social and economic value creation cannot on its own resolve the conflict regarding whether individuals should profit from solving social problems. The history of the co-operative movement demonstrates the long-term tendency for enterprises with both commercial and social goals to 'degenerate' into ones that are primarily commercial (Somerville, 2007). This, of course, reflects a long-standing normative debate about which goods and services should be provided by social enterprises and which are not really 'social goods'.

Zahra et al. (2009) illustrated three types of social entrepreneur, according to how they identify opportunities, mobilise resources and impact on society. These are discussed, in turn, below:

1 *'Social bricoleurs'*. They usually focus on discovering and addressing small-scale local social needs. Social bricoleurs have intimate knowledge of both local environmental conditions and locally available resources. Typically, they do not require external or specialised resources, and they often rely on whatever resources are readily harnessed. Such independence enables them to operate more freely and more flexibly. Community entrepreneurs are typically social bricoleurs (Somerville and McElwee, 2010). Overall, social bricoleurs identify local opportunities, mobilise local resources and have predominantly a local impact.

2 *'Social constructionists'*. They identify social needs that are inadequately addressed by existing institutions, businesses, non-governmental organisations (NGOs), and government agencies. Social constructionists develop products, goods and services to meet those needs. They create organisations to match the scale and scope of the social needs they seek to address, which can be local, regional, national, or global. Further, they aim to remedy social problems by planning and developing formalised or systemised scalable solutions, which can meet growing needs, or be transferred to new and varied social contexts. The scope of the social needs to be addressed usually requires developing fairly large and complex organisations with considerable financing and staffing needs. This means that they can be driven to some extent by the need to attract and please large funders. Overall, social constructionists identify unmet needs within the system, mobilise resources to meet those needs, and help to make the system work better.

3 *'Social engineers'*. They identify systemic problems, such as inadequate or entrenched governments and business elites, which they address through revolutionary change. 'The large scope and scale of their ambitions, as well as the deficits of legitimacy they might

face, require Social Engineers to harness popular [political] support to fulfil their missions' (Zahra et al., 2009: 531). Zahra et al. (2009) describe the example of Muhammad Yunus, the founder of the Grameen Bank, and another example from Bangladesh is that of Fasle Hasan Abed, who founded BRAC (Smillie, 2009). Overall, social engineers identify opportunities to change the system, mobilise large populations to make that change, and create and grow new institutions to replace those that have been found wanting.

10.3 The nature of social value

Social entrepreneurship is distinguished from commercial entrepreneurship by its social purpose and social value, and social entrepreneurs are then those who identify the opportunities and mobilise the resources to create that value. The key issue is the *nature of that social purpose and value*. However, social value itself remains undefined. *Social value* is related to social justice and the resolution of social problems, or intangible outcomes such as happiness and well-being as distinct from tangible outcomes such as products, clients served or funds generated that relate to economic value (Zahra et al., 2009). Many of the products and services that social entrepreneurs provide are non-quantifiable. For instance, it is problematical to measure the social value of clean water in remote villages, the adoption of orphans from war-torn nations, or the empowerment of women entrepreneurs in oppressive societies (Zahra et al., 2009). Considering such examples, it seems clear that social value cannot be measured in economic terms but only in terms of ethical and political priorities. Devising a *formula of 'total wealth'*, which involves the summation of economic and social value, does nothing to solve this problem of incommensurability. This is because we cannot simply add social value to economic value, or tell whether a social enterprise has created more or less social value than economic value, even if we were able to measure the economic, opportunity and social costs incurred in creating that total value (Zahra et al., 2009). Alternative approaches are needed.

This question might usefully be addressed by considering Zahra et al.'s (2009) typology of social entrepreneurship. In the case of the social bricoleurs, social value relates to the good of the locality as a whole, and the fair allocation of that good around the locality. Operationalising this notion seems to require the existence of a democratic body for the locality responsible for deciding what is the common good for the locality, and to whom the social bricoleurs could if necessary be held accountable (e.g., to explain how the social value they generate adds to that common good). There seem to be greater problems in holding social constructionists to account because of the different scales on which they operate. This group could also be held accountable to democratic governments at the different levels, as well as to their various stakeholders, and they could be required to follow democratically established rules of good governance. Where appropriate, this democratic regulation could be supported through established processes of social audit. In the case of social engineers a different approach may be called for, and the way forward is likely to be less clear and highly contentious. Zahra et al. (2009: 536) asserted that:

'Champions of radical change and leaders of social movements are often individualistic and may even hold values that others consider toxic to society at large. Some of these entrepreneurs may even be socially deviant, manipulative and unrelenting in the pursuit of their own idiosyncratic agendas. The changes these entrepreneurs champion to remedy existing problems can also lead to a new set of societal challenges that reduce or even harm public good. Social Engineers usually marshal great resources and create momentum for wide-ranging societal change. They are usually driven by a missionary zeal and unbounded belief in the righteousness of their causes. Sometimes, it takes this dedication to transform a community or society. There are times, however, when these behaviours create, intensify and perpetuate social tensions, conflicts and acrimony rather than harmony and prosperity. Given their passion and charisma, monitoring and constraining visionary Social Engineers can be a challenge.'

These observations raise a number of questions relating to who provides the necessary monitoring, who decides when and how to constrain the social engineers, how value conflicts are to be managed and resolved, and whose value is to count in the long run. Addressing these challenging questions probably involves entering into more explicitly political debates, which are beyond the scope of this chapter. In the next section, we focus upon the appropriate institutional arrangements for social bricoleurs.

10.4 Understanding the production of local social value

Social bricoleurs operate within a local community. The social value they produce depends largely on how they relate to that community. An important variable for identifying the nature of this social value is eligibility for membership of the local social enterprise. The following four institutional arrangements can be envisaged.

- First, membership could be open to all but only those who live in the local community (i.e., Peredo and Chrisman's (2006) model of community enterprise). Here, the possibility exists for the distribution of social value to all, provided only that they take up the opportunity of membership offered to them.
- Second, membership of the enterprise could be open to all those who have a stake in that enterprise, including people and organisations outside the community (i.e., employees who live elsewhere, customers, contractors, supporters, and others affected by its activities). This means that the enterprise is embedded in a community of stakeholders, as in the case of a multi-stakeholder co-operative or a non-profit venture, and social value is distributed in a way agreed by the community.
- Third, membership of the enterprise could be restricted to certain members of the local community, who are selected by the social bricoleur(s). In this case, although the enterprise is embedded in the local community, there is a risk that it may be biased in favour of a certain section or sections of that community, and that other sections of the community may not benefit from its activities. In such circumstances, the social value created is likely to be partial and limited, and may also be inequitably distributed. On the other hand, such exclusivity may serve to protect the enterprise from adopting what the social bricoleurs see as suboptimal or even self-destructive courses of action. In this scenario, social value is conserved and possibly enhanced.
- Fourth, members of the enterprise could be selected by the social bricoleurs from a wide range of stakeholders. Under this arrangement, there may be difficulties in ensuring that the social bricoleurs remain committed to the local community, and that the enterprise's activities continue to bring clear benefits to that community.

In the first institutional arrangement, the balance of interests inside and outside the community is not an issue. Clear priority is assigned to community interests. Here, it seems that the enterprise can be fully inclusive of its community. On closer inspection, the situation presents certain problems. For example, there is likely to be inequality in the stakes held by different community members; those held by the social bricoleurs are typically far higher than those held by others. Consequently, it can seem unfair to those with higher stakes in the enterprise that their views should carry no more weight in decision-making than those with lower stakes. Also, communities can be deeply divided internally, and what counts as the 'community interest', or as social value for the community may be highly contested. Such a situation can lead to the adoption of the third institutional arrangement, which seems exclusionary and even elitist, but, it can protect the high stakes of a minority against the risk of plunder by the majority (whose stakes are much smaller). The third arrangement, like the first, assigns priority to interests within the community but, unlike the first, it implies that these interests may not be those of the community as a whole. With the second and fourth arrangements, in contrast, the balance of interests inside and outside the community is of crucial importance. The key question relates to whose interests or whose social value the enterprise serves.

The degree of local community control of an enterprise is less important than its overall purpose and function. For any decision made by social bricoleurs, we need to ask not so

Entrepreneurship in action 10.3
The wider stakeholders in a social enterprise: Cafédirect

The collapse of the International Coffee Agreement in 1989 sent market prices plunging, putting the lives of millions of smallholder farmers around the world in jeopardy. In response, three coffee growing communities – in Peru, Costa Rica and Mexico – each shipped a single container of coffee, loaned on trust, to the UK. The beans were roasted and sold through church halls, charity shops and at local events.

Cafédirect was born. Since then Cafédirect has been a pioneer in ethical business. It began trading three years before the Fairtrade Foundation mark was first used in the UK and was the first coffee brand to carry the mark. In 2004, it successfully executed the UK's biggest ethical public share issue to become a publicly listed company, raising £5 million from 4,500 investors. The opportunity enabled grower partners, consumers, employees and founders to own a share in the company and to be directly connected to each other. Today Cafédirect works with 40 grower organisations across 14 countries, encompassing over 260,000 farmers and directly improving the lives of more than 1.6 million people.

Cafédirect is the innovative result of Oxfam, Equal Exchange, Traidcraft, and Twin Trading's decision to bypass the conventional market and buy coffee direct from disadvantaged growers in developing countries. In the past five years alone, Cafédirect has invested more than £3 million of its profits directly into the businesses and communities of our growers, and paid more than £7.5 million over and above market prices for our raw materials.

Pioneering grower initiatives and consumer engagements for more than 18 years, Cafédirect has developed and works to its own Gold Standard, consistently setting the bar for ethical business leadership. In 2009 it won the coveted Ethical Business of the Year Award at the Triodos Bank 'Women in Ethical Business Awards'.

Cafédirect is unlike any other coffee brand. Growers own shares in the business, sit on the board and get over half the profits back as investments into their businesses.

Source: http://brewing.cafedirect.co.uk/.

much how representative the decision-making process was of the local community, but rather what benefits that decision brought for that community. However, given the basic tenet of a social enterprise, it is important that benefits should not just accrue to the community as a whole, or to one or more sections of it, but should also be distributed fairly among community members (i.e., on the basis of need). Achieving such a distribution does require a democratic process, but it is one that lies outside the enterprise itself, in the political arena. It follows that, although democratic principle may not be essential for driving a local enterprise, it is vital for ensuring that the enterprise generates social value for the local community as a whole.

The creation of social value by social bricoleurs depends upon their embeddedness in a community of equals, whether these be members of a co-operative, a community of supporters, or a community of some other kind, bound together by common residence, interest or identity (see the example of Cafédirect in Entrepreneurship in action 10.3).

For any given community enterprise, it is not essential that all sections of the community are represented within it, nor does it require high degrees of community participation, so long as the wider community within which that enterprise operates is democratically governed. The 'community' here must be seen as in one sense a political community, with structures and processes of democratic government.

10.5　Looking forward

This chapter has examined the nature of social entrepreneurship and in particular, how it differs from commercial entrepreneurship. Building on Austin et al.'s (2006) typology of *mission, opportunity, resources and impact*, it has argued that the distinctiveness of social entrepreneurship lies in its aim to create social value, and in its mobilisation of resources of a different kind to realise that value. The nature of social value, however, is contested, both in its meaning and its measurement. If it is really different from economic value, then it cannot be reduced to the sum of the utilities of individuals, and realising social value must go beyond stakeholder satisfaction. There is a twofold problem. On the one hand, commercial entrepreneurship creates a certain amount of social value, for example, through networking, organisation building, etc. Consequently, in practice, commercial entrepreneurship seems to involve a certain amount of social entrepreneurship. On the other hand, it has already been established that social entrepreneurship involves the production of economic value as much as social value. Therefore, social entrepreneurship may involve a substantial degree of commercial entrepreneurship. Commercial and social entrepreneurship are not fundamentally different but are situated along a continuum, stretching perhaps from anti-social commercial entrepreneurship at one end to anti-capitalist social entrepreneurship at the other. In the former case, social value is actually destroyed rather than created (environmental pollution might be a good example of this), while in the latter case profit-making is eschewed in favour of altruistic action, organisational innovation and institutional reform.

The key distinction, then, is not between commercial and social entrepreneurship, but between economic and social value, and between the characteristically different ways in which these two types of value are created. The nature of social value remains vague. It is possible, however, to identify different kinds of stakeholder that are involved in its creation, for example, willing participants rather than or as well as hired hands, supporters and beneficiaries as well as customers, investors of human capital instead of economic capital, and so on.

In lieu of a satisfactory definition of social value, a distinction between different kinds of social entrepreneur, or different kinds of context in which social entrepreneurs operate, would appear to have some merit. Zahra et al.'s (2009) concept of *social bricoleurs* shows that it is possible to identify social value by reference to the relationship between the criteria for membership of a local social enterprise and its local community. Broadly speaking, more inclusive and more equal memberships have potential to produce greater local social value. However, this does not rule out the possibility that, in some cases, more restrictive memberships may be expedient, particularly where a variety of social enterprises are operating in the same locality, and where a common forum or assembly exists in which such variety is represented. Analogous arguments could be made in relation to Zahra et al.'s (2009) concepts of *social constructionists* and *social engineers*. It seems unlikely that social entrepreneurs of these latter two types are creating social value of a different kind from that provided by social bricoleurs. Nevertheless, they are working in different kinds of institutional contexts, and perhaps with different political purposes. Social constructionists aim to meet specific social welfare needs, while social engineers seek nothing less than a transformation of the institutional environment, which can include changes in the political system.

So far, attention appears to have been devoted to elaborating on the conceptual dimensions of social entrepreneurship and the creation of social value. Further research is needed that considers the *processes* of social value creation.

Discussion questions

1 To what extent do you agree with the view that it is not possible to identify a social enterprise as a distinct form of ownership?

2 Under what conditions is it more appropriate to engage in social entrepreneurship rather than traditional commercial entrepreneurship?

3 What difficulties arise in defining social value?

4 Discuss the challenges in distinguishing between economic and social value in social enterprises.

5 Discuss whether it is possible to separate the notion of social entrepreneurship from the community context in which a particular social enterprise operates.

Recommended further reading

Austin, J. E., Stevenson, H. and Wei-Skillern, J. (2006). Social and Commercial Entrepreneurship: Same, Different, or Both? *Entrepreneurship Theory and Practice*, 30 (1): 1–22.

Townsend, D. M. and Hart, T. A. (2008). Perceived Institutional Ambiguity and the Choice of Organizational Form in Social Entrepreneurial Ventures. *Entrepreneurship Theory and Practice*, 32 (4): 685–700.

Zahra, S., Gedajlovic, E., Neubaum, D. O. and Shulman, J. M. (2009). A Typology of Social Entrepreneurs: Motives, Search Processes and Ethical Challenges. *Journal of Business Venturing*, 24 (5): 519–532.

Chapter 11

External environmental context: Drivers and barriers

Contents

Learning objectives

- Appreciate that local external environmental conditions (i.e., an exogenous determinant) can provide stimuli and resources that enable individuals to establish and grow new firms.
- Consider that local external conditions shape entrepreneurial behaviour and performance.
- Illustrate the theories explaining the growth in business start-ups and regional variations in new firm formation (NFF) rates.
- Consider the problems associated with a non-selective policy of encouraging NFF and growth with no regional targeting built into policy.
- Analyse the motivations of practitioners seeking to foster clusters of new firms and localised knowledge spillovers.
- Appreciate how practitioners can provide supportive institutional environments (i.e., Science Parks) to promote NFF and development.
- Consider the relevance of theories relating to entrepreneur location decisions with regard to the provision of services provided by owners of Science Parks.
- Evaluate why some entrepreneurs select a 'managed' rather than a 'non-managed' Science Park environment.
- Consider the wider relevance of the 'entrepreneurial performance hypothesis'.
- Appreciate new firm formation and development issues relating to emerging and transition economies.

11.1   Introduction

The study of entrepreneurship is deficient if it focuses exclusively on the characteristics and behaviours of individual entrepreneurs and treats the social, economic, and political infrastructure for entrepreneurship as externalities (Van de Ven, 1993). External environmental conditions need to be considered when exploring the entrepreneurial processes, since these will influence both whether entrepreneurship takes place at all, and the form it takes, including whether it makes a positive contribution to society, or is destructive if it involves corruption and criminality (Baumol, 1990). Global Entrepreneurship Monitor (GEM) studies have pointed to marked differences in the incidence of entrepreneurship between countries across the globe, much of which are attributed to differences in environmental conditions (GEM, 2004). Yet detailed theoretical and empirical studies exploring whether local external conditions shape entrepreneurial behaviour remain scarce (Rocha and Sternberg, 2005). Nevertheless, studies suggest that family firms in the United States are more prevalent in less prosperous regions, and they play an important role in local economic development (Chang et al., 2008). External environmental conditions (i.e., an exogenous determinant) can be viewed as a key variable that should be taken into account when examining the behaviour and performance of entrepreneurs.

The external environment context, which can be viewed from a locational and/or an industrial perspective, can provide stimuli and resources that enable individuals to establish and grow new and small firms. The external environment may deterministically (Hannan and Carroll, 1992) promote (or retard) enterprising behaviour, but this view has been questioned (see Section 3.8.2). Some entrepreneurs can adapt and improve their chances of accessing and leveraging resources required to circumvent barriers to new firm formation (NFF) and development. However, individuals in society differ in their willingness to supply themselves as new firm founders (Armington and Acs, 2002). For example, an individual's resource pool can shape their propensity to pursue a career in entrepreneurship (see Chapter 4). Studies monitoring regional variations in NFF rates need to consider the resource profiles of the population living in a locality (i.e., endogenous/supply-side issues), and the external environmental context (i.e., exogenous/demand-side issues).

Policy can proactively provide a supportive environment for enterprise (see Chapter 2). Practitioners recognise that some localities with 'munificent' resource pools are associated with high rates of NFF and superior firm performance (Wang and Ang, 2004), whilst other more 'hostile' localities (Covin and Slevin, 1989) associated with narrower pools of resources report lower NFF rates and smaller enterprise stocks. A hostile external environmental context can shape entrepreneur location selection decisions and behaviour, as well as firm performance. Competition and other barriers to resource access and utilisation can retard entrepreneurial behaviour in some localities. To promote NFF and development, particularly in hostile environments, governments can directly (or indirectly) support local level initiatives that reduce uncertainty for entrepreneurs, and/or provide resources (Birley and Westhead, 1992) to enable more people to circumvent attitudinal, resource, operational, and strategic barriers to enterprise formation and development (DTI, 2004).

Practitioners have sought to foster enterprise at a local level through the creation of 'clusters' (which can be termed 'industrial districts', 'agglomerations', 'growth poles', 'industrial complexes', 'technopoles', etc.) associated with geographically localised, related and interdependent firms (Desrochers and Sautet, 2008). To generate creativity, innovation, efficiency, productivity, wealth creation and job generation benefits, practitioners are supporting 'cluster strategies' (such as Science Parks and incubators) (Aernoudt, 2004), which promote NFF in specialised (i.e., technology-based) industries. Firms located in 'industrial districts' may more easily circumvent barriers to firm development. Businesses with limited resources, no track record and no established professional procedures and routines (i.e., potentially associated with the 'liabilities of newness and smallness') may improve their ability to secure and use essential exogenous resources for firm development by positioning themselves in a cluster (Chung and Kanin, 2001), which encourages firms to innovate in order to remain competitive. Regions associated with industry clustering have been found to be associated with firms that possess performance advantages due to superior access to knowledge spillovers (Gilbert et al., 2008).

Audretsch (1995) has presented a knowledge spillover theory of entrepreneurship that challenges an assumption implicit to the knowledge production function – that firms exist exogenously and then endogenously seek out and apply knowledge inputs to generate innovative output. Rather, it is the knowledge in the possession of economic agents that is exogenous, and in an effort to appropriate the returns from that knowledge the spillover of knowledge from its producing entity involves endogenously creating a new firm. Audretsch and Keilbach (2006: 288–289) asserted that:

> entrepreneurship is an endogenous response to opportunities created, but not exploited, by the incumbent firms . . . knowledge spillovers are geographically bounded and localised within spatial proximity to the knowledge source.

Other theorists question whether there is conclusive evidence supporting the existence of localised knowledge spillovers, let alone the positive externalities they are assumed to generate. Desrochers and Sautet (2008: 814) asserted that:

> a 'successful' policy push toward specialisation might contain the seeds of its own demise by leaving regional economies more vulnerable to cyclical downturns and less likely to support the emergence of innovative practices and behaviour, such as the development of interindustry linkages and new combinations of existing technologies and materials ('Jacobs externalities').

Rather than policies that promote local industrial specialisation (i.e., clusters), Desrochers and Sautet (2008: 814) have presented a case for spontaneously developed industrial and economic level diversity. They have provocatively claimed that entrepreneurial activity is the source of regional development. Regions reporting high rates of NFF are associated with higher levels of job generation and wealth creation (van Stel and Storey, 2004). Practitioners recognise that enterprise can be shaped by external environmental conditions. By encouraging entrepreneurship (i.e., NFF and self-employment) practitioners assume that they can promote local and national economic development (Carree et al., 2007), and reduce place and people poverty. Some practitioners are seeking to raise local rates of NFF to national levels (One NorthEast, 1999; see the example of Scotland's Birth Rate Strategy in Entrepreneurship in action 2.5) to promote local job generation and wealth creation (see Chapter 2).

This chapter summarises the evidence relating to the external environmental factors that can promote and/or retard NFF at national and local levels. Resource issues relating to the entrepreneur (i.e., supply-side) and the external environmental context (i.e., demand-side) shape NFF activity. We illustrate that the pool of resources in a nation or a locality can be linked to a growth in business start-ups and variations in NFF rates. Theories explaining the growth in business start-ups and regional variations in NFF rates are summarised. Institutions such as Science Parks have been built to provide sponsored environments for new technology-based firm (NTBF) formation and development. Studies focusing on the location decisions made by entrepreneurs are summarised, and a distinction is made between 'managed' and 'non-managed' Science Parks. This discussion illustrates that the local context and the type of support it provides can enable some entrepreneurs to adapt, and address barriers to enterprise. Issues relating to the formation and development of new firms in emerging and transition economies are then discussed.

11.2 New firm creation: Theoretical insights

11.2.1 Growth in business start-ups

Theories have been advanced to 'explain' the growth in business start-ups in developed economies (Westhead and Moyes, 1992). Recession-push theory, large firm fragmentation theory, structural theories, and 'enterprise economy' theory are discussed, in turn, below.

In addition, theories explaining spatial variations in new firm formation rates have been presented (Keeble and Wever, 1986). Structural theory, socio-cultural theory and economic theory are summarised below. Self-employment studies are discussed elsewhere (Parker and Robson, 2004).

11.2.1.1 *Recession-push theory*

Recession-push theory suggests that people 'pushed' into entrepreneurship after redundancy or unemployment establish new firms (Storey, 1982). Recessions can increase NFF in several ways (Binks and Jennings, 1986). First, through the provision of cheap second-hand plant and machinery from businesses that have closed or gone into liquidation. Second, potential market niches may be opened up by large firms withdrawing from what they perceive to be peripheral and possibly less profitable activities (see the example of Dawn Hardy in Entrepreneurship in action 11.1).

11.2.1.2 *Large firm fragmentation theory*

Growth in new firm numbers is, in part, due to the deliberate fragmentation policies by large firms under conditions of technological and market uncertainty, and increasing difficulty of control over the labour process (Shutt and Whittington, 1987). 'Fragmentation methods' that encourage NFF relate to: decentralisation of production to smaller firms which remain in the ownership of the large firm; a shift in production to small firms from large ones through franchising and licensing; and the disintegration of production to independently-owned small firms through outsourcing, subcontracting, corporate venturing, and management and employee buyouts (see Chapters 8 and 9).

Entrepreneurship in action 11.1

Dawn Michelle Hardy: An entrepreneur creating a business during a recession

Hardy is the founder of Dream Relations, a public relations (PR) and literary consulting agency located in Brooklyn, New York in the United States, which was started during the recession. She has a Bachelor of Science in Marketing International Trade. Hardy's business, Dream Relations, offers publicity, book tour and promotional services to mainstream and independent authors. Hardy commented she was devastated after being being made redundant ten days before Christmas. She worked for a small publishing company where she oversaw production and served as a personal assistant to the chief executive officer (CEO). While working for the CEO, Hardy learned all she could about the publishing industry, and had hands-on experience in drafting publishing contracts, proofing manuscripts and press coverage. She has used this knowledge and learning to develop her own business. Hardy says her start-up costs were approximately $150, and this finance was used to purchase a business license. Further, Hardy reflected that she now enjoys the freedom and peace of mind that was never felt when she worked for someone else. Hardy commented there is now no limit on the amount of money that can be made. She has to 'wear numerous hats' which may, however, restrict business development. So far, Hardy makes two-and-a-half times her last salary, which was $42,000. She uses interns in her business and temporary assistants in order to satisfy increasing workload demands. Hardy feels that being responsible and hardworking provides a good foundation for her business. Yes, she's having fun!

Source: http://www.articlesbase.com/entrepreneurship-articles/business-flying-without-a-net-entrepreneurs-starting-businesses-during-the-recession.

11.2.1.3 *Structural theories*

Structural changes in the composition of the economy can encourage NFF (Keeble and Wever, 1986). The technological change view sees the growth in NFF being linked to the growth in major technologies such as micro-electronics, computers, telecommunications and information technologies. The introduction of new scale-down production equipment suited to small-batch production and the emergence of a 'thoughtware economy' has enabled new and small firms to create and to take advantage of new opportunities. Increased NFF can also be linked to the rise in real incomes. The break-up of the mass market has led to increased demand for more varied, short series, customised, better quality and more sophisticated products. Numerous potential market niches have appeared which require short production runs and flexible production processes, which small firms have traditionally exploited better than large firms.

11.2.1.4 *Enterprise economy theories*

Measures taken to create an 'enterprise economy' may increase NFF. Such measures are aimed at freeing up market imbalances that unfairly disfavour small firms relative to large firms. These policy actions include 'hard' (i.e. financial support) and 'soft' support measures (i.e., advice and training) (Bridge et al., 2003) to encourage individuals to become self-employed, or to start businesses that employ people.

11.2.2 Regional variations in (New Firm Formation) NFF

11.2.2.1 *Structural theory*

Some regions have a reputation for adaptability and growth and are characterised by a high proportion of small firms and sectoral concentration (Acs, 2006). This is often referred to as flexible specialisation. It is characterised by an organisation of economic activity that is both adaptable and robust. Economic activity is specialised on a narrow range of goods or services.

Structural theory suggests that sectoral and plant size structures shape the geography of NFF. Traditional heavy industrial urban areas associated with high proportions of firms with mature production technologies, high barriers to entry, and low market growth report lower NFF rates (Cross, 1981). Some regions have industrial structures that do not foster enterprise (Johnson, 2004). Environments with employment generally in large firms report lower rates of NFF (Acs, 2006). New firm founders may have received more appropriate experience and training for entrepreneurship in small establishments than in large (Storey, 1982).

11.2.2.2 *Socio-cultural theory*

The geography of NFF can be shaped by the existing socio-economic mix of a locality, and the (entrepreneurship) human capital profiles of residents (i.e., supply-side issues) (Audretsch and Keilbach, 2004b). The resident population of a locality can shape the supply of entrepreneurs. Two socio-cultural explanations explaining regional variations in NFF have been proposed. The occupational structure of the local population, especially with regard to the relative concentration of non-manual, managerial or professional workers, possessing higher educational qualifications can increase the supply of potential new firm founders in a locality (Gould and Keeble, 1984). Founders with the latter characteristics have the 'human capital', financial capital and social and business networks to establish new firms. These processes are apparent in environmentally attractive, previously unindustrialised, rural localities that have benefited from environmentally-influenced in-migration. As a result, some localities have increased their supply pool of potential entrepreneurs.

The second explanation argues that high rates of NFF in more agriculturally-based rural regions stem from a local tradition of self-employment, enterprise and indigenous economic initiative. Conversely, low rates of NFF in industrial areas associated with a legacy of externally-controlled nineteenth century industrial specialisation on coal, steel, shipbuilding and heavy engineering (Checkland, 1981) have not fostered the emergence of an 'indigenous business class' of local entrepreneurs.

11.2.2.3 *Economic theory*

Economic theory focuses on the local availability of factors of production such as premises, labour, technology and capital (Galbraith et al., 2008). People located in munificent areas with resources may be more likely to establish new firms than individuals located in sparse environments associated with intense competition for limited resources. Economic theorists suggest that local demand for new firm products or services can shape the geography of NFF (Acs, 2006) and firm development (Braunerhjelm and Boargman, 2004). Differences in the level, nature and growth of local and regional demand for goods and services, therefore, can promote regional differences in NFF and development (Reynolds and Maki, 1990). Local market growth can reflect a variety of processes including large firm restructuring, public sector spending (e.g., health, education, fire service, police, etc.) and population trends reflecting the 'livelihood principle', and environmentally influenced migration.

Urban areas (i.e., agglomerations) may have advantages as incubators for new firms (Parr, 2002). These include the relative ease of access to customers and the inputs required (i.e., capital, labour, suppliers, etc.) to produce the goods or services. Urbanised contexts are frequently a source of entrepreneurs, such as educated individuals with business experience in their early and middle adult years. However, the costs associated with most inputs (i.e., physical space, wages and transportation) are higher in urban areas.

Government through local spending on infrastructure (i.e., schools, health care, roads, police and fire service, etc.) may indirectly increase the demand for goods and services provided by new firms. Expenditure on local community infrastructure may improve the status of particular locations and consequently makes them more attractive to potential entrepreneurs to move to, in order to establish new firms. Government programmes, in addition, provide direct assistance to new and small firms (Keeble and Walker, 1994), and may encourage firms to be established in localities.

11.3   Regional variations in NFF: Evidence

11.3.1   Spatial variations in NFF rates

The underlying processes associated with the geography of NFF rates were explored in a study of seven developed economies (Reynolds et al., 1994). Each country study focused on two dependent variables relating to firm births in all economic sectors in regions, and manufacturing firm births in regions. The following two methods were used to control for the differing sizes of regions:

1 Number of new firms in a region (1980 to 1990) per 100 firms in that region (1979) (i.e., the 'ecological approach' that analyses the extent to which the business sector is being rejuvenated (Johnson, 2004)).

2 Number of new firms in a region (1980 to 1990) per 10,000 population in that region (1979) (i.e., the 'labour market approach' that explores how entrepreneurial a region's people are (Johnson, 2004)).

The study found considerable variation in NFF rates between EC countries on both these measures.

11.3.2   Entrepreneurial processes and NFF rates

Table 11.1 indicates the relative importance of seven entrepreneurial processes underlying NFF from the demand and supply-side examined by Reynolds et al. (1994). The figures in brackets in Table 11.1 show the number of countries where one or more of the 'explanatory' indicators of the entrepreneurial process could be included. The indicators of the processes ranged from 1 to 7 in the different countries. A high level of 'explanation' was recorded in all the countries apart from Italy, averaging about 70 per cent for the models of NFF rates in all economic sectors, and between 40 and 50 per cent for NFF rates in manufacturing. This suggests the selected entrepreneurial process variables were linked to NFF in each country.

The analysis indicated that NFF is most strongly encouraged by:

- Growth in demand generated by income and population growth – theory explaining business start-ups: structural theory.
- Urbanised/agglomeration context reflecting the advantages of agglomeration, presumably including the benefits of access to customers, source of supply, as well as awareness of competitors' actions – theory explaining regional variations in NFF rates: economic theory.
- Small firms skills, expertise and knowledge context – theory explaining regional variations in NFF rates: structural theory.

Table 11.1 Overview of results from the cross-national study

Entrepreneurial process	All economic sectors	Manufacturing only
Demand growth	Positive (6)*	Positive (6)
Urbanisation/agglomeration	Positive (6)	Positive (5)
Unemployment	Positive (4)	Mixed (5)
Personal, household wealth	Positive (3)	None (4)
Small firms/specialisation	Positive (6)	Positive (7)
Political ethos	Positive (2)	Positive (2)
Government spending/policies	None (4)	Positive (1)
Predictive success (average – median – explained variance)		
Births/10,000 people	78%	60%
Births/100 firms	65%	32%

* Indicates the number of countries where one or more indicators of the process could be included.

Source: Reynolds et al. (1994, Table 4: 451).

Other processes, related to unemployment, personal wealth, liberal political climate, or government actions had weak or mixed impacts.

In all economic sectors, the most significant process was growth in demand. Two processes had a consistent positive effect encouraging NFF: urbanisation/agglomeration and the presence of small firms and specialisation. A weak positive effect was recorded from measures of personal household wealth. The presence of a liberal political ethos (as reflected by socialist voters) had a mixed effect, and there was no statistically significant impact from government action (i.e., local spending or programmes of assistance). Further, the role of unemployment in shaping NFF rates was not simple, or consistent. Increase in unemployment was significantly positive in only one study (i.e., promoting NFF), significantly negative (i.e., retarding NFF) in two studies, and not significant in three studies. With regard to the absolute unemployment level, significant results were recorded in only three studies (i.e., promoting NFF), while the other three studies found no significant relationships.

A slightly different pattern of relationships was detected with regard to manufacturing firm birth rates. Most notably, a strong positive effect was found from the presence of small firms (presumably reflecting some specialisation) in the region. A consistent positive effect from growth in demand was detected. Weak positive impacts were found from processes associated with urbanisation/agglomeration, a liberal political ethos and government spending/policies. A mixed pattern was detected with regard to unemployment. Personal household wealth had no impact.

New firm births rates in all economic sectors were principally associated with the processes associated with consumer oriented commerce – population growth, urban context, or availability of small amounts of capital. In contrast, the major customer for manufacturing firms are other businesses, often other manufacturing firms, and ease of access to large human populations was less significant than other factors, such as input costs. Measures of personal wealth – related to housing and land values – or urbanisation or agglomeration had little value in predicting manufacturing firm birth rates.

11.4 NFF regional variations: Policy and practitioner implications

11.4.1 Focus on quantity of entrepreneurs and new firms

Regional disparities in NFF rates reflect major shifts in population and resources (Reynolds et al., 1994). Reducing regional disparities in NFF rates may require policies that constrain (or discourage) migration across regions, compensate for differences in demand across regions, or develop programmes for rural areas that compensate for the natural advantages found in some urban areas. The costs, political and financial, of achieving equality across regions in NFF rates may be substantial (Johnson, 2004). Only the political process can resolve the value of subsidising declining regions to achieve parity in NFF rates and economic well-being.

Governments can stifle the efforts of those attempting to start new firms through onerous bureaucratic requirements, complex regulations or merely a slow reaction to requests for decisions required to form a new firm. Also, government can introduce policies that enhance the capacity for all firms to function effectively. They can provide an efficient, effective infrastructure (i.e., transportation, education, etc.). Government can reduce the transaction costs for firms and minimise bureaucratic complications. General measures to expand business activity (i.e., all ages and employment sizes) may be the most cost-effective strategy. Nationally applied policies to increase capacity for NFF in all regions may indirectly favour more prosperous and socially and economically well-endowed regions.

A non-selective policy of encouraging NFF and growth, with no regional targeting built into it, may enhance regional differences by proving relatively more modest impacts in regions with existing resource shortages. In the short term, national and local governments have limited policy freedom to encourage NFF across all regions without massive capital expenditures. Reynolds et al. (1994) found that government enterprise policies had modest impacts on predicting NFF rates. Explanatory variables found to best predict NFF were those not easily affected by government action. One way to reduce the overall cost would be to restrict assistance to certain regions, seen as having unusually high or low potential, or to new firms in certain industries – those seen as having the highest potential for NFF and growth such as technology-based activities. However, differential allocation of public resources is controversial.

11.4.2 Focus on quality of entrepreneurs and 'high potential for growth firms'

Instead of spending vast sums, which are necessary to raise the NFF level, policy-makers could identify new and established firms in localities that have the greatest ability to increase employment and to export their goods and services outside the local region (i.e., to reduce the problem of new firm displacement) (see the example of Scottish Enterprise in Entrepreneurship in action 11.2). Policies to assist entrepreneurs and firms to survive business development barriers may be more amenable to policy intervention. Targeted

---

Entrepreneurship in action 11.2
Scottish Enterprise and regional job creation

In April 2010, Scottish Enterprise announced assistance worth £6 million to help a leading energy industry manufacturer to expand its output, and to secure up to 400 local jobs. BiFab was offered £2 million of Regional Selective Assistance (RSA), plus a £4 million commercial loan from Scottish Enterprise to help finance a new 12,000 square metre facility on the Fife Energy Park in Scotland. The investment anchored BiFab to the Fife Energy Park and provided a major economic boost to the region. This external support to enterprise sought to ensure Scotland's leading position in the global development and deployment of offshore renewable energy generation. BiFab was viewed as an excellent example of a proven company with expertise in deep water oil and gas exploration, which had the ability to diversify into the offshore renewables sector. The new manufacturing facility would secure hundreds of local jobs, and would act as a driver through supply-chain opportunities to create new jobs in other local firms. Scottish Enterprise argued that resource investment into this big opportunity would support the accumulation of offshore wind capabilities, and ambitious local firms involved in the supply chain of this renewable sector would accumulate capabilities and knowledge, which would enable them to exploit opportunities beyond Scotland. This investment also supported the Scottish government's drive to create a low carbon economy. The funding allowed BiFab to ensure long-term employment opportunities for its workforce, and to provide additional jobs and apprenticeships in Fife when sales orders increased.

Source: Scottish government, eGovmonitor, 13 April 2010.

assistance toward 'types' of entrepreneurs and firms is a politically controversial strategy, for it amounts to excluding most firms from gaining access to external support (see Chapter 2). Reynolds et al. (1994) concluded that the focus of public policy in geographical areas with high NFF rates (and business stocks already at their carrying capacity levels) should emphasise the quality of the existing firms (i.e., promote high-flying 'winner' entrepreneurs and firms). The focus of public policy in geographical areas with low NFF rates (and business stocks below their carrying capacity levels) should encourage NFF (i.e., introduce initiatives that ease the hurdles nascent entrepreneurs face).

11.5 Local institution to support NTBFs: Science Parks

11.5.1 The nature of Science Parks

Science Parks are sponsored environments that seek to reduce external environmental barriers to the formation of NTBFs such as premises, legitimacy, finance, skills, etc. (see Chapter 6). The following criteria have been used by the United Kingdom Science Park Association (UKSPA) to define a property-based Science Park initiative (UKSPA, 1999):

- encourages and supports the start-up and incubation of innovation-led, high-growth, knowledge-based businesses;
- provides an environment where larger and international businesses can develop specific and close interactions with a particular centre of knowledge creation for their mutual benefit; and
- has formal and operational links with centres of knowledge creation such as universities, higher education institutes (HEIs) and research organisations.

The ownership structure and management strategy of a Science Park, in part, shapes the types of support provided and the types of entrepreneurs attracted to the Science Park. A distinction can be made between the following types of management strategies (Grayson, 1993):

- *University led and funded strategy*: Park established and developed and managed by a HEI on its own (this is the least common model).
- *Joint venture company strategy*: Science Park run as a separate legal entity. This mechanism ensures a continuing positive role for the HEI and other investors in the joint venture company.
- *Co-operative venture strategy*: Partners work together within a flexible and informal framework. A local authority or development agency usually leads the development. Least input from the HEI but is the most common strategy.

11.5.2 Theoretical insights concerning location decisions made by entrepreneurs

11.5.2.1 *Context*
Guided by theoretical insights concerning the location decisions made by entrepreneurs, Science Park owners have considered the needs of entrepreneurs. The various theoretical rationales for Science Parks are discussed below.

11.5.2.2   *Neo-classical location theory*

Early studies focusing upon location decision-making and industrial development were positioned within a neo-classical economics paradigm (Section 3.8.1), which assumes entrepreneurs seek to maximise wealth (i.e., a focus on cost reduction). Location of individual firms is influenced by direct economic costs (Smith, 1981) relating to distance from markets, transport costs, labour costs, and agglomeration economies (or external economies of scale). Factors more recently identified (Flynn, 1993) relate to the cost and availability of premises, cost and availability of skilled labour, availability of financial grants and subsidies, provision of complementary services to overcome an entrepreneur's weaknesses in core business skills, environmental quality, and the presence of a local university or HEI. From this perspective, Science Parks may facilitate the lowering of a new firm's transaction costs (Tan, 2006).

11.5.2.3   *Behavioural location theory*

Behavioural location theorists have highlighted the role played by uncertainty (or lack of full information) in entrepreneur decision-making. Satisfying basic requirements rather than profit-maximising can be a key factor shaping location decisions made by entrepreneurs (Autio and Kauranen, 1994). An entrepreneur who does not have established mechanisms to deal with uncertainty may prefer a location where there is a mediator who can channel information and resources to an organisation with limited legitimacy. Gate-keepers (i.e., Science Park managers) can act as a formal mechanism to reduce uncertainty (and associated costs) for entrepreneurs. A gate-keeper can enhance the reputation of inexperienced entrepreneurs (i.e., those with limited social and business networks), and enable entrepreneurs to gain access to an uninterrupted supply of crucial resources from a variety of organisations including HEIs, banks, venture capitalists, and enterprise agencies. Gate-keepers have a role in generating the human and social capital of entrepreneurs.

11.5.2.4   *Structuralist theory*

Structuralist theorists suggest that the structure of an entire industrial system can play a key role in influencing the location of economic activity. They have sought to explain locational agglomeration. Structuralists have developed the notion of an industrial district (Piore and Sabel, 1984). They suggest that non physical resources, proximity, relational capital and co-operation and learning influence the development of territorial synergy (Saxenian, 1994). The combination of clusters of science-based knowledge, together with institutions and skilled labour can encourage innovation (Castells and Hall, 1994). By reducing uncertainty and transaction costs, as well as enabling entrepreneurs to take full advantage of commercial and technical information, it is assumed that Science Park gate-keepers provide and gain access to structural elements that encourage synergy between NTBFs. Institutional factors within a Science Park locale can provide a context for acquiring knowledge and experience as well as for the routinising of activities (Thrift, 1996).

11.5.2.5   *Network theory*

Theorists recognise the role of social capital embedded in entrepreneurs' networks can shape entrepreneur location decisions (Tötterman and Sten, 2005). Utilising the concept of 'borrowed size', Phelps et al. (2001: 614) asserted that there is a:

> need to move away from thinking of the relationship between small firms and external economies purely in terms of the characteristics of individual localities and toward an emphasis upon the interactions between businesses in groups of localities.

By joining networks and forming alliances, SMEs can expand their social capital networks, and subsequently utilise knowledge and value-creating resources that a firm cannot create independently. SMEs can create a capital of trust through effectively utilising their institutional and social networks. An alliance with a large organisation may enhance the social legitimacy of a new firm, as well as enable firms with more limited resources to address customer, financial, technical, manufacturing, marketing and/or distribution obstacles to firm development (Folta et al., 2006).

Johannisson et al. (1994) have proposed a model of emerging networks for Science Parks with regard to the relational structure of exchange between individuals. A Science Park is viewed as a formal institution that is deliberately created to deal with collective concerns. The Science Park's formal administrative structure and management agreement provides an institutional context for the provision of supportive services (i.e., resources) towards tenant firms.

Links with universities play an important network role in relation to Science Parks (Phan et al., 2005). Westhead and Storey (1995) for the United Kingdom, Lindelöf and Löfsten (2004) for Sweden, and Link and Scott (2004) for the United States have examined the links with universities by firms located on or off Science Parks. The latter studies offer insights into the differences between NTBFs and research based spin-off firms according to the nature of the links. These studies suggest that the strength of the link is associated with the proximity and richness of the university research environment, R&D output and survival. Bøllingtoft and Uhløi (2005), using evidence from Denmark, identified a network business incubator based on territorial synergy, relational symbiosis, and economies of scope. In contrast to top-down incubators, this model is bottom-up where the new ventures themselves have developed and managed the incubator in order to best develop and exploit networking opportunities.

11.5.3 Supportive services provided by Science Parks

Guided by insights from studies that have focused on the location decisions made by entrepreneurs, Science Park developers make the following assumptions:

- firms desire high specification and flexible premises;
- firms desire landscaped environments;
- firms benefit from shared resources;
- firms are concerned with business image and want to increase their credibility and status;
- firms want to be linked to a local HEI;
- firms want to co-operate with other tenants; and
- firms are prepared to pay a 'rent premium'.

The management of a successful Science Park should go beyond tenant selection, lettings, rent collection and rent review negotiation (Lee and Osteryoung, 2004) (see the example of the No.1 Nottingham Science Park in Entrepreneurship in action 11.3). Science Parks can respond to changing property needs. Science Park owners provide flexible premises of various sizes, which can enable firms to reduce their costs in line with their actual space requirements. To ensure rental growth and minimise business closures, Science Park managers generally provide a supportive environment (Tan, 2006). Jointly used services can help firms to reduce their fixed overhead costs (Sternberg, 1990). Rent-free periods for new

No.1 Nottingham Science Park is a property-based initiative that has won awards for its architecture and environmentally sustainable infrastructure. The initiative seeks to inspire creativity and to increase both productivity and quality of life for the tenant knowledge and technology-based firms. This striking industrial space has over 42,000 square feet of flexible accommodation. The property initiative seeks to increase the credibility of tenant firms seeking to attract and retain the best employees and customers. This Science Park provides the following benefits and services to enable knowledge and technology-based firms to address several barriers to business formation and growth:

- Awarding winning property design;
- Park is a member of the UK Science Park Association;
- Inspirational location for information and communication technologies (ICT), low carbon technology research and development (R&D) and technology generation and exploitation;
- Land available for bespoke design and build solutions from around 25,000 square feet;
- Flexible space ranging from 1,000 to 42,000 square feet;
- Flexible premises ranging from Grade A to bespoke solutions;
- High quality meeting rooms and break out areas;
- Located in the heart of the Nottingham science city cluster;
- Adjacent to Nottingham University;
- Environmentally attractive landscaping;

- Award winning sustainability, low carbon footprint, near carbon neutral biomass woodchip heating system, brown roof for natural insulation and biodiversity, optimized light and ventilation for a happier and healthier environment, adiabatic comfort cooling, sustainable urban drainage system, and green transport initiatives; and
- Low tenant running costs.

Tenants include: 121 Systems, which provides solutions for transport organizations that operate logistics intensive businesses who require visibility and control over their vehicle fleets and business processes. Energy is a young dynamic firm that works for large infrastructure companies located throughout the world. Its innovative cooling systems enable customers to save money and energy. Advance Comms is an independent company that provides business telecom solutions over global system for mobile communication (GSM) gateways relating to the transmission technologies for the delivery of voice over IP (VoIP) communications covering IP networks such as the Internet or other packet-switched networks. Meerkat provide a billing platform and marketing materials for asymmetric digital subscriber line (ADSL), symmetric digital subscriber line (SDSL), and wide area networks (WAN's). Changan Automotive is a Chinese car company researching R&D electric cars. Chinook Sciences are renting a larger space, researching waste to energy reduction.

Source: http://www.nottinghamsciencepark.co.uk.

firms are provided by some Science Parks, for example, in emerging markets such as China (Wright et al., 2008b). A Science Park may provide intellectual and physical infrastructure that includes the built environment, its immediate surroundings as well as communications, telecommunication, IT, business services and business support services. Further, Science Park management may actively support the transfer of technology, and for their smaller firm clients, business skills. Science Parks can proactively stimulate technology transfer and promote links between the local HEI and tenant firms through informal contacts and visits from an HEI's Industrial Liaison Officer. Increased awareness of the HEI's resources and skills can be disseminated to firms on the Park through seminars and magazines developed by the local HEI. Informal contacts between employees in the HEI and

Science Park firms can be facilitated by shared social and recreational facilities. Science Parks can provide business advice and services related to financial and marketing skills to tenants. Science Park management may provide business advice and training itself. Also, Science Park management may utilise the skills of external training providers. Science Park management can guide and encourage tenants to utilise the local HEI's library service in order to gain access to the latest technical and commercial information. Moreover, Science Park management can act as brokers (and finance providers) advising tenants how to gain access to finance from private and public sector sources. Advice from the Science Park manager (i.e., gate-keeper) can legitimise the activities of inexperienced (academic) entrepreneurs, and can increase and diversify an entrepreneur's commercial, professional and social networks.

Westhead and Batstone (1998) found that Science Park firms in the United Kingdom were significantly more likely than comparable off-Park firms to report the following reasons for selecting their locational context:

- 'prestige and image of the overall site';
- 'provision of on-site management and common services';
- 'access to facilities of HEI/centre of research';
- 'prestige of being linked to the HEI/centre of research';
- 'scope for attracting graduate HEI staff'; and
- 'friendly atmosphere among tenants on site'.

Respondents in off-Park firms were significantly more likely to report 'the firm was already based in the area'.

11.5.4 'Managed' and 'non-managed' Science Parks

Science Parks are not a homogeneous entity. Variation in sponsored environments is, in part, shaped by the goals of the owners of the Science Park, the management structure adopted and the munificence of the local external environmental context associated with the Science Park's location. Utilising an asset complementarity perspective, Wright et al. (2008b) illustrated that the 'type' of Science Park location selected by entrepreneurs is linked to the entrepreneurs' need to acquire or access assets or capabilities they do not possess or control, but which are central to NFF and development. Galbraith et al. (2008) have asserted that the strategy selected by an entrepreneur shapes the type of location selected to pursue a business opportunity.

Entrepreneurs with limited resources may select a 'managed' (i.e., a Park generally with a full-time manager on-site whose principal task is to manage the Science Park) rather than a 'non-managed' (i.e., a Park which does not have a full-time manager on-site) Science Park (Westhead and Batstone, 1999). Firms located on 'managed' Science Parks are not a homogeneous entity. Similarly, a heterogeneous group of firms are located on 'non-managed' parks. Westhead and Batstone (1999) compared the profiles of firms located on 'managed' and 'non-managed' Science Parks in the United Kingdom. They found that firms located on 'managed' Science Parks were generally located in assisted areas for regional assistance; were highly dependent on a small number of customers; and were providing products/services that may be perceived to be risky because they are based on leading-edge knowledge. To overcome resource dependency problems, and to increase their legitimacy in depressed local external environments, entrepreneurs had opted to locate on 'managed' Science Parks.

The latter type of Park provides businesses with low-cost producer services. 'Managed' Parks have gate-keepers that actively expand the social and business networks of their tenants. The latter initiatives increase the status and legitimacy of new and small tenants.

Older and larger technology-based firms generating income from manufactured products, and protecting their established products with patents (rather than investing high proportions of their total sales revenues towards developing new products/services), had selected 'non-managed' Science Parks. More established and resource rich technology-based firms were, therefore, less likely to have sought the gate-keeper roles provided by 'managed' Science Park managers. Firms located on 'non-managed' Science Parks, nevertheless, still generally appreciated that a Science Park provided status, prestige, links with a local HEI, and encouraged the development of diverse social and business networks.

Westhead and Batstone (1999) noted that firms located on 'managed' Science Parks in the United Kingdom had, on average (i.e., mean) used twice as many facilities as firms located on 'non-managed' Parks (i.e., 6.7 facilities compared with 3.3 facilities). Over 41 per cent of valid responding firms, on 'non-managed' Science Parks, reported that they had used conference rooms and the restaurant/cafeteria. No statistically significant differences were detected between firms on 'managed' and 'non-managed' Science Parks with regard to the use of 16 facilities since locating on the Science Park. Over 41 per cent of valid responding firms in the 'managed' Science Park sample had used the following facilities: reception, conference rooms, mail service, building services: maintenance and installations, photocopying services, restaurant/cafeteria, audio-visual equipment, telephone answering/message taking service, and fax/telex service. A larger proportion of firms on 'managed' rather than 'non-managed' Science Parks had used secretarial/word processing services, office cleaning, and finance services.

Respondents on 'managed' Parks suggested that the Science Park manager/director had a markedly high level of involvement with regard to the following roles: 'approachability: how easy is s/he to talk to in person', 'accessibility: how easy is s/he to get to see', 'does s/he run the science park efficiently on the whole', 'how effective has the management been in responding to your property needs', 'how well informed is s/he on subjects of interest to your firm', 'does s/he provide a useful range of services for companies on site', and 'does s/he provide a useful facility to sources of information'. On the downside, Science Park managers/directors on managed Parks were regarded as being much more effective in responding to the property needs of firms than in either providing signposting facilities to sources of information, or in providing a useful route to the HEI services/skills.

Westhead and Batstone (1999) also asked entrepreneurs to report the aspects of the current location that were of importance to the running of their firms. For entrepreneurs located on 'non-managed' and 'managed' Parks, a Science Park location was generally perceived to provide a 'prestige address'. Both groups of respondents suggested the 'possibilities for expansion into additional/adjacent units' was a benefit. Respondents on 'managed' Science Parks were significantly more likely to have valued: 'the unit itself: its facilities and standard of finish', 'access to communal space', and 'access to HEI facilities' than firms located on 'non-managed' Parks. Although of less importance to respondents on 'managed' Parks, entrepreneurs located there were significantly more likely to have valued its: 'communal atmosphere', 'secretarial/business support services', and 'the management/ business service' than respondents located on 'non-managed' Parks. Respondents located on 'non-managed' Science Parks were particularly concerned with reducing their fixed costs. Further, some entrepreneurs suggested their rents were too high.

11.6 Entrepreneurial performance hypothesis

Knowledge spillovers (such as Science Parks) have been associated with enhanced local economic development in several countries (Alcacer and Chung, 2007). An 'entrepreneurial performance hypothesis' linked to the local external environmental context selected by entrepreneurs has been presented. Audretsch and Keilbach (2006: 298) have suggested that:

> The performance of knowledge-based start-ups should be superior when they are able to access knowledge spillovers through geographic proximity to knowledge sources, such as universities, when compared to their counterparts without a close geographic proximity to a knowledge source.

Firms accessing localised knowledge spillovers are assumed to exhibit superior performance. This view has been tentatively empirically supported (Audretsch et al., 2006). With reference to a sample of U.S. based initial public offering (IPO) firms (i.e., unique subgroup of all firms), Gilbert et al. (2008) noted that IPOs founded in locations associated with high levels of industry clustering reported higher product innovation and sales growth than IPOs founded in locations with limited industry clustering. Contrary to expectation, Gilbert et al. (2008: 406) concluded that:

> our findings challenge the notion that technological spillovers contribute to the superior performance of cluster firms and suggest that the literature may give too much emphasis to technological knowledge spillovers at the expense of other factors which may be similarly or even more important.

There is evidence suggesting that firms located in Science Parks report superior levels of firm productivity (Siegel et al., 2003a, b) (see Section 6.2). The performance of firms on Science Parks may, however, be contingent on the nature of the entrepreneur and the firm. Wright et al. (2008b) noted that returnee entrepreneurs in China who had academic knowledge in the form of patents transferred from abroad, enjoyed stronger growth in employment in non-university Science Parks, while those returnees with commercial experience in multinational enterprises (MNEs) abroad performed better in university Science Parks. The wider applicability of the entrepreneurial performance hypothesis, therefore, needs to be explored beyond knowledge-based entrepreneurs, NTBFs, Science Parks and IPOs.

11.7 Emerging and transition economies

The United States and Europe have provided the contexts within which to ground the theoretical foundations of most entrepreneurship studies but:

> researchers should not assume that findings in a developed economy will be equally applicable in an emerging economy (Bruton et al., 2008: 2).

A country's culture and institutional context can shape people's attitudes, access to resources and behaviour with regard to opportunity exploitation (see Case 17, Rad-Amer Intourist: American entrepreneur opportunity recognition and exploitation in Moscow). The emergence of market economies from former centrally planned economies, in particular, such as China, raises opportunities for entrepreneurship in environments where entrepreneurship has previously been difficult, if not illegal. The change in environment to one in which the institutions of a market economy are either undeveloped or are missing introduces the issue of whether entrepreneurship is either destructive (for example, organised crime and corruption), or constructive (Baumol, 1990). The development of market institutions may encourage new entry to entrepreneurship by individuals not previously engaged in it (see Case 18, *The Fleet Sheet*: New firm creation in a transition economy). Further, it may encourage returnee entrepreneurs into entrepreneurship, that is to say, people whose ancestors were entrepreneurs prior to the advent of communism. There may also be the formalisation of previous grey and black market activities. For example, because of chronic shortages in former centrally planned economies, many manufacturing organisations would employ individuals with the connections to obtain the materials they required to enable them to meet production targets.

Entrepreneurship is unlikely to instantly appear fully fledged and it is more likely to emerge with regard to a number of stages. Estrin et al. (2006) show that at the beginning of the transition the heritage from central planning meant that state-owned firms provided the basis for entrepreneurs to develop. Former communist party members typically have the connections to political and economic elites, which enable them to take entrepreneurial actions in the chaotic conditions involving weak legal and institutional frameworks that typify the start of the transition process. Privatisation of enterprises also provides the possibility for incumbent managers to acquire firms on favourable terms that they can then restructure, but the extent to which this occurs can be linked to the form that transition takes (Filatotchev et al., 1999). As greater political and economic stability is established, including the enforcement of property rights, more normal entrepreneurial behaviour can appear (see Case 19, BCH TeleCommunications). A major challenge to the development of entrepreneurship is that often the legislation to enable markets to function may be enacted but poorly enforced. For example, the development of commercial institutions has been greater in the countries of Central Europe than in the countries that constituted the former Soviet Union, with resultant effects on the nature and extent of entrepreneurship in these countries. In the absence of fully functioning markets and institutions (i.e., institutional voids), entrepreneurs may develop substitutes through networks and more informal and personal credit sources.

11.8 Looking forward

Studies are generally positioned within an endogenous/supply-side view of entrepreneurship, and they fail to appreciate that the external environmental context can shape attitudes to enterprise, access to resources, and competition for resources. Numerous studies fail to appreciate that the regulatory regime can promote (or retard) enterprise (Tan, 1996). An overtly optimistic view of the 'power' of the entrepreneur is widespread, and the assumed view is that the entrepreneur has the ability to adapt to any external environmental context. Many studies solely focus on supply-side issues relating to entrepreneur and firm resources, skills, competencies and knowledge. However, people finding it difficult to establish and develop firms suggest deficiencies in the external environment (i.e., market failures relating to premises, information, finance, technology, skilled labour, etc.) retard their ability to fully exploit identified opportunities. Business closure studies detect that entrepreneurs suggest firm closure is due to problems in the external environment (Hall, 1992). This chapter has highlighted that a broader appreciation of the entrepreneurial process can be achieved if studies consider the varying nature of external environmental conditions (i.e., exogenous/demand-side issues). It has also illustrated that external environmental decisions can shape the choices made by entrepreneurs to establish and grow their ventures as well as firm performance.

Future studies need to gather more information on wealth creation and the behaviour of entrepreneurs, and the patterns exhibited by entrepreneurs and their organisations in a variety of industrial, regional, national and cultural settings. Limited research has been conducted exploring the proactive and reactive entrepreneurial behaviour in relation to opportunity identification and exploitation in contrasting external environmental settings. Studies need to explore why particular 'types' of entrepreneurs and organisations are more prevalent in particular environmental settings (i.e., portfolio entrepreneurs and family firms in rural areas) (see Chapters 5 and 7). The profiles and behaviour of entrepreneurs (i.e., academic entrepreneurs compared with private sector entrepreneurs) who select contrasting sponsored environmental settings for enterprise (i.e., state university-sponsored incubators compared with private university-sponsored incubators) deserves more rigorous empirical scrutiny (Siegel et al., 2003a, b; Phan et al., 2005) (see Chapter 6). Additional studies are warranted that explore the selection of appropriate competitive strategies (Galbraith et al., 2008) by different 'types' of entrepreneurs (and organisations) located in hostile and munificent environments (i.e., link between Themes 2, 3 and 5 in Figure 1.1 in Chapter 1). Despite recent progress, the development and testing of an integrative model of the links between entrepreneurship and external environmental conditions is still required (Theme 5). Additional research is warranted surrounding the acquisition and leverage of social capital to circumvent barriers to firm formation and development in developed and developing country contexts by types of traditional commercial enterprise as well as types of social enterprise (see Chapter 10). Entrepreneur behaviour in different 'types' of environment (i.e., university and non-university Science Parks) may illuminate fresh insights that can guide practitioner resource allocation decisions (Wright et al., 2008b). Studies need to recognise that contrasting external environmental conditions exist for entrepreneurship. More studies need to focus on how to channel entrepreneurial talent and vision into more productive (i.e., constructive) activities rather than criminal and destructive activities. Additional studies are warranted that explore whether theories and key findings relating to North America and Europe are applicable to developing country contexts (Robson et al., 2010, 2011). A replication and extension of previous studies in contrasting geographic and cultural context is needed to present robust relationships, and evidence-based research is required that can guide local resource allocation decisions by practitioners. As will be highlighted in Chapter 14, additional studies are still urgently required focusing upon the relationships between the entrepreneur, the organisation, the external environment and organisational performance in terms of financial and non-financial indicators (i.e., links between Themes 2, 3, 4, 5 and 6 in Figure 1.1).

Discussion questions

1   What are the major environmental barriers to new firm creation?

2   Discuss theories that have been advanced to explain the growth in business start-ups and regional variations in new firm formation (NFF) rates.

3   Critically review empirical evidence relating to factors found to be associated with regions reporting high (and low) rates of NFF.

4   Can government intervene to reduce regional variations in NFF rates?

5   Will non-selective policies widen the gap between localities reporting high and low NFF rates?

6   Should policy-makers consider new firm 'quality' as well as 'quantity' at a local level?

7   Why are practitioners seeking to foster clusters of new firms and localised knowledge spillovers?

8   How do owners of Science Parks encourage the formation and development of new technology-based firms (NTBFs)?

9   What industrial location theories have been used by owners of Science Parks to provide supportive environments for NTBFs?

10   Are Science Parks a homogeneous entity? Discuss the profiles of entrepreneurs selecting 'managed' and 'non-managed' Science Parks.

11   What is the 'entrepreneurial performance hypothesis'? Is there any evidence to support the hypothesis?

12   What unique challenges face entrepreneurs in emerging economy environments compared to developed economy contexts?

Recommended further reading

Aernoudt, R. (2004). Incubators: Tool for Entrepreneurship. *Small Business Economics*, 23 (2): 127–135.

Audretsch, D. B., Keilbach, M. and Lehmann, E. (2006). *Entrepreneurship and Economic Growth*. Oxford: Oxford University Press.

Desrochers, P. and Sautet, F. (2008). Entrepreneurial Policy: The Case of Regional Specialization vs Spontaneous Industrial Diversity. *Entrepreneurship Theory and Practice*, 32 (5): 813–832.

Flynn, D. M. (1993). A Critical Exploration of Sponsorship, Infrastructure, and New Organizations. *Small Business Economics*, 5: 129–156.

Reynolds, P., Storey, D. J. and Westhead, P. (1994). Cross-National Comparisons of the Variation in New Firm Formation Rates. *Regional Studies*, 28 (4): 443–456.

Rocha, H. O. and Sternberg, R. (2005). Entrepreneurship: The Role of Clusters. Theoretical Perspectives and Empirical Evidence from Germany. *Small Business Economics*, 24 (3): 267–292.

Chapter 12

Entrepreneurial finance

Contents

Learning objectives

- Discuss the problems in obtaining finance for entrepreneurs and entrepreneurial firms.

- Highlight the different forms of finance available for entrepreneurs and entrepreneurial firms.

- Discuss the operation of venture capital firms in terms of providing insights into the lifecycle of the venture capital process.

- To provide an appreciation of the nature of business plans, which entrepreneurs need to provide in order to particularly attract venture capital finance.

12.1   Introduction

Many entrepreneurial firms that are innovative, growing and seeking to internationalise encounter problems in obtaining sufficient finance. A long debate has surrounded the existence of a possible *market failure* in the provision of finance to entrepreneurial firms. This alleged *market failure* (see Chapter 2) is seen as creating a so-called *finance gap* for new and growing firms, and more specifically a gap relating to the ability of some entrepreneurs and firms to attract *equity finance*. As a result, there have been calls for policy intervention to resolve the problem. Although some new and small firms may be unable to obtain finance, this is not in itself an indication of a market failure. If markets are working efficiently, firms that do not have viable products or markets or are inefficient with no competitive advantage will face difficulties in obtaining finance. However, a market failure may indeed occur if viable businesses are unable to obtain the amounts of finance they need. This may be because of problems arising from an unwillingness by the suppliers of finance to take the risks that would be involved, or it may be the result of the challenges financiers face in obtaining the information about a firm, which they need in order to be able to make an informed investment decision.

In this chapter, we examine the challenges to entrepreneurs in obtaining finance for their firms. Most entrepreneurs seeking to obtain finance for their ventures will need to prepare a business plan. Below we discuss the role and content of a business plan. We then outline the different sources of finance that can be used by entrepreneurs. This is followed by a discussion of the take-up and utilisation of informal business angel finance, and formal finance provided by venture capital (VC) firms. A brief review of several government initiatives to address financing gaps for new, smaller and growing firms is then presented. Finally, financing issues facing entrepreneurial firms are highlighted.

12.2   Business plans

The *business plan* is a key document for attracting the initial attention of a financier such as a bank, local enterprise development agency, business angel, or a VC backer. VC firms, for example, generally fund a very small percentage of the large number of business plans they receive each month. Consequently, the business plan must clearly highlight that the entrepreneur seeking finance has a credible investment opportunity, which offers the potential for a significant return on investment. The business plan should cover the following issues: all major activities of the business, financial projections, a detailed and coherent strategy for achieving projected performance, details of the funding which is sought, and the expected timing and nature of returns for the investor (Table 12.1). The entrepreneur may need to leverage professional and independent advice, which can be used to shape the plan as well as support the projections stated in the plan. This external validity can be used to sell the entrepreneurs investment proposition to a VC firm. However, the VC firm will want to see the entrepreneur's (or entrepreneurial ownership team's) ideas and expertise clearly reflected in the business plan, and not those of someone else. The major areas of weaknesses in business plans relating to NTBFs have been found to relate to marketing and the management team, followed by financial aspects.

There is some debate about the usefulness of business plans, especially for early stage businesses where the product may still not be well-defined, and the market is yet to be determined. Honig and Karlsson (2010) noted that new ventures in Sweden are subject to institutional pressure to produce written business plans. Notably, they are expected to plan, they are encouraged to imitate other successful organisations, or they are told to plan. Honig and Karlsson failed to find a link between business plan writing and superior new venture survival or profitability. Burke et al. (2010) have asserted that the impact of business plans depends on the purpose for and circumstances in which they are being used. They noted that firms in England that had written business plans reported superior employment growth.

Table 12.1 Elements of a business plan

Section	Key features
Executive summary	Short summary of the purpose and key aspects of the plan, including the funding sought to achieve them (i.e., milestones)
The business	Brief business history, progress and organisation which is relevant to future development
Management and employees	Details of the management team's past experience and future role; gaps in management that need to be filled; employee numbers and skills mix
Products/services	Description of products or services; distinctive competence of products/services in the market; state of technology involved; range of products/services (current and future)
The market and competition	Size and expected market growth; domestic and international mix; market segments; current and expected customers
Marketing	Current and expected approaches to marketing and pricing
Operations and production strategy	Existing production facilities and future developments; suppliers
Investment proposal	Amount of funding sought; expected ownership stakes, valuations and returns; timing and nature of realisation of future gains for investors
Financial information	Up to three years' historic financial information and up to three years' detailed financial projections, including cashflow statements; banking arrangements; state of order book; sensitivity analyses and assumptions underlying them; nature of financial control systems
Risks and milestones	Main areas of risk and milestones and how they will be addressed
Appendices	Details of management curricula vitae, patents, etc. as appropriate

One potential problem with business plans is that they are static documents, which may be severely undermined when the assumptions on which they are based come into contact with the reality of the market-place. Therefore, it may be important for an entrepreneur to develop a *business model*. The more dynamic approach should describe how the business would create, deliver and capture value. Further, the business model should illustrate how each part of the business fits together to produce the product/service, how supplies will be accessed, how the product/service will be distributed to customers, and how revenues will flow into the business over time (see Entrepreneurship in action 12.1 for a comparison between business plans and business models).

Entrepreneurship in action 12.1
Business plans versus business models

I was catching up with an ex-graduate student at Café Borrone, my favorite coffee place in Menlo Park. This was the second of three 'office hours' I was holding that morning for ex-students. He and his co-founder were both PhD's in applied math who believe they can make some serious inroads on next generation search. Over coffee he said, 'I need some cheering up. I think my startup is going to fail even before I get funded.' Now he had my attention. I thought his technology was potentially a killer app. I put down my coffee and listened. He said, 'After we graduated we took our great idea, holed up in my apartment and spent months researching and writing a business plan. We even entered it in the business plan competition. When we were done we followed your advice and got out of the building and started talking to potential users and customers.' 'Ok', I said 'what's the problem?' He replied, 'Well the customers are not acting like we predicted in our plan! There must be something really wrong with our business. We thought we'd take our plan and go raise seed money. We can't raise money knowing our plan is wrong.' . . . These guys had spent 4 months writing a 60-page plan with 12 pages of spreadsheets. They collected information that justified their assumptions about the problem, opportunity, market size, their solution and competitors and their team. They rolled up a 5-year sales forecast with assumptions about their revenue model, pricing, sales, marketing, customer acquisition cost, etc. Then they had a 5-year P&L [profit and loss] statement, balance sheet, cash flow and cap table. It was an exquisitely crafted plan. Finally, they took the plan and boiled it down to 15 of the prettiest slides you ever saw. The problem was that two weeks after they got out of the building talking to potential customers and users, they realized that at least ½ of their key assumptions in their wonderfully well crafted plan were wrong . . .

As I listened, I thought about the other startup I had met an hour earlier. They also had been hard at work for the last 3½ months. But they spent their time differently. Instead of writing a full-fledged business plan, they had focused on building and testing a business model . . . This team had spent their first two weeks laying out their hypotheses about sales, marketing, pricing, solution, competitors, etc. and put in their first-pass financial assumptions. It took just five PowerPoint slides to capture their assumptions and top line financials. This team didn't spend a lot of time justifying their assumptions because they knew facts would change their assumptions. Instead of writing a formal business plan they took their business model and got out of the building to gather feedback on their critical hypotheses (revenue model, pricing, sales, marketing, customer acquisition cost, etc.). They even mocked up their application and tested landing pages, keywords, customer acquisition cost and other critical assumptions. After three months they felt they had enough preliminary customer and user data to go back and write a PowerPoint presentation that summarized their findings. This team had wanted to have coffee to chat about which of the four seed round offers they had received they should accept.

Source: Steve Blank, No Plan Survives First Contact With Customers – Business Plans versus Business Models, 8 April 2010, available at http://steveblank.com/2010/04/08/no-plan-survives-first-contact-with-customers-%E2%80%93-business-plans-versus-business-models/.

12.3   Sources of finance

The main sources of finance available to entrepreneurial firms are summarised in Table 12.2. Certain sources of finance may only be available as the firm develops (Figure 12.1).

12.3.1   Equity finance

Finance for entrepreneurial firms may be provided in the form of straightforward ordinary and preference *shares*. Ordinary shares generally do not involve a commitment to pay a dividend and hence hold attractions for early stage ventures, which are typically 'burning' cash to develop the product and to establish operations. Preference shares will have higher ranking rights in the event of a winding up of the company than ordinary shares, and will normally have rights to a fixed and cumulative dividend.

Entrepreneurs may be able to provide some start-up capital. At this early stage, entrepreneurs often rely on obtaining contributions from contacts in their social network, relating to

Table 12.2 Types of finance

Short term	Long term
Overdraft	Initial equity
Short-term loans	Retained profits
Trade credit	Long-term loans
Hire purchase	External equity
Leasing	Business angel funding
Factoring	Venture capital
Invoice discounting	
Credit cards (business and/or personal)	

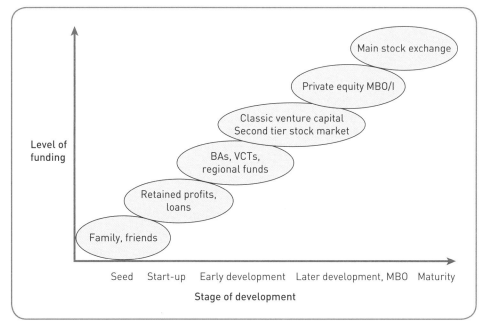

Figure 12.1 Finance over lifecyle stages

the so-called *3Fs of 'family, fools and friends'* (see Case 20, UFO Pictures: The challenges of film production). In return, these providers of finance may take an equity stake in the venture, which provides for long-term involvement, and avoids the need to pay out much-needed cash on dividends or interest payments. Beyond this source of finance, entrepreneurs may approach business angels and formal VC firms for larger amounts of finance. Business angel finance is discussed in Section 12.5, whilst formal VC is discussed in Section 12.6.

Raising *equity finance* through a stock market flotation (or initial public offering (IPO)) is unlikely to be feasible for entrepreneurs seeking small amounts of finance. Entrepreneurs seeking to raise equity finance will need to have a track record of profitable trading, or demonstrate that the business, even if not revenue generating, has very significant growth prospects.

All forms of equity finance require current firm owners to give up part of the ownership and control of the firm, which many entrepreneurs are averse to doing because they see the firm 'as their baby'. This reluctance to sell equity to 'outsiders' can impose a major constraint on firm growth unless the entrepreneur can obtain debt finance.

12.3.2   Debt

Most smaller firms tend to rely on *bank debt* rather than venture capital as their major source of external finance (Keasey and Watson, 1992; Scherr et al., 1993). Often this debt is in the form of short-term loans and overdrafts. Evidence indicates a limited role for debt finance in many high-technology entrepreneurial firms such as spin-off firms from universities (Roberts, 1991). The use of debt in entrepreneurial firms depends on the taxable income expectations the investment has, or will shortly have, as well as the collateralisable assets. These conditions are more likely to arise where the venture has products that have become established, which for innovative high-technology ventures may take many years. Debt may be secured with regard to a fixed charge over a firm's property and/or a floating charge over a firm's movable assets and general undertaking. The amount of debt advanced may be linked to a multiple of the business's earnings before interest and tax, or to its free cashflow.

At its simplest, the servicing of a *secured loan* may involve payments, which include both interest and capital repayment. However, where there is a need to restructure the business it may be preferable to delay repayment in order to retain cash inside the firm. In such cases, types of debt may be used which have either a one- or two-year repayment holiday, and/or instruments that are only repayable in one payment when the firm is sold or floated at a predetermined date.

Typically, *various accounting and non-accounting covenants* will be put in place by debt providers. Accounting covenants typically relate to the need to keep within certain predefined levels of key accounting ratios such as interest coverage (Citron et al., 1997). The triggering of these covenants is designed to provide an early warning of problems.

Convertible loan stock may be used in entrepreneurial finance as an alternative to redeemable preference shares. Options are typically linked to the convertible loan stock, enabling all or part of the loan to be converted into equity in the future, at a price decided at the time of the investment.

12.3.3   Other forms of finance

If an entrepreneurial firm is being acquired either from a family or an existing corporation, the vendor (i.e., seller) may provide an element of finance to ensure that the transaction can be completed. This form of finance can be useful in bridging the gap between the price the vendor seeks and the finance that can be raised from the management, VC firms and/or banks. It may be difficult to place a robust valuation on a firm, for example in uncertain market conditions, or where a division of a larger corporation has not previously traded as an independent profit centre. Vendor finance can take the form of a deferred payment, which may be either fixed or variable according to future firm performance (i.e., an 'earn-out'). Alternatively, an equity stake may be retained with the vendor benefiting from a share of the gains when the management buyout (see Chapter 9) is subsequently sold. A third possibility is for vendor finance to take the form of a loan on favourable terms.

Once a business has become established and is generating revenue from products, retained profits provide a major source of finance for future firm growth. Property sale and lease-back, where the firm has sufficient assets and where conflicts with the security required by debt providers can be avoided, is a further source of finance for more established ventures. Plant leasing and hire purchase can be used in respect of specific assets. Factoring and invoice discounting can be an effective means of accessing working capital. Security provided by the fixed or current asset, respectively, mitigates problems in risk assessment of innovative and growing firms.

Many entrepreneurial firms rely on trade credit provided by suppliers. This can be an expensive form of finance if the firm foregoes early payment discounts. Further, paying late can put a strain on relationships with suppliers. This is because suppliers are in effect financing their customers' operations and chasing outstanding debt is time-consuming and expensive. The uncertainty inherent in late payment makes it difficult for the firm extending trade credit to plan their cashflows to ensure business survival and development. Government financial assistance schemes also provide access to funds, and they are briefly discussed in Section 12.7.

12.4 The entrepreneur's choice between different forms of finance

The entrepreneur's need for finance can be analysed using the *pecking order hypothesis* (Watson and Wilson, 2002). This hypothesis assumes that internal funding is preferred over external sources of finance. If an entrepreneur is confronted by insufficient internal funds, bank debt is generally a preferred source of finance because it does not lead to the selling of the firm's equity to 'outsiders' (i.e., ownership dilution). Entrepreneurs that do not provide complete information about themselves, the business, and their competitors may find it difficult to secure debt finance. *Information asymmetries* (i.e., one party has more information about the likelihood of the businesses success than the other) between entrepreneurs and the bank may have negative consequences for the provision of bank finance, which may result in *credit rationing* to particular types of entrepreneurs and firms (i.e., one firm may be given finance whilst another firm is not provided with finance) (Stiglitz and Weiss, 1981). Evidence from the United Kingdom (Cressy, 1996) indicates that the constraint may not be as severe as generally accepted. Nevertheless, many banks seek to reduce their exposure to *moral hazard* (i.e., if the bank is taking the risk, less care may be taken by the entrepreneur with regard to risky projects). Today, many bank lending decisions are based on evaluations of an entrepreneur's human capital (i.e., experience, knowledge and track-record), and the amount of their own collateral (i.e., personal assets of the entrepreneur (i.e., house, car, jewellery, antiques, etc.) they are seeking to invest in the venture. This information can be used to ameliorate the negative impact of information asymmetries.

The pecking order hypothesis suggests that innovative NTBFs facing severe financing constraints (Westhead and Storey, 1997) will look for different forms of internal financing complemented with debt financing before they seek finance from VC firms. From a policy perspective, this hypothesis indicates that in order to stimulate NTBFs, initiatives need to be introduced to make internal and debt financing easier, as well as mechanisms that encourage entrepreneurs to adopt business practices that encourage VC firms to support ventures with significant growth potential. With regard to the context of spin-off firms from universities (Chapter 6), evidence suggests that in contrast to the pecking order theory, technology transfer officers (TTOs) see VC finance as being more important than internal finance with regard to the early stages of development of these firms (Wright et al., 2006).

Business angels and formal VC firms are two of the most important sources of finance for entrepreneurial firms, as opposed to smaller firms in general. Their activities are discussed in detail in the next two sections.

12.5 Business angels

Business angels are individual private equity (PE) investors, or clubs of 'baby venture capital funds' who invest their own funds. For entrepreneurs, business angels can be difficult to identify unless they are a member of a *network*. A number of networks have been developed in recent years to address this problem. These networks vary considerably in their format, and with respect to the degree of screening of entrepreneurs and angels that they provide. Some networks are sponsored by government agencies, while others are privately organised. Networks can involve circulation of newsletters with details of entrepreneurs seeking funding, online networks and conferences where entrepreneurs have opportunities to pitch their proposals to groups of angels.

There is some debate about the nature of business angel investors, which seems to be, at least in part, influenced by whether studies have focused upon angels who are part of publicly supported networks, or private networks. The former appear to have smaller amounts available to invest than the latter. Studies from different countries suggest that business angels in Japan are, on average, considerably older than their counterparts elsewhere. Business angels are quite heterogeneous in terms of their background, their motives for investment, and the returns they seek (Mason and Harrison, 1994; Stevenson and Coveney, 1994). Business angels may be entrepreneurs who have sold their businesses and are looking to invest some of their gains, but do not want to run a business full time, while others may still own a portfolio of businesses. Some angels are successful corporate managers or professionals (i.e., accountants, lawyers, dentists, doctors, etc.) with considerable wealth to invest directly in riskier entrepreneurial ventures. Also, some angels may wish to invest without being involved in the running of the business, while many others may want to seek an active role in the ventures in which they invest. Further, some angels are looking for capital gain on their investment, others seek an income stream, while others claim they invest for 'fun' and they are not too concerned about the monetary returns.

A business angel's own networks, primarily business associates and friends, can be used to identify attractive firms (i.e., *deals*) that are seeking external finance and are prepared to sell equity to 'outsiders' (Mason and Harrison, 1994). Accountants and other finance professionals provide a secondary tier source of potential business deal referrals. Organised networks that attempt to bring angels and entrepreneurs together tend to provide relatively few deal opportunities, especially in terms of those that would make attractive investments. This low level of attractiveness of opportunities from this source may be because these networks are attracting entrepreneurs that have failed to find finance from other sources.

The issues shaping the investments decisions of business angels are not strictly the same as those reported by formal VC firms (Fiet, 1995). Business angels are less concerned about the market risk because they tend to invest in known sectors. Formal VC firms are more concerned with market risk because they typically have less knowledge about a market sector than the entrepreneur. However, some financiers such as VC firms focusing upon particular industrial sectors may have more accurate information about the risks and possibility of success because they have broader knowledge of industries, markets and other firms (de Meza and Webb, 1987). Business angels are more concerned about agency risk, that is with problems relating to the entrepreneur not acting in the angel's interests, and thus tend to seek to limit investments to entrepreneurs they know. Formal VC firms are less concerned about agency risk because they can protect themselves through contractual devices (see Section 12.6.6). Business angel investments may not be appropriate in the case of university-based intellectual property (IP) (Mason and Harrison, 2004). Most angels appear to lack the requisite experience in high level science and engineering research and development to make a confident assessment of commercial potential.

Some business angels are serial investors because they make more than one investment. A study of active business angels in the United Kingdom estimated that 65 per cent were serial investors, and they had made, on average, 7.3 investments (Van Osnabrugge, 1998). Serial angel investors often use their experience to try to reduce market risk, in part due to a negative previous investment experience in an unknown sector (Kelly and Hay, 1996).

Business angels' involvement with their investments is quite varied, ranging from helping to develop strategies, acting as a sounding board for the entrepreneur's ideas, monitoring performance, finding customers and further sources of finance, helping to develop marketing plans and new opportunities, and dealing with crises. Entrepreneurs report that they find the most useful aspects of business angel involvement to be acting as a *sounding board* (Mason and Harrison, 1994).

Business angels may be more appropriate for smaller investments and investments that, while viable, have lower internal rates of return than those that would be of interest to formal VC firms. Business angels have lower transaction costs relating to investment selection and monitoring than formal VC firms. Further, business angels are less constrained than formal VC firms with respect to the timescale over which they need to make returns for their investments. Studies suggest that business angels have fewer investments on which they lose their money compared to early stage VC firms. However, business angels report fewer investments that earn high returns (Mason and Harrison, 2002). Serial business angels do appear to earn higher returns than one-time investors (Van Osnabrugge, 1998).

12.6 Venture capital

12.6.1 Context

Venture capital involves the provision of equity (i.e., risk) type finance to entrepreneurial firms (see Wright et al., 2003 for a collection of articles covering the main lifecycle stages of venture capital). In contrast to interest payments on bank loans, the return provided by

Entrepreneurship in action 12.2
Lloyds Development Capital Fund

As part of a wider UK strategy to further improve SMEs' access to growth capital, LDC has committed £100 m over the next three years to back businesses requiring £10 m of equity funding or less. Ian Podmore, investment director for LDC, said the fund is designed to help unlock the potential of quality businesses and ambitious management teams. He said: 'Since its inception almost 30 years ago, LDC from its regional base has supported hundreds of

small and mid-sized companies, providing equity investment to assist their growth aspirations. Providing access to the necessary funding and expertise to help businesses achieve their potential is a key mandate for LDC.' In 2007 LDC completed the £67 m buyout of Tredegar-based Penn Pharmaceutical Services.

Source: S. Barry, *The Western Mail*, 7 May 2010.

entrepreneurial firms to the VC firm is in the form of a dividend, and principally a capital gain on the realisation of the investment (i.e., the sale of the entrepreneurial firm). Independent and semi-independent VC firms typically raise a limited life fund (usually with a ten-year life) to invest in a specific type of project (see Entrepreneurship in action 12.2 relating to the Lloyds Development Capital Fund).

12.6.2   Sourcing deals

VC firms need to obtain access to viable projects that can be funded at entry prices, which will generate target rates of return. *Deal generation* is closely linked to the VC firm's *preferences* with respect to investment stages and deal size, as well as to the availability of information. Competitive pressure on VC firms has led them to become proactive in identifying potential investment candidates, rather than reacting to business plans mailed or brought to them.

When an investment is being considered, VC firms are faced with a potential adverse selection problem (i.e., high risk firms are more willing to sell equity in their firms to 'outsider' VC firms, whilst low risk firms may not be willing to sell a high proportion of equity to 'outsiders'). These problems arise because there may be difficulties in verifying the entrepreneur's performance in the enterprise prior to deal completion. To reduce this problem, VC firms screen all potential investments.

12.6.3   Screening

The nature of the screening problem may vary with the stage and sector of an investment. The problems of obtaining access to full information may be highly problematical in complex high-technology/bio-technology NTBFs. This is because the nature of the product and the market may be more difficult to establish. In development capital situations, it may be difficult to judge whether the entrepreneur's previous performance will continue in the future where their equity stake is diluted by the introduction of venture capital. With regard to a management buyout context, VC firms may be guided by incumbent management's experience in post, and their knowledge of the business. Incumbent management seeking to obtain the most favourable terms may, however, have an incentive not to reveal full information to a VC firm. With regard to a management buyin context, the potential new owners are not members of the firm's existing management teams, and there may be problems identifying and assessing their true skills and knowledge.

The most important criteria used by VC firms in screening investment proposals relate to the entrepreneur's personality and experience, with less emphasis placed on the investee firm's market, product and strategy. Trade-offs are made between various criteria during the screening of investments (Muzyka et al., 1996). VC firms may prefer to select an opportunity, which offers a good management team and reasonable financial and product market characteristics, even if the opportunity does not meet the overall fund and deal requirements of the VC firm.

Many deal plans are rejected because they do not fit the VC firm's investment focus, or because they have shortcomings on one or more of the criteria applied in the process. Studies suggest that VC firms invest, on average, in only two to three per cent of the business plans received, and of these less than only ten per cent of supported deals are highly successful for the VC firm.

Murray and Lott (1995) concluded that VC firms in the early 1990s in the United Kingdom preferred not to invest in NTBFs. By the end of the 1990s, this reluctance to support NTBFs was less prevalent (Lockett et al., 2002). VC firms became more flexible but technology was still viewed as a more important risk factor than stage of investment. Entrepreneurial firms, particularly NTBFs, need to be in a pre-prepared state (or 'investor ready'), which enables VC firms to evaluate them more easily (Zacharakis et al., 1999).

12.6.4 The entrepreneur's selection of venture capital firm

Entrepreneurs need to screen potential VC investors. The ten most important characteristics of VC firms considered by entrepreneurs, in order of descending importance, are the equity stake offered, personal chemistry, speed of decision, the price of the deal, commercial awareness, capital contribution, decisiveness, professionalism, whether voting control is sought, and reputation. Personal chemistry appears to be more important for entrepreneurs than is the case for VC firms.

12.6.5 Valuation

12.6.5.1 *Context*

VC firms place considerable emphasis on the specific attributes of a potential investee company when assessing its value, and the rate of return to be expected from it. While *accounting information* is an important element in deal screening and in arriving at a *valuation* and a *target rate of return*, VC firms place most emphasis on a very detailed scrutiny of all aspects of a business, typically including *sensitivity analysis* of financial information, discussions with personnel, and accessing more unpublished and subjective information (Wright and Robbie, 1996). Later stage investors are more likely to be interested in the market acceptance of a product, whilst early stage investors focus upon a range of product strength and market growth characteristics. This is because early stage transactions are technology based with little available data on market acceptance.

12.6.5.2 *Valuation methods*

Discounted cash flow (DCF) methods of valuation, while theoretically correct, pose particular problems in a VC investment context (Wright and Robbie, 1996). With regard to the

DCF approach, it is difficult to forecast future cashflows in the typically highly uncertain environment of a start-up. Complications may arise in valuing early stage investments that may require several rounds of finance.

In practice, venture capital projects are typically valued by applying one or more valuation techniques to the financial and accounting information relating to the potential investee typically contained in the business plan submitted by management to the VC firm (Manigart et al., 1997). Forward-looking information in the business plan may be subject to *sensitivity analysis* both by management and their advisers, and by the VC firm according to the expected influence on future performance of other information. Indeed, the VC firm's own *due diligence* report is the most important source of information in preparing a valuation.

VC firms typically place greatest emphasis on one particular valuation method but use others as checks. Most importance appears to be attached to *price earnings multiples based valuation methods*, particularly among later stage investors. VC firms also make frequent use of recent transactions prices in the same sector as a benchmark valuation. In comparison, moderate use is made of DCF techniques.

12.6.5.3 *Target returns*

VC firms generally measure their target returns in terms of an *internal rate of return* (IRR) on their investment. In general, the IRR that is sought increases with the riskiness of an investment. Hence, as the stage of investment moves from later (development) stage, to buyout to buyin and finally to early stage, the required rates of return become progressively higher.

Target rates of return vary across countries. Manigart et al. (1997, 2002) found higher required rates of return by VC firms located in the United States and United Kingdom compared with those located in France, Belgium and the Netherlands. In part, variations are due to differences in institutional, legal and cultural context. They suggested that more developed capital markets, such as the United States and the United Kingdom, required more frequent valuation of investee firms. Consistent with the resource-based view (RBV) of the firm (Chapter 3), Manigart et al. (2002) noted that specialist VC firms focusing on early stage deals requested higher rates than those focusing on deals with later stage firms. Deals relating to technology-based firms are viewed to be riskier than deals relating to later stage projects. VC firms generally use a higher target rate of return to assess technology-based deals. It is the stage to which the technology has been developed that is important in determining how risky the venture is likely to be, and hence the return that is sought by investors (Lockett et al., 2002). VC firms may set standard benchmark rates of return that individual proposals have to meet, which are sufficient to reflect the overall returns expected by investors in VC funds. In practice, many VC firms adopt a more flexible approach. They base target returns on the particular circumstances of each deal, or on the risk band of a particular investment. Also important are general economic conditions, the industrial or product sector of the investment, and the expected gearing ratio when the finance is structured. Changes in returns on quoted equities and gilts and changes in interest base rates are relatively unimportant. The rate of return sought is unlikely to vary according to whether or not the VC firm owns the majority of the equity in the investee firm.

12.6.6 Due diligence

VC firms do not take the entrepreneur's business plan at face value. Once they have decided that the proposal is potentially interesting, VC firms subject the proposal to detailed scrutiny, or *due diligence.* Due diligence is an essential part of the VC investment process designed to reduce various *adverse selection* problems arising from *asymmetric information* between the entrepreneur and the investor. Firms seeking smaller investments can be put off by the costs relating to conducting due diligence (Harvey and Lusch, 1995).

Commercial due diligence is aimed at establishing the reliability of the information contained in the business plan, assessing whether the project will achieve the kind of *returns* that the VC firm is seeking, and assessing the *downside risks* if targets are not met. This due diligence will focus on the following four main areas of the business: the entrepreneur, products and/or services, markets, and operations. Various sources of information are used in this process. The most important source is the VC firm's own market evaluation, with considerable reliance also being placed on personal references. Independent market reports are generally less important, partly because of time constraints, though they may be useful in specialist sectors. Due diligence will focus on factors both 'hard' (i.e., objective factors, such as management's qualifications, details of the customer base, age, and state of equipment) and 'soft' (i.e., subjective factors, such as the chemistry between the VC firm and the entrepreneur, customers' perceptions of the product, etc.). The VC firm will interview the entrepreneur, visit the premises, and talk to previous employers, customers and suppliers in order to obtain the detailed information that is required.

Accounting and financial due diligence will be undertaken to obtain a view on the reliability of these aspects of the business plan. The analysis focuses on an examination of the following key elements of financial information contained in the business plan: cashflow forecasts, historic and forecast profit and loss accounts, and balance sheets. In addition, analysis will include verification of the state and adequacy of financial control systems, which may be especially rudimentary in new firms (see Case 21, New Covent Garden Soup Company: Contributions made by venture capitalists). Tax, insurance and other actual or contingent liabilities are checked. The analysis is conducted in order to check the realism of assumptions about the market, sales and pricing, and their consistency with findings from commercial due diligence. This analysis helps establish the consistency of forecasts with both historical performance and the VC firm's own perceptions based on the commercial due diligence. Examination of current management accounts and variances, where they exist, may provide an indicator of the reliability of short-term forecasts. The realism of costs and expected gross margin percentages can be verified as well as the timing of improvements in performance. For early stage investments in particular, the length and expense of developing commercial production are frequently underestimated in business plans. Such timing issues are critical to a decision to invest or not, to whether financing needs to be staged, to the expected timing of the VC firm's returns, and to the nature of the financing structure. Although a business plan may contain sensitivity analyses, its realism needs to be checked both in terms of the extent of worst and best case scenarios, and crucially, the effects of timing differences in expected cashflows of any sensitivity analyses contained in the business plan.

The combination of commercial and financial due diligence will enable the consistency of the business plan with existing facilities, systems and management to be established. A critical issue concerns the verification of the *state of the order book,* and the validity of contracts. Entrepreneurs may claim that they have a certain level of orders but not all of these may be certain. In small, new, private companies with limited control systems, establishing the state of the order book may be especially difficult (Robbie and Wright, 1995). VC firms will use both their own due diligence as well as an accountant's *'Long Form Report'*, which includes the following: a full background report on the company, a review of the management accounts since the last audit, and a separate opinion on the compilation of the forecasts contained in the business plan.

Legal due diligence is carried out to check legal ownership of shares and other assets such as property, IP rights, etc. Checking ownership of IP rights may be especially important in NTBFs involving a number of patents (see the cases of spin-off firms in Chapters 6 and 8). Legal due diligence also focuses on identifying potential exposure to liabilities and problems relating to such issues as disputes with customers and suppliers, claims and contingent liabilities, regulatory authorities (i.e., environmental, health and safety), etc. These areas are likely to be the basis for *management warranties*.

The level of due diligence that is carried out will be influenced by time restrictions relating to when a deal has to be completed, cost constraints, and situational factors. The cost of due diligence in relation to the transaction value may be prohibitive. This is one of the reasons why VC firms aim to invest in a smaller rather than a larger number of portfolio companies.

Due diligence may be a particular problem in the management buyout segment of the VC market where corporations are seeking to dispose of subsidiaries in a controlled auction. Auction procedures may not allow sufficient time for VC firms to carry out their normal due diligence. Detailed due diligence, including direct access to incumbent management and to an 'information room' prepared by the vendor, may only be possible after a VC firm's initial bid has been accepted.

12.6.7   Financial structure

VC firms use various *contractual and relational mechanisms* to encourage entrepreneurs to perform and to reveal accurate information (Kaplan and Strömberg, 2003). An important feature of many VC firm investments, especially early stage ones, is the *staging of financing* over several rounds. Under these arrangements, entrepreneurs would typically be set *target milestones for the development of the business*, which they have to meet before a further round of finance would be provided. The staging of financing introduces a number of important issues that need to be addressed. In particular there is a need, first, to identify mechanisms for agreeing whether milestones have been achieved. Secondly, if a further VC investor is to be introduced in subsequent financing rounds, there is a need to ensure that a valuation is agreed. This should provide the original investors with a fair return on their investment, whilst at the same time it does not disadvantage the incoming investor, who may be less experienced and who does not have the benefits of having been associated with the investment from the beginning. Other mechanisms include convertible *financial instruments* (i.e., *'equity ratchets'*), which may give financiers control under certain conditions. For example, the entrepreneur's remuneration linked to value created, mechanisms to put pressure on entrepreneurs to distribute capital and profits, and powers written into *Articles of Association* which require approval for certain actions to be sought from the investor(s).

These conditions may be incorporated in specific types of shares such as *Convertible Redeemable Participating Preferred Ordinary Shares* (CRPPOs). The conditions attached to these shares enable the VC firm to obtain a regular dividend, a share in capital gains, and to increase (or decrease) management's equity stake. The holder has a prior right to a fixed, and usually cumulative dividend, as well as a participating dividend in remaining profits above a certain level. The shares may be converted into ordinary shares, or redeemed according to predetermined criteria. Their redemption, in part or in whole, may be a means by which an equity ratchet increases the management's equity stake.

The VC firm and the entrepreneur may fail to agree on the timing of the investee firms ability to be profitable. Such differences may arise because of differing views of an uncertain situation. This problem can be addressed through the use of *equity ratchets* in the financing structure, which provide entrepreneurs with an incentive to perform. The equity ratchet may be triggered if specific performance targets (e.g., cumulative profits over a particular period, market capitalisation on exit within a specified time period, redemption of financing instruments, etc.) are met. Management's equity may increase in discrete jumps, so-called *'cliff-edge' ratchets*, as firm performance increases, or along a continuum. Equity ratchets may pose major problems in terms of specifying the contract concerning the definition of financial performance to be used, manipulation of information by managers, and the timing of the crystallisation of the ratchet. One means of minimising these problems is for ratchets to be structured along a defined continuum rather than being 'cliff-edge'.

VC firms may also make use of debt finance in structuring their investments, especially in later stage development capital and management buyouts where firms are likely to be generating cashflow. Various types of bank finance were summarised in Section 12.3. With regard to larger amounts of debt being requested by an entrepreneur, more than one type of *senior debt* may be provided to reflect different layers of risk. In such cases, the 'A' layer loan may typically have a seven-year life, while the 'B' and if applicable 'C' layer loans generally have longer maturity and nominal amortisation prior to repayment of the 'A' loan. Higher interest rates are associated with 'B' or 'C' senior debt.

As an alternative, or in some cases a supplement to secured bank debt, *mezzanine debt* may be used. This is finance with a level of risk intermediate between senior debt and equity with a commensurate intermediate return and risk. Mezzanine debt may be used where there are too few assets to enable sufficient secured debt to be provided, and/or where the amount of equity that would have to be used to replace debt means that the returns to equity providers would be diluted to unacceptable levels. The strength of cashflow is key to the provision of mezzanine debt. Cashflow will be needed to meet debt servicing costs. Mezzanine debt is unlikely to be entirely unsecured but may involve a secondary charge on assets. Moreover, mezzanine debt can take various forms, ranging from simply a layer of finance with a higher rate of interest than senior debt, through to a combination of a higher rate of return and an *'equity-kicker'*.

A further type of finance relates to payment-in-kind instruments (either debt or equity), which do not receive interest or dividend in the form of cash. The holder, however, obtains a return by being able to convert them into another financial instrument.

12.6.8   Entrepreneur's equity

The percentage equity stake held by the entrepreneur (or the entrepreneurial ownership team) in a VC investment varies according to the nature of a particular transaction. With regard to early stage investments, the entrepreneur is likely to have a controlling equity stake. A key part of negotiating and structuring the finance in these cases revolves around how much equity the entrepreneur is willing to cede to the VC firm, and how much the VC firm needs in order to meet its target rates of return. In these cases, an equity ratchet mechanism may be used (see Case 21, New Covent Garden Soup Company: Contributions made by venture capitalists).

With regard to management buyouts, management typically hold little if any of the equity in the firm prior to the buyout transaction. The amount of equity management are able to acquire will depend on their personal resources, the nature of the transaction, and their negotiating power. With regard to larger management buyouts, the management team's personal financial resources will generally enable them to contribute a smaller proportion of the total purchase price. Consequently, management generally obtains a small share of the equity in the purchased firm. With reference to small management buyouts (i.e., a transaction value of less than £10 m) management teams, on average, have to contribute about one eighth of the purchase price. Management generally obtains, on average, 60 per cent of the equity in the purchased firm. However, with regard to relatively large deals (i.e., a transaction value above £10 m) management teams, on average, have to contribute about 3 per cent of the purchase price for an average equity stake of about 30 per cent (CMBOR, 2009). There are wide variations around these averages. Within management buyout teams, there can be diversity of equity holdings according to seniority and individual wealth. There is a need for management to agree an acceptable degree of dispersion of their equity holdings.

12.6.9 Monitoring investee companies

The *involvement of VC firms in their investments* has often been portrayed as a choice between a *hands-on or a hands-off role*. In the former, the VC firms take a close and active involvement in the direction of the investee firm. In the latter, the VC firm takes a more passive role. However, this is something of an oversimplification, as all VC firms will want some form of *monitoring activity*.

The level of involvement in VC investments relates to the nature of the operating business, as well as to the choice by the VC firm with regard to the general style it seeks to adopt. By their nature, early stage and high-technology investments call for more specialist skills. VC firms may become closely involved in developing strategies and control systems in investee firms with incomplete management teams and entrepreneurs. At a later stage, VC firms may become involved in identifying potential acquisition targets, and guide the entrepreneur through the acquisition process.

VC firms may, in general, have a less hands-on relationship in investments that are more developed and presumably less risky. Management buyouts, where the business is typically well-established with a strong market position, for example, may require less VC firm involvement. Management buyins, in contrast, often require significant restructuring with there being a need for greater involvement by VC firms. VC firms may intensify their monitoring activities as the need dictates, becoming more involved if a deal is not developing according to budget, or more drastically requires turnaround actions such as firing the entrepreneur (Lerner, 1995).

In order to carry out their monitoring role, VC firms typically require accounting information flows on a more regular and more detailed basis than the statutory requirements for quoted companies. VC firms may require investee firms to develop their accounting information systems so that they provide a sound control mechanism for the company, but also information in the form required by the VC firm (Mitchell et al., 1995).

In addition to the regular provision of accounts, *board representation* is one of the most frequent methods of monitoring the companies supported by VC firms. The VC firm may also seek to appoint a non-executive chairperson with appropriate industry experience.

Although VC firms will put in place formal monitoring mechanisms, there is a need for flexibility through personal relationships in the monitoring of VC investments. The frequency of these personal interactions between the VC firm and the entrepreneur depend on the entrepreneur's new venture experience, the venture's stage of development, the degree of technological innovation being pursued, and the extent to which the entrepreneur and the VC firm agree about the goals for the business (Sapienza and Korsgaard, 1996). Even when the two parties are clear about the supported firm's goals, in an uncertain new business environment the appropriate course of action may be difficult to chart. Considerable and frequent exchanges of information generally help to identify the appropriate course of action.

Formal powers are used sparingly to ensure they are effective. To act precipitously may destroy carefully nurtured relationships and commit the VC firms to unknown amounts of time to put matters right. However, involvement is not costless and, especially for smaller investments, there is a need to weigh these costs against the potential benefits.

VC firms and business angels differ with regard to their monitoring practices (Ehrlich et al., 1994). VC firms are more likely to impose stringent controls, have reporting requirements that are more frequent, have a tradition of supplying more verbal feedback, and have performance targets that are more difficult. They provide more feedback when targets are not met. VC firms are viewed by entrepreneurs as being more helpful in installing management systems. However, business angels are more flexible and require less time to be spent in reporting. VC firms are more active in selecting management. The choice of a business angel or a formal VC firm investor, in part, is shaped by the managerial skills of the entrepreneur. Entrepreneurs need to appreciate the long-term costs associated with each type of financial investor because the costs may exceed the short-term benefits.

12.6.10 Exiting

12.6.10.1 *Context*

VC firms obtain the bulk of the return in their investment from *realising a capital gain*. They will seek a means to *exit their investments*. There may be an attempt to identify the trajectory to exit at the time of the initial investment, but there may be a need to respond opportunistically to changing stock market conditions, or unsolicited offers from firm acquirers. The conditions relating to the company itself, the stock market and takeover market, as well as the objectives of management and financiers can change significantly over the period of an investment. VC firms generally maintain a flexible approach to the timing and form of exit.

In order to achieve timely exit, VC firms are more likely to engage in closer monitoring of their buyout investments and to use exit-related equity-ratchets on management's equity stakes. The greater the conflicts in the objectives of the parties that had to be suppressed at the time of the VC investment transaction, the greater the need for flexibility over exit arrangements. Even so, exit arrangements will largely be influenced by the relative bargaining power between VC firms and entrepreneurs. Entrepreneurs may have substantial bargaining power even where they have relatively small equity stakes. This is because a high proportion of the investee firms value may depend on their hard to replace entrepreneurial and managerial skills.

12.6.10.2 *Flotation or Initial Public Offering (IPO)*

VC firm backing provides a certification effect, or signal, to the stock market suggesting the supported firm has considerable assets and potential for future growth. Experienced VC firms appear to be particularly good at taking companies public near market peaks, while less experienced VC firms may be more prone to exit their investees somewhat prematurely. This may be because of the need to demonstrate an exit track record in order to be able to raise further funds (this has been termed 'grandstanding') (Gompers, 1996).

Secondary and tertiary tier stock markets provide access to equity finance for newer firms with short or weak performance track records but which, nevertheless, are deemed to have significant growth prospects. These markets also provide opportunities for VC firms to obtain an exit, for example, on the Alternative Investment Market (AIM) in the United Kingdom.

12.6.10.3 *Trade sale*

Despite the attention and glamour surrounding an IPO, sale to a third party is often the most commonly preferred and actual form of exit. This is principally because a threshold for an IPO is not reached, or because an attractive but unforeseen acquisition proposal is received. Whilst a trade sale provides more immediate full liquidity of an investment than is possible in an IPO flotation, the objectives of the entrepreneur may not be satisfied. Partial trade sales may involve the sale of an equity stake in the investee firm to either a strategic or a financial investor. Sale of an equity stake to a strategic investor may provide the opportunity to access new markets and technologies whilst retaining the company's independence.

12.6.10.4 *Secondary buyouts and buyins*

Secondary buyouts and buyins have been discussed in Chapter 9. They can involve changes in ownership by management and VC investors. A secondary buyout may also be a means of transferring ownership to the next generation of management, if the original managers wish to retire. Secondary buyouts and buyins have become more common as an exit route because the trade sale and IPO options have become more difficult, especially for management buyouts.

12.6.10.5 *Other exit routes*

Other forms of exit involve refinancing of an investment, either because it has been more successful than expected, or because there has been a major under-performance, as in the case of 'living dead' investments. With regard to refinancing underperforming investee firms, there is a need to ensure that problems outside the control of managers are removed from assessing managers' performance. Also, there may be a need to introduce revised remuneration mechanisms to ensure that they are adequately incentivised to turn the business around. This has been a particular issue in the credit crisis of 2008 to 2009 where the shares of entrepreneurs in venture backed management buyouts and buyins, in particular, have become worthless as firms struggle to service their heavy debt burdens (Wilson et al., 2010).

12.6.10.6 *Exits from early stage ventures*

In seeking exits from early stage investments, VC firms generally prefer a trade sale followed by buy-backs and then IPOs (Murray, 1994). Exit by means of a trade sale can enable an attractive price to be obtained with reference to developed proven technology. Besides enabling gains to be realised in cash, they can be associated with potential purchasers who can be quickly identified. Early stage companies may represent rather small acquisitions for trading groups seeking to obtain economies of scale and/or scope. However, they may be attractive if purchasers are seeking to gain access to new technology or product innovations. A stock market flotation is generally viewed as a hope rather than an expectation. This is because few early stage investments display the levels of growth required to be attractive to stock market investors. Depending on stock market conditions, companies in such sectors as biotechnology may be floatable even though they have note generated viable products (see the example of Renovo in Entrepreneurship in action 6.1). *Share buy-backs* are generally associated with less successful transactions. VC firms may need to offer this option to entrepreneurs who are reluctant to cede equity. If the investee firm has not performed well, the entrepreneur may have difficulty raising the funds to effect a 'buy-back'.

Exit by sale to a next stage VC firm is the fourth most preferred exit route. Problems that may arise to restrict this form of exit concern potential conflicts of interest between exiting and entering VC firms especially in relation to setting a sale price. Initial VC firms may have the benefit of knowing the current state of development of the company, which a potential new investor does not. Where the investment has not yet begun to demonstrate significant growth but needs further funds, initial investors may be in a relatively weak negotiating position. Early stage investments may in any case still be too undeveloped and too risky to be attractive to a potentially incoming development stage VC firm.

12.6.11 Reinvesting in exited entrepreneurs

Habitual entrepreneurs have been highlighted in Chapter 5. VC firms may receive proposals from entrepreneurs who have exited from their own or other VC firms' portfolios. In considering reinvesting in entrepreneurs who have exited from their own portfolio, VC firms are potentially faced with a situation in which the entrepreneur is now more aware of the effectiveness of the VC firm's monitoring, and how (dis)advantageous their initial contract was with a VC firm (Wright et al., 1997). As a result, the entrepreneur may attempt to negotiate a larger equity stake compared with their first VC investment. VC firms have to convince themselves that the entrepreneur still has the motivation to make the commitment to a new venture. There are also potential dangers that the benefits of prior business ownership experience may be offset by fixations on repeating past (successful) behaviour. As a result, VC firms may be cautious about reinvesting in entrepreneurs drawn from their own portfolio of supported firms. Experience alone is not the key factor in the decision to invest again in an entrepreneur. The major difficulties to be dealt with concern whether the entrepreneur has been able to identify another investment, which offers attractive returns, and whether this meets the VC firm's investment criteria.

12.6.12 Effects of venture capital investment on investee companies

Several studies have explored the links between the provision of VC backing and the subsequent performance of supported entrepreneurial firms. Hellmann and Puri (2000) analysed the link between type of investor and whether portfolio firms in the United States followed innovator or imitator strategies. They found that innovators were more likely to be financed by VC firms than imitators. VC backed firms, especially innovators, reported a faster time to market. However, other evidence regarding the relationship between VC backing and firm performance, particularly in terms of growth, is rather mixed. Engel and Keilbach (2007) noted that VC backed firms in Germany generated faster employment growth. In contrast, Burgel et al. (2000) detected that VC backing had no impact on firm growth in Germany and the United Kingdom. Studies comparing the growth of VC and non-VC backed firms that went to IPO also show mixed results. Jain and Kini (1995) and Audretsch and Lehmann (2004) detected VC financing increased firm growth, but Botazzi and Da Rin (2002) failed to detect a significant link. Colombo and Grilli (2008) noted in Italy that once an NTBF received VC backing the role of founders' skills became less important, whilst the skills of VCs became more important in contributing to firm growth. More sophisticated longitudinal studies conducted by Bertoni et al. (2008) in Italy and Alemany and Marti (2005) in Spain revealed that VC-backed start-ups were associated with higher growth. Further analyses showed that it is not just VC backing that is important. The amount of finance is also important (Heirman and Clarysse, 2005). NTBFs in particular need significant amounts of funding to establish the commercial value of the technology, and to identify and penetrate large markets.

VC backing can facilitate the internationalisation of investee firms. VC firms can provide the knowledge-based resources needed to know how to internationalise (Zahra et al., 2007). Also, VC firms can provide the resources to increase the scale of the business to facilitate internationalisation, and to further increase international revenues once internationalisation has occurred (George et al., 2005). The nature of the VC firm's involvement (i.e., monitoring versus added value) in influencing internationalisation varies according to the stage of investment. Lockett et al. (2008) found that monitoring resources were most effective in promoting export behaviour for late-stage ventures, whilst value-added resources were important in promoting export behaviour in early-stage ventures.

Studies have attempted to ascertain what aspects of VC firm involvement contribute to superior firm performance. Dimov and Shepherd (2005) noted that it is not simply the amount of human capital provided by the VC firm that is important. They detected that the *nature of human capital* was important. General rather than specific human capital was linked to an increased proportion of investee firms being publicly listed. Specific human capital, however, was linked to an increased proportion of investee firms going bankrupt. Bottazzi et al. (2008) detected that VC firms whose partners had prior business experience were significantly more active in investee firms. Having more venture experience increased the likelihood that an executive would be put in charge of supervising portfolio firms. They also found more investor activism increased the likelihood of exit performance.

Syndication by VC firms can help access greater expertise and provide for risk spreading (Wright and Lockett, 2003). De Clerq and Dimov (2008) found that investing in industries in which a VC firm had more knowledge, and investing with more or familiar syndicated partners, increased the performance of investees. Access to the knowledge provided through syndication is most important when there is an incongruity between what the investee firm knows, and what it intends to do.

12.7 Government assistance

Several types of government assistance for new and small firms have been introduced (DTI, 2004). Schemes have been introduced to provide loan guarantees to entrepreneurs with no or limited collateral. Also, tax incentives schemes have been introduced to encourage individuals to invest directly (or indirectly) in entrepreneurial firms. Other approaches have involved consideration of a statutory right to receive interest on trade debt to help smaller firms who may particularly encounter problems in obtaining payment from larger companies. Schemes have, in addition, been developed to encourage the provision of more long-term finance to replace overdrafts on which many smaller firms rely heavily. To enhance entrepreneur demand for finance, government schemes have been introduced to increase the availability of information surrounding the sources of financing for smaller firms, and to encourage the take-up of financial skills training programmes (DTI, 2004). While these initiatives have been focused on smaller firms in general, the funding problems facing new entrepreneurial high-technology ventures have led to six types of specific measures targeted at this sector. These are discussed, in turn, below.

First, some governments have created public funds with the specific aim of financing (high-technology) spin-off firms at a very early stage, such as the Finnish fund 'Sithra' which provides additional coaching to improve business plans and to finance market research activities. A second category of policy initiatives involve the establishment of public–private partnership funds, a specific category of which are the university funds, such as the University Challenge Fund (UCF) in the United Kingdom. A further example concerns the availability of innovation vouchers (see Entrepreneurship in action 12.3), where concerns about awareness

Entrepreneurship in action 12.3
'Vital' innovation vouchers already available for small businesses, WAG insists

Innovation vouchers that were urged as 'vital' for the Welsh economy are already in place, the Welsh Assembly Government (WAG) said yesterday . . . Welsh business leaders have called on WAG to introduce the vouchers for small businesses to invest in partnerships with higher education institutions as a way of stimulating innovation. But a WAG spokesperson, defending its record on innovation, said that it has an innovation voucher scheme in place to encourage new ideas in business, using European structural funding. The response came after business leaders yesterday urged the Welsh Assembly Government to introduce innovation vouchers that had been running in English regions and had attracted widespread support from universities.

Vouchers of up to £5,000 are made available to SMEs to invest in research at universities within the region where the businesses are. In a survey by Universities UK of participating institutions in England, 88 per cent of those asked said that the vouchers had forged new relationships with SMEs and 86 per cent said that they had stimulated further collaborations.

A WAG spokesman said: 'Our Business Innovation Support Programme is designed to support businesses at all stages of the innovation process. The programme provides an integrated package of innovation support advice . . . This support includes approximately £1 m of innovation voucher funding annually. Innovation vouchers are worth up to £10,000 and can fund up to 50 per cent of project cost. They enable business to procure expertise from the private sector as well as universities and colleges.' . . . So far there have been 154 applications received and 127 offers made since the programme was launched last year, with the amount offered nearly two-thirds of the £1 m available. But Russell Lawson from Federation of Small Business (FSB) Wales said the current model is 'extremely well hidden' and that businesses were only 'vaguely aware' of the existence of the unit. He said: 'It just highlights that if we have not heard of this scheme then businesses are likely not to have heard of it either . . . If you have 150,000 small businesses in Wales and provide only £1 m to finance the scheme then it goes without saying that not going to take on many projects. With such a paltry amount it is understandable that it is not known . . . The fact that businesses have barely heard of the innovation unit is simply because WAG keeps it so quiet – it is down to them not promoting them and it won't happen with another £1 m.'

Source: G. Henry, *The Western Mail*, 7 May 2010.

of the scheme also illustrate a major challenge to the take-up of this kind of funding. A third set of initiatives, inspired by the United States Small Business Investment Companies (SBIC) scheme, involves VC firms investing in a (high-technology) spin-off firm being able to co-finance its investment by a loan granted by the government, which is reimbursed at a fixed below-market rate. A fourth set of measures aim to reduce the risks faced by VC firms through guarantee schemes. If a start-up fails, the government can reimburse the VC firm, which qualifies for the scheme for (part of) its lost investment. The potential problem with these schemes is that they may give an incentive to VC funds to let their portfolio companies go bankrupt, in order to recover at least part of their money invested, instead of trying to save supported companies. Fifth, 'fiscal incentives' provide tax reductions on capital gains created by investments, or they allow investors in VC funds that qualify for the scheme to offset (parts of) their investment against taxes (for example, Venture Capital Trusts in the United Kingdom). Sixth, business incubation schemes provide infrastructure and management support for NTBFs but may not directly provide capital (e.g., the German EXIST programme).

12.8 Looking forward

Despite considerable debate, major challenges remain in accessing the finance needs for entrepreneurial firms that are innovative, growing and seeking to internationalise. These challenges arise due to the attitudes, preferences and behaviour of entrepreneurs (i.e., *demand-side issues*), as well as the potential providers of finance (i.e., *supply-side issues*). Access to all appropriate information poses particular problems for entrepreneurs and financiers alike. The traditional approach to reduce the asymmetric information problem has been to encourage entrepreneurs to write detailed business plans surrounding the potential risks and rewards associated with the business. Recent developments have questioned the traditional business plan approach whose written document is supposed to encapsulate all the information about a business. First, there is growing appreciation of the need to focus on precisely how the venture will make money illustrated in business models. Additional analysis needs to be reported relating to the feasibility of each proposed business model. Second, there is a need for greater attention to due diligence issues, which traditionally have solely focused on objective aspects relating to the business. Adherents of the business model approach suggest there is a need for due diligence to uncover how the business works, which may include the need to understand more subjective or tacit aspects of the business. Notably, it needs to be more widely appreciated that the returns on early stage VC investments are generally very low. Investor experience can promote superior growth in returns.

Several questions need to be explored. Additional research is warranted to examine the links between the characteristics of both ventures (and their entrepreneurial ownership team members) and VC investors who shape whether a venture receives financial investment, and the extent and effectiveness of the value-adding and/or monitoring behaviour provided by VC investors. The human and social capital profiles of ventures and VC investors need to be explored. Other issues concern the heterogeneity of investor types, the origin and stage of ventures receiving support, and the technological and industrial sectors in which the ventures operate. Considerable attention has focused on the behaviour of independent VC firms, especially those located in the United States. Independent, corporate, and public VC investors differ in terms of investment objectives, time horizons and capabilities to assist the development of their portfolio of supported firms. Additional research attention is warranted to explore the profiles, preferences, behaviour and wealth generation contributions of a broader spectrum of actors in the VC industry. Further detailed analysis is needed to explore how investment objectives, time horizons and capabilities shape the value-adding activities of each type of VC investors, both in terms of the degree to which they engage in them, and the effectiveness of their actions.

Discussion questions

1 Why does a so-called equity gap for entrepreneurial firms exist?

2 What factors influence an entrepreneur choosing between business angel and formal venture capital finance?

3 What are the main problem areas facing an entrepreneur when preparing a business plan? How might these challenges differ between a business plan prepared for a bank loan and one prepared to try to obtain venture capital?

4 Discuss the roles of contractual mechanisms with regard to venture capital firm financing.

5 To what extent do you think that a venture capital firm's requirement to realise a capital gain on its investment in a portfolio company may affect the way in which the entrepreneur runs the company?

6 What factors are most important in influencing how venture capital firms add value to their portfolio companies?

Recommended further reading

Department of Trade and Industry (DTI). (2004). *A Government Action Plan for Small Business. Making the UK the Best Place in the World to Start and Grow a Business: The Evidence Base*. London, DTI, Small Business Service.

Manigart, S., DeWaele, K., Wright, M., Robbie, K., Desbrieres, P., Sapienza, H. and Beekman A. (2002). Determinants of Required Returns in Venture Capital Investments: A Five-Country Study. *Journal of Business Venturing*, 17: 291–312.

Wright, M., Sapienza, H. and Busenitz, L. (2003). *Venture Capital Volumes I to III*. Cheltenham: Edward Elgar.

Chapter 13

International entrepreneurship

Contents

Learning objectives

- Consider traditional internationalisation theories and emerging international entrepreneurship theory to explain how private firms internationalise.

- Appreciate that some firms have competitive advantages that enable them to be international new ventures (INVs) (or 'born globals') from the outset.

- Illustrate the profiles of firms that are not likely to internationalise relative to those that are more likely to internationalise.

- Appreciate that there are internationalisation 'states' rather than 'stages'.

- Consider that modes of internationalisation can be linked to strategy, risk, control and cost issues.

- Highlight that the domestic environmental context (and linkages to larger organisations) can 'push' and 'pull' firms into internationalisation, as well as provide resources that can be leveraged to circumvent barriers to internationalisation.

- Consider the entrepreneur and not solely the firm as the unit of analysis for academic and policy debate.

- Appreciate the economic benefits associated with firms that internationalise.

13.1 Introduction

International entrepreneurship (IE) is the process of creatively discovering and exploiting opportunities that lie outside a firm's domestic market in the pursuit of competitive advantage (Zahra and George, 2002). Autio et al. (2000) noted that the growth in international sales reported by SMEs was associated with earlier initiation of internationalisation, and greater knowledge intensity related to learning behaviour. Yet insights from these kinds of firm may not be appropriate for the vast majority of firms that do not offer products and/or services relating to substantial value added based on a process or technology breakthrough. Insights from other perspectives need to be considered to understand the factors influencing firms engaged in a broad array of industrial activities to internationalise.

Two broad theoretical streams have emerged to help explain how firms internationalise. First, *traditional internationalisation theories*, such as stage theory (Johanson and Vahlne, 1977) have focused on the factors influencing internationalisation, especially in larger firms. These traditional internationalisation approaches have been the subject of considerable criticism (Jones and Coviello, 2005). Second, the inability of traditional internationalisation theories to explain why some SMEs internationalise from the outset has been highlighted in the emerging *IE theory* (Autio, 2005; Oviatt and McDougall, 2005; Zahra, 2005; Keupp and Gassmann, 2009; Dimitratos et al., 2010). Entrepreneurship related aspects of internationalisation have been developed as a counterpoint to the received wisdom of traditional internationalisation theories.

The novel contribution of IE theory to knowledge and policy debates is still not clearly positioned by its advocates who acknowledge that a unifying and clear theoretical direction has not been presented (McDougall and Oviatt, 2000; Young et al., 2003; Gabrielsson et al., 2008). Attempts to address this issue are beginning to recognise the restrictive nature of the

IE perspective. First, O'Farrell et al. (1998), focusing on the service sector, recommended a flexible theoretical approach to explore internationalisation by SMEs. They suggested that theory should consider the strategic choices open to entrepreneurs, and that the home region context may influence foreign market decisions. Second, Jones and Coviello (2005) note that while contemporary understanding of internationalisation is informed by integrating multiple theoretical perspectives, there remains a need to incorporate entrepreneurial behaviour into models of internationalisation. This represents recognition of the need for conceptual models to be flexible to accommodate a range of conditions that might shape a firm's internationalisation decision, its actions and its dynamic processes. Indeed, the scope of IE has broadened since the initial work of Oviatt and McDougall (1994, 1995), who emphasised small, international new ventures. Researchers now view IE as a more general phenomenon, which also encompasses the entrepreneurial qualities of larger, established firms (Zahra, 2005; Cumming et al., 2009; Keupp and Gassmann, 2009).

Table 13.1 summarises the conceptual insights from the key theoretical perspectives associated with SME internationalisation and IE (Wright et al., 2007). A distinction is made between *traditional internationalisation theory* (i.e., stage theory and internationalisation/transaction costs theory) and *IE theory* (i.e., strategic choice theory, learning and knowledge theory relating to *international new ventures (INVs) or born globals*, and resource-based/network theory) with regard to seven themes. We also suggest that the industrial sector and the tradability of the goods or services should be considered. This framework is used to guide the following discussion relating to the key themes in the internationalisation of private SMEs.

13.2   Timing of internationalisation

The timing of internationalisation is an important distinguishing factor between traditional internationalisation studies and IE studies. Within the latter theoretical perspective, *INV theorists* guided by strategic choice theory and learning/knowledge theory question the stage model theory. Notably, INV theorists suggest that many new private SMEs can internationalise from the inception of business operations (Autio et al., 2000).

INVs are viewed as organisations which, from inception, seek to derive *significant competitive advantage from the use of resources* and the sale of output to multiple countries. Theorists assert that many firms no longer regard international markets as simple adjuncts to the domestic market. SMEs with specific *competitive advantages linked to their technological level and product and/or service characteristics* may be alert to opportunities in international markets from the outset (Oviatt and McDougall, 1994). *Opportunity-driven firms* do not follow an incremental internationalisation path (see Case 22, AAC Limited: Entrepreneurial team dynamics). Firms that internationalise from the outset may be associated with the *asset of newness*. New SMEs do not have to unlearn procedures focused on developing a domestic market presence (Autio et al., 2000). McDougall et al. (1994) have asserted that international entrepreneurs try to avoid domestic path-dependence by establishing ventures which have routines for managing multicultural workforces, for co-ordinating resources located in different nations, and for targeting customers in multiple geographic locations simultaneously.

Evidence from Finland suggests that the time from the establishment of a firm to the time of the first export delivery is becoming shorter (Luostarinen and Gabrielsson, 2004). Some technology and non-technology-based firms may ground their international

Table 13.1 Theoretical perspectives relating to SME internationalisation

Theme	Traditional internationalisation theories		International entrepreneurship theories		
	Stage theory	Internalisation/ transaction cost theory	Strategic choice theory	Learning/knowledge theory[1]	Resource-based/ network theory
1 SMEs can internationalise from the outset	No, build resources and experience first in domestic market	Depends on transaction costs	Depends on motivation and relationships with clients	Yes	Possibly, if have internal or external resources
2 Once SMEs internationalise, they continue to do so	Unilinear	If transaction costs increase, exit. Role of sunk costs	The need to redirect scarce expert resources means complex strategic choices; influenced by ability to obtain repeat business and evaluation of experience	Increased learning leads to increased internationalisation [implicitly if learning is negative, may reduce internationalisation]	May exit if resources depleted
3 SMEs can enter through high control entry modes	Firms move from low to high control modes as they develop experience and commitment	Depends on transaction costs and cost of resource commitment	Past experience influences form of servicing in a particular foreign market; different motivations affect choice of entry mode	High control from start increases learning	Depends on nature of resource access required
4 Domestic environmental factors provide spillovers that can be leveraged by SMEs to internationalise	Domestic market provides basis for resource and expertise accumulation		Domestic market demand and supply context can be projected into foreign market	Restricted domestic market	Domestic market provides resources to internationalise. May use domestic resources initially overseas if are geographically fungible

Continued overleaf

Table 13.1 (*continued*)

Theme	Traditional internationalisation theories		International entrepreneurship theories		
	Stage theory	Internalisation/transaction cost theory	Strategic choice theory	Learning/knowledge theory[1]	Resource-based/network theory
5 SMEs can leverage external resources		Joint ventures provide middle range control	Importance of sustainability of relationships with clients, in some cases to pull firms abroad	Build links with networks of larger firms to obtain knowledge	Depends on nature of resource access required
6 Focus on the firm rather than the entrepreneur	Firm	Firm/transaction	Firm	Firm/entrepreneur	Firm/entrepreneur/network
7 SMEs that internationalise outperform	Yes	Depends on transaction costs	Depends on motivation	Yes	Depends
Representative articles	Johanson and Vahle (1997)	Buckley and Casson (1985)	O'Farrell et al. (1998)	Autio et al. (2000); McDougall and Oviatt (2003); Oviatt and McDougall (2005); Zahra and George (2002); Zahra (2005)	McDougall et al. (1994); Bloodgood et al. (1996); Westhead et al. (2001a)
Industrial sector	Depends	Depends, but main focus on manufacturing	Depends	High technology firms	Depends
Tradability of goods or services	Develops over time	Depends on transaction cost	Depends	High technology firms	Depends

Note: Learning and knowledge theory is especially linked to international new ventures (INVs) and born global (BG) ventures.

Source: Wright et al. (2007, Table 1: 1016).

competitive pattern on unique resources (i.e., human capital resources such as entrepreneurial capabilities relating to entrepreneurial orientation, alertness, information search and processing, cognitive mindset, etc.) (Obrecht, 2004). INVs generally offer products and/or services that involve substantial value added based on a breakthrough in process or technology. Given the relatively short lifecycle of such products/services, these firms may seek to maximise sales by serving multiple markets.

INV theorists may have encouraged a growing policy belief that more new private firms can internationalise, and that they can do so from the outset (EIM, 2005). The development of policy based on these notions may apply only to a distinct subgroup of SMEs. If practitioners only contextualise support toward knowledge and technology-based firms, this support may not be appropriate for the vast majority of SMEs that do not offer products and/or services that involve substantial value added based on a process or technology breakthrough. Insights from other perspectives need to be considered by practitioners seeking to encourage more of the latter types of firms to internationalise. *Findings and relationships detected with regard to INVs may not be universally applicable to other 'types' of SMEs for the following reasons.*

First, some SMEs may produce goods and services that are *not tradable*. Some firms' markets may be restricted to the local domestic environment because of local tastes, distribution costs, or because they are unable to offer competitive advantage over domestic suppliers in foreign markets. It is necessary to understand the distinction between those cases where the goods and services are not tradable and those where they are tradable in principle, yet the firm does not engage in internationalisation. This may be attributable to the attitudes, resources and behaviour of the entrepreneurs and firms involved. The *majority of non-exporting SMEs may not have the inclination and/or ability to export.* Many non-exporting private firms do not export because they are *focusing on their domestic market* (Westhead et al., 2002). Firms (and entrepreneurs) may not internationalise because they are reluctant to *commit their (limited) resources* to enter foreign markets (Westhead et al., 2001b). Most SMEs *'stay at home'* (Acs et al., 1997). Westhead et al. (2002, 2004b) found that only a minority of SMEs in the United Kingdom engaged in several manufacturing and services industries were exporters, and the exporters only exported a small proportion of their sales. A similar pattern is apparent in the European Union where only 18 per cent of SMEs were found to be exporters (EIM, 2005). Consequently, while practitioners may hold the belief that internationalisation is desirable, they need to acknowledge that *attitudinal barriers* need to be addressed if the pool of internationalising private SMEs is to be increased. Barriers to exporting are highlighted in Entrepreneurship in action 13.1.

Second, the findings from several empirical studies may be associated with low external validity. Some studies are restricted to small countries where *high-technology firms* may have to internationalise if they are to identify sufficient customers.

Third, the nature of the *industrial sector* selected by the SME to operate in may be important. Westhead et al. (2004b) detected that younger and manufacturing firms in the United Kingdom were more likely to be exporters, and they reported higher internationalisation intensities. Further, Bell et al.'s (2004) evidence relating to 15 'knowledge-intensive' and 15 'traditional' manufacturing firms located in three regions in the United Kingdom suggests that whilst 'traditional' firms generally followed an incremental approach both domestically and internationally, 'knowledge-intensive' manufacturing firms were more likely to have reported an international orientation from inception, and they internationalised rapidly.

Entrepreneurship in action 13.1
Small firms put off overseas trade by 'perceived' barriers

Almost one in three small UK firms is selling to overseas customers, but many more are put off international trade by concerns about currency, payment and language, research by Lloyds TSB has found. Of the two-thirds of small businesses not exporting, only six per cent have any plans to do so in the future. But the survey suggests more businesses would be prepared to sell internationally if they were less worried about barriers to exporting.

Problems cited by respondents included concerns about late payments and currency fluctuations, language barriers and uncertainty about expertise or resources. But these can all be overcome, said Lloyds TSB commercial spokesman Stephen Pegge. 'In the survey, 39 per cent of respondents who do not export said that there would not be demand for their product or service, and this may be true of some – for example, a hairdresser,' he said. 'However, there are many small firms that are being held back by their own perceptions of what the difficulties and risks are, without thinking through how they will overcome those,' Pegge continued. Also, he stated that, 'Exports tend to be cloaked in jargon and it feels very high risk, but often it is easier than people think and all the perceived barriers can be addressed.'

Among the measures that could be adopted by small firms to counter their exporting fears, Pegge suggested: using letters of credit, international invoice discounting and factoring to manage payments; covering currency risks with formal exchange contracts; language training; taking exporting training courses run by bodies such as UK Trade and Investment and British Chambers of Commerce; and talking to the international service manager at your bank.

The measures could also benefit firms that have started to export without a clear strategy. 'Many of the small businesses that export are just firms with websites that have taken orders from overseas, and they don't necessarily see themselves as exporters,' said Pegge. 'In fact, they could benefit from targeting certain markets and having information on their website in another language.'

UK Trade and Industry (UKTI) spokesman Jamie Oliver said that although it takes effort for small firms to export, those that do so tend to be more profitable. 'The UK is a small island with a relatively small population, so to ensure long-term growth, firms should at least research their opportunities overseas,' he said. Further, 'UKTI runs courses where you can work out whether it's worth trying to export. We also offer grants and support in terms of trade shows, to dip your toe in overseas markets. Businesses should take a chance and not be put off by perceived barriers, as exporting is potentially profitable,' he added.

Source: The Marketing Donut, www.marketingdonut.co.uk, 8 June 2010.

Fourth, there is a need to consider the *nature of the support system*, which may be an important source of knowledge leveraged by the new firm to *circumvent attitudinal, resource, operational and strategic obstacles to internationalisation*. With regard to NTBFs from universities located across Europe, Clarysse et al. (2005) concluded that an incubator model involving heavily resourced and intensive activities over a considerable period of time and based on world class science was needed to promote firms that have the potential to internationalise. Studies have tended to ignore this potentially important influence on the timing and extent of internationalisation (Autio et al., 2000).

Fifth, the notion of SMEs internationalising from the outset ignores the potential impact of the changing international competitive landscape, and the associated *corporate restructuring*. The reassessment of the scope of larger corporations in response to changing market pressures is leading to the outsourcing of activities, and the divestment of modestly-sized subsidiaries and divisions to management and leveraged buyouts that have greater discretion to select their markets and customers (Wright et al., 1990). These developments raise opportunities for SMEs that may have been domestic-market oriented (or heavily dependent on trading with their former parent) to become niche players with a specialised set of customers on a global scale.

13.3 Intensity and sustainability of internationalisation

IE scholars have highlighted the importance of more dynamic aspects associated with the *acquisition and assimilation of new knowledge* (De Clerq et al., 2005). A firm's ability to import can shape its propensity to export (Holmlund et al., 2007). Autio et al. (2000) found that the growth in international sales reported by SMEs was associated with earlier initiation of internationalisation, and greater knowledge intensity related to learning behaviour. A development of stage model theory is exhibited by the latter theorists who appreciate the *role of knowledge and learning as well as entrepreneurial strategic choice*. The implicit implication from the latter studies is that more knowledgeable firms, and firms that have learnt from their successes (i.e., intelligent learning from mistakes) will increase their commitment to internationalisation. This argument is, however, problematical for the following reasons.

- Many entrepreneurs (and firms) discover barriers/hurdles to internationalisation only after experiencing the internationalisation process (EIM, 2005). Some exporting SMEs may withdraw from exporting and possibly re-enter the exporting arena at a later point in time (Westhead, 2008). Others perhaps should exit but do not.
- Some SMEs only *export when there is limited demand in the domestic market*, and then stop exporting when domestic market conditions improve. Crick (2004) distinguished between 'disappointed firms' (i.e., firm has exported in the past but is not currently engaged in exporting and does not plan to export in the future) and 'disinterested firms' (i.e., firm has exported in the past but is not currently engaged in exporting but it plans to export in the future) (Westhead, 2008).
- O'Farrell et al. (1998) distinguished between business service and manufacturing firms, arguing that the former may be more likely than the latter to enter into a *'suspended state' of internationalisation* as projects are completed, and firms seek repeat business or new clients. There may, therefore, be a need to focus on *internationalisation 'epochs' and 'states' rather than 'stages'* (Bell et al., 2003). O'Farrell et al. (1998) have presented a strategic decision framework that can be utilised to evaluate an exit decision.
- A firm's (perception of) *sunk costs* can lead to continued exporting. These costs relate to the establishment of production and distribution networks, as well as the costs of acquiring information on overseas customers, suppliers and regulatory environments, etc.

A firm may continue exporting not because of knowledge accumulation and learning but because exporting is seen as an *irreversible investment* (Requena-Silvente, 2005). Existing approaches to the sunk cost issue may benefit from considering learning effects. The sunk costs of acquiring overseas information and building distribution networks in one market may be reduced by the learning benefits associated with such activity. Further, the sunk costs of establishing overseas production and distribution facilities can be reduced where these can be divested to another firm, which may be more feasible with the development internationally of corporate asset markets that include increased sell-offs between company groups. The latter behaviour is feasible if there are open markets in corporate assets.

The extent and rationale for exit from internationalisation is not well understood, yet it holds important policy implications relating to the following issues: the provision of support for assessing international market opportunities prior to entry, the appropriate mode of entry to support, and the extent to which support is provided for internationalisation post-entry. The IE perspective relating to learning/knowledge theory does not explicitly analyse the conditions under which learning might lead to exit. This perspective rests on the assumption that firms can learn from their international experiences. Learning from experience may not, however, be automatic. Indeed, Sitkin (1992) asserts that learning from success may be particularly problematic because the firm is not forced to understand and question what led to that success.

13.4 Mode of internationalisation

The *mode of internationalisation* selected by a firm is an important *strategic choice* that can influence its position in the selected markets, and its ability to gain access to vital information and acquire resources. Firms internationalise through a variety of modes (O'Farrell et al., 1998), and each mode is associated with risk, control and cost issues. The *most frequently reported modes* by private SMEs relate to direct exporting without an overseas base, or establishing an overseas base through some form of foreign direct investment (FDI) associated with a greenfield site, an acquisition or a joint venture (Solesvik and Westhead, 2010) (see Case 23, *Model Kit World*: Firm growth through geographic expansion relating to the market entry mode used by a firm in Hong Kong). The case of Bon Bon Buddies Limited in Entrepreneurship in action 13.2 illustrates that after sales growth in the domestic market the firm began to export sales abroad, and then established subsidiaries abroad. *Stage model theorists* who suggest a unilinear evolutionary internationalisation process, with incremental stages and a well-defined mode of internationalisation at each stage, have attracted extensive criticism (Bell et al., 2004).

Entrepreneurship in action 13.2
Bon Bon Buddies eyes more European growth

Fast-growing confectionery and biscuits company Bon Bon Buddies has set its sights on European expansion as the company continues its strong growth strategy. The firm, based in Oakdale near Blackwood [in Wales], now has sales of more than 50 per cent in its markets on mainland Europe, with targets to achieve further growth in the next three years.

Bon Bon Buddies, founded by Chris and Pauline Howarth 16 years ago, now has centres in France, Poland and a recently opened office in Copenhagen in Denmark. The company also recently made an acquisition of Teepee Creative (out of administration), which has pan-European rights to Disney toys with confectionery and 'surprise' confectionery products.

The future for the firm is looking a bright one, according to managing director Mr Howarth, who is looking to lead further expansion in the next 12 months. He explained: 'The business has a pan-European strategy for growth . . . This will be the first year when we have sold more than 50 per cent of our total sales outside of the UK and we now have three full-blown subsidiaries in Europe . . . Our Polish business, which we established this year, is doing very well in local markets and we have now set up Bon Bon Buddies in Copenhagen.'

Bon Bon Buddies is a leading supplier of licensed confectionery and novelty biscuits, including seasonal and year-round product lines. Its innovative design, development and licensing team create a wide product range based on popular teen and children's characters licensed from the copyright holders. The confectionery and biscuit ranges feature characters such as Dr Who, Disney Princess, Toy Story, Hello Kitty and Sponge Bob Square Pants. Mr Howarth said: 'It is quite complex because we sign licence agreements with the children's brands such as Disney and Nickelodeon and some of these licence agreements cover specific countries. But more and more we are signing on a pan-European basis.'

The company says its success is in the combination of the right popular character with an appealing confectionery novelty or gift concept, looking to gain shelf space in a market that is already highly competitive. 'Our skill-set is licensing other people's brands and utilising them within the confectionery arena,' said Mr Howarth. 'To establish your own brand is a huge and challenging task . . . The reality is that more than 80 per cent of brands launches fail, that is even with multi-million-pound brand launches by companies such as Mars, Nestlé and Cadbury . . . Our expertise is in managing the complexities of design, product-sourcing and manufacturing for the most popular children's brands.' It is through this that Bon Bon Buddies has continued to trade successfully and enjoy strong sales through the recession. Mr Howarth said: 'In recession, people tend to cut back on big luxury items, but still carry on with affordable treats – such as confectionery and particularly gift confectionery for children . . . The total confectionery market has remained pretty solid through the recession and while licensed

novelty confectionery is a relatively small part of that sector, we have still seen pretty strong growth.'

Mr Howarth said the company is on track to deliver a turnover of more than £27 m in its current financial year, which will be 17 per cent up on last year's figure, and 'a good level profit' on that revenue. Bon Bon Buddies is also committed to its Welsh base, being headquartered in the South Wales Valleys and at present employing 53 people in the UK, with 17 at its overseas operations. Much of its success, Mr Howarth stressed, is down a strong management team which includes his ex-wife and business partner Pauline – the firm's licensing, design and innovations director, and her team. He said: 'Pauline and her department drive the product innovation and that drives the growth. We have made some really good licensing deals over the last year . . . We are very well placed to capitalise on trends from around the world and the licence team are very good at recognising strong brands coming down the track and whether they are appropriate for our type of business.' With this strategy in place, Mr Howarth expects the company to achieve £50 m turnover in the next three to four years, with good profit margins on that.

As the company continues that growth, it will look at any acquisitions that are a potential good fit, such as the recent Teepee Creative buy. 'Our plans are fairly straightforward – consistent, profitable growth,' said Mr Howarth. 'We have got a strong balance sheet and we will look to make opportunistic acquisitions along the way where they fit in with our business . . . We have got a clear plan over the next three years and the plan is to continue growth, not just here but overseas and we are pretty good at managing that aspect. As we continue to expand in the coming year we will be hoping to take people on and add to our workforce.'

Looking at the achievements of the last year, Mr Howarth pointed to the prestigious Licensing Award it won for the second year in a row. 'That was a great achievement,' he said. 'It's for all food products and we have beaten multinational companies in doing so . . . We are really pleased with that, it's an outstanding accolade to our licensing, design and product development teams, who have done a fantastic job.'

Source: A. Blake, *The Western Mail*, 16 December 2009.

NTBFs are able to develop networks that raise the probability of selecting a joint venture to enter the foreign market (Dana and Wright, 2004). Growing enthusiasm for internationalisation by NTBFs has led to a general perception that all SMEs, irrespective of industrial activity, can enter foreign markets through FDI (EIM, 2005). The latter mode may only be applicable to the internationalisation of a small subsample of SMEs engaged in knowledge and technology-based activities.

O'Farrell et al. (1998) have suggested that the internalisation/transaction cost framework of internationalisation is inappropriate when exploring business services SMEs. This is because business services firms need an understanding of what is required to best support collaboration with clients. They asserted that the transaction cost framework is unable to handle complex choices among alternative modes, and it is difficult to differentiate between experienced and inexperienced business service firms.

The *modes of entry into foreign markets are likely to differ on key dimensions* such as the amount of resource commitment, higher transaction costs and costs relating to acquiring resources, the extent of risk, the potential for returns, and the degree of managerial control. Zahra et al. (2000) found important relationships between the international mode of entry and learning in NTBFs. They detected that foreign acquisitions and other higher control modes of entry facilitated greater breadth and speed of technological learning than low control modes such as international export and licensing agreements. The latter modes may not be appropriate for all SMEs. The case of Ablynx in Entrepreneurship in action 13.3 illustrates the importance of developing global strategic collaborations and alliances for NTBFs that need access to the resources of larger firms.

Entrepreneurship in action 13.3
Ablynx: Internationalisation through strategic alliances

The biotechnology company Ablynx is a spin-off from the Flemish Biotechnology Institute (VIB) and the Vrije Universiteit Brussel (VUB). In 1993, a research group at VUB discovered an unique type of antibodies that occur in certain animals belonging to the Camelidae (e.g., camels and llamas). Later findings showed that these antibodies offer several advantages over conventional antibodies because they have a simpler structure, they are easier to isolate, and small-scale production is feasible. By 2000, the research group in collaboration with a multidisciplinary team at VIB had created a technology platform, which could be used for the discovery and development of therapeutic drugs. Subsequently, a business plan was developed and Ablynx was founded in 2001. Ablynx started with ten employees including five former VUB researchers. The researchers facilitated technology and knowledge transfer from the VUB group to the newly founded company. Professional

head hunters were recruited to identify an experienced management team, and this contributed greatly to the raising of start-up capital of €5 m from an international consortium of venture capitalists that specialised in biotechnology. By mid-2004, Ablynx entered into its first collaboration agreement promoting discovery and development with the leading pharmaceutical company Procter and Gamble Pharmaceuticals in order to develop Nanabody®-based drug candidates. Collaboration agreements were also signed with other large and established companies such as Johnson & Johnson and Novartis. In 2007, Ablynx announced the creation of a global strategic alliance with Boehringer Ingelheim to further develop the discovery of Nanobodies® against agreed targets across multiple therapeutic areas including immunology, oncology and respiratory. Both parties proposed target opportunities for the collaboration with the goal of bringing

Nanobody®-based products rapidly to patients. Boehringer Ingelheim will be exclusively responsible for the development, manufacture and commercialisation of any products resulting from the collaboration. Ablynx will have certain co-promotion rights in Europe. This strengthened the existing relationship with Boehringer Ingelheim, and it was hoped that the strategic alliance would provide the opportunity for Ablynx's to grow its own product pipeline.

Source: Clarysse, B., Bruneel, J. and Wright, M. (2011). Growth, Value Creation and Resources in Young High Growth Technology Based Firms: the Impact of Environmental Contingencies. Strategic Entrepreneurship Journal (forthcoming).

Westhead et al. (2002) found that the most important mode of entry reported by private SME owners was *direct exporting*. Owners of firms engaged in traditional manufacturing and service activities rarely reported joint ventures and partnerships. The reported preferences regarding mode of entry reflected their limited social and business networks, as well as their desire to have greater control over their resources (O'Farrell et al., 1996).

A broader resource-based perspective would suggest that the appropriate mode of entry depends on the nature of foreign market resource access that is required. Firms that internationalise may be exploiting their existing resources, or may seek to enhance their resources. If a firm has resources that are geographically fungible, *low resource access modes of entry*, such as exporting, may be selected to utilise existing resource pools. Some SMEs are able to internationalise through low resource access modes if they *build links with larger companies*, and are drawn to internationalise on the back of these linkages (Le Galès et al., 2004). If a firm's resources are location-specific, *high resource access modes* (i.e., FDI, acquisition and greenfield entry) may be necessary.

13.5 Domestic environmental context

Firms *accumulate resources in domestic markets* and resources can be leveraged to internationalise their activities. Resource-based theorists (see Chapter 3) suggest that some firms gain a competitive advantage based on the quality and distinctiveness of their products and/or services rather than low price alone. These advantages can accrue to individual SMEs when many firms specialising in the various levels of the production chain are clustered together in a geographical locality (see Chapters 6 and 11). Certain localities may acquire a global strength that *enables individual SMEs located in the cluster to leverage a broad range of resources* (i.e., legitimacy, technological and marketing knowledge, brand name, etc.) that can be used to circumvent obstacles to internationalisation. Local government or local business associations have an important role in supporting specialised clusters by facilitating the accumulation and spread of local collective competition goods, particularly knowledge, between various actors in a cluster (Le Galès et al., 2001).

Resource scarcity in 'rural' peripheral domestic markets may stimulate owners of rural SMEs to exhibit greater proactive entrepreneurial behaviour (Moen, 1999). There is limited evidence to suggest that domestic environmental conditions provide the basis for learning and knowledge accumulation, which can provide a *positive platform for internationalisation* (Préfontaine and Bourgault, 2002). Westhead et al. (2004c) found no significant differences between 'urban' and 'rural' firms in the United Kingdom with regard to their propensity to export, the proportion of total sales exported, reported obstacles impeding export activity, or reasons reported for exporting. Westhead et al. (2004b) also noted that SMEs' perceptions of environmental turbulence were not significantly associated with the propensity to export, or the intensity of internationalisation.

However, there may be important *spillover effects from the domestic market* (Hewitt-Dundas et al., 2005). Dimitratos et al. (2004) noted that firms in Greece internationalised primarily to *reduce the perceived uncertainty associated with domestic environmental conditions*. Some SMEs may be located near other (larger) organisations in order to borrow size and resources (i.e., legitimacy, finance, technology, marketing capabilities, etc.) (Phelps et al., 2001), and to leverage local demand through input–output multipliers (McNaughton and Brown, 2004). *Local customers and other organisations can act as conduits* to increase the pool of SMEs reporting the propensity to internationalise.

The importance of the domestic environment may be sector and country specific. O'Farrell et al. (1998) have suggested that important regional influences shaped the internationalisation of business service SMEs in the United Kingdom. The volume and quality of home region demand and supply conditions may enable responsive business services firms to develop tradable skills, notably where international comparative advantage can be developed for multinational enterprises (MNEs). Requena-Silvente (2005) also found regional spillover effects on exporting with regard to a measure of region–industry concentration of employment. Luostarinen and Gabrielsson (2004) concluded that INVs drawn from large countries globalise mainly because of the demand-based pull forces in global markets for their products. Conversely, INVs drawn from small and open economies such as Finland do so due to the push and pressure forces related to the smallness and openness of domestic markets, and the fear of expected future competition coming from INVs located in large countries.

13.6 Leveraging external resources

A firm's ability to internationalise can be shaped by the acquisition and leverage of external resources (Bloodgood et al., 1996; Autio et al., 2000). Firms that are members of a *network* can gain access to external tangible and intangible resources that aid internationalisation. Inter-firm relationships can shape both market selection and the internationalisation mode utilised by SMEs. Networks may involve large and small firms in a symbiotic relationship that facilitates internationalisation (Dana and Wright, 2004). Some SMEs find it difficult to market their activities to the global economy, even when local support agencies and associations try to develop their competencies. Barriers to internationalisation can be circumvented when one or more large firms move into an area and *make the connections from local to global with smaller firms becoming the suppliers of corporate prime-movers* (Le Galès et al., 2004). SME internationalisation can be facilitated when large firms provide designs, technology support, quality control mechanisms, and established brand names. SMEs with smaller resource pools may be able to *borrow size* (Phelps et al., 2001) *and resources from (larger) organisations* located elsewhere.

To retain existing customers in domestic markets, SMEs with limited resources may be *'pulled' into foreign markets* by the internationalisation activities of larger network partners, such as domestic clients who have established relationships with organisations in foreign markets. In order to defend or maintain a position in a business network, a firm may be *'pushed' into becoming an exporter*, particularly if the major customers have entered foreign business networks. This is consistent with the 'piggy-back' mode of entry. Some SMEs internationalise because they are *reactive exporters* with a larger partner organisation obtaining the contract to service foreign customers (O'Farrell et al., 1996). By joining networks and forming alliances particularly with larger organisations SMEs, for example, those located in developing economies associated with local resource deficits can expand their social capital (Pisano et al., 2007; Robson et al., 2011). SMEs can subsequently utilise knowledge (Yli-Renko et al., 2002) and value-creating resources that cannot be created independently.

There may be major constraints on the ability of some SMEs to develop broader social and business networks. The case of Helax AB in Entrepreneurship in action 13.4 illustrates how links can be used productively to internationalise. Firms that are inexperienced at internationalisation may not have the human capital or financial resources to identify potential partners and build networks with larger organisations. Many SMEs want to remain independent and in control of their operations. They are reluctant to co-operate with international partners (EIM, 2005), particularly large organisations that they fear will 'acquire' their intellectual property (IP) and then dump them. This may pose particular issues in

Entrepreneurship in action 13.4
Helax AB: Born global using network links

Helax started in 1989 and is a leading supplier of systems for the integration of radiation oncology departments. A decade later Helax employed 100 people. In total, 50 were employed in Uppsala in Sweden, which is a leading centre for R&D in medicine. Helax sold products in 40 countries and 95 per cent of its sales were abroad. The company developed wholly-owned subsidiaries in Germany, France, Norway, the United Kingdom, and the United States. In 1999, the core personnel were the research group that started the company. Helax's founder studied physics at Uppsala University in the 1960s. He became involved with a research team involved in computer physics, with his task being to evaluate different types of research projects. One of the projects focused on new radiation techniques and involved an attempt to visualise and simulate what happens in the human body with the aid of a computer. The project developed well and a collaborative agreement was signed in 1993 between Uppsala University and Siemens in Germany. In the company's first year, the first systems were sold to reputable university hospitals in Sweden. In 1989, Helax

sold a system to a hospital in Oslo. Links had been established between Uppsala and Oslo University hospitals, and they assisted the marketing of Helax. These links encouraged the introduction of a referral system. Helax then sold the product to other Norwegian and Danish university hospitals. In 1993, Helax established a subsidiary in Norway. Earlier in 1989, Helax's founder had used his social ties to identify a clinic in Glasgow that subsequently bought a Helax system. In 1990, a subsidiary was established in the United Kingom, which employed personnel from Siemens. The former managing director (MD) of Siemens UK became the MD of the subsidiary. Subsequently, he leveraged his contacts with the MD of Siemens France, and this led to the sale of a Helax system to a French hospital. In 1992, Helax acquired a subsidiary in France. Using similar social ties, Helax has developed its entry strategy into other countries including Germany and the United States.

Source: This is an edited extract of the case of Helax in Sharma, D. D. and Blomstermo, A. The Internationalization Process of Born Globals: A Network View, *International Business Review*, 2003, 12: 739–753.

some fast-moving sectors where long-term survival of an SME depends on full or partial acquisition by a larger firm, which can provide specialists resources but where the owners are reluctant to give up control. The network links with larger firms may not be symbiotic. Rather, the resource dependence perspective suggests that there may be an asymmetry of interdependence (Pfeffer and Salancik, 1978). The individual SME may be dependent on resources controlled by other (larger) firms (O'Farrell et al., 1998), and an SME may be at a disadvantage. There is a risk that the larger firm may hijack the innovation (Acs et al., 1997). Further, SMEs typically need to meet strict quality, delivery and cost requirements when dealing with larger customers, and these requirements may be exacerbated in an international context.

Network linkages between a smaller firm and a large organisation may only be facilitated in receptive environments, which may need to be created (Clarysse et al., 2005). Mechanisms for learning may need to be introduced (Etemad, 2004). There is, therefore, growing appreciation that SMEs can be 'pushed' as well as 'pulled' into foreign markets, and the activities and resources of (larger) organisations can impact their internationalisation behaviour.

13.7   Unit of analysis

Traditional internationalisation theories exclusively focus on the *firm as the unit of analysis*. This literature may direct practitioner attention toward firm issues to the detriment of entrepreneur issues relating to the entrepreneurial creation and/or discovery of opportunities in foreign markets. Similarly, *IE scholars professing the INV perspective* focus on the accumulation of knowledge by the firm rather than the individual entrepreneur. Indeed, most IE studies generally *fail to consider entrepreneur-specific variables*. Although Autio et al. (2000) considered owner-managed firms, they did not consider the internationalisation experience of the entrepreneur. Zahra et al. (2000) considered internationalisation experience but only at the firm level. However, during the early stages of private firm development, owner(s), not organisation, characteristics play a pivotal role in shaping export performance (Kunda and Katz, 2003). In many SMEs, *the owner(s) is the key resource*. They can accumulate human capital and social capital leading to industry and management know-how; physical and financial capital needed to develop a venture (see Chapter 4); and the organisational capital that enables the competitive production of goods and services offered by a firm (Brush et al., 2002) (see Chapter 3) in both domestic and international markets. It is reasonable to assume that entrepreneurs (and entrepreneurial teams) can acquire and leverage foreign business knowledge, foreign institutional knowledge, and internationalisation knowledge (Eriksson et al., 1997).

An *entrepreneur's resource profile* can shape firm performance (see Chapter 14). Firm level analyses may ignore important dimensions that impact on the internationalisation process, and the performance of internationalising SMEs. Previous experiences (Reuber and Fischer, 1997), resources (Bloodgood et al., 1996), capabilities, knowledge and learning mobilised by an entrepreneur (or entrepreneurial team) may lead to the creation, discovery and exploitation of opportunities in foreign markets. The entrepreneur's expertise and cognitive processes may be highly influential in international opportunity exploitation (see Chapter 4). Jones and Coviello (2005), in their *model of entrepreneurial internationalisation*, incorporated three constructs relating to the *entrepreneur, which comprise their philosophical view as well as their social and human capital.*

Some entrepreneurs who have been *exposed to foreign markets* may, as a result of this personal experience, develop an international orientation whereby they are positively predisposed to internationalisation. Owners of firms may have *owned previous firms* where they gained experience of internationalisation. This experience as an owner–manager may be qualitatively different from that gained as a manager in a larger firm. Also, this experience may or may not have been associated with firm success. Entrepreneurial experience adds to individuals' specific human capital by providing valuable episodic knowledge (see Chapter 5). This experience can offer entrepreneurs an opportunity to learn and assess their ability in the entrepreneurial domain, in turn influencing subsequent activities. *Episodic knowledge* acquired through business ownership experience such as managerial experience, enhanced reputation, better access to finance institutions and broader social and business networks (Shane and Khurana, 2003) can be leveraged to identify and exploit international business opportunities. This knowledge may include the identification of opportunities to internationalise products and services that may not previously have been regarded as tradable. For example, the growth of United Kingdom residents acquiring property abroad may provide scope for local craftspeople in the United Kingdom to provide these services overseas.

Some recent SME internationalisation studies have focused on the *entrepreneur as the unit of analysis.* Human resources have been found to be the most important resources associated with internationalised firms (Brush et al., 2002). Independent firms with older principal founders, with more resources, denser information and contact networks and management know-how were more likely to be exporters (Westhead et al., 2001a). Firms with principal founders that had industry specific knowledge, as reflected in starting their businesses in the same industry as their last employers and had previous experience of selling goods or services abroad were more likely to be exporters.

Robson et al. (2010) explored the exporting behaviour of novice, serial and portfolio entrepreneurs in Ghana. They found that respondents reporting 'innovation not tried' reported lower exporting intensities, whilst those that had made investments in product and services innovation and process innovation (i.e., distribution and work practices) reported higher exporting intensities. Notably, they detected that the nature rather than the extent of prior business ownership experience was linked to higher exporting intensities. Habitual (i.e., serial and portfolio) entrepreneurs reported higher exporting intensities than novice entrepreneurs. Further, they found that portfolio, rather than serial entrepreneurs, reported higher exporting intensities.

There is, therefore, a need to consider the role of the owner/entrepreneur/entrepreneurial team in the internationalisation process. There may be important behavioural and *learning* differences between experienced (habitual) and novice entrepreneurs (see Chapter 5).

13.8 Internationalisation and firm performance

There is no clear and consistent relationship between an SME's propensity to export and ability to report superior firm performance (Aspelund and Moen, 2005). There is *no consensus surrounding how to measure internationalisation performance* (Katsikeas et al., 2000).

The variety of performance indicators used makes comparison across studies difficult (see Chapter 14). Results may be affected by the sectors analysed and the timeframes of analysis. Indeed, many studies have failed to consider inter-industry differences between non-exporters and exporters.

McDougall and Oviatt (1996) noted that firms that had increased international sales *superior performance* in terms of both relative market share and return on investment (ROI). Further, Bloodgood et al. (1996) found that internationalisation was marginally significantly associated with firms that reported higher profits. Burgel et al. (2001) detected that exporters reported higher levels of productivity and sales growth but not employment growth. These three studies focused on internationalising firms engaged in new technology-based sectors.

In contrast, Lu and Beamish (2001) found with reference to a sample of listed Japanese SMEs covering 19 industries that the proportion of sales exported reported *lower returns on assets*. With regard to firms in the United Kingdom engaged in several manufacturing and services industries, Westhead et al. (2001a) detected that the propensity to export was only significantly associated with superior operating performance relative to competitors. The propensity to export was not found to significantly encourage subsequent sales and employment growth, or firm survival. Similarly, Westhead et al. (2004b), utilising a weighted average firm performance score to control for industry differences, found that the propensity to export variable was not significantly associated with superior performance of United Kingdom firms.

The studies reviewed above suggest that the *relationship between the propensity to export and firm performance may be context (i.e. country, region and industry) specific*. Studying the relationship between internationalisation and firm performance could be fraught with several methodological problems. For example, it may be difficult to establish a causal relationship between internationalisation and firm performance if studies rely on cross-sectional evidence. Even when longitudinal evidence is analysed (McDougall and Oviatt, 1996; Westhead et al., 2001a), the results are still inconsistent. This may be partly due to the role of context discussed above, and/or differences in the time lag used to explore the impact of internationalisation on firm performance. Lu and Beamish (2001) highlighted the importance of time by demonstrating that FDI activity was initially associated with a decline in profitability, but later greater levels of FDI was associated with superior performance.

Another important consideration relates to the possibility that the relationship between internationalisation and performance is *moderated by other strategic variables*. This may be particularly relevant to SMEs in small open economies, whereby SMEs pursuing a growth strategy may be more likely to expand by entering foreign markets. With reference to the United States context, McDougall and Oviatt (1996) detected that increased international sales in NTBFs required simultaneous strategic changes in order to enhance firm perform-ance. Further, Lu and Beamish (2001) found that exporting moderated the relationship FDI had with firm performance. They detected that pursuing a strategy of high exporting concurrent with high FDI was less profitable than one that involved lower levels of exporting when FDI levels were high.

Studies exploring internationalisation intensity that exclude non-internationalising firms in their analysis may suffer from selection bias. Appropriate econometric models that correct for such bias need to be used (Robson et al., 2010).

Looking forward

The IE literature has placed considerable emphasis on the role of learning but relatively little attention has been devoted to *how* firms learn. Absorptive capacity is important for learning, but how absorptive capacity and dynamic capabilities for internationalisation are acquired and built is poorly understood. This is an important omission in the literature, especially for ventures that are developing through the early stages of their lifecycle, when the expertise and absorptive capacity of their founders may be reaching their limits. Firms that have developed organisational capabilities to acquire new knowledge will be better able to translate that knowledge to firms which have not developed such capabilities. For example, firms that have developed capabilities in establishing research partnerships can build on these capabilities to launch new (overseas) partnerships focused on the commercialisation of innovation.

Little understanding exists on the decision to exit from international entrepreneurship activity. Some exploratory studies have explored the profiles of firms that exit from exporting (Crick, 2004; Westhead, 2008). Additional work on this topic is warranted.

Greater attention to the entrepreneur in IE research would enhance understanding of the origins of international efforts, and the consequences for individual entrepreneurs, as well as aid in understanding firm-level processes and outcomes. Indeed, cross-level studies are critical to the advancement of entrepreneurship theory, as the process itself often evolves from individual to group to organisation (Cumming et al., 2009).

International business research has often focused on international knowledge transfer promoted by firms that select a FDI strategy. An IE perspective draws attention to the mobility of labour and entrepreneurs. The increase in *returning entrepreneurs* from developed economies back to their countries of origin such as China and India provides a potentially important means of international knowledge transfer, which may contribute to the internationalisation of entrepreneurial ventures located in their countries of origin. Again, an emphasis on entrepreneurs themselves seems to be important. Preliminary evidence from China suggests that the mobility of returning entrepreneurs with global networks is more important in accelerating internationalisation than the movement of former employees drawn from MNEs (Wright et al., 2008b). There is limited evidence relating to the internationalisation behaviour of returnee entrepreneurs. There may be different 'types' of returnee entrepreneur according to their institutional context, their prior experience, the type of venture they found, and other potentially important sources of heterogeneity. *Transnational entrepreneurs* represent an equally interesting dimension of mobile labour that is little understood. They are individuals that migrate from one country to another, concurrently maintaining business linkages between their country of origin and the newly adopted countries and communities. Drori et al. (2009) have positioned transnational entrepreneurs within the entrepreneurship domain, and they have presented an extensive research agenda. As with returnee entrepreneurs, transnational entrepreneurs may be heterogeneous, yet we currently know little about this heterogeneity, and the links between the strategies pursued and outcomes generated by subtypes of entrepreneurs involved in IE.

Prior experiences of entrepreneurs, especially their international business experiences, have been identified as having an important influence on IE. Such experience may have been gained in MNEs, but it may also have been obtained from prior business ownership.

The extent and nature of prior business ownership experience can shape opportunity identification and exploitation behaviour in ways that are qualitatively different from employment in an MNE. Notably, MNEs may have offered associated support structures and resources, but their idiosyncratic world views may prove inappropriate in new contexts and countries (Zahra, 2005). As discussed in Chapter 5, habitual entrepreneurs may be able to leverage prior knowledge to enhance their internationalisation activity compared to novice entrepreneurs (Robson et al., 2010). The nature of prior business ownership experience is heterogeneous. Currently, little theory exists to predict how different configurations of prior entrepreneurial knowledge and experience will shape internationalisation activity.

To reduce problems associated with new firm displacement, to encourage competitiveness and to foster wealth creation and job generation in local domestic markets, practitioners are encouraging more new and small firms to internationalise. This discussion has highlighted that research relating to private SME internationalisation is emergent, and associated with several methodological problems. Some studies are not keyed into debates relating to the internationalisation of private smaller firms as opposed to larger MNEs. There are several concerns surrounding the size and representativeness of samples, the techniques used, and the validity and reliability of measures operationalised in SME studies. Particular problems relate to establishing whether there is a causal link between internationalisation and superior firm performance. On the basis of cross-sectional analysis, it is unclear whether any causal link runs from internationalisation to superior performance, or vice versa. Some firms develop their activities over time, and they adapt their modes of internationalisation at different points in time as part of the process of learning and development. This suggests a need for deeper understanding of the determinants of internationalisation if the assumed benefits associated with internationalisation can be more widely generated. Resource deficient SMEs can circumvent barriers to internationalisation by developing links with larger organisations already linked into global markets. Additional research is warranted to provide further insights into the nature of these small and large firm relationships and how the international context presents additional issues, which are different from those exhibited when exploring relations between small and large firms in domestic contexts alone. Research is warranted to explore the internationalisation behaviour of smaller private firms located in developing countries that accumulate resources and select strategies to overcome local resource deficits (Pisano et al., 2007; Robson et al., 2011). Further, studies could explore why and how small entrepreneurial private firms in emerging economies internationalise from emerging to developed economies (Wright et al., 2005; Yamakawa et al., 2008).

With reference to internationalisation, as well as other themes highlighted in this book, there is, therefore, a need for longitudinal datasets and the application of panel data estimation techniques. In such analysis, there is also the need to consider the nature of the lag between internationalisation and any improved firm performance. This additional research can provide an evidence base which can guide policy with regard to resource allocation decisions and the targeting of groups for assistance (or customised support to each type of entrepreneur/organisation) (see Chapters 2 and 4). Identification of the time lags between internationalisation and superior firm performance effects in particular has implications for the timing and duration of policy support. While some work is emerging that uses longitudinal data, evidence from these studies can be problematical if they explore online datasets constructed for different purposes and utilise proxies for key variables that are too blunt (Requena-Silvente, 2005). This suggests a need for research that either uses specifically designed questionnaires administered over time (Autio et al., 2000), and/or the combination of these instruments with archival data (Zahra et al., 2000).

Discussion questions

1 Why do some practitioners want to encourage more private SMEs to internationalise?

2 Discuss the profiles of private SMEs that do not internationalise.

3 Critically discuss the applicability of traditional internationalisation theories.

4 Does the emerging international entrepreneurship theory solely explore issues facing a small subtype of private SMEs?

5 Are all private SMEs 'pulled' into internationalisation?

6 What resources are required by private SMEs to internationalise?

7 Discuss the sources of resources that are used by private SMEs to internationalise.

8 Does private SME resource acquisition and leverage shape the selected mode of internationalisation?

9 Should the entrepreneur be the unit of analysis in internationalisation studies?

10 What can returnee and transnational entrepreneurs add to the ability of entrepreneurial firms to internationalise?

11 Do private SMEs that internationalise consistently report superior levels of performance?

Recommended further reading

Bell, J., McNaughton, R., Young, S. and Crick, D. (2003). Towards an Integrative Model of Small Firm Internationalization. *Journal of International Entrepreneurship*, 1: 339–362.

Cumming, D., Sapienza, H., Siegel, D. and Wright, M. (2009). International Entrepreneurship: Managerial and Policy Implications. *Strategic Entrepreneurship Journal*, 3 (4): 283–296.

Jones, M. and Coviello, N. (2005). Internationalization: Conceptualising An Entrepreneurial Process of Behaviour in Time. *Journal of International Business Studies*, 36: 284–303.

Katsikeas, C. S., Leonidou, L. C. and Morgan, N. A. (2000). Firm Level Export Performance Assessment: Review, Evaluation, and Development. *Journal of Academy of Marketing Science*, 28: 493–511.

Keupp, M. and Gassmann, O. (2009). The Past and Future of International Entrepreneurship: A Review and Suggestions for Developing the Field. *Journal of Management*, 35: 600–633.

McDougall, P. P. and Oviatt, B. M. (2000). International Entrepreneurship: The Intersection of Two Research Paths, Special Research Forum. *Academy of Management Journal*, 43: 902–906.

Wright, M., Westhead, P. and Ucbasaran, D. (2007). The Internationalization of Small and Medium-sized Enterprises (SMEs) and International Entrepreneurship: A Critique and Policy Implications. *Regional Studies*, 41 (7): 1013–1029.

Chapter 14

Outcomes: Enterprise barriers, growth and performance

Contents

Learning objectives

- Appreciate the array of resource, skill, expertise and external barriers to enterprise development.
- Consider that a firm's internal and external environment can shape firm survival and performance.
- Illustrate that a range of measures can be used to monitor firm and entrepreneur performance.
- Understand the key dimensions of alternative stage models of business development.
- Recognise that most firms do not report linear growth over time.
- Consider the key dimensions of alternative theories (i.e., industrial economics theory, stochastic models, strategic management perspective, resource-based theory and population ecology theory) that have been proposed to 'explain' firm survival, growth and superior performance.
- Illustrate evidence from studies that have monitored firm performance.
- Appreciate that entrepreneur as well as firm performance needs to be monitored to fully assess entrepreneurial activity.
- Recognise that firm exit is not always a negative outcome and there are alternative definitions of business closure (or failure).
- Appreciate that the performance of habitual entrepreneurs needs to be assessed with reference to all the firms they have owned.

14.1 Introduction

Numerous new private firms are 'born to die young' and many surviving firms are 'born small and stay small' (see Section 2.2.1). At the other extreme, as we saw in Chapter 2, only a small proportion of new and small firms make significant contributions to economic development. Storey et al. (1987) detected that the fastest growing 4 per cent of firms generated 50 per cent of all the employment generated by the firms in their sample over a decade. These fast-growing small private firms have been described as *'gazelles', 'fliers', 'growers'* and *'winners'*.

In this chapter, barriers to firm development are illustrated. Internal and external reasons reported by entrepreneurs for growing their firms are then discussed. Several *'hard' economic firm performance outcomes* monitored by entrepreneurs, practitioners and academics are identified. In the following section, theoretical lenses used by academics to examine issues relating to firm growth are summarised with regard to several *growth models and theories*. The evidence base relating to superior firm performance and growth as well as entrepreneur performance is then discussed. In Chapter 2, it was highlighted that enterprise agencies in many countries have introduced universal national schemes (or 'blanket policies') to aid the conversion of nascent entrepreneurs into practising entrepreneurs. Practitioners have introduced 'soft' (i.e., information, advice, training, etc.) and 'hard' (i.e., premises, finance, etc.) support measures to address barriers to firm formation and development. Issues relating to *'targeting'* support and *'picking winners'* were raised in Chapter 2. The firm and entrepreneur performance evidence base discussed below is warranted to guide resource allocation decisions to 'pick winners', 'avoid losers', and/or provide 'customised support' to each 'type' of entrepreneur or firm. Finally, areas for additional research attention are illustrated.

14.2   Barriers to enterprise development

For many entrepreneurs, growth of their firm is not an objective. Only a small proportion of entrepreneurs have the inclination, the expertise or the resources to grow their private firms (see Case 24, Upstart Graphics: Merger and acquisition issues). Many entrepreneurs are concerned with maintaining their independence (Birley and Westhead, 1994) rather than firm growth. O'Farrell and Hitchens (1988: 1375) have asserted:

> a policy of survival is frequently preferred to one of growth. Furthermore, a growth strategy almost inevitably involves dilution of ownership through external equity investment, a price which many owner-managers and partnerships are not prepared to pay in order to secure growth . . .

Some entrepreneurs may be discouraged from pursuing a growth strategy because they fear this will attract attention from larger competitors who may take over their firm (see Case 24). Many entrepreneurs do not aspire to, or are not capable of, owning and managing large employment sized firms. Some entrepreneurs form and grow their firms to a point that allows them to maintain control of the organisation and the supervision of labour issues.

Attitudinal, resource, operational and strategic barriers to firm formation and developed (i.e., *market failures*) were alluded to in Section 2.1.1. The University of Cambridge Small Business Research Centre (1992) conducted a major study focusing upon the major constraints on the ability of over 2,000 independent firms to meet their objectives (also see Cosh and Hughes, 2000). Four types of businesses were identified: *'micro'* (1 to 9 employees), *'small'* (10 to 99 employees), *'medium'* (100 to 199 employees), and *'larger'* firms (200 to 499 employees). Fast growth firms were classified as firms that reported employment growth of more than 75 per cent over the 1987 to 1990 period. Respondents were asked to rank 11 possible constraints on their ability to meet their business objectives.

Table 14.1 shows that respondents in most firms perceived constraints in the *'external'* environment as being barriers to development. Finance barriers were most frequently reported as the most important constraints on the ability of firms to meet business objectives. Issues relating to the overall growth of market demand and increasing competition were frequently perceived as constraints (see Case 25, Private health practice: Limits to growth). Of less importance were constraints relating to managerial skills and shortages of skilled labour. Technological problems were generally regarded of modest importance, whilst few respondents mentioned the availability of premises. Fast-growing firms emphasised the importance of constraints relating to finance, employment and markets. Most notably, fast-growing firms highlighted constraints relating to finance and those relating to internal and employment matters; such as access to marketing and sales skills or management skills.

In a later study, Atkinson and Hurstfield (2005) detected that the greatest obstacles to firm success reported by entrepreneurs in the United Kingdom were competition (16.2 per cent), regulations (14.5 per cent), the economy (12.0 per cent), cashflow (9.9 per cent), taxation (9.4 per cent), recruiting staff (6.4 per cent), and availability/cost of premises (4.1 per cent). Many entrepreneurs believe that 'external' environmental issues, rather than themselves (i.e., internal motivation, commitment, skill and knowledge issues), are the major barriers to business development, which contradicts the views of practitioners.

Table 14.1 Constraints on the ability to meet business objectives by size and growth of firms

Constraints	Mean rank[a]					
	All in the sample	Micro[b]	Small[c]	Medium[d]	Large[e]	Fast growth[f]
Availability/cost of finance for expansion	4.95	5.20	5.06	4.49	4.07	5.17
Availability and cost of overdraft finance	4.90	5.06	4.97	4.58	4.29	5.16
Overall growth of market demand	4.67	4.18	4.87	4.81	4.92	4.24
Increasing competition	4.33	3.90	4.33	4.99	4.92	4.03
Marketing and sales skills	4.12	3.81	4.24	4.34	4.20	4.43
Management skills	3.85	3.20	3.95	4.39	4.68	4.29
Skilled labour	3.42	2.73	3.66	3.75	3.70	3.58
Acquisition of new technology	2.32	2.07	2.39	2.56	2.37	2.42
Difficulties in implementing new technology	2.16	1.78	2.25	2.55	2.46	2.34
Availability of appropriate premises or site	2.09	2.26	2.16	1.70	1.50	2.53
Access to overseas markets	1.89	1.58	1.98	2.02	2.06	1.85
Total responses (no.)	1,933	517	1,054	178	169	401

Notes:
(a) These are means of ranked data on a score from '0' indicating that the factor was completely unimportant and '9' indicating that it was highly important.
(b) Micro firm (1 to 9 employees).
(c) Small firm (10 to 99 employees).
(d) Medium firm (100 to 199 employees).
(e) Large firm (200 to 499 employees).
(f) Fast growth firm (i.e., employment growth of more than 75% over the 1987 to 1990 period).

Source: Cambridge Small Business Research Centre (1992, Tables 3.1 and 3.2).

14.3 Internal and external motivations for firm growth

Some entrepreneurs report the following *'internal'* and *'external'* reasons for firm growth:

● *Internal entrepreneur (and family) motivations.* To satisfy an entrepreneur's need for achievement; to increase an entrepreneur's desire for control and independence; to generate a store of wealth for the entrepreneur and their family; to provide employment positions for family members; to ensure the survival of an independent firm that can be transferred to the next generation of family members; to spread risks across products/services and/or markets; and to make a contribution to the development of the local community where the entrepreneur lives.

● *External motivations.* To increase the status and legitimacy of the owner(s) and the firm in social and business networks; to ensure external resources are leveraged to address the liabilities of newness and small size; to proactively consider current and future competitive threats; and a growth and competitiveness focus that enables the firm to adapt and to remain competitive irrespective of market, technological and/or regulatory conditions.

14.4 Firm performance outcomes monitored

The *'economic outcomes'* sought by practitioners (i.e., job generation, sales growth, profit maximisation, internationalisation, etc.) may not be the outcomes sought by entrepreneurs who may consider other *'non-economic'* or *'satisfying outcomes'* (i.e., maintain ownership, control, independence of the firm, protect a management comfort zone and lifestyle, combine family and business agendas, societal and environmental agendas, etc.). The following *'hard' economic firm performance outcomes* are monitored by entrepreneurs, policy-makers and/or practitioners (Cooper, 1993; Davidsson et al., 2006):

- number of customers;
- sales turnover growth;
- market share;
- return on investment;
- productivity;
- profits;
- profitability relative to competition;
- share value;
- net worth;
- new products/services;
- innovations, patents, copyrights, etc.;
- size of premises;
- customer satisfaction;
- ability to be an exporter/proportion of sales exported; and
- employment size and growth.

Studies have generally monitored firm performance with regard to several performance indicators. No single performance measure is universally accepted and monitored.

14.5 Theories to explain firm growth

14.5.1 Context

There is no comprehensive theory to explain which firms will grow, or how they grow. Despite numerous theoretical and empirical studies there is limited understanding of the drivers of firm growth. Alternative theories from several theoretical lenses have been presented to illustrate issues relating to firm growth (see O'Farrell and Hitchens, 1988; Freel, 1999). The following perspectives are discussed, in turn, below:

- stage models of business development;
- industrial economics theory;
- stochastic models of firm growth;
- strategic management perspective of small firm growth;
- resource-based theory; and
- population ecology theory.

14.5.2 Stage models of business development

14.5.2.1 *Context*

Stage models of business development suggest that the nature of a firm changes as it grows. Issues at the heart of each stage may differ from the issues central to other stages (Bridge et al., 1998). A linear set of stages is assumed with organisational characteristics exhibited at each stage. Types of problems encountered at each stage and the abilities required by entrepreneurs and managers to deal with critical incidents to move to the next stage are illustrated. There is no generally accepted stage model of business development. Greiner's (1972) 5-stage model, Churchill and Lewis's (1983) 5-stage model, and Scott and Bruce's (1987) 5-stage model have been presented. Each model is briefly summarised, in turn, below.

14.5.2.2 *Greiner's 5-stage model*

Greiner's (1972) model suggests a linear firm growth with periods of incremental trouble-free growth (i.e., evolution) punctuated by *crisis points* (i.e., revolution). Each growth stage is associated with attributes, but each growth stage is associated with a crisis that has to be dealt with. Greiner's 5-phase model is summarised in Table 14.2. Freel (1999: 204) succinctly summarised Greiner's model as follows:

- *Crisis of leadership.* The shift from a Phase 1 firm to a Phase 2 firm is triggered by a crisis of leadership. More sophisticated knowledge and competencies are required to operate larger production runs and manage an increasing workforce. Capital must be secured to underpin further growth and financial control must be put in place. The business must hire additional executive resources and restructure to meet these challenges. *Growth is achieved through creativity.*
- *Crisis of autonomy.* The control mechanisms implemented as a result of the first crisis become less appropriate as the physical size of the business increases. Line employees and managers become frustrated with the bureaucracy attendant upon a centralised hierarchy. Further, line staff are more familiar with markets and machinery than executives and become torn between following procedures and taking initiatives. It becomes necessary for the owners of the business to delegate to allow sufficient discretion in operating decision-making. *Growth is achieved through direction.*
- *Crisis of control.* Top executives begin to perceive a loss of control as a consequence of excessive discretion resting with middle and lower managers. Problems of co-ordination

Table 14.2 Greiner's stage model of business growth

Attribute	Phase 1 Creativity	Phase 2 Direction	Phase 3 Delegation	Phase 4 Co-ordination	Phase 5 Collaboration
Management focus	Make and sell	Efficiency of operations	Expansion of market	Consolidation of organisation	Problem-solving and innovation
Organisation structure	Informal	Centralised and functional	Decentralised and geographical	Line staff and product groups	Matrix of teams
Top management style	Individualistic and entrepreneurial	Directive	Delegative	Watchdog	Participative
Control system	Market results	Standards and cost centres	Reports and profit centres	Plans and investment centres	Mutual goal-setting
Management reward emphasis	Ownership	Salary and merit increases	Individual bonus	Profit sharing and stock options	Team bonus
Crises	Crisis of leadership	Crisis of autonomy	Crisis of control	Crisis of red tape	Crisis of ?

Source: Derived from Freel (1999, Table 9.1: 205).

may be exhibited across divisions, plants or functions. Top management regain control by using (undefined) special co-ordination techniques. *Growth is achieved through delegation.*

- *Crisis of red tape.* The 'watchdog' approach adopted by senior management and the proliferation of systems and programmes leads to a crisis of confidence and red tape. Further, the business is too large and complex to be managed through an extensive framework of formal procedures and controls. Movement to the next Phase is only achieved through a shift towards 'interpersonal collaboration'. *Growth is achieved through co-ordination.*

- *The next crisis!* No consistently identified crisis in Phase 5 was identified by Greiner. He suggests the crisis will revolve around the psychological saturation of employees. *Growth is achieved through collaboration.*

14.5.2.3 *Churchill and Lewis's 5-stage model*

Churchill and Lewis (1983) presented a 5-stage model where transition from one stage to the next has no explicit trigger. Their model is summarised in Table 14.3. They highlight issues relating to management style, extent of formal systems, and major strategy pursued. Their model suggests that a firm's internal organisational structure progressively exhibits increasing horizontal and vertical complexity. This is reflected in greater managerial sophistication and delegation. A strength of the model is that it recognises the initial role of the original firm owner can diminish over time from a central to a peripheral role when a firm has reached 'resource maturity'. Table 14.3 suggests that firms move from informal and ad hoc birth, through a quasi-functional state, culminating in the highest level of managerial and organisational refinement. This model makes the following distinctions:

- *Stage 1*: Organisational existence (i.e., staying alive by funding products or services and customers).
- *Stage 2*: Organisational survival (i.e., establishing the customer base, demonstrating viability).
- *Stages 3-D or 3-G*: Either success-disengagement or success-growth (i.e., confidence in its market position, options for further growth (for example, Stage 3-D firms or 'comfort firms' have achieved economic viability but they choose not to proactively seek further growth); further growth can be achieved providing managerial incompetence is avoided and the environment does not change to destroy the market niche(s) being served).

Table 14.3 Churchill and Lewis's lifecycle growth model

	Stage 1 Existence	Stage 2 Survival Disengage	Stage 3-D Success – Growth	Stage 3-G Success –	Stage 4 Take-off	Stage 5 Maturity
Management style	Direct supervision	Supervised supervision	Functional	Functional	Divisional	Line and staff
Extent of formal systems	Minimal to non-existent	Minimal	Basic	Developing	Maturing	Extensive
Major strategy	Existence	Survival	Maintaining profitable status quo	Get resources for growth	Growth	Return on investment

Source: Freel (1999, Table 9.12, p. 207; derived from Churchill and Lewis, 1983).

Table 14.4 Scott and Bruce's 5-stage model of business growth

Stage	Top management role	Management style	Organisation structure
1 *Inception*	Direct supervision	Entrepreneurial, individualistic	Unstructured
2 *Survival*	Supervised supervision	Entrepreneurial, administrative	Simple
3 *Growth*	Delegation/co-ordination	Entrepreneurial, co-ordinate	Functional, centralised
4 *Expansion*	Decentralised	Professional, administrative	Functional, decentralised
5 *Maturity*	Decentralisation	Watchdog	Decentralised functional/product

Source: Scott and Bruce (1987, Table 1: 48).

- *Stage 4*: Take-off (i.e., opting to go for growth).
- *Stage 5*: Resource maturity (i.e., the characteristics of a large, stable company).

14.5.2.4 *Scott and Bruce's 5-stage model*

Scott and Bruce's (1987) 5-stage model is summarized in Table 14.4. They highlight issues relating to top management role, management style and organisation structure associated with each stage. Scott and Bruce suggest that a firm moves from Inception (stage 1) through to maturity, which is the fifth and final stage.

14.5.2.5 *Critics of linear stage models of firm development*

Linear stage models of firm of development have been criticised (Birley and Westhead, 1990a). Some models are discursive and wisdom based classification schemes rather than conceptualisations of the processes underlying firm growth (O'Farrell and Hitchens, 1988). Further, some models unrealistically assume steady firm growth despite the fact that many firms die young, or are *born small and stay small*. Many firms cease to trade within three years (Storey, 1994), and never move beyond Stages 1 and 2. A theory of firm growth should be able to account both for the rarity of the process and for the tendency for most firms, once they have survived infancy, to plateau and remain essentially the same size for years (O'Farrell and Hitchens, 1988). Some firms move to a 'survival stage', but the owners do not have the inclination to further develop the firm. Firm growth may be associated with numerous discrete steps rather than a steady even progression. Not all firms start at Stage 1 and move to Stage 5, even if they continue to trade. Vohora et al. (2004), in their analysis of the phases of growth of spin-off firms from universities, identified an iterative, non-linear process of development as ventures may need to revisit and adapt the routines and processes introduced in earlier phases to enable them to address unanticipated challenges of later phases (see the example of Optical in Entrepreneurship in action 14.1).

A firm may have a management style that is more or less advanced than the stage (i.e., its organisational structure). Stage models do not explain what is happening inside a firm. They only describe its situation, and models illustrate symptoms not causes. Stage models do not help in predicting what will happen next to a firm. Theorists assume that movements from one stage to another are 'triggered' by a point of crisis, or critical juncture. Additional research is warranted to test the latter assumption. Many stage models do not incorporate an explicit spatial dimension that appreciates that there are alternative local contexts for enterprise associated with contrasting levels of resource munificence and

---

Entrepreneurship in action 14.1
Optical: A university spin-out firm traversing the stages of development but needing to adapt

Optical [a fictitious name] is a spin-out firm involved in the design and manufacture of telecommunications network equipment. A surrogate [external] entrepreneur championed business development. During the initial research phase, the academic team were focused on maintaining their worldwide reputation. The academic entrepreneurs published their scientific research findings relating to the application of fibre optics technology in material and telecommunications. The opportunity framing phase involved a surrogate entrepreneur who had worked in the telecoms industry. He recognised the opportunity almost by accident while engaged with the academics in the design of applications for their technology. The external surrogate entrepreneur commissioned a feasibility study into the potential market applications of the technology developed by the academics. During the pre-organisation phase, the surrogate entrepreneur used his network of contacts to gain access to necessary resources. The senior academic entrepreneurs did not want to leave their university posts. However, the surrogate entrepreneur was strongly committed to commercialising

the technology to ensure firm development. The academic and surrogate entrepreneurs realised that they needed to form a strong team. They needed to put the building blocks in place to ensure the team reached the credibility threshold required to attract financial support from a venture capitalist. A business plan was prepared, and an initial investment of £1 million was secured from a venture capitalist. The company entered into a reorientation phase because the early prototypes failed due to design mistakes and a shift in the market. The team had developed sufficient intellectual property (IP) and market intelligence to realign the firm's strategy towards new opportunities. The company was reorganised with changes in human resources to reflect requirements of the new strategy. Further, the company reached a sustainable returns phase, the business is profitable and continues to grow, exploiting new IP created by its engineers and the university. The venture capitalist reinvested £6 million.

Source: Derived and adapted from Vohora et al., 2004.

---

competition for resources that promote (or impede) firm development (see Chapters 11 and 13). Stage models need to be empirically validated with reference to large samples of firms in a variety of national and cultural settings. Longitudinal studies testing the applicability of stage models still need to be carefully conducted.

14.5.3 Industrial economics theories

Industrial economics scholars exploring firm growth have focused on the development of large firms. The nature and scale of issues facing smaller private firm have generally been ignored. Nevertheless, Downie (1958) insightfully suggested that the rate of firm growth is shaped by:

- financial and demand factors;
- capital required to expand capacity; and
- customers required to absorb production.

Industrial economics theorists assume that capacity varies directly with the rate of profit, whereas the rate of profit varies inversely with the rate of customer expansion and growth of demand. An upper limit to the rate of expansion of a firm is discussed but this perspective fails to identify an upper limit to the absolute size of a firm. Penrose (1959) suggested that firm growth might be retarded by *managerial constraints* (i.e., the '*Penrose effect*'). She asserted that the supply of managerial services and management capacity shape firm growth (see Section 3.8.2.2). Penrose claimed that growth rate of a firm is constrained and not the ultimate size of a firm.

14.5.4 Stochastic models of firm growth

The size distribution of firms in an economy is highly skewed with a few large firms and a large proportion of firms being small firms. Cumulative random shocks due to a stochastic process can promote a skewed distribution of firms. Gibrat's (1931) '*law of proportionate effect*' discusses the process of random growth leading to a skewed distribution of firms with regard to the following three assumed effects:

1 constant growth rate (of the market) which is common to all firms;
2 systematic tendency for the growth of a firm to be related to its initial size; and a
3 random growth term.

This law is difficult to test and conflicting evidence surrounding its applicability has been presented. The stochastic model perspective suggests that many factors shape firm growth, and there can be no dominant theory to explain small firm growth (O'Farrell and Hitchens, 1988).

14.5.5 Strategic management perspective

Within the strategic management perspective, resources, capabilities and strategies leveraged by an entrepreneur can shape firm development (see Section 3.8). Entrepreneur aspirations and behaviour are, in part, shaped by their social context and human capital (see Section 4.2). How quickly the entrepreneur can adapt and learn from the experience of dealing with its internal (i.e., 'resources of the entrepreneur and the firm') and external environments (i.e., competition for resources outside the firm) can shape firm development (Milne and Thompson, 1992). Internal environment resources relate to the firm and the entrepreneur. The '*external environment*' (see Chapter 11) relates to the:

- nature and extent of demand growth for products/services;
- degree of dependency upon a small number of suppliers and customers;
- extent of complexity in the market(s) served;
- strength of competition;
- threat of potential entrants;
- sectoral trends;
- regulation and levels of business and personal taxation;
- interest rates and exchange rates; and
- government policies to address 'market failures' facing new and smaller enterprises.

The local environment where the firm has its main operational premises can shape a firm's ability to acquire and leverage resources required for firm development (Vaessen and Keeble, 1995). Strategic management theorists appreciate that entrepreneurs need to continually collect and leverage entrepreneur and firm resources. Entrepreneurs and their firms need to adapt and to continually select strategies that ensure competitive advantage and profitable business operation.

Information, for example, is a key resource that needs to be accumulated and leveraged by an entrepreneur (Cooper et al., 1995). Many entrepreneurs do not have detailed information about products or services and markets, and this can act as a barrier to firm development. Firms seeking to enter new markets may benefit from policy initiatives designed to promote business survival and growth (see Section 2.3). External professional advisors can provide advice and counsel, as well as a breadth of knowledge to the principal entrepreneur not necessarily available from 'inside' partners or managers. External professional advisors can identify (and secure) critical resources from the external environment that might not otherwise have been secured. Also, they can draw to the attention of entrepreneurs a variety of opportunities. Local enterprise agencies can provide 'hard' (e.g., financial assistance) and 'soft' support (e.g., technical assistance) to encourage firm development. Provokingly, Robson and Bennett (2000) noted that weaker performing firms were more likely to seek external support in order to ensure firm survival rather than to promote rapid firm development.

14.5.6   Resource-based theory

14.5.6.1 *Context*

Resource-dependency theorists view organisations as entering into transactional relationships with external environmental actors because the entrepreneur cannot generate all necessary resources internally (Pfeffer and Salancik, 1978). More recently, resource-based view (RBV) of the firm theorists suggest that firm formation, survival and development is linked to the entrepreneur's and the firm's ability to gain access to a predictable uninterrupted supply of critical resources (see Section 3.8.3.2). The external environment (or locality) can be viewed as a pool of resources (i.e., customers, suppliers, finance, land, property, machinery, technical information, etc.) and new firm formation (NFF) and development can be linked to the degree of local resource abundance. If entrepreneurs do not secure through proactive and/or reactive strategies essential resources, they can be forced to close their firms. RBV of the firm theorists suggest that firm survival and development is encouraged by differentiation and diversification.

Cooper et al. (1994) asserted that principal entrepreneurs with more diverse levels of human capital have the ability to develop relevant skills and contacts, and they are able to tap into dense resource and information networks to circumvent barriers to firm development. They focused upon the following categories of the principal entrepreneur's human capital:

- general human capital;
- specific human capital – management know-how (i.e., managerial capabilities);
- specific human capital – specific industry know-how (i.e., technical capabilities);
- specific human capital – prior business ownership experience (i.e., entrepreneurial capabilities); and
- specific human capital – ability to acquire financial capital.

An entrepreneur's demographic characteristics and their *'general' and 'specific' human capital* can shape the ability to establish and grow a firm (see Section 4.2.2). This distinction is used below to illustrate the profiles of principal entrepreneurs linked to superior firm performance.

14.5.6.2 *Entrepreneur demographics*

Female entrepreneurs generally have fewer opportunities to develop relevant experience, have fewer contacts, and greater difficulty in assembling resources such as bank loans (Carter and Rosa, 1998). Women owners are less likely than male owners to solely pursue economic goals (Brush, 1992). Due to the disadvantages they face, and the low-barriers-to-entry competitive industrial sectors they select, some females are unable to capitalise on identified market opportunities.

Ethnic entrepreneurs generally trade within their own cultural niche markets. Entrepreneurs from ethnic minorities may draw upon their parents' social and business networks. Because many immigrant parents are likely to have established dense social and business networks (for example, outside the current domestic context), it is expected that second or more generation ethnic entrepreneurs will seek to exploit these contacts and 'break-out' into foreign markets (Ram and Hillin, 1994).

Principal entrepreneurs drawn from backgrounds where their parents had owned businesses (i.e., role models) can accumulate management know-how (see Chapter 7). Further, older principal entrepreneurs are more likely to have financial security, particularly in terms of owning their own homes (Cressy and Storey, 1995). They generally have wider social and business contacts, as well as considerable experience to enable their firm(s) to survive. Older principal entrepreneurs are able to capitalise on their wider social and business networks to exploit identified opportunities.

14.5.6.3 *Entrepreneur general human capital*

Firms owned by principal entrepreneurs who have been awarded a university degree generally have had their expectations raised. Education is related to knowledge, skills, problem-solving ability, discipline, motivation and self-confidence. These attributes enable highly educated entrepreneurs to cope better with problems.

Debate surrounds whether entrepreneurs' management know-how is a source of general or specific human-capital. Management know-how, as distinct from industry-specific know-how (see below), is a form of general human capital representing the non-economic knowledge accumulated by individuals that has a direct impact on individual economic behaviour. Here, managerial work experience is viewed as a dimension of general human capital if acquired outside a business ownership context. The central resource of a firm, the principal entrepreneur, can acquire resources based upon their management know-how, and their ability to identify appropriate partners, investors and advisors, which can be nurtured to supply the firm with necessary resources (Carter et al., 1997) (see the example of Lilias Cruikshank in Entrepreneurship in action 14.2). The level and breadth of prior management experience provides the opportunity to cultivate skills for monitoring diverse functions, and to develop contacts with potential suppliers and customers (Cooper et al., 1994). Entrepreneurs who have held managerial (or professional) positions prior to start-up may be able to introduce better human resource practices, undertake more promising competitive strategies, and identify more promising market opportunities.

14.5.6.4 *Entrepreneur specific human capital*

Previous experiences and beneficial close relationships can accumulate a principal entrepreneur's industry-specific know-how with specific customers and suppliers. Entrepreneurs with pre-business ownership experience in the same industry as their current firm provides them with detailed knowledge of the task environment. Industry-specific experience can

Entrepreneurship in action 14.2
Lilias Cruikshank: Entrepreneur's general human capital

Lilias Cruikshank left school at 16 with no formal qualifications. She was able to work her way up the managerial ladder in a variety of recruitment consultancies. At the age of 44, Lilias was made redundant from her managerial role in a management recruitment agency, which was in a highly competitive industry. She decided to start her own business rather than to seek an employment position. Lilias believed that she had accumulated considerable industry-specific and managerial know-how, and she had the personal skills to run a people-related business. Her sister-in-law, with no prior business ownership experience, was a nursery nurse who also wanted to work for herself. Lilias decided to start a nursery day-care business using her sister-in-law's industry related expertise. With the pooling of their accumulated managerial knowledge and talents, Lilias believed that they had sufficient resources to establish and run an efficient and professionally managed nursery business.

Source: Westhead, P., Ucbasaran, D., Wright, M. and Martin, F. Habitual Entrepreneurs in Scotland. Glasgow: Scottish Enterprise, 2003.

allow entrepreneurs to become acquainted with a customer base, and to develop more appropriate market niches (Chandler, 1996). Entrepreneurs' prior experience in the industry has been linked to subsequent business ownership success. Drawing upon industry-specific know-how, some principal entrepreneurs are able to identify resources and market opportunities to ensure the survival and development of their firms (see the example of Mike Kosic in Entrepreneurship in action 14.3).

As illustrated in Chapter 5, the skills, competencies, knowledge and networks accumulated during a previous business ownership experience can influence the decision to identify

Entrepreneurship in action 14.3
Mike Kosic: Entrepreneur's specific human capital

Mike Kosic left school at 16 with no formal qualifications. He joined the family bakery business owned by his father. Moreover, he ran the business for over ten years before his father died. Mike and his younger brother took over the management of the business. Drawing upon his work experience as well as the reputation and resources of the family firm, Mike had been able to purchase equity stakes in a snack bar and a confectionery manufacturing business. With the assistance of his brother, Mike made several changes to the family bakery in response to intense competition from the larger supermarkets. They decided to close down the retail bakery and set up a property company. They refurbished their retail shops to generate additional, more profitable, rental income streams. Mike has a close relationship with his bank manager who values the professional management systems Mike has put in place to monitor the development of his portfolio of businesses. Contacts seeking financial and managerial expertise are now presenting Mike with additional business opportunities. Before investing in any venture, Mike carefully screens the applications that are presented to him.

Source: Westhead, P., Ucbasaran, D., Wright, M. and Martin, F. Habitual Entrepreneurs in Scotland. Glasgow: Scottish Enterprise, 2003.

and exploit new opportunities. Habitual, particularly portfolio, entrepreneurs, more aware of potential market opportunities, may seek to capitalise on their existing skills and competencies in new markets.

The presence of partners increases the legitimacy of an organisation and they reduce some of the liabilities associated with newness and small size. Partners provide a firm with greater depth of expertise. Firms owned by teams of partners have wider social and business networks. Moreover, firms owned by partners have more diversified skill and competence bases to draw upon, which can be used to identify and obtain more resources from their external environment. Firms owned by teams with greater breadth and depth of expertise generally start off with more financial resources because the team are able to accumulate larger resources (Slevin and Covin, 1992). External investors are also more likely to regard firms owned by teams as being more credible. These human capital resources may be leveraged to address financial barriers.

A principal entrepreneur's ability to obtain financial resources can act as a buffer against random shocks (Brüderl et al., 1992). An over-reliance on personal savings alone can reduce new firm survival chances and employment growth prospects (Westhead and Birley, 1995). The availability of capital can allow entrepreneurs to learn and to overcome problems (Cooper et al., 1994). More capital can enable a firm to pursue a broader range of activities and more ambitious projects. Credible habitual entrepreneurs with successful track records may find it easier to obtain additional finance (on more favourable terms) than inexperienced novice entrepreneurs (see Chapter 5). Habitual entrepreneurs, particularly portfolio entrepreneurs, establish their firms with larger amounts of finance which is drawn from several sources. Firms that are undercapitalized from the outset generally report poorer survival chances (Brüderl et al., 1992).

14.5.7 Population ecology theory

Population ecology theorists suggest that the processes of *density* (and *'carrying capacity'*), *legitimation* and *competition* play a determining role in the size of organisational populations (Hannan and Carroll, 1992). These processes influence the ability of firms to survive and grow. Within this framework, firms have to change rapidly in order for an appropriate organisation–environment relationship to develop. Firm survival and growth is linked to the availability of resources and the ability to gain legitimacy and competitive advantage in potentially saturated markets. To survive and grow, firms may move into new market niches (or markets) with higher levels of munificence and/or less competition for available resources. This perspective suggests that the external environmental may *deterministically* promote (or retard) enterprising behaviour.

14.6 Firm performance and exit: Evidence

14.6.1 Firm performance

'Hard' economic firm performance outcomes have individually or collectively been monitored in firm performance studies. Factors found to be associated with one firm performance indicator may not be the same as those associated with another performance indicator (Birley and Westhead, 1990a). Firm performance needs to be explored with regard to a range of performance indicators (Cooper, 1993). Several statistical techniques have been used to 'explain' firm performance, and there is no universally used multivariate statistical technique to monitor firm performance. Growth has been widely used as a measure of entrepreneurial firm performance. There is a low correlation between different measures of growth, principally sales and employment growth (Delmar et al. 2003), suggesting different underlying relationships. Delmar et al. (2003) show that growth patterns among high growth firms differ according to organisational characteristics (i.e., age and size) and industry (i.e., manufacturing compared with service industry). Davidsson et al. (2006) found that 31 per cent of studies used sales revenues as a measure of growth, while 29 per cent used employment as a growth measure. Although it could be argued that growth is not a good measure of performance (Davidsson et al., 2009), these measures are widely used because it is often difficult to gain access to profit based performance measures relating to smaller private firms, especially high-technology firms that may take many years before they earn profits. Some studies have used entrepreneurs' 'satisfaction-with-performance' measures and these have been found to be reliable (Chandler and Hanks, 1993).

Insights from the RBV of the firm, human capital theory, and the strategic management perspectives suggest that a variety of 'internal' and 'external' environmental factors may be linked to superior firm performance. Storey (1994) presented a categorisation that identified the following three broad components linked to superior firm performance:

1 *starting resources of the entrepreneur(s)* (i.e., the personality, behaviour, attitude and capabilities of entrepreneurs);
2 *firm* (i.e., the structure of the firm); and
3 *strategy* (i.e., the goals of management and the decisions made to deal with internal and external environmental issues).

Storey (1994) suggested the following factors can be identified at various points in time:

- *characteristics of the entrepreneur* (i.e., identifiable before firm start-up);
- *characteristics of the firm* (i.e., identifiable post firm start-up); and
- *characteristics of the corporate strategy* (i.e., identifiable post firm start-up relating to the extent of complexity in the market(s) served).

Storey identified several factors that had been found in previous empirical studies to be significantly associated with growing firms (i.e., in terms of employment, sales, profits, etc.). These factors are summarised in Table 14.5. Storey (1994: 122) argued that:

> the three components – the entrepreneur, the firm and strategy – all need to combine appropriately in order that the firm achieve rapid growth.

With reference to the 15 elements related to *'the entrepreneur and access to resources'*, Storey (1994; 137) concluded that:

> although fifteen elements of the background of the entrepreneur have been identified and examined in a number of studies, the impact which this background has upon the subsequent performance of the firm looks to be relatively limited. Of course, if all fifteen elements were simultaneously included within a single study, then a more accurate assessment could be made of their relative impact. This, however, has not been undertaken and so we are forced to conclude, albeit on the basis of incomplete information, that some variables appear to be more significant than others.

Table 14.5 Factors associated with small firm growth

The entrepreneur/resources	The firm	Strategy
1 Motivation	1 Age	1 Workforce training
2 Unemployment	2 Sector	2 Management training
3 Education	3 Legal form	3 External equity
4 Management experience	4 Location	4 Technological sophistication
5 Number of founders	5 Size	5 Market positioning
6 Prior self-employment	6 Ownership	6 Market adjustments
7 Family history		7 Planning
8 Social marginality		8 New products
9 Functional skills		9 Management recruitment
10 Training		10 State support
11 Age		11 Customer concentration
12 Prior business failure		12 Competition
13 Prior sector experience		13 Information and advice
14 Prior firm size experience		14 Exporting
15 Gender		

Source: Storey (1994, Table 5.6: 123).

Of the fifteen elements, the motivation for establishing the business appears to be of some importance, with individuals who are 'pushed' possibly through unemployment, into establishing businesses being less likely to found a rapidly growing firm than those attracted by a market opportunity. The evidence also suggests that individuals with higher levels of education are more likely to found rapidly growing firms, as are those with some prior managerial experience. More rapidly growing firms are more likely to be founded by groups, rather than single individuals. Finally, middle-aged owners are most likely to found rapidly growing firms . . . Prior to start-up, the identikit picture of the entrepreneur whose business is likely to grow is extremely fuzzy.

With reference to the 6 elements related to *'the firm'*, Storey (1994: 143) concluded:

firm specific characteristics are generally more consistent and definitive than those relating to the background and resources of the entrepreneur. The pattern which emerges is that younger firms grow more rapidly and that there are sectoral differences. Legal form also appears to have an influence on growth, with limited companies having faster growth than either sole traders or partnerships. The direction of causation in this relationship is, however, somewhat unclear.

The evidence also suggests that there are differences in small firm growth rates according to where the firm is located, with those located in accessible rural areas in the United Kingdom having higher employment growth rates than those located either in urban areas or in inaccessible rural areas.

Probably the most complex results relate to the impact of firm size. Here it is clear that the smallest firms are the least likely to grow. Nevertheless, it also seems to be the case that few firms, once they have achieved MES [minimum efficient size], continue to seek further growth. In the United Kingdom the growth group appears to be those with between two and twenty employees.

With reference to the 14 elements related to *'strategy'*, Storey (1994: 154) concluded that:

there are four elements, or groups of elements, which stand out as important. The first, element 3, which indicates that growing firms are much more likely to have owners who share equity with external individuals or organisations. This demonstrates that the willingness to share equity is central to the achievement of growth.

The second fairly consistent finding is that rapidly growing firms have often made a conscious decision on market positioning – element 5. They have chosen to occupy particular niches or segments where they can exploit any quality advantage which they have. Very often this quality advantage is reflected in greater technological sophistication and willingness to introduce new products.

Thirdly, the introduction of new products – element 8 – is important in the balance of cases.

Finally, the ability of the small business to grow must be influenced by the willingness of the owners to devolve decisions to non-owning managers – element 9. The selection, motivation and retention of these individuals in the creation of a strong managerial team is likely to be important, but our research-based understanding of this issue remains weak.

The predictive modelling approach to 'explain' firm performance may have reached an impasse (Cooper, 1993). Freel (1999: 218) asserted that:

> The factors influencing growth are innumerable and are likely to defy classification in a simple, usable model. Attempting to isolate those where evidence of effect is 'consistent' appears fruitless.

Many predictive models are statistically significant but they 'explain' a relatively small proportion of the variance in the dependent variable (Westhead and Birley, 1995). Additional research is required that shifts the focus away from categorical variables towards a more dynamic analysis of firm survival and performance (Cooper et al., 1994). Research is required which considers the processes of adaptation and learning by (experienced) entrepreneurs and firms (Chapter 5). Also, research is required to focus on 'types' of organisations and entrepreneurs that have high growth potential.

Chapters 5 and 6 highlighted entrepreneur heterogeneity, whilst Chapters 7 and 10 illustrated organisation heterogeneity. Factors associated with firm survival are not exactly the same as those associated with superior performing firms. Broad and unfocused policies to encourage all firms to survive risk being ineffective if the aim of public policy is to encourage the growth of new and small firms. Practitioners may adopt a *'policy of avoiding losers'* rather than *'picking winners'* (Storey, 1994) because the 'losers' are easier to identify (Westhead, 1995). Nevertheless, practitioners need to appreciate more fully the needs and resources of each 'type' of entrepreneur (and firm) when they are formulating policies. Rather than provide 'blanket support' to all entrepreneurs, irrespective of their need or ability, there may be a case to *customise support* to each 'type' of entrepreneur (Westhead et al., 2004a). *Blanket policies* risk being ineffective if the objective of public policy is to foster the maximum level of economic development with the minimum amount of public support.

Recent research has shed important further light on the impact of the external environment (see Chapter 11) in which the firm operates on firm growth and value creation. While Romanelli's (1989) work on a population of start-ups within one industry showed that firm survival was based on addressing customer needs from the beginning, this study solely focused on one environmental configuration (i.e., low uncertainty and low complexity). Recently, Clarysse et al. (2010) found that although firm growth takes place in different environmental contingencies, the relation between the nature of the value creation process and the kind of growth that results is significantly different in each environment. Structuring the firm's resource portfolio so that it matches the environmental contingencies can create value. Depending upon the uncertainty and complexity in the environment, emphasis can be placed on either elaborating the technological part (i.e., low uncertainty and high complexity), the product part (low uncertainty and low complexity), or the market delivery (high uncertainty and high complexity) aspect of the value proposition. To realise this, technical expertise has to be built up internally if the technology proposition is the core, product experience has to be cumulated if the product proposition is key, and technical expertise has to be acquired if the market approach is central.

14.6.2 Firm exit

An important outcome of the entrepreneurial process is the issue of 'firm exit' (Birley and Westhead, 1990b). There is no universally accepted definition of firm closure (or 'failure'), and several definitions have been utilised (Westhead et al., 1995). Notably, there is no universally accepted definition of the point in time when a firm can be said to have closed (or 'failed') (see the example of the reasons relating to the closure of John Pimblett and Sons Limited in Entrepreneurship in action 14.4). The development of management buyouts of companies in receivership suggests that although a firm may have 'failed' in terms of one configuration of resources, it may be possible to resurrect it in another form (see Chapter 9). Keasey and Watson (1991) found that statistical models using firm-level data were able to predict the probability of firm closure better than human decision-makers using the same information sets. They believe that there may be a need to develop specific models for different 'types' of firm failure (Ucbasaran et al., 2010). The major problem, however, is being able to obtain appropriate and representative samples of failed and non-failed firms. Brüderl et al. (1992) examined the contributions of human capital theory and organisational ecology explanations of new firm failure. Their analysis suggests that variables reflecting the latter approach, such as number of employees, capital invested and organisational strategies, are the most important determinants of firm survival. Characteristics of the founder, notably years of schooling and work experience, were also found to be important determinants.

Entrepreneurship in action 14.4
Bakers Pimbletts goes into administration

Renowned St Helens firm Pimbletts has gone into administration with the loss of 60 jobs – the company employed 140 people and is famed around the country for the quality of its pies. Its 10 retail outlets dotted around St Helens [Lancashire in England] and the surrounding areas have been sold by administrators Paul Flint and Brian Green from KPMG Restructuring to Waterfield's [another bakery firm]. That move will safeguard 80 jobs but means the John Pimblett and Sons Bakery in College Street will be axed, along with 80 jobs. The company was founded by John and Mary Pimblett in 1921 and remained a family-run operation. It went on to become one of St Helens' most recognisable exports, with pie-lovers travelling from far and wide to stock up on their famed Pimblett meat and tatties. But the company has recently fallen on hard times, and earlier this year was forced to sell off and lease back its College Street headquarters in an attempt to ward off the effects of the credit crunch. Those efforts, ultimately, were in vain. Staff were told on Friday afternoon that the company would be going into administration and that a number of jobs were likely to be lost.

KPMG's director Paul Flint said, 'The tough trading conditions currently experienced by retailers up and down the country, coupled with rising food prices, have unfortunately led to John Pimblett & Sons being placed into administration.' He also commented, 'While we are pleased to have saved approximately half of the jobs with the sale of the shops to Waterfield's Bakery Limited, it is with regret that we have had to close the Pimblett bakery with the loss of 60 staff.'

Source: A. Moffat, Bakers Pimbletts Goes into Administration, *The St Helens Reporter*, 5 December 2008.

The entrepreneur's decision to exit from the current business may not strictly be the result of 'failure' or poor financial/economic performance (Hall, 1992; Wennberg et al., 2010). Ronstadt (1986) noted that 43 per cent of sampled firms exited due to liquidation, but a further 46 per cent of respondents exited by selling their firms. Entrepreneurs can leverage prior business failure experience to establish additional new firms (see Section 5.3.6.9). Conversely, the emotional effects associated with prior business 'failure' may retard an individual's subsequent ability to establish or purchase a further firm (Shepherd, 2003). Failure at a specific task can reduce an individual's belief in their ability to successfully undertake that task in the future. Habitual entrepreneurs who had experienced a 'business failure' may pursue more opportunities than those with no 'business failure' experience. Entrepreneurs with prior 'business failure' experience may perceive they are in a loss situation. Prospect theory (Kahneman and Tversky, 1979) suggests that when confronted with a loss situation, individuals exhibit risk-seeking behaviour. The latter individuals may pursue more opportunities to 'catch up'. Alternatively, if entrepreneurs view the outcome of a firm as one of many (in the past, present or future), they may adopt an options perspective (McGrath, 1999) whereby they have 'small bets' on more opportunities, and they accept that some opportunities will fail.

Exit from a firm may depend on an entrepreneur's own threshold of performance (Gimeno et al., 1997). Wennberg et al. (2010) noted that entrepreneurs exited their firms due to liquidation or sale, irrespective of firm performance (i.e., financial distress and superior firm performance), and strategies were linked to an entrepreneur's human capital profile. An entrepreneur may choose to close or sell a firm that may not be a total economic failure. Firm survival, therefore, depends on an entrepreneur's own threshold of performance which is determined by human capital characteristics such as alternative employment opportunities, psychic income from entrepreneurship, and the switching costs involved in moving to other occupations (Gimeno et al., 1997). If economic performance falls below this threshold, the entrepreneur may exit the firm, but continue in business if performance is above this threshold (see the example of an entrepreneur exiting a career in entrepreneurship in Entrepreneurship in action 14.5).

A distinction can be made between economic firm failure (i.e., firm bankruptcy), and failure because the firm did not meet expectations (i.e., closure/sale of a firm whose performance was too low in relation to the entrepreneur's expectations). With regard to the latter distinction, Ucbasaran et al. (2010) noted that despite exposure to more learning opportunities through multiple business ownership experiences, habitual entrepreneurs not experiencing business failure were more likely than novice entrepreneurs to report comparative optimism. This finding questions the ability of entrepreneurs to learn solely from positive experiences. Some experienced habitual entrepreneurs appear to be prone to the liabilities of success. Ucbasaran et al. (2010), in addition, detected that only portfolio entrepreneurs (and not serial entrepreneurs) experiencing business failure were less likely than novice entrepreneurs to report comparative optimism. They inferred that the circumstance under which business failure is experienced is linked to how the entrepreneur responds to, and learns from that experience. Ucbasaran et al. suggested that entrepreneurs who have experienced business failure are heterogeneous. They asserted that entrepreneurs reporting business failure experience should not be aggregated into a single crude business failure group that does not differentiate economic business failure from failure to meet an entrepreneur's expectations.

If we accept the perspective that entrepreneurship relates largely to the recognition and exploitation of opportunities (see Sections 3.6.3 and 3.6.4), it follows that opportunities

Entrepreneurship in action 14.5
Exiting entrepreneurship: Reflections made by a business pundit

A business pundit, Rob May, made the following comments: 'It has been more than two years since I left my last full-time corporate position. In that span I've started a small business, written a chapter for a book, taught a few college courses, been paid to blog, and launched a few web projects. I've loved it, but it is time to do something more financially rewarding for awhile . . . I've had to take a hard look at my long-term goals (start and run an artificial intelligence company) and decide what things I need to do today to get there. Sure, I could start and run my own business just for the sake of running my own business, but that isn't what I want. I want to do something I love . . . It's hard to find a job after doing your own thing, but I managed to get several great offers. Four of the five were with very young companies, two pre-funding startups, two older startups with some

funding, and a rapidly growing corporate spinoff. I ended up with a young company that does wireless software (bluetooth, WLAN, UWB, etc.) with a focus on embedded platforms . . . I'm one of three people on the 'business' side, and I get to have a role in defining my tasks and job scope, which is cool. I also get to see lots of great technology that is coming down the road, as our primary customers are companies developing new products . . . I still intend to go back to entrepreneurship someday, but honestly, this job has all the fun and excitement plus a steady paycheck, so I don't really feel like I'm in the big company grind. I'm very satisfied with helping drive this company to the next level.'

Source: http://www.businesspundit.com/why-i-quit-entrepreneurship-and-got-a-real-job/.

may emerge at any time, and in various forms. The option to exit from a firm may also be viewed as the exploitation of a strategic window of opportunity by the entrepreneur. Hence, the entrepreneur may choose to sell a firm if an attractive offer is put forward. Alternatively, the entrepreneur may choose to exit a firm if a more appealing venture (i.e., opportunity) is accessible. There is a need, therefore, for additional research to explore the various reasons for exiting a firm and the 'modes' of exit selected by entrepreneurs (Birley and Westhead, 1993b).

14.7 Entrepreneur performance

Empirical studies have monitored various 'hard objective' financial and non-financial indicators to measure firm-level growth and performance. Due to the focus on 'winning businesses' rather than 'winning entrepreneurs', relatively few studies have monitored the performance of entrepreneurs (i.e., *the entrepreneur rather than the firm as the unit of analysis*) with regard to entrepreneur performance indicators. Entrepreneurial performance is a subjective concept, depending on the personal expectations, aspirations and skills of the individual entrepreneur. Given the heterogeneous nature of entrepreneurship in terms of motivational diversity, different types of entrepreneurs and organisational forms, measuring entrepreneurial performance is inevitably a challenging task (Davidsson et al., 2006). Davidsson and Wiklund (2001) suggest that in order to distinguish what is truly attributable to the individual entrepreneur from the idiosyncrasies of the particular opportunity, the individuals must be studied across several new firm efforts. Rosa (1998) has called for a measure of entrepreneurial performance in which aggregate value is assessed over all firms owned by the entrepreneur, not just any single existing firm under study. Most notably, the performance of portfolio entrepreneurs should be assessed with reference to all the firms in which they currently have an ownership stake (Carter et al., 2004). 'Entrepreneurial career performance' in terms of the number and proportion of successful new enterprise processes, or the total net worth created, may be an effective means of avoiding the mismatch between independent and dependent variables (Davidsson and Wiklund, 2001).

Habitual entrepreneur studies have monitored entrepreneur rather than solely firm performance (see Chapter 5). Entrepreneur performance can be assessed with regard to an array of indicators relating to the desire to grow the surveyed firm; desire to increase the total employment size of the surveyed firm; the amount of money drawn out of the surveyed firm; household income (Rønning and Kolvereid, 2006); satisfaction with the surveyed firm; standard of living today compared to when they first established/owned the surveyed firm; and willingness to start or purchase a business again in the future (Flores-Romero and Blackburn, 2006; Kolvereid and Isaksen, 2006). However, many studies fail to appreciate the diversity of entrepreneurs and organisations owned by entrepreneurs. Consequently, very few studies have focused upon 'which type of entrepreneur' (and which 'type of organisation') shape several performance outcomes. This diversity raises opportunities for entrepreneurship research in that there is a need to learn more about how 'type' of entrepreneur (and/or type of organisation) acts as a 'moderator' in shaping relationships between explanatory variables and performance (Chandler, 1996). To understand and separate the contribution of individual entrepreneurs (as well as teams of entrepreneurs) with regard to the entrepreneurial process and entrepreneurial performance, there is a need for more theory building qualitative studies.

14.8   Looking forward

Several theories have been presented to explain the growth of firms. Each theory has its strengths and its limitations. Bridge et al. (1998: 184) made the following realistic conclusion:

> given the complexity of entrepreneurs and of small businesses, and the complexity and diversity of markets in which they operate, any attempt to produce a comprehensive theory or any meaningful analysis of growth may be unrealistic, at least in the short term. One may also add that there is no single correct management of growth and that growth itself, as has been noted, is not a simple linear process: rather, businesses are growing, contracting and growing again several times and at different rates.

Nevertheless, an entrepreneur's ability to acquire and leverage resources and to deal with issues relating to the firms' internal and external environments cannot be ignored. Resource-based variables (such as human capital variables) have the advantage of being visible, and relatively easy to assess by entrepreneurs and practitioners. Variables relating to the ability of an entrepreneur/firm to acquire resources are amenable to public policy intervention (Westhead, 1995; Ucbasaran et al., 2010), unlike variables such as business age and size that have been found to be associated with growing firms (Storey, 1994). Doubts surround whether new and smaller private firms need special policy help to address barriers to enterprise development (see Section 2.3.3). Practitioner benefits (i.e., economic and non-economic) associated with promoting NFF and firm development are acknowledged. Assuming an interventionist stance to maximise these benefits, debate surrounds the merits and the ability to 'picking winners' and/or to 'avoiding losers'. A balanced policy agenda that encourages NFF and firm development fostered by customised support to each 'type' of entrepreneur (and/or firm) may be appropriately contextualised to each local environmental context (see Chapter 11). To guide future resource allocation decisions, an evidence base is required to explore the research questions discussed in Section 11.8 relating to the themes illustrated in Figure 1.1 in Chapter 1.

Discussion questions

1 What are the most frequently reported barriers to enterprise development?
2 Discuss the strengths and weaknesses of a selected stage model of business development.
3 With reference to a selected stage model of business development, discuss the types of problems encountered at each stage, and the abilities required to progress to the next stage.
4 Do all firms report linear development over time? Discuss.
5 Population ecology theorists suggest that the external environment deterministically promotes (or retards) enterprising behaviour. Critically discuss and make reference to alternative theories to illustrate the array of themes assumed to be associated with firm growth.
6 To what extent is firm development shaped by the ability to adapt and to assemble and leverage resources?
7 To what extent is a firm's strategy the main factor promoting superior firm performance?
8 What factors have been found in empirical studies to be associated with superior performing firms?
9 Can practitioners identify the profiles of 'winning businesses' and 'winning entrepreneurs'?

Recommended further reading

Cooper, A. C. (1993). Challenges in Predicting New Firm Performance. *Journal of Business Venturing*, 8: 241–253.

Cooper, A. C., Gimeno-Gascon, F. J. and Woo, C. Y. (1994). Initial Human and Financial Capital Predictors of New Venture Performance. *Journal of Business Venturing*, 9 (5): 371–395.

Davidsson, P., Delmar, F. and Wiklund, J. (2006). *Entrepreneurship and the Growth of Firms.* Cheltenham, UK: Edward Elgar.

Gimeno, J., Folta, T. B., Cooper, A. C. and Woo, C. Y. (1997). Survival of the Fittest? Entrepreneurial Human Capital and the Persistence of Underperforming Firms. *Administrative Science Quarterly*, 42: 750–783.

O'Farrell, P. N. and Hitchens, D. M. W. N. (1988). Alternative Theories of Small-Firm Growth: A Critical Review. *Environment and Planning A*, 20: 1365–1382.

Storey, D. J. (1994). *Understanding the Small Business Sector.* London: Thomson Learning.

Case studies

Case study 1

IPS Communication – Distribution: Claude Guinet's career in entrepreneurship*

Joëlle Piffault and Louis J. Filion

Summary

This case describes the entrepreneurial career of Claude Guinet. He acquired survival skills during the German occupation of Paris in the Second World War. Guinet learned the printing trade in his father's business, but his mother, a sales representative for a women's lingerie company, also had a profound influence on his life. He began his career as a salesman for a printing firm and gradually moved towards advertising and communication. In 1968, he purchased a stationery store that specialised in office supplies. He then transformed IPS Communication – Distribution. The company focuses upon office supply distribution, communications and retail sales. The family firm employs 100 people and has an annual turnover of CAN$20 million. Looking forward Guinet needs to consider issues relating to ownership succession and the future of the family business.

Introduction

Claude Guinet was an only child, born on 14 May 1929. His father, like his grandfather before him, came from the Savoie region of France. Both were entrepreneurs. Young Claude grew up surrounded by entrepreneurs and enterprising people on both sides of his family. His father was joint owner of a print shop known for its use of leading-edge technologies relating to offset and lithography. His mother was a sales representative for a

ladies' underwear company. During the Second World War, Claude was a teenager living in Paris, France, where he developed his defence and survival mechanisms. Claude Guinet recalled:

> 'We had to protect our lives and that meant forming a very close-knit family structure. After each bombing, we had to repair and clean up our living quarters. . . . We became farmers in the classical sense, raising rabbits and chickens, growing potatoes and peas, carrots and cauliflowers. As for the rest, we gathered what we could from the fields after the harvest, and scavenged wood or coal for the fire. Life was a precarious thing. We had to accept that and devise our own methods of self-preservation.'
>
> (Claude Guinet in Montreal on 8 May 2000 and in Paris 29 June 2000.)

The effects of the war were not just negative. It was a time when Claude Guinet was able to choose and build foundations for his fundamental values, forging a system of 'self-defence and adaptability' that would serve him well throughout his life. Surveying an area, assessing an environment, sensing an atmosphere and choosing his contacts became second nature to him, and this had a tremendous impact on his adult personality.

At school, young Claude received a classical education. Outside school, the need to 'be operational in the field' taught him to fend for himself. This day-to-day dichotomy in his life created what he described as an 'extraordinary personal dynamic'.

Whilst still at school, he began work in his father's print shop. He learned the printing trades relating to lithography, typography, offset printing, the rotary press and computer-assisted publishing (CAP). Claude became familiar with the different types of services offered to the shop's customers. Notably, technical documentation for

*The full case is reported in Piffault, J. and Filion, L. J. (2002). Claude Guinet: l'art des Rencontres. In L. J. Filion *Savoir Entreprendre*. Montréal: Presses de l'Université de Montréal, pp. 129–166. This case was translated from the French by Benjamin Waterhouse.

drugs, business registers, brochures, posters and straight-forward lithography and typography.

The dangers he had experienced during the war had also taught him that it was best to have two irons in the fire. Through sport he discovered the Scout movement, which in France has strong values and is affiliated with the Catholic Church. For Claude Guinet, becoming a Scout meant resuming contact with the Christian values and faith he had set aside during the war to live what he describes as a 'utilitarian' life. In the Scout movement, Claude discovered a world organised around a team focus, together with a certain systemic continuity with which he felt comfortable. He threw himself into it. From troop leader, he soon became district commissioner. Typically, his weekends were divided between sports and Scout activities.

When Claude left high school, he worked full time and enrolled in evening classes at the National Institute of Graphic Arts and Industries. His field of interest was printing, a changing profession. Claude completed his academic studies while working in his father's printing shop.

Between 1945 and 1949, Claude Guinet became a fully-fledged member of the print community, working for his father but also spending time in other local print shops. Printing was a business based on contacts and communication, and it was this that most attracted his attention. Moving from firm to firm, he built up his business expertise and developed a network of personal contacts that led him, in 1968, to purchase and develop his own firm. Claude Guinet was first and foremost 'a developer and an organiser', and would remain so throughout his life, according to the people closest to him. Others have described him as a 'winner', adding that he has 'preserved the intense sporting culture that he developed as a child'.

Claude Guinet had to do military service. The military authorities quickly seized on his talents as a group leader, and he says he spent 'two fabulous years' in military service, organising camps and sports for different companies, organising choirs and setting up inter-regiment meetings. He even hosted theatre troupes.

He was 21 years old when he left the military. His courses at the National Institute of Graphic Arts and Industries were coming to an end, and he needed a job. His Scouting activities and life in the army had taught him that he needed to live and develop in an environment that would bring him into contact with people.

Claude had also learned a lot about himself and knew he would be more comfortable in a situation where he could be a business developer in the broader sense. There were several possibilities open to him. Which would he choose? He began by getting married. Claude and his first wife would have a son and a daughter.

A developer through and through

Claude knew all about the printing trade, and was also familiar with life on the shop floor – he had, after all, worked there since the age of 15. Thanks to his family environment, Claude had developed a certain expertise in a trade that required a high level of perfectionism to be successful. However, as he himself freely admits, he felt much more at home with the business know-how acquired from his mother – the need for contacts, a pleasant manner and sales. As a teenager he had been a member of the CGT, a major French trade union with communist leanings that dominated the print community. If he wanted to work on the shop floor, he would have to join it again. In his mind, though, the implacable union logic was synonymous with 'standardisation', which went against his developer's temperament and prevented him from ever returning to his original trade.

But which path should he take? Claude arranged an interview with the president of Rouchet, a large print shop whose products he knew well from his work experience with the company. He offered his services as a salesman, because he felt he would be 'happier and more successful' in a sales career. Unconsciously, he had returned to his own 'logic and security'. In choosing his first career, Claude showed how well he had assimilated the culture of his parents – printing and sales – and also demonstrated an excellent capacity to listen to his own inner voice. There is an old Arab proverb that says, 'The man who practises his father's trade is invincible'. Claude Guinet, practising the trade of both his father and his mother, would be doubly invincible.

As Claude learned more about the craft of selling, he introduced new techniques and changed employers. From his first position as a pure salesman, he went on to become a communications consultant and then a commercial director. After the adhesive labels, he sold continuous paper for computer printers, and then advertising boards. Claude also tried his hand at design, working for a firm selling advertising and mechanical print products. It was here that he realised the importance of expressing a message when producing documents:

> 'I understood that it wasn't a matter of producing for the sake of it, but of producing to express a message. From then onwards, I brought designers and graphic artists into my work teams. I introduced many different design structures, right up to the day I launched my own business. I moved from firm to firm until I eventually changed the course of my career, when I decided I should stop being a printer and start being a designer.'

An entrepreneur is born: Information, Publicity, Service (IPS) Communication – Distribution

In May 1968, Claude Guinet took a gamble and bought a small business with ten employees, located at Place de la Porte Champerret in the 17th *arrondissement* in Paris, and known as the Sauvion Champerret Printing and Paper Company. The firm, with its strategic geographical location, offered several advantages. Notably, many French and foreign businesses moved their headquarters to this neighbourhood. The stationery store, specialising in office supplies, had been in operation for 80 years. Behind the store was a small print shop very similar to the one his father ran.

Claude Guinet found the transition from commercial director (his position at the beginning of May 1968) to business owner of Information, Publicity, Service (IPS) Communication – Distribution (his position at the end of May) difficult, because it involved several important decisions. He sold the print shop assets, kept the stationery store and created a communications department. Claude also hired a managing director, so that he himself would be free to develop the business.

In his new role as business owner, Claude wasted no time in structuring his distribution department, basing it on the model of major French distributors Guilbert and Gaspard. Although he had some accounts outside the city, Claude decided not to develop a network to serve them, since the resulting structure would be much more cumbersome than the one he already had. In opting to concentrate his activities in Paris and its suburbs, he was able to institute a rigorous system that allowed him to offer same-day delivery, within four hours of the order being placed.

By keeping the store, he knew his short-term cashflow was secure, and by delivering orders directly to his customers' offices he was able to maintain his medium-term cashflow. This in turn allowed him to develop the graphic design component of his firm, which would produce revenues in the longer term. He subcontracted all his printing work.

The store served private individuals as well as businesses, offering a wide range of stationery products, a specialised accounting bookshop and a printing and photocopying service. The ground floor displayed general stationery, educational supplies, a children's corner, gifts, cards, diaries and pens, as well as computer supplies. Office supplies, filing supplies and the general stockroom were in the basement. The products were placed on shelves so that customers were easily able to find what they wanted; as everyone knows, a satisfied customer will come back for more. The windows were reorganised and redecorated regularly to attract new customers. In subsequent years Claude Guinet added a second and then a third store, in Levallois-Perret, a Paris suburb close to Porte Champerret. When asked if he ever thought of developing a retail chain, his answer was a categorical 'no':

> 'Every time I opened a new store, it required an additional investment and was a heavy corporate charge in a country where corporate charges were already very heavy. I preferred to find markets where I could subcontract printing work, to cut down on costs and overheads. I designed, I composed, I did the page layout and then I subcontracted the rest. I opted for the least cumbersome formula possible and then developed it to the maximum.'

His subcontractors were a series of smaller structures serving the needs of the distribution and design departments. Although independent, the subcontractors worked closely with IPS. When Claude eventually decided to move onto foreign markets, he chose the same formula. In 1968, the communications department was still fairly small, comprising Claude Guinet and three designers working from the cramped quarters formerly occupied by the print shop. However, the world of graphic communications was changing fast. For Claude Guinet, a former communications consultant, the time had come to play a more proactive role in the process by developing the marketing aspect of printed matter. Paper, until then the main vehicle for graphic communication, was gradually replaced by computers and sophisticated software packages. On-screen design and digital printing eclipsed some of the traditional printing techniques. Claude Guinet describes the radical transformation of his sector as follows:

'I understood that a document was only of interest if it was nicely laid out, with appropriate graphics and headers. I set up a design studio with designers and graphic artists, and I started doing intelligent page layout that served as a basis for developing the communication and marketing aspects.'

He also needed customers. This is how he went about recruiting them:

'It quickly became clear that I needed two regular sources of supply, namely a daily revenue from the store, and recurrent orders payable at 30, 60 and 90 days for the medium term. I went to see organisations like the Bank of France and other major French financial institutions, because they had excellent financial capabilities and guaranteed terms of payment. I offered to transform their written communications and market their products. That enabled me to seek out markets for the longer term.'

The longer-term markets he mentions here were the accounts of some of France's largest corporations, including SNCF (the national railway company), EDF and GDF (Électricité de France and Gaz de France, the country's electricity and gas utilities), and Vivendi and Alcatel. Smaller accounts were managed by a team of salespeople, each responsible for a territory covering several Parisian *arrondissements* or suburbs.

IPS Communication – Distribution in 2000

IPS operates in two separate sectors, namely communication and distribution. Its total annual turnover is around CAN$20 million. Distribution accounts for 80 per cent of sales, whilst the communication sector generates 20 per cent of sales.

Between 1968 and 1985, when he finally retired, Jacques Croué, 'a salesman and organiser', was the company's general manager. He was succeeded by Maurice Cognard with a background in general administration, but he stayed just under a year. In 1986, Claude Guinet asked Pierre Le Floc'h to take over as general manager, a position he still held in 2000. Le Floc'h had been employed as a helicopter pilot in the French Air Force. He had taken a postgraduate course in international trade, and held several management positions with major French corporations prior to joining IPS.

IPS is not unionised, but it does have an enterprise committee, as required by law in France for firms with more than 50 employees. The company's headquarters and the communications department offices are located in Paris at Place du Général Kœnig.

The distribution department's main building is the warehouse located at Colombes, near La Défense, in western Paris. Containing approximately 9,000 office supply and print items, it stocks around 70 per cent of the products sold in the stores. The rest, including cards, diaries and gifts, are obtained from specialist suppliers who deal directly with the store managers. Sales are divided over three major market segments, namely major accounts, which bring in around 30 million francs per year [around CAN$6 million], the small and medium-sized business sector, which brings in 40 million francs, and the very small business sector, which brings in 10 million francs. To ensure that it offers the most competitive prices possible, the company is a member of a buyers' co-operative with between 150 and 200 other firms.

The distribution team is composed of more than 70 people. The upper floor of the warehouse is set aside for logistics, and commercial manager Jean-Marie Croué (the son of Jacques Croué) also has his office there. Fifteen salespeople cover the Paris area and suburbs. Office-based account executives administer sales and deal with telephone and fax orders. The Internet and Intranet have grown significantly in importance over the last few years, and around 20 per cent of orders now arrive by e-mail. The ground floor of the warehouse is used to prepare and ship orders. The company has its own fleet of trucks, and hires additional vehicles when necessary. Deliveries can also be made by pool cars when a more personalised service is required.

The distribution sector has undergone some fundamental changes since the early 1990s. The massive use of computers and the increasingly important role played by the Internet have modified some of the rules of the game, and mergers and acquisitions by major international groups have added to the turmoil. In the case of IPS, the changes have resulted in reduced profit margins. Indeed, over the last decade its profits have fallen from 40 to 42 per cent to 33 to 34 per cent.

Pierre Le Floc'h has this to say about the situation in the distribution department when he first joined the company:

'When I first arrived in 1986, there were two stores and a distribution section, and they all functioned like relics from the Middle Ages. Nothing was computerised, and it quickly became clear that we couldn't develop the existing setup. We replaced the staff in its entirety. Jean-Marie Croué, who wasn't even 30 years old at the time, was brought in with the primary task of developing this aspect of our operations. His job included computerisation, referencing all the products, and recruiting and implementing an entirely new organisation, especially for the commercial sector. Things went well; from an initial figure of around 25 million francs, we now have a turnover of 80 million [2000].'

(Pierre Le Floc'h interviewed in Paris on 27 May 2000.)

The two stores, which employ ten people, are under the authority of the distribution department. Nicole Guinet, Claude's wife, manages the Levallois Perret store and oversees daily operations at the Porte Champerret store.

The communications department, employing around 30 people, is managed by Philippe Guinet, Claude's son, who was born in 1952. The department oversees communications relating to publishing, creation and layout of documents for printing, and also has an Internet section that hosts websites. It serves several major public and private sector accounts, including the national police force. The communication and advertising sector has undergone some major changes in recent years, due to the transformation of the media industry and the increasingly important role of the Internet.

During his military career, Pierre Le Floc'h 'did a lot of human resources work' and acquired extensive experience of human beings and human relationships. This, along with his age, has been an asset in his business career, and he cultivates it carefully:

> 'I'm not in charge of the company. Claude Guinet is. He's the major shareholder, and he can decide to continue for another year or two, or stop . . . I don't want to talk about private affairs, that's something between Claude Guinet and his son. It's a delicate subject, both privately and professionally. Obviously, it's difficult to build their father–son relationship into things as well. If I were to say all was well between father and son, it simply wouldn't be true. But I've known them both for many years – I met Claude in 1973 and Philippe not long afterwards. I know them through the business and as private individuals. I know their respective qualities, and we manage to work together . . . I knew Philippe, like I knew Claude, before I came to work for the firm. Two different worlds . . . and we manage to compromise.'

Claude Guinet's business philosophy

Claude Guinet is aware that the dynamics of his designers are very different from the dynamics of his distribution team. Yet, by combining the two units under the same brand image and a logo with carefully selected colours and an evocative catchphrase, he has managed to create a business philosophy that everyone can embrace (see Figure 1). This is how he describes the process of creating the firm's brand image:

> 'I chose three elements right away: the colours, the logo and the catchphrase. The Ferrari colours, red and black, seemed to offer the strongest dynamic. Red is a warm colour. The contrast between red and black gives both colours strength, and I used them in my IPS logo back in the 1970s. I repeated the process 30 years later, when I modernised the logo as part of a study for Montreal's Multimedia City. It's now the 'Eye of Multimedia'. The problem is to make sure your graphic design doesn't become dated; in my own case, I don't think it has. On the other hand, I do need a new catchphrase, because the one we currently use – Stationery at the Heart of the Firm – has served us well over the years but doesn't really apply today, in the e-commerce era. I have 15 or so possibilities in mind, and I'll have to choose one of them soon.'

Claude Guinet knows the relationship with his colleagues and employees is important. He considers the selection and training of people who will work with him to be a priority, because 'there are only 24 hours in a day and you have to be able to delegate'. He also pays considerable attention to his firm's 'image of moral health', so that his employees 'can experience success and security'. The working relationship must be able to recreate the human warmth that is so essential to the pleasure of being with someone else. According to Claude, 'the employees must be able to recognise themselves in the image you create. For me, a company culture is first and foremost a social culture, where people share the same values and the same needs.' To reach this balance, Claude visits the warehouse, the stores and the design office on a regular basis. Claude 'adjusts the engine every day, because nothing is ever perfect.' He talks to his employees and supports them through their personal dramas.

Claude Guinet considers the role of entrepreneur and owner-manager to be a difficult and demanding one, because:

> 'An entrepreneur has to take care of his standing at the bank; the firm's reputation with its suppliers and

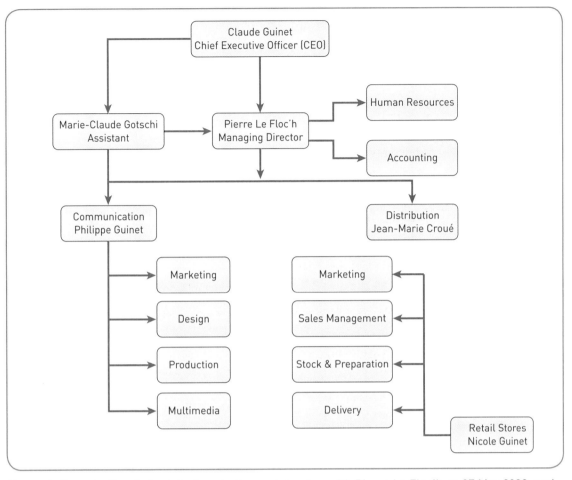

Figure 1 Organisational chart designed after an interview with Pierre Le Floc'h on 27 May 2000, and revised by Claude Guinet

employees depends on it. Pay cheques always have to be issued on the same day, at the same time. You can't accept anything else.'

To help protect his 'standing', Claude opened an account with the Bank of France. It is not a current account, since his payment capability is limited. However, it does provide him with a cushion, in case he ever needs extra funds.

Claude Guinet is a man of action who tends to follow his instincts, but he is well aware that he sometimes needs to curb his enthusiasm. He uses a business plan to guide his activities, but he questions its limitations, believing that if a business plan is followed to the letter, it can lead to managerial rigidity and loss of contracts. Sometimes a chief executive officer (CEO) can lose confidence in

himself or the people around him. However, he must never let this show, because the business environment changes so quickly that doubts can disappear overnight.

Has he ever thought of splitting the company into two separate units? There was a time when this might have been interesting. By 2000, he was no longer thinking along those lines, because it would not have been a good decision financially. Experience has shown that the distribution and communication sectors are not governed by the same economic cycles. During the war, Claude Guinet learned never to put all his eggs in one basket; it was a question of survival. He talks of this characteristically prudent approach:

'I don't know why, but it's never worked systematically. Distribution works when communication doesn't, and vice-versa. I've always been able to rebalance my accounts, precisely because I had three strings to my bow: distribution of office supplies, communications (publishing) and the stores. Now [2000], with the addition of multimedia to the communications sector, I have four main strings and two main departments. The logic isn't the same.'

Who is Claude Guinet?

Claude Guinet reflects:

'I wasn't really interested in the printing trade, but I'm very grateful to my father for helping me to understand the concept of continuity, a fundamental value that's been very useful to me in everything I've done. It was my father who taught me to think of a career as a linear thing. The line between a man and his destiny is composed of many different elements, but they all lead towards the same end result, the image of that man and how he constructs his destiny. The trick is to know where to find the way out. Sometimes you realise you've lost sight of it, and this can be especially true today, with the Internet. The process is a bit like mushroom picking. You set off to pick mushrooms and suddenly you come across some wild fruit that you just have to taste. The trick is to know how to get from the mushrooms to the fruit, and back . . . Sometimes, you're so interested in all these peripheral elements that you lose your focal point. My father gave me a focal point when he gave me a trade . . . It's also a role play between intelligence and instinct, learning to use fundamental intuition, inspiration and rational logic all together, at the same time, all the time.'

Pierre Le Floc'h comments:

'Because he's a winner, in both sporting and financial terms, he could never accept, for example, that his firm was losing money. Claude has a profound sense of humanity. Someone he knew got cancer. Claude was probably the person who did the most for him. He gave him moral support. Thanks to his contacts in the medical community, he tried to direct him to the best hospitals and the best specialists. It's his "regimental father" side.'

Nicole Guinet reflects:

'Claude has always been a passionate man. He's also very generous. He has a lot of principles. He has deep religious beliefs, a true Catholic . . . He's continued to develop, change and take charge of his destiny. He needed to enjoy himself, to travel, to do things, to climb mountains.'

Robert Gagnon remarks:

'Claude has the ability to be able to judge people fairly easily, and he's ready to act on those judgements. It's always been like that in our relationship.'

Claude Beaulieu suggests:

'There are no limits with Claude. He always has to go a bit further, a bit bigger.'

Maurice Cognard a longstanding colleague comments:

'[Claude] was interesting to meet because he had ideas. Advertising people always had really brilliant ideas. However, when it came to putting them down on paper and handing them over to the printers, they often didn't work, because they were technically impossible to achieve. You need the technology to do things. It was always the printers' fault if things didn't work out. Some young, up-and-coming printers, including Claude Guinet, took things in hand and began to incorporate design and creation into the printing trade so as to control the technical process and satisfy their customers' expectations. Instead of bottom-up integration, they did top-down integration. These youngsters were the driving force behind a revolution in the printing community, offering their customers a complete product, including both creation and production.

[Claude] is well aware that the market is changing and it's now much harder to get money out of customers than it used to be. Before, you could count on having customers and getting your money; now, you have the customers, but the money is a different story! He realises the need for some strategic thinking, and he feels the answer may not be to do what we've always done. So we know that he's evolved from the tradesman he used to be to the entrepreneur he is now. He may not master all the techniques and technologies, but he's a businessman. So he hasn't wasted his time.

His wife, his partners and his close colleagues all describe Claude Guinet as a man of ideas with a surprising ability to analyse. His commercial flair, developed over the years, enables him to identify his customers' needs. A problem is never a problem for long, because he always ends up 'realising that in the middle of it all is a question of concept' that he can use to find a satisfactory solution. His life is shaped by his ability to listen, his ability to understand and his ability to learn. However, Claude Guinet's life is not just a series of ideas and analyses. He also needs to be in contact with people who can provide him with a varied intellectual, artistic and professional input. These contacts create 'breaks' in his rhythm and act as 'human and intellectual crossover points' that allow him to recharge his batteries.

Claude Guinet likes to play a role in educating future generations, and is always willing to share his experience, know-how, self-awareness and vision of the future. He loves to learn from and talk to students, whether at HEC-Paris, where he is part of the HEC-Entrepreneurs programme created by Robert Papin, or at HEC Montreal, where he is a frequent visitor. His favourite subjects include market development, the Internet and new business methods. He finds his contacts with business students to be very stimulating. Claude Guinet now lives in the Eastern Townships region of Quebec (Canada). In 2001, he was appointed Officer of the Legion of Honour, the highest distinction awarded to individuals for service to France in the course of their personal or professional lives.

The future

How does Claude Guinet see his future? The future of his family? The future of his company? One thing is certain, retirement is not an option. Indeed, the word has been banished from his vocabulary. Nevertheless, he is aware that he will have to make some major decisions in the next few years. The very nature of his business, which operates in two sectors currently undergoing extensive changes, means that he will soon have to choose between several options.

He could sell all or part of the company, but his need for activity and human contact is such that this would cut him off from 'a wonderful source of contacts'. This need to develop contacts, activities and business in its broader sense does not seem to have declined over the years. On the contrary, with the current technological transformation in the communications sector, it has become much stronger.

Mergers and acquisitions have become commonplace in recent years in the office equipment and supply sector, and he could easily sell the 'distribution component' of his company. However, in doing so he would run the risk of cutting himself off from a source of information on the new economy. Yet, maintaining his distribution activities is risky too, because as a small player he may well find himself completely alone in a world controlled by giants.

Keeping the communications component, which has always interested him and continues to stimulate him, is a definite possibility, because the multimedia sector is expanding rapidly. However, there are fewer applications, and the risks are greater.

Although the majority shareholder, Claude Guinet is not the sole owner of IPS Communication – Distribution. His son Philippe, who is nearly 50 years old, is also a shareholder. What about his daughter, who has never been involved in the company? And Nicole, his wife, does she want the retail stores to become a separate unit? Or is she thinking about retiring? Claude seems to have a significant emotional investment in the *Domaine de la Cressonnière* company. Would he like to spend more time on it? Or would he rather work with other partners on projects aimed at the American market? Should he spend more time promoting the arts that are such an important part of his life? Should he continue exactly as he is? Or should he simply sell the company and set out on a new adventure? Claude Guinet may well be at a crossroads in his life!

Questions and issues

1 Can IPS Communication – Distribution be viewed as a family firm?

2 What enterprising skills and resources has Claude Guinet accumulated?

3 What family firm assets have been accumulated by IPS?

4 What issues need to be faced by Claude Guinet?

Fickle Rooster Productions: Turning a hobby into a profitable business

Kirk Frith

Summary

It is the dream of many would-be entrepreneurs to slide seamlessly from their pursuit of a favourite hobby into the establishment and operation of a business based on their favourite pastime. The creative industries, including arts and crafts, designer fashion, film, theatre and the performing arts, broadcast media and recorded music (Henry and Johnston, 2005) are a particularly fertile area for the extension of personal hobbies into new businesses. Indeed, being a creative micro-business 'seems to be the ultimate role model in business nowadays' (Poettschacher, 2005: 177). Focusing on one of the creative industries, recorded music, this case explores the motivations, early setbacks and accomplishments of a business founder within the first three years of trading, as well as providing an account of a business's changing trading focus over time. This case highlights the many and various challenges faced by a new business owner, and suggests that business development is often beset by discontinuous and critical incidents.

Introduction

From an early age, Eddie Mangoldt found music to be an important part of his life.[1] He played in a number of local bands from the age of nine onwards, and managed two small bands from the age of 17. Both of his parents were keen musicians and, as he himself suggests, he inherited their interest in music:

> 'I suppose being interested and involved [in music] was inevitable given my parents', well, almost obsessive passion for music.'

[1] All names have been changed.

With the encouragement and support of his parents, Eddie decided to put his interest in music to one side and to go to university. Eddie's choice of course, BA Media Production would, he felt, enable some use of his skills as a musician, but would also provide him with a valuable qualification to fall back on should a career in music not materialise upon the completion of his studies.

Towards the end of his course, Eddie decided to launch the Fickle Rooster Productions business. Established in 2003, Fickle Rooster Productions was set up as a media production company, specialising in writing and recording music for television and radio. Eddie co-founded the business with two colleagues, Scott and John, whom he had met and worked with successfully throughout his studies. Despite the business opening and operating as a partnership, Eddie wrote and produced the music, whilst Scott and John undertook the more supportive roles of website development and accounts (Scott), and marketing and sales (John). However, they struggled to generate enough business in their chosen market and, as a consequence, had to branch out and find work in a number of diverse but related areas, including website development for other companies, part-time lecturing, school evening classes, and the occasional weekend working as disc jockeys at local pubs and nightclubs. Eddie noted:

> 'It was a difficult time, financially. We really were scraping the barrel so to speak; it didn't matter what we found or what we were asked to do, we did anything that would bring money into the business.'

In February the following year, despite developing good relationships with a number of local firms and having a growing portfolio of productions to their credit, Fickle Rooster Productions ceased trading. John was forced to leave the business for personal reasons, and Eddie and

Scott reached the conclusion that they did not want to continue working together. However, Scott did agree to allow Eddie to retain the trading name Fickle Rooster Productions, which he officially relaunched in March 2004. Eddie remarked:

'To be honest, I'm a little bitter about the fact that the business was folded so early . . . six months in business is absolutely nothing. Everyone knows that the first six months are always the most difficult, but I felt that we were really beginning to make some headway. It was a difficult blow to take.'

The closure of the Fickle Rooster Productions partnership left Eddie in a difficult position. Premises from which he was working (i.e., a university-supported incubator) were lost. He was left with a £10,000 bank loan to pay back. In addition, Eddie missed the camaraderie and the challenges associated with working in a team, and the shared feeling of accomplishment that they had felt when they had achieved a breakthrough. For a short time after Scott's departure, Eddie contemplated folding the business for good. Eddie commented:

'I thought long and hard about closing the business; it was a difficult time both financially and emotionally. To be honest, if it were not for the close support of my partner and family, I don't think I'd have tried again.'

A long-held ambition to be a full-time music composer, coupled with a belief that there would be no better opportunity to start his own business, meant that Eddie decided to persevere. Eddie remarked:

'I decided that was the time to do it, this was the time to risk it, whilst I'm still young, whilst I can still walk away from this and not really have to worry about things like mortgages, kids . . . I'm young and relatively free to do as I please and if I make mistakes, well, if I make some mistakes on the way then that's not the end of the world.'

Sole trader

Becoming a sole trader presented Eddie with a number of new difficulties and challenges, not least of which was finding the motivation to push the business forward. Eddie commented:

'That's one of the biggest challenges I've faced since going solo, just making sure that I get up in the morning, making sure I get the work done. I've set myself a goal of trying to do at least one thing every day that will benefit my business, whether that means getting in touch with a new customer, joining a website, composing a new track whatever it is, I always try and do something that will benefit my business so that at the end of the day I know that I've been productive.'

Becoming a sole trader also meant that Eddie had to assume all the responsibilities that had been formerly undertaken by his partners. Previously, Scott and John had taken care of the accounts and marketing. After they had left, Eddie found himself responsible for every aspect of the business, a realisation that was met with both alacrity and alarm. Eddie reflected:

'It has been difficult and time-consuming but rewarding at the same time. I've definitely acquired new skills from taking on these extra responsibilities that I would not have acquired otherwise . . . I've found that I now make more grounded, more realistic decisions and I think that that's good news for me and for the business in the long run.'

Business early stages

Although Fickle Rooster Productions was established as a media production company specialising in music production for television and radio, basic survival requirements had meant diversification into a far wider range of activities. The initial six months' trading had been sufficient to generate a small but steady supply of work writing and recording radio advertisements. Although this was not of sufficient volume to secure the business financially, it generated enough cash for Eddie to be more selective with regard to the work that he undertook. One of the activities that Eddie chose to continue with was his work at a local community centre where he taught young people how to disc-jockey and how to compose music using computer software packages. Eddie reflected:

'I really enjoy working with kids, especially from disadvantaged areas. It's by no means the most lucrative work that I do, but I feel that I benefit from it in a number of ways. Firstly, I feel that it keeps me in touch with what people are listening to, you know, I get to hear music that I wouldn't normally come across in my day-to-day activities. Secondly, it gives me a real sense of satisfaction, being able to use music to give something back to the community. Finally, and I don't want this to sound as though I am exploiting the situation, it really does help boost my business's profile – newspaper, radio and local television stations have all run stories on what I do and that has helped promote my business quite substantially.'

Major difficulties

Marketing and promoting Fickle Rooster Productions has been the major difficulty faced by Eddie with regard to the development and expansion of the business. He was initially reluctant to engage in the marketing and promotion side of his business. Eddie's first thought was to find an agent who would promote his music, thereby enabling him to concentrate exclusively on producing new music. Eddie noted:

'I've never really been much of a salesman; I've never enjoyed selling, I've never really been into that side of things, it's just not something that I feel particularly comfortable doing.'

After contacting a number of agents, Eddie learnt that they were reluctant to take on a new client who had very little market exposure. Eddie reflected:

'I've been in touch with a few agents now and they've said that although they like my music it's not worth their while until I've got a name, name that the industry recognises . . . It's a bit of a chicken and egg situation.'

Eddie recognised that he had no other choice and he began to actively promote and market his business. He developed and released a royalty-free CD, which he distributed to interested clients at a set price of £50 per unit. Although it meant contacting potential clients through cold-calling, and despite the fact that the production and distribution of royalty-free CDs was not in Eddie's long-term plans for his business, he felt at the time it was the only way that he could generate enough market exposure to get bigger clients interested in his work. Eddie commented:

'It was difficult in the beginning, but after a short time, I found a selling strategy that I was comfortable with, you know, I adopted a relaxed and friendly approach that I found worked quite well for me and despite the fact that the production and selling of a royalty-free CD wasn't where I wanted the business to go, wasn't what I wanted to do, I felt it was the only way of taking the business forwards at the time . . . it was really just about getting my name out there . . . it was a platform.'

Another difficulty faced by Eddie was finding and obtaining assistance from business support providers. After the failure of the partnership, the debts that he had previously accrued meant that cashflow was very tight. Consequently, he had few resources available to develop and grow the business. Furthermore, the loss of the skills that his fellow partners had brought to the business, notably the website work of Scott, meant that Eddie was forced to look for a way of overcoming his own skills shortages. Eddie reflected:

'I recently went for a grant to help creative businesses like mine with things like marketing, website development and so on, but I was let down because of my postcode area. The grant was only available to businesses in specific postcodes and because I'd had to move premises, I was no longer eligible to apply. It was a real shame as they were really excited when they talked to me, you know, things were really looking promising but then as soon as they knew my postcode, that was it, it was all over.'

The time and effort involved in applying for the grant meant that failing to obtain it was particularly demoralising. Eddie's considerable scepticism of the role played by business support providers is illustrated in the following comments:

'I'm not really interested in that avenue any more. I think it's better to look after my own interests and not to rely on other people or organisations to support my business.'

Throughout the course of his studies, being asked to write and record soundtracks for his fellow students gave Eddie a high level of confidence in his abilities. Eddie commented:

'I found that a lot of my friends who were studying media would ask me to produce soundtracks for them, it gave me a bit of a self-belief, you know, I suppose that was when I first realised that I could make a living from music production.'

However, Eddie recognised that he is quick to take compliments about his work, but he finds it difficult to take any form of criticism. Eddie reflected:

'If I write a piece of music that I'm not particularly happy with and someone else criticises it, then I don't find that to be a problem, but if I write a piece that I'm really happy with and someone else doesn't like it, I tend not to take their comments on board. I know that that's probably not the best way to go about things, but I'm so precious about my work that I find it difficult to accept any form of criticism.'

Eddie's reluctance to accept any criticism is in stark contrast to his constant search for positive feedback. He takes his music with him wherever he goes, and he asks everyone to comment on what they do and do not like about his music. Eddie remarked:

'I'm forever showing people, taking my music to their houses, to their parties, getting as many people to listen to [it] as possible, you know, I love to see people's reactions, even if they say that they hated it, you know, even then I enjoy the fact that my music causes a reaction.'

Eddie finds criticism only slightly less difficult to accept if it comes from people whose views he either values (such as close friends and family members) or respects (such as industry professionals). Eddie said:

'Although I find it difficult to accept any criticism, if it comes from someone who is close to me I trust their judgement more than I might that of a stranger, I feel that their comments are meant to help me rather than to undermine me. To a degree, that's also true of people with industry experience although there have been times when I thought the criticisms made of my work were neither accurate nor helpful – you have to know who to listen to and who to ignore and that can be a difficult judgement call.'

Major breakthroughs and business development

Eddie's big breakthrough came in late 2005, when an international publishing house approached him and asked if he would be interested in signing for them. Despite the fact that such an approach had always been a dream of Eddie's, it was received with a mixture of feelings. Eddie stated:

'It was difficult, signing meant that I would have to give them a big say in what kind of music I produced, I would lose the sense of ownership that comes from running your own business. On the other hand, signing would have given me a level of exposure both nationally and internationally that I couldn't possibly achieve on my own, at least not at anytime in the near future; it was a really difficult decision to make.'

After sitting down with the company's representatives and discussing how their relationship would work, Eddie decided in consultation with his parents and some close friends that he was not ready to sign. Fickle Rooster Productions was, at the time of approach, growing at a reasonable rate, although Eddie was still engaged in a number of peripheral activities to keep cash coming into the business. However, the amount of time he was able to spend writing and recording his own material was increasing every month. The signs were that some of the contacts he had made within the industry were close to securing him more work, and more profitable work. Eddie noted:

'The big benefit of being approached was that, because they're such a prestigious company, as soon as they said that my music was good it gave me the confidence that I needed, you know, when someone that renowned says that you're producing good stuff then it really does make a difference to how you feel about what you're doing, the music I was producing. It made me realise that I was good, that I did have talent, that it wasn't just me thinking that, you know, people in a position to judge were telling me that my music was good and that was important to me.'

Conclusions – where next?

Eddie's belief in his abilities, reinforced with the encouragement of friends and family as well as big industry players, was vindicated in the first half of 2006 when he was approached to write and record the music for two national advertising campaigns. He was also asked to write the soundtrack for a locally produced and aired radio show. Fickle Rooster Productions was still in operation in November 2006. After the recent commercial success, the business has not developed in line with Eddie's expectation. Nevertheless, he remains confident that the business will continue to expand. His growing reputation within the industry has generated increased business confidence as reflected in the following comments by Eddie:

'I have a feeling that last year was really the breakthrough year for me. My name is being circulated at much higher levels than ever before and the number of people contacting me and asking me to write them pieces of music is growing every year.'

From the original business idea to the current business situation has been a long and difficult road, and has involved many unexpected twists and turns throughout the three years of trading. Eddie remarked:

'My vision when I was writing the business plan was completely different to what I'm doing now, there have been things that I've tried and that just haven't worked and there have been things that I've had to do which I wasn't expecting. It's been a bit of a rollercoaster for me but the business is still going and, at the end of the day, I really feel that I'm now on track to achieve my longheld ambition to make my living from the writing and production of music.'

Questions and issues

1 What barriers to business formation and development need to be addressed by entrepreneurs?

2 How can an entrepreneur ensure that assumptions relating to the viability of the business idea are valid?

3 How can an entrepreneur implement changes without compromising the original business idea?

4 What measures might a novice entrepreneur (i.e., with no prior business ownership to leverage) deploy in order to speed up both personal and business development?

References

Henry, C. and Johnston, K. (2005). Introduction: special issue: entrepreneurship in the creative industries – an international perspective. *International Journal of Entrepreneurship and Innovation*, 6: 141–142.

Poettschacher, E. (2005). Strategic creativity: how values, beliefs and assumptions drive entrepreneurs in the creative industries. *International Journal of Entrepreneurship and Innovation*, 6: 177–183.

The Recording Room: Ben Wallace's musical ventures

Ed McMullan

Summary

Ben Wallace was a young musician and he tried to make the most of his interests, talents and opportunities. This case discusses why and how Ben established a business, which he called 'Guitar Lessons, Will Travel'. He taught students from his home and the students' homes. Ben recognised the limited potential of this business to grow and to satisfy his financial and creative expectations. Technological change was providing new opportunities to record audio. Ben perceived a gap in the market relating to the provision of computer audio engineering. He learnt the skills relating to emerging computer audio engineering and decided to establish a home-based audio production studio called 'The Recording Room', using computer technology. This new technology facilitated the quicker processing of client work. Over time, Ben found that clients liked the image (i.e. the boxes and lights) associated with less technologically advanced recording studies. This case illustrates that Ben found it difficult to generate sufficient work to cover the costs incurred purchasing the computer equipment. Further, the case illustrates issues relating to market research, service differentiation, pricing and advertising. To ensure business survival and growth Ben, in the end, identified a checklist of issues to be addressed. These issues could have been considered before he established the new audio studio.

Introduction

Ben Wallace was 22 years of age when he established a music production studio in 1999. He invested 800 hours and $19,000 (Canadian dollars) in order to establish the studio. Ben reflected:

'I figured that since I had been successful with guitar lessons I could do the same with recording. So I was confident about it at the time.'

After 18 weeks of operation, the studio had generated very modest sales revenue income. The debt was growing relating to the equipment and software purchased to establish and operate the studio. Ben wanted to make a decent living from the studio but he had no clear perspective on how to develop the business. He was concerned about the viability of the business to satisfy his personal and financial goals.

Personal and business background

When Ben Wallace was 15, after four months of playing guitar, he told his mother that he knew he wanted to be a musician and a composer. He learnt classical music and then flamenco, jazz and finally pop guitar. Teachers told him that he was a gifted musician and he had an excellent ear for music. Ben recalled:

'Frequently I can play back a song from memory even after only hearing it once – even a song with many changes. Given a bit more time I can recreate pretty well any song by ear.'

He dreamed that he would have a successful career writing music for film sound-tracks in the style of Angelo Badalamenti (i.e., best known for his collaboration with David Lynch in films such as *Twin Peaks*, *Blue Velvet*, *Wild at Heart* and *Lost Highway*). Like many other artists, Ben wanted to make a living from the music he composed and loved. His closest friend was a graduate in computer technology and he was expecting to start a new job with a salary around $35,000 a year. Ben wanted a similar income from his own business.

During the last year of high school, Ben began teaching music to earn an income. Ben reflected:

'Teaching guitar was so much better than being a sales clerk or working in a burger joint. For me, teaching seemed like a natural extension from busking and playing in restaurants for money.'

Ben's love of music resulted in him studying music for two years at a post-secondary Junior College. Ben established a business, which he called 'Guitar Lessons, Will Travel'. He taught students from his home and the students' homes. He offered the first hour free. People could try him out without risk. Ben charged around $29 for a 45-minute lesson from his home, but when he delivered a lesson in a student's home he charged $46 for a one hour lesson. Ben commented:

'I didn't know of anybody else who was travelling to homes to do guitar lessons. To some parents the extra cost was worth more than having to drive their kids back and forth every week.'

To ensure he was paid, Ben requested post-dated cheques typically covering a period six months in advance. Ben stated:

'When people gave me the post dates I still offered them the opportunity to cancel at any time. For some reason those who gave me post dates were much more reliable and tended as a whole to stay the duration. Perhaps this was the most important trick I learned making this business work for me.'

Not knowing any other way, Ben began promoting his teaching by placing posters on telephone polls and display walls around the city of Calgary in Canada. Ben commented:

'It is a tiresome business going out every few days to put up more posters because they get torn down or covered up. I even had people phone me saying how I was destroying the image of the community with my posters all over the place.'

Subsequently, Ben promoted the business in local magazines, specialty newspapers, and the White and Yellow Pages of the telephone book. He advertised his business, now called 'Guitar Lessons, Will Travel 607-AXES', on the side of his upgraded and prized, red Mazda RX7 sports car.

To begin with Ben enjoyed driving his car around the city to students' homes. This strategy generated several students drawn from wealthy families. Ben remarked:

'Some of my clients were from the families of top Chief Executive Officers of major companies, including CP Rail. It was nice. You go to their house and because you are teaching their son they treat you like you are royalty. A maid comes up to you with a silver goblet and a silver platter. You get freshly squeezed orange juice and the choice of any fruit you might like.'

Over the next three years, from September to June, Ben made $2,000 or so a month from teaching. During the summer vacation this business typically died off. Ben did not need much money because he was still single and living at home with his father and stepmother. Ben commented:

'I found the teaching business attractive for a number of reasons. It allowed me to stay with music. It provided me with enough income – on an hourly basis. I was doing much better than most of my friends. My life was my own. I got up when I wanted. I went to bed when I wanted. I had plenty of time to pursue my interests – creative and otherwise. Even some of my students became personal friends. I felt that I was becoming pretty well spoiled for employment. Even university had limited appeal because I couldn't see it giving me anything better. The only thing that bothered me was the apparent ceiling on earnings. Was this business going to provide what I needed over a longer time frame?'

Audio engineering: the technology

Technological change was constantly impacting on the type of equipment used in recording studios. For many years analogue tape had been used but it had gradually been replaced by digital tape (i.e., ADAT). Computer hard drives were beginning to replace digital tape. Ben reflected:

'As a kid I had spent large amounts of time on the computer. In general, I know what computers can do. I know that all the movies are done on computers. I watched someone do digital sound engineering five or six years earlier. I had known about digital audio since the eighties. I knew that DDD [Digital record, Digital mix, Digital play] went back to 1987. I knew that the ideal CD [compact disc] was DDD, so obviously you want to go with a digital medium. I didn't even know there were people using digital tape. That would have seemed totally absurd to me. Why would somebody even think of using digital tape when a computer is available? It was actually kind of a shocker to find out that the majority of studios were still using digital tape.'

As far as Ben was aware, most of the experienced audio engineers in Calgary were still using analogue or digital tape technology. He reasoned that once engineers became proficient using audiotape, and were committed to their expensive equipment, few of them would be willing to learn new skills and spend considerable amounts of money upgrading to use new computer technology. Ben was not intimidated by the new computer technology. He stated:

'Those racks of peripherals looked so impressive you could see guys just needing to buy them. Computer recording, in contrast, was nothing to look at – no eye candy other than the monitor.'

Peripherals were typically in video recorder style metal boxes stacked one over the other in metal racks. All the displays and dials emitted beams of light. These numerous boxes were replaced by computer audio and sophisticated software. During the summer of 1998, Ben decided to try his hand at computer audio engineering. Both his stepfather and his father encouraged him to learn the skills relating to emerging computer audio engineering. His stepfather was a successful independent contractor in the roofing business, whilst his father was a professor with independent business ownership experience. They both encouraged Ben to develop a successful business that was related to his interests and talents. He identified an opportunity to establish a home-based audio production studio to record his compositions, as well as generate money recording other people's music. Ben commented:

'At the outset I felt what was nice about this business is that even if it doesn't work out I still get to keep all the equipment for my own use.'

His stepfather offered to cover 50 per cent of the initial costs to establish the production studio. Ben stated:

'It was a great deal and I wanted to take full advantage of it.'

Ben needed $19,000 to equip a 'decent studio'. His stepfather provided $9,000 to establish the studio. Ben was aware that computer recording was becoming more available to artists seeking to record their own material. He appreciated that a second-hand 4-track recording and mixing machine could be purchased for $500. Ben recognised there was going to be competition. Nevertheless, he wanted to establish a profitable business that would provide him with an income. Ben remarked:

'My stepfather said he also wanted to see me make a return on the investment.'

Previously, he had found it difficult to find other musicians who were willing to be musical collaborators on his compositions. He hoped that ownership of a production studio would make it easier for him to attract musical collaborators. Ben remarked:

'For a couple of years I had been looking for musicians of my calibre to record my music, or to just find someone who had a common interest in music. I always had trouble though. I found that they were unreliable, or they were with a band, or they were playing a different style.'

About this time, Ben became increasingly aware that he was spending a vast amount of time travelling to student's homes in order to provide music lessons. He began to consider the costs incurred, and the relatively limited financial return he was receiving per hour worked. Ben reflected:

'I would often start work around 15.30, the beginning of rush hour. The travel time between student's houses was usually half an hour, and frequently upwards of 45 minutes. Over time, I was considering the driving time more frustrating than the teaching time. Even if I was charging more per hour I wasn't earning more, especially after you removed the cost of the car. I thought it would be . . . an advantage to encourage students to take lessons in a recording studio. I started the production studio to encourage students to come to my house for lessons. I learned that recording student work helped them appreciate the importance of rhythm and tonality.'

Ben began acquiring the hardware and computer programs he required for a successful business. He commented:

'It was really exciting and intriguing to learn all this new software and realize how much more power you have with the sound than you had before. I knew then that I could do anything a big studio could do. I just had to learn the interface.'

Ben calculated that he spent about 800 hours over the next nine months learning how to use several computer programs prior to the launch of his audio recording studio business in April. His friend, who was a self-taught audio engineer, provided 100 hours of one-on-one instruction. While studying audio engineering, Ben developed his ideas relating to how to set up the production studio. He converted his bedroom and a spare bedroom into a control room and an acoustic recording room.

To the human ear, the sound quality of computer audio is no better than digital tape, but they are both superior to analogue tape. A production job using computer audio would, on average, take half the time required to conduct a comparable job using tape. Computer technology provided time and cost savings because there was no need for cueing and rewinding tape. Effects could be applied and tweaked very quickly with computers. In marked contrast to computer technology, analogue and digital tape technologies did not support the Musical Instrument Digital Interface (MIDI), which is the use of synthesizers and other selected devices such as drum machines and effects processors. Using computer technology, therefore, provided additional advantages during the recording process.

With regard to a variety of sources, Ben discovered that studios using tape technology required production equipment that cost at least $100,000. Computer production equipment was cheaper, and the sound quality was just as good as that produced on digital tape. He believed that the bigger studios might have better recording rooms and isolation chambers, but they did not have better mixing equipment. Further, he believed that the big studios had enough equipment to record symphony orchestras, but they could not outperform the small studios with regard to projects with fewer musicians, or when the musicians were recorded sequentially. Better acoustics can provide benefits but Ben believed that most of the real difference was generated by the art of the audio engineer. Ben asserted that a poor engineer with the right equipment was like having a poor cook who was unable to use all the best ingredients in the kitchen. He recognised that the engineer should know what to do with the music. Ben commented:

'Few of those guys are musicians although some of them may really understand certain genres of music.'

He hoped that the timesaving provided by the computer technology studio equipment, especially with regard to editing and mixing, would translate into savings for clients, and higher profits for his business. There was, however, a problem convincing clients that computer audio was better than tape audio.

By December 1998, an experienced audio engineer suggested that Ben was a professional in the field of audio engineering. He appreciated that he had reached the mark, but there was always more to learn. Ben believed that a great audio engineer should have the following attributes: proficiency with appropriate equipment; the fine ear of a good musician with appreciation of notes and rhythm; a good ear for sound (i.e., more the ear of a conductor than of a musician); and knowledge of what affects the target audience in each particular genre.

Estimating the time that a job would take was a tricky business for Ben. The following issues impact on recording time: the proficiency of the musicians (i.e., number of recording takes); how clear the clients were on what they were doing (i.e., number of recording takes); whether the clients knew and could communicate the sound they wanted (i.e., time spent mastering each track, which is the effects processing time spent by the audio engineer after the track(s) have been recorded by the musicians); and how fussy the musicians are about the 'finished' product (i.e., time spent mastering each track).

Promotion

The initial name for the recording studio business was 'Extreme Studios' because Ben liked the image the name projected. After a couple of months, he changed the name to 'The Recording Room'. Discussions with his 'Guitar Lessons, Will Travel' clients revealed that 25 per cent of them had sought his services in response to advertisements in the White Pages of the telephone book. In order to generate clients for his new business, Ben decided to place an advertisement in the White Pages of the telephone book. However, he missed the March cut-off date relating to the next issue of the telephone book. His business was listed as 'Recording Room, The' in the September issue of the telephone book.

Ben conducted research relating to where and how his competitors advertised. He advertised his new business in the *FFWD* (i.e., fast forward) free weekly paper targeted to the arts community. Approximately 24,000 papers were circulated each week, and it was distributed at trendy locations around the city. A line advertisement in this paper cost him $15 per month. After six weeks of running the line advertisement, he followed the advice of his stepfather. Ben asked *FFWD* to design a 2-inch by 2-inch display advertisement, which cost $25 per week. He selected a picture of a microphone in the advertisement to draw attention to the fact that his new venture was a recording business. Also, a line advertisement that cost $15 per month was placed in another free weekly paper (*Calgary Straight*, circulation 27,000) targeted at young people. Ben thought that it would take him six months or more to identify what mode of advertising worked best.

Market research

Before starting his own studio, Ben was considering producing his own album. He visited the home studio of a producer who primarily used computer audio technology. The producer's house and car suggested he was financially successful. This producer had been in the industry for 30 years and he gave off an aura of success. Ben was provided with a guided tour around the studio, and the cost of each piece of equipment was highlighted. In total, the equipment would cost $250,000. Ben reflected:

'It was an impressive looking place.'

Ben subsequently discovered that most of the equipment was 'just for show' and not used by the producer, who had almost entirely shifted to computer production. The producer indicated that he typically charged about $10,000 to produce a CD. Ben's stepfather knew the producer and he believed the producer made more than $100,000 a year. In addition to recording musicians, the producer provided telephone audio restoration work for the police, and recordings for a psychologist to support his seminars.

Ben noted that the city of Calgary with a population of 850,000 people had 24 audio production studios listed in the Yellow Pages or *The Bargain Finder*. Pretending to be a potential client, Ben contacted nine out of the 24 studios. Three firms contacted were omitted because two specialised in soundtrack production and did not record for the general public and one was a record label. He collected information about pricing and production capabilities. A surveyed company was one of the two top studios by reputation in the city (i.e., the first listing in Appendix 1). Many of the firms contacted were basement operations, and it was frequently difficult to talk to representatives from these firms on the telephone. Ben noted that studio 6, the studio with the lowest costs, could record but it had limited ability to edit and master. He reflected that the average client would not recognise the limitations of the services provided by studio 6. Ben wondered how his studio would survive when an alternative studio was offering less but seriously underpricing him. However, in marked contrast to 'The Recording Room' studio, none of the six surveyed potential competitors provided computer editing and mastering.

Ben conducted a telephone survey of musicians to explore the needs of potential clients, and to increase client awareness of his new studio. However, this market research was delayed. He thought that this time-consuming research could be of modest value relative to the effort invested.

Over the May to July period, Ben conducted about $2,000 worth of recording work mostly at $39 per hour. With the exception of a piece of work from a student, all the work had been generated by the advertisement in *FFWD*. Despite the uncertainty involved, Ben was beginning to get a feel for how long different jobs would take. His work included:

- single song for a local rock band ($200);
- audio restoration of a talk track ($120);
- audio mastering and recording for an established jazz musician ($550);
- two songs for a local alternative folk musician with Ben composing and performing a melodic bass line ($320);
- a song for a folk-rock musician ($200);
- two songs for a rhythm and blues (R&B) duet ($500);
- vocal recording for a rap/death metal band ($75);
- vocal tracks over two cover songs ($200); and
- removal of vocals from one song on a finished CD for a play company that wanted to use their own singer ($80).

The last of these clients was a city playwright who liked Ben's compositions. The playwright asked Ben to do some sound effects and musical compositions for his plays in the future. He told Ben that he had been searching for a composer for some time because composers were really hard to find in Calgary. The playwright indicated that he was looking for a government grant to help fund the play.

Through his father Ben met Andrew Hugh, who was recording engineer with a Masters in Business Administration (MBA). After two years in the business, Andrew told Ben that he would not record any more musicians. Andrew recorded clients who advertised on the radio. His business also provided multi-media audio recording for computer-based training software. Andrew told Ben:

'It's hard to make money in this business. Musicians who want the recordings don't have any money, but when they do, they want a well-known studio that charges them big bucks for a job that probably isn't any better. They don't care about saving money because the record company is putting the cash out. They might even spend $80,000 or more on a single album.

Nowhere in the world do these businesses get over 100 employees. They just don't grow.'

Even though Andrew's business exclusively used computer audio he still owned a couple of racks of peripherals for the image. Andrew suggested the peripherals made his studio look real to clients. Andrew suggested to Ben that his best chance for making money was to produce soundtracks for small independent filmmakers because they typically had bigger budgets than musicians. Filmmakers were more interested in the quality of the final product rather than the ability of a studio to have large racks of audio peripherals. Andrew indicated that 10 per cent of a film's budget was typically allocated to the provision of a soundtrack. He told Ben that he knew of a one-person studio, similar to Ben's, which was successfully making soundtrack compositions for films in the city.

Ben had solely focused on developing client relationships with musicians. With Andrew's help, Ben was able to identify in more detail the following five market segments by customer type:

1 *Musicians* with record deals were encouraged to use record company-owned studios, or they used well-known and prestigious studios headed by reputable producers. However, musicians with no record deal and limited money typically wanted demos. This latter group of musicians were inclined to do more of the recording themselves, and sometimes they only wanted professional mastering.

2 *Advertising agencies* required audio work for radio and TV commercials as well as corporate videos. Andrew suggested the advertising agencies were very demanding. Recording studios had to have the right image, which tended to rule out a home-based operation. Money was required for interior design and other image related factors. Advertising agencies kept the end customer at a distance.

3 *Production companies* required produced TV and radio commercials, videos and in some cases films.

4 *Law firms, the police and courts* required the sound quality on recordings (e.g., telephone calls) to be improved for court appearances.

5 *Self-help albums* were requested by individuals and businesses that required sales and educational tapes to support in-house training and seminars and to better communicate with the general public.

Another initiative

In addition to recording his own music, Ben used the studio to record some of his own telephone comedy. To distribute his work, Ben set up a webpage.

Where to go from here?

Ben wondered whether he should solely pursue the audio recording business opportunity, or solely pursue the soundtrack composition opportunity. Ben did not like some of the issues he had recently learnt of relating to the recording business. He remarked:

> 'Frequently people don't keep their appointments. They make lots of false promises. Many callers are checking on me as competition only. Some callers just want me to burn their CDs because they were doing their own recording. I get a higher percentage of closes in teaching than with the audio engineering. My students also tend to appreciate me a whole lot more than most of the recording clients.'

It seemed to Ben that audio engineering was more competitive than he originally anticipated, and the clients were less reliable than the students he had been used to dealing with. The audio business was less certain and more confusing than it had first appeared.

Ben had allowed his student clientele to decline to three per week due to his focus on developing the audio production studio. In part due to the reduction in student teaching income, and the expenses incurred purchasing equipment for the studio, his debts had increased. In addition to his car loan, he had a $4,500 balance on his Visa account. Ben realised he was now in a bad financial situation. Studio work was not coming in quickly enough. He was low on money and running close to the borrowing limit on his Visa.

What was he to do? With help from his family, Ben began to compile the following list of issues that required his attention:

- construct a business plan;
- promote his services in other venues;
- complete his research on musicians;
- prepare a brochure and business cards;
- spend two hours every day meeting people and informing them about his recording services;
- place the emphasis back on the lessons and rebuild the teaching business while the recording studio was being developed;
- make a demo recording;
- change the advertising on his car to 'The Recording Room';

- offer to co-produce albums with selected individuals or groups in exchange for partial ownership of each album;
- check the web for audio businesses and create a web-page for 'The Recording Room';
- survey playwrights around Calgary, or even Alberta, in order to identify composition and sound effects opportunities;
- provide the local TV station with a demo and more proactively seek to obtain work with independent film producers in the region;
- advertise on the Jazz Hour on CKUA radio, which promoted local artists in Alberta;
- determine a better pricing strategy;
- determine in detail what he should say when a potential customer telephoned;
- contact, know and understand the (successful) entrepreneurs behind other production studios in the city;
- broaden his knowledge relating to the composition as well as the business and technical sides of audio engineering;
- spend more time composing and recording his own work;
- conduct more collaborative musical projects with other like-minded people;

- find out more about successful composers and how they had developed their careers;
- begin acquiring audio-peripherals to get the 'right look' for the business (even if they were not used at all);
- submit grant applications to provincial funding agencies on behalf of his clients (i.e., one agency provided up to 50 per cent of album recording costs, while another agency provided grants up to $1,000 towards recording costs); and
- investigate the market for audio restoration.

Questions and issues

1 What are the main differences between the music teaching business and the audio production studio?

2 What are the competitive advantages of 'The Recording Studio'?

3 What are the competitive disadvantages of 'The Recording Studio'?

4 At the end of the case, Ben identified a list of 'issues' to develop 'The Recording Studio'. What advice would you provide to Ben?

Appendix 1 Competitive analysis

Studio	Rate	Other rates	Packages	Format	Effect processing	Number of staff	Equipment	Channels	Number of recording rooms	MIDI?	Burn CDs
1	$50+(20,25)	MSTR $200/sng?	Day ($550)-10AM-12AM + Engineer$	Analog R-R	Rackmount	4	Tonnes/high quality		2(1Lg)	No	No, but claim YES
2	$55/hr			A/D Tape/No comp but claim comp	Rackmount	1	Tonnes/high quality	32 Rec/Playback	3 Rm, no line of sight	No	Don't know
3	$400/6hrs + $50/hr after, Editing ($250/ 4hr + $50 thereafter)	$275/Day for venue, DAT $20, CD $25		Masters to DAT or CD-R		1		2 Rec, More Playback	No room	No	
4	$35.00/hr			Digital tape		1	Mid range	24 Rec/Playback		No	
5	$60/hr	$600/10 hours day includes finished master tapes +40 for tapes?		Digital tape, no MIDI (Insecure)	Rackmount	1		32 Rec/Playback		No	Yes
6	$50 upfront, $25/hr		$600 for 5 songs Recording Only (no Time limit)	Tape/Digital Tape/Claims computer	Rackmount, software?	1	Mid range	7 or 8	1 small room	No	Not yet apparently
The Recording Room	$45/hr	$400/10 hrs		Digital computer	Software + 2 rack	1	Excellent/ many effects	14 Rec/Unlimited Playback	1 small room	Yes	Yes

Portable Patient Lifts, LLC: Patent and start-up issues

Gerard M. Campbell

Summary

This case looks at the development of a business started up by the inventors of a device for transferring a person from a bed to a wheelchair. It traces the development of the enterprise from the planning stage to business reality. Design modifications and patent protection issues as well as the role of the Internet in product development, marketing and sales are discussed. The case shows how initial plans were modified over time and highlights lessons for future innovative entrepreneurs.

Introduction

In the summer of 1996, Gerry C. invited Alex B. to meet at a restaurant to discuss the possibility of collaborating on an invention for transferring a person from a bed to a wheelchair. The need for such a device became apparent to Gerry after he and two other men had struggled to help transfer a friend whose illness had left him too weak to stand up by himself. Gerry had been good friends with Alex from the time they had studied mechanical engineering together as undergraduates 14 years earlier. Since then, Gerry had switched fields into operations management. Alex, on the other hand, went on to obtain a Master's degree and continued to work in the automation engineering field. At the restaurant, Gerry was delighted that Alex expressed interest in collaborating on the design of a patient lift.

Although the two had no practical experience as entrepreneurs, they outlined plans to design a lift, obtain a patent for it, and start a company to bring it to market. They encountered many challenges along the way. The product was developed and brought to market with relatively little capital outlay. However, the resulting product and business were not what the pair had initially envisioned. The lift is now receiving accolades from those who have purchased it.

Designing the lift

A review of patent search results relating to the keywords 'patient' and 'lift' on the United States Patent and Trademark Office website (www.uspto.gov) reveals that the problem of patient transfer has captured the imaginations of many inventors over several decades. Perhaps the most successful of these inventors is Ted Hoyer, whose 'Hoyer lift' is the most popular type on the market today. Examples of this type of lift include those marketed by companies such as Invacare and Hoyer (see www.dmeonline.com/ptlift.html). With a typical Hoyer lift, the patient is seated in a canvas sling, which is attached to an overhead boom via chains or straps. The boom is attached to a vertical mast, which connects to a U-shaped base on wheels. A hydraulic or motorised lifting mechanism raises and lowers the boom. A major advantage of the Hoyer lift is its simplicity of design, which translates into relatively low manufacturing costs.

Despite its advantages and popularity, Gerry and Alex believed Hoyer lifts suffered from the following disadvantages:

1 they are large and heavy, which makes them difficult to transport and store;
2 it can be difficult to get the sling onto and off the patient; and
3 the dangling position of the patient could result in discomfort and may be considered undignified by some.

Focusing on disadvantages 2 and 3, Alex and Gerry designed a lift. This lift's most distinguishing characteristic is its retractable steel 'wings' to support the patient. These wings were designed to be positioned one at a time beneath a patient's buttocks. Twelve months after their initial discussion, Gerry and Alex invited two friends over to Alex's house to review the design, and sign an invention disclosure as witnesses. Although the friends were polite, it was clear that they were not impressed with the initial design. Dubbing it the 'butt butterfly', they had many questions regarding how the positioning of the wings would be accomplished. The less-than-enthusiastic response sent Gerry and Alex back to the drawing board.

At this point, the pair of inventors focused their attention on the first set of disadvantages listed earlier for Hoyer lifts (i.e., their size, weight and lack of portability). Considering this, and the desire for a more dignified position for the patient, Alex and Gerry eventually arrived at the 'Compact Portable Patient Lift' shown in Appendix 1. Several plastic and wooden mock-ups were built as the design was being refined. Little money went into the project, but countless hours of effort were expended. It is difficult to describe how intense the design process was over a period of several months. Many ideas were developed and subsequently discarded on the way to the configuration shown in Appendix 1.

Following guidelines detailed in *Patent it Yourself* (Pressman, 2002), Alex and Gerry continued searching the United States Patent and Trademark Office website to ensure that key features of the new lift had not appeared in prior patents. They eventually took the design and results of their prior art search to a patent attorney for an initial consultation. To ensure completeness, they engaged him at a cost of $500 to conduct a more formal patent search, and to advise them on the scope of protection they could expect to achieve if they decided to pursue a patent. Although the likely scope of what they could claim was narrower than the inventors had hoped, the attorney confirmed that certain features of the new lift did not appear to be taught by prior art. The attorney provided a quote of $1,800 to help Gerry and Alex file a Regular Patent Application. To save money, they decided to do as much as they could themselves. Alex and Gerry put together a Provisional Patent Application (PPA), and two years after their initial discussion they filed it with the United Sates Patent and Trademark Office. The PPA, which essentially describes the current invention, is less complicated than a Regular Patent Application (RPA), which must include specific claims that detail the scope of what is to be protected. After filing a PPA, inventors have one year to file a RPA for the same invention. Gerry and Alex thought they could use that time to explore marketability, and develop a business plan for the new lift.

Planning the business

The Internet played a major role in enabling Gerry and Alex to obtain feedback on their lift design. Alex incorporated CAD drawings of the lift onto a website to introduce the Portable Patient Lift (PPL) invention. The website, which was registered with various Internet search engines, included a request for feedback from visitors. Many encouraging comments were received, including the following:

'A great looking concept. Would buy tonight for my mother's care. As previous medical director for a 14 bed Acute Rehap Unit, would have recommended numerous times, instead of substantially more awkward devices. What are you waiting for??? DO IT!.'

'I have found your site on-line, and am very interested in this product. I am a rehabilitation nurse, and work at the VA San Diego Spinal Cord Injury Center. We might be potentially interested in working with you on this, as a clinical trial site, and also to provide you feedback on potential product improvements. I am also interested in this personally as we are in need of a lift such as this for my mother . . . .'

'I am a manufacturer's representative in Upstate New York and have been in the healthcare field as a dealer, distributor and manufacturers representative for 31 years. I currently represent manufacturers of both floor lifts and ceiling lifts. Your product looks very interesting from the standpoint of portability. Current lift configurations make it very difficult for those who might have the ability to travel to do so . . . .'

'Would like information on availability date; being a beta test; for this product. Also, location of sales person closest to Atlanta, GA.'

'Wish this lift was available.'

'Exactly what we are looking for/needing for a recent amputee with no muscle strength for transfer. Please advise of availability. Great idea!!!.'

'I'd like to know the price of your PPL. Thank you.'

This positive feedback encouraged Gerry and Alex to invest nine months later about $3,000 to cover the cost of producing a prototype. With the outlay of this amount of money, their determination to start a business took on a greater level of intensity. This was further fuelled by the fact that Alex had recently left his full-time job because he did not want to relocate from Connecticut to Georgia. Alex had enough severance pay and savings to last several months, but after that he would require an income. With this in mind, Gerry and Alex put together the four-phase start-up plan shown in Appendix 2.

The first phase of the start-up plan included drafting a formal business plan. As an input, the partners found data showing that approximately 24,400 lifts per year were reimbursed by United States Medicare insurance. Data regarding the size of the non-Medicare market was not available. Financial projections were based on an assumption of eventually achieving 2 per cent of the Medicare market, which translated to about 40 lifts per month. Unfortunately, Medicare provided reimbursement for rentals, not purchases, which meant capital laid out to produce lifts for Medicare patients would be paid back over a longer period than for lifts sold outright. Consequently, additional capital and loans had to be built into the business plan.

Gerry and Alex met with a representative of the Connecticut Small Business Development Center to review their business plan. He offered encouragement and put them in touch with an attorney, who provided useful start-up advice and emphasised the need for liability insurance. The best quote they could obtain for the insurance was $5,300 per year. Based on advice from the attorney, and information in a book entitled *Form Your Own Limited Liability Company* (Mancuso, 1999), Gerry and Alex put together an 'Operating Agreement for Member-Managed Limited Liability Company'. In doing so, one of the delicate issues to be worked out was the fact that Alex, as the primary design engineer, had put in many more hours on the project than Gerry. How to divide the company to reflect this was a complicated matter that nearly led to the dissolution of the partnership. In the end, a 50:50 initial ownership split was agreed upon, with the following option for Alex (quoted from their Operating Agreement):

> *First Additional Capital Contributions*: Additional capital contributions will be required during the first quarter of the year 2000. The total of these additional contributions shall be agreed upon by unanimous vote of the members. The portion contributed by each member shall be determined by Alexander B. by his choosing one of the following as his resulting percentage interest in the LLC: 50%, 67% or 75%. For example, if the total additional contributions is $20,000 and Alexander B. chooses his resulting percentage interest as 67%, then the breakdown of the additional contributions would be:

> Alexander B. $23,000 \times .67 - 1500 = \$13,910$
> Gerard C. $23,000 \times .33 - 1500 = \$6,090$.

> Subsequent additional capital contributions shall be made in proportion to the percentage interests of the members.

The Operating Agreement was signed on 12 November 1999. Shortly afterwards, the necessary papers were filed with the State of Connecticut, and Portable Patient Lifts, LLC was officially in business. The company's name has been changed for the purposes of this discussion.

Before Gerry and Alex made additional capital contributions, they wanted to know more about how the lift would be received by potential customers. Focusing on nursing homes in Connecticut, Alex and Gerry contacted health care professionals who might be willing to review the prototype. After a few showings, the reception was disappointing. Especially discouraging was a showing before a group of home care nurses, which ended with suggestions regarding what Gerry and Alex might invent instead, such as a device to enable easier oxygen portability.

Four months later, Alex and Gerry had come to a crossroad. Having accepted a new job in another city, Gerry was looking at major changes for himself and his family. At this point, he was not prepared to lay out the capital necessary to begin lift production, especially after the lukewarm reception to the prototype. Alex was disappointed, but understanding. Gerry sold Alex his ownership interest in Portable Patient Lifts, LLC. However, Gerry remained as an inventor on the Regular Patent Application they had filed themselves on 18 January 2000 (U.S. Patent # 6,430,761, which issued on 13/8/02), but other than that Alex was now on his own.

Production begins

Before going into production, Alex decided to modify the lift design once more to respond to feedback obtained during prototype showings. The base was widened to add stability, and several additional refinements were made. A significant hurdle Alex faced in bringing the lift to market was ensuring compliance with United States Food and Drug Administration (FDA) guidelines for medical device manufacturers. To register with the FDA, practices such as product labelling, quality control, and design verification and validation had to be documented. Once FDA registration requirements were accomplished, Alex began production by ordering enough parts for 10 lifts from the same local job shop that had produced the prototype. A separate manufacturer was lined up to produce slings. Alex would handle assembly and testing himself. The production side of the business was ready, but how the lift would be received in the market-place was still an open question.

Because he was on his own, Alex scaled back the start-up plan to a level that entailed lower capital outlay, and less risk. Knowing it would be a while before the scaled back business would realise enough sales to enable a salary, Alex found full-time employment as an engineer with a nearby semiconductor equipment manufacturer.

Alex redesigned the company's website to accept orders for lifts. Payment was accepted by check or credit card, and lifts were shipped via United Parcel Service (UPS). Several of the initial sales were to people who had made inquiries based on the earlier website. The company's website was registered with several Internet search engines. Alex decided not to advertise through other websites, or in print outlets such as *New Mobility* magazine. With a full-time job keeping him busy, Alex was satisfied with a relatively slow stream of initial orders.

The price of the lift has stayed at $1,800 (sling included), while per unit manufacturing costs have dropped from an initial level of $1,500 in year one of production to $1,300 in year four of production.

From all indications, customers have been highly satisfied with the lift, as demonstrated by the following examples of customer testimonials:

'We are very pleased with the lift we ordered from you. We have used it several times to put my daughter in the car. Can't tell you how much we appreciate your help . . . The joy has come back into Tammy's life, thanks to the Portable Patient Lift. She likes nothing better than to go for a ride in the car.'

'Lift received in good condition . . . tried it on myself and it looks as though it will be a godsend to us . . . daughter that we purchased this for lives in home about 70 miles from us . . . lift will enable us to bring her home more often . . . Thank you so very much.'

Alternatives for the future

Alex has been considering several options for the company's future. Advertising and trade shows could be used to increase awareness of the product. Another possibility is to pursue relationships with sales people

and distributors. This option could be combined with the development of a rental programme for the lifts, which would bring it in line with Medicare reimbursement policies. So far, all revenues have come from sales to customers with sufficient personal funds.

The realisation of additional market share could make the company an attractive acquisition prospect. Alex has looked into this possibility with a few potential suitors, but it appears that sales need to increase substantially before this could be a serious option. The investments of capital and work required to accelerate sales would be substantial, and there is always the risk that higher sales may never materialise. Alex believes there are good reasons to continue the company as is. Because the lift is truly helping the handicapped people who purchase it, Alex considers the prospect of closing the business to be an option of last resort.

Questions and issues

1 In the process of starting the company, what were the major milestones? What was done well? What could have been done better?

2 Considering the alternatives mentioned in the last section of the case (and any others you might add), what recommendations would you give Alex at this stage of the company's life?

3 Assume Alex is talking with other medical equipment manufacturers who are considering purchasing his company to add to their product lines. How should Alex arrive at a reasonable asking price for the company?

4 Consider the claims shown for U.S. Patent # 6,430,761 on the United States Patent and Trademark Office website (www.uspto.gov). Which aspects of the lift design are protected by these claims, and which are not?

References

Mancuso, A. (1999). *Form Your Own Limited Liability Company*, 2nd edition. Berkeley, CA.: Nolo Press.

Pressman, D. (2002). *Patent it Yourself*, 9th edition. Berkeley, CA.: Nolo Press.

Appendix 1 Drawings of the Compact Portable Patient Lift

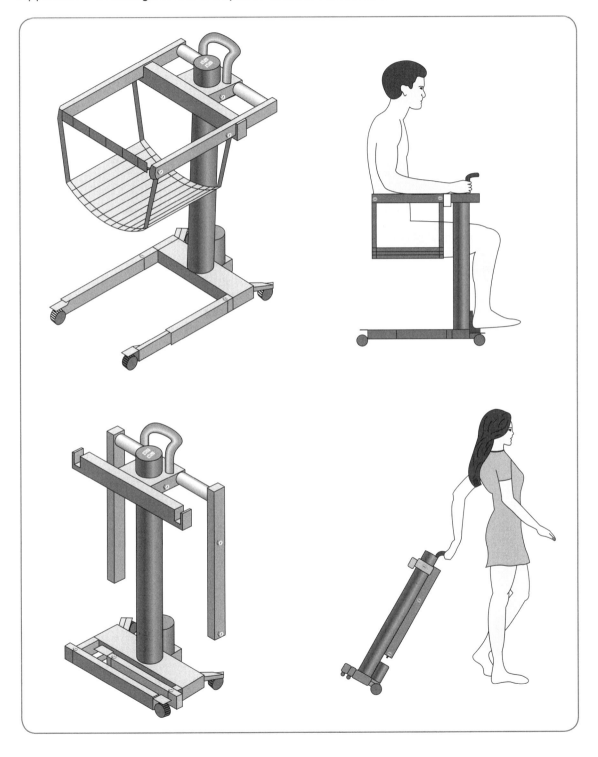

Appendix 2 Four-phase start-up plan

**Phase I: Pre-incorporation   1st October –
1st December 1999**
- Build and debug prototype
- Prototype
- Draft business plan
- Write pre-incorporation agreement.
- Learn about FDA and insurance rules and
  regulations.
- File papers to start business.
- Prepare Regular Patent Application.

**Phase II: Prototype evaluation   1st December 1999 –
1st February 2000**
- Test prototype on individuals.
- Commit to Phase III/provide major capital funding
  (e.g., approx. $20,000).
- Obtain endorsements from patients and medical
  professionals.
- Line up several job shops to enable volume flexibility
  (emphasise short lead times).
- Set-up commercial website.
- Establish bookkeeping system.
- File Regular Patent Application.

- Obtain liability insurance.
- File Medicare supplier application.
- Take orders for initial batch.

**Phase III: Batch production   1st February –
1st June 2000**
- Sell product through website and direct contacts.
- Produce in batches (e.g., order sizes of 10) using
  multiple job shops.
- Obtain Medicare supplier approval.
- Build sales volume.
- Show lift at trade shows.
- Gather data to evaluate in-house manufacturing.
- Further refine product design.
- Look for new product ideas.

Phase IV: Volume production   1 June 2000 onwards
- Volume at 40 lifts per month.
- Revenue stream sufficient for Alex to draw salary.
- Evaluate make versus buy decision.
- Reduce production costs to achieve higher margins.
- Add new models to the product line.
- Develop new products.

Original Voddy Company Limited

Andy Corcoran

Summary

This case discusses the launch of a new alcoholic spirits company. Operational, financial, marketing and strategic issues relating to new firm formation and development are illustrated. The case highlights the difficulties faced by entrepreneurial organisations when implementing their ideas in a mature competitive market with large incumbent players. The Original Voddy Company (OVC) story illustrates that, even if the company has an award-winning product and expertise within its executive team (many of whom are investors), difficulties can be exacerbated by management decisions.

Background and inspiration

In 1999, the two founders-to-be of Original Voddy Company (OVC), Peter Bayliss and Bertrand Jack, were sitting in a bar drinking Red Bull™ and vodka. One turned to the other and said:

> 'I like the effect but it really doesn't taste very nice.'

From this short conversation, the germ of the idea grew, resulting in the creation of a company selling two brands of vodka, one containing caffeine (i.e., 'Tara Red') and the other containing elderflower and other ingredients (i.e., 'Tara Blue'). This was the conception and the embryonic stage of OVC. Active trading and fund-raising began a few years later.

Entrepreneurs

The above conversation took place while Peter and Bertrand were studying for an MBA at Cranfield University's School of Management. The two entrepreneurs lived in the south-east of England, but their backgrounds were dissimilar. Bertrand had worked in information technology (IT) positions for British Telecommunications (BT), a French Bank and the BBC. His functional business skills were in IT systems development and the marketing processes connected with these systems. Bertrand works full time in the OVC business and has taken on the role of the Chief Executive. Peter is the Financial Director, working part time to reduce costs. In addition, he worked for his father's civil engineering company. Peter had previous financial experience in Thames Water (a water utility company). He had stood for selection as a Conservative Party candidate. The two entrepreneurs thought they had identified an opportunity that existing products and brands were not exploiting. After informal focus group sessions and desk research, they estimated that the potential market could be 3 per cent of the United Kingdom's total vodka market, which was valued at £1.6 million (Mintel, 2005a). Their research involved casual conversations with friends and colleagues. The market estimates were deduced from market research reports on the World Wide Web.

Product

The idea was simple – to create a product that had a similar effect to that obtained by drinking vodka mixed with Red Bull™, or a similar brand of drink. Red Bull™ and similar products are classed as 'energy drinks'. They contain high levels of sugar and caffeine and are part of the 'functional drinks' category. This sector was valued at £1 billion (Mintel, 2005b). Bertrand Jack reflected:

> 'Red Bull™ is a success story since its launch in 1995 and it is estimated that 40 per cent of its volume is drunk with vodka.'

Once committed to their idea, the entrepreneurs started to develop the product. They chose the name 'Alice Extraordinary Vodka' because their grandmothers were both named Alice. It was decided that this would be the umbrella brand name for a distinctive and original family of vodka brands. The unique selling proposition (USP) would be the added ingredient(s) in each of the vodkas. These additions would be designed to target particular groups of customers. As noted above, the first phase of product development created two vodka brands. 'Tara Red' contained the functional ingredients that would allow it to compete in the market for energy drinks mixed with vodka. 'Tara Red' contained natural caffeine, guarana, creatine and D-ribose, whereas 'Tara Blue' contained hops, chamomile and elderflower. During the product development stage, the entrepreneurs took the products to several trade shows at large venues such as London's Earl's Court, and they also exhibited them at the International Wine and Spirit Fair in 2005. 'Tara Blue' was awarded a coveted medal at this Fair because of its distinctive flavour. The entrepreneurs recognised that the ingredient levels in 'Tara Red' needed to be safe, and the amounts of creatine, caffeine and guarana were carefully controlled. The vodka is distilled from English grain grown in Norfolk and Suffolk. Further, it is milled and then blended with yeast and fermented. The resulting substance is distilled five times to form the base spirit.

Raising finance

To complete the product development and to prepare for a product launch, the entrepreneurs decided to sell part of the company to raise funds. An initial funding round offered 25 per cent of the company and raised £100,000, valuing the fledgling organisation at £400,000. The founders knew that they would need further expertise, and during the first 'funding round' of financing they approached certain individuals with knowledge of the alcohol business. These individuals were offered non-executive directorships. They were brought into the project for their specific skills and competences, and they worked in the company on a part-time basis. This initial funding round generated sufficient capital to allow a 'pilot' launch to take place.

Initial launch

Initial marketing efforts generated a small number of orders from pubs, bars and hotels. The products were also placed on sale in an online environment through third-party websites. One of these, www.drinkon.com, retailed the 50 ml bottle at £12.95 for either 'Tara Red' or 'Tara Blue'. Export market orders were received. The

company signed up to the United Kingdom Trade and Investment (UKTI) export programme entitled 'Passport to Export', which offered matched funding (i.e., the UKTI invested the same amount of money in the project as the company) and a free export consultant for one year. This activity generated orders from Sweden and interest from Malta, the Canary Islands, several Caribbean Islands and Canada. In Canada, the Ontario Liquor Board had refused a listing application because of the ingredients in 'Tara Red'. The agent in Canada was still interested but he was considering launching the product in Alberta, which did not have a Liquor Board. In Canada, the various state Liquor Boards can decide whether or not an alcoholic drink can be sold in their territory. Branding materials were developed and, in return for some equity and professional fees, RISE-UP Marketing was established as the marketing agency for the brands. This organisation supervised the various activities and events that were designed to promote the brands.

Customers and bars provided feedback after the initial launch. Their responses were recorded, and the management of OVC identified the following issues:

- The base cost of the product was too high, especially for the export market. At this time, the business model proposed spending £1 producing one 50 cl bottle of either vodka, which would then retail for £2 to £3 per bottle before duty and taxes.
- The supplier of the bottles used had increased the minimum-order quantities. This increase was significant and prevented smaller orders being placed.
- Additional competitors had entered the premium vodka market during this period. Often, large companies with considerable funds to invest in marketing campaigns supported these competitors.
- Bars wanted to stock 70 cl bottles rather than the 50 cl bottles in which 'Tara Red' and 'Tara Blue' were available.
- The Portman Group, the self-regulating body for the alcoholic beverages industry in the United Kingdom, had raised some regulatory issues.
- The branding, especially for 'Tara Red', was not well received by the target market, which comprised single 18 to 25-year-olds.

Change of direction

Following the initial launch, the board decided to redesign and rebrand the bottles, using lower-cost materials. The redesign would be communicated using public relations as a promotional tool. This public relations activity would be developed to support one of the brands. At this time, the company had 9,000 bottles with the original branding in stock. Although these bottles had not been filled and sealed, they represented an existing cost and, because of the rebranding, a decision needed to be taken about whether they should be disposed of, and the cost taken on the profit-and-loss accounts of OVC. This option was something that the company could not afford. It was decided that the United Kingdom market would use the new size (70 cl) rebranded bottle, while the original bottle (50 cl) would be sold to the export market.

Notably, they decided to focus the company's efforts on 'Tara Red' rather than both brands. Merchandising materials were accordingly developed for that brand, and further relaunch events were planned.

The test of the new design was carried out in Manchester from 30 May to 3 June. Five venues were found and a variety of activities were organised. One venue, 'Bedlam', sold two 12-bottle cases on the first night. A satisfactory result, according to one of the non-executive directors, considering the usual performance of the company's new product launches and other industry launches. After the test, three of the venues agreed to continue listing the product. The entrepreneurs interpreted this as an indication that the market opportunity for 'Tara Red' did exist, and additional finance was needed to support marketing activity.

Second financing round

The changes and the amount of time it had taken to develop the brands to this stage had stretched the financial resources of the founders and the company. In June, after the test launch of the new designs, a brief prospectus was sent out offering shares in OVC. The offer was 20 per cent of the shares, with a valuation of £100,000, valuing the company at £500,000. It should be noted that the company had only one class of share. It was trying to structure the offer under the United Kingdom government's Enterprise Investment Scheme (EIS), designed to allow investors to reduce their tax burden.

OVC's application for approval within the EIS was not in place at the time of the share offer. The purpose of this finance round was to generate enough funds to market the 'Tara Red' brand, with 50 per cent of the new funds allocated to the acquisition of new personnel

with the required expertise, and 50 per cent to the marketing activities. The company would also undertake factoring and under bond sales to reduce working capital requirements. The founders were still very positive and compared their opportunity to that of BLAVOD plc, which had developed an innovative vodka and, within five years, had gone to an initial public offering (IPO) and created a company with a market capitalisation of £30 million.

Current situation

The entrepreneurs appear to have chosen a market that was in a growth phase. The quotation below illustrates the market growth noted in the premium section of the drinks market:

> 'Demand for premium products in pubs is denting sales of established brands across several categories.'

Based on data from 20,000 pubs ordering products from wholesaler Matthew Clark, the *Morning Advertiser* compiled a snapshot of what was selling well across the market. The gap was mainly widening in the spirits and bottled beers markets. Meanwhile, the rise of cocktails has nurtured a plethora of products:

> 'Marie Brizard liqueurs sell well as does the juice carton range Sunpride. Sparkling wine and champagne sales continue to increase as consumers no longer perceive these products as being reserved for special occasions.'

> (*Morning Advertiser*, 7 September 2006.)

Other companies have entered the market. According to *Marketing Week*:

> 'Richmond Marketing is gearing up to take on Absolut and Smirnoff with the launch of Marx, a red-coloured herbal vodka. Marx is the first red-coloured vodka to be launched in the UK.'

> (*Marketing Week*, 31 August 2006.)

The OVC products, despite positive reviews and pockets of good sales performance, had not taken off. As this case study is being written, the company is looking to make a trade sale because the funds have started to dry up, and further investment funding cannot be found. The founding partners are considering an exit strategy. The options available to them at this stage are to: undertake a trade sale, an option in which one of the non-executive directors has expressed an interest; to conduct a management buy-out; or to seek an injection of cash from a venture capital firm.

Questions and issues

1 Consider Porter's (1980) Five Forces to analyse Original Voddy Company's sources of competitive advantage at an industry level. Given the information provided in the case, indicate how these barriers and opportunities might be easier to overcome or exploit for a large organisation rather than for smaller organisations such as partnerships or sole traders.

2 The Original Voddy Company (OVC) raised finance by selling one class of shares in two funding rounds. This enabled the OVC to raise at least £100,000. What other options for funding were available to the company in the first round of funding, and what are the different implications for the entrepreneurs?

3 To what extent did the lack of detailed research at the start of the venture cause problems for the OVC at a later stage?

4 Does the branding and the brand image of a product solely relate to the creative design on the bottle and the merchandising, or are other elements more important in the creation of a brand?

5 The OVC started with one idea but produced two brands. One brand (i.e., 'Tara Red') entered a crowded market space against larger competitors, and the other (i.e., 'Tara Blue'), an award-winning brand, offered a new approach to the market. 'Tara Blue' positioned vodka alongside brandy and whisky as a drink to savour, rather than as a social drink to be mixed or used in cocktails. What are the pros and cons of positioning two new brands simultaneously?

6 The OVC launched two products into domestic and international markets. Given the small size of entrepreneurial firms, what lessons can be learned from the problems faced by the OVC?

References

Mintel. (2005a). White Spirits UK. Rockville, MD: Mintel, March.

Mintel. (2005b). Energy and Stimulant Drinks UK. Rockville, MD: Mintel, July.

Porter, M. E. (1980). *Competitive Strategy: Techniques for Analyzing Industries and Competitors*. Free Press, New York: Free Press, p. 5.

Additional reading

Andersson, S. (2000). Suppliers' International Strategies. *European Journal of Marketing*, 36 (1), p. 2.

Brassington, F. and Petit, S. (2000). *Principles of Marketing, 2nd edition.* Harlow: Prentice Hall.

Christensen, C. (2001). The Past and Future of Competitive Advantage. *Sloan Management Review*, 42 (2): 105–109.

Churchill, N. C. and Lewis, V. L. (1983). The Five Stages of Small Business Growth. *Harvard Business Review*, 61 (3): 30–50.

Johnson, G., Scholes, K. and Whittington, R. (2005). *Exploring Corporate Strategy.* Harlow: FT Prentice Hall, Harlow, pp. 78–87.

Keller, L. K. (2003). *Strategic Brand Management, International Edition.* Paramus, NJ.: Prentice-Hall PTR.

Pickton, D. and Broderick, A. (2005). Integrated Marketing Communications, 2nd edition. Harlow: Prentice Hall.

Porter, M. E. (1980). *Competitive Strategy: Techniques for Analyzing Industries and Competitors.* New York: Free Press, p. 5.

Alba Adventures: An entrepreneur pushed into entrepreneurship

Marlene Mints Reed

Summary

This case discusses the behaviour of an entrepreneur pushed into entrepreneurship after redundancy. The case illustrates the difficulties an entrepreneur with technical competence but no managerial experience faces in establishing a new business. Important economic and marketing concepts such as opportunity cost of time and resources, identification of profitable target markets and determining appropriate promotional strategies to reach lucrative segments are highlighted. This case suggests that entrepreneurs constantly need to accumulate and leverage resources, and they need to select an appropriate strategy to ensure firm competitiveness and business development.

Introduction

Alba Adventures was a three year-old company based in Glasgow, Scotland. The company provided outdoor adventures such as canoeing, archery, gorge-walking, rock-climbing and abseiling (repelling) to social and community groups. John Johnston, the owner, had done a good job of organising the outdoor activities. After three years in business, he perceived that he needed to define a strategy for the future. He would need to consider the following issues: identification of appropriate customer groups; development of a profitable pricing policy; selection of adequate staff to carry out the strategy identified; and the need to define a marketing strategy that would reach the identified customer groups. John wondered where he could find the resources to assist him with these decisions and their implementation. John commented to his partner:

> 'Sandra, I've been thinking, and it occurs to me that necessity is a great motivator; and the fact of the matter

is there is now a necessity for me to try to concentrate my efforts on managing Alba Adventures better than I have in the past.'

John Johnston's long-term companion and the mother of his children had heard this many times before, but at this point John seemed more intent than ever on evaluating the state of his business.

Alba Adventures had been born out of necessity, and now it seemed that necessity would shape the future of the business. John knew the business had been a good idea. No one else had thought of starting a private company that would take troubled young people, or those with problems, on adventures into the remote areas of Scotland. The trips encouraged participants to realise their potential, to act independently, and to shape their own destiny. The problem was that these trips had been sponsored by governmental agencies, and the fees were limited because of the limited funds available to these agencies. John had recently been pondering the idea that there might be other customer groups that would be interested in his services. However, he had not been able to identify in his mind exactly who these new customers might be, and how he could reach them. John was worried about the seasonality of his business, which until now had been dependent upon the holiday schedule of schools. Cashflow had not been steady. He needed consistent funds to support his three children. John also wondered if he had been pricing his services appropriately, or if there were some other way to optimise his pricing strategy.

Beginnings of Alba Adventures

John Johnston was a rugged individual who had always loved the outdoors. As a child, he had grown up with a passion for playing in the beautiful rolling hills around

Glasgow, and the north-western part of Scotland. After leaving school, he had many jobs, and he focused on working outdoors. For the past ten years, he had been actively involved in working with various charitable and non-charitable organisations as an activity leader. This work had primarily been with young people from varied backgrounds, but mostly teenagers from the inner cities and drug rehabilitation centres. As an activity leader he provided the groups with an introduction to the outdoors through rock-climbing, abseiling (repelling), canoeing, mountain-biking, archery, gorge-walking, caving, orienteering, skiing, snowboarding and hill-walking activities. The charitable organisations that he worked for paid for his services with grants that they had obtained from the government.

His employer made John redundant three years ago and he decided to become self-employed. In the back of his mind, John had always thought that he would like to start his own business; but it was this traumatic experience that caused him to make a decision about the future that he might otherwise have delayed for years. John looked logically at his skills and interests. Linked to his work experience, he decided to open a business that would provide the same types of outdoor activities that he had been providing for the organisations he had formerly worked for. Alba Adventures was selected as a business name because 'Alba' is the Gaelic name for Scotland.

John began contacting governmental social agencies that he had worked with. His business sought to service the needs of troubled young people. He decided to price his services on a cost-plus basis. John estimated the cost of providing the services required by the agencies with regard to the number of reservations requested and then just added a fee on top for himself. He suggested that the minimum number of campers should be eight. John had never stopped to explore why eight was the magic number, but it just seemed like an appropriate minimum number of campers for a group. When deciding upon the cost of an outing, he would estimate the cost of hiring the required number of freelance employees who were familiar with outdoor activities, the cost of petrol for his mini-van, and any costs for food that would be needed by the group. He would then add an additional fee for the firm over and above the costs involved.

At this time, John was using two freelance employees to help with his outdoor adventures. He had selected people who had certificates from the appropriate associations to be involved in his outdoor activities. Among the freelancers that he used the most were two young people, Ronnie and Zoe. Ronnie was still at Glasgow University but was able to devote part of his time to help John. Zoe worked part time in other jobs, but she loved the work she did with Alba Adventures. John was the only full-time employee of the company at the time, and he did not foresee adding any additional full-time employees in the near future.

John decided that the best way to advertise his services would be through the Yellow Pages in the Glasgow Telephone Directory, through brochures and flyers, and through a website, http://www.albaadventures.co.uk/about-us.php. He bartered for the services of a website developer by offering to furnish the website company with outdoor adventures in return for the development of Alba's site. The website that was developed bore the address: www.albaadventures.co.uk. It contained information about the types of activities the Alba provided.

John found that repeat work with government agencies accounted for the majority of his business. Because Alba Adventures was not a charitable (i.e., non-profit) organisation, it did not receive direct grants from the government. The only money that came into the business was generated by its activities. During the first year of operation, the gross receipts were £22,000. John's business had broken even, but he had not yet been able to take out a salary for himself. He would normally take out about £100 per week from the business to pay his mortgage. After three years in business, John had begun to see the light at the end of the tunnel. John made the following remarks to Sandra with regard to the finances of the business:

> 'I could probably get a job somewhere else and make more money, but that would be a step backward for me. I do know there is very little full-time work that I could do in the Glasgow area. If I were to work for another company, I would expect to earn somewhere between £15,000 and £20,000 a year. However, I would have to uproot you and the children and move and also give up this lifestyle, and I would not like to do that.'

When his friend Paul had asked John what were the primary rewards of owning his own business, John suggested:

> 'The irregular meals, the strained relationships, the high blood pressure and the receding hairline. But I wouldn't have it any other way.'

Alba Adventures delivered several different types of outdoor adventures. One type was called a 'Day Taster', and this series of activities lasted for only one day. A 'Residential' would normally involve an outing of three to five days depending upon where the clients wanted to go. With the 'residentials', John would arrange all of the accommodation for the group in a house or a bunkhouse. He would also organise all of the meals for the group. See Appendix 1 for a summary of three different outings with income and expenses.

Steps required to open Alba Adventures

In order to operate Alba Adventures, John had to secure a government licence, public and employer's liability insurance, and various qualifications. Associations relating to sporting and camping activities granted qualifications. For example, he had to qualify for a permit from the Scottish Canoeing Association, as well as several other associations. The examinations upon which the permits were issued were designed to ensure the safety of camping and outdoor activities within Scotland. John was glad to comply, and he applied for all of the required permits.

In addition to meeting these standards, John had applied to the Glasgow North Local Development Council (LDC) for new firm start-up assistance. Although he had worked out of his home during the first six months of operation of the business, John now realised that he needed an office, and more storage space for the equipment that he was accumulating. The LDC had taken out six leases in an office building named Ardoch House on Ardoch Street near the heart of Glasgow. It then subleased the offices in this building to new firms that needed start-up assistance. John secured an office that had a great deal of storage space in the basement. Also, he had secured a parking place for his minivan to keep it out of the weather. There was no time limit on the lease. The LDC subsidised the cost of the lease with regard to the first year. There was less pressure on John to make the business survive in the first few years.

John had recently become involved with some training courses that the LDC offered. The one he was currently taking was called 'Strategic Planning'. A professor from Glasgow University taught the class one night a week to new business owners. The participants were supplied with a notebook, some readings and cases that were discussed in a classroom setting. Some of the topics covered were: developing a mission statement, strategic plan and action plans; performing a strengths, weaknesses, opportunities and threats (SWOT) analysis; use of Porter's Five Forces Model (Porter, 1980,

1985); and other related topics. John was optimistic that the knowledge he was acquiring on strategic planning would be invaluable in running his business. The LDC also helped Alba Adventures with computer and financial training, and some marketing assistance.

Site selection for outdoor activities

Most of the sites for John's outdoor activities were within an hour's drive of Glasgow. He identified small lochs (i.e., lakes) for canoeing and country parks for walking and climbing. John had often commented that he was 'spoiled for choice' for outdoor activities in Glasgow. The north-west section of the country provided many beautiful sites. For most of the public parks and forests that John used, he asked permission from the Forestry Commission. This was primarily for the sake of courtesy.

Competition

John believed his major competitors were swimming pools, ice-skating rinks, theme parks and golf courses because they all competed for disposable income allocated for 'outdoor' exercise. However, he noted that only a few firms directly competed with Alba Adventures. One of these was an organisation called the 'Outdoor Resource Unit', which was government-subsidised and worked exclusively with community groups. The Outdoor Resource Unit offered activities similar to those that John offered, and they had often hired him to work for them as a freelance employee because they could not accommodate all of the business they obtained from community groups.

Challenges for Alba Adventures

As John rubbed his tanned forehead, leaned back in his chair, and gazed out of the glass windows that covered the entire front of his office on Ardoch Street, he continued to speculate on the state of Alba Adventures in the spring of 1999. John was approaching his 38th birthday. He had just looked at the income statement and the balance sheet for the past year that his accountant had delivered to him. He wondered how he could increase the bottom line of his business. See Appendix 2 for the income statement and Appendix 3 for the balance sheet. John reflected:

'Sandra, I believe the greatest challenge for me in this third year of the business is deciding on some strategy for the future. I must determine if my customers in the future will be the same customers that I have today. If that is true, this business will always have to live with seasonality. I have to plan all of the activities around the school holidays and summer breaks. That means that I have many months during the winter when I have virtually no business at all. If I do decide on another market to reach, I know I must decide on a way to reach them. I have already suggested on my webpage that I would like to work with businesses, but I just don't know how to get their attention. Perhaps the methods I am presently using may not be effective with other customers . . . I also know that I need more personnel for the business, but I don't know exactly what kinds of skills I need for them to have. I can't seem to decide if I should continue to be heavily involved in the outdoor activities and hire a business manager and continue to use a couple of freelance outdoors people, or if I should become the business manager myself and hire someone to do the outdoor activities for me. So far I have been a jack of all trades and master of none. I also don't know if there is a better way to price the services of my business or not. I'm not sure that I am paying myself enough for the time that I put into the business as the owner. I wish I had someone to develop a strategic plan for me that would include pricing and personnel selection. Perhaps I can get a couple of student interns from one of the universities to help me during the summer to develop such a plan.'

Questions and issues

1 Discuss the personality characteristics possessed by John Johnston that are consistent with the research on successful entrepreneurs.

2 List the pros and cons of John's technical and organisational competencies. How can John compensate for any weaknesses?

3 Develop a strengths, weaknesses, opportunities and threats (SWOT) analysis for Alba Adventures.

4 Using Michael Porter's Five Forces Model (Porter, 1980, 1985), develop a viable future strategy for Alba Adventures.

5 Discuss the 'four Ps of marketing' (i.e., product, price, place (distribution) and promotion) and their application to a viable strategy for Alba Adventures.

6 Discuss the resources that John Johnston has to accumulate to ensure that he has appropriate organisational skills.

7 Explain how the economic term 'opportunity cost' applies to John's use of his time.

References

McClelland, D. (1961). *The Achieving Society*. Princeton, NJ: Van Nostrand Publishing Company.

Porter, M. E. (1980). *Competitive Strategy: Techniques for Analyzing Industries and Competitors*. New York: Free Press.

Porter, M. E. (1985). *Competitive Advantage: Creating and Sustaining Superior Performance*. New York: Free Press.

Timmons, J. A. (1990). *New Venture Creation: Entrepreneurship in the 1990's*. Homewood, IL: Irwin Publishing Company, pp. 165–170.

Appendix 1 Summary of three different outings offered by Alba Adventures

Client	Service	Group size	Cost to customer	Staff	Expenses
Outing 1–21 May					
Falkirk College (customers for four years)	Hillwalking and abseiling	18	£250	3	Wages for staff (2 × £50.00). John did not pay himself for the outing. Use of the minibus to transport staff and equipment to and from site (about 100 miles). It cost £0.40 per mile to run the minibus. Little time was spent organising the day because this group came once or twice each year and the programme never changed. A few phone calls and about two hours sorting out equipment. The equipment depreciated at 25 per cent per year. The cost of all equipment used on this trip (including the van) was around £4,000.
Outing 2–3 June Stage party before the wedding	Climbing, abseiling, canoeing, gorge-walking	15	£450	2	Wages to one staff member at £50. John was the other staff member. The trip was around ten miles in the bus. A great deal of equipment was used. Alba's calculation of the cost to hire all of the equipment for the day was about £500.
Outing 3–5 June Television company	Company required Alba to furnish abseilers for a film it was making	–	£3,400	2 on 4 June, 6 more on 5 June	Wages to staff totalled £850. All other expenses were taken care of by the television company (fuel, ferry fares, food, accommodation, etc.). Alba put in about three-quarters of a day's work before the event to cover safety issues.

Appendix 2 Alba Adventures income statement (£s)

Income:

Sales	28,247	
Equipment hire	30	
Total income		28,277

Cost of sales:

Wages	4,471	
Social Security	225	
Vehicle hire	1,125	
Residential courses	487	
Other course costs	3,767	
Promotional expenses:		
Clients	373	
Catering for course delegates	1,305	
		11,753
Gross profit:		16,524

Expenditures:

Telephone	1,472	
Post & stationery	452	
Advertising	1,300	
Travelling	106	
Motor expenses	3,074	
Licences & insurance	122	
Repairs & renewals	164	
Sundry expenses	128	
Accountancy	482	
Legal fees	685	
Donations	40	
Entertainment	50	
Bad debts	840	
Rent	819	
Rates & water	1,315	
Insurance	1,132	
Light & heat	260	
		12,441
		4,083

Finance costs:

Bank loan interest	66	
Loan	230	
Bank charges	343	
		639
Carried forward		3,444

Depreciation:

Plant & machinery	847	
Fixtures & fittings	5	
Motor vehicles	704	
Computer equipment	416	
		1,972
Net profit:		1,472

Appendix 3 Alba Adventures Balance Sheet (End of year) (£s)

Fixed Assets:

Plant and machinery	3,262
Fixtures & fittings	10
Motor vehicles	1,789
Office equipment	656
	5,717

Current Assets:

Prepayments	1,200
Bank current account	3,910
Cash in hand	1,810
	6,920

Current Liabilities:

Cliff Giddings	(1,535)
Ronnie Bruce	90
Social Security & other taxes	(298)
Deposits received in advance	(100)
Accrued expenses	(5,463)
Glas. North loan repayable 12 months	(902)
Bank loan payable within 12 months	(474)
	(8,682)

Financed By:
Long-term liabilities:

Glasgow North loan 1 to 2 years	1,300
Bank loan 2 to 5 years	(356)
Glasgow North loan	688
	1,632

Capital Account:

Net profit	1,470
Capital introduced	5,047
	6,517

Less:

Drawings	(4,082)
Taxation	(80)
National Insurance	(32)
Net Capital:	2,323
	3,955

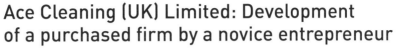

Case study 7

Ace Cleaning (UK) Limited: Development of a purchased firm by a novice entrepreneur

Mark Freel

Summary

Mary Anderson, a former contracts manager in Ace Limited, purchased the assets of her employer after the business had failed (i.e., gone into liquidation). She immediately changed the name of the purchased business. This case illustrates issues relating to the early stage development of Ace Cleaning (UK) Limited, which was owned and managed by a novice entrepreneur with no prior business ownership experience to leverage. Further, this case illustrates that an entrepreneur's social context background, personality, experience and knowledge can shape firm development. Also, this case illustrates that external environmental conditions (i.e., resource availability, competition, and the support provided by enterprise and development agencies) can shape the decisions made by entrepreneurs as well as impact on firm development.

Introduction

After 14 years of continuous employment as a contracts manager in Ace Limited, which was a contract cleaning company, Mary Anderson found herself without permanent employment and means of support. Due to debt accumulation Ace Limited in Scotland had been forced into liquidation and the firm closed.

Mary Anderson was a 52-year-old single parent and she perceived it would be difficult to regain a job. Recognising this dearth of opportunity and, in light of her previous experience, she perceived a business opportunity relating to a familiar market. Mary was determined to investigate the concept of salvaging contracts previously secured by Ace Limited in order to start her own business, which she subsequently called Ace Cleaning (UK) Limited.

Formation of Ace Cleaning (UK) Limited

Ace Limited had gone into receivership with debts in excess of £80,000. Mary, in acquiring their contracts list and goodwill, was required to take on board the debts of the former company. The debt referred specifically to leasing and purchasing agreements for equipment and stock. Ace Limited had been a labour-intensive contract cleaning business. The value of the assets of Ace Limited related to the contracts list and customer goodwill. Contract lists have a certain sale value. By taking responsibility for the £80,000 debt accrued by her former employer, Mary ostensibly purchased the plant and equipment required to take over Ace Limited.

In addition to the £80,000 that it had cost to purchase the contracts list from her former employer, the new company – Ace Cleaning (UK) Limited – required working capital for wages and stock. Contract cleaning employees were generally paid on a weekly basis, while invoice turnover and customer payment had a minimum cycle of 30 days. In addition, turnover on stocks was associated with a lag period of between four and eight months. Mary required a small amount of finance to purchase the capital equipment. However, the endeavour she proposed was not envisaged to be immediately self-financing.

Financing

A nominal funding package in excess of £100,000 was required to finance the launch of Ace Cleaning (UK) Limited. This figure was greater than any personal savings held by Mary Anderson. However, she was able to negotiate the phased payment of accrued debts by offering a director's guarantee to cover outstanding debt. The £80,000 debt was to be repaid from monthly sales turnover over a two- to three-year period.

By offering this director's guarantee to creditors, Mary was also able to ensure the continuation of previous leasing and supply agreements. However, there still remained the requirement for operating capital in the region of £30,000 to £40,000. Mary contacted the bank to discuss an overdraft facility but she met with some initial resistance. Although Mary was in a position to invest £5,000 from private means, the shortfall she had hoped that the bank would provide in the form of an overdraft (£25,000) would result in Ace Cleaning (UK) Limited being relatively highly geared. Mary offered her house as collateral to the bank. The bank valued her house and the housing equity (£25,000) was accepted as collateral by the bank. Mary faced further difficulties securing additional finance. Ace Cleaning (UK) Limited was heavily in debt and the new firm had few or no tangible fixed assets/capital. Mary had bought Ace Limited's contracts list in order to guarantee some orders. Nevertheless, the bank required assurances with regard to cashflow and customer payment. The bank informed Mary that the provision of the overdraft facility would only be provided if Ace Cleaning (UK) Limited factored its invoices.

Mary initially had difficulties in securing a factoring agreement. Many of the leading factoring companies were not prepared to accept the risk. An agreement was eventually reached with a factoring company whereby 100 per cent of her invoices would be factored at a cost of 4 per cent of the total invoice value. With this agreement in place the bank provided Mary with a £25,000 overdraft facility. Ace Cleaning (UK) Limited was now in a position to begin trading.

Premises

Ace Cleaning (UK) Limited had little scope when choosing premises at start-up. Mary chose to occupy the premises previously leased by Ace Limited. The premises were far from ideal but necessity dictated that they would suffice for initial trading purposes. By staying in the same premises Mary Anderson believed that Ace Cleaning (UK) Limited would secure the goodwill and contracts of the former clients of Ace Limited. Mary perceived the former premises of Ace Limited provided visibility and continuity benefits for the new company.

Marketing and client acquisition

Mary Anderson had previously been the contracts manager in Ace Limited. She sought to retain the custom of all the key clients of her former employer. Mary contacted several former customers of Ace Limited, and she expected that these contracts would generate sales turnover of approximately £200,000. These contracts would cover 75 per cent of the wage bill. Mary Anderson went 'cap-in-hand' in order to secure the contracts from former clients. She offered these former clients continuity of former service provision. Further, as a result of her employment with Ace Limited, Mary had been able to establish a considerable network of personal contacts with industry and clients groups. This standing and visibility (i.e., credibility) was leveraged to secure former Ace Limited customers within the geographical confines of her immediate market.

No specific activities were undertaken to directly market the new company and its services. The contract cleaning industry was associated with intense competition. It was felt that it would be extremely difficult to compete on non-price factors (quality being the exception, but not demonstrable prior to sales). The firm had a limited budget. Consequently, a sophisticated marketing campaign was not perceived to be viable or cost effective. Mary used direct marketing and a personal approach to generate customers. By using industry contacts and public information boards (e.g., newspapers, television, local authority contracts, bulletins, etc.) Mary subsequently appreciated the existence of a broader range of potential customers. She made direct speculative enquiries to potential customers generated from these sources. Mary offered free quotations to potential customers to ensure that initial contact was gained.

A further operational practice which can be viewed in some way as an extension of the marketing activities of Ace Cleaning (UK) Limited was the decision to undertake the contract cleaning of private dwellings. This latter activity generated an even lower profit margin than commercial cleaning. Nevertheless, Mary chose to pursue this type of work in order to generate more lucrative contract cleaning contracts (i.e., a 'loss leader' strategy used by supermarkets to get customers through the door to buy other goods). Domestic cleaning contracts increased the visibility of the new firm. The vans of the company could be seen out and about. Mary hoped this activity would increase word-of-mouth recommendation and referral business. People who could afford domestic cleaning services were often in positions of relative authority within commerce, and they could recommend Ace Cleaning (UK) Limited to their employers. As a result of these activities, Ace

Cleaning (UK) Limited gained its first significant contract independent of the goodwill and contracts list purchased from Ace Limited. A commercial cleaning contract was secured with Hilton Hotel at a major UK airport. The contract, worth £45,000, provided the young company with a broader foundation to develop in the future.

With regard to customer maintenance, or the securing of repeat custom, Mary appreciated that her business, in common with all service sector endeavours, required a strong customer orientation. From the outset, customer care, quality and thoroughness were viewed as essential to success. Mary personally visited each individual corporate client to allow them to identify the managing force behind Ace Cleaning (UK) Limited. Customers could, therefore, complain or make suggestions directly to the top of the organisation.

At the end of the first year, Ace Cleaning (UK) Limited's sales turnover had risen to over £354,000. Through the activities described above, the company was beginning to enjoy the benefits of referral business.

Management structure and style

Ace Cleaning (UK) Limited employed in the region of 70 staff when it was established. Including Mary Anderson the firm employed three office staff. Excluding Mary, the office staff was primarily concerned with administrative and clerical tasks, and they had no management responsibility *per se*. The firm employed staff and the latter staff steadily increased in line with client retention and acquisition. With regard to the field staff, there were two supervisors supervising the large body of cleaners. Low profit margins made it difficult for the firm to employ essentially non-productive members of staff in supervisory or management positions.

Mary projected a dictatorial (or autocratic) managerial style. The firm's organisational structure was, in part, shaped by Mary's desire to maintain a high degree of direct, personal and regular communication with clients. This structure did not lend itself to the devolution of responsibility. The firm did not have any middle managers who could insulate (or separate) Mary from the two line supervisors and field employees. Any empowerment of employees exercised was limited to low level on-site tasks. As a result, Mary's time was concerned almost exclusively with the daily operational issues of her company (i.e., fire fighting), leaving little scope to consider strategic options. Although business planning was undertaken, this was more often a mental activity on the part of Mary with little time available to establish a formal planning process.

Early stage growth

During the first two years of trading Ace Cleaning (UK) Limited enjoyed steady, if unspectacular, growth. The sales turnover increased from £354,565 relating to the first year of trading to £380,772 relating to the second year of trading. During the first year of trading the firm generated a net profit of £12,925 but during the second year a loss of £4,495 was generated. Over this period, the personal drawings of Mary Anderson were dependent on the capital needs of the company. Mary's salary was reduced if the firm needed funds to purchase or maintain plant or machinery. In effect she was paid, directly, what the company was able to afford.

Despite the reluctance (or inability) to pursue formal marketing activities, Ace Cleaning (UK) Limited reported relative sales turnover success over the first two years of operation. The firm had increased the customer base beyond the list of clients purchased from Ace Limited. Mary felt that, in the absence of product differentiation capabilities, the vigour and determination of the direct approach to potential customers had played a significant role in gaining additional custom. Everything she owned was on the line, and as such her motivation to succeed was strong. This initial growth was further reflected in the relocation of Ace Cleaning (UK) Limited to new premises towards the end of the second financial year.

Relocation

Mary was made aware of the availability of alternative premises. The local Enterprise Agency was the agent leasing the new premises in the industrial estate. These new premises were of a considerably superior quality to those inhabited from start-up, and at a significantly reduced rate (i.e., the first three months of occupancy being rent-free with the following three months at half-rent). The relocation of the business encouraged Ace Cleaning (UK) Limited to develop a closer relationship with the local Enterprise Agency (i.e., information, advice, support, etc.).

The Value Added Tax (VAT) dilemma

After two years' trading with relative success, Ace Cleaning (UK) Limited may have reasonably expected to have gained a degree of security. However, at the end of the second year the firm was faced with closure. With reference to the sales generated Ace Cleaning (UK)

Limited had charged their clients value added tax (VAT) on behalf of the government. The firm had generated sales above the VAT threshold and was now liable to repay the VAT income collected to the government's Revenue and Customs department (HMRC). That is to say, the company had been charging clients the requisite 17½ per cent for VAT and, through naivety, had failed to transfer this revenue to HMRC. In Mary Anderson's words the company had been overtrading. Mary had been under the mistaken impression that she would be able to pay the VAT owed by the company late. She had used all incoming revenue to promptly, or even early, pay, suppliers. The company was requested to pay in full in one week the £18,000 owed to HMRC. This may appear a small sum for a company generating a sales turnover in excess of £380,000. However, due to insufficient attention to cashflow control, the company did not have £18,000 in cash. The company did not have any assets that could be secured against a loan.

In retrospect, Mary believed that this situation forced her to 'face up to some home truths'. Until then she had been 'the boss', enjoying the power without the responsibility. Due to this crisis, Mary realised that the role of the managing director was to manage and to direct the business, and not 'to boss'. Mary recognised she had responsibilities to her employees, creditors and customers. She reflected that the business idea was sound but the firm had suffered due to her poor management. Mary was

determined not to let others endure the consequences of her failings. If the business failed Mary stood to lose everything but, more importantly to her, Mary's staff (now in excess of 200) would lose their jobs.

The profit and loss account for Ace Cleaning (UK) Limited relating to year one of trading is summarised in Appendix 1, and the balance sheet in Appendix 2. Further, the profit and loss accounts for Ace Cleaning (UK) Limited relating to year two of trading is summarised in Appendix 3, and the balance sheet in Appendix 4.

Questions and issues

1 What is the main activity of Ace Cleaning (UK) Limited with regard to the idea/and market?

2 Why is Ace Cleaning (UK) Limited established (i.e., push and/or pull factors)?

3 What are the key characteristics of the entrepreneur that established Ace Cleaning (UK) Limited (i.e., personality, skills and knowledge relating to management and industry know-how as well as prior business ownership experience, etc.)?

4 What issues relating to enterprise formation and development were inadequately considered by the entrepreneur?

5 Is there any entrepreneurial learning exhibited by the entrepreneur?

Appendix 1 Financial accounts of Ace Cleaning (UK) Limited: Profit and loss account for the year Ending 31 August, year one

Turnover		£354,565
Cost of sales		£269,730
Gross Profit		£84,835
Administrative expenses		
Staff costs	£15,813	
Depreciation	£9,437	
Other operating charges	£46,660	
		£71,910
Net operating profit		£12,925
Interest payable		£1,603
Profit on ordinary activities before tax		£11,322
Tax on ordinary activities		£1,912
Profit on ordinary activities after tax		£9,410
Statement of retained earnings		
Retained profit for the year		£9,410
Retained profit carried forward		£9,410

Appendix 2 Financial accounts of Ace Cleaning (UK) Limited: Balance sheet for the year ending 31 August, year one

Fixed assets		
Tangible assets		£43,007
Current assets		
Stock and work in progress	£10,090	
Debtors	£31,286	
Cash at bank and in hand	£783	
	£42,159	
Creditors: Amount Falling Due Within 1 Year	£60,165	
Net current assets		(£18,006)
Total assets less current liabilities		£25,001
Creditors: Amount falling due after 1 year		£4,841
		£20,160
Capital and reserves		
Share capital		£10,750
Profit and loss account		£9,410
		£20,160

Appendix 3 Financial accounts of Ace Cleaning (UK) Limited: Profit and loss account for the year ending 31 August, year two

Turnover		£380,772
Cost of sales		£292,369
Gross profit		£88,403
Administrative expenses		
Staff costs	£20,346	
Depreciation	£8,836	
Other operating charges	£63,716	
		£92,898
Net operating profit		(£4,495)
Interest payable		£3,925
Profit on ordinary activities before tax		(£8,420)
Tax on ordinary activities		(£1,912)
Profit on ordinary activities after tax		(£6,508)
Statement of retained earnings		
Retained profit for the year		£9,410
Retained profit carried forward		£2,902

Appendix 4 Financial accounts of Ace Cleaning (UK) Limited: Balance sheet for the year ending 31 August, year two

Fixed assets		
Tangible assets		£41,886
Goodwill		£13,591
Current assets		
Stock and work in progress	£10,412	
Debtors	£39,641	
Cash at bank and in hand	£8,832	
	£58,885	
Creditors: Amount falling due within 1 year	£76,951	
Net current assets		
		(£18,006)
Total assets less current liabilities		£37,411
Creditors: Amount falling due after 1 year		£8,509
		£28,902
Capital and reserves		
Share capital		£26,000
Profit and loss account		£2,902
		£28,902

Case study 8

The OffQuip saga: Partner entry and exit dynamics

Louis J. Filion

Summary

This case is drawn from real life. The names of the people, company and location as well as the dates have been changed. David Rose bought his father's used furniture business. With a partner, in addition, he created a new company, OffQuip, which sold used office equipment. An additional partner was introduced who held a minority equity stake in OffQuip; the two partners left OffQuip and David became the sole owner. After their departure, OffQuip ran into financial difficulties. To avoid bankruptcy, discussions were conducted with two new potential partners. A new partnership agreement was drawn up between the three partners. New difficulties emerged in the new partnership.

Part A: From glory to decline

David Rose was introduced to the business world very early in life. His father had launched a company that bought and sold used furniture. As a child David loved going to auctions with his father. Throughout high school, David worked part time in the family business. His father had bought an old barn in the countryside, 50 km north of Toronto in Canada, which was used as the company's warehouse. A huge flag fluttered outside in the wind, announcing: 'Rose Furniture – antique and modern – low priced furniture for all tastes.'

In 1981, when David was 21, his father retired. David bought the company. He was unable to obtain enough supplies from auctions. David then began to purchase office furniture from bankrupt businesses and businesses that had gone into liquidation. He quickly realised the potential provided by the latter search activity. In 1983, he went into partnership with John Lucas, a friend of his father, who owned a similar business. The pair knew each other fairly well, and had been

going to auctions together for several years. They decided to open a used office furniture store in Scarborough. The new company specialised in the sale of used office furniture, and was named OffQuip. In addition, they each kept their own previous businesses.

The pair needed a manager to run the new business. David met Ron Livingstone, an old high school friend, at a golf tournament. After several subsequent discussions, David and John offered Ron a job. Ron, however, wanted to be a partner. He negotiated a 20 per cent holding in OffQuip and the position as general manager. Ron had limited knowledge of the furniture sector. He had been a shoe salesman and was very good at sales.

The following year passed uneventfully. Ron and David knew each other well and often played golf together. They developed a close working relationship. John, feeling somewhat left out, gradually began to lose interest in OffQuip. His relationship with Ron became difficult, and he decided to withdraw from OffQuip. David and Ron talked about how they would divide up the shares. They agreed that David would hold 60 per cent of the shares and Ron would hold the remaining 40 per cent.

OffQuip prospered between 1985 and 1987. David decided to sell Rose Furniture. He bought a large, two-storey warehouse store located on a major commercial street near OffQuip's existing store. David rented the ground floor to OffQuip, and the company moved into the new premises in April 1988. The second floor became the base for a new venture, solely owned by David, which sold new office furniture. The new company was called NewQuip. This new company obtained its supplies from the most popular manufacturers. NewQuip soon became the main dealer–distributor for a well-known product line, which was similar to the Westinghouse office furniture system. The line was new to the market.

The situation in OffQuip began to deteriorate. The two partners began to argue constantly. They could not agree the amount of rent that OffQuip should pay (i.e., to David) for the leased premises. The receptionist, hired to work for both partners, received half her salary from Off-Quip, and the other half from NewQuip (i.e. David). Ron believed the receptionist spent too much time working on David's personal business interests. Also, Ron complained about David's numerous absences, especially during the golf season. The number of unresolved disputes increased. They decided to break up the partnership. In November 1988, David became the sole owner of OffQuip. He abolished the name NewQuip. David combined all his activities under the name of OffQuip. Ron became a partner in a competitor firm.

OffQuip's sales continued to increase. Stock rotation figures exceeded those of the best-known furniture stores. Sales turnover increased by more than 1,000 per cent in five years, and profits were above the industry standard. Between 1989 and 1994, the workforce grew from eight to 32 employees. David was on the fast track, and he thought big. He bought two trucks and an $80,000 (Canadian) computer system. OffQuip was expanding. David considered himself a successful businessman, and he drove a big BMW. His two teenage children, Isabel and Hugh, were interested in the company and they worked part time in the business. His wife was a nurse who worked the night shift every other week. David had become a keen – and frequent – golfer, and liked good company. He was frequently spotted in the restaurant of a reputable golf club, in the company of a female office supply representative. David often asked his receptionist to send flowers to women. Rumours began to spread about his 'private' life. David dismissed them and claimed that he was only maintaining good relations with suppliers. He spent less time working for OffQuip. Although David was an excellent salesman, he now spent most of the little time left dealing with administrative issues. David became a connoisseur of expensive wine.

Despite a turnover of $4 million in 1994, David's high standard of living had eaten into the profits. Expenses were poorly controlled. Business pressures began to increase. In 1995, David suffered a burnout and he had to take nearly three months off work. That year, OffQuip recorded a loss of $150,000. In 1996, sales continued to drop. The bank threatened to withdraw the company's line of credit unless a new source of capital could be found. David mortgaged the building and paid $200,000 to absorb the losses incurred in 1994 and 1995.

The company accountant suggested hiring a comptroller to enable David to conduct the sales job he enjoyed. However, David decided to hire a sales manager. David soon came to the conclusion that the new recruit had no aptitude for management. The sales manager reflected:

'He's a great salesman, but he doesn't know how to manage.'

In fact, the two did not get on. David fired the sales manager after three months.

In December 1996, OffQuip was on the brink of bankruptcy. David was considering winding up the firm, or even bankruptcy. He gradually laid off the staff. OffQuip had only four employees; one salesperson on each floor, one receptionist, and a delivery person with a truck. An accountant came in to do the books one evening a week. David mortgaged his home and his warehouse to the hilt. He had used up all his resources and could not go on. Examining options with his accountant and lawyer, David came to the conclusion that he would have to find a new partner if he wanted to stay in business. He knew it would be difficult for him to share power with someone else. David knew he had acquired a lifestyle and habits that would be difficult to change. He wondered if it might be easier simply to shut down and take a job as a salesman with another business. David reflected:

'I could easily earn over $100,000 per year as a salesman, but the problem is, I don't know how I'd live without the freedom I'm used to. I'd have to give up my golf tournaments and a lot of other activities that I enjoy.'

David faced a dilemma in late 1996 and was unsure what to do.

Part B: Salvation through partnership?

David's morale was at its lowest ebb. His company was on the brink of bankruptcy. It was the first time in six years that he had not gone to Puerto Rico for his traditional January golfing week. In early 1997, he turned his energies towards finding a business partner. In mid-January, David went out to dinner with Felicity, a sales representative for one of his suppliers. They talked about a partnership. They had known one another for around ten years, but they had never spoken much.

Felicity was 40 years old. She had once been a star in the contract sales field (i.e., the sale of office layouts including furniture). The business she worked for at the time had gone bankrupt. Subsequently, she had become a sales representative for a small furniture manufacturer, earning a reputation as a good seller. Felicity wanted to move back into contract sales, and felt David's situation would be a good opportunity for her. If David's offer was accepted, she could develop the contract sales sector. Felicity was a prudent and reserved person, and she set one condition relating to the proposed partnership. She wanted Robert, one of her former bosses, to join them. Robert had proven enterprise recovery skills as well as considerable experience in the office furniture sector. Robert had been the sales manager of the company that employed Felicity at the height of her sales career. In fact, Robert had hired and trained Felicity. He was a good motivator and sales team leader. Robert had become a victim of his own success. He had worked hard to develop the company, but the more profits he made, the more expensive the owner's lifestyle became. His former employer went into bankruptcy in late December 1996. Robert was unemployed and seeking a new challenge.

Partnership negotiations began in late January, and they were difficult. David was asked frequently about his previous partnership experience. He had to explain the previous partnership failures. This aspect was discussed extensively, but no real conclusions were reached.

Felicity had begun her career as a secretary with a law firm, and later moved into sales. She liked persuading people and was not afraid of hard work. Felicity lived alone and her social life revolved entirely around work. Her success was due to her determination and passion. She enjoyed being an active player. Felicity devoted considerable energy developing good working relationships.

Robert was more inclined to play a background role. He was organised and conservative. Robert was known as an entrepreneur rather than a manager. While he did not directly involve himself in sales, he enjoyed sales management. Robert loved to work on development. His hobby was taking part-time courses. He liked to say his success was due to the fact that he had encouraged the people around him to develop. Now 49 years old, Robert wanted to be his own boss. He wanted to run a company on his own or with partners. David, Felicity and Robert discussed several possible scenarios. A plausible scenario was identified. Felicity would be the sales manager. She would develop the contract sales sector and with Robert's help she would recruit a salesforce. David would take care of in-store sales of new and used furniture, and would have the title of president. Robert would organise the administration and accounting, and he would then draw up a strategic plan. He would hold the position of general manager. Robert would ensure the strategic plan was implemented.

Robert would have his office alongside David's, at the southern end of the second floor. Felicity would be located on the opposite end of the same floor, near the reception desk, where offices already existed for sales representatives. She regarded this area as her territory.

Task distribution was not clearly agreed, and a number of grey areas remained. Issues remained relating to accounting for the purchase and sale of used furniture conducted on the ground floor under David's sole responsibility.

By early March, David was worried. After talking for several weeks without reaching a clear agreement, he wondered if the potential partners would be able to forge a sufficiently close working relationship that would put OffQuip back on its feet with a new impetus. After further discussions, David began to consider whether he wanted to share power and become a team player. He wanted a partnership that benefited every partner but allowed him to retain his freedom.

Part C: Recovery, hope and disillusionment

An agreement was reached. The company's lawyers drew up a detailed and complex shareholder agreement, which was signed by the three partners at the end of March 1997. OffQuip paid the $6,000 bill. Felicity and Robert each paid $1 to become partners. They were given a year to make a financial commitment and exercise their right to each purchase one-third of the shares. In fact, they had wanted more time to assess the situation before committing themselves. During the first year, Felicity and Robert would each receive a salary of $60,000.

A few working sessions were held and the discussions were long and laborious. Felicity and Robert went into action and combed the contract sales sector to recruit salespeople. Within a few weeks, the news had spread like wildfire. Everyone was talking about OffQuip. Felicity and Robert received an avalanche of applications. A constant stream of would-be representatives filed through their offices, looking for jobs with the company whose star was rising. They discussed hiring designers to support the representatives, generating opportunities with companies and business groups, and paying sales commissions in excess of the 50 per cent generally offered in the sector.

David was impressed by the procession of salespeople offering their services. He was responsible for negotiating and signing the final employment agreements, which often contained 'special arrangements' relating to expense accounts linked to sales turnover, secretarial support, bonuses relating to particular types of contracts, and so on. OffQuip aimed for fast growth. The partners were prepared to be flexible in order to accommodate good people.

A month later, the company had more than a dozen salespeople with differing levels of ability, but the same high level of motivation. David knew nothing about contract sales, yet he often made decisions without consulting his partners, which caused them some problems. For example, the representatives quickly understood that it was easier to make sales with David's support, because he would give discounts to customers even when it was not necessary to do so. Felicity and Roger became frustrated when they realised that David held the most power. During the early days of the partnership, the partners held weekly meetings. Several questions were raised. Relations between Felicity and David became tense and they were unable to speak to one another. The meetings were cancelled in June.

Robert transformed the company's physical appearance. Everything was clean and ordered. He introduced an accounting system and fired the truck driver, who had spent much of his time doing nothing. Robert sold the truck and eliminated a number of expenses. At the same time, he produced the first draft of his strategic plan. The partners could not agree a strategic plan.

Situation at the end of 1997

Throughout 1997, finances were tight. The $150,000 line of credit was always used to the maximum. By October, the company was in the throes of a cash and leadership crisis. Three of the representatives were generating 50 per cent of the sales, while the others were generating considerably fewer sales. The break-even point was sales of $425,000 per month. The desired profitability level was 4 per cent of sales turnover. On several occasions, the bank told David that they wanted to close OffQuip's account. The company was not profitable enough and its cashflow development was too slow. The bank gave OffQuip until January 1998 to add a net value of $100,000, failing which the company would have to find a new financial institution.

Robert wanted to manage the entire company. However, his process analysis charts and new work planning methods failed to generate the anticipated sales growth.

David expressed doubts about these approaches and he described them as 'bureaucratic nonsense'.

Deterioration of relations between the partners

The three partners were unable to establish a shared vision for OffQuip. The culture and language of each partner were very different, and this made communications difficult between the partners, particularly with David. Words had different meanings for each partner. By the end of the year, the partners had not managed to agree on a single issue. Relations had deteriorated. David had generated enough sales to cover his salary. He pushed the other partners to do the same. David was becoming increasingly successful in the contract sales field. He was the only partner to make full use of the potential offered by the company's dual activities, by including nearly new used furniture in his contract sales. David drew on the expertise of the contract sales representatives to develop his own skills in the sector. By the end of the year, David was reporting better results than Felicity and most of the representatives.

The week before Christmas, David telephoned his accountant and asked him to organise a meeting with the three partners. David commented:

> 'Look, we have to move quickly. The bank has pulled a gun on us. I've just received a written notice giving me ten working days to transfer the account to another bank. It's Monday now. The three of us have to agree on the involvement of the other two before Friday.'

The accountant met each partner separately. He learned that Felicity and Robert did not want to keep paying rent for in-store sales stocks. Many of these sales were paid directly to David, in cash, and the money was never seen again. For Felicity, there was no question of doing anything with David. Her solution was to separate the contract sales from the in-store sales. Felicity wanted to set up a new business in collaboration with Robert that would concentrate exclusively on contract sales. For David, there was no question of doing anything with Felicity. His options were to go into partnership with Robert, who would manage the contract sales while he would make sales, or to dissolve the partnership. Robert did not want to go into partnership with Felicity. He proposed the following three options: reduce the number of partners to two (himself and David) with no sales role played by himself, but he would help the building of a contract sales team; dissolving the partnership; or reviving the existing partnership by creating an advisory committee, or quasi-board. The accountant is now in the process of preparing the meeting with the three partners, and he is wondering what to do.

Questions and issues

1 How entrepreneurial was David in how he went about creating a new business in the office furniture field?

2 To what extent does David learn from his previous experiences?

3 What are the strengths and weaknesses of how David selected each partner? What are the strengths and weaknesses of each partner selected?

Iain Russell and Arran Aromatics Limited: Portfolio and serial entrepreneurship

Carol Craig and Frank Martin

Summary

This case discusses the behaviour of Iain Russell. He makes a major career change in leaving an elite part of the police force in England in order to move to the island of Arran in Scotland. Iain wants to bring his family up in an island environment. He is very disenchanted with the police force and its regimented procedures. Iain goes through a series of crises and recovery situations trying to start various businesses on the island. The case explores the process of trying to make something out of nothing. This case illustrates a single-minded entrepreneur who often offends more people than he should. Success is eventually achieved. Iain, with skills inputs from his wife, does succeed in making a good living for his family. He is still not satisfied with his situation and the case ends with Iain contemplating new business opportunities.

Introduction

In 1989, Iain Russell established Arran Aromatics Limited. It was a small company based on the island of Arran in Scotland making a range of gift soaps and toiletries. In its first year, the sales turnover was £200,000. Six years later, sales had risen to £2 million. The company was taking regular orders from up-market stores, such as Heal's and Habitat. It was also receiving similar orders from companies based in the United States.

In the spring of 1996, Iain Russell was the managing director of Arran Aromatics. He was 52 years old and had lived on the island for 23 years. Iain was in an enviable position. His order book was growing each day. His daily drive to the office started at his luxury home in Arran's Whiting Bay, and took him to Brodick along a beautiful coastal road. He could spend weekends and evenings sailing his yacht off Arran. For Russell, another of Arran's attractions was its proximity to Glasgow. Within two hours of leaving his 'haven', he could take his seat on the board of the Glasgow-based Scottish Design Council.

Arran Aromatics was essentially a lifestyle business where quality of life was paramount. From his office window, once the Home Farm for Brodick Castle, he could watch sheep grazing, and on fine days draw inspiration from the legendary Goatfell, which towers over the island. So why did Russell, sitting in his Home Farm office in May 1996, proclaim that setting up in Arran had been a '*catastrophic mistake*', the '*worst business decision*' of his life? What had led him to this view, and was there anything he could do to rectify the position he was now in?

Police years

Iain Russell grew up in the midlands of England. His father was a policeman. When Iain left school with few qualifications he had no clear idea of what he wanted to do. Joining the police was an obvious option. His father wanted his son to follow in his footsteps but instead of joining the police force, he went to work for the Midland Bank. After a few years spent in what he describes as a 'Dickensian' organisation, Iain relented and joined the police force.

Russell spent the first few years of his police career in uniform. He graduated to the criminal investigation department (CID), and then to the Fraud Squad. To his dismay he soon discovered that, like the bank, the force too was '*stuffy and hierarchical*', and promotion was more likely to go to those who '*toed the line*'. Russell believed his job restricted his imagination, creativity and innovative tendencies.

After an interview for the Police College, Russell was told, 'Many are called but few are chosen'. His dreams of making it to the higher echelons were smashed, and he lost interest in his police career. He knew he had to get out and he needed to do something different. Russell liked the idea of setting up a business because it would give him the independence he craved. However, Russell had no capital or business knowledge.

In part due to his family circumstances, Russell was reluctant to take risks. His wife, Janet, had recently given birth to Andrew, their first son. Janet was the same age as her husband and came from a Methodist Shropshire family. Unlike Iain, Janet had stayed on at school and acquired a State Registered Nurse qualification. By the time she left nursing to start a family she was a Ward Sister.

During a summer holiday on Arran, his father's birthplace, Iain felt frustrated with the CID and Birmingham, which he thought was not a suitable place to raise a family. He was being pushed towards giving up a secure, well paid job and starting a new life. Iain considered moving the family to Arran in order to start a new life in '*the unspoilt haven*'.

Given the limited employment opportunities on a small island like Arran, the Russells' only hope was to start their own business. They had no capital other than what they could generate from selling their house in Birmingham. After several unsuccessful attempts, they managed to buy a petrol filling station and accompanying shop in Arran's Whiting Bay. In January 1973, they moved to the island.

Early days on Arran

According to Iain Russell, the first few weeks on Arran were '*pretty bleak*'. Industrial disputes were bringing the country to a standstill. Petrol prices doubled and the future was uncertain for anyone running a petrol filling station. They soon discovered that Janet was pregnant again. This had not been part of the plan.

After paying off the mortgage on their house in Birmingham, they were left with £6,400. The petrol filling station business cost them £6,000 to buy outright. They managed to rent a house for £500 per annum. To tide them over until the tourist trade started later in the year, Iain planned to take up the offer of a temporary job driving a lorry. This job fell through and they had no money to live on. He sought unemployment benefit but was refused. Iain then used his considerable powers of persuasion and was provided with unemployment benefit for eight weeks.

Within months the business they had dreamed about began to take shape. They rented out some of their new premises to a hairdresser. Further, they opened their own craft shop. They also bought a few bicycles and a rowing boat to hire out to the tourists. Janet gave birth to their second son, Duncan.

The sales turnover in the first year was £28,000, and the declared profit was £1,300. They had money to feed themselves but not enough to clear their debts. A solicitor's bill for £700 landed on their doormat, and they could not pay the bill. Iain went to see the lawyer immediately in order '*to come clean and tell the truth*'. He always believed that if '*you're open and honest, people will go a long way for you*'. They eventually paid the bill and no long-term damage was done. The following year they bought a dilapidated croft, which was renovated in their spare time. The croft generated rental income. In 1976, undaunted by cashflow problems, Iain rented an additional craft shop located on Brodick pier.

Within a few years, both shops were doing well. However, Russell was finding it difficult to source suitable craft items to sell. In the early 1980s there were several craft workers on Arran, but many of them did not want to sell their goods to Iain. They resented Russell making profits on what they had produced. Arran Canners, an important supplier, closed down and in the process triggered the next phase of Iain Russell's entrepreneurial career.

Cutting the mustard

Iain was aware that food was the only item in his craft shops that seemed to be '*recession proof*'. Tourists with limited funds would still buy gift food items.

Iain contacted the former foreman at Arran Canners, and asked him to demonstrate how wholegrain mustard was made. Back in the early 1980s, mustard meant nippy English mustard. They put their new wholegrain mustard in ceramic and glass containers, and it was an instant success at the Ingleston Craft Show outside Edinburgh. The Arran Mustard Company was born. The Highlands and Islands Development Board (HIDB) (now called Highlands and Island Enterprise) provided grants to set up a new factory. Janet recruited the staff to work in the factory.

The new purpose built factory was established in Lamlash on Arran. The first mustard was produced in March 1981, and the sales turnover for the first year was £125,000. By March 1982, sales had risen to £200,000. The Russells were beginning to struggle for money to keep this level of business going. Iain had to make a strategic decision relating to the kind of business being built. They sold their Whiting Bay craft shop for £93,000 and the money was ploughed into their new manufacturing business.

Russell was confident that the mustard business would take off. Within a month of the factory opening, a jam-making company wanted to buy the The Arran Mustard Company. Iain declined the offer. The jam-making company copied their mustards and sold the mustard for half the price charged by The Arran Mustard Company. Iain soon realised that he had to get serious if he wanted his company to survive. He realised that his business needed to diversify. Janet Russell had always been involved in all the businesses established by Iain. She was happy to accept that the ideas were Iain's and that he made all the big decisions. Now, her skills were required. Janet was drawn from a traditional English family, which made its own jam. It was a tradition she had kept up as a housewife. Janet read her recipe books and she soon came up with several quality preserves that could be produced in their factory. Arran Mustard Company was subsequently renamed as Arran Foods.

The Russells also realised they needed to pay more attention to the look of their products. They employed professional designers. The Russells opted for a 'handmade' look with the mustards and preserves being sold in attractive glass bottles and jars. Looking back, Iain reflected that some of their products were more like '*kitchen ornaments*' than food.

The high-street chain Boots placed an order for £70,000 and this, on top of the export orders being generated, began to create problems for the Russells. By 1984, the sales turnover was £400,000 and the business was overtrading. Iain reflected:

> 'We just didn't have the money to keep that level of business going.'

To begin with the Russells faced no difficulties hiring factory workers, but when they started to employ more than 30 people in the factory they faced recruitment problems. At the turn of the nineteenth century Arran had a population of 8,000, but by the 1980s this had declined to 4,500 people. Many Arran residents were fairly prosperous, and they had retired. Few Arran residents wanted to work in a factory. If the Russells had opened their factory on the Ayrshire Coast adjacent to Arran, labour would have presented no problems. Many people on the Scottish mainland were unemployed manual

workers. Moving people from the mainland to Arran was out of the question. It would be too expensive and time-consuming for people to commute from the mainland. Potential workers could not move to Arran because there was no social or low-priced housing on the island.

Selling out

In December 1985, a large food and drink company began to diversify into the specialist food sector. Robertson & Baxter bought Arran Foods for £625,000. The new owners employed Iain Russell on a lucrative five-year contract. Iain became the Group Managing Director of their new Food Division. In addition, this company bought a company making a range of oatcakes and craft biscuits in Livingston on the mainland. The new owners provided Janet with a job in the Arran factory. She was in charge of product development and personnel.

For the first time in their lives, the Russells had serious money to spend. They bought a Porsche and a yacht and made more improvements to their home in Whiting Bay. The takeover and subsequent expansion of Arran Provisions, as it was then called, generated more local labour problems. In August 1989, *The Glasgow Herald* published an article about Iain Russell and Arran Provisions. The article focused on Arran's poor infrastructure and the skill shortages on the island. Russell told the Herald:

> 'I'd like someone to look at the big picture now . . . If the present momentum on Arran is to be kept up, we need to look seriously at the ferry link, housing, schooling, even the water supply and sewage treatment.'

Iain soon felt he was paying a high personal price for the money he made from selling Arran Provisions. He was away from Arran a lot and he spent too much time in Glasgow hotels. His new bosses ignored his advice. Iain found it frustrating that they did not understand what Arran Foods was all about. According to Iain Russell:

> 'Arran Foods was a gift company, not a food company – our new owners never understood that.'

His five-year contract was not yet up but he knew he had to get out.

Dreams into reality

Iain had always admired Crabtree & Evelyn. He was impressed by the way they successfully combined food and toiletries in a coherent, well-designed range of gifts. These items had been sold in the gift shops owned by the Russells. When he was running Arran Foods Iain wanted the company to become the Scottish Crabtree & Evelyn. Iain suggested to the owners of Robertson & Baxter that Arran Provisions could increase its sales if the company diversified into toiletries. His new bosses rejected the idea. Iain started toying with the idea of setting up his own value-added soap and toiletries business in the old Home Farm at Brodick Castle. To qualify for grants, the HIDB insisted that Iain had to obtain the blessing of Robertson & Baxter. Iain's relationship with his employer became increasingly strained. It was mutually agreed that Iain could leave Arran Provisions after another year's consultancy, on the condition that Iain sold his remaining shares in Arran Provisions to Robertson & Baxter.

Robertson & Baxter paid Russell £60,000 for a year's consultancy. This work was quickly conducted and Iain was able to spend time developing his idea for Arran Aromatics. At the end of 1987, Iain did some consultancy work for the Overseas Development Agency (ODA). He advised several Indian food companies and travelled a lot. This consultancy work generated considerable income and the money was used to start his new manufacturing venture.

In November, Iain bought the premises for Arran Aromatics. He started renovating Home Farm, which is located on the outskirts of Arran's main town, Brodick, and a busy tourist route to Corrie and Lochranza. Russell believed Home Farm had great commercial potential. After renovation, Home Farm was an attractive stone-built courtyard development, and was subdivided into commercial units. A section of the building housed Arran Aromatics' offices. The rest was let out. Over the years, it housed up-market gift shops, a café, a seafood restaurant, and a small cheese-maker. Iain let one of the shops to a woman who had previously worked for him. They verbally agreed that her shop would mainly sell items produced by Arran Aromatics and it would function as the Arran Aromatics' factory shop.

Getting Arran Aromatics off the ground

The Russells invested £400,000 of their own money to establish Arran Aromatics in 1989. In addition, they obtained a £70,000 grant and £100,000 loan from the HIDB. The Russells employed a chemist to teach them the principles relating to the manufacture of soap and various 'wet products'. It was then up to Janet to devise

Table 1 Arran Aromatics: Sales versus profits

Year	Sales (£s)	Profits (£s)
1989	200,000	−20,000
1990	420,000	20,000
1991	801,000	50,000
1992	1,401,000	100,000
1993	1,440,000	170,000
1994	1,604,000	220,000
1995	1,650,000	293,000
1996	2,275,000	384,000
1997 (budget)	3,100,000	650,000

a range of items for Arran Aromatics to sell. She experimented on her kitchen table with various scents and colours. Janet rediscovered some of the traditional preparations her family had used when she was a child.

The first Arran Aromatics products were similar to the Body Shop's in that they were sold in plastic bottles. Table 1 shows that the sales turnover for the first year was £200,000. Consultancy income for the ODA was used to cover the £20,000 loss in the first year. Iain and Janet had watched people spending money in their gift shops. They knew what would sell and for what price. Both believed they had developed an intuitive feel for the gift market. However, with regard to Arran Aromatics they knew they were not getting it right. To increase sales, they decided to improve their presentation and to inject more added value. In 1990, they improved the presentation using attractive glass rather than plastic bottles. Sales subsequently doubled and the business began to make a small profit.

Products

Despite being made by a machine, Arran Aromatics' products had the quality and appearance of hand-made items. Some products were hand-finished in order to provide a personalised look. For example, some of the soap bars were hand-tied with raffia. Like most soaps and toiletries sold in the 1990s, Arran Aromatics marketed its products as natural and environmentally friendly. Iain believed that by giving them a hand-finished look they:

'. . . added value by the implied care and attention which makes the product desirable as a gift, reflecting as it does the esteem of the giver for the recipient.'

He believed that the company was genuinely committed to quality; that they only used high quality formulations; and customers benefited from using the products. The Russells serviced a varied range of potential customers and outlets. By 1996, Arran Aromatics produced 200 individual products in three different collections relating to Janet Russell, Apothecary and Earthwise.

Market

Over time sales increased (Table 1). During the early 1990s, slightly more than half of Arran Aromatics' products were sold in the United Kingdom, mainly to independent retailers such as gift shops, garden centres and department stores. Eighteen per cent of home market sales was commissioned for own brand sales by a range of up-market retailers such as Habitat, Heal's, Liberty, House of Fraser and Debenhams, as well as more middle-range stores such as Boots the Chemist and British Home Stores.

In 1995, almost half of all sales were exported outside the United Kingdom, of which 70 per cent was exported to the United States. Over the years, Arran Aromatics had generated an increasing amount of business with major store groups in the United States such as Pier 1 Imports and T. J. Maxx. Initially American buyers visiting United Kingdom trade shows generated this business. In the 1996 marketing plan for the United States Iain Russell wrote:

> 'We have always followed these leads up quickly and efficiently and have visited our customers in America about once a year. Significantly some of them visit us on a regular basis on Arran. We have formed strong personal and business bonds with these customers. We have found them to be straightforward, plain speaking, and quick decision-makers. Much less egotistical than the United Kingdom store groups and much more budget-minded. I have nothing but praise for them.'

Arran Aromatics' appeal in the United States led the Russells to turn their attention to increasing their sales in the United States. In January 1996, they exhibited at the New York Gift Show. The response was very positive and they took several orders from small independent retailers and department stores. In addition, links were made with ten major players in the United States who in the long-run might place contracts for individual orders ranging from £500,000 to £1 million.

In January 1996, to capitalise on their success in New York, they set up Arran Aromatics Inc. The company was incorporated in the State of California and Lifestyle Resources, an existing American Company, was appointed as their agent. Russell took these first steps on American soil because he was convinced that there was a potentially huge market for their products in the United States. However, he was not convinced that he could adequately exploit the opportunity. Difficulties were being posed by the Arran location and poor infrastructure on the island.

The Arran problem

As soon as demand for Arran Aromatics products increased in the early 1990s, the island location became a problem. In 1993, Iain realised that the factory needed additional space to keep up with the rising orders. He began to consider whether it made sense to expand the factory on Arran. Iain had constantly faced problems recruiting labour on the island. He considered establishing a new factory on the mainland Ayrshire coast. Iain met staff from Enterprise Ayrshire and they encouraged a move to a new factory in Ardrossan beside the Arran ferry terminal. He was attracted to this proposition. It would allow him to keep his office and home on Arran and he would have a purpose-built manufacturing base on the mainland where labour was plentiful.

However, the £70,000 grant from the HIDB had specified that production had to be conducted on Arran. Iain realised that if he moved production to the mainland he would have to repay some of the original grant. In the end, Russell dropped the mainland option. The HIE (formerly called the HIDB) agreed to build additional factory space on the Home Farm site. The new factory building was funded by the HIE and leased to Arran Aromatics for £25,000 per annum. By the end of 1995, the 9,500 sq. ft. premises would be operational. For various reasons, the new premises were operational 12 months later than planned. This delay created serious production problems for Arran Aromatics. Production had to peak in spring in order to fulfil the orders for the forthcoming Christmas season.

Decision time

In May 1996, Iain's dissatisfaction with his Arran location increased. He asserted that setting up in Arran had been a 'catastrophic mistake' and the 'worst business decision' of his life. Iain wanted to rapidly grow Arran Aromatics. He felt frustrated.

Iain Russell was now 52 years of age. He was beginning to get bored with the daily grind of Arran Aromatics and he hankered after a new adventure.

In 1995, he could have walked away from the company. Someone offered to buy Arran Aromatics for £700,000. In addition, rental income from the Home Farm site would have generated additional income and would have supported a new life. Iain knew it was not a good offer for a business that had made a profit of almost £400,000 that year alone. Iain and Janet were both tempted to say 'yes'. Their eldest son, Andrew, was made redundant by his employer. Andrew had sales experience and knowledge and he now wanted a job in Arran Aromatics. Iain and Janet refused to sell the business. In January 1996, Andrew started work as Arran Aromatics' Marketing Manager.

Once they had turned down the offer, the Russells threw themselves into developing the American side of their sales. But recurrent difficulties with the island location were undermining Iain's confidence relating to his ability to fulfil the orders to the United States. Iain sat in his office reflecting upon these opportunities and threats, and asked himself, '*What next?*'

Questions and issues

1 Should Arran Aromatics relocate?

2 Assuming that Arran Aromatics does not satisfactorily increase its productivity and manufacturing output, what activities should be conducted to grow the business? Discuss the pros and cons associated with each identified activity.

3 What are the pros and cons associated with Iain Russell developing the Home Farm site, or opening other shops on Arran?

4 Discuss the strengths and weaknesses of Iain Russell's personality.

Marine Products Limited: Confronting barriers to innovation

Povl Larsen and Alan Lewis

Summary

This case study highlights the barriers to innovation encountered by a managing director (MD) of a micro firm seeking to turn his idea into a commercially viable product. Barriers to the exploitation of an innovative product are discussed. The idea was awarded a 'Millennium Product' award by the UK Design Council for its 'ground-breaking' innovativeness. This case explores whether the new product development processes adopted by the firm is an exemplar to other firms considering new product development. The case relates to an actual firm but all names are pseudonyms.

Introduction

From the age of ten, the MD of Marine Products Limited had been messing about with boats. He has a semi-engineering background and had provided training for the Ministry of Defence. In 1986, with a friend, he started from home a retail business selling boats, water skis, surfboards, and marine accessories. The business was located in a seaside tourist resort far away from any industrial estate or assisted area that would enable government grants to assist the formation and development of the firm. The MD noticed that a product that assisted medium and large boats was not currently provided to the owners of small boats. He was confident that he could produce a product that would fill the gap in the market.

Barriers to innovation

Eight barriers to innovation were identified. The first barrier to innovation was determining whether the risks involved in developing the idea into a commercial product were worth taking. The second barrier related to whether the idea could be developed into a suitable product. The third barrier related to how to protect the idea. Patenting the product in the UK would be expensive and there could be the need for costly patents in foreign countries. The fourth, fifth and sixth barriers faced by Marine Products Limited were interrelated. The MD had no previous experience of new product development, he had limited knowledge surrounding current manufacturing methods, and he had no experience of employing people. The seventh barrier related to the selection of the most appropriate marketing strategy. He considered the following questions: Should the firm sell directly to the boating fraternity and/or to marine chandlers? Should the firm start off slowly and build up the business through word-of-mouth? Should the firm organise a major advertising campaign in the national press, television and/or boating magazines? Should the firm use marketing consultants or take care of promotion themselves? The eighth barrier related to the finance required to develop the idea, and to manufacture and market a new innovative product. Sufficient finance was required to develop the idea in parallel with the marketing plan. The MD sought to reduce the lead-time between product development and exploitation. To reap first-mover advantages, he aimed to take the product quickly to market. Additional finance would enable the firm to advertise heavily as well as build up stock, which could immediately satisfy even large orders. To address the finance barrier, Marine Products Limited sought finance from several sources including the Small Firms Loan Guarantee Scheme (SFLGS) (i.e., a system whereby the government underwrites 75 per cent of the risk of monies lent to a business (now available under the New Enterprise Finance Guarantee Scheme)), local enterprise agencies and venture capital firms.

Addressing barriers to innovation

To address the first attitudinal barrier, the MD reviewed the market potential of his idea with regard to national and international markets. The MD commented:

'The bigger the risk the bigger the reward; because the potential was greater than the risk I thought it was worth risking everything.'

The MD believed that the second attitudinal barrier could be addressed. Drawing upon his engineering skills and knowledge of boats, the MD believed he could produce an innovative workable product. He asserted:

'It all comes down to pushing back the boundaries. Questioning why not to change this or not to do that. People are trained to be limited in their thinking – they cannot see the wood for the trees.'

The third barrier was addressed by patenting the product in the UK. The MD attended a trade show in the United States and the product was well received. The firm then applied for a patent in the United States. However, the ability to patent the product in other markets was constrained by the availability of finance.

The ability to address the sixth barrier enabled the firm to simultaneously address the fourth and fifth barriers. People are required to manufacture a product. Employees are protected by health and safety legislation. The associated paperwork with employee National Insurance, tax and pension plans can be a burden on business. The MD, with no experience of employing people, decided to subcontract out the manufacture of the product to other firms. However, he faced problems identifying manufacturers that would produce a quality product for the 'right price' The decision to subcontract manufacturing reduced the Marine Products Limited MD's exposure to risk, and the need to attract additional financial resources to invest in manufacturing the product. Also, this decision enabled him to secure the skills of people with previous experience of new product development (barrier 4), and detailed knowledge relating to current manufacturing methods (barrier 5). Advice provided by subcontractors relating to improving product quality as well as reducing manufacturing costs was considered, and if appropriate adopted by the MD of Marine Products Limited. His openness to new ideas is reflected as follows:

'I've designed it, now you make it – no matter what, make it like I've designed it.'

The design drawings for the product were taken to a toolmaker and he suggested modifications to the design and materials used in the product. Marine Products Limited adopted the suggestions because they were seeking to sell a cheaply-produced, high-quality product. The MD remarked:

'When you talk to specialists they will tell you what needs to be considered. If you listen to them and take note, then when you go back and show them your revised drawings it all goes smoothly. If you do not take heed of their views, then on your return they will make life difficult and cause major headaches and worse still, they will charge you for it!'

Before Marine Products Limited could deal with the seventh barrier the firm needed to secure additional finance. Initially, the firm looked for government grants but the company was not located in an assisted area where specific grants and initiatives are made to entrepreneurs establishing and developing new private firms.

The firm applied for finance from the national SFLGS. Marine Products Limited received all the literature and went through it in detail. The firm had the assets to secure funding from the scheme. Market research had been conducted, and the patent protected the IP surrounding the product. The MD contacted a SFLGS adviser in Sheffield relating to the scheme, and they both went through the application. A couple of weeks later a SFLGS officer contacted the MD in Marine Products Limited by telephone. The SFLGS officer required additional information relating to the size of exporting activity suggested in the application. Marine Products Limited indicated that due to the small size of the UK market the firm planned to export between 70 and 80 per cent of all its products to customers in the United States, Australia and South Africa. The SFLG officer thanked Marine Products Limited for the additional information. A week later Marine Products Limited received a letter from the SFLGS, which indicated that the application had been declined because the majority of the firms' sales were for export markets.

An enterprise agency then contacted Marine Products Limited and they encouraged the firm to seek venture capital. Although disheartened by the failure to secure finance from the SFLGS, the MD agreed to meet a representative of the enterprise agency. The MD indicated that the patented product worked and had been 'tested to destruction'. The enterprise agency representative requested a sample of the product, which would enable a design consultant to prepare an independent report. A grant was provided to cover the £200 cost of the independent report. The enterprise agency expected the report from the design consultant to agree with the information provided by Marine Products Limited. The market statistics were not open to dispute. The American Marine Manufacturing Association and the United States coastguard had supplied the information to the MD. This independent report suggested that the product required further investigation surrounding its design. The enterprise agency was then not willing to introduce Marine Products Limited to venture capital firms. A feasibility study costing £5,000 was requested by the enterprise agency. The MD of Marine Products Limited remarked:

> 'Talk about risk aversion – five grand and keep your fingers crossed!'

Rather than waste any more time and resources to secure external finance, the MD of Marine Products Limited decided to use the firm's own assets to fund the exploitation of the new product. The MD appreciated that the firm had to carefully monitor its cash flow, and the survival of the business should not be put in jeopardy by overstretching the firm's financial commitments.

Due to the failure to secure additional external finance Marine Products Limited did not have the funds to invest in several parallel processes. The MD had planned to develop the product concurrently with an appropriate marketing and sales strategy (barrier 7), but due to financial constraints this was not possible. The firm did not have the funds to employ a marketing consultant. To reduce costs, a do-it-yourself approach marketing strategy was selected, which involved the firm selling the product via the Marine Products Limited webpage. This approach was associated with several advantages. Notably, the firm obtained feedback relating to product design and quality as well as quality of service direct from its customers. Profits from the initial sale of the product were then envisaged to cover the costs relating to the proposed more sophisticated marketing and sales strategy. The MD believes that the above events delayed the launch of the product by 18 months, and left the company in a weakened position.

Questions and issues

1 Marine Products Limited was not located in an assisted area where grants and assistance is provided

for new and growing private firms. Should the MD have moved the firm to an assisted area location to exploit the new product?

2 Marine Products Limited faced problems securing external finance. Discuss the reasons why the firm faced difficulties in securing external finance.

3 The Patent Office in the UK suggested that before an individual or company files a patent application they must be sure that the design has not been made available or disclosed to a third party in any way. What sources of external advice should be considered by owners of private SMEs seeking to convert an idea into a commercially viable product?

4 The UK Design Council 'Millennium Product' award is awarded to micro firms that have successfully addressed barriers to innovation. Is Marine Products Limited an exemplar to other micro firms surrounding how to circumvent barriers to the innovation process?

References and additional reading

Beaver, G. and Prince, C. (2004). Management, Strategy and Policy in the UK Small Business Sector: A Critical Review. *Journal of Small Business and Enterprise Development*, 11: 34–49.

Birley, S. and Niktari, N. (1995). *The Failure of Owner-Managed Businesses: The Diagnosis of Accountants and Bankers*. London: Institute of Chartered Accountants in England and Wales.

Brown, R., Lewis, A. and Mumby, A. (1996). *Enhancing Design Effectiveness in Very Small Companies*. Cardiff: Design Engineering Research Centre.

Bruce, M., Cooper, R. and Vazquez, D. (1999). Effective Design Management for Small Businesses. *Design Studies*, 20: 297–315.

Cooper, R. (1996). From Experience: The Invisible Success Factors in Product Innovation. *Journal of Product Innovation Management*, 16: 115–133.

Deakins, D., Levinson, D., Paul, S. and O'Neil, E. (1996). *The Use and Impact of Business Consultancy in Scotland*. Paisley: PERC, University of Paisley.

Department of Trade and Industry (DTI). (2005) accessed 4 February 2005, http://www.dti.gov.uk/sflg/pdfs/sflg_booklet.pdf.

Foley, P. and Green, H. (1995). A Successful High-technology Company: Plasma Technology (UK) Ltd. In P. Foley and H. Green (eds) *Small Business Success*. London: Paul Chapman Publishing.

Freel, M. S. (2000). Barriers to Product Innovation in Small Manufacturing Firms. *International Small Business Journal*, 18: 60–80.

Hadjimanolis, A. (2000). A Resource-based View of Innovativeness in Small Firms, *Technology Analysis and Strategic Management*, 12 (2): 263–281.

Hall, G. (1989). *Lack of Finance as a Constraint on the Expansion of Innovatory Small Firms*. In J. Barber, J. Metcalfe and M. Porteous (eds) Barriers to Growth in Small Firms. London: Routledge.

The Patent Office (2005) accessed 4 February 2005, http://www.patent.gov.uk/patent/howtoapply/index.htm.

Tidd, J., Bessant, J. and Pavitt, K. (1997). *Integrating Technological, Market and Organisational Change*. Chichester: John Wiley and Sons.

Walsh, V., Roy, R., Bruce, M. and Potter, S. (1992). *Winning by Design*. Oxford: Blackwell Business.

Woodcock, D. J., Mosey, S. P. and Wood, T. B. W. (2000). New product development in British SMEs. *European Journal of Innovation Management*, 3: 212–221.

Wren, B. M., Souder, W. E. and Berkowitz, D. (2000). Market orientation and new product development in global industrial firms. *Industrial Marketing Management*, 29: 601–611.

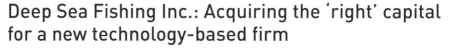
Deep Sea Fishing Inc.: Acquiring the 'right' capital for a new technology-based firm

Alf Steinar Sætre and Truls Erikson

Summary

This case discusses a new technology-based firm searching for the right investors to fund the venture's development. The entrepreneur behind the technology of Deep Sea Fishing Inc. developed a new type of plug, combining explosives and pyrotechnics with traditional technology, for uncorking offshore oil wells. The firm's owners had mixed experiences with government funding, before finding the right investors. When they finally entered the market, competitors had all but caught up, and they had to redevelop their technology to market a disappearing plug. This required more capital than initially expected because their revenue stream had been delayed.

Introduction

Deep Sea Fishing Inc. is a Norwegian offshore fishing company seeking informal venture capital. In late April 1999, Odd Suldal, inventor of the 'fishing equipment' technology, and the two Velure brothers, who invested in the project at a very early stage, who owned the company, sat in their makeshift offices and turned down an offer for almost €1 million for a 35 per cent stake in their fledgling business. At this point, their initial capital had all been spent and they did not have a paying customer. Their decision to retain ownership of the firm paid off. The firm now employs 20 people.

The company 'fishes up' equipment that has become stuck in offshore oil wells. Their technology is a unique and patented fishing tool, which combines traditional offshore fishing equipment and explosives. The technology enables Deep Sea Fishing Inc. to do in one run (a run down and up an oil well) what usually requires two to three runs. This technology can save two days of downtime on each job. Downtime on an offshore oil rig

costs between €140,000 and €430,000 per day. The following statement by Tor Velure, Deep Sea Fishing's CEO, illustrates the concept's potential:

> 'There is a tremendous amount of money to be saved. Tests have been performed on various types of equipment and they have been 100 per cent successful. So we have our first hire that we will do for Statoil at one of their oil fields, where they have spent over €12 million and they still have not got it. But they have spent all this money and there still are two problems that they cannot get up [from the well]. We attached to it in Stavanger with Statoil at the Stavanger research centre, and 'it' got it out on the first attempt. So we are going to do this over Christmas, a real baptism by fire. What nobody else has managed, we get to try . . . What is kind of unique is that we have actually not discussed a price yet, not at all . . . We have only discussed technical solutions.'

> (Tor Velure, 25 October 1999.)

Odd Suldal, who has a broad base of experience from the Norwegian Army, offshore oil exploration and construction work generated the business idea. He has owned and operated a diving firm. Odd acquired experience dealing with high explosives across several industries. He also has experience in underwater work, and this experience was leveraged to develop the 'fishing tool' technology behind Deep Sea Fishing Inc. His skills with explosives turned out to be a key competency when the company faced the technology redevelopment challenge. He stated:

> 'The clue behind the idea is that you have a bit of insight into quite a number of things. I have worked with explosives underwater, in the army, and in construction and so forth. I have a broad experience; I know a little something about a lot of things.'

> (Odd Suldal, 20 January 2000.)

Brief history of the company

DeepSea Inc. and Deep Sea Fishing Inc. were founded on 28 March 1998. DeepSea Inc. was owned by the Velure brothers, who each owned 40 per cent, and Odd Suldal, who owned 20 per cent. At that time, Deep Sea Fishing Inc. had 50,000 shares valued at €0.136, with a total of €7,000 in equity. This equity capital was, later that same year, boosted to €40,000 by the founding trio, with their relative equity positions in the company remaining unchanged.

DeepSea Inc. owns Deep Sea Fishing Inc., which is a subsidiary company that owns the commercial rights to Odd Suldal's patent. These rights were purchased for €200,000. At the same time, the equity in Deep Sea Fishing Inc. was increased by €40,000 to €47,000. The Velure brothers contributed this capital, and Odd Suldal received shares as part of his compensation package. In October 1998, Deep Sea Fishing Inc. held a private share offering, open only to individuals who had been key contributors during the start-up and early product testing phases, and they paid €23,000 for 9 per cent of the shares, at a rate of €1.5 per share. In 1999, still in the product development stage, Deep Sea Fishing Inc. required more capital than the owners could provide. The owners identified three potential investor groups relating to a City Industry Development Group (CID), a mechanical shop and its owner, and two private investors, Fredrik Ravn and Hans Frost, associated with the Ravn Group.

The Ravn Group made an initial offer of €930,000 for 35 per cent of the stock to be issued at a private offering. DeepSea Inc. rejected the offer after careful consideration for several reasons. The owners felt that 35 per cent of the stock was a very large portion of the company to 'give away'. They did not believe that they needed as much as €930,000. Later experience taught them that there was a need for much more capital. After a final round of negotiations, a revised offer was accepted. New stock was issued for €785,000 in a private offering, and the owners sold some of their stock for €145,000. In April 1999, €145,000 worth of new shares was transferred to the Ravn Group, who acquired control of 35 per cent of Deep Sea Fishing Inc., at a rate of €5.14 per share. Fredrik Ravn purchased 20 per cent of the stock and Hans Frosta acquired a further 15 per cent. After the second offer, the original owners cashed out €145,000 instead of issuing new stock for the same amount.

In October 1999, shares were sold on the unlisted ('grey') stock market at a rate of €14 per share. People working in the oil industry who knew of Deep Sea Fishing Inc. and its technology bought these shares. This stock price put the market value of the company close to €7 million even before Deep Sea Fishing Inc. secured its first 'fishing' job from the North Sea oil fields.

Due to the substantial costs associated with testing and verification, as well as product development, the need for further capital arose in May 2000. Another private offering was made to the current owners, bringing in another €500,000 at €15 per share. Equity stakes held by the owners altered somewhat after this offering. DeepSea Inc. now held 50.3 per cent of the shares in Deep Sea Fishing Inc., whereas they had previously held 56 per cent of the stock. The Ravn Group increased its relative stake in Deep Sea Fishing Inc. correspondingly. The private offering of December 2000 involved Ravn Group putting up €570,000 in cash, and a royalty agreement between DeepSea Inc. and Deep Sea Fishing Inc. for 15 per cent of the turnover until August 2002 was valued at €570,000. After this offering, the relative position of the owners remained unchanged. Subsequent funding totalled €2.35 million over the following years, largely from the Ravn group. Development of equity capital in Deep Sea Fishing Inc. is summarised in Table 1.

Regarding the two people with offshore-related expertise who invested in Deep Sea Fishing Inc. in October of 1998, Tor Velure made the following comments:

> 'It was expertise we were after that time, to get co-players, the capital we collected was twofold. It was really saying thanks for the help . . . The €47,000 was spent [on technical tests at the Trondheim Research Centre] so there was not much capital left in October of 1998.

> (Tor Velure, 25 October 1999.)

This statement suggests there were three reasons for 'allowing' the two individuals to invest in Deep Sea Fishing Inc. First, they had expertise that the company needed. Second, they had both made significant contributions to the company but they had not been compensated. Third, Deep Sea Fishing Inc. needed fresh capital at that juncture because the existing equity capital had been spent on technical tests. Several conversations with the principal owners of Deep Sea Fishing Inc. revealed the shares were sold to secure the competencies and expertise of the two 'investors' who were trusted and respected, combined with the need for cash.

Table 1 Development of equity capital in Deep Sea Fishing Inc.

Date	Amount (€s)	Price (€s)	Investor(s)
March 1998	7,000	0.14	Anders Velure (40%), Tor Velure (40%), Odd Suldal (20%)
June 1998	40,000		same as above
October 1998	25,000	1.50	Two key individuals who contributed to the start-up with financial/strategic and industry expertise. One works in offshore law, the other runs an offshore related business (9%)
April 1999	785,000	5.14	Fredrik Ravn (20%), Hans Frosta (15%)
May 2000	500,000	15.00	Ravn Group increased their share to 50.3%
December 2000	570,000	15.00	Owners maintained their equity stakes

Suldal had tried for nine years to find funding for his project before he identified the Velure brothers and founded DeepSea Inc. and Deep Sea Fishing Inc. In his quest for funding he contacted, without much success, agencies funded and operated by the government, aimed at stimulating new entrepreneurial ventures. These experiences are discussed below.

Experiences with state-funded government agencies

Over a period of ten years, Odd Suldal had endeavoured to commercialise his idea. He started with government agencies such as the Norwegian Industrial and Regional Development Fund (SND) and the States Advisory Council for Inventors (SVO). Suldal's experiences with government and state agencies are fairly typical as indicated in the following quote from him:

'It was a struggle. They have something fancy called an inventor something or other, where you can get financial support. But it is really for people with funding and backbone [infrastructure]. I know for a fact that several people in Statoil have been funded, and they have had Statoil behind them all the way. A regular guy like me does not get that. So I was met by a cold shoulder all the way. It is those state-funded things; I have a very strained relationship with them.'

Odd Suldal indicated he was frustrated with state-funded agencies. He remarked:

'I tried SND and SVO. When it is state funding, it is only those who have resources who get funded. Those who do not have resources, but have the solution, they don't get anything. If you invent something and need it funded, you can't finance it over your pay cheque, so

that idea is stillborn. First they take half your pay cheque in taxes. Are you to finance the idea and your family with the other half? That won't work. But when you go and ask, you don't even have enough resources to push it through their system, because the system is too cumbersome. There should be one guy who says 'yes' or 'no'. But they have 50 people to give their opinions, and you get 50 different answers.'

Odd Suldal did not have the best of experiences with state-funded agencies whose role is to stimulate new venture growth. He feels that these agencies are bureaucratic and they do not have sufficient resources and clout to push an application through the bureaucratic system.[1] Odd Suldal did not possess the managerial, technical or networking expertise to navigate his applications successfully through the bureaucratic maze. He feels his ideas were good but he did not have sufficient resources to pursue the applications. According to Odd Sulhal, the quality of the idea has little or nothing to do with whether or not an idea is funded by a state-operated agency.[2] Even after acquiring additional finance and expertise funding from the Velure brothers, Odd Suldal's inability to secure outside finance from state-operated agencies was also exhibited

---

[1]Suldal's statements should be considered as an indication of his frustration level, rather than a well-founded criticism of the state-funded agencies. He may lack the patience, skills, and knowledge to complete the application form in the required manner.

[2]Many entrepreneurs with underdeveloped ideas suggest outside investors are unable to see the potential behind the idea. Suldal subsequently received funding from private investors. The latter may have broader business experience than people employed in state-funded agencies.

by DeepSea Inc., with a new set of problems. Tor Velure explains:

'We had a presentation for the Ravn Group, and we had one for CID [City Industry Development].[3] We had actually got the furthest with them in our discussions. CID made an offer which was horrible, to put it mildly. It was killing all initiative and entrepreneurial spirit, and it was taking over everything, and controlling everything, even if they did not own everything, and it is a horribly wrong approach for stimulating anything. They wanted to put up some money, but wanted to have a lot of shares. They wanted the right to buy more at a given price if [the venture became] successful. They wanted to have the CEO; they wanted to decide everything. It was that simple. There were so many frightening clauses that we never seriously considered it. It is a pity that it is this way with this kind of company, because it could have been very useful. But I call it robbery, coming in and taking control of everything. The offer from CID was totally unacceptable.'

(Tor Velure, 25 October 1999.)

The contrast between what CID called a 'standard' offer and what they received from the Ravn Group was stark. Tor Velure explains:

'But after we read it [the offer from CID] they lost outright, because it was not stimulating. What we got from the Ravn Group was much more professional. So everything that the Ravn Group offered was much better. We have the chairman of the board, and we are in control. They are professional in managing. I have only positive things to say about them; they are very professional in the way they work.'

(Tor Velure, 25 October 1999.)

The issue here was not gaining access to capital, the problem was that CID,[4] for some unspecified reason, used a standard investment contract from which it could not, or would not, deviate.[5] This standard contract contained clauses that Deep Sea Fishing Inc. felt would kill their motivation and entrepreneurial spirit. CID's desire for complete control over further development of the

company made CID an unacceptable partner for Deep Sea Fishing Inc.

Deep Sea Fishing Inc.'s experiences with government agencies have not all been negative. Before conducting the final tests at the Trondheim Research Centre, they were awarded 35 per cent of the test costs from SND Invest. The Velure brothers personally, however, had to provide a guarantee of €71,000.

Relationship with the private investors from the Ravn Group

CID's posture is in sharp contrast to that exhibited by private investors involved in the Ravn Group. The Ravn Group's business lawyer stated:

'We wish to have a minimum share of 34 per cent, either alone or together with partners. On the other hand, it is important that we do not seize an unreasonably large portion at the expense of the entrepreneurs. They should have plenty of incentives and ownership to work hard for the company.'

(Eivind Elgseter, 18 December 2000.)

Tor Velure's earlier statement suggests that Deep Sea Fishing Inc. is pleased with the Ravn Group's attitude. In light of the offer that Deep Sea Fishing Inc. received from CID, Ravn Group's request for one-third of the shares and two of the four board members was viewed as a demanding but an acceptable offer. Eivind Elgseter's statement above demonstrates that the Ravn Group places demands on the companies in which it invests. Both Ravn and Frosta are well-known investors who receive numerous investment opportunities each year, but Deep Sea Fishing Inc. appeared to be an attractive investment opportunity. Eivind Elgseter remarked:

'When it came to DeepSea, they were pretty far along in the process when we got involved. They appeared believable, in that they had an inventor who clearly had a high degree of product knowledge, and he was very creative. In addition, they had a management team [the Velure brothers] that had a very relevant financial background, which made the project appear credible.'

(Eivind Elgseter, 18 December 2000.)

When Eivind Elgseter speaks about the Ravn Group's general investment strategies, and of the entrepreneur in general terms, he uses the singular to describe the entrepreneur, but when he speaks about Deep Sea Fishing Inc. he uses the plural. The Velure brothers are viewed as an integral part of the entrepreneurial ownership

---

[3]CID, or City Industry Development Inc., was a company owned and run by SND Invest, Vesta and others. SND Invest is the dominant owner and CID is not strictly speaking a 'government agency'.

[4]The entrepreneurs perceived CID as an extension of SND Invest but it can be viewed as a venture capital fund.

[5]CID (and other government agencies) may not have sufficient competencies to identify good investment opportunities.

team. It was the collective competencies and experiences of the entrepreneurial ownership team that were evaluated by the Ravn Group.

Investors are not the only actors with demands. The entrepreneurs in Deep Sea Fishing Inc. were seeking financial and non-financial support from a potential investor. The initial offer from the Ravn Group was rejected but they were seen as attractive investors and business partners as indicated by Tor Velure:

'Ravn and Frosta are considered hitters in our region. They are very professional and we are very pleased . . . With regard to going to Statoil to introduce ourselves, it gives us credibility to have them onboard. They are involved in offshore already. They are smart people with the right connections.'

(Tor Velure, 25 October 1999.)

The fact that Ravn and Frosta invested in Deep Sea Fishing Inc. gave the company 'instant credibility'. Legitimacy and superior networking skills provided by Ravn and Frosta were valued by the entrepreneurs seeking to reduce the 'liabilities of newness and small size' associated with their technology-based firm. The Norwegian oil business is conservative and many of the large oil companies have a policy limit of 100 suppliers. With the Ravn Group behind Deep Sea Fishing Inc., the task to secure contracts becomes easier. The Ravn Group provided an important financial investment but the legitimacy, skills, knowledge and networking contributions by the investors is of further value to the venture.

The supply side: Investment decision considerations

In addition to the usual business issues such as profit potential, risk, cash flow and the like, investors are concerned with the integrity and other personal attributes of each entrepreneurial ownership team member. Eivind Elgseter explains:

'Before we invest, it is important that we feel secure in relation to the entrepreneur on a personal level. This is extremely important. In particular, there are three

qualities that we [seek] for openness and competency. By competency I mean that he must have some insight into what he is doing, the technical aspects of the product must be solid, and he must show an understanding of the appropriate market actors.'

To reduce risk, investors require information relating to the honesty and integrity of each entrepreneurial ownership team member as well as an understanding of each member's entrepreneurial, managerial and technical skills and competencies. Elgseter elaborated:

'Furthermore, it is important that he does not show greed, or take eggs out of the basket to enrich himself. By that I mean that the entrepreneur must show that he has faith in the project, and that the capital that we provide goes towards commercialisation, and not for a new fur coat for the wife.'

(Eivind Elgseter, 18 December 2000.)

Investors need to trust and respect each member of the entrepreneurial ownership team in which they are investing. Elgseter speaks of these things in general, indicating that it is a matter of routine to evaluate these issues prior to making an investment decision. Comments from Elgseter suggest that the entrepreneurial ownership team of Deep Sea Fishing Inc. satisfied the Ravn Group's requirements. The fact that the Ravn Group investors have continued to invest in Deep Sea Fishing Inc. through multiple rounds of investment and technology redevelopment shows the high level of trust they placed in the supported entrepreneurial ownership team.

The development of Deep Sea Fishing Inc.

Over the years, Deep Sea Fishing Inc. has required approximately €3.75 million in risk capital. Despite this investment, sales revenue growth has been slower than anticipated. After entering its initial market, Deep Sea Fishing Inc. had to redevelop its technology. Subsequently sales revenues began to rise. Sales revenues and operating results for Deep Sea Fishing Inc. over a six-year period are summarised in Table 2.

Table 2 Sales revenues and operating results (€) for Deep Sea Fishing Inc.

	2001	2002	2003	2004	2005	2006
Revenues (€s)	0.00	0.00	966,125.00	539,000.00	1,924,875.00	4,049,750.00
Operating results (€s)	−210,375.00	−481,250.00	−108,250.00	−508,875.00	−294,625.00	512,500.00

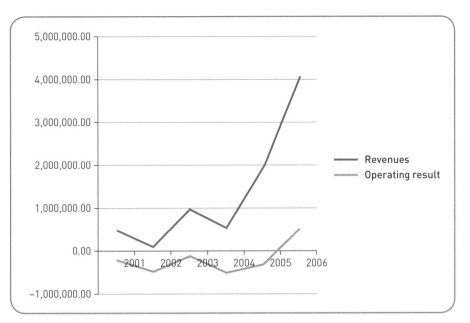

Figure 1 Sales revenues and operating results (€) for Deep Sea Fishing Inc.

Figure 1 shows that the operating results lag behind the growth in sales revenues. Substantial capital is, therefore, required to service the shortfall in revenue income during the early phases of product development and exploitation. Capital is also required to invest in the further redevelopment of the technology and the business.

Questions and issues

1 What are the founding entrepreneur's distinctive demands? Is the founding entrepreneur solely seeking finance? If not, what other resources and competencies are sought from a potential investor?

2 The resource-based view (RBV) of the firm suggests that a firm's resources can shape firm performance. Barney (1995) argues that firms have a competitive advantage when their resources relating to assets, capabilities and/or processes are valuable, rare, difficult to imitate, and well organised. There are different 'types' of resources (also termed capital). Resources can be financial, physical, social and/or intellectual (Nahapiet and Ghoshal, 1998; Ulrich, 1998). They can be quantitative or qualitative and tangible or intangible. A firm's bundle of different types of resources enables the firm to identify and exploit an opportunity and to have a competitive advantage. What resources are sought by the founding entrepreneur? What

resources are then sought by the first entrepreneurial ownership team? Are financial resources the only issue here? If not, what are the other issues and resources illustrated by Deep Sea Fishing Inc (DSF)? What can we absorb from the inductive and deductive knowledge-generating methods?

Suggested reading

Barney, J. B. (1995). Looking Inside for Competitive Advantages. *Academy of Management Executive*, 9 (4): 49–62.

Nahapiet, J. and Ghoshal, S. (1998). Social Capital, Intellectual Capital and the Organizational Advantage. *Academy of Management Review*, 23 (2): 242–266.

Ulrich, D. (1998). Intellectual Capital = Competence × Commitment. *Sloan Management Review*, 39 (4): 15–27.

Supplementary readings (on the role of informal investors)

Erikson, T. (2007). Discriminating 'Schumpeterian' from 'Austrian' Informal Investors. *Journal of International Entrepreneurship*, 5 (1-2): 1–10.

Erikson, T. and Sørheim, R. (2005). Technology 'Angels' vs Other Informal Investors. *Technovation*, 25 (5): 489–496.

Additional reading

Barney, J. B. (1991). Firm Resources and Sustained Competitive Advantage. *Journal of Management,* 17: 99–120.

Barney, J. B. (1995). Looking Inside for Competitive Advantages. *Academy of Management Executive,* 9 (4): 49–62.

Barney, J. B. (2001). Is the Resource-Based 'View' a Useful Perspective for Strategic Management Research? Yes. *Academy of Management Review,* 26 (1): 41–56.

Chrisman, J. J. (1999). The Influence of Outsider-Generated Knowledge Resources on Venture Creation. *Journal of Small Business Management,* 39 (4): 42–58.

Erikson, T. (2002). Entrepreneurial Capital: The Emerging Organization's Most Important Asset. *Journal of Business Venturing,* 17 (3): 275–290.

Nahapiet, J. and Ghoshal, S. (1998). Social Capital, Intellectual Capital and the Organizational Advantage. *Academy of Management Review,* 23 (2): 242–266.

Penrose, E. (1995). The Theory of the Growth of the Firm. *New York: Oxford University Press* [a reprint from the 1959 edition].

Sætre, A. S. (2003). Entrepreneurial Perspectives on Informal Venture Capital. *Venture Capital: An International Journal of Entrepreneurial Finance,* 5 (1): 71–94.

Ulrich, D. (1998). Intellectual Capital = Competence × Commitment. *Sloan Management Review,* 39 (4): 15–27.

Painotalo Ltd and Rakennuspalvelu Ltd: Family business transfer issues

Ulla Hytti, Kirsi Peura and Pekka Stenholm

Summary

This case study explores the need for firm owners to consider issues relating to business ownership transfer. The challenges facing families, family firm owners and potential successors are raised. The two cases discussed have fictitious business names and they illustrate alternative business transfer processes. The Painotalo Ltd case relates to a context where internal family successors could be identified, while the Rakennuspalvelu Ltd case relates to a context where the incumbent owner had no internal family successor.

Introduction

One early winter morning, Reino and Sisko Lehtinen are sitting at the kitchen table. They take the opportunity to talk about transferring their company to their children, Risto and Maija. Sisko asks her husband:

'Have we done everything we need to? I hope we haven't forgotten anything important! I don't want to think we are getting the kids into a big mess.'

Reino replies:

'You're right. We need to think this through again. I've talked with the accountant and she has reassured me that all the legal stuff has been taken care of, but I suppose there is more to this than just paperwork.'

Company background

Painotalo Ltd is a first generation family business and the company was established in 1980. The company specialises in the printing of signs, decorations and placards and is located in Riihimäki in southern Finland. In total, the company has six full-time employees and one part-time employee.

The printing industry is rapidly developing towards a fully digital business. As a result, the company has made some changes and investments over the past few years to keep pace with this development. Risto and Maija have mainly initiated these investments. They have seen the need to move away from the old system of doing things because they do not want to engage in time-consuming manual work. Reino and Sisko have assessed the projected costs of the investments. In Risto's and Maija's opinion, their mother was not always fully supportive of the investment decisions. Due to the new investment the company has secured its competitive advantage. The firm's market area is the whole of Finland. During the past year, the company reported a sales turnover of €2,270,000, which is higher than the €1,690,000 reported the previous year (Appendix 1). This growth is due to the new investments, which has attracted new customers and retained existing customers. The family believe the company will continue to grow.

The family

The Lehtinen family is strongly involved in the business. The father Reino (56 years old), mother Sisko (55) and their two children, Risto (31) and Maija (33) work in the firm. In addition, Maija's husband works in the business. Reino and Sisko have a third child, Riitta, but she is not directly involved in the firm. Riitta is a teacher in a primary school.

Business transfer process

The succession planning regarding the transfer of ownership was started very early. No major problems have been encountered or are foreseen. Risto and Maija own 90 per cent of the company between them, and they each own 45 per cent of the company. The business transfer process was started in the 1980s with the assistance of an accountant and a legal adviser. The firm's independent accountant has been a key player. She is the same age as the parents and she is expected to retire in the near future. Maija knows that the accountant's daughter is taking an accountancy degree and she believes the daughter will take over her mother's business.

With regard to the succession plan, Reino will retain a small ownership stake in the company, but he will retain the majority of voting shares. It is planned that the transfer of the business will take place during the next six years.

Currently, the family is investigating ways in which the remaining 10 per cent of the ownership can be transferred. Sisko, the mother, is of the opinion that the children should not be forced to pay too much for the 10 per cent ownership stake. Reino supports his wife, but he thinks at the same time that they need to find a solution which will not harm the business, but will ensure the parents have some financial security after their retirement from the business. They plan to split the business activities and the real estate into two separate businesses. One child will own 51 per cent of the printing business and the other will own 51 per cent of the real estate. When the share capital of the company was raised, Sisko and Reino donated the funds to their children. Sisko and Reino (i.e., family firm incumbent owners) have tried to avoid making it necessary for their children to borrow money to develop the printing business. According to Sisko:

> 'We did not want to tie up the whole family into raising the capital. There would have been in-laws also . . . If they have to take big loans and so . . . As a mother it is quite scary, of course.'

Risto and Maija have been working in the firm for several years, and are now both committed to developing the business. This has not always been the case. Prior to joining the family business they both obtained employment in other printing firms. The parents encouraged them to acquire skills and knowledge in other firms. The children's main reasons for returning to work in the family business were so that they could carry it on. Also, they wanted to obtain a thorough knowledge of the firm, which they already partially owned. Roles within the firm are shared in such a way that the successors (i.e., Risto and Maija) can replace the incumbents (i.e., Reino and Sisko), if and when necessary. They are all responsible for the key tasks in the firm as well as its development. However, the successors have been assigned their own areas of responsibility. Risto is in charge of digital printing, selling and marketing, while Maija looks after selling, marketing and some aspects of financial management. Reino is currently fully in charge of accounting and financial management. He is responsible for cost calculations and pricing. Also, Reino has the final word in decision-making. The key customers have learned to know and trust Risto and Maija over the years, although many of the oldest customers still prefer to contact Reino or Sisko. Risto is more knowledgeable about digital printing than his father. Reino commented:

> 'They learn to deal with Risto. I know nothing of computers but I am in charge of pricing. It does not really matter who takes the job because I can calculate the price afterwards.'

Risto and Maija want their parents to trust them more with regard to business issues. Reino and Sisko agree that they have not given up all the responsibility that their children would like to take. According to Risto and Maija, the employees work in a self-directed way, and because they work mostly outside the firm there have not been any problems, so far. Currently, Reino makes the final decisions if he is around. Risto and Maija believe that because they have worked in the company for many years the employees have become accustomed to them.

After the final ownership transfer, Reino and Sisko plan to take some time off from the company in order to spend more time in their summer house. The parents wonder whether they will ever be able to completely stay away from the business. Reino remarked:

> 'We will come here to see how things are run. It will not be easy to leave for good. We've done this for 30 years already.'

Risto and Maija do not have a clear idea of what the future will bring. They feel that they still have enough time (i.e., six years) before the final transfer and there is no need to worry about everything at this stage. However, Maija is concerned about how she will be able to combine work and family life after the ownership transfer. Risto does not see any major changes except that he will become fully responsible for the financial management of the company. He does not believe that his work will change in the future.

Summary of the situation

The transfer of ownership from the incumbents to the second generation (i.e., Risto and Maija) was initiated in the 1980s. The process has taken a long time and no major problems have been experienced, and none are foreseen. Yet the Lehtinen's still think that they have not dealt fully with all the challenges involved. There are still some issues that need to be discussed and more decisions need to be made.

Rakennuspalvelu Ltd

Matti Virtanen is an entrepreneur with a long history in the construction business. He looks at his two 'heirs', Mikko and Tero, and says to a fellow entrepreneur:

'Well, they're quite young and like all young people today maybe they are not fully aware of all the realities in this world. But they are top of their class and I hope that they'll get a hang of things during the next few years.'

Company background

Rakennuspalvelu Ltd was set up in 1984 in Helsinki in Finland. Apart from the owner, Matti Virtanen, there are seven employees, including five trainees. The company operates in the construction industry providing services for real estate renovation and redevelopment. The sales turnover for the last financial year was €539,000, and this is lower than the €771,000 reported in the previous year (Appendix 2). Matti expects that the company will grow moderately in the future. When he started to plan for retirement, Matti owned 100 per cent of the company. At the time, he set himself the goal of completing the business handover in three to six years. Within this timeframe, Matti believed that he would be able to find suitable successors, and to train and motivate them to follow in his footsteps. Matti reflected:

'It'll definitely take more than three years for me to retire. After that I still might hang around looking after the successors and what they'll be up to. The best case is to leave the business gradually, to be available for the lads and share my experience with them whenever needed.'

Business transfer process

There are no family members working in the firm and Matti (55 years old) does not have a suitable family to take over from him. Matti is reluctant to see his life's work go down the drain when he retires. Due to the lack of family successors, Matti contacted a local vocational institute in order to locate possible candidates who might buy the company and develop the business after his retirement. With this in mind, Matti employed two trainees directly from the institute (Mikko, 22 and Tero, 23) with a view to preparing them to take over and develop the business in a few years' time. Both Mikko and Tero are committed to the firm. Matti, Mikko and Tero contacted a consultant and an accountant to prepare a plan to transfer ownership of the business. The idea was to transfer ownership of the company to Mikko and Tero (i.e., the successors), but with Matti (i.e., the incumbent owner) remaining in the company as the chief executive office (CEO) to support Mikko and Tero. Matti and both the successors find the financial issues relating to the business transfer process very complex. Further, Matti suggests that other issues merely have to be 'talked through'. In 2003, a major development impacted on the business transfer process. Mikko and Tero purchased 50 per cent of the shares in the company and they became officially involved in the business.

Mikko and Tero are both still quite young and, according to Matti, because of their youth and lack of experience, they do not fully understand the issues involved in running a business. Matti has supported the young men vocationally and personally on their way to becoming entrepreneurs. He visited their homes and met their parents and girlfriends. Matti has openly explained his future plans for the business to the young men. He is aware that the change that lies ahead is dependent on how motivated Mikko and Tero are. Matti wants both young men to be really committed to developing and running the business. He wants Mikko and Tero to consider how owning and running a business will impact on their work and family relationships. Matti commented:

'The boys have to understand that their girlfriends might not necessarily understand what it takes to be in the business. They might not understand the financial as well as personal investments involved. But I've said to the boys, remember the business stays but the girlfriends might change.'

Mikko and Tero share the same tasks in the company, but according to them, the distribution of work is clear. Mikko is better at handling paperwork. Tero is more open and sociable and he can deal with customers. Moreover, Matti is encouraging both of them to develop their managerial skills as well as their personal abilities. Matti has a strong personality and he wants to cultivate his own kind of determination in Mikko and Tero. He has offered his help as a mentor and a teacher. He is emphasising to the young men that personal success affects the business and vice versa. Matti is ready to offer his support with regard to anything they may need. He sees himself as a sort of stepfather, and is striving to prevent the disappearance of his lifelong work and achievement when he retires. Matti has acquainted Mikko and Tero with the suppliers. Mikko and Tero appreciate the assistance provided. In addition, Matti has taken them to a construction business fair and he introduced them to importers and manufacturers. Matti is proud that his customers have already expressed satisfaction with Mikko and Tero, and their work.

Summary of the situation

Officially, the transfer of ownership started a year ago, although from the point of view of the incumbent the process has taken somewhat longer. Matti has invested time to find suitable successors. He also expended time and effort making them familiar with the business. For Mikko and Tero, the process has been much shorter. Both successors have been able to 'grow' in the company and they have gained valuable business experience. However, because they are young and at the beginning of their professional and personal adult lives, various issues remain to be discussed and resolved.

Questions and issues

This case is intended to be used for a *group discussion and role playing* relating to the *business ownership transfer process*, particularly in small, private, independent firms. A group of students should play the role of the *incumbent firm owners*, while another group of students should play the role of *potential successors* (and/or acquirers). Students should raise issues prior to the business ownership transfer process, during the process, and after the process (i.e., before, during and after the transfer of business ownership). The two groups (i.e., incumbent owners and potential successors) are invited to discuss their agendas with each other as if in a *family/business meeting*. This discussion relates to the following general question:

1 What issues and procedures need to be considered with reference to the business ownership transfer process in a small private (family) firm?

A teacher may facilitate the discussion by asking the following additional questions.

Discussion between the incumbents and successors

2 Are both sides aware of their respective plans and personal wishes?

3 Have there been discussions relating to ownership transfer of the business between the incumbents and successors? Is the larger family included in these discussions (i.e., spouses or children other than the successors)? Are they aware of the issues to discuss? Is there a need for assistance?

The transfer of the business or withdrawal from the business

4 What to give up and how? Is there a need for external assistance (e.g., the transfer of contracts)? Is there trust and openness between the incumbents and successors?

5 Are there any possible conflicts between the incumbents and successors?

6 When should responsibilities be transferred (i.e., customers, suppliers, employees, etc.)?

7 After the business transfer will any incumbents remain in the business? Is the incumbent's future financially secured? Is the incumbent's future socially interesting?

Employees, customers, suppliers

8 When and how inform to different shareholders in the firm (i.e., openness, continuity of information, etc.) with regard to the business transfer process?

9 Will the customers, suppliers, employees and financiers know and trust the successors?

Financial and legal issues

10 What is the financial situation of the firm (i.e., viability, possible solutions to improve the financial situation, etc.)?

11 What financing issues need to be considered (i.e., contacts with different financiers, need of financing, financing of tax claims (for incumbent and successor), etc.)?

12 How and who will calculate the net worth of the firm (i.e., factors influencing the worth, need for external assistance, etc.)?

Tax issues

13 What tax issues need to be considered (i.e., capital gains tax, inheritance tax, etc.)?

14 What are the tax implications associated with different business transfer options?

Future of the business

15 What business planning and strategy issues need to be considered before and after the business ownership transfer?

16 What role do incumbents and successors play in the planning process?

17 Do the successors have complete information and knowledge of the business and its markets?

18 Will the successors be able to leverage the good name and reputation and trust of the former owners of the business?

Planning the transfer of the business

19 Is there a need for a written plan relating to the business ownership transfer (i.e., timing, roles of the different parties, contracts, financing and taxation, different areas that need to be focused upon, etc.)?

20 What potential unforeseen changes need to be planned for (i.e., sudden death or accident relating the incumbent)?

Additional reading

Barach, J. A., Gantisky, J., Carson, J. A. and Doochin, B. A. (1988). Entry of the Next Generation: Strategic Challenge for Family Business. *Journal of Small Business Management*, 26 (2): 49–56.

Barnes, L. B. and Hershon, S. A. (1976). Transferring Power in the Family Business. *Harvard Business Review*, 54 (4): 105–114.

Brockhaus, R. H. (2004). Family Business Succession: Suggestions for Future Research. *Family Business Review*, 17 (2): 165–177.

Cadieux, L. (2007). Succession in Small and Medium-Sized Family Businesses: Toward a Typology of Predecessor Roles During and After Instatement of the Successor. *Family Business Review*, 20 (2): 95–109.

Carlock, R. S. and Ward, J. L. (2001). *Strategic Planning for the Family Business – Parallel Planning to Unify the Family and Business*. New York: Palgrave.

Churchill, N. C. and Hatten, K. J. (1987). Non-Market Based Transfers of Wealth and Power: A Research Framework for Family Businesses. *American Journal of Small Business*, 11 (3): 51–64.

Fédération des Experts Comptables Européens. (2000). *Keeping it in the Family. SME Family Business Succession. Planning for yourself, your business and the next generation*. Bruxelles: Fédération des Experts Comptables Européens.

Fox, M., Nilakant, V. and Hamilton, R. T. (1996). Managing Success in Family-Owned Business. *International Small Business Journal*, 15 (1): 15–26.

Handler, W. (1990). Succession in Family Firms: A Mutual Role Adjustment Between Entrepreneur and Next-Generation Family Members. *Entrepreneurship Theory and Practice*, 15 (20): 37–51.

Hunt, J. M. and Handler, W. C. (1999). The Practices of Effective Family Firm Leaders. *Journal of Developmental Entrepreneurship*, 4 (2): 135–151.

Ibrahim, A. B., Soufani, K. and Lam, J. (2001). A Study of Succession in a Family Firm. *Family Business Review*, 14 (3): 245–258.

Ip, B. and Jacobs, G. (2006). Business Succession Planning: A Review of the Evidence. *Journal of Small Business and Enterprise Development*, 13 (3): 326–350.

Kets de Vries, M. (1993). The Dynamics of Family Controlled Firms: The Good and the Bad News. *Organisational Dynamics*, 22 (3): 59–72.

Lambrecht, J. (2005). Multigenerational Transition in Family Businesses. A New Explanatory Model. *Family Business Review*, 18 (4): 267–282.

Lansberg, I. (2002). The Succession Conspiracy. In C. E. Aronoff, J. H. Astrachan and J. L. Ward (eds) *Family Business Sourcebook*, 3rd edition. Family Enterprise Publishers, pp. 45–59.

Le Breton-Miller, I., Miller, D. and Steier, L. P. (2004). Toward an Integrative Model of Effective FOB Succession. *Entrepreneurship Theory and Practice*, 28 (4): 305–328.

Levinson, H. (1971). Conflicts That Plague the Family Business. *Harvard Business Review*, 49 (2): 90–98.

Morris, M. H., Williams, R. W. and Nel, D. (1996). Factors Influencing Family Business Succession. *International Journal of Entrepreneurial Behaviour & Research*, 2 (3): 68–81.

Stavrou, E. T. (1999). Succession in Family Businesses: Exploring the Effects of Demographic Factors on Offspring Intentions to Join and Take Over the Business. *Journal of Small Business Management*, 37 (3): 43–62.

Stavrou, E. T. and Swiercz, P. M. (1998). Securing the Future of the Family Enterprise: A Model of Offspring Intentions to Join the Business. *Entrepreneurship Theory and Practice*, 22 (2): 21–40.

Stenholm, P. (2003). *Yrityksen sukupolvenvaihdos ja sen tukeminen (Succession in a Firm and the Ways to Promote it*. In Finnish). Edita Oy: Helsinki: Ministry of Trade and Industry, Studies and Researches, 7/2003.

Trow, D. B. (1961). Executive Succession in Small Companies. *Administrative Science Quarterly*, 6 (2): 228–239.

Venter, E., Boshoff, C. and Maas, G. (2005). The Influence of Successor-Related Factors on the Succession Process in Small and Medium-Sized Family Businesses. *Family Business Review*, 18 (4): 283–303.

Appendix 1 Painotalo Ltd

Income statement (€ '000s)	2001	2002	2003
Turnover	1808.7	1692.9	2270.9
Value added	943.1	996.5	1219.2
Salaries	896.2	907.6	981.4
Rents	0.0	0.0	0.0
Gross margin	47.0	88.9	237.8
Financing costs	46.4	36.9	98.4
Taxes	0.7	0.9	0.0
Income before extraordinary items	−0.1	51.1	139.4
Depreciation	54.8	46.5	215.5
Net income	−55.0	4.5	−76.1
Extraordinary items	−1.9	0.0	0.0
Profit	−53.0	4.5	−76.1

Balance sheet (€'000s)	2001	2002	2003
Fixed assets	629.5	583.0	1102.5
Current assets	329.0	356.4	563.4
Current assets	958.5	939.4	1666.0
Own capital	73.3	77.8	98.5
Loan capital			
– with interest	807.0	754.5	1231.9
– without interest	78.2	107.1	335.6
Liabilities and capital	958.5	939.4	1666.0

Appendix 2 Rakennuspalvelu Ltd

Income statement (€'000s)	2001	2002	2003
Turnover	573.0	771.4	539.4
Value added	200.6	226.5	284.6
Salaries	151.1	196.3	178.4
Rents	0.0	0.0	0.0
Gross margin	49.5	30.2	106.2
Financing costs	0.0	0.0	−18.0
Taxes	10.5	2.3	32.5
Income before extraordinary items	39.0	27.9	91.7
Depreciation	12.9	21.0	12.8
Net income	26.1	6.9	78.8
Extraordinary items	0.0	0.0	0.0
Profit	26.1	6.9	78.8

Balance sheet (€'000s)	2001	2002	2003
Fixed assets	38.6	63.0	38.5
Current assets	70.5	62.1	172.5
Current assets	109.1	125.1	211.0
Own capital	71.4	71.1	144.0
Loan capital			
– with interest	16.7	8.2	39.8
– without interest	21.0	45.9	27.2
Liabilities and capital	109.1	125.1	211.0

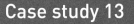

Case study 13

Spin-offs at Tremcar: Partnerships for growth

Caroline Mireault, Danielle Luc and Louis J. Filion

Summary

This case discusses the behaviour of Jacques Trem-blay, who acquired and grew the Tremcar business, and who selected the spin-off process to ensure firm growth. Three spin-offs relating to Citernes Hébert & Son, JC Tanks & Repair and Raynox were launched. These spin-offs enabled Tremblay to concentrate on his core business activities relating to the manufac-ture of tankers to transport comestibles. This case describes the spin-off philosophy of Jacques Trem-blay as well as the context in which the three spin-offs were created. The profile, management and development of each spin-off is discussed.

Introduction

Jacques Tremblay has sharp instincts. He has learned to recognise the employees he can count on and to whom he can entrust additional responsibilities, including business management. The person he is looking for must not only be able to run Tremcar's new repair shop in the United States, but also be willing to be Tremblay's partner in the venture. Three successful spin-off experiences to date have convinced him that this is the right way to go. His fourth spin-off presents an additional challenge, that of distance. For the first time, he cannot choose an employee from his Iberville (30 km south of Montreal), Canada plant. Instead, he must try to assess the potential of the employees at his Champlain plant, located some 50 km south of Montreal, in New York State in the United States.

Jacques Tremblay

French is the main language spoken in Quebec. All the principal players in this case study, speak, work and live in French. Jacques Tremblay has entrepreneurial blood in his veins. His father built a concrete products factory and managed it jointly with Jacques' older brother. When his older brother died in 1959, Jacques Tremblay (17 years old) abandoned his education and took over his brother's role in the family business. The firm employed ten peo-ple. In 1966, health problems forced Jacques' father to cut down his activities, and Jacques (by then 24 years old) acquired the business. The factory employed 15 people but this figure would triple within five years.

In 1985, Tremblay went into partnership with a long-time friend who worked in the concrete sector. The alliance strengthened the production capacity of both firms, which together had nearly 150 employees. By the time he sold his shares to his partner, 30 years after the initial acquisition, the firm had two plants in Quebec and another in Miami, Florida.

Tremblay completed his high-school education with some additional courses in small business management, concrete technology and workplace psychology. His wide reading relating to economics and politics encouraged him to be politically active. In 1985, he was elected Mem-ber of the National Assembly for his home region of Montérégie. Tremblay was appointed president of a par-liamentary standing committee, and he became the assis-tant to Daniel Johnson, then Minister of Industry and Commerce and who was to succeed Bourassa as premier.

Tremblay was missing his business life. Although Tremblay trusted his partner, he was finding it increas-ingly difficult to manage his businesses from a distance, and the pull of entrepreneurship became stronger and stronger. Like his father before him, Tremblay wanted to work with his three children to prepare his succession. He reorganised his affairs, and decided to focus his efforts on Tremcar.

Tremblay considers it extremely important to in-volve his employees in defining the firm's mission. He exhibits a visionary, participatory and consensual management style. When Tremblay has an idea, he submits it to others to see what they think. In all his decisions, he tries to assess the long-term impact based on the general environment in which the firm operates. He provides a number of programmes to motivate managers and employees. Tremblay commented:

> 'Spin-offs are also a kind of motivation, since they convey a message of trust and openness to the employees.'

Tremcar: Concentrating the firm's central activities

The Tougas brothers, welders by trade and handymen by nature, started Tremcar in 1962. They began to produce handmade tanks for the dairy farmers in Quebec. They were better as craftsmen and inventors than managers. A successor could not be found to take over the family business. They decided to sell the firm to 'local lad' Jacques Tremblay who had very little knowledge about tankers and agro-food transportation. His accountant assured him that this was a golden opportunity. In 1987, the Tougas brothers sold Tremcar to Jacques Tremblay and his partner. The company employed 30 people and reported sales of CAN $3 million. Tremblay realised that steel tanker production and maintenance is highly specialised, and the firm was not being operated to its full potential. The two partners managed Tremcar as a unit in a group of highly disparate enterprises put together almost at random, relating to a concrete products manufacturer, a hardware store, a plastics plant, a car dealership, and a wood sector plant. Tremblay decided to focus his activities. His partner had not shown much interest in Tremcar. In 1989, they decided to sell Tremcar. Potential purchasers were identified, and negotiations were begun. Tremblay changed his mind and he acquired complete control of the company from his partner in exchange for other assets. He believed that transportation sector firms, unlike concrete firms, were not dependent on a single region. Tremblay wanted to expand his horizons.

In 1992, Tremblay acquired his only direct competitor in Quebec, a company located in Drummondville. The following year he acquired a competitor in Toronto. He closed the production unit but retained the service department. In 1999, he purchased a plant in Champlain in New York State in the United States. After consolidating his new acquisitions, Tremblay began the process of restructuring. The milk tanker market was

saturated. He decided to extend his range by producing stainless steel tankers to transport liquid, chemical and agro-food products. In 1998, the firm introduced a line of aluminium tankers for dry goods. Each tanker was custom-made to meet the client's own particular specifications and they complied with stringent state or provincial regulations. The firm's production capacity rose from 40 tankers a year in 1989 to 600 in 1999. The firm sells its products to a whole range of clients and has made inroads into the United States market, which now accounts for 50 per cent of its sales. When the Tougas brothers owned the firm, 90 per cent of sales were in the Quebec market. In the early 1990s, the firm's annual sales turnover was under CAN $3 million. By 2001, the enterprise employed 275 people and reported sales of CAN $40 million.

Spin-offs as key elements in Tremcar's growth strategy

For Tremblay, the spin-off process offers many benefits that are consistent with his business philosophy. Tremblay reflected:

> 'I am very much in favour of active employee participation in the organisation of work . . . As much as possible, I try to remain close to my employees. However, the firm has grown quickly and now employs a lot of people, with the result that it is becoming increasingly difficult for me to spend as much time on this aspect. The spin-off process allows me to convey a message of trust and to reinforce employee commitment to the firm.'

He knows he could simply have subcontracted his repair shops and after-sales services. But in his opinion:

> '. . . a subcontracting arrangement does not have the same solidity or consistency as the relationship of trust required for a partnership. The strength of the relationships between me and my three partners could not have been achieved in any other way.'

Tremblay is the first to admit that the shift from employee to partner requires an adaptation and personal growth, both for him and for his partners. It requires the capacity to adapt because:

> '. . . the new entrepreneurs cannot concentrate on making profits at the expense of their ties with Tremcar. They have to maintain a perpetual balance between the short-term and the long-term vision.'

The repair shop spin-off produced some unexpected strategic benefits. It is a showcase for Tremcar. Further, the client base provides information on competitors' products. The shop repairs tankers built by Tremcar's competitors. Tremcar has acquired knowledge surrounding the strengths and weaknesses of its competitors' products.

Tremblay suggests success is related to the partners he has selected. He suggests people must:

'. . . have what it takes – in other words, the entrepreneurial qualities that will enable them to succeed in business. They must exhibit leadership, energy, dynamism and the will to succeed. They must also be flexible, willing to compromise and open to discussion.'

Tremblay is guided by a sense of trust and honesty in his potential partners. He insists on clear roles for everyone concerned. In the three spin-offs, his partners all became president of their respective companies, and inherited the duties and responsibilities of that position. Tremcar and its president are much more than financial partners; they play an instrumental supporting role both technically and managerially in the spin-off companies. By handing the entrepreneurial flame to other people in his entourage, Tremblay has made his own life easier by creating an organisational and psychological support system that will help him face up to and overcome the competition.

First spin-off experience: Handing over the service function

Tremcar's growth was virtually exponential and the firm quickly outgrew its premises. In 1993, Tremblay purchased a repair shop in Saint-Athanase and appointed employee Louis Hébert to manage it. All Tremcar's tanker repair and after-sales service activities were transferred to the new premises. Eight months later, he sold the repair service to Hébert and another employee, both of whom had been with Tremcar for many years.

Tremblay knew that Louis Hébert, with more than 25 years of experience in the firm, had become an acknowledged expert in tanker sales and repairs. Hébert had been involved in the tanker development process. He had held welder, foreman, appraiser and salesman positions. Hébert had built up a reputation outside the province, in Eastern Canada and the northern United States. Tremblay sought to retain his expertise for Tremcar. He commented:

'As the firm developed and grew, I realised how important it was to protect our distinctive skills. They were the reason our clients came to us.'

Tremblay sold all his shares in the subsidiary to his two employees, taking steps to transfer ownership, drawing up a business plan, asking his own lawyers to prepare the sales contract, and even financing the equipment purchase himself. He viewed the decision as an investment that would pay off in a few years' time.

The new firm, Citernes Hébert et Dugas, inherited all Tremcar's after-sales service activities along with its spare parts sales service for Eastern Canada. Hébert continued to work as a sales agent for Tremcar products, mainly in the milk transportation sector, and the firm's stainless steel tanker specialist. The spin-off firm also offered a Tremcar tanker rental service for firms in temporary need of tanker trailers.

The following year, Hébert's partner withdrew and Tremblay bought half of the firm's shares. The financial ties between Hébert and Tremblay strengthened their partnership. Trust was a significant element in the tacit agreement between the two men. The relationship between the two firms remained basically unchanged. However, meetings became more frequent, and the new partner was able to offer extensive business management advice. Tremcar offered Citernes Hébert employees training. Technical advice was also provided. Citernes Hébert was, and still is, of great strategic importance to Tremcar. It would be virtually impossible for Tremcar to sell its tankers without the high level of after-sales service provided by the spin-off company.

Citernes Hébert's customer base grew, and the parent company now accounts for only 25 per cent of its sales turnover. The ties between the two companies go far beyond figures. Each is dependent on the other, and each has a strong interest in the other's success. In 2000, Citernes Hébert had approximately ten employees, mostly welder mechanics. The firm can now repair six tankers at a time. Unlike Tremcar, Citernes Hébert has several competitors in the Quebec market.

Jacques Tremblay regards this first spin-off experience as being extremely positive. Citernes Hébert is currently preparing its succession. To the delight of both partners, Louis Hébert's son has joined the repair shop team, thus ensuring some future stability. This new step in the firm's development was marked by a change of name to Citernes Hébert and Son.

Second spin-off experience: Improving the supply system

In 1991, Raynald Ostiguy joined Tremcar as a welder. According to Tremblay, he always displayed leadership, dynamism and creativity. Tremcar grew very quickly and the three assembly shops sometimes faced difficulties obtaining components. Suppliers could not always offer the desired quality at the right price and time, and this restricted production growth. With senior management's blessing, Tremblay hired employees to produce components on site. In autumn 1995, Tremcar's president offered Ostiguy a partnership arrangement, which would involve building a specialised component manufacturing unit able to supply the three assembly shops. Ostiguy had always wanted his own business. In April 1996, he became general manager of Raynox, and owned 20 per cent of the firm's shares. Tremblay financed all the equipment purchase and installation costs.

The second spin-off was more complicated than the first spin-off. This time, it did not just involve transferring a client list. A factory had to be built, the component production line had to be moved, and new staff had to be trained. Negotiations lasted several months. The new firm's goals, the shareholders' agreement and the details of the partners' relationship were negotiated simply, man to man. Throughout the preparatory period, a number of people including the local industrial commissioner and the mayor of Saint-Césaire offered their help in identifying new premises, which were finally acquired in April 1996. Production began in May.

Initially Raynox manufactured only two products, and had two employees. By 2000, the firm employed more than 40 employees and manufactured more than 5,000 different parts. Tremcar's rapid growth had a direct impact on Raynox, which had no choice but to keep up with its principal client's production growth. Tremcar accounts for nearly 90 per cent of all Raynox's sales, and 35 of Raynox's 37 employees work exclusively on Tremcar contracts. Because Raynox is of such strategic importance to Tremcar, the partners have agreed to limit the development of its external client base. Tremblay reflected:

> 'Raynox would be more stable if it had more external clients, but any development would [have to not be] detrimental to Tremcar, which must always be its absolute priority. Also, the average age of its employees is a reflection of the firm's youth. Raynox still needs to increase its critical mass of experience to ensure its survival.'

Close ties have been forged between the two firms and the two partners. They talk regularly about the development of Raynox. Tremcar's doors are always open to Raynald Ostiguy, who utilises its engineering, financial and administrative specialists.

Third spin-off experience: Expanding the service to other areas

In 1993, Tremblay entered into a majority partnership with a Toronto competitor. He closed the factory but retained its after-sales service department, which served Western Canada. Managing at a distance was difficult. The management style of the previous owner, who was appointed to manage the new subsidiary, was not compatible with Tremcar's style and culture. Complaints with the service were recorded. Tremblay decided to purchase all the firm's shares and looked for a new manager. He approached Jean-Claude Robillard. Robillard had been with Tremcar for 20 years. He had extensive experience in tanker production and sales. Robillard had held a range of positions in Tremcar, and he had been its representative in Western Quebec and Ontario.

Tremblay applied the same procedure as with Hébert and Son. He asked his own lawyers to draw up the partnership agreement papers. Tremblay does not believe in complicated shareholders' agreements. His contracts are simple and are based on trust. Robillard was given half the shares in the new firm, called JC Tanks & Repair. Tremcar's president financed all the equipment purchases.

The two shareholders agreed on the services to be provided and the responsibilities of each party. JC Tanks & Repair took over exclusive responsibility for Tremcar's after-sales service and purchased warranties in Western Canada. Robillard also continued as Tremcar's representative in that area. In return, Tremblay made Tremcar's entire administrative and technical expertise available to his new manager and partner. He was unable to visit the new company as often as he had done with regard to Hébert and Son. Despite the distance, the trust remained strong.

In a few years, Tremcar's contribution to the Toronto firm's sales turnover fell to about 25 per cent of its total turnover. JC Tanks & Repair faces a very different market dynamic from its counterpart, Hébert and Son. The firm has a larger customer volume and more competitors. The firm with its eight employees has carved itself a niche in the sector.

Although their career paths are similar, Hébert and Robillard have very different personalities, along with their own particular strengths and weaknesses. They both have extensive experience of the tanker sector. This expertise was sought and leveraged by Tremblay.

Next spin-off: The first in the United States

Tremblay has great plans for Tremcar. He knows it has a unique potential that needs to be preserved and exploited. Tremcar's products have a good reputation in Canada and the United States. Tremblay is well aware that to conquer a market he has to offer reliable after-sales service. In 1999, the firm's sales in the United States were concentrated in the border states, because the market is still dominated by United States Midwestern manufacturers. Tremblay would like to move into the more southerly states of the United States. He has signed subcontracting agreements with two service centres in Illinois and Wisconsin. For his next spin-off, Tremblay will need to select a partner located a long distance away. The obstacles are more numerous and the uncertainty greater, but this has not shaken his confidence in the spin-off process to ensure the growth of Tremcar.

Questions and issues

1 What was Tremblay's rationale for spinning-off ventures?

2 What are the benefits of spinning off activities to enable growth?

3 How important is trust versus contractual agreements in pursuing a spin-off strategy?

4 What key lessons did Tremblay learn from his initial spin-off that helped in developing subsequent ones?

Wemas International Limited: Purchase and turnaround of an existing business by Brent Lybbert

Ed McMullan

Summary

Brent Lybbert was 33 years of age and a student on the University of Calgary's Enterprise Development Master of Business Administration (MBA) programme in Canada. Although he had limited business experience and cash of his own, he found himself in a position to purchase a medium-sized steel fabrication firm located in Calgary. Wemas International Limited was a 42-year-old company that employed 40 people and its sales revenues were nearly $4,000,000 (Canadian dollars). Brent had limited knowledge surrounding the firm's industry, markets and products. He sought to arrange a deal to buy the loss-making company. The consolidated net loss for both the holding company and the operating company was $64,000. Much more challenging was the need for the firm to generate extra money to pay out the owners over a ten-year period (i.e., $2.5 million and accumulated interest). Brent thought about failure but refused to accept the possibility.

Introduction

Brent had recently been offered a management consultant job in a big four accounting firm, which would pay him an $85,000 salary plus bonuses that could raise his total income above $100,000. If Brent accepted the position, he would be involved in transformation projects with large public companies, and he would work with three impressive people. Also, he was offered a job with Finning's Materials Handling Division in Vancouver. A salary of $85,000 with perks was offered. The perks related to the payment of house rent for a year, a $100,000 interest-free loan to buy a home, a notebook computer, a vehicle allowance, and an all expenses paid trip for his family to visit Vancouver for a week. With Finning,

Brent would have been the manager of growth, helping to position the division to grow to the next stage. Brent and his wife had two children aged three and nine. His wife wanted him to select a job that was going to make him happy. Brent sought independence and he wanted to provide a high quality of life for his family, as well as help the less fortunate in society.

In addition, Brent applied for investment banking jobs with Scotia Capital Markets and CIBC Wood-Gundy. Both employers indicated that they would provide Brent with an employment position in the autumn when an upturn in the market was anticipated. In both firms, Brent would be an associate analysing mergers and acquisitions and initial public offering (IPO) deals. A new MBA graduate would earn a base salary of around $75,000 plus bonuses relating to a further $30,000 with regard to normal conditions. Brent could make up to $150,000 during the first year with regard to good conditions. After four years, he could expect to be earning between $300,000 and $400,000, whilst after ten years some directors earned well over $1,000,000 in Calgary. Brent knew that employers sought aggressive and competitive people with high academic grades who had the ability to do deals. Doing deals meant being a good salesperson. Brent believed he had all these qualities.

Brent had identified an opportunity to purchase and transform a loss-making business in Calgary on his own. He had to make a career choice to accept an employment position, or to pursue a career in entrepreneurship as a business owner and transformer.

Before his MBA

Brent grew up in a small town in northern Alberta where his parents had accumulated ranching land before selling it to a developer for over a million dollars.

They then began buying, upgrading and selling apartment buildings and office warehouse buildings in Edmonton. Brent recalls his mother being a very creative person, always coming up with product and business ideas. Brent reflected:

'It almost became part of our family culture. At the same time she wasn't particularly inclined to financially back her ideas. Although both my parents were supportive, they didn't particularly encourage my getting involved in entrepreneurial activities.'

In 1991, immediately after Brent finished his undergraduate degree in commerce, he went to work for the Royal Bank. His training related to ten policy manuals and his knowledge of policy was constantly tested. Within two months, Brent realised that he hated his customer services teller job.

His wife of five years was a dental hygienist. She kept telling Brent about the horrors of dental business management. After conducting some research, he identified a viable business opportunity relating to management consulting for health care practices. Brent talked to some dentist friends. He identified the leading management consulting firms, and the services they offered. Brent then telephoned some of the consulting companies to find out what they did, and asked them to send him their packages. He discovered that all the consultancy firms were selling a standard approach, which did not necessarily take the client into consideration. Brent perceived a gap in the market. He quit his job with the Royal Bank and established a new company to exploit the opportunity. A cold calling strategy was followed and his first call generated a client.

With regard to his second client, Brent claimed that he increased the revenue per hour by 62 per cent in two months. Brent discovered that receptionists, dental assistants and dental hygienists all contributed to the success of a practice. They, however, required different types of financial incentives. His company offered consulting products. Notably, his company provided a productivity gain-sharing incentive programme. For the first year-and-a-half he worked with a manual product. Brent's friend was an experienced Windows programmer, and his knowledge was leveraged to write software for a computerised training product. During the first year, he earned $14,000 from his company and this increased to $28,000 during the second year. With regard to the third year and beyond, he earned about $60,000 per year from his company.

Brent knew that his dental practice management business would never be as big as he wanted it to become. He recognised that his skills and knowledge would be enhanced if he obtained a MBA. Brent wanted the skills and qualifications that would enable him to obtain a highly-paid corporate finance, management consulting or senior management position in a large corporation.

The MBA experience: Finding three different business takeover opportunities

During the first year of his MBA, Brent worked in teams with his classmates to address problems faced by companies. Brent reflected:

'I got more of a feel for management responsibilities and of the complexities associated with running a firm with $125 million in revenue. In addition, I reinforced the feeling that the people running these larger businesses were just normal people. Apart from their specialized industry knowledge, they received their information from the same source as everyone else.'

He applied the concepts and tools nurtured in his classes to real businesses. Brent gave a presentation surrounding his dental practice management business and the software he offered to clients. A classmate, who turned out to be a dentist, identified an opportunity to establish a company to market Brent's software. Brent sold him the software program for $14,000 plus a 5 per cent royalty on sales revenue over a five-year period starting from the first sale.

By February of his first year on the MBA, Brent considered acquiring a company. Brent began to question the analysis and conclusion made by his classmates relating to a firm being discussed. He identified different issues and solutions. Brent considered the exit strategy options open to the business owners. Further, he considered whether the existing management of the firm had the skills to ensure firm growth. He began to appreciate that the absence of financial know-how within a firm could constrain firm development. Brent recognised that the industrial refrigeration market was maturing and becoming increasingly competitive. He talked to the course instructor who confirmed that the owner of the firm being discussed was potentially looking to sell the firm. Brent contacted the owner of the firm, and many of his views relating to the firm were confirmed.

The MBA tutor encouraged Brent to pursue the identified opportunity. He was encouraged to acquire the company, which employed 125 people and reported a sales turnover of $20 million. Up to that point, Brent had mixed feelings surrounding his idea. Brent commented:

'The professor's response was that little bit of extra motivation I needed to further pursue the buyout possibility.'

Brent had practically no money to invest. His professor encouraged him to meet with a venture capitalist who was helping out on the first year MBA programme. The venture capitalist reviewed Brent's takeover proposition. He referred Brent to a merchant banker whose investment profile aligned with Brent's proposition. After discussions with the merchant banker, Brent discovered that he could buy a company with little to no money of his own. He then learned about vendor take-back.

The pursuit of the acquisition target was conducted during the summer and the autumn. Brent remarked:

'I didn't let it go even though it was an on-again, off-again affair.'

During the second year of his MBA, Brent decided to take the firm acquisition project forward. After several meetings he concluded that the owner of the company was not fully committed to selling the business. Brent decided to look elsewhere for other opportunities.

Robert Kulhawy, a successful Calgary entrepreneur, provided advice to the MBA students. He was impressed by Brent's presentation. Robert offered to mentor Brent. Brent indicated he wanted:

'. . . a leveraged buyout with vendor take back terms.'

Notably, he wanted to pursue a leveraged buyout of a company that had a number of the following features:

- Private firm which would enable Brent to secure vendor take-back terms;
- Strong asset base that could be leveraged;
- Owners who had not identified an alternative exit strategy;
- Stable financial history that would be appreciated by the banks;
- Currently stagnant performance, which would enable Brent to capitalise on the upward potential;
- General manager who knew the business and this knowledge could be transferred to the new owners;
- Owners who had not been heavily involved in the day-to-day running of the company, and if they left

the business there would be no detrimental implications for existing employees, customers or suppliers; and/or

- Brent's expertise was required to realise the businesses growth potential.

Robert Kulhawy initially advised Brent to telephone as many business brokers as he could in order to identify alternative business acquisition prospects. After finding seven business brokers in the Yellow Pages telephone directory listing business names, Brent telephoned all of them. At this point, Brent realised he lacked credibility. The first three brokers he contacted made the following negative response:

'Who are you? You want to buy a company? You are an MBA student with no money? Oh yeah.'

He considered gaining assistance from people affiliated with the MBA programme in order to raise his credibility.

Brent changed his line of approach with regard to the fourth broker. He alluded to having access to people affiliated with the MBA programme who had access to capital. The fourth broker told him to come back with letters of support from a couple of credible individuals who would provide finance. Brent supplied the fourth broker with letters of support he had obtained from the entrepreneur in residence in the Business School, and his new mentor. Brent then signed a confidentiality agreement with the broker. His broker began to divulge information. He provided the broker with his selection criteria relating to an ideal leveraged buyout.

Brent began to consider a business acquisition possibility relating to a building products manufacturer, which employed 60 people and reported a sales turnover of $14 million. During the winter term of the second year of his MBA, he initiated negotiations with this firm. Brent remarked:

'During that period I was working about 120 hour weeks; getting almost no sleep between trying to maintain my grade point and properly analyze the deal. During that period I rarely saw my wife or children. I felt that this was a period where I was both energized and exhausted at the same time. My eyes were constantly bloodshot. My ability to do fifteen minute power naps at different places within the university may have saved me.'

He spent 50 hours a week negotiating the business acquisition, whilst the remaining time was spent pursuing his MBA studies.

In April 1999, Brent presented the deal to Robert Kulhawy, and he agreed to fully finance the deal. During their third meeting, Robert elaborated the terms he was willing to accept. Brent would receive around 30 per cent of the total equity. His mentor suggested that they needed to consider four or five deals before they found the right one. Robert Kulhawy's business partner was willing to invest in a business acquisition deal, but only if the company had potential to go to the United States (US). Research revealed that the building products manufacturer did not have the potential to go to the US. The second potential business acquisition deal was killed.

In March 1999, the broker that Brent had worked with previously provided some preliminary oral information relating to Wemas International Limited, which employed 40 full-time employees. He suggested that Brent would not be interested in this poorly performing firm. Kevin, the broker, personally introduced Brent to the unlisted company. The broker also gave him information relating to the profile of the company, as well as the financial statements.

Wemas International Limited

Wemas International Limited was a 42-year-old steel fabrication company specialising in a variety of products (i.e., structural steel components for commercial buildings, stainless steel brewery vats, steel heater and air-conditioning cabinets, and other light gauge steel products). The firm had approximately 600 customers. On 30 April 1999, the company reported sales revenues of $3.6 million, a drop from the $4 million reported the previous year (see Appendices 1 and 2). The company reported a book loss of $64,000, which was the first significant loss posted in five years.

The business related to a holding company that owned the land and two buildings assets and an operating company. Assets of the holding company were valued at $1.4 million by an independent real estate broker. The book value of the operating assets, less assumed liabilities, was $1.1 million. Brent and his broker placed the overall value of the company at $2.5 million.

Brent went to the Industry Canada website and gathered information relating to four segments of the metal products fabrication industry. The average revenue per employee across the four industry segments was $140,000 with a gross margin per employee at $68,000. Wemas's revenue per employee was $85,000

per employee and the gross margin was $27,000. Brent concluded that Wemas was performing well below the industry standard. He perceived the potential for significant efficiency and productivity improvements.

The two elderly owners (i.e., 70 and 72) of Wemas had emigrated from Germany and Denmark, and they had established the company in 1957. Both had been metal workers before moving to Calgary. One owner spent only a few hours a week working in the company, whilst the other occasionally dropped in from time to time to say hello to employees. Their joint take-home pay in the form of management fees and dividends ranged from $90,000 to $180,000 depending on how well the company was performing.

The Wemas deal

Brent believed that Wemas had a good asset base, which could be leveraged to attract bank finance. His broker agreed with Brent's assessment of the situation. Brent completed his MBA course work. At the end of April 1999, Wemas's owners, the broker and Brent attended meetings to discuss the business acquisition deal. During the first exploratory one hour meeting, Brent sought to gather information relating to the flexibility and purchase price sought by the owners. He went up to the white board and wrote the figure $2 million on the board. Brent commented:

> 'I said that I realized that we wouldn't agree on a price right away but that I did some preliminary cash flow valuation and concluded that this was a good starting price. I asked them what they thought the company was worth and they said over three million dollars. We left with good feelings and a date for the next meeting. Before the end of June after two more meetings, each lasting about an hour and one-half, we agreed on a price of $2.5 million.'

The first oral agreement between the parties was structured as follows: $1.4 million cash on closing the deal to the owners along with $1.1 million of preferred shares to the owners with an agreement to buy them back over a five-year period. During July and August the deal evolved, and it emerged from the year-end financial statement that the company was making a loss. The owners then decided to pull out of the deal. Brent thought that the business acquisition deal was dead.

Brent tried a number of other arrangements with different banks but they were not interested in the business acquisition deal. He went back to Wemas's owners and highlighted the lack of interest from the banks with regard to the deal. Both owners suggested that Brent was the person to run the company, and they were willing to do whatever it would take to make it work. Brent reflected:

> 'Then we came up with the new structure. Still a $2.5 million purchase price but with a demand note collateralised by security of $1.4 million on the buildings.'

Brent would have to make monthly payments of $15,000 over ten years with an effective interest rate of 6.25 per cent. The other $1.1 million, also backed by a note but with no interest rate, was to be payable annually at the rate of $110,000 per year over ten years. Brent was not allowed to pre-pay the $1.4 million demand note before he had paid the $1.1 million unsecured note.

Brent's understanding of the Wemas business

Brent considered the following issues:

Clients and products

Wemas provided a lot of quotes for fabrication work but they only won 20 per cent of the contracts. The general manager suggested that they failed to win bids due to the high prices tendered by Wemas. Many of the steel fabrication projects provided by the firm were small (i.e., mean and median order sizes of $1,500 and $420, respectively). The firm had relatively few big clients. One competitor had Nortel as a client.

Union

Several employees told Brent that they did not want to be part of a union. The impression he gained was that the union was primarily supported by older employees, and would over time become a decreasing force. Brent perceived that the union was resistant to change and their actions reduced the flexibility of the company to take advantage of new opportunities. He asserted that the firm's labour cost base was raised by the Union. Brent claimed: 'Instead of paying someone six dollars an hour you have to pay ten since they have to be a member of the union.' Consequently, Brent recognised he had to negotiate with the union to ensure more appropriate work practices were adopted.

Inventory system

The existing inventory system unnecessarily tied up crucial cash. In one case, the company pre-manufactured $140,000 worth of product for a customer, and it remained in the inventory for four months. Material suppliers were close by and the company was on good terms with them. The firm had the potential to operate a more efficient just-in-time inventory system.

Increase productivity

When Brent realised that the revenue per employee and the gross margin per employee were well below the industry standard he knew the firm's cost base had to be reduced. Some staff had to be sacked. Production was being conducted in two buildings adjacent to one another. To reduce duplication costs and to generate efficiency and productivity gains, Brent sought to streamline and consolidate production.

Consolidating operations in the south building

Brent appreciated that space was poorly utilised (i.e., empty space or space with junk stored in it). He sought to ensure that more space was used to enhance the manufacturing capacity of the firm.

Streamlining manufacturing

Brent noticed two computer-controlled punch machines side-by-side located in a secluded pocket. These two machines were typically located at the front-end of the fabrication process. He wondered why they were grouped together away from the other machines. Brent appreciated that the current positioning of machinery contribution to a production bottleneck. Prior to closing the business acquisition deal, Brent began to research the productivity benefits associated with computerised equipment. He gathered information from the Internet and contacted tool and industry representatives. Over the next three years, Brent planned to provide high quality and efficiently manufactured products, which would be produced by a fully integrated, technologically advanced steel fabrication facility unlike anything that existed in western Canada (as far as he was aware).

Rental of the north building

Brent considered renting the north building, which would lead to a reduction in the costs associated with taxes, utilities and the mortgage. Brent thought that he could rent out the 14,260 sq. ft. for a gross rent of approximately $6 per sq. ft. By consolidating production to the south building, he anticipated cost savings with regard to supervision and equipment.

Accounts receivable

The general manager admitted to Brent that he had not been very aggressive with regard to the accounts receivable. He felt that it was difficult to be both a salesperson and a bill collector. Late payment of trade bills was a serious problem. In total, $200,000 of trade bills had not been paid within 60 days, of which $70,000 had not been paid within 90 days. The previous year, the company had written off $78,000 worth of bad debts, of which $40,000 related to one client who had fallen into difficulty after they supplied the firm with products. Brent considered how he could use the legal process to recoup some of the bad debt owed to Wemas.

Sales approach

For 42 years (in Brent's opinion) the company had been an order taker. Two salespeople had been sitting at desks waiting for customers to call. A third salesperson had been recently hired. Brent believed that Wemas should more proactively seek new customers, and the salespeople currently working for hourly wages should be incentivised to generate more sales.

Transactions

Unsolicited or repeat business over the telephone generated approximately half of all sales. A further 25 per cent of sales came from winning quotes from bidder (i.e., tender) lists, whilst salespeople making calls generated 25 per cent of sales. Brent saw the potential to increase sales by an incentivised, proactive sales team making more calls. Efficiency and productivity gains would lead to a reduction in production costs, which would enable the firm to price its products more competitively.

Promotion and marketing

Brent perceived that Wemas did very little promotion or marketing. An outdated folder with colour pictures of products that had been built in the past was used to promote the activities of Wemas. To increase sales, Brent recognised the benefits of professional promotion and marketing practices. He sought to introduce these practices. Brent sought to further develop and utilise the recently developed company website (www. wemas.com).

Tracking projects

Three months earlier the company had attempted to utilise new computer software to track each project with regard to time and profit margin. People on the shop floor, however, refused to use the computer programme. This issue had to be addressed by Brent. He was concerned that profit margins were 'eaten up' during the product design phase. Brent believed that the company had to reduce any cost implications associated with design error, particularly with regard to small projects. Further, the company had to more appropriately charge for prototypes produced for large projects, and any changes subsequently requested by the client had to be paid for by the client.

Employee layoffs

The business acquisition agreement stated that Brent had to rehire all Wemas employees. He would be liable to pay the redundancy costs associated with the dismissal of any staff members. These costs, however, could be discounted from the amount he owed the sellers. With regard to the cashflow statement, he sought to reduce labour wages and benefits by $500,000. Brent laid off 13 out of the 40 employees. Four employees were on disability and they were not receiving a salary. One of them had resigned, and the other three would not be returning to employment. A further nine employees layed off by Wemas had been employed for two years or less.

Other product possibilities

To increase sales by $3 million a year, Brent identified some new product possibilities. He considered manufacturing stainless steel sinks and air-conditioning equipment.

Cashflow, short-term

Brent required cash to pay for all the costs (i.e., lawyers, accountants and broker) incurred relating to the business acquisition process. He also required funds to purchase the new equipment, and to cover the redundancy payments of the people he had sacked. The latter costs were to be discounted from what he owed the sellers (see above). Brent identified several potential short-term sources of finance. First, he would sell off excess equipment after operations had been consolidated in the south building. Second, he could make money renting the north building. Third, he could sell excess steel that was sitting in the yard, which had not been part of the inventory. Fourth, he could repossess some property that was in use even thought it had not been paid for. Fifth, there were savings associated with employee layoffs.

Context and environment

Approximately 75 per cent of Wemas's sales were sold to local customers in the Calgary market with a further 15, 5 and 5 per cent sold to customers in Alberta, Saskatchewan and the United States, respectively. The business was exposed to volatility in the Calgary construction market, and the oil market. In total, 30 per cent of Wemas's sales was generated by the oil market.

Conclusion

Brent could have selected a prestigious, secure and well-paid job provided by a large organisation. However, he wanted to be his own boss. Brent enjoyed identifying and exploiting business opportunities and negotiating business deals. He believed that owning his own company would generate the financial returns offered by an investment banking firm, but being his own boss would provide a higher quality of life.

Question and issue

What issues need to be considered by an entrepreneur seeking to purchase an existing business?

Appendix 1 Wemas International Limited balance sheet ending 30 April 1999 (unaudited)

Assets	30 April 1999	30 April 1998
Current assets		
Cash	$(0)	$-
Accounts receivable	747,231	679,169
Prepaid expenses	9,508	12,775
Refundable income tax	887	887
Inventory and work in progress	640,984	780,351
Total current assets	1,398,610	1,473,182
Investments	92,783	167,587
Fixed assets		
Automotive equipment	67,500	67,500
Machinery and office equipment	1,478,128	1,442,977
Minus accumulated depreciation	1,170,081	1,070,646
Total fixed assets	375,547	439,831
Total assets	1,866,940	2,080,600
Liabilities		
Current liabilities		
Bank overdraft	193,449	92,846
Accounts payable and accrued liabilities	276,326	387,310
Deferred income taxes	8,913	8,913
Current portion of long-term debt	117,120	117,120
Total current liabilities	595,808	606,189
Long-term debt	67,094	191,114
Total liabilities	682,857	797,303
Shareholders' equity		
Share capital	1,087,818	1,087,818
Retained earnings	116,265	195,479
Total shareholders' equity	1,866,940	2,080,600

Appendix 2 Wemas International Limited statement of earnings 12 month period ending 30 April 1999 (unaudited)

	1999	1998
Sales	$3,602,727	$3,939,251
Cost of sales		
Materials handling 1 May 1998	349,576	372,015
Work in process 1 May 1998	430,775	280,244
Total opening inventory	780,351	652,259
Materials purchases	864,316	1,394,199
Total materials and work in progress	1,644,66	2,048,458
Less ending inventories		
Material	357,740	349,576
Work in progress	283,243	430,775
Total ending inventory	640,984	780,351
Cost of materials used	1,003,683	1,266,107
Gross profit on sales	2,599,043	2,673,144
Shop expenses		
Wages – shop	1,003,847	1,001,355
Subcontract work	289,200	263,318
Small tools and supplies	156,786	187,229
Wage – benefits	115,095	127,878
Repairs and maintenance	36,819	32,614
Vehicle expenses	14,455	13,656
Total shop expenses	1,616,202	1,626,050
Operating income (loss)	982,841	1,047,094
Administrative expenses		
Bad debt	70,469	13,591
Business tax and licences	17,104	18,649
Miscellaneous office expense	8,015	11,354
Insurance	33,591	32,572
Legal and accounting	18,313	17,359
Advertising and promotion	13,158	2,986
Repair and maintenance – building	14,252	19,270
Utilities	49,335	45,336
Telephone	9,963	11,434
Courier	1,401	4,312
Education and training	5,358	3,117
Building rent	60,000[1]	60,000
Computer lease	20,731	1,503
Repair and maintenance – office equip.	2,545	2,095
Fees and dues	129	408
Salary benefits	59,398	59,785
Salary and wages	423,178	362,570
Consulting fees	13,473	25,373
Stationary and office supplies	16,525	15,412
Vehicle mileage	954	1,982
Depreciation	99,434	114,950
Interest and bank charges	33,804	33,648
Management fees	90,926	184,000
Total administrative expenses	1,062,055	1,041,706
Net earnings (loss) after tax	**$(79,214)**	**$4,075**

[1]This figure was paid to Wemas Holdings and was enough taxes and depreciation with $14,680 left over.

Case study 15

Seagate Technology

Mike Wright and Angela Loihl

Summary

This case study highlights the issues involved in considering whether an entrepreneurial firm presents an opportunity for a management buyout. The case involves examination of issues relating to management, the market, the product, investment needs, and financial issues. Also, the case provides an opportunity to examine the scope for management buyouts beyond traditional areas of firms in mature sectors with stable cash flows and low investment needs.

Introduction

Seagate Technology Inc. designs, manufactures and markets products for storage, retrieval and management of data on computer and data communications. Their products include disc drives and disc drive components, tape drives and software. Seagate is the world's largest manufacturer of disc drives and disc drive components, magnetic discs and read-write heads, an innovator in tape drives, and a leading developer of Business Intelligence software. The firm's major customers include original equipment manufacturers, distributors, resellers, dealers, systems integrators and retailers. Seagate is based in Scotts Valley, California, but has operations throughout North America, Europe, and Asia, and employs more than 87,000 people worldwide.

Seagate's storage products include a comprehensive line of disc drives for the desktop personal computer (PC) market, higher performance PC and workstation drives, and higher-capacity drives for the storage and performance-intensive network server, disc array, and audio-visual markets. Their Internet Solutions Group targets emerging markets and applications that are storage-intensive, specifically in the areas of consumer electronics, commercial and services opportunities related to web-based applications. The Removable Storage Solutions group offers a broad line of tape drives for backup on networks, multi-user systems, workstations, desktops and portable PCs. Seagate Software is a majority owned and consolidated subsidiary of Seagate Technology, which develops and markets software products and provides related services enabling users to store, access, and manage enterprise information.

The company has pursued a strategy of vertical integration with regard to its core product line of rigid disc drives and related components. Over the years, they have broadened their strategy to additionally address the markets for storage, retrieval, and management of data. In order to pursue this broad strategy, the company has acquired, invested in, and formed strategic alliances with complementary businesses. Seagate's approach includes acquiring companies that posses technology and development personnel which provide long-term growth potential to their business.

Seagate Technology was founded as a disc drive manufacturer in 1979 by industry legends Al Shugart, Tom Mitchell and Finis Conner. In 1980, they introduced the industry's first 5.25-inch disc drive, which was 'instrumental in turning the original IBM PC into a serious business tool, and drove the company to a dominating presence in the early PC industry' (Silicon Valley.com, March 2000). Founder Al Shugart was instrumental in the invention of the disc drive, and pioneered the development of the floppy drive during his 18 years with IBM, prior to forming his own company. Shugart and his Seagate associates are credited with having led the way in the PC revolution. Seagate floated on the New York Stock Exchange in 1981.

From its beginnings in 1979, Seagate has grown both organically and through a number of acquisitions and investments. At their peak in 1997, Seagate controlled an estimated 50 per cent of the market for disc drives in PCs, with more than 100,000 employees, and sales that approached $9 billion a year. Seagate, however, has demonstrated a critical vulnerability to the cyclical trends that plague the high-tech industry. T. Quinlan (2000) asserted that:

> 'Although Seagate officials had a tendency to announce that they had broken the cycle at the end of every downturn – by acquiring software companies or other disc drive companies as the opportunity presented itself – it was a pattern that would constantly afflict the company.'

Seagate had a breakthrough year in 1984, with sales of $344 million and profits of $42 million. By the following year, sales had fallen to $215 million with profits of only $1 million. Seagate suffered from the cyclical nature of the industry again in the late 1990s when revenues fell from $8.9 billion in 1997 to $6.8 billion in 1998, with profits declining from $658 million to a $530 million loss in 1998. A series of layoffs associated with the latest downturn has left the company with an estimated 60,000 employees, and ultimately resulted in Shugart being forced from the company he created and led for nearly 20 years. In addition to the dangers of operating in a cyclical industry, Seagate has struggled as a result of intensely competitive market conditions and pressure from PC companies to make bigger disc drives at lower prices. While their drives have increased dramatically in size, their prices have fallen, leading to a declining profit margin.

Management team

Seagate Technology was founded in 1979 by Alan F. Shugart, David (Tom) Mitchell, and Finis F. Conner. Al Shugart joined IBM in 1951, the day following graduation from university. In 1969, he left IBM to work for Memorex Corp., taking with him approximately 200 engineers. A few years later when Memorex was experiencing troubles, Shugart, along with several loyal followers, launched Shugart Associates, which was responsible for pioneering the floppy drive. Finis Connor, who had started at IBM as Shugart's gofer, was among the group. In 1974, the company ran into problems and Shugart's venture backers fired him. Four years later, Connor approached Shugart with the idea of developing small hard drives for PCs. With $1.5 million in start-up capital, Shugart, Connor and four associates formed Seagate. With the enormous surge in the PC market, Seagate prospered and reported revenues of $344 million by 1984.

The following year, amid brutal price wars, the tides were turning. While Shugart insisted on making disc drives from scratch, Connor disagreed, arguing that buying parts involved less risk. This conflict represented an apparent pervasive divergence in corporate strategy between the two founders, and Connor left Seagate to launch a rival disc drive company, Connor Peripherals. Compaq Computer Corp. backed Connor Peripherals, and sales rocketed to $113 million in the first year. Connor's company was so successful that in the late 1980s he considered buying Seagate. Connor's success, however, was short-lived, and, in the end, Shugart's strategy of vertical integration was vindicated. In 1993, the demand for PCs had exploded, and key components became scarce. Companies like Connor's that followed an outsourcing strategy, suffered and every drive maker except Seagate lost money. Seagate acquired rival Connor Peripherals in 1996, boosting their market share to 33 per cent of the then $25 billion industry.

Following Connor's departure, Seagate was run by Shugart, co-founder Mitchell, and Douglas Mahon. Shugart, already a famous figure in the industry, was the company's public face, the 'emblem on the car', in the words of a former executive. Shugart is said to have achieved success the old-fashioned way, defying the era's common management wisdom. A true entrepreneur, Shugart apparently enjoys dabbling in other businesses. He has owned a gourmet restaurant, an air charter service, and funds a publisher of quirky books. When Shugart launched Seagate he was in his 50s, ancient by Silicon Valley standards. He is said to have come to work in a short-sleeved polyester shirt, without a tie, and answered his own telephone calls. In a recent interview, he described himself as a 'street guy' and a 'regular guy' and not a corporate executive. He even tried to run his dog Ernest for congress, an antic that raised $3,000 and involved buttons, a campaign committee, and press releases. Despite his unique management style, Shugart's presence in the disc drive business has been likened to Bill Gates' in software. Shugart is said to have been popular with his employees, winning tremendous loyalty. This loyalty got him in trouble in 1994 when he was sued by his former employer, IBM, for hiring away the engineer who was heading up its development of magneto-resistive heads.

With charismatic Shugart at the helm, Mitchell was in charge of operations, and Mahon was in charge of product design and technology. Mitchell, an ex-marine, is said to have run the company with an iron grip, driving the business forward with what he used to boast was 'management by intimidation'. Described by one analyst as 'the Darth Vader of the industry', Mitchell is said to have made people work through the Christmas and Thanksgiving holidays. He had a reputation for being a demanding, driven perfectionist, and during his leadership as president and chief operating officer Seagate had an extraordinarily high turnover rate. Many of the employees who stayed on, however, became very rich, and Seagate became the world's largest disc drive manufacturer. Where Shugart has been described as rumpled, affable, and blunt, Mitchell has been portrayed as polished, charismatic and brutal. As a result of these differing management styles, and after a failed bid to become the chief executive officer (CEO) in 1991, Mitchell left Seagate and went on to join forces with Connor, as CEO, at Connor Peripherals.

Shugart is credited with transforming Seagate into a more mature and stable company after taking over the day-to-day operations following Mitchell's departure. He made a concerted effort to distance himself from the management style imposed by Mitchell, improving the company's reputation with employees. According to Phil Devin, chief analyst of the industry for Dataquest Inc., Shugart:

> 'runs the company in a more conservative down-to-earth business manner rather than engaging in egotistical bashes to become the market leader.'
>
> (Levander, 1995.)

Shugart demanded hard work, but also recognised the restorative value of having a good time, and has been famous for holding impromptu staff meetings at local bars. Whereas Mitchell was considered a demanding tactician, Shugart is described as a strategist and a delegator who takes pride in freeing people up to do their jobs. While being technically astute, colleagues have credited Shugart's success to his managerial style, and he is said to balance his no-nonsense approach with 'a huge appetite for fun'. Today, however, Seagate still possesses its high-pressure reputation and company nicknames include 'Slavegate' and 'Stressgate'.

In 1993, Stephen J. Luczo, former investment banker from Bear, Stearns & Co., joined Seagate as senior vice president of corporate development. As the chief planner of Seagate's expansion into software, Luczo was appointed as chairman and chief operating officer in September 1997. At the time of his appointment, Luczo was viewed as the executive most likely to succeed Shugart, despite Wall Street's criticism of his apparent lack of experience in manufacturing operations. Less than a year later, in July of 1998, the company's board of directors fired Al Shugart, as he apparently refused to acquiesce to a quiet succession plan. Company officials justified Shugart's forced resignation, at age 67, as the latest effort by the company to survive in an increasingly competitive hard drive industry. Shugart was fired because it was deemed time to accelerate the pace of change in the company. Stephen Luczo was promoted to CEO and appointed to the board of directors following Shugart's dismissal. Shugart maintained that the company failed to give him a reasonable explanation for his ouster, other than wanting changes in leadership. Despite being in his late 60s at the time of his ousting, Shugart claims no plans for retirement and reports that he has received requests to join company boards and review business plans.

Firm performance

The dramatic downturn in the high-tech industry in the late 1990s resulted in slim margins and intense competition, decimating profits for both Seagate and its competitors. Seagate, however, was hit particularly hard. Revenues declined from $8.9 billion in 1997 to $6.8 billion in 1998, with profits of $658 million in 1997 declining to a record loss of $530 million in 1998. The company blamed poor results on the continuing decline in the average unit sales price of their products as a result of intensely competitive market conditions, coupled with a lower level of unit shipments reflecting continuing weakness in demand for disc drive products. In addition, Shugart's strategy of vertical integration was partially blamed for the losses. In their annual report, company officials site the strategy as incurring a high level of fixed costs, which requires a high volume of production and sales to be successful. Consequently, during periods of decreased production, as witnessed in 1998, the high fixed costs associated with vertical integration apparently had an adverse effect on operating results and financial conditions. This strategy has also been blamed for delays in the company's ability to introduce new products.

When Luczo became chief operating officer in 1997, one of his boldest moves was to challenge Shugart's strategy of backwards integration, arguing that the policy was out of date. Luczo contended that outsourcing would be cheaper and would allow the company to take advantage of new technologies and products developed elsewhere. Luczo also worked hard to rationalise costs, which involved cutting more than 10,000 jobs and consolidating the company's design centres from five to three. Arguably, as a result of Luczo's takeover of the daily operations of Seagate, the financial results for 1999 were slightly improved. Revenues for 1999 were pretty flat compared to 1998, but profits increased to $1.2 billion. The recovery in profits, however, came only minimally from operations, and was predominantly a result of a gain related to the selling off of part of their software division. In June 1999 Veritas, which makes programmes to protect computer data, bought the software unit of Seagate, paying for it with $2.7 billion of Veritas shares. Subsequently, Veritas shares gained enormously in value, such that by March

2000 Seagate's stake had ballooned to $21.7 billion. Seagate's stake in Veritas, a third of the company, became worth more than Seagate itself. The problem for Seagate was that none of their investment in Veritas was reflected in their own market capitalisation, which stood at $15 billion. During the period from January 1999 to January 2000, the market price of Veritas shares rose 800 per cent, while the market price of Seagate common shares did not significantly increase (see Figure 1).

As Veritas shares soared, Seagate needed to find a way to let its own shareholders benefit from the wealth. If the Veritas shares were distributed to Seagate's shareholders, the transaction would incur double taxation, once for the corporation in realising its gain, and a second time for individual shareholders. With corporate taxation rates between 36 and 41 per cent, the effect would be significant.

Although the disc drive industry, having suffered through years of price competition and slim margins, has shown signs of recovery, it continues to lag behind the enormous stock market success of other high-tech sectors. Like other public manufacturers of computer components, Seagate's share price has been

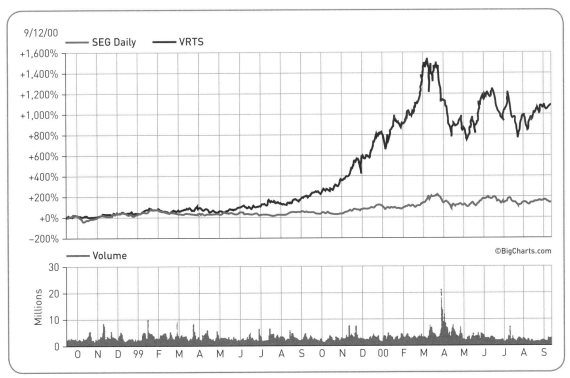

Figure 1 Comparison of daily share prices for Seagate and Veritas

Figure 2 Seagate share price compared to the NASDAQ composite

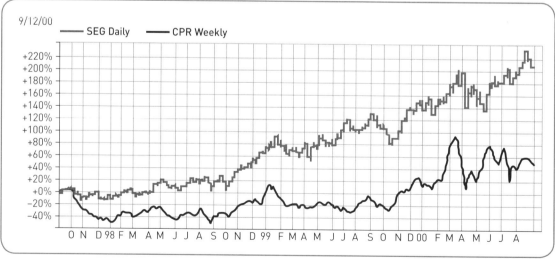

Figure 3 Seagate's performance relative to the computer index

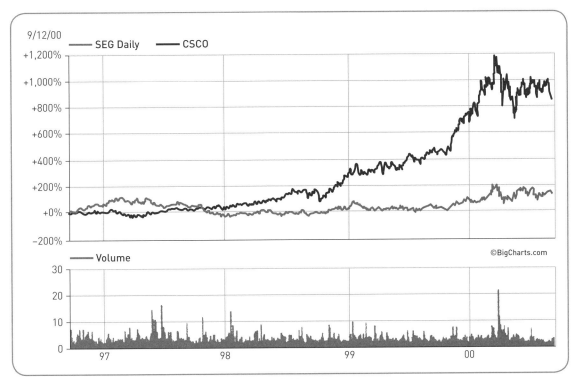

Figure 4 Changes in share prices for Seagate and Cisco Systems

highly volatile, suffering if investors' expectations were not met. Although Seagate's share price rose 60 per cent in the three years prior to the buyout agreement, their shares have lagged significantly relative to the NASDAQ Composite. Figure 2 shows Seagate's change in share price relative to that of the NASDAQ Composite.

Seagate's performance has lagged even more significantly over the last three years when compared to its industry (Dow Jones Computer Index, CPR). Figure 3 shows share price fluctuations for Seagate relative to its industry. A table of ratio comparisons between Seagate, the computer industry, the technology sector, and the S&P 500, is presented in Appendices 1 and 2, showing that Seagate has underperformed both its industry and sector in many areas.

According to McNamee:

'The public market has not been patient with the storage industry, and being private will allow Seagate to make investments in product development to be more successful than it was in the past decade.'

Seagate CEO, Luczo, claims the motivation for transaction arose because the market undervalued Seagate's underlying business, such that shares were trading at a substantial discount relative to the value of the company's assets. Seagate trades on the NYSE at just 18 times earnings, compared to Cisco Systems Inc., whose technology is seen as more central to the Internet, which trades at 205 times earnings. Figure 4 shows changes in Seagate's daily share price, relative to Cisco Systems.

Questions and issues

1 What aspects of Seagate suggest that it might provide an opportunity for a management buyout?

2 What aspects of Seagate would cause you concern about undertaking a management buyout?

3 Focusing specifically on the management in Seagate, what skills do you think the management team have to undertake a successful management buyout, and what skills do they lack?

4 Assuming a management buyout bid was attempted, how would you undertake it?

5 What strategic actions would you seek to undertake after the management buyout in order to make it successful? Distinguish between those that involve improving efficiencies and those that are more entrepreneurial.

Appendix 1 Annual balance sheet

In millions of U.S. dollars (except for per share items)	As of 06/30/00	As of 07/02/99	As of 07/03/98	As of 06/27/97	As of 06/28/96
Cash & equivalents	875.0	396.0	666.0	1,047.3	503.8
Short-term investments	1,140.0	1,227.0	1,161.0	1,236.3	670.3
Cash and short-term investments	2,015.0	1,623.0	1,827.0	2,283.6	1,174.1
Trade accounts receivable, net	678.0	872.0	799.0	1,040.8	1,066.5
Other receivables	–	–	–	–	–
Total receivables, net	678.0	872.0	799.0	1,040.8	1,066.5
Total inventory	430.0	451.0	508.0	808.3	790.8
Prepaid expenses	–	–	–	–	–
Other current assets	386.0	366.0	481.0	419.6	367.9
Total current assets	**3,509.0**	**3,312.0**	**3,615.0**	**4,552.3**	**3,399.3**
Property/plant/equipment – gross	3,754.0	3,533.0	3,242.0	3,058.4	2,404.5
Accumulated depreciation	(2,146.0)	(1,846.0)	(1,573.0)	(1,271.8)	(1,004.7)
Property/plant/equipment, net	1,608.0	1,687.0	1,669.0	1,786.6	1,399.9
Goodwill, net	353.0	144.0	169.0	199.1	274.0
Intangibles, net	–	–	–	–	–
Long-term investments	1,122.0	1,745.0	0.0	0.0	0.0
Other long-term assets	575.0	184.0	192.0	184.9	166.4
Total assets	**7,167.0**	**7,072.0**	**5,645.0**	**6,722.9**	**5,239.6**
Accounts payable	707.0	714.0	577.0	863.1	715.4
Accrued expenses	689.0	782.0	777.0	902.8	670.9
Notes payable/short-term debt	–	–	–	0.0	0.0
Current port. LT debt/capital leases	1.0	1.0	1.0	1.1	2.4
Other current liabilities	81.0	43.0	20.0	69.3	49.4
Total current liabilities	**1,478.0**	**1,540.0**	**1,375.0**	**1,836.4**	**1,438.1**
Long-term debt	703.0	703.0	704.0	701.9	798.3
Capital lease obligations	–	–	–	0.0	0.0
Total long-term debt	**703.0**	**703.0**	**704.0**	**701.9**	**798.3**
Total debt	**704.0**	**704.0**	**705.0**	**703.1**	**800.7**
Deferred income tax	1,020.0	1,103.0	435.0	478.8	351.5
Minority interest	–	–	–	–	–
Other liabilities	119.0	163.0	194.0	230.1	185.6
Total liabilities	**3,320.0**	**3,509.0**	**2,708.0**	**3,247.2**	**2,773.5**
Redeemable preferred stock	–	–	–	–	–
Preferred stock – non-redeemable, net	–	–	–	–	–
Common stock	3.0	3.0	3.0	2.5	2.1
Additional paid-in capital	1,960.0	1,991.0	1,929.0	1,902.8	1,132.3
Retained earnings (accum. deficit)	2,539.0	2,355.0	1,298.0	1,947.0	1,390.3
Treasury stock – common	(708.0)	(736.0)	(238.0)	(318.6)	0.0
Other equity	53.0	(50.0)	(55.0)	(58.0)	(58.7)
Total equity	**3,847.0**	**3,563.0**	**2,937.0**	**3,475.7**	**2,466.1**
Total liability & shareholders' equity	**7,167.0**	**7,072.0**	**5,645.0**	**6,722.9**	**5,239.6**

(*continued*)

Appendix 1 (*continued*)

In millions of U.S. dollars (except for per share items)	As of 06/30/00	As of 07/02/99	As of 07/03/98	As of 06/27/97	As of 06/28/96
Shares outs. – common stock	229.25	228.72	244.76	244.55	213.43
Total common shares outstanding	**229.25**	**228.72**	**244.76**	**244.55**	**213.43**
Employees (actual figures)	60,000	82,000	87,000	–	–
Number of common shareholders (actual figures)	5,700	6,990	–	–	–

Appendix 2 Annual cash flow statement (indirect method)

In millions of U.S. dollars (except for per share items)	12 Months ending 06/30/00	12 Months ending 07/02/99	12 Months ending 07/03/98	12 Months ending 06/27/97 Reclass. 07/02/99	12 Months ending 06/28/96
Net Income	310.0	1,176.0	(530.0)	658.0	213.3
Depreciation/depletion	693.0	696.0	664.0	607.0	416.9
Deferred taxes	(121.0)	661.0	(33.0)	96.0	(84.5)
Non-cash items	(568.0)	(1,478.0)	467.0	235.0	132.8
Changes in working capital	(241.0)	145.0	(68.0)	284.0	(106.7)
Total cash from operating activities	**73.0**	**1,200.0**	**500.0**	**1,880.0**	**571.7**
Capital expenditures	(580.0)	(603.0)	(709.0)	(941.0)	(906.9)
Other investing cash flow items	1,573.0	(103.0)	(139.0)	(591.0)	22.0
Total cash from investing activities	**993.0**	**(706.0)**	**(848.0)**	**(1,532.0)**	**(885.0)**
Financing cash flow items	–	–	–	–	(0.1)
Total cash dividends paid	–	–	–	–	–
Issuance (retirement) of stock, net	(585.0)	(761.0)	(38.0)	(498.0)	(27.2)
Issuance (retirement) of debt, net	–	0.0	(1.0)	691.0	(15.6)
Total cash from financing activities	**(585.0)**	**(761.0)**	**(39.0)**	**193.0**	**(42.8)**
Foreign exchange effects	(2.0)	(3.0)	6.0	2.0	1.1
Net change in cash	**479.0**	**(270.0)**	**(381.0)**	**543.0**	**(355.0)**
Cash interest paid	52.0	52.0	52.0	26.0	64.4
Cash taxes paid	577.0	(109.0)	(1.0)	59.0	207.8

Hill Holt Wood: Community-owned social enterprise

Kirk Frith and Gerard McElwee

Summary

This case discusses Hill Holt Wood (HHW), which is a community-owned social enterprise. The enterprise relates to a 14-hectare deciduous woodland. Karen and Nigel Lowthrop purchased HHW. Nigel felt that he needed to secure a project that would enable him to apply his ideas in practice, and to prove that his concept had genuine potential. Nigel's concept of economic conservation was applied to woodland that was in poor condition.

Introduction

The previous owners had worked to strip the deciduous woodland of its natural resource endowments, and they failed to consider the resulting environmental degradation. After the extensive logging, invasive rhododendrons had taken hold (replacing the natural understory), the drainage system had been severely damaged, and there was a consequent lack of biodiversity across the site. Hill Holt Wood (HHW) presented a perfect case for demonstrating to others, notably the Forestry Commission (i.e., the United Kingdom government's department responsible for the protection and expansion of forests and woodlands), that alternative approaches to conservation were possible and, indeed, should be considered preferable. Nigel's experience with working with the Forestry Commission, both as a ranger as well as a private contractor, had left him with the impression that their approach to woodland conservation was not effective, or efficient. Nigel felt that the Forestry Commission's approach to woodland management would prove unsustainable over the long-term. This dissatisfaction with the existing state of affairs was the primary driver in Karen and Nigel's decision to develop HHW. They had to demonstrate that their beliefs were correct. Further, they had to restore and manage this ancient woodland more efficiently and effectively than their government counterparts.

Karen and Nigel felt that the sustainability of the Forestry Commission's approach to woodland management was compromised due to the emphasis on environmental aspects and the almost total disregard for the social and economic relevance of woodlands to the general population. The relatively narrow focus of the Forestry Commission's approach to the protection and expansion of woodlands at that time, coupled with their inefficient use of public monies, was sufficient to suggest to Karen and Nigel that the development of a more effective approach was not only possible, but actually an environmental, social and economic imperative:

> 'They [the Forestry Commission] get so much money and the return just isn't there. People either don't have access to the woodlands, or simply aren't interested in visiting them. It's a real waste.'

Karen and Nigel felt that the Forestry Commission's approach to the management of woodlands represented a missed opportunity in terms of integrating the protection and expansion of existing woodlands with the specific needs of local communities. Rather than adopting a top-down approach to the management of HHW, Karen and Nigel felt that eliciting and integrating the views and requirements of the local community such that the development of a shared vision for and approach to the conservation of HHW might emerge would be the most effective approach to take. Lloyd (2007: 79) asserted that:

> 'the social economy has the potential to empower and integrate people . . . create the conditions to mobilise goodwill and free volunteer labour . . . it brings on board

the special ability of the social economy to mobilise social capital through reciprocal relationships that integrate a dimension of service to the community.'

At the core of Karen and Nigel's idea was the view that the long-term prospects of conservation projects were almost entirely dependent on their ability to prove the project to be self-sufficient. In the case of HHW, the journey to self-sufficiency was composed of two distinct but related components: interaction with and integration into the local community, and the development of a genuine and sustainable income stream, sufficient to cover the immediate needs of their family as well as the needs related to the restoration of the woodland.

Both Karen and Nigel felt that it was imperative that they should move onto the woodland itself to prove to themselves, and to the local community, that they were fully committed to the project. Moreover, they were prepared to invest everything that they owned into making HHW a success. Karen and Nigel immediately applied for planning permission to build a permanent dwelling on the site. They had moved into a large American caravan on the site as soon as they had sold their family home. Given the strict planning regulations, Karen and Nigel knew that planning permission would not be granted lightly. The planning committee initially refused the application, arguing that a permanent dwelling had no place in the woodland. They countered this argument by claiming that a permanent dwelling was essential in giving them the shelter that they needed to commit as much time and effort as possible to the conservation of HHW. In response, the planning committee argued that Karen and Nigel had to demonstrate that they could earn a living wage from the forest's primary product, timber. The planning committee felt that this stipulation would ensure that Karen and Nigel were genuinely interested in turning HHW into an environmental conservation site rather than simply looking to build a new house in an idyllic setting. They knew that to earn a living wage from the sale of timber would be impossible given the total acreage of the site, and given that the previous owner had felled the majority of saleable timber. In response, Karen and Nigel argued that the economic returns of woodland environments should no longer be derived solely from the extraction of raw material. They claimed that the project would be associated with wider benefits (i.e., the delivery of services to the local community, the provision of local amenities, landscaping efforts, and other projects). The planning committee accepted Karen and Nigel's argument that forestry need not be the principal revenue-generating activity taking place at HHW. Further, the planning committee agreed to grant planning permission subject to a number of environmental and sustainable caveats (i.e., the house could not be built on permanent foundations, it was not allowed to be on-grid, and the materials used in the house's construction were required to be environmentally-friendly). The period from the initial planning application to the completion of the house was ten years.

> 'It was really difficult convincing the planning committee that we weren't just here to make a quick buck, but that we were genuinely interested in making a difference in the local community. On the other hand, I think that all the dialogue with the planning committee really helped us to hone or shape our vision for Hill Holt Wood and the role it could play in the local community. From that point of view, although the planning committee were tough, I think that they were really helpful.'

Social mission statement

HHW's social mission statement aims relate to running a locally valued social enterprise by:

> Providing amenities, facilities and access to local people and organisations within a safe, accessible, supportive and informative site . . . Providing education, training and employment preparation advice to excluded school children, young offenders and unemployed or otherwise disadvantaged young people . . . Developing and implementing structures, which facilitate community control . . . Using local goods, materials and services.

Whilst social enterprises have always played an important role in terms of the delivery and management of social and labour market services, the decline of the welfare state coupled with other systemic and structural shifts has re-emphasised the importance of the contribution of social enterprises to a wide range of individuals and stakeholders. Noya and Clarence (2007: 9) have suggested that:

> 'Social [enterprises] have moved to fill the gaps left by the market and the state, and have shown themselves to be innovative, adaptable and responsive to local needs when provided with the opportunity and environment which enables them to fulfil their potential.'

In part, the diverse needs and requirements of such individuals, coupled with their limited access to resources, makes it difficult for public and private sector organisations to create effective and efficient service offerings. Businesses that cater for genuine social needs also reap economic rewards as a direct consequence (Crowther and Aras, 2008).

Social responsibility is translated at HHW as a continuing commitment to all the groups and individuals who might affect or be affected by or through the achievement of the organisation's aims. The local community were initially very suspicious regarding the aims and intentions of Karen and Nigel in terms of their purchase of HHW:

> 'People thought we were barmy, you know, they thought that we might be tree-huggers and that we'd fill the woodland with those types of people. I think that, in the first instance, the local people weren't too happy about our purchase of Hill Holt Wood.'

In order to overcome this initial suspicion, Karen and Nigel felt that it was essential that they meet with as many local people as possible, and share with them their ideas regarding the future of HHW. This meant that Karen and Nigel spent a great deal of time going to local meetings, meeting their neighbours, joining local committees, and becoming involved in a whole range of other activities that would enable them to break down those initial barriers. They felt that this interaction with the local community enabled them to build bridges, to share and gain support for their ideas, as well as providing them with the opportunity to listen to the needs of the local community so that they could then integrate these into their vision for the woodland:

> 'We heard that people would like to use woodland environments more often as a place to take picnics or to walk their dogs, but that there were access and safety issues that made this difficult for them. We decided that we could help resolve this need by opening Hill Holt Wood to the public, by building pathways through the woodland and by developing little clearings where people might take rest or enjoy picnics with their families.'

In demonstrating to the local community their intentions towards providing free, safe and easily accessible facilities, the local community began to change their opinions of their ideas. Karen and Nigel sought to identify new ways to utilise the site:

> 'We started having volunteer days on which local people would come along, usually a Sunday, and help us with clearing the woodland or building new pathways that they might subsequently use. We provided tea and biscuits and they provided that extra muscle. I think the

people that came along had a thoroughly fun time . . . the rewards of their labour were immediately obvious and immediately enjoyable.'

When Karen and Nigel opened the woodland, they found that they had an opportunity to talk to people about their ideas for HHW, and how those ideas might be successfully integrated with their own intentions for the site. Visitors working with disaffected and disengaged local youths suggested that the woodland might make a perfect site for activity away days.

> 'We thought it would be really great if we could help in some way. Karen suggested that we might run training courses in the wood with content geared around conservation and environmental protection. We then got in contact with this visitor and asked if he might help us arrange a training day later that month, which he did and which proved to be both popular and successful.'

In early 1998, another social enterprise, Groundwork in Lincolnshire, approached Karen and Nigel and asked if they might assist with the delivery of a New Deal for Young People programme. The delivery of this programme became a regular fixture at HHW. Young people from the local area were taken to the site to be educated about the environment and to be taught about the responsibility associated with the protection of woodland sites. The success with which these training courses were met gave Karen and Nigel the confidence needed to take on the contract that Groundwork in Lincolnshire had originally won, but had decided to offload. The training development council appreciated that young people had acquired new confidence and skills, as well as improved their career prospects. From Karen and Nigel's perspective, the opportunity to be paid for related to the management of a permanent team of workers onsite. Classes were provided with the equipment and tools that they needed to perform particular tasks (i.e., removal of the rhododendrons, the building of new pathways, etc.). HHW received a number of local, regional and national awards relating to its achievements in relation to enterprise and its contribution to developing new approaches to helping young offenders finding ways of working, team-building and responsibility sharing.

In early 1998, the local education authority approached Karen and Nigel and asked if they might replicate their service for young children who had been permanently excluded from mainstream education due to behavioural problems. This meant employing more staff, and the development of a bespoke education pro-gramme. The local education authority promised Karen and Nigel a renewable contract that would provide HHW with a constant and sizeable income:

'It was a no-brainer, really. It met all of our goals in terms of making a positive contribution to the local community and it meant that the woodland would be restored in a time far shorter than we had envisaged at the start of the project.'

After winning this contract, Karen and Nigel were able to reach out to the community in different ways. The hard work that the youths were putting into the site meant that HHW benefited from an increase in path-ways, outbuildings, information signs, composting toilets, and a range of additional amenities which improved access to and interest in the activities and de-velopments taking place in the woodland. More people learning and working on the site increased the profile of HHW in the local community. Karen and Nigel invited people to become members of the woodland, and to contribute their time and private resources to support the organisation's objectives. In late 1998, they estab-lished a management committee for HHW. In opening up the management of the site to a wide range of indi-viduals, the project was able to benefit from a range of knowledge and insights. They felt that the establish-ment of a management committee would help to: im-prove the overall transparency of the project; establish the groundwork for making HHW a social enterprise; create a sense of shared ownership within the local community; and validate (internally and externally) the relationships that had developed over the previous two years.

At the heart of Karen and Nigel's approach to their management of HHW was the notion of transparency. They felt that in order to develop open and trusting re-lationships with the local community, they had to adopt an open-door policy, not only to the woodland, but to the details of the business itself, including financial ac-counts, strategic objectives, and all other information that businesses traditionally keep very private:

'I had the director of operations for the forest enter-prise next to me and all these other senior people around the table and the words were, justice, trans-parency, openness, trust, and I thought, this is all non-sense! But now, two years on, I use those words in reports that I write and use them to explain how we de-veloped the trust of the local community and that's

what gave us planning permission and gave us the com-munity support . . . and that's why I'm always telling people everything about the business and involving as many people as possible, you know, I'm sticking to my principles, I'm saying that we are open and transparent and we will tell people how much the site is worth, how much we earn, how much the business turns over, anything!'

Transparency ensures stakeholder involvement and ac-cessibility to third-party individuals or organisations. Further:

'Transparency is of particular importance to external users of such information as these users lack the back-ground detail and knowledge available to internal users of such information . . . and equally can be seen to be part of the process of recognition of responsibility on the part of the organisation for the external effects of its actions and equally part of the process of transferring power to external stakeholders.'

(Crowther and Aras, 2008: 16.)

The development of a management committee pro-vided the groundwork for transferring ownership of HHW to the local community, which, according to Karen and Nigel, was one of their most important objectives:

'We weren't aware at the start of the project of the pos-sibility of creating a social enterprise, but having had discussions with a wide range of people we began to recognise that making Hill Holt Wood a social enter-prise, giving ownership to the local community, was imperative in terms of the achievement of both short- and long-term goals. The move into becoming a social enterprise was primarily driven by considerations of sustainability; it helps to make the business more sus-tainable, it helps to make the community link more sta-ble. The real difference is that now the business is becoming less dependent on me, I mean, it won't be long now until it is totally independent of me . . . it could survive probably without me now, but would struggle. If Karen and I left, it would be borderline at the moment but in another year or so I think it would be fine, it might even do better!'

In relinquishing ownership, Karen and Nigel felt that under social ownership the woodland would be man-aged in the most effective fashion given the needs and demands of local stakeholders. Transfer of ownership of HHW to the local community took place in 2002. They were made manager and director, respectively. Karen and Nigel were allowed to portion off a small area of the woodland for their own private residence. HHW is now owned and controlled as a membership organisation limited guarantee. In the United Kingdom, a company limited by guarantee is associated with the following characteristics:

- Does not have a share capital;
- Has members (not shareholders);
- Members are guarantors instead of shareholders, usually guaranteeing to pay £1 on dissolution;
- Can hold property and can borrow money in its own name;
- Must have a minimum of one member (national or overseas);
- Must have a secretary.

Environmental statement

HHW's environmental statement aims relate to running environmentally sustainable woodland by:

> Managing horticulture, permaculture and animal husbandry on a sustainable basis . . . Sustainable management of the woodland . . . Monitoring the progress of flora and fauna to increase biodiversity . . . Developing and applying alternative/appropriate building, energy generation and manufacturing technology.

When Karen and Nigel first purchased HHW, it was clear to them that the previous owner had taken little environmental care as reflected in the negative impact of their actions. The environmental aspect of HHW was the primary driver in the conception and development of the project. Intensive restoration work over several years was required to restore the woodland to the pre-felled condition. While the social and economic dimensions were important to both Karen and Nigel, environmental conservation remained the primary objective:

> 'We love having the kids here, it's great. But the first thing we tell them is that the woodland comes first. The importance of conservation, of caring for the environment is paramount and so if anyone comes on site and is not willing to give to the environment the same level of care and attention [of] my staff and myself then they are asked to leave. It's that simple.'

In addition, consideration of and for the environment has an impact on how the business is run and on the profits that the business makes. In contrast to more traditional organisations, environmental rather than economic profit is the primary goal and so decisions are taken at HHW that might leave more hard-nosed business people somewhat aghast:

> 'There is a limit to what we can do here at Hill Holt Wood. We already employ more than 20 people in various capacities and we have more than that again in on-site learners and you have to remember that Hill Holt Wood's only a tiny site, relatively speaking. There is a capacity, an operating capacity that if we exceed will result in us doing more damage to the woodland than good. We do want to make more money so that we can do more good, but we are not prepared to compromise our environmental aims. We are now looking with the management committee at ways of moving up the value chain in those activities in which we are already engaged and we are also looking for sister sites that might take on and develop the model that we've worked so hard to validate here at Hill Holt Wood.'

Economic statement

HHW's economic stated aims relate to running an economically viable social enterprise by:

> Achieving an annual surplus for investment and innovation . . . Maintaining a diversity of income streams, clients, products and services . . . Manufacturing and selling woodland added-value products . . . Delivering consultancy services.

The economic dimension, or the ability to generate revenues in excess of costs, shapes social enterprises' survival and growth. The ability to generate profits that can be used to help achieve organisational objectives (Leadbetter, 1997) is of fundamental importance to social enterprises:

> 'I hate that term "not-for-profit", because we are all about profits, not one profit, however, but three. We are all about social, environmental and economic profit. The difference between what we do as a social enterprise and what is done in the private sector is that we count all three forms of profit as contributing towards our bottom-line whereas private sector enterprises are only interested in the economic returns.'

Social enterprises seek economic profits with consideration of, and regard for, social and environmental impacts. Also, some private sector enterprises consider the social and environmental impacts of their activities. Awareness of, and commitment to, issues of social and environmental consequences often help to define the particular opportunities that social enterprises identify and/or respond to. When multiple opportunities for profit are identified, consideration of social and environmental impacts may direct a social enterprise towards pursuit of the opportunity, which promises the most advantageous outcomes in relation to social, environmental and economic goals. In contrast to private sector enterprises that have to answer to shareholders (i.e., commonly required to seek to exploit the most profitable opportunities), social enterprises observe a different set of requirements and they do not solely focus on profit-maximisation. Other important commitments can be pursued by social enterprises:

'I think that there's a limit to how far conventional businesses can go, they have to be more "green-minded", there's been a shift in attitudes that has ensured that, but they need to make economic profits above all else, but in our case, there are no profits to be shared . . . everything is retained by the business, we have no shareholders and we don't want any. The key, the bottom-line, is that social enterprises need to be very good at what they do otherwise socially- and environmentally-minded normal business will simply step into that market and push the social enterprises back out again, so you've got to be as good [as] or better than mainstream business to succeed. This is about real business, this is about making money, it's just that we do it in a way that is socially and environmentally aware.'

Social enterprises must periodically reconcile competing obligations. They must make judgements with regard to their social, environmental and economic obligations over both short- and long-term horizons. Greffe (2007: 91) asserted that they are:

'. . . not committed to maximising financial profit, social [enterprises] can take into consideration the values and expectations of actors in the field . . . and the long-term effects of decisions.'

Although the primary income stream generated by HHW relates to the training and teaching contracts with local educational and vocational boards, the management committee and, in particular, Karen and Nigel are continually on the lookout for new opportunities:

'It's essential that we diversify, that we generate income from a wide range of activities. I like to think about it as an issue of sustainability, you know, at present we're excessively dependent on our training and teaching courses and the income that we earn from them. As a result, we're exposed to significant risk if one or both of those contracts are withdrawn. From a sustainability point of view it's the same as an animal eating only one foodstuff – if the crop fails, you're done for! We are busy

increasing our income in a range of other areas, including consultancy, landscaping, building projects and litter collection – we're even toying with the idea of offering an eco-burial site here. Providing the opportunities that we respond to are in line with our environmental and social commitments, we're more than happy to give them a go!'

Rather than having a clear sense of their product or service, the management team at HHW are happy to respond to new opportunities as and when they emerge. This responsiveness allows the participants engaged in HHW to explore new opportunities, and to test the water with new ideas. There have been some setbacks. However, the majority of new ideas have been welcomed and proven to be successful extensions of the core product/service message developed by HHW.

Due to an active interest in generating profits, the enterprise has conducted social audits. Developed originally as an accounting practice, social audits allow for the full economic benefits of an organisation to be fully monitored. This auditing process allows positive externalities to be measured, and this information can be recorded in a social enterprise balance sheet:

'I see social and environmental accounting as being really important not only to see how successfully we are working but for investment as well. I have a big concern about making sure social enterprise is allowed to be enterprising. Having the social audit, the LM3[1] indicators and the SROI[2] work will allow us to go back to potential investors and say "here's the (social and environmental) dividend, invest in it and grow your dividend".'

The social audit allows the management committee to discuss the array of benefits provide by HHW. It also enables comparisons to be made with similar and dissimilar projects, which in turn, helps to provide an information platform for potential investors (private and public sector) to use when considering the level of involvement with and commitment to HHW.

Due to growth, the initial vision (or mission) associated with a social enterprise may be obscured by

---

[1]The Local Multiplier 3 (LM3) tool can be used by organisations to measure the extent of their contribution to and impact on the local economy.

[2]The Social Return on Investment (SROI) tool can be used by organisations to more effectively evaluate their achievements against their objectives, to manage their performance levels and to communicate their results.

responses (and adaptations) to emerging challenges and new opportunities. Social enterprises need to retain a degree of flexibility in order to address contingent circumstances and emerging stakeholder needs (Leadbetter, 1997). Excessive flexibility may be detrimental to an enterprise if it results in a loss of strategic focus and organisational direction. Some social enterprises lack focus because they seek to consider, incorporate and implement disparate ideas and views from a wide range of stakeholders:

> 'We've always listened and we've always tried to do what we can to include the comments and suggestions of our employees, customers and clients. However, everything that we do is always in alignment with our primary objective of proving the value of ancient woodland in the 21st century.'

Social enterprises need to find ways to achieve a healthy balance between the external requirements that are levied upon them as a result of their interaction with local communities and stakeholders, and the demands associated with ensuring that internal competencies and identities are developed and maintained.

Future contributions

The community within which HHW is situated undoubtedly benefit from the freely provided amenities. HHW now functions as a retreat for vulnerable young adults and children who cannot function effectively in mainstream society. Due to the experiences at HHW, their attitudes are positively altered. This can be viewed as the most substantial benefit to the community. Although unexpected, the help and support of the community, through the development of a management committee and eventually full ownership of the project,

has proven pivotal in making HHW a success now, and in the foreseeable future.

Questions and issues

1 How important is it that social enterprises take into consideration the needs and requirements of the communities within which they are based?

2 Given the competing obligations associated with a triple bottom-line commitment, can social enterprises always make profit-seeking decisions?

3 It is often difficult for new businesses to develop the crucial social links that they require to overcome the liabilities associated with newness? What might be the best, or more effective, means of breaking down these barriers and building ties with local communities?

References

Crowther, D. and Aras, G. (2008). *Corporate Social Responsibility*. London: Ventus Publishing.

Elkington, J. (1997). *Cannibals with Forks: The Triple Bottom Line of 21st Century Business*. Gabriola Island: New Society Publishers.

Greffe, X. (2007). The Role of the Social Economy in Local Development. In A. Noya and E. Clarence (eds) *The Social Economy: Building Inclusive Economies*. Paris: OECD Publishing, pp. 91–118.

Leadbetter, C. (1997). *The Rise of the Social Entrepreneur*. London: Demos.

Lloyd, P. (2007). The Social Economy in the New Political Economic Context. In A. Noya and E. Clarence (eds). *The Social Economy: Building Inclusive Economies*. Paris: OECD Publishing, pp. 61–90.

Noya, A. and Clarence, E. (2007). *The Social Economy: Building Inclusive Economies*. Paris: OECD Publishing.

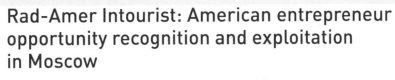

Case study 17

Rad-Amer Intourist: American entrepreneur opportunity recognition and exploitation in Moscow

Zafar U. Ahmed, Peter Robinson and Leo Paul Dana

Summary

In the mid-1980s Paul Tatum, a United States (U.S.) citizen, sought investment opportunities. Economic and political reform associated with *perestroika* and *glasnost* raised the potential for business opportunities to be identified and exploited in Russia. However, the culture, the institutional context and the lack of a business infrastructure in the country were barriers to enterprise. Tatum identified an opportunity to establish a Western-style business centre attached to a high quality Western hotel in downtown Moscow. Tatum and his company Americom initiated a joint venture between Intourist (i.e., the Soviet national tourism organisation), Radisson Hotels International and Americom to establish a new hotel and business centre in Moscow. The joint venture was called Rad-Amer Intourist. Intourist would own the building, Radisson would manage the hotel's rooms and restaurants, and Americom would manage the retail shops, office space and other services. Tatum's dream became a reality but during the chaotic climate of post-communist Russia he was assassinated. This case illustrates that cultural and institutional factors can shape the business formation and development process in a transition economy.

Introduction

From an early age, Paul Tatum showed enterprising traits. During his undergraduate studies at Oklahoma State University, he persuaded his friends to pool their money in order to send him on the Semester-at-Sea Program, which is an educational voyage of the Institute for Shipboard Education. On this trip, his life turned a corner in Tunis, where he identified a business opportunity.

He purchased some goods and then sold them on the street. In two days, he made $2,700 (U.S.) and reported a 300 per cent profit. Paul Tatum recalled:

'I got a feeling for international markets.'

When the boat docked in Casablanca, Paul Tatum made another $1,000 by selling his camera. He decided that there was no need to go back to Oklahoma State University. Instead, he spent the next 20 years conducting a series of risky deals and the stakes got bigger and bigger.

When Paul Tatum dropped out of college after his junior year, he made what was, for a young person, a clever but genuinely odd career move. He borrowed $10,000 and donated the money to the Republican National Committee in the United States. He was rewarded with a 'Republican Eagle' award, and this guaranteed him some access to the higher echelons of power. Paul spent the next decade establishing his political consulting firm, and he made money in real estate and oil deals. But Tatum's affairs took a turn for the worse in 1983 with the collapse of Oklahoma City's Penn Square Bank. He lost approximately $1 million. Paul left Oklahoma City with several small outstanding lawsuits pursued by creditors.

In 1985, during an Oklahoma trade mission to the former Soviet Union, Paul Tatum fell under the spell that Mr Gorbachev's (i.e., the communist president of the USSR) *perestroika* had cast on much of the West. He identified a market of nearly 250 million Soviets hungry for Levi jeans and Detroit cars with automatic transmission. Tatum took special note of the bewildered foreign business people negotiating million dollar deals on crackling phones in drab Soviet hotel rooms. He believed that foreign investors needed a business centre adjacent to a shiny Western-style hotel in Moscow.

Business people could then get a room, buy a drink, rent an office and do their business deals. Tatum stated:

'It was as if I found myself standing on a mountaintop from which I could see everything; my past, my present and my future.'

Tatum did not have sufficient financial resources to exploit the identified opportunity on his own. A presidential decree in the USSR had just legalised joint ventures as the only way Westerners could penetrate the Russian market. Tatum, therefore, sought a Soviet partner to exploit his idea. He also needed a Western partner with financial resources and expertise relating how to build and manage a hotel. Tatum leveraged his Republican Party contacts. In 1989, Paul Tatum formed a company called Americom Business Centre. Tatum developed links with H. Haldeman, Nixon's former chief of staff, who was involved in Apollo Acquisitions, which was a small, publicly trading holding company based in Florida in the United States. Americom Business Centre and Apollo Acquisitions merged. Tatum put together a team of dealmakers consisting of Haldeman, Bernie Rome (i.e., an international businessman), and Robert Schmidt (i.e., then the vice chairman of Control Data Institute). In 1991, Tatum fired Schmidt from the board of directors. Haldeman died in 1992, and Rome withdrew to a consulting capacity. By 1995, Tatum was the president and chief executive officer (CEO) of Americom and he owned a controlling share of the company's stock.

Cultural and institutional context for enterprise in Russia

In an attempt to understand how some people in Russia conduct business, it is useful to examine the historical development of entrepreneurship in the former USSR, and specifically in Russia. There is a long history of entrepreneurship in Russia (Hisrich and Grachev, 1993). From the fourteenth century, trade became increasingly concentrated in the hands of specialists. During the next four centuries, many people in Russia were engaged in some form of commercial activity. Russian entrepreneurs were oppressed, heavily taxed, treated as powerless individuals, and regarded as the bottom echelon of society. This situation changed little in the eighteenth and nineteenth centuries. Peter the Great attempted to create a class of Russian industrialists. However, his programme did little to develop entrepreneurs, or to establish the foundation for entrepreneurial activity.

During most of the twentieth century individual enterprise was not promoted by the Communist Party. With regard to state-owned enterprises, Communist Party entrepreneurs were joined by Red Directors (i.e., individuals with a strong engineering background). During the Second World War, the military power of the USSR increased and massive investment in weapons promoted a new group of Soviet entrepreneurs, notably, innovators drawn from the scientific and technical intelligentsia.

Entrepreneurs in Russia faced several barriers to enterprise formation and development. First, they faced attitudinal and psychological barriers to enterprise. The communist culture did not promote individual enterprise. People were not encouraged to be independent, creative, to generate vast personal wealth, and to create and grow their own businesses.

Second, the government and the institutional context restricted the activities of entrepreneurs. Government saddled successful entrepreneurs with burdensome obligations; demanded special contributions from entrepreneurs during times of emergency or war; repealed previously granted rights and privileges whenever it was expedient to do so; demanded punctual and exact fulfilment of obligations; and confiscated property when these obligations were not met.

Third, the legal system promoted state-owned enterprises. It was difficult for individuals to assume risk and to establish independent companies to exploit identified business opportunities. Consequently, some enterprising individuals established illegal new ventures in the 'second' or 'shadow' economy. Most of these opportunistic entrepreneurs identified and exploited gaps in the market, and most of them did not innovate to create and exploit business opportunities related to scientific knowledge. Entrepreneurs engaged in the 'shadow economy' pursued highly risky (i.e., illegal) activities, and some of them reaped high financial returns from their speculative investments.

Fourth, the long-term isolationism and separation of Russian enterprises from their Western counterparts resulted in people in Russia having limited knowledge of Western entrepreneurial and management techniques.

Fifth, foreigners seeking to invest and exploit opportunities found the rules and regulations for business in Russia were very difficult local barriers to enterprise to address. Entrepreneurs had to deal with a complicated infrastructure and poor distribution channels established by Soviet central planning regimes. Further, the communication network was archaic, overloaded and unreliable. Roads and railways were inadequate and in disrepair, and airline travel was unreliable.

In 1985, President Gorbachev announced that the USSR was going to enter a new period of its history. He called it *perestroika*, which means 'rebuilding' or 'changing'. Gorbachev acknowledged that over the previous 20 years industrial production had declined, whilst corruption had increased. He wanted the unemployed receiving state benefits to be provided with opportunities to work. During the subsequent transition period, the state would recognise private enterprise in the form of co-operatives, individual labour activity, and joint ventures using foreign capital. Post-1987, these changes led to an unprecedented growth in new business creation.

In 1987, two pieces of legislation under *perestroika* opened the door for foreign direct investment into the USSR. Article XIX of the Law on Soviet State Enterprise declared that foreign economic entities of Soviet enterprises had the right to establish joint ventures directly with foreign partners. Further, the Law on Joint Ventures stipulated the conditions for creating and operating foreign ventures in the USSR. Joint ventures were envisioned to be activities between partners engaged in manufacturing or services based on shared ownership and joint management of the enterprise, as well as shared risks and division of any profits generated. Joint ventures with foreign partners were granted special legal status by the Soviet government. They would enjoy numerous privileges and exemptions from several laws applying to domestic Soviet enterprises.

In 1989, the government introduced an act entitled 'On Measures Concerning the Creation and Development of Small Enterprises'. This act promoted a new free market economy, and it made it possible for Russians outside the centralised economic system to legally start and own new ventures. This act ensured that several elements of the former centralised economic system were altered. Some of the most important included: the reduction or elimination of subsidies to unprofitable state enterprises; the introduction of competition within the system, often from outside the country; the breakdown of Gosnab (i.e., the centralised or state supply system to all enterprises); the elimination of Gosplan (i.e., the centralised or state planning of the economy); and the introduction of market forces. Despite these legal and institutional changes, the new culture of enterprise had to fight the long-standing habits, routines and mindsets associated with a communist culture. In 1992, due to structural and attitudinal reasons, the state still owned 95 per cent of the country's industrial capacity, and by 1994 the state still owned 50 per cent of the means of production.

In 1993, the country was still operating under the old Communist constitution, which had no provision for private property, including businesses. There was no legal or formal contract law. Also, there was no legal system to enforce the presidential decrees that had been put in place to encourage and support the fledgling market system. This, along with the win-lose attitude, made it acceptable for the government to change the rules at any time if it they thought they could get away with it, and they could get more out of the deal. In essence, there was no concept of the rule of law, only the rule of people. There are many examples of negotiated deals with retail shops, hotels, government entities, factories, charter airlines or shipping companies, in which, well after a final agreement had been reached, the state-owned Russian businesses came back and tried to change the conditions of the contract.

Exploitation of a business opportunity in Russia: Post-perestroika

In 1989, Paul Tatum sought to exploit the business opportunity he had noticed in Russia. Tatum identified a grey, half-finished building located on Moscow's Berezhkovskay Embankment, facing east toward the Moscow River. It was owned by Intourist, the Soviet national tourism organisation, which had the monopoly over all services used by foreign travellers in the country. Intourist wanted to erect a new hotel that could increase foreign currency earnings. Tatum started talking to big U.S. hotel chains, and he found that Radisson Hotels International was keen to enter the Soviet Union, which before *perestroika* had been a closed market. Tatum and his company Americom initiated a joint venture between Intourist, Radisson Hotels International and Americom to establish a new hotel and business centre in Moscow. The joint venture was called Rad-Amer Intourist. Intourist would own the building, Radisson would manage the hotel's rooms and restaurants, and Americom would manage the retail shops, office space and other services. Radisson and Americom received 10 per cent and 40 per cent of the shares in the joint venture, respectively. Intourist, their Russian partner, received 50 per cent of the shares. Radisson would receive 4 per cent of hotel revenue and an incentive fee, whilst Americom would receive income from the business centre revenue and an incentive fee. The two partners from the United States negotiated a $33 million credit deal to finance further construction of the hotel and the business centre. Intourist agreed to defer rent payments for several years.

By March 1989, a business plan for the joint venture was written. A rental agreement relating to the building leased from Intourist was agreed in October 1990. The land was owned by the City of Moscow. The Rad-Amer Intourist joint venture faced several hurdles to development. In 1991, the Soviet Union collapsed. Uncertainty surrounded property rights and the validity of contracts agreed during the Soviet period. The new Russian Federation regime struggled with issues relating to tourism. Doubts were cast surrounding who owned the land and the building relating to the hotel leased by Rad-Amer Intourist. After months of wrangling, ownership of the property was transferred to Moscow City Council. Tatum had a new Russian partner. In response to this change, and increased uncertainty, Tatum's bankers in the West withdrew their promise to provide commerial loans relating to $20 million.

Problems faced by Paul Tatum and Rad-Amer Intourist after the collapse of the USSR

By mid-1992, more than 5,000 enterprises from 65 countries had been registered in the former USSR. Foreign and Russian directors of joint ventures reported deterioration in the situation for joint ventures between mid-1991 and mid-1992. They raised concerns relating to the the the increase of 'typically Soviet' behaviour that interfered with business activity in Russia. Notably, they complained about unclear and often contradictory legislation, the complicated tax structure, incompetent officials, and the increasing demand for hard-currency deals.

For Tatum, the disaster started on 29 May 1994, when the contract of general director Vladimir Draizer expired in Rad-Amer Intourist. Tatum asked him to vacate his office in the hotel. This request was based on the following assessment by Tatum:

'He (Draizer) has outgrown his capabilities in this position. Because of his mismanagement and incompetence, I estimate that the joint venture lost over $7 million in profits during 1993.'

Draizer had previously resided in the US for 15 years before returning to the USSR. Representatives from the GKI (GosKomImuchestvo – State Property Agency) and then MosIntour (Moscow branch of Intourist) encouraged Draizer to 'adopt their point of view' with regard to the operation of Rad-Amer Intourist. In 1992, he began transfering funds from Rad-Amer Intourist to 'Russian representatives' and himself. Tatum commented:

'It was our discovery of this, and confrontation with him on the subject, coupled with his desire for a personal ownership share of our enterprise, that brought about his hiring of armed guards to stop me from entering the property after the expiration of his term as general director. He knew that only Americom was opposed to him continuing as general director for another term and that if he could embarrass me, it might win him employers, partners, and bring him continued success.'

Draizer did not want to leave his office, and he reacted by bringing security reinforcements from a private company to deny Tatum access to the hotel and business centre. With the assistance of more than a dozen bodyguards Tatum regained entry to the hotel and his third floor office. After this event Tatum commented:

'It is amazing how it's easier to change status quo illegally in this country today than through legal channels.'

The City of Moscow decided to expropriate the business. The Rad-Amer Intourist joint venture was very profitable, and it attracted business travellers and government officials from all over the world to use its services. In response, Tatum wrote several open letters to Intourist, to the Russian government, and directly to President Yeltsin to complain about what he perceived as an abuse of power.

The Russians wanted to remove Tatum from the board of the Rad-Amer Intourist joint venture, but they did not know how to remove him. In April 1995, Mr Djaibrailov issued an order to evict Tatum from his hotel rooms and office. If Tatum refused to leave the rooms, they were to be sealed. According to Djaibrailov, the reason for the eviction was Tatum's unpaid rent relating to $500,000.

Independent lawyers hired by Americom concluded that Americom had the right to use the office for a period of 36 months starting from 1 July 1994, with an option to extend for another three years. Also, they pointed out that the lease agreement stated that Americom had to pay $3,500 per month. Therefore, Paul Tatum owed only $21,000 to the Rad-Amer Intourist joint venture. Tatum claimed that Djaibrailov's order was illegal. He decided to stay in his room and he waited for his personal guard service to arrive the next day. The issue was subsequently dealt with by several courts.

Demise of Paul Tatum

Paul Tatum was stubborn and he refused to play along with the unwritten Russian business rules. Instead, he did the opposite. He wrote to President Yeltsin suggesting the need for the creation of a new ministry to assist Western businesses, the need to establish a new institution under the auspices of Presidential Office support, and the need to create and implement new tax laws. What he should have done was to learn the unwritten rules of his environment by observing what was happening around him. For example, in 1993, the foreign partners of several joint ventures were asked to give up their shares. Further, he should have appreciated the new Russian patriotism, and the desire to remove expensive foreign employees from partnerships. Russian employees were cheaper and they did not argue with the management. Tatum received several messages from 'powerful' people, and they warned him to leave the country for his own safety. One of his bodyguards was stabbed and instructed to tell his boss to go home. Tatum started to wear a bulletproof vest, and he stopped using a car because he thought that the crowded Moscow public transport system was safer. Nevertheless, using the media he continued to raise his visibility. In 1996, Paul Tatum was shot dead in Moscow.

Questions and issues

1 What enterprising skills and behaviour did Paul Tatum exhibit?

2 Why did Paul Tatum establish a joint venture to exploit the business opportunity identified in Moscow?

3 What weaknesses did Paul Tatum exhibit with regard to the development of Rad-Amer Intourist?

Reference

Hisrich, R. D. and Grachev, M. V. (1993). The Russian Entrepreneur. *Journal of Business Venturing*, 8: 487–497.

Case study 18

The Fleet Sheet: New firm creation in a transition economy

Marlene Mints Reed

Summary

This case describes the start-up and development of an English language publication that summarises political and economic news for international companies operating in the Czech Republic. The news summary was relayed primarily by a one-page fax, which was distributed at 8.00 each weekday. A one-page e-mail was later distributed as a marketing tool to potential customers. The case discusses issues relating to new venture creation in a transition economy; issues relating to the development of a strategic plan; the intricacies of using discount pricing among various market segments; and the challenges faced by firms with 'first mover' advantage.

Introduction

On 22 February 1992 Erik Best established *The Fleet Sheet*, which is an English language publication that summarises political and economic news for international companies operating in the Czech Republic after the Velvet Revolution. The firm provided at 8.00 each weekday a news summary primarily in the form of a one-page fax. A one-page e-mail was later distributed as a marketing tool to potential customers. The paper had generated a reputation for honest, straightforward evaluation of the Czech economy and government that had made it highly popular with foreign companies and their managers. During the summer of 2007, Eric reflected on the viability of his business relating to its organisational and legal structure. Changes in technology and greater access to news through the Internet also posed challenges to the survival of the business.

Education and early work experience

Erik was born in North Carolina in the United States and when he was 11 years old, his family moved to Montana. He wrote for the high school newspaper and was a part-time staff sports writer for the local *Missoulian* newspaper. Near the end of his senior year in high school, Erik was offered a journalism scholarship to Vanderbilt University. He turned the offer down because he wanted to be involved in business and/or politics. Erik attended Georgetown University and in 1985, he graduated with a degree in Foreign Service. Whilst pursuing this course, he studied Russian during the summer vacation at Middlebury College in Vermont and in 1985 he was awarded a Master's Degree. A four month period of study in Moscow had the greatest impact on his life. In 1987, Erik was awarded an MBA degree from the University of North Carolina at Chapel Hill.

Move to Prague

Erik, who could speak Russian and several Slavic languages, became fascinated with the historic changes taking place in Eastern Europe. Centrally-planned socialist economies in Eastern Europe were seeking to make the transition to free market economies. In February 1991 he joined the MBA Enterprise Corps to work in Prague in what was then Czechoslovakia. Erik immediately fell in love with the country and found the Czech language very similar to Russian. In explaining his love of Prague, Erik stated:

'I have always loved music, and there is no city in the world so rich with music as Prague. There are classical concerts daily in concert halls, churches, town squares, on the breathtaking Charles Bridge, private chambers, large public halls and under street arches. There are musicians playing violins and accordions on street corners and in Metro stations. I have heard that there are more musicians per capita in the Czech Republic than anywhere else in the world. After all, it was in Prague that Mozart wrote the opera "*Don Giovanni*" and found greater acclaim than in his own Austria. It was also the home of composers Dvorak and Smetana. This is one of the reasons I feel at home in this city.'

Eastern Europe situation

In the early 1990s, the break-up of centralised socialist economies was occurring all over Eastern Europe. Simultaneously, there was a rapid growth of the private sector in Russia as well as Poland, Czechoslovakia and Hungary. One of the challenges in the burgeoning market economies was the privatisation process associated with the creation of small businesses out of large enterprises, as well as the establishment of de novo new ventures. Auctions of small businesses and the restitution of property led to the restoration of some family firms. The development of a small business sector was the most successful manifestation of the movement to a market economy.

Numerous problems faced the new private ventures. Entrepreneurs faced growing inflation rates, whilst employees suffered stagnant wage rates. To deal with unfair and cumbersome legal procedures in the regulatory environment and/or to avoid the attention of the Mafia or corrupt officials, many entrepreneurs were forced to operate illicitly. Secure contracts to lease property were difficult to obtain, and the banking system was not equipped to deal with the needs of small businesses. Further, entrepreneurs lacked prior managerial experience relating to running private businesses. The MBA Enterprise Corps was a Western organisation with consultants that aimed to promote a free market economy.

Idea

After working in Prague for a year, Erik noticed that international companies with offices and operations in the Czech Republic required accurate and timely information on political and economic trends in order to make appropriate business decisions. Drawing upon his management consultant work experience, Erik knew that busy decision-makers required concise information written in English. Erik generated the idea of an inexpensive one-page fax news summary solution to the problem. The name of the firm relates to Fleet Street in London, where all major English national newspapers had been published 'on time' before they moved to the Docklands area of London.

On 22 February 1992, Erik published the first issue of *The Fleet Sheet*. He believed that if he had four or five subscribers in the first month, the product would be successful. In fact, 15 subscribers signed up during the first month and by the spring of 2007, there were approximately 1,000 subscribers. Erik believed that the lifecycle of his product would be short and the operation of the firm would be easy to manage. He did not prepare a business plan and he adopted a sole proprietorship mode of operation. The firm employed eight members of staff. Some staff arrived very early in the morning and they reviewed and translated the news from Czech newspapers into English. Staff members that arrived after 7.30 engaged in distribution and client support.

Erik picked out the most important news to be translated and distributed in *The Fleet Sheet*. He believed a key competitive advantage was the firm's emphasis on a quality product relating to useful Czech economic and political news. If *The Fleet Sheet* provided inaccurate information it was promptly retracted and a public apology was made. Erik recognised the needs of his customers and listened to any customer complaints.

Pricing strategy

Erik immediately realised that a major publication constraint would be the number of people he could physically fax copies of *The Fleet Sheet* to in a short period of time. The firm was constrained by the limited number of telephone lines. He recognised that larger multinational companies with larger budgets would pay a higher price to acquire information very early in the morning, whilst many smaller firms dealing with fewer complicated decisions would only require information once a week, and they would prefer to pay a lower price if information was sent later in the day. A graduated pricing strategy was devised. Customers in large companies and lawyers for whom 'time is money' were charged, on average, $3 to $4 per day, for *The Fleet Sheet* faxed early in the morning. They were guaranteed a pre-9.00 faxed delivery, and if *The Fleet Sheet* was delivered late, which never occurred, the publication would be free. Information enabled customers to make astute and timely decisions based upon realistic information. A discounted price was offered to customers that requested information to be sent later in the day. Customers in smaller firms requesting *The Fleet Sheet* faxed once a

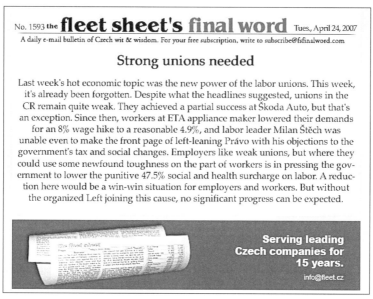

No. 1593 the **fleet sheet's final word** Tues., April 24, 2007

A daily e-mail bulletin of Czech wit & wisdom. For your free subscription, write to subscribe@fsfinalword.com

Strong unions needed

Last week's hot economic topic was the new power of the labor unions. This week, it's already been forgotten. Despite what the headlines suggested, unions in the CR remain quite weak. They achieved a partial success at Škoda Auto, but that's an exception. Since then, workers at ETA appliance maker lowered their demands for an 8% wage hike to a reasonable 4.9%, and labor leader Milan Štěch was unable even to make the front page of left-leaning Právo with his objections to the government's tax and social changes. Employers like weak unions, but where they could use some newfound toughness on the part of workers is in pressing the government to lower the punitive 47.5% social and health surcharge on labor. A reduction here would be a win-win situation for employers and workers. But without the organized Left joining this cause, no significant progress can be expected.

Serving leading Czech companies for 15 years.

info@fleet.cz

Figure 1 *The Fleet Sheet*'s Final Word, http://www.fleet.cz/

week were charged, on average, $0.50 to $0.75 per issue. The graduated pricing strategy enabled more people to purchase the product, and it also made the product easier to distribute.

Marketing strategy

The marketing of *The Fleet Sheet* was multi-faceted. Erik advertised in English-language publications such as the *Prague Post, Business Central Europe* (published by *The Economist*), *The American Chamber of Commerce Newsletter*, and in the Czech press read by the elite. Subscribers were drawn from English-speaking countries as well as Dutch- and French-speaking, and subscribers. People in Czech companies realised the time and economic benefits associated with abbreviated news.

Fleet Sheet also engaged in direct marketing. Potential new subscribers were identified through personal contacts, word of mouth and company names provided by the American Chamber of Commerce. The benefits of *Fleet Sheet* were immediately drawn to the attention of potential subscribers. Positive referrals from satisfied subscribers generated new customers. *Fleet Sheet* provided analysis of key issues rather than a simple reporting of the news. Satisfied customers made the following comments on *The Fleet Sheet* website:

'Nearly the entire finance community in Prague is reading *The Fleet Sheet*, so I must too. I find I rely on it more than I probably should.'
(Jiri Kunert, Chairman and CEO, Zivnostenska Banka.)

'Most people can translate the headlines. *The Fleet Sheet* is successful because it understands the Czech market and gets to the real issues. It tells me what I need to know.'
(William D. Harter, General Manager, Seagram.)

'I read *The Fleet Sheet* before anything else in the morning. My Czech colleagues also find it useful.'
(Ian Ferguson, Managing Director, Tabak.)

'I read *The Fleet Sheet* because it's the first source of news for the foreign community in the Czech Republic, and I find it extremely important to know just what it is that everyone else knows.'
(Jiri Pehe, Political Analyst.)

Fleet Sheet now uses e-mail to whet the appetite of potential subscribers (see Figure 1 – '*The Fleet Sheet*'s Final Word'). Anyone that e-mailed Erik was immediately added to a mailing list, and twice a week they were sent a summary of *The Fleet Sheet*'s articles. Benefits associated with daily faxes of *The Fleet Sheet* were drawn to the attention of potential subscribers. Understanding the animosity some people have to receiving 'junk e-mails', Erik made the following point at the bottom of the e-mail:

'If you do not wish to receive such messages in the future, please simply let us know and we will remove your name from our list.'

Few people asked for their names to be removed, and many became regular subscribers. The e-mail was only sent to individuals whom Erik believed would be interested in Czech news.

In the late 1990s, Erik developed a website for *The Fleet Sheet* (http://www.fleet.cz) as a marketing tool. A sample of the news provided by *The Fleet Sheet* was listed on the webpage to attract interest from potential subscribers. Erik believed the webpage had the potential to generate even more subscribers than the e-mail synopses.

Erik had offered *The Fleet Sheet*'s entire archives on disk for a $500 subscription per year. He decided to list all the archives relating to the previous eight years on the website. People that registered could access the material for free. They were also sent e-mail synopses, which would encourage them to subscribe to the daily faxed service. Rather than selling archives as the *Wall Street Journal* had done, Erik believed in the long-run that *The Fleet Sheet* could make more money by using its archives as a marketing tool to generate more subscriptions.

People asked Erik why he had not solely selected e-mail as the medium for publishing and distributing *The Fleet Sheet*. His response was:

'There is the problem of protecting intellectual property. Unless you can encrypt it, you may have a copyright infringement of your material. In fact, Stephen King's most recent story that was published originally on the Internet was encrypted, but someone broke the code. Another problem with encryption is that the message can only be sent to a specific person – not a company. Therefore, there are some real problems with encrypting the information on the Internet.'

Barriers to business development

Unlike most start-up businesses, *The Fleet Sheet* was immediately profitable. To reduce costs, Erik made an early decision to rent office space and computers. He only purchased necessary equipment when *The Fleet Sheet* was a financially viable business. Concerning the success of the company, Erik mused:

'The revenues of the company have grown every year because the Czech Republic was seen early as the darling of the West, and they also received a great deal of media attention. Under more realistic conditions, many of the companies would not have come here.'

During the late 1990s, *The Fleet Sheet* faced a reduction in subscriptions. This was, in part, due to increased competition. With regard to this barrier, Erik commented:

'We have had to fend off six or seven competitors who began to offer the same service that we were offering – a faxed bulletin with important political and economic news. It was a blatant rip-off of our product. The success of *The Fleet Sheet* drew other companies into the market.'

Erik speculated:

'The drastic price reduction the competition offered in the beginning served to lower the overall revenue size of the market. I have often wondered if there is a big enough market to support ONE such publication over the long-run, much less numerous competitors in a smaller revenue pool.'

However, he observed:

'The reason we survived was due to the overall quality of the paper. Business people know quality when they see it, and they immediately know that *The Fleet Sheet* is professionally done.'

Government regulations, which had been devastating to many businesses in the Czech Republic, had been minimal for *The Fleet Sheet*. Unlike large pharmaceutical companies operating in the Czech Republic, *The Fleet Sheet* did not require a large number of costly and time-consuming licences or drug approvals. *The Fleet Sheet*, however, had to deal with distribution issues generated by government bureaucracy. The government requested *The Fleet Sheet*, at its own expense, to send its publication to hundreds of libraries in the Czech Republic. Open access could have eroded the firm's customer base and *The Fleet Sheet* would not be profitable. They took a risk and only sent the paper to selected libraries where they believed potential subscribers would subsequently purchase the product for themselves. The regulation was changed in early 2000, and *The Fleet Sheet* was no longer required to freely distribute the publication to libraries.

In the late 1990s, Erik decided to add an advertisement to *The Fleet Sheet*. The advertisement was priced at $400 a day, and was rotated among four or five different companies' advertisements. If another advertisement was added, *The Fleet Sheet* would need an additional faxed page. Faxing charges are relatively small; additional labour to prepare the page would add to the unit cost of production. Erik was concerned about whether people would read two pages, and whether the advertisement would weaken the company brand associated with relevant and concise news information sought by discerning and loyal readers. Erik worried that a new two-page format would reduce, rather than increase, the number of subscribers. In the spring of 2007, *The Fleet Sheet* had approximately 1,000 subscribers paying, on average, $2.50 each per day to receive the publication. Each additional subscriber was associated with a 90 per cent rise in profits and only a 10 per cent increase in variable costs.

Erik had always used Adobe Acrobat to format the paper, and this ensured the faxed paper was easy to read. If he solely adopted e-mail publication of the paper, there could be text format issues that could make it difficult to publish on only one or two pages. Erik was considering whether the changes would also impact the integrity of the product. The concise format of a one-page fax was established and well received. He was concerned about whether people would read lengthy e-mails on their computers and would they still prefer a fax that they could hold in their hands. Erik speculated:

'If you could produce the same experience of reading a newspaper on the Internet, it would be good. However, our present computer monitors prevent this from occurring.'

Erik wondered how *The Fleet Sheet* could build a brand name and attract a loyal readership over the Internet. He was concerned that customers using the Internet would have to click through many pages to identify the desired material, and some customers would object to time-consuming searches with potential high opportunity costs.

When Erik began *The Fleet Sheet*, he firmly believed it would be a short-term operation until other sources of information became available. He had spent little time pondering the relative merits of alternative business legal structures. Erik had not considered the risk reduction and potential financial leverage benefits associated with limited liability company status for his business. When he established the business, Erik had not appreciated the need to develop a business plan to ensure business survival and growth. Erik began to wonder whether it was too late to adopt a limited liability company status for *The Fleet Sheet*, and whether

he should write a business plan associated with a formal long-term strategy for the business. If the latter options were selected, he knew he would have to fill out some forms and notify the U.S. government of his actions. Erik also wondered if the legal structure of *The Fleet Sheet* would have capital gains tax implications if he decided to sell the business. It had taken two weeks for Erik to launch the business; he never assumed that *The Fleet Sheet* would last this long, and he would have to spend more time planning than launching the business.

Erik's dilemma

Erik wondered if *The Fleet Sheet* could survive indefinitely into the future. He started to consider the factors that could ensure the survival of the business as a 'going concern'. Some foreign companies had already begun to close their offices in the Czech Republic because of the difficulties of doing business there, and some German banks were beginning to focus on economic development in Germany. Even if the multinationals decided to stay in the country and there continued to be a market for *The Fleet Sheet*, he wondered what format it might take in the future. Erik was concerned about the growing use of the Internet. The potentially quick, free and easy access to data on the Internet could make the service provided by *The Fleet Sheet* obsolete.

Erik also thought about future competition. Would other businesses try to offer the service offered by *The Fleet Sheet* at a lower price? Would subscribers be attracted by lower price even though the quality of the product might be inferior?

When Erik established *The Fleet Sheet* he believed that his former employer did not provide an adequate salary. After establishing the firm, he often speculated that it would be easy to close the business and to work for someone else. By the spring of 2007, the business was doing so well and he was making a very good salary, and this remuneration package could be difficult for an alternative employer to match.

Questions and issues

1 What are the difficulties associated with starting a private new business in a transition economy?

2 Prepare a strengths, weaknesses, opportunities and threats (SWOT) analysis relating to *The Fleet Sheet*.

3 Using Michael Porter's Five Forces Model, analyse the competitive position of *The Fleet Sheet*.

4 What are the key success factors associated with *The Fleet Sheet*?

5 What experience and skills did Erik Best accumulate and leverage to establish *The Fleet Sheet*?

6 How did Erik Best use discriminatory pricing with *The Fleet Sheet*, and upon what variable was the discount pricing based? Name other companies and industries that regularly use discount pricing strategy and identify variables (time, personal characteristics of customers, age, sex, etc.) upon which they base their

discounts. What possible inefficiencies or illegal activities by customers can develop as a result of such strategies?

7 How would you assess whether a venture is a 'going concern' or not? How will that consideration affect Erik Best's relationship to the business in the future?

8 Erik Best did not prepare a business plan when he established *The Fleet Sheet*. Under what circumstances would a business plan be imperative, and when would a business plan not be absolutely necessary?

BCH TeleCommunications
Marlene Mints Reed

Summary

This case discusses the start-up of a telephone call-back service company in the Czech Republic initiated by two Americans. The case outlines the problems associated with developing a new business overseas, particularly a firm perceived to be not fully legal in a transition economy context where the legal, financial and economic infrastructure was in a state of flux.

Introduction

For as long as he could remember, Jeff Welker had wanted to go into hospitality management. He completed high school in Glendale, California in the United States. Jeff decided to enter the programme at the University of Nevada at Las Vegas (UNLV). During his time at the university, he established many close relationships, including friendships with managers and directors of hotels in Las Vegas. With the conclusion of his work at UNLV, Jeff accepted a job as Assistant Convention Director at a Sheraton Hotel located in the Los Angeles area. Within the next three years, Jeff was promoted several times. He reflected:

> 'Part of it was being in the right place at the right time, and part of it was giving 120 per cent of myself. I had the people skills, the work ethic, morals, flexibility and ability to change when that was needed.'

Early entrepreneurial speculations

Jeff's family had some wealthy friends in California who commented:

> 'If you are ever going to be involved in some venture, come and talk with us. We would like to help with the financing.'

He filed this away in the back of his mind just in case something interesting did come along. After a couple of years, Jeff was transferred to the Sheraton Hotel in San Diego. He soon became friends with an older man who was a real estate developer in Los Angeles and Hawaii. In part, due to discussions with this man about opportunities in Hawaii, Jeff began contemplating putting together a project for a hotel there. For the next two years, Jeff worked concertedly on this plan. He even selected a parcel of land in Hawaii, talked to the owner of the land about his interest in putting a hotel there, and developed an aerial-shot video of the land to show to potential investors. In addition, he had a graphic artist overlay a sketch of the proposed hotel onto a photograph of the land. Jeff was now 26 years old, he had enough pledges to build a hotel in Hawaii, and he envisioned that his lifelong dream was about to become a reality.

However, this dream was not to be. He had made friends with a young lawyer from New York named Charles, who was tired of the gruelling hours in the large law firm in which he worked. Charles planned to quit his job in order to start his own business. Jeff was understandably startled when Charles asked him one day:

> 'Have you ever thought of building the hotel somewhere else for about 100 times less money? . . . Do you know anything about the Riviera – the Yugoslavian Riviera?'

Jeff admitted that he knew almost nothing about Yugoslavia, and he certainly did not know it had a Riviera. By a strange twist of fate, the travel section of the local newspaper had a 12-page article on the Yugoslavian Riviera the following weekend. Jeff read each word carefully and began doing some research on this part of the world. He went back to his investors and told them about this new opportunity, and they also became excited. Charles and Jeff began applying for visas. Unfortunately, a war had broken out in Yugoslavia before they could get there. This forced them to scrap the whole idea.

Four months later, Charles suggested that they should continue to concentrate on Eastern Europe where doors of opportunity were beginning to open for entrepreneurs. Charles proposed the idea of starting a bar and grill in Prague in what was then Czechoslovakia, which was viewed as the gateway between Eastern and Western Europe. Although he had never been there, Jeff had some knowledge of Czechoslovakia. Other circumstances in his life at the time caused him to rethink the future. He had moved from Sheraton Hotels to Marriott Hotels but now Marriott was in the process of restructuring. Jeff became uncomfortable with the changes he saw taking place. He decided Charles's idea was not so bad after all. Jeff quit his job and began serious research on the new project.

Research for the venture in Prague

Although a formal business plan was never developed, Jeff and Charles did spend some time researching the proposed project in Czechoslovakia. Charles had decided that in addition to the bar and grill that Jeff would run, he would like to start an import–export business in Prague because he had always been enamored by this type of operation. He had a hunch that this business might work in a country newly opened to Western goods.

Charles needed to know about the types of goods not available in Czechoslovakia. First, at home in the library of the University of California at San Diego, they did some research on Czechoslovakia. Also, they visited the Czech Consulate in Los Angeles. Then they flew to Washington, D.C. and talked to the Czech Embassy, the United States Commerce Department, the EXIM (Export–Import) Bank, and the IMF (International Monetary Fund). They searched for information relating to the economic climate in Czechoslovakia. The Czech Consulate and Embassy told them there was a demand for used blue jeans and used computers. This was before widespread utilisation of the Internet. Research had to be personally conducted in libraries and people's offices. Charles's law firm had a one-person office in Prague, and that lawyer provided knowledge about Czechoslovakia.

Jeff and Charles began exploring names for their embryonic company, and decided to use an acronym for the company name. After days of brainstorming they selected the acronym BCH, which was an abbreviation for 'beach', a place where Jeff had spent some of the best years of his life. Later that year, Jeff and Charles arrived in Prague to launch their business operations. Jeff secretly wondered just where BCH Enterprises would take these two entrepreneurial friends.

Economic developments in Czechoslovakia

In November 1989, Czechoslovakia experienced what would later be referred to as the 'Velvet Revolution'. In response to the pleas of students and nurses, the socialist government finally stepped down and handed the country over to the people. Great social, political and economic changes subsequently occurred in the newly freed nation. The disintegration of the former Council for Mutual Economic Co-operation (Comecon) was one of the most significant factors for change. The National Assembly elected Vaclav Havel as President of Czechoslovakia on 29 December 1989.

The primary constraint to any reform efforts on the part of Vaclav Havel and his new government was the fact that all industrial and agricultural production was owned by the state or state-dependent collective farms. The new Minister of Finance, Vaclav Klaus, proposed in February of 1990 a coupon privatisation project. By paying only a small administration fee, all Czechoslovakian citizens were given the opportunity to obtain a coupon book, which could be used to purchase shares in certain privatised concerns. The first coupon books were sold on 18 May 1992, with the result that 70 per cent of the population became shareholders. Following this, there was a project entitled 'Small Privatisation', which singled out smaller service and trade premises from state property and sold them at auction.

Another constraint to reform was the less than rapid integration of Czechoslovakia into the community of Western European states. Exporters in the Western European countries were delighted with the new opportunity to sell their goods in Czech markets, but they were disinclined to buy Czech goods. The former socialist economy was strongly oriented towards Comecon (a planned economy) and the Soviet Union. This had a negative effect on domestic production and caused the country to be non-competitive in world markets. The central planning commission stressed heavy industry and neglected the service sector entirely. Because of this, the Czech economy suffered a decrease in exports when Comecon was dissolved, and there was a loss of Eastern markets for their goods (Radomin, 1999).

Somehow the Czechoslovakian economy survived the breakup into the Czech Republic and Slovakia on 1 January 1993, and the collapse of markets in Eastern Europe. The country began to develop a greater orientation toward the markets of Western Europe, and more foreign firms began to enter the domestic Czech market (Pokorny, 1994).

The government bureaucracy had become a major barrier to the creation of new enterprises. The former state-owned banks were very slowly being privatised and new banks from other countries were beginning to enter the country. However, the experience of one company in what was once Russia is very similar to experiences of entrepreneurs in the Czech Republic. This new small business received the required 27 documents, many requiring notarisations, after a loan approval and before the money could be disbursed (Wallace, 1996).

Two separate Czech economies appeared to be developing by the middle 1990s. One was the economy in which new Czech entrepreneurs were attempting to establish new ventures. They had great difficulty obtaining bank loans. They obtained bank loans if they were prepared to accept a 30 per cent interest rate. Also, they had to break through the 'old boy network', which was a residual of the socialist state. And the other sector, which represented companies from Western countries that had access to banks outside the Czech Republic and well-skilled lawyers to assist with the bureaucracy, was experiencing great success.[1] It was within this economic climate that Jeff and Charles hoped to start a business.

Hurdles for the new business

Many foreign companies that made investments in the Czech Republic became frustrated with the difficulty of getting things taken care of in a timely manner. Every contract or piece of paper needed a stamp by someone to make it official. Sometimes the stamps were paper stamps that could be purchased at a post office, and sometimes they were the imprint of a rubber stamp.

[1]Conversation with Weston Stacey, Managing Director of the American Chamber of Commerce in the Czech Republic on 10 April 2000.

Jeff decided very early that he would not be daunted by such hurdles. He said to himself:

'Look at yourself. You're no longer in America. You must do everything on your own and accept that.'

Jeff believed that philosophy had saved him from many hours of anxiety fretting over the difficulty of moving processes along in his new country.

However, there were the hurdles that became insurmountable. With the import–export business, the hurdle was the incorrect information they had received from sources with whom they had consulted before entering the Czech Republic. Although they had been told by Czech sources that there was a great need for used computers in the Czech Republic, when they arrived they found that most people who wanted a computer already had one. In addition, although there was a great demand for used blue jeans as had been suggested, any jeans that were imported were either stolen at the border or, if they made it past the border, were burdened with a heavy duty being placed upon them by the Czech government. Therefore, BCH could not make a profit with prohibitive duties on their products.

With the restaurant business, there were insurmountable hurdles with the renovation of the building to house the eating and drinking establishment. Jeff and Charles signed a contract for a stated amount with one construction company only to have them come back later and suggest:

'We forgot to put doors and windows in our contract; and also there is water damage in the walls, and we have to fix that.'

They let this company go and signed a contract with another construction company who later said to them:

'Oh, we must add an additional $80,000 to the contract for electrical wiring, elevators and stairs.'

Jeff and Charles began to understand that the signing of contracts meant nothing, and the project would go well beyond their budget. They knew they could not continue to ask their investors to pour money into a black hole, so they gave up on the whole project. Jeff and Charles lost more than $40,000 on this project. Their deal with investors was that they would put $250,000 into the project, but they wanted Jeff and Charles to invest (and be willing to lose) the first $50,000. Jeff wondered if part of their problem might have sprung from the fact that neither of them spoke the Czech language and depended upon translators for all transactions.

An introduction to callback services

Jeff began doing some hospitality management consulting in Eastern Europe. Tourism had become a big business after the demise of communism. He identified that a substantial expense was the cost of telephone calls. The Czech Republic had a metered charge for local and long-distance calls. At the time, the long-distance calling fee was $3.50 USD a minute. Jeff first used AT&T, then Sprint, then another carrier, but the costs were still quite high.

On a trip back to the United States, Jeff read in a magazine about a 'Callback Service for International Calling'. As soon as Jeff landed, he called a representative of the company, WorldLink Callback, and asked him to explain the meaning of 'Callback Services'. This representative commented:

> 'You call from Prague to our computer in New York to a specially assigned telephone number, and you hang up before our computer answers. After this, the computer calls you back and offers you a dial tone, and then you dial as if you were in the United States . . . International rates in the United States are so much cheaper than the rest of the world, that they give you discounted rates.'

When Jeff tried the process, it did not work exactly in the way stated by the representative. In 1992, only one out of ten phone calls worked in Czechoslovakia. Moreover, 99 per cent of telephones in Czechoslovakia had rotary dials. When Jeff and Charles signed up for the service, they needed a touch-tone phone; but they had to bring one with them from the United States. Then they had to obtain an adaptor to make it work.

One day the Chief Executive Officer (CEO) of the company that offered callback services called them, and he asked if they would like the licence for the service with regard to Eastern Europe. Jeff immediately responded that they were not interested because:

> 'Your service doesn't work; and if you want to know why, I will be glad to tell you.'

The CEO responded:

> 'Would you be interested if we got the service working?'

Jeff said they might be interested. The CEO provided an engineer to listen to their complaints. When Jeff hung up the telephone, he said to Charles:

> 'When people call you peddling a service, it turns you off. I have never liked selling, and I certainly didn't come to Prague to be a salesman.'

Unlike Charles, Jeff was doing some hospitality consulting. Jeff believed income could be generated by a new consultancy venture. Because the new venture would be primarily speaking with representatives from Western companies, the lack of fluency in the Czech language would not be a hindrance. The growing number of Western companies doing business in the Czech Republic provided an excellent customer base for this service.

As much as Jeff hated the idea of calling people and convincing them that they needed to buy their product, he and Charles reluctantly accepted the licensing and marketing agreement for the callback services in Eastern Europe. WorldLink Callback would be the first company to offer this service in Eastern Europe.

Charles began immediately working on the project in the May of 1993. Within four months, he had signed up 60 people. Charles went back to the United States for two weeks and he asked Jeff to contact the firms he had sent information to relating to their services. Jeff made the follow-up calls. He telephoned people who had recently signed up for their service and asked, 'How is the service doing?' At the time, the service provided by Czech Telecom (the former Czech monopoly) was poor. It took ten tries to get one call through. However, people using the service provided by Charles and Jeff reported a call got through seven out of ten times. His customers were very pleased with the service. All the companies that had received information from Charles indicated that they wanted to sign up for the service. All of this happened within 30 minutes, and Jeff was astounded.

After completing the calls, Jeff picked up the English language newspaper named the *The Prague Post*, which provided a synopsis of what was going on in Prague. He saw some advertisement placed by large multinational companies doing business in the Czech Republic. On a whim, Jeff randomly called some of the companies in order to explain the callback services provided by Charles and Jeff. The common response to his calls was:

> 'How fast can you send information and have a meeting with us?'

Jeff hurriedly sent the information to the companies, met with them soon afterwards and very quickly signed them up for the service.

After Charles's return, Jeff decided to focus on the large multinational companies while Charles would focus on the smaller companies. Charles concurred with this suggestion. At this juncture, the name 'BCH TeleCommunications' (see Appendix 1) was allocated to the business dealing with callback services.

Competition faced by BCH TeleCommunications

The company's biggest competitor was Czech Telecom, which was the state-owned telephone company. In the former centrally-planned economy of Czechoslovakia, the government had a monopoly in all industries. There was no private enterprise. Unlike the situation in the United States where a Consent Agreement had been signed by AT&T in the early 1980s to break up the company (i.e., monopoly) into a number of smaller regional local calling companies, which promoted competition with regard to the long-distance calling market. The transition in Czechoslovakia was slow because the legal and economic infrastructure necessary to move to a free market system was cumbersome. Czech Telecom refused to believe that it would be possible for another company to compete with them.

Soon after BCH TeleCommunications began offering callback services, the Czech government and Czech Telecom contacted Jeff and Charles, and threatened to deport them. They presented the young men with official documents with the required number of stamps on them and said:

'You must leave the country in 60 days.'

Jeff and Charles consulted with their Czech lawyer who said:

'They may make your life more difficult, but you have done nothing wrong.'

These two relatively naive young Americans soon discovered that competition may come in several guises, and some may actually threaten your well-being. Jeff mulled over the view that every entrepreneur must know the competition and understand how to survive in the midst of competition.

Often when Jeff would give information about their company to potential customers, they would ask:

'This is great. Does it break any laws?'

Jeff would assure them that it did not. However, when potential customers called Czech Telecom, they would assure them that BCH TeleCommunications was breaking the law. Some potential customers believed that the new firm was an illegal operation.

Jeff became aware later that other countries, including the United States, did not always view this new process as enthusiastically as he did. Often the established operator community in a country publicly and legally took a dim view, claiming in various ways that the services actually constituted a wire fraud. Revenues they were unable to collect relating to the use of their assets troubled the operator community. Also, they suggested that it circumnavigated their international conventions for settlement. Operators in Argentina and several African states had attempted to block the switching techniques that enable callback hardware to capture identification codes and re-route calls (Liebmann, 1997).

Jeff was aware that there was a growing interest, even in the Czech Republic, in substitute products such as e-mail and fax messages, which were low-cost alternatives to long-distance calling and competitors for callback services. He appreciated that the telephone companies had a bright future. Unlike his company they were not tied to one long-distance communication product. Moreover, the market for communication was growing. In 1995, the world spent 60 billion minutes communicating by phone, fax and data, four times the amount spent just a decade ago (Morton, 1996).

An issue raised by BCH TeleCommunications operation was international comity. International comity is based on the principle of respect.

'Comity is implicated where domestic and foreign laws conflict. When a conflict occurs, a country must decide whether to respect the foreign law or to enforce its own domestic law. In making such a decision, the domestic body balances domestic public interests against international considerations. The domestic body is under no obligation to abide by the foreign law; the decision of whether to respect foreign law is entirely discretionary.' (Silber, 1996.)

Jeff reasoned that these potential problems might put a constraint on callback services.

The company grows and takes on more staff

BCH TeleCommunications soon began to represent other telecommunications companies such as Sprint, Direct Net, Axcom, and Dial International (DIT) who did not have a representative in Eastern Europe. They expanded the operations of BCH TeleCommunications into Poland, Slovakia and Hungary. In addition, Jeff expanded his hospitality management consulting into

Slovakia and Hungary. The Office of the Ministry of Finance identified BCH as one of the top new companies in the Czech Republic (see Appendix 2). They sought Jeff's advice surrounding how to help Czech entrepreneurs succeed.

Jeff speculated that the success of BCH TeleCommunications was due to cheaper telephone services offered, and the good technical support provided to their customers. The company hired an engineer just to work on technical problems and help with future business expansion plans. Jeff noted that over 50 per cent of their new business came from referrals by satisfied customers.

BCH TeleCommunications had excellent staff. Ivana Svobodova, for example, started as a receptionist and within months she was a sales associate before becoming a director of the company. She was the person that Jeff relied upon to give a realistic assessment of the operations in the Czech Republic. Ivana was a Czech and she knew better than Jeff what would work and what would not work in the Czech Republic. She was a native speaker and could assist with Jeff's learning of the Czech language. Also, Ivana was a trustworthy translator.

Crisis for Jeff Welker

Jeff Welker noted that their callback service operations had grown by 150 per cent since he and Charles had become involved with them two years ago. He had heard that callback services in general were growing at a rate of 15 per cent a month. BCH TeleCommunications operations were growing in Poland and Hungary, and Charles wanted to take over the business operations in Poland. However, Charles became increasingly unhappy and frustrated in the business and with his relationship with Jeff. He left a letter for Jeff telling him that he was leaving the business and that he was taking around $150,000 in cash with him. Jeff felt that the rug had been pulled from underneath him. He normally had a very positive outlook on life but this setback seriously upset him.

With no money in the bank and all of his legal documents gone, Jeff considered filing for bankruptcy. Under the former Socialist state, 'bankruptcy' was a word that no one mentioned. Central planning had always provided an easy way out for money-losing enterprises. Under the new government, bankruptcy was beginning to play a role; however, the process was not working well. Usually, for struggling companies, a hint

of the possibility of insolvency meant scrambling to hide assets before creditors noticed. The 1991 Bankruptcy Act was based on rules dating back to the Austro-Hungarian Empire. It had been amended ten times, and parliament, bankers and unions were discussing additional amendments.

Jeff had to take a hard look at the future of the callback service. Although the offering of this service had been extremely profitable, he wondered about the growth of alternative means of communication. Jeff read that the total revenues for callback would increase from $200 million in 1994 to $2 billion by 1998. A recent article suggested the problem of market saturation. In 1990, there had been only six callback operations in North America but this had increased to over 200. They all offered consumers in numerous countries cheaper (and even illegal) international phone and fax calls (Scheele, 1995).

The Federal Communications Commission in Washington in the United States was aware of the disparity in international dialling rates. They were considering new pricing rules that would force foreign carriers to lower their rates or face possible punitive measures. Increased competition for callback services was viewed as a mechanism to encourage other countries to comply (Shiver, 1996).

Jeff walked to the Metro station near to his office and took the train to the Mustek Station and got off. He heard the strains of Mozart floating from a nearby music shop, and he thought what a rich cultural town this was and how he would hate to leave it. Jeff wondered to himself how he could survive and make the business prosper with no money to pay his staff and creditors. He also wondered if this would be a good time to move into a related business that would have greater prospects for profitability in the future. Jeff recognised that the Czech Telecom monopoly (with 27 per cent of the equity owned by Swiss and Dutch investors) could be broken up, and competition from other companies would be welcomed.

Questions and issues

1 Explain the advantage of preparing a business plan before launching a new business.

2 List and discuss the key success factors relating to BCH TeleCommunications.

3 Jeff hated selling, but he loved representing the callback services operation. What is the difference?

4 Charles has left the country and taken all the company's liquid assets with him. What should Jeff do now?

5 What concerns does this case raise for people considering starting a new business in a foreign country?

References

Liebmann, L. (1997). The Siren Song of Callback Services. *International Business*, March, pp. 37–38.

Morton, P. (1996). Dialing for Dollars: Callback Companies Give Consumers Great Long Distance Rates, But They Pluck Revenues from Foreign Phone Systems. *Financial Post*, 19 October, p. 16.

Pokorny, J. (1994). *The Czech Lands 1918–1997*. Prague, Czech Republic: Prah Press, pp. 4l–46.

Radomin, J. (1999). An Overview of the Czech Republic. *Czech Republic Business Guide*, pp. 2–6.

Scheele, M. J. (1995). You Can't Beat the Price. *Telephony*, March, pp. 65–70.

Shiver, J, Jr (1996). FCC, Phone Firms Take Notice as Callback Industry Expands. *The Los Angeles Times*, 13 September, p. D-1.

Silber, S. C. (1996). The FCC's Call-Back Order: Proper Respect for International Comity. *The George Washington Journal of International Law and Economics*, pp. 97–125.

Wallace, E. (1996). *Financial Institutional Development – The Case of the Russian Small Business Fund. Small Business in Transition Economies.* London: Intermediate Technology Publications Ltd, pp. 76–84.

Appendix 1 BCH TeleCommunications DirectDial Services

BCH **DirectDial** services are international telephone services that can save up to 42% on your international calls.

There are many added values when using BCH DirectDial Services:
• Best rates.
• No monthly fees.
• Direct Dialing to all countries worldwide.
• 24 hour unbeatable customer service.
• Many different kind of connections to fit the needs of customers.
• Detailed call record every month for free.
• Easy billing in CZK, USD or by major credit card.

Joining **BCH DirectDial** Service is easy. We will need only this information:
• Where the client wishes his billing information to be sent.
• The currency the client wishes to pay with.
• The local numbers to be connected.

This routing creates two legs for each call:
• The first is charged by the local telecom.
• The second charged by BCH at tremendous discounts.

BCH DirectDial Service is one of many top-quality services offered by BCH TeleCommunications. Please call us for more information about **DirectDial** and the many other attractive products and services available from Central Europe's leader in discount international telecommunications.

BCH Corporate Business Center * Sokolovska 156 * 180 00 Praha 8 * Czech Republic Tel. (420 2) 683 1310 * Fax (420 2) 683 5052 * E-mail: bch-tel@ini.cz

Appendix 2 Financial history of BCH TeleCommunications ($000s)

1992	
Revenues from restaurant	0
Revenues from consulting	0
Total revenues	0
Expenses of restaurant	$15,000
Profit (Loss)	(−$15,000)

Note: Restaurant – there never was any money generated from the restaurant because contract disputes prevented the building from being completed. The owners spent much of this year finding a place to develop (location, architect, contractor, etc.). General – they used most of their time getting themselves established in the business community (networking and getting involved in the expatriate community).

1993	
Revenues from consulting	$10,000
Revenues from telecom	50,000
Total revenues	$60,000
Expenses of restaurant	35,000
Expenses of telecom	12,000
Expenses of consulting	1,000
Profit (Loss)	$12,000

Note: Consulting – the company established a hospitality and communications consulting arm of the firm. The primary targets were the hospitality industry and the service industry (i.e., real estate, law firms, and grocery stores). Telecom – at the beginning of this year, the company broke into the telecom market offering discount callback services. BCH was the first to offer such services in the region, and they gained about 100 customers in their first year. They worked out of Jeff's apartment and began a full advertising/marketing campaign.

1994	
Revenues from consulting	$ 25,000
Revenues from telecom	105,000
Total revenues	$130,000
Expenses of consulting	$ 3,000
Expenses of telecom	154,000
Profit (Loss)	(−$27,000)

Note: Consulting – this part of the business grew well and kept Jeff busy all of the time. The company expanded its activities into Slovakia and Hungary (for specific clients). Much of this revenue (which was almost pure profit) was supporting loans, paying many of the company's past bills and financing the marketing efforts of the telecom division. Telecom – this project continued to grow very rapidly. At the end of the year, the partners decided to work on their own. Instead of making a commission for another firm, BCH would actually buy and sell their own international time from large telecom carriers. In addition, they took on a third partner for additional expansion. He was an expatriate who had lived in Prague for two years. Four full-time sales staff were added and they moved into a large office complex. One postgraduate (from graduate school) was added on a one-year internship to assist with the think-tank process of expanding. They were actively marketing their services in Hungary.

1995	
Revenue from consulting	$31,000
Revenue from telecom	175,000
Total revenues	206,000
Expenses of consulting	3,000
Expenses of telecom	217,000
Profit (Loss)	$(-\$14,000)$

Note: Consulting – this continued to generate revenue that was used to support the expansion efforts of the telecom division. The partners had decided that it was not necessary to continue to grow this division. They sought to maintain it and use it as a networking effort to further support the telecom division. Telecom – the company moved to a private office from the office complex where they obtained more space at a cheaper rental cost. BCH added two more post graduates (from graduate school), which were on one-year internships. They expanded their services portfolio to include an international calling card. This proved to be successful for the next two to three years. The sales team grew by an additional two staff, and then they added two full-time customer service staff. At the end of the year, the third partner was asked to leave the firm. This added a large financial burden to the bottom line in order to pay his severance costs. The company expanded into Poland and established a full office. One of the partners was stationed in Poland 85 per cent of the time. BCH began working with three telecom service providers. These were firms through whom they bought and sold telecom time. This allowed BCH to add more services to its portfolio.

1996	
Revenues from consulting	$17,000
Revenues from telecom	180,000
Revenues from glass/crystal	3,000
Total revenues	200,000
Expenses of consulting	1,000
Expenses of telecom	39,000
Expenses of glass/crystal	70,000
Profit (Loss)	$ 90,000

Note: This year was associated with considerable change. Consulting – this division wound down its activities. The company began to concentrate all of its efforts on the telecom division. This had been very enjoyable for Jeff and a good money maker, but he no longer had enough time for all of its activities. Telecom – there was considerable unrest in this division as it continued to grow. All three interns left the firm because they were disgruntled with the overall direction and management of BCH. One of the primary partners – Charles – decided to leave BCH permanently; he removed all his financial assets in the firm when he left the country. This generated an enormous financial burden on the company operations. At the end of the year, there were only two employees on the payroll. Three additional employees stayed on for four months without any pay. Class/crystal – BCH decided to start up a new project of exporting glass and crystal to the United States and Canada.

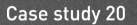

Case study 20

UFO Pictures: The challenges of film production

Marlene Mints Reed

Summary

This case describes the decisions that Jefe[1] Brown, a United States expatriate[2] living in the Czech Republic, had to make concerning the raising of money to fund his small film production company. This case also illustrates the decisions he made relating to the most efficient and cost-effective way to distribute his films. Jefe had grown up in Texas and attended Texas A&M University where he received a degree in European Art History. Jefe had been enamoured of art films since he was a teenager and longed to produce some small films himself. He relocated to the Czech Republic after the Velvet Revolution and taught English for a while. Then he began to put together a small film production company. By the summer of 2007, Jefe had already produced several films that had been critically acclaimed. He used finance from family, friends and his own personal savings to fund his films. However, Jefe knew that these sources of finance would not be sufficient in the future if he intended to continue making films. Jefe also realised that he needed to be able to control the distribution of his films more ably than he had done in the past.

Introduction

On 21 June 2007, Jefe Brown put down his copy of the *Prague Post* and looked into the large cup of latte sitting in front of him, and he wished it were a crystal ball. Jefe knew he was at a crossroads with his film production company. He folded the paper and walked out of the door of the Ebel Coffee House near Old Town Square ('Staromeska') in Prague in the Czech Republic, and tried to develop in his mind a plan for raising money in the future. Jefe had just turned 36 and he loved film production. He had to figure out a way to fund and make money on future films by the end of the year, or else he would be forced out of the industry.

Jefe Brown's background

Jefe Brown grew up in Arlington, Texas. After completing high school, he entered Texas A&M University in College Station, Texas, where he pursued a degree in European Art History. Jefe was never a stereotypical Texas college student. His tastes and interests were not consistent with those that often characterised young men in the southern part of the United States. The majority of A&M students, or 'Aggies' after the 'A' in A&M which stood for 'Agricultural and Mechanical', spent countless hours collecting wood for the famous A&M bonfire before the (American) football game with Texas University. In contrast, Jefe initiated a protest to stop the bonfire, which he perceived as being dangerous to those who put it together. Whereas most college students were interested in the latest Hollywood films shown in the College Station Metroplex, Jefe was driving to Houston, Dallas, or Austin to see the latest films shown in the few art houses located in those cities.

Jefe was greatly influenced by the Czech New Wave films of the 1960s. This group of protest films preceded and greatly influenced the Prague Spring uprising.[3] Two Milos Forman films, *Closely-Watched Trains* and *Loves*

---

[1] Prounounced 'Hefa'. A Spanish word meaning 'boss'.
[2] One who has left their country of birth and nationality to live in another country.

[3] The 'Prague Spring' occurred in February 1968 and was an unsuccessful student-led uprising against the communist government in Czechoslovakia.

of a Blonde (both Oscar winners for best foreign film) were influential in shaping Jefe's interest in the small film. American and European independent films also influenced him.

Jefe believed he could not live with a 9 to 5 job. His two brothers lived in Germany and he wanted to travel. While at high school, he travelled to the United Kingdom and Europe in order to play soccer. This whetted his appetite for more travel.

During his years at A&M, Jefe helped run a programme out of his house called 'Students for Czechoslovakia'. This programme sent students to Czechoslovakia to teach English.

Jefe's roommate had gone to Prague in the early 1990s, and he decided to follow his lead. He packed up his belongings and left for Czechoslovakia in September 1993. Jefe ended up in Jablonec and Nison, a Bohemian town in the mountainous area of northern Czechoslovakia. He taught business and conversational English in a private language school to employees of businesses in the town. Most of the money he had made from his job was spent on travelling around the country.

His arrival in the country in 1993 coincided with the breaking up of Czechoslovakia into the Czech Republic and Slovakia. Czechoslovakia had experienced the Velvet Revolution in 1990. This resulted in the Czech communist president turning over the keys of government to Vaclav Havel, the outspoken writer who had been a political dissenter for many years.

After a couple of years, Jefe secured a teaching position at a pedagogical university in Brno named after Thomas Masyryk, the first president of Czechoslovakia after World War I. Brno was a much larger town than the one where he had lived when he first arrived in the Czech Republic. At Masyryk University he taught language, literature and a translation class. He remained in Brno for four years. While teaching in Brno, Jefe co-created a CD Rom entitled *Czech for Foreigners* with a freshman at Masyryk University. Many of these CDs were sold to businesses.

During two summers while he was teaching in Brno, he went to Bosnia and worked with the Organisation for Security and Co-operation in Europe (OSCE), which was similar to the United Nations in its mission. Jefe worked as an election observer for two elections for the OSCE. He was there during and after the war between the Serbs and Croatians. Jefe decided to produce a documentary on the war, which he named *Collateral Damage*. The film dealt with the damage suffered by

surrounding countries such as Bulgaria, Romania, Macedonia and Serbia precipitated by the bombing in Bosnia. The film cost him $10,000 to produce, and it was previewed at the United Nations Human Rights Festival.

In 1999, he contributed articles to Central Europe Online (CEO), which was a well-visited website. Jefe accepted the job as editor-in-chief and he moved to Prague, the capital of the Czech Republic. He ran a small operation for them. Jefe was more interested in being in the field than being in an office. CEO covered stories in the Czech Republic, Poland, Hungary, Romania, and the Balkans. Later the stories published on this site were written by news agencies encapsulating the news. Because his documentary script for *Collateral Damage* was so well received at a number of film festivals, he left CEO and went out on his own as a small film producer.

Literary influences on the Prague Spring

For many years, Czech writers had been philosophers. They often commented on public affairs to a greater extent than politicians could, or would, because their consciences demanded it. The same was true of progressive film-makers and other people in the theatre and arts in the middle years of the twentieth century. The following key cultural developments supported a 'critical thinking' philosophy:

- The emergence of a 'new wave' in the Czechoslovakian cinema;
- The dispute about the recognition and understanding of Franz Kafka (the free-thinking writer);
- The emergence and flourishing of modern Czechoslovakian drama and of a modern concept of the theatre; and
- The discussions about the essence of a socialist 'cultural policy'.

UFO Pictures

From 2000 to 2003, Jefe spent time as a script writer for commercials and small films and he was the production assistant on these films. It soon became clear to him that he needed to produce some films on his own. Jefe worked on a Cuban film project with a friend, David Rauch. David was a Czech who had been born in Cuba. He had worked on an earlier film named *Kolya* that won the Oscar in 1994 for Best Foreign Film.

Jefe had raised some money to produce the Cuban film, but he later decided to invest the money in another film project called *Rex-Patriots*. This film was a mockumentary (mock documentary) about a group of expatriates who left Prague but returned for a second chance of success there. Jefe described the shooting of *Rex-Patriots* in this way:

'A lot of the film was guerrilla shooting. We didn't have time to get the proper permissions, so cast and crew would quickly descend on a spot and film the scene.'

The film premiered at the Rome Film Festival and received good notices from CNN and *Variety*. It was a hit in Prague because most of the expatriate community who were not in it came out to see who *was* in it.

In 2002, Jefe formed a limited liability company (LLC) in Texas called Peligroso. Then in 2003, Jefe formed UFO Pictures with two other film producers. In addition, he worked on projects outside the confines of UFO. He independently raised the finance to fund the relatively small scale *Rex-Patriots* production, which involved 30 actors and 10 crew members. The film cost approximately $40,000 to produce.

UFO Pictures also produced a number of interesting musical films including the Nick Cave (a rock star) concert film entitled *The Myth* and *Call of Dudy: Bohemian Bagpipes Across Borders*.

Peligroso Productions raised money for a film that Jefe produced in 2004 named *Shut Up and Shoot Me*. The film was an association of three production companies, namely, Storitel, Peligroso Productions and UFO Pictures. UFO did the 'service production', which means they got the crew together and organised the physical production. UFO Pictures did not raise the money or distribute the film. Jefe decided that UFO Pictures would solely produce any future significant production.

Jefe likened his films to two American cult films, *The Rocky Horror Show* and *Spinal Tap*. These films were shown in a limited number of theatres but had had a strong following since their premières.

Shut Up and Shoot Me was a British–Czech black comedy about a suicidal Englishman, Colin, who hired a down-on-his-luck Czech to kill him. The film won the Best Film Award at the Cherbourg International Film Festival, and the Variety Critics' Choice at the Karlovy Vary International Film Festival. It was also granted the privilege of being positioned as the Opening Film at the Galway International Film Festival. The writing and direction for the film was by Steen Agro, and a strong working relationship between Agro and Jefe was established.

Jefe found it best to shoot his productions on Super 16 rather than 35 millimetre film. To ensure high quality footage he shot on cellular and not digital. A producer was required to blow up Super 16 to 35 millimetre for the theatre. However, Super 16 was half as expensive to shoot. If television acquired the distribution rights to a film, it would be shown on Beta, and the producer would not have lost money on a 35 millimetre shoot. Jefe believed that the two most difficult aspects of running a small film production company related to raising finance and finding a good distributor. These issues are discussed, in turn, below.

Raising seed finance

Jefe learned a great deal about how people feel about money when he sought to raise finance for his films. He first invested his own savings, and then he went to family and friends; and the experience was like riding a roller coaster. Jefe felt like he was asking for a handout, but it was an exhilarating trip when the money came in. The bottom line was that he had to ask himself:

'Who could I talk to and they wouldn't freak out? Who had money and the right attitude – who could get excited about the project? They were investing in my learning, and they respected that. There is nothing more risky to invest in than films. People usually invest in everything but films.'

He soon found that raising finance for a small film was similar to raising finance for any small start-up venture (see Figure 1).

Finding a good distributor

Normally a producer would hire a sales agent to find distributors for a film in different countries. Film distributors were independent companies, which acted as the final agent between a film production company, or some intermediary sales agent, and a film exhibitor. The primary agenda of the distribution was to convince the exhibitor to rent or 'book' each film in its theatre or theatres. In order to achieve this goal, the distributor often arranged industry screenings for exhibitors to convince them that the film would be profitable to show.

After the booking was accomplished, the distributor then secured a written contract that would state the amount of gross ticket sales to be paid to them. This was usually a percentage of the gross sales after the exhibitor had deducted a 'floor', which is called a 'house allowance'. Then the distributor would collect the amount due and audit the exhibitor's ticket sales to ensure that the amount reported for gross sales was accurate.

During the early part of the twentieth century, the large studios used the studio system. Under this system, the large studios produced and distributed their own films to the theatres they also owned (i.e., vertical integration). Today, large holding companies rather than the studios now own the theatres.

Jefe found that the sales agents were very difficult people to deal with. Small films had to go to film festivals to get a viewing. However, sales agents did not want to take films to festivals because the expenses of doing so came out of their fees. Sales agents usually had a film on the top shelf for about four months. During that time, they vigorously pushed the film to distributors. After that, the film went in their catalogue and received very little attention.

The normal process in distributing a film relates to the producer, the sales agent and then the distributor. Sometimes the sales agent would package a desired film with two undesirable films to encourage the distributor to take all the films. However, sometimes a well-known producer was able to go directly to the distributor and avoid the sales agent. Jefe learned a painful early lesson with regard to paying a sales agent up front for distribution rights to one of his films. After collecting the money, there was no incentive for the sales agent to continue pushing the film to distributors. Normally payment went to the sales agent after the film had been shown. Therefore, the real challenge for a small film producer is to ensure their name is known in the industry. Producers with high levels of credibility can take their films directly to distributors in order to reduce the costs and delays associated with employing sales agents.

The independent film production industry

Funding an independent film

The film-makers Ascher and Pincus suggested that:

'Independent film-making is usually defined as working outside a studio or other large organisation that bankrolls and controls your work. But even if you're on salary with a large corporation, you may still need to convince others to fund your project. Raising money can be one of the most arduous and painful parts of making a movie.'
(Liehm, 1967.)

There was a considerable difference in funding for a small film production company and a major production company such as Columbia Pictures or Paramount.

A small film company may be only able to raise finance for a proposed film from personal savings and friends and family. Conversely, a film producer working for a large company such as Paramount may simply propose a plan for a film and then compete with other producers for funding. The major studios spend an average of $20 million per picture, and they fund about eight to fifteen pictures a year. They fund and distribute their movies. A small film producer, however, has to secure a sales agent who then finds a distributor for the film. The sales agent and the distributor take a percentage of each film's revenues, and a small proportion of the revenues are left for the independent film-maker.

Guy Kawasaki, who worked for Apple Computer and developed the Macintosh Computer using the resources of that company, suggested that in every industry there are a number of differences between being an entrepreneur in a start-up venture and an entrepreneur exerting an entrepreneurial influence in a large company (Kawasaki, 2004).

Before seeking finance for a new venture, the film-maker has to first develop a budget for the project. The rule-of-thumb percentages in the motion picture industry relating to film expenses (Russo, 1989) are shown in Table 1.

Once the budget has been developed, the independent film producer has to seek the funding for the project. Sometimes seed or development money can be obtained to develop the idea or a script. Personal savings and friends and family are generally used (see Figure 1). Some independent producers contact business angel investors and/or formal venture capital firms who invest in ventures associated with high levels of profitability. Approximately a third of all film projects supported by venture capital firms make money for the investors.

In order to raise finance, some independent producers form a limited liability corporation (LLC). The investors supply the finance but the film producer retains

Table 1 Expenses in the motion picture industry

Item	Percentage of expenses
Story and screenplay	5
Producer and director	5
Cast	20
Studio overheads	20
Crew and materials	35
Taxes	5
Contingencies	10
Total	100

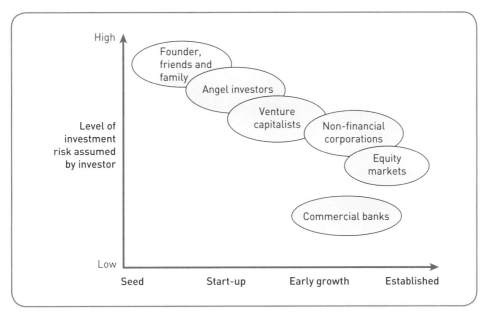

Figure 1 Sources of finance for each venture stage

Source: Van Osnabrugge, M. and Robinson, R. J. (2000). *Angel Investing*. San Francisco, California: Jossey-Bass Publishing Company, p. 37.

control of the project. A limited partnership (LP) is another option for raising finance. In this type of arrangement, at least one partner has to be a general partner with unlimited liability. In addition, one or more limited partners have liabilities in the company limited to the amount of their investment. A limited partner does not have a voice in running the company.

Government grants are sometimes provided to fund small projects. In the European Union (EU), the EU Media Net allocates grants to film-makers to produce films. These grants are for film development and not film production. In the United States, some states grant money to film producers to encourage the filming of movies in those states. In the Czech Republic, Slovakia and Poland, for example, governments have provided funds to movie producers to encourage film production in their countries in the early years of the twenty-first century. Some countries have also provided tax incentives to film producers; unfortunately, the Czech Republic did not do this.

Distribution of revenues from independent films

The distribution of revenues from independent films has always been a complicated affair. Novice film producers quickly learn the difference between 'gross' and 'net' revenues. If a producer signed a contract that

promised them 50 per cent of the net earnings of the film, that producer received half of the money left over from the ticket sales after the distributor paid off all the office help, their salary, advertising costs, printing and promotion, travel expenses for the distribution representative to foreign film festivals, cab fares, business lunches, and expensive dinners (Schmidt, 1995). Figure 2 shows the typical process of distribution of revenues from a film relating to an independent film producer.

Jefe ponders his decision

As Jefe walked along the cobblestones of the Old Town Square in Prague, he remembered the words of the renowned film director Marcel Carne:

> 'The problem is that to be a producer, one must be a gambler. And the greatest French producers were gamblers.'

Jefe wondered if he was a gambler, or simply someone who was willing to take a reasonable risk. He speculated on the difference between an entrepreneur and a gambler.

Jefe knew the next few years would be critical ones for his career. He could not imagine returning to the United States at this point in his life. His life seemed firmly planted in the Czech Republic where the film industry was still fun. However, the only way he could stay here as

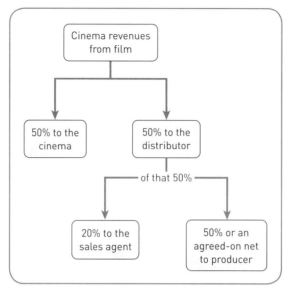

Figure 2 Distribution of revenues from independent films

a film producer would be to devise a plan to secure funding for his films, and a more stable process for their distribution. At this point in his film career, Jefe knew he had exhausted the funds available from his own savings, family and friends for underwriting his films in the future. He passed in front of the Town Hall as the astronomical clock began to strike the hour, and the apostles gallantly marched forth from their hiding place behind the face of the clock. The chiming of the hour reminded him once again how quickly he had to formulate his plan.

Questions and issues

1 How did Jefe Brown's background (i.e., personality, education, hobbies and organisations) equip him to be an international entrepreneur? Which, specifically, do you think had the greatest influence?

2 Discuss Jefe Brown's method of raising finance. Was a typical method of raising finance for a new firm followed? Did the type of venture being pursued impact on the obstacles he faced raising finance?

3 What are the greatest challenges facing a typical small film producer?

4 Outline a plan of action that Jefe Brown might follow with regard to raising finance for his film productions in the future.

5 Describe a strategy that Jefe Brown could pursue to ensure his films are distributed in the future.

6 Compare the finance raising and film distribution of a small film producer with the same activities of a producer working within the organisation of a large production company such as Paramount or Columbia.

7 How does your answer to Question 6 compare to the experience of an independent entrepreneur trying to secure funding and distribution of a new product (i.e., Guy Kawasaki, who worked within the structure of Apple Computers to develop and distribute the Macintosh)?

References

Ascher, S. and Pincus, E. (1999). *The Filmmaker's Handbook*. New York: Penguin Books USA, Inc., Frontispiece.

Kawasaki, G. (2004). *The Art of the Start*. London: Penguin Group.

Liehm, A. J. (1967). *Speech at the 4th Writers' Congress*.

Russo, J. (1989). *Making Movies*. New York: Dell Publishing.

Schmidt, R. (1995). *Feature Filmmaking at Used-Car Prices*. New York: Penguin Books USA, Inc., Frontispiece.

Van Osnabrugge, M. and Robinson, R. J. (2000). *Angel Investing*. San Francisco, California: Jossey-Bass Publishing Company.

Case study 21

New Covent Garden Soup Company: Contributions made by venture capitalists

Mike Wright

Summary

This case discusses the New Covent Garden Soup company, a new company seeking to develop its management team and scale-up its operations. The case illustrates the role of the venture capitalist in investing in an early stage venture which, after a period of major problems, subsequently showed significant growth.

Introduction

The entrepreneur, Andrew Palmer, did not have any experience in the food processing industry. He had previously worked as a stockbroker in the City of London. Palmer's main hobby was sailing his single-person dinghy. Whilst living at home with his mother and sister, he had the idea for the soup in his bath. Unlike tinned or dried soups, New Covent Garden Soup (NCGS) is a fresh soup. The soup is sold in supermarkets and can be eaten chilled or heated. The soup is named after London's main wholesale vegetable market. His company had begun to develop a management team. Palmer obtained advice from a consultant. In return, the former consultant was given shares worth £30,000 in the business, and he had been allocated the general manager position. NCGS also had a production director but he did not have a background in operations management.

Product development and launch

Two-and-a-half years of product and process development conducted between 1985 and 1987 was followed by production trials. In early 1988, the product was launched into independent retail outlets. By mid-1988, the first multiple retail outlet customer was obtained. Other key major retail grocery chains, such as Tesco and Waitrose, were added throughout the year. At this point, NCGS was operating out of leased premises and employed 17 people. The company was selling 8,500 cases of soup per month with the break-even point being 11,000 cases per month.

The initial development work for the soup was conducted in the entrepreneur's mother's kitchen using fresh, seasonal, vegetables. Subsequently, production moved to modestly-sized leased premises. In order to expand production, equipment had to be acquired, which was capable of producing sufficient quantities of the soup to appropriate levels of hygiene. Given the newness of the product concept, the required equipment could not simply be purchased. Commercially available equipment had to be adapted. Once this production problem was resolved it was thought that attractive production economics were available for high volume continuous output production as well as low volume batch production.

The entrepreneur's sister, who had design experience, designed the initial packaging for the soup. NCGS was able to test the market for the new flavours of soup. They promoted each flavour as a 'soup of the month'. A soup was withdrawn if it was associated with poor sales.

Bacterial infection in pre-prepared fresh foods is a major concern to retailers. An important technical advance was made by NCGS with regard to the preparation of the soup. The company developed a mechanism which signalled and warned the consumer if the soup was no longer edible.

Market growth

By the end of 1988, NCGS had become the clear brand leader in an emerging market due to quality product, technological innovation, and strong brand identity and design. The product provided home-made quality and due to the innovation noted above, for which a patent application was pending, it offered an extended shelf life with no use of preservatives.

In the United Kingdom, the manufactured soup market was well established. Some 92 per cent of households served soup regularly, with canned soup taking

44 per cent of the market and dried package soup taking a further 26 per cent. Soup products were highly accepted by households but market analysis suggested the market was stagnant. However, in the United Kingdom many households increasingly had two adults working full time. It was thought that there might be a market opportunity to sell an attractive, quickly prepared food product. The general chilled ready meals market had grown at an estimated 20 per cent per annum in the mid-1980s. Euromonitor, the consulting firm, estimated that fast growth would continue in the 1990s.

Financing issues

At the end of December 1988, NCGS reported a trading loss of £248,000. Fixed assets totalled £150,000, stock totalled £45,000, trade debtors totalled £143,000, and cash totalled £49,000. Trade debtors related to a small number of reputable supermarket customers who generally paid within approximately 40 days at current sales levels. Trade creditors amounted to £115,000. NCGS had a bank overdraft (i.e., line of credit) of £47,000. The company relied on the involvement of senior management to ensure that cash was collected from customers and creditors were paid. The gross profit margin on sales (i.e., sales less ingredient costs) was 64 per cent. At this time, the factory was working 5.5 days per week and 10 hours per day. Ingredient costs tended to be relatively stable. Labour and machinery efficiency had been low during the start-up period, and had been made worse by the poor layout of the factory. The company has no fixed asset register, no perpetual stock records, and no formal system for recording liabilities. It was projected that over the next three years, sales would rise from £350,000 in 1988 to £5,200,000 in 1991, and from about 310,000 litres of soup in 1988 to 4,000,000 litres in 1991. It was anticipated that the current net margin on sales would increase from a loss of −8.3 per cent to a positive 21 per cent by 1991. Further, stock turnover would fall from 43 days to 10 days, and debtor days as a percentage of sales would rise from 39 days to 45 days.

In early 1989, Palmer contacted a venture capitalist and requested funding worth £1.2 million in return for 20 per cent of NCGS's equity. The new funds were to be invested in the building of a new factory in a new location. A factory with an appropriate layout would facilitate the utilisation of new production technology, and more production capacity. The intention was to expand the range of soup recipes. The aim was to develop a microwave pot version for the snack market, which would be launched in 1989. In addition, NCGS aimed to 'roll out' distribution to a wider range of major supermarkets in the United Kingdom, Europe and the United States. To reduce costs and increase efficiency and productivity, there was a perceived need to introduce computerised control systems with regard to the manufacturing process as well as administration. Also, there was a perceived need to strengthen the operational experience of the management team.

The existing financing structure of the company included ownership stakes by the entrepreneur, his family, and a number of other minority shareholders. It was thought necessary to construct a financing arrangement that would reward the investment made to date by the initial investors, meet the entrepreneur's requirement for continued control, and enable the venture capitalist to obtain a return on funds invested which was commensurate with the risks involved.

In the first year following the venture capitalist's investment, the company purchased freehold property and a new production plant. As a result of continuing difficulties with the process, production volumes were significantly behind plan. Consequently, both sales and profit before tax were behind plan (Table 1). The entrepreneur approached the venture capitalist for a further investment of £475,000 in convertible unsecured loan stock.

Table 1 NCGS performance (£'000s)

	1989 Plan	1989 Actual	1990 Plan	1991 Plan
Sales (£m)	1,967	1,269	3,256	5,225
Profit before tax (£m)	(16)	(366)	277	1,063

Questions and issues

1 Put yourself in the position of the venture capitalist approached to fund the company. What factors would you try to check before making a decision to invest, or not to invest? How would you check these factors?

2 At the time of the initial venture capital investment, what conditions would you require as a condition for your investment?

3 At the time of the approach for the second round of investment, what would be your conditions for further investment?

4 How would you envisage realizing your gain in this venture if you were (a) the entrepreneur and (b) the venture capitalist?

Case study 22

AAC Limited: Entrepreneurial team dynamics

Eva Jarošová and Joan Winn

Summary

This case discusses the behaviour of Dagmar and Hedvika, who decided to quit their factory jobs in order to establish a glass-bead manufacturing company. Dagmar is the designer and she is young, easy-going, childless and recently divorced. Hedvika is the operational and financial manager and she is strong-willed, divorced and has older children. Hedvika's daughter Michaela works as the company's sales manager. After three years, the company is profitable, but Michaela wants to start marketing the firm's products abroad. Michaela wants to make personal sales calls, which is more costly than the current Internet-based marketing. She is seeking the approval of her mother and Dagmar to change the firm's marketing strategy.

Introduction

Hedvika Horská, the co-owner of AAC in Železný Brod in the Czech Republic, stated:

> 'When you start a company you have to know and complement each other.'[1]

AAC, s.r.o.[2] produces and sells glass 'lamp' beads and costume jewellery. Hedvika and her business partner Dagmar Kůtková founded the company. They established their firm in Železný Brod and this locality has existing competitors. The region of Jablonec and Nisou, which includes Železný Brod, is famous for its tradition of glass and costume jewellery manufacturing.[3]

---

[1] Železný Brod ('Iron Town') is in the Jizera region of northern Bohemia, about 100 km north-east of the capital city of Prague, in the area known as the Czech Paradise (Český Ráj). Železný Brod has been known for its iron and glass works since the sixteenth century.

[2] s.r.o. is equivalent to Limited Liability Company.

[3] See http://www.mestojablonec.cz/.

Hedvika and Dagmar reflected after three years of operating the firm:

> 'We must always try new things because of the strong competition in this industry. We must continually invent new things to offer to our customers.'

They hoped that they could maintain the successful trajectory of the company, whose revenues had tripled over three years (see Appendix 1), but they knew that more competition, higher costs, and increasing market uncertainties lay ahead. Success is attributed to their different personalities and their trust in each other's abilities. Neither of them knew how to cope with seasonal sales fluctuations in demand, which has made production scheduling difficult. As the company grew in size, managing work schedules became easier, because more workers could pick up slack if someone was ill or on vacation. Declining demand taxed both women's management skills and placed the company's financial health in jeopardy. They wanted to find other markets for their products. However, they did not want to spend money on fancy marketing brochures or expensive international trips, which had little guarantee of success. Both founders recognised that they would have to do something different to stay ahead of the competition.

Dagmar and Hedvika: Testing business and friendship

Dagmar and Hedvika had known each other for ten years before they decided to start a business together. As co-workers at the Liglass Company in Líšný, not far from Železný Brod, they had worked together making handcrafted glass. Dagmar worked in a division that made lamp beads, whilst Hedvika worked with glass stones and gems. Dagmar lived in Turnov, and had graduated from the arts-glass-craftsman high school in

Železný Brod before going to work for Liglass. Hedvika moved to Železný Brod from nearby Hradec Králové in 1976, when her husband was offered a job that included housing. She had studied glass craftsmanship in high school, and worked at the Vertex Company in Litomyšl, where glass fibre was made. The couple divorced, and Hedvika remained in Železný Brod with her three children. Both women had moved up to heads of their departments at Liglass. They enjoyed the opportunity to experiment with new technologies in glass-making. Dagmar supervised design and production teams and handled purchase orders for glass bars. Hedvika managed employee relations and timesheets, production flow and client invoices.

Liglass brought in a new management team and they decided to cut costs by reducing their research in glass technology development. Hedvika and Dagmar were unhappy with this change. They decided to leave and start their own business, which would focus on innovation and creativity and new process technology. Hedvika reflected:

'My company was a present to myself for my 50th birthday.'

Hedvika's children had grown up and she felt free to take a risk. Dagmar was 27 years old, married with no children. Both women believed that the 'timing was right'. They were both in a position to take a risk that would not jeopardise their families. Both founders knew that it would take time for their business to be profitable. They wanted their new firm to break even within two years. Both founders recognised the need for careful planning.

The women knew each other well, and respected each other for their professional experiences and complementary skills. Dagmar was a designer, eager to use her creativity in her own way. Hedvika knew how to manage people and set up production systems. They believed that their personalities and skills complemented each other. Both founders felt confident that solving disputes would not be a problem. However, they recognised that running a company together could jeopardise a good friendship. From the beginning, they carefully laid out roles and responsibilities and involved each in any major decision-making. Dagmar commented:

'Hedvika is a good money manager, so I knew I could count on her to keep close track of the company's finances. I don't care about money, partly because I've never had to struggle and I haven't had to worry about supporting a family.'

Both partners suggested mutual understanding was a key to success. Dagmar reflected:

'Our advantage is the age gap between us and the difference in our personalities. If our personalities were similar we could not conduct business with each other. We are completely different from each other and we use our differences in dealings with customers. Somebody prefers a young woman; someone else may prefer an experienced person at her or his own age.'

Hedvika commented:

'Our personalities complement each other. When I get upset, Dagmar is able to calm me down. On the other hand, I give the impulses to move forward. When we deal with each other, Dagmar completely understands what I have in mind and sometimes can even say it instead of me. It is only natural that we sometimes have different opinions about how to approach some business problems.'

Dagmar emphasised that it was crucial for business partners to talk through and successfully resolve different views and opinions. She emphasised that opinions should be discussed with factual arguments and not personal ones. An agreed view was sought relating to key decisions. Hedvika stated, with a laugh:

'Till now we have always agreed on everything. If we could not solve our dispute we just tossed a coin.'

Dagmar commented:

'Both of us do our work with pleasure and both of us have the same goal. We have our vision, our own path and we go for it. We don't do it for huge profits, but we do it because we like doing it; we believe in it. We try to keep the quality of production and level of service to our customers with a personal approach.'

Launching the business

Dagmar had wanted to set up the company with each woman being her own independent contractor. Hedvika had bigger plans and she reflected:

'I really wanted to create an enterprise . . . I did not want to be self-employed, working on my own. I knew how to manage people and I knew I could do a better job than the new bosses at Liglass. I also wanted to incorporate so that we could meet EU [European Union] standards and set ourselves up for international distributorships.'

Hedvika's arguments prevailed and Dagmar was convinced that incorporation was a wise move. Their partnership was reflected in the name (i.e., AAC) of their limited liability company, which came to existence coincidently when one customer said that they were a company of two As, meaning two women who were number one in their field.

At the outset, both partners doubted that they would receive any support or loans. They did not want to indebt themselves. Confident of future success, they decided to finance their business with their own savings, which they treated as a loan to the company. Dagmar had to borrow money from her parents to match the amount that Hedvika was willing to put into the company. In order to pay themselves back, they took a low salary for 18 months after firm start-up, gradually paying themselves back until the debt was repaid within two years. They were able to finance construction of workshop space and offices for the company's manufacturing facility with the first year's earnings.

Starting the business was very time-consuming. They both spent 12 hours per day working including frequent weekends. This busy schedule affected Dagmar's marriage, which finally ended in divorce 16 months after establishing the company. Dagmar reflected:

> 'Having the business was a good distraction for me . . . Hedvika was my sounding board, and my best supporter during this difficult time.'

The main focus of the business was the production and sale of lamp beads (i.e., beads made from rotating long tubes of coloured glass on an oxygen-rich flame). Drawing upon their work experience, they recognised that a sales emphasis was essential. Dagmar designed original patterns with which they hoped to attract potential customers from an already saturated market. Both partners knew it would not be easy to establish themselves in the market. They sought to differentiate their firm from existing competitors by making different and better beads than their competitors.

Hedvika's daughter Michaela became AAC's sales manager. After finishing high school Michaela had worked in the foreign sales department of Preciosa (i.e., a maker of cut glass and costume jewellery).[4] In addition to helping her mother at AAC, Michaela attended the University of Economics in Prague, where she studied diplomacy and politics. Michaela commented:

> 'Perhaps I should have studied marketing . . . But I learned a lot about culture differences and negotiations, which has really been valuable in working with AAC's

customers. My boyfriend is studying marketing, so he has helped me understand the competitive issues, and is teaching me about promotion and distribution.'

Hedvika, Dagmar and Michaela believed that the basis for good relationships with their customers lay in the close interaction between production and sales. They prided themselves on listening to their customers. Hedvika and Dagmar created a sophisticated system of pricing for the lamp beads, based on the time and materials needed to create each bead. This system enabled them to justify the price to the customer when there was a difficult order at hand. It also served as the basis for the piece-rate wage system for the workers. Hedvika and Dagmar were careful to create a wage system that was open and transparent, which would increase productivity. Some beads required particular skills. Consequently, they carefully assessed wage rates based on the time and difficulty of each bead. The production of lamp beads required previous experience of working with glass and a high level of manual dexterity.

While there were many people with glass experience in the region, it was difficult to find suitable workers. During the whole first year, the company faced recruitment problems. There were few workers available who had the qualifications AAC needed for the intricate mixing of colours and types of glass that went into Dagmar's designs. Those who were not skilful enough to create the difficult beads often left the company after only a short time at AAC. Another factor that influenced the recruitment process was that other manufacturers with similar products offered work to the employees of AAC. Competitors suggested that AAC would not survive and the new hires would soon be without work. Two years after establishing AAC, the situation improved after the closure of a nearby company that had produced glass puppets. Employees made redundant were happy to join AAC, despite the additional training they needed to meet AAC's skill requirements. For people used to a factory production facility (i.e., wages relating to hourly work), AAC's piecework system was hard to adjust to. Many workers were previously used to a slow pace that did not affect their salary. Training and acculturating workers to this new system took a lot of close supervision during the first two years.

Competing in a global market-place

Železný Brod is a town of approximately 7,000 inhabitants situated in an area called Jablonecko, and is well known for its long history of costume jewellery and

---

[4] See http://www.preciosa.cz/.

glass making. Glass has been produced in north-east Bohemia from the fourteenth century, and costume jewellery from the eighteenth century. The knowledge of glass making was passed from generation to generation, and was taught in local glass craftsman schools. There were about 200 manufacturers of glass, ranging from large companies such as Bižuterie-Česká Mincovna in Jablonec, Nisou and Crystalex in Nový Bor, and Železnobrodské Sklo in Železný Brod, to small companies and independent craftspeople. Most of the locally-produced costume jewellery was exported. Because the region was well known for its glass, many importers came directly to Železný Brod to place orders.

The leading exporter of fashion jewellery in the north Bohemian region was Jablonex Co. Ltd.[5] Founded in 1952, Jablonex specialised in glass beads and costume jewellery, as well as hand-painted blown-glass vases and receptacles, decorations, artificial flowers and gift items. Jablonex had 12 foreign offices and a network of agents in 42 countries around the world. In addition to in-house design and manufacture, Jablonex relied on more than 200 suppliers. Jablonex had 410 employees and generated CZK 2,445.9 m in sales.[6]

Despite the fact that AAC sold about 30 per cent of its bead production to Jablonex, Hedvika and Dagmar considered Jablonex their strongest competitor. Both women acknowledged that AAC could only be profitable if they dealt directly with foreign customers. Michaela conducted a worldwide search on the Internet. She sent potential business partners an e-catalogue showing photos of AAC's distinctive lamp bead designs. Three months after business start-up, AAC's had only one foreign customer. After two years, AAC had attracted many foreign customers (i.e., U.S., Canada, Australia, South America, and Western Europe), and the company employed ten full-time employees.

Seasonal surges in increased demand were handled by offering contracted services to experienced glass craftspeople, such as women on maternity leave or pensioners. Slumps in seasonal demand put pressures on their existing workforce, who had learned to work efficiently in order to maintain their salary expectations. Hedvika and Dagmar were not sure how to cope with the sales volatility problem. They thought about expanding their costume jewellery assortment, which accounted for only

2.2 per cent of AAC's sales. Roughly 20 per cent of the beads were sold to manufacturers; the remaining bead sales were sold to resellers (i.e., on-line distributors and retailers). They contemplated emulating other large distributors like Jablonex, partly to spread out the production highs and lows, but also to reduce the service demands associated with small custom orders. Another option under consideration was to explore other markets for beads and costume jewellery, such as Russia or countries in the Middle East. Michaela explained:

'We see strong competition coming from China and India, so it's difficult to see our future in ten years . . . We know there's a space on the market now, but the Chinese are good students and they can easily copy standard bead designs and make them cheaper. Silver jewellery is different, and our beads are specialised designs that adapt well to silver settings. But jewellery is sold differently [to] loose beads. Retailers and galleries that sell high-end jewellery don't sell on the Internet and they don't respond to my e-mails. I can go to Prague to talk with retailers personally, but I need to convince my mother to travel abroad with me to approach potential foreign customers face-to-face.'

Michaela put together a strengths, weaknesses, opportunities and threats (SWOT) analysis that showed AAC's strengths and weaknesses in relation to the competition (see Appendix 2 and 3). The strong Czech currency made Czech goods less attractive to buyers in the United States, but now that the Czech Republic was a member of the EU Michaela believed that AAC was in a good position to sell to other EU countries. Michaela was excited about the possibility of European expansion, especially in costume jewellery. She believed that AAC's dependence on Jablonex, their Czech distributor, made them vulnerable. Michaela was afraid that if AAC did not start to market itself aggressively the future growth of the company was in jeopardy.

Maintaining the partnership

Michaela outlined a plan for visiting Frankfurt or London in February, but she knew that her mother would be hard to convince. Dagmar was excited about the possibility of visiting boutiques and galleries and showing off her new designs, and February was a low time in their production cycle. Hedvika, on the other hand, wanted to wait until spring, when the company's sales started to pick up. Michaela commented:

'Dagmar is easy going . . . But convincing my mother is a lot harder. Maybe it's part of the mother–daughter

[5] http://www.jablonex.cz/.

[6] http://www.krolomoucky.cz/podnikatele/dokumenty/ katalog_exporteru_2004/en/en/firms/74/00000892.html.

relationship, but I need to lay things out in a precise and logical way so that she understands the plan and sees that it will have good results. I guess it is a good thing for me to carefully put together my arguments. It keeps me focused on what's important.'

After nearly three years of doing business together, Hedvika and Dagmar recognised that to sustain their position in a highly competitive market would require reliable relationship with business partners, and the maintenance of customer and brand loyalty. Also, both partners recognised the need to find new ways to ensure that their current customers did not switch to domestic and/or foreign competitors. They hoped that their customers recognised the quality and originality of the goods offered by AAC. Also, they wanted them to appreciate the personal approach and the flexibility with which they could adjust to any demand from any customer.

The women wanted to grow the business. Their labour force understood the technological aspects of production, were efficient with their manual skills, and they worked well together contributing ideas for new designs and product lines. Dagmar and Hedvika thought about Michaela's ideas about travelling abroad to directly approach potential customers using a personal sales team. Hedvika wanted to expand the business, but she was concerned about the time and expense for the company that such trips would entail. Dagmar was amenable to a trip to Frankfurt because she enjoyed visiting galleries, but she knew that Hedvika needed to be convinced that the trip would generate customers. The company had generated limited success selling jewellery in Western Europe, despite letters, calls, and e-mails. AAC had sold beads to a Japanese distributor. Dagmar believed that expanding their sales in Asia might be a better bet.

As Michaela constructed a marketing plan, she thought about the company's current position, and the pressing issues that needed to be solved. The company needed to expand in order to reduce its dependence on loose beads and small distributors. It also needed to manage seasonal swings in demand to ensure enough work for their employees throughout the whole year. Michaela had been successful with the Internet and telephone contacts, but she had exhausted these possibilities. She believed that a personal approach was needed to break into new markets. Knowing the personalities and priorities of Hedvika and Dagmar, how could she convince them to change the strategy and marketing approach?

Questions and issues

1 What have Dagmar and Hedvika done to ensure the success of their business partnership?

2 What differences between entrepreneurial ownership team partners encourage firm formation and development?

3 How have Dagmar and Hedvika worked out differences of opinion in the past? How should Michaela approach them about her plan for a new marketing strategy?

4 What advice would you give to Dagmar and Hedvika for prioritising business issues? What factors are the most important to consider so that the partnership and the business will continue to operate successfully in the future?

Additional reading

Baron, R. A. and Markman, G. D. (2003). Beyond Social Capital: The Role of Entrepreneur's Social Competence in their Financial Success. *Journal of Business Venturing,* 18: 41–60.

Collins, C. J., Hanges, P. J. and Locke, E. A. (2004). The Relationship of Achievement Motivation to Entrepreneurial Behaviour: A Meta-Analysis. *Human Performance,* 17 (1): 95–117.

Fisher, R., Ury, W. and Patton, B. (1991). *Getting to Yes! Negotiating an Agreement Without Giving In.* London: Random Century Limited.

Lukeš, M. (2004). Psychologické přístupy k podnikání. In H. Kopalová (ed.) *Adaptační a rozvojové procesy firem po vstupu do EU.* Praha VŠE, pp. 279–302 (ISBN 80-245-0678-5).

Robbins, S. P. and Hunsaker, P. L. (2003). *Training in Interpersonal Skills, 3rd edition.* Englewood Cliffs, N.J.: Prentice Hall.

Schein, E. (1980). *Organizational Psychology, 3rd edition.* Englewood Cliffs, N.J.: Prentice-Hall, Inc.

Thomas, K. W. (1976). Conflict and Conflict Management. In M. D. Dunette (ed.) *Handbook of Industrial and Organizational Psychology.* Chicago: Rand McNally.

Whetten, D. A. and Cameron, K. M. (2002). *Developing Management Skills,* 5th edition. Upper Saddle River, N.J.: Prentice Hall.

Appendix 1 AAC financial performance

	Year 1	Year 2	Year 3
Gross receipts[1]	**1,543,147**	**2,659,074**	**4,695,256**
Loose beads[2]	1,520,147	2,612,074	4,592,000
Jewellery	23,000	47,000	103,256
Total expenses	**1,539,147**	**2,573,074**	**4,204,927**
Fixed costs (rent)	106,678	126,318	126,318
Variable (materials) costs	47,895	96,993	286,769
Marketing and advertising	21,000	24,000	160,000
Salaries and contract wages	473,583	833,269	1,488,883
Taxes and insurance	123,825	267,656	707,700
Gross margin from sales	20%	20%	20%
Net profit	**4,000**	**86,000**	**490,329**
Return (profit/costs)	2.6%	3.3%	12%

[1] All figures relate to Czech crowns (CZK) with approximately CZK 25 = USD $1 in 2004 and CZK 33 = USD $1 in 2002.
[2] includes both direct export and Jablonex sales.

Source: AAC records, Year 3.

Appendix 2 Competitive strengths and weaknesses of AAC

	AAC	Competitors
Strengths	• Original designs • Professional and personal approach to customers (we are a reliable and timely partner) • Our customers can understand our pricing because of personal visits to our company (they can even try production) • High quality of products • We are enthusiastic and we have initiative • Highly flexible communication, send samples • Good payment conditions (no deposit before production, differentiated approach, home currencies of customers – Japan, New Zealand, Czech Republic)	• They have tradition (broader range of clients, financial reserves, they are better able to attract new employees) • Bigger companies can create a good corporate image • Lower prices (classic beads and jewellery) • They make more commodities (good against seasonal variations) • Lots of small hobbyists can copy any design for local stores
Weaknesses	• Vulnerability (narrow range of clients) • Higher prices • No systematic personnel policies (we lack recruiter for hiring glass technicians) • Limited production (small team of skilled workers) • Location (not close to clients and distributors) • Low knowledge of final customers and their priorities • Low marketing budget, lack of defined marketing plan	• Low innovation • Not flexible to their clients (currency assortment, currency and marketing) • Demand deposit before production • Lower quality of products

Source: Michaela Horská, AAC strategy presentation, Year 3.

Appendix 3 External analysis relating to ACC

	AAC	Competitors
Opportunities	• Costume jewellery – growing demand in the Czech Republic and abroad • Increasing demand for big pieces and jewellery • Increasing importance of EU trade • Jewellery market is open everywhere; high margins • Fashion cities, boutiques – London, Paris, Milan	• Change in Jablonex strategy toward production of non-company designs • Increasing demand for big pieces and jewellery • Increasing importance of EU trade
Threats	• Strong Czech crown (CZK) • Asian countries (especially China) are increasing the production of classical lamp beads • High taxes in the Czech Republic • Seasonal demand fluctuations • Potential change in Jablonex ownership • Wars, catastrophes (always followed by decreasing sales) • External perception of Czech-made goods (not 'high fashion')	• Strong Czech crown (CZK) • Asian countries (especially China) are increasing the production of classical lamp beads • High taxes in the Czech Republic • Exclusive trends – it will be possible to compete with China only with distinctive products • Decrease in the price of standard goods (mostly from Asia)

Source: Michaela Horská, AAC strategy presentation, Year 3.

Model Kit World: Firm growth through geographic expansion

Alex S. L. Tsang, Wai-Sum Siu and Gloria H. Y. Ting

Summary

This case illustrates why and how a small Hong Kong magazine publisher entered the mainland Chinese market. Wai-Chuen Lai, the chief editor of the *Model Kit World* magazine recognised that the local market in Hong Kong was saturated. Identifying and exploiting an opportunity in the larger and growing mainland market addressed this constraint on product growth. This case illustrates issues relating to market selection, market entry mode and the formulation of a marketing and pricing strategy.

Introduction

Wai-Chuen Lai reflected:

> 'I made my first plastic model when I was six. Initially, I liked making military models; but in 1980, after I saw a Japanese science-fiction (sci-fi) animation called *Mobile Suit Gundam,* I was fascinated by sci-fi models . . . I was working in the printing industry; however, this sector had been gradually declining since the mid-80s; so, I had to look for alternative business opportunities. I thought, because I was a Gundam fanatic and had extensive social networks in the publishing industry, I could start my own model magazine.'

In October 1990, Wai-Chuen Lai launched the *Model Kit World* magazine in Hong Kong. Under his able management, the magazine generated satisfactory sales reaching the break-even point between 1994 and 1995. He realised that the potential for market expansion in Hong Kong was limited. To ensure business development, there was a need to sell the magazine beyond the local market. In 2000, he decided to enter the mainland Chinese market to expand the readership of the magazine. However, the mainland market was more complicated than the local Hong Kong market.

The plastic model kit market

Model kits are modular toys, usually replicating airplanes, cars, tanks, castles or spacecraft. These models can easily be reduced in scale and divided into parts to enable hobbyists to enjoy the assembly process. Sci-fi models dominate the model market in Hong Kong as well as Japan. The most popular sci-fi models are robot models originating from the animated series *Mobile Suit Gundam.* Most of the model magazines in Hong Kong, Japan and Taiwan contain stories about 'Gunplas'. Gunplas relates to 'Gundam plastic models' and is the official name used in the model community. Model hobbyists living in mainland China generally favour military models but younger hobbyists increasingly prefer Gunplas. The Gunplas licence was awarded to Bandai, a major worldwide toy manufacturer with its headquarters located in Japan. Models range in price and technical difficulty to make. The majority of models sold relate to the High Grade series and the Master Grade series. They retail for between HK$50 and HK$250 (Hong Kong dollars). The retail price for models in mainland China is very similar to the price charged in Hong Kong, which makes it difficult for young mainland hobbyists to afford them.

Over the last 40 years, the Hong Kong and Japanese model markets have developed and they are more mature than the mainland Chinese market. After ten years of continuous growth, the Hong Kong model market is nearly saturated. The market is relatively small and has an ageing population. There is, therefore, limited local market growth potential. Hong Kong's market decline can be attributed to younger hobbyists being attracted to an increasing number of other recreational activities that provide immediate consumer satisfaction. For example, building a good model can take between a few days to several weeks. In contrast, other recreational activities such as computer games, Karaoke and movies can provide immediate satisfaction. In response to these changes, Bandai introduced the easier to assemble Gunplas series. It was hoped that reductions in time and effort required to build the models would increase the market attractiveness of the Gunplas series. However, this attempt to counter the market trend cannot be viewed as a sustainable long-term strategy. Recognising this, Bandai has introduced exquisitely painted and preassembled kits relating to the Mobile Suit in Action (MIA) series and the Gundam Fix Figuration (GFF) series. Hobbyists can now own their favourite Gundam models with little or no time or effort. This latter strategy suggests that Bandai does not feel very positive about the long-term growth of Gunplas.

Model magazine survival

The 1980s were the golden era for models. There were many hobbyists creating many business opportunities for model magazines. This golden era was followed by an economic recession in Japan, and a depression in the model industry in the early 1990s. Hong Kong's model market also went into recession. Over this period, labour costs began to rise. Nearly all the model magazines published in Hong Kong went out of business.

At the start of 2000, the model magazine market in Hong Kong experienced an Indian summer. Some enthusiasts, like Lai, established small magazine publishing houses. They displayed their talents by publishing new model magazines such as *Hobby Mix* and *Toy Box*. At the same time, competitors from Japan and Taiwan entered the 'magazine war'. For example, the *Hobby Japan* and *Dengeki Hobby* magazines were published in Japan, and the *All Dimensions (Creased)* and *Model Grand Master* magazines were published in Taiwan. Due to intense competition and the model market recession, several of the new Hong Kong magazines barely survived.

Model Kit World's major competitors were the Japanese magazines that provided rich contents, and were associated with elegant printing. However, Japanese magazines were written in Japanese and they were more expensive (i.e., HK$60 and HK$80). Exchange rate fluctuations could also dramatically increase the price of the magazines from Japan. *Model Kit World* was a superior product because it was written in Chinese, and was cheaper. The magazine was sold for only HK$20, which made it more affordable for secondary school students.

In 2003, the Japanese publisher decided to publish a Chinese edition of *Dengeki Hobby*. A small amount of news about Hong Kong model trends was inserted and some premiums were attached on an irregular basis. Its selling price was HK$38. The price was slightly higher when the premiums were attached. Also, the prevalence of the Internet allowed model manufacturers and retailers to construct their own webpages. The latest information about models could be instantly announced online. Model hobbyists created their own webpages, and newsgroups shared their best conversion techniques and exchanged ideas. Lai believed that increased Internet use would reduce *Model Kit World*'s 20 per cent market share in Hong Kong. He decided to sell the magazine to a growing market beyond Hong Kong.

Entering a new market: Market selection issues

Lai faced many difficulties in choosing an additional market for the long-term development of *Model Kit World*. He went to Taiwan, Japan, and the Guangdong Province of mainland China to assess market potential. He found that each market was associated with particular problems.

Lai did not have any detailed knowledge of the publishing business in Japan. He would incur costs relating to translating the magazine into Japanese. Further, he would have to deal with intense competition from local Japanese magazines. After several trips, Lai perceived that the publishing industry in Taiwan was very conservative. Many of the people in the publishing businesses were older and cautious surrounding product offerings. Lai perceived a culture of protectionism and ethnocentrism that did not encourage foreign investment. He concluded that it would be unwise to invest in Japan or Taiwan.

Lai decided to enter China's Guangdong Province. He strongly believed that mainland China had high market potential, and operational costs on the mainland could be kept low. Lai was concerned about the serious corruption and complicated human relationship issues that he had heard about. After he entered the market, Lai found that corruption was not as serious as he had been led to believe. Further, the political situation was stable. He also found that the publishing industry was similar to Hong Kong's. Lai believed he could reduce his risk exposure by networking and building partnerships with local firms on the mainland.

Market entry

Market background

Economic growth can stimulate increased demand for cultural products. The annual expenditure on educational, cultural, and recreational services in China increased from RMB $112 (i.e., Renminbi is the official currency of the People's Republic of China and the currency is legal tender in mainland China but not Hong Kong) per capita in 1990 to RMB$1,033 per capita in 2004 (*China Statistics Yearbook*, 2004). In 1990, expenditure on educational, cultural, and recreational services was 11 per cent of consumption, but by 2005, it had increased to 14 per cent. Over this period, the demand for books, comics, newspapers, and magazines increased.

The publishing industry in China is highly profitable. The industry is always ranked as one of the top five most profitable industries. Evidence from the CEI China Industry Development Report (2005) suggests that 7,000 publishing units in 2003 serviced the requirements of 1.3 billion people in China. The average expenditure on magazines was RMB$22 per person. The number of magazines in China increased from 2,801 titles in 1981 to 9,490 titles in 2004 (Table 1). In 2003, approximately 66 per cent of the magazines were published monthly or bimonthly (Table 2). Almost half of

Table 1 Number of magazines in China, 1981 to 2004

Year	No.	Year	No.	Year	No.
1981	2801	1989	6078	1997	7918
1982	3100	1990	5751	1998	7999
1983	3415	1991	6056	1999	8187
1984	3907	1992	6486	2000	8725
1985	4705	1993	7011	2001	9015
1986	5248	1994	7325	2002	9029
1987	5687	1995	7583	2003	9074
1988	5865	1996	7916	2004	9490

Source: CEI China Industry Development Report (2005).

Table 2 Frequency of magazine publication, 2003

Frequency of publication	%
Monthly	34.7
Bimonthly	31.5
Quarterly	24.6
Other	9.2
Total	100.0

Source: CEI China Industry Development Report (2005).

Table 3 Magazine content, 2003

Magazine content	%
Natural and practical science	49.6
Philosophy and social science	25.2
Culture and education	10.7
Miscellaneous	6.3
Literature and art	5.9
Junior reading	1.5
Graphics	0.8
Total	100.0

Source: CEI China Industry Development Report (2005).

the magazines focused upon natural and practical science, whilst only 6 per cent were miscellaneous magazines (Table 3). In 2003, 17 magazines published more than one million copies. Magazines can be grouped into general interest household magazines, magazines published by the Communist Party, students' reading, government magazines on current issues, and industry magazines.

A study conducted by Sinomonitor International suggests that publishing firms in China will need to deal with change (Zhu, 2006). In 2002, an amendment was made to the Regulations on the Administration of Publication, which made it easier for new firms to enter the market. Lower entry barriers will encourage more competition between publishers. Also, the Chinese government has reduced the budget allocated to government departments and state-owned enterprises that can be used to purchase communist magazines. Consequently, there is reduced demand for such magazines.

Legal issues

The publishing industry in China is highly protected. In the past, only state-owned enterprises could publish magazines. Since the amendment to the Regulations on the Administration of Publication, local firms have been allowed to participate in the industry. Foreign companies have to follow a different set of regulations. According to the Measures for the Administration of Foreign-Funded Distribution Enterprises of Books, Newspapers, and Journals, foreign companies are allowed to enter the Chinese market under the World Trade Organisation (WTO). In fact, foreign companies can only enter the magazine wholesale and retail markets. Foreign companies require initial capital of not less than RMB$30 m to establish wholesale businesses, and they require not less than RMB$5 m to establish retail businesses. These changes did not assist existing firms in Hong Kong such as *Model Kit World* to enter the mainland market.

Lai found a partner on the mainland (i.e., a state-owned enterprise) to help him sell his magazines on the mainland. He faced a legal problem relating to the acquisition of a 'serial number'. The Administration of Publication requires that all published materials have to be supervised by the Bureau of Press and Publication (or equivalent body) in each city, or province. These local regulators require all magazines to have a serial number before they are published. To maintain quality standards, these local regulators do not easily issue legal serial numbers. Usually only established companies with a long history and sufficient capital can obtain legal serial numbers. The regulations do not allow people to sell or transfer serial numbers. People who do this are generally prosecuted. Entrepreneurs, particularly small foreign investors, unable to obtain legal serial numbers may engage in illegal publishing activities. Illegal activities relate to using false serial numbers, using numbers registered in foreign countries, and using a number to sell posters with free magazines attached. Some companies purchase a serial number for one type of magazine but print a different type of magazine (i.e., using the serial number for a military magazine to sell a fashion magazine).

Lai stated that using a leased serial number was risky and potentially costly. Residents of Hong Kong can use their identity card to register a business and to obtain a business registration certificate. Successful applicants can then publish materials. A serial number (or publisher's code) in Hong Kong can be acquired free of charge. However, on the mainland a serial number is a commodity that can be traded. For example, in the Guangzhou Province, a serial number could be sold for between RMB\$200,000 and \$300,000. High market entry costs make it very difficult for low volume publishers to operate. To address this issue, Lai established a partnership in 2004 with a mainland wholesaler. He has used a VCD serial number to publish his magazine. Lai reflected that it is a strategy of 'buying a VCD and getting a magazine'.

The publishing industries in Hong Kong and mainland China are totally different. Hong Kong has a free market economy offering a high degree of publishing freedom. The mainland publishing industry is, however, under strict government supervision and is tightly controlled.

Table 4 *Model Kit World*'s timeline

December 1990	Wai-Chuen Lai established the *Model Kit World* magazine in Hong Kong
1994 to 1995	*Model Kit World* magazine broke even
2002	First issue of the mainland edition of *Model Kit World* was launched in the Guangzhou Province of China
April 2003	The Japanese magazine, *Dengeki Hobby*, launched its Chinese edition in Hong Kong
March 2005	*Model Kit World* magazine was issued nationwide in China on a trial basis

Adaptation – Magazine contents, pricing, and promotion

The *Model Kit World* magazine (mainland edition) was issued nationwide in China on a trial basis in March 2005 (Table 4). Lai selected a cross-subsidising strategy. Profits from the operation in Hong Kong were used to support investments in the mainland. *Model Kit World* is a derivative of Gunplas products, and sales of the magazine are highly related to the popularity of Gunplas. Lai believed that the popularity of Gunplas on the mainland might only last for three or four more years. Consequently, the mainland edition of *Model Kit World* was expanded to include military models. The magazine was sold at a lower price on the mainland compared to Hong Kong because of the former's lower per capita income. The mainland edition, however, could not be markedly cheaper because the lower cost could jeopardise sales of the Hong Kong edition. The mainland edition was sold for RMB\$18, which was two dollars lower than the Hong Kong edition. In order to avoid direct competition between the Hong Kong and mainland editions, the mainland edition was sold one or two months after the publication of the Hong Kong edition. Lai appreciated that bookshops and magazine kiosks would not place newly introduced magazines in the best locations to attract readers' attention. To address this issue, Lai advertised in other model magazines in order to raise product awareness among Gunplas hobbyists with regard to the publication of the *Model Kit World* magazine.

Decisions to be made

Post 2004, the Japanese model magazine market was associated with increased competition. The two giants – *Hobby Japan* and *Dengeki Hobby* – used numerous premiums to entice readers. These practices are beginning to shape publishing behaviour in Hong Kong. Lai recognises the threat of new forms of competition. The selection of an appropriate marketing strategy will shape the success or failure of *Model Kit World*. Lai is now considering what he should do in order to increase his firm's foothold in the mainland market.

Questions and issues

1 What threats did *Model Kit World* face by solely operating in Hong Kong?

2 What opportunities did Lai identify to grow *Model Kit World*?

3 Did Lai underestimate the issues relating to geographic expansion in mainland China?

References

CEI China Industry Development Report. (2005). *China Economic Information Network*. Economy Publishing.

China Statistic Yearbook. (2004). *National Bureau of Statistics of China*.

Zhu, X. D. (2006). "*The Future of the Magazine Industry under the Challenge of New Media*". Blue Book of China's Media. Social Academic Press.

Upstart Graphics: Merger and acquisition issues

Donald M. DePamphilis

Summary

This case study illustrates how a disciplined acquisition process can be applied to resolve growth issues in the context of an aggressive entrepreneurial business. The focus is on a business which chooses to pursue growth through acquisition after examining a range of options. The first two stages of the process relate to the development of business and acquisition plans. Additional stages relate to the search, screening, first contact, negotiation, integration planning, closing of an acquisition deal, and post-merger integration and evaluation.

Introduction

In the late 1980s, an emerging technology called multimedia, the integration of sound, video and text on compact disks called CD-ROMs, caught David Duncan's imagination. David believed that CD-ROMs would revolutionise entertainment by allowing users to interact easily with the new media. For almost two years, David evangelised about the virtues of multimedia through his company Upstart Graphics (UG).[1] To energise the growth of multimedia usage, David convinced Apple, IBM, Sony and others to fund his efforts to promote their multimedia technologies.

With a small staff and increasing revenues, David had the perfect niche but he was aware that his success was likely to be short-lived. As CD-ROMs loaded with multimedia applications were becoming common, the need for UG's promotional activities would end. His dream, that multimedia CD-ROMs would become the mainstay of the interactive entertainment industry and the reference manuals of the future, appeared to be coming true but to survive he had to find a new niche.

Building the business plan: Analysing options

David and his staff of nine met to define their place in the evolving multimedia industry.[2] Figure 1 summarises David's assessment of the competitive dynamics in the electronic publishing industry. Relating to a modified 'five forces' model (Porter, 1987) Figure 1 summarises the major determinants of the intensity of competition and of cashflow/profitability in the industry.[3] Content was king and content owners were in a position to license it to the highest bidder. UG's limited cash position put it at a distinct disadvantage in dealing with content owners. Moreover, competition for multimedia programmers was intense. UG had to rely more on the prospect of striking it rich by offering potential employees stock options, which could be exercised when UG was publicly listed. However, UG could not afford the salaries being offered by the larger, more established firms such as Microsoft and Activision. In contrast to several of the firm's competitors, UG lacked access to reasonably priced content and distribution. While UG had some degree of brand recognition, it was in a relatively narrow market niche, which limited long-term growth potential. UG's products (largely consisting of putting the work of artists on music CD-ROMs)

---

[1] The names of the individuals, companies, the financial data used, events described, and the final outcomes are fictitious. However, the information is based on the author's experience in managing 30 transactions, several of which are represented in the case study.

[2] See Chapters 4 and 5 in DePamphilis (2008).

[3] Figure 1 represents a modification of the traditional 'five forces' model developed by Porter. The figure includes an expanded array of factors that impact both the competitive intensity of an industry, as well as its profitability and cashflow.

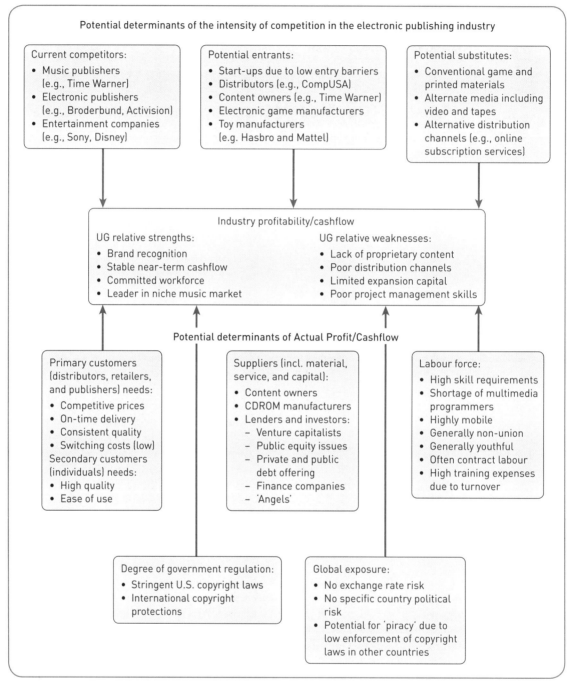

Figure 1 Upstart Graphics competitive market dynamics

were perceived by customers to be high-quality, but UG had relatively little pricing power due to the slow acceptance of its product. Converting the dream into reality required considerable hard work and money.

David decided to address the firm's limited access to content first. Although options were limited by the lack of funds, he could develop the content internally, and then pay a licence fee to use the artist's name. He realised that this would require substantial time and effort to hire the right talent, and to negotiate licence arrangements. David thought he could solve this problem and the lack of a cost-effective distribution channel by directly contacting major music publishing companies. The latter companies, which frequently owned the rights to certain music libraries, were in a position to convince the artist to promote the CD-ROM. In addition, they had the financial resources to aggressively advertise new CD-ROM products. In January 1993, David signed a contract with a major music company. By late 1993, UG had introduced several new CD-ROMs. Sales doubled between 1993 and 1995. In 1995, revenue and net income reached $6.8 million and $450,000, respectively. Cashflow was almost $800,000, and the company had little debt.

To fuel high growth, UG had to continue to sign more artists, expand staff, increase the size of their facility, and augment their promotion and marketing budget. By late 1996, industry-wide sales began to slow. UG's market niche was not immune because other companies were selling similar products. Due to high product quality and excellent brand recognition UG was able to sustain strong sales and profit growth. However, David knew that UG could not continue to grow faster than the market for very long. Increasing capital outlays and working capital requirements caused operating cashflow to deteriorate.

A review of what successful players in the industry were doing convinced David that he had to change UG's formula for success. High Flyer Technology (HFT), the fastest-growing industry participant, and Megamedia, Inc., the largest player, were continuing to grow. Unlike others, they were focusing primarily on programing while allowing others to manufacture the disks. Marketing was conducted largely through alliances with major software companies, such as Broderbund. David believed that decelerating growth, at least in certain market segments, would require consolidation to survive. The cost of developing, buying, or licensing

content was becoming too great for the smaller players to survive. David carefully considered other options such as the sale of all or a portion of his company to a larger company. But he wanted to retain control. In late 1999, his worst fears were realised when Megamedia, Inc. acquired a small competitor for $15 million. Industry consolidation was underway.

Upstart Graphics looks to grow through acquisition

As outlined in UG's business plan, the primary strategy was to gain market share by extending its existing product line capabilities into related markets. The means of accomplishing this was through the medium of the CD-ROM. An acquisition was viewed as the best way to rapidly implement the business strategy. David enlisted the aid of a respected regional investment banking firm's senior partner, Brenda Bernard. He proceeded to develop an acquisition plan as the primary means of realising UG's business plan. The acquisition plan highlighted issues relating to financial and non-financial objectives, UG's resource limitations, further definition of the target industry, and management's preferences with respect to the acquisition effort. UG sought to identify other related companies with proprietary content or access to proprietary content, effective distribution channels, and excellent design and production capabilities.

Defining management preferences

UG's board and management knew how much risk they were willing to accept. They did not want to invest too much because a single mistake could bankrupt the business. Notably, they defined what they were willing and not willing to do with regard to an acquisition. They identified the following guidelines:

- UG would not be willing to pay more than $100 to $200 million for an acquisition;
- The minimum acceptable rate of return would be UG's 15 per cent cost of capital;
- Financing the transaction would not violate existing loan covenants, or materially increase UG's borrowing costs;
- Only friendly transactions would be considered;
- Current competitors would be considered as potential target partners;
- UG would own at least 51 per cent of the acquired firm's outstanding equity;

- The maximum price-to-earnings ratio (P/E) of the acquired company could not exceed 30 times the current year's earnings;
- The fixed payment (i.e., interest, lease, and principal payments) coverage of the combined companies could not fall below the industry average of 1.0; and
- A maximum of one-half of the present value of projected cashflow resulting from synergy would be included in the purchase price.

Initiating the search for acquisition candidates

With Bernard's assistance, UG's management team set about determining appropriate criteria for selecting potential acquisition candidates. The primary selection criteria included the target industry, size, price range, profitability, and growth rate. In establishing secondary selection criteria (i.e., those used to reduce the long list developed by applying the primary criteria), Bernard advised UG to focus on targets whose cashflow, asset base, or lack of leverage could be used to finance the acquisition.

A short list of potential acquisition targets was identified following a search of Bernard's in-house database of companies, a review of industry literature, and confidential inquiries to UG's board members as well as law and accounting firms. Current competitors and potential entrants into the market were given particular consideration. With this information in hand, Duncan was prepared to initiate 'first contact' with firms on the short list. Whenever possible, contact would be made through a trusted intermediary such as a UG board member, the company's law or accounting firm, or Brenda Bernard. Secrecy was of paramount importance. David did not want to create concern among UG's employees, suppliers, or customers. In addition, he did not want the market-place to get wind of his intentions, which could drive up market values of potential acquisition targets (DePamphilis, 2008).

First contact

After a somewhat frustrating two-month search, UG reduced what had been a lengthy list of 12 candidates down to two firms. After being rebuffed by the first firm contacted, David asked Donna Franklin, one of UG's board members, to contact one of her former business associates, Barry Beecham, the chief executive officer (CEO) of HFT. Beecham said that HFT might be willing to be acquired under 'the right conditions.' Brenda

Bernard recommended further research into HFT's competitive market position, and the goals of major shareholders and management before approaching HFT with a formal proposal.

HFT's success reflected its ability to outsource programing activities to service bureaus employing armies of highly skilled, but relatively inexpensive software programers in India and the Philippines. HFT was able to diversify into other types of content in order to expand its product offering. This generated significant software development savings. Moreover, HFT had developed good marketing relationships with some major software companies.

After further conversations between Franklin and Beecham, David believed that it was time for a face-to-face meeting with Beecham. At that meeting, David presented the argument that together their two companies could present an effective counterweight to Megamedia, Inc., and he wanted to play to Beecham's concerns. David asserted:

'Individually, their competitive positions were problematic in the long run given the apparent slowdown in industry demand. But together they could benefit from UG's growing content library and HFT's lower cost of designing, developing, and marketing CD-ROM products.'

Beecham seemed to be impressed by Duncan's compelling logic.

Parties exchange data

David and Barry agreed to sign a confidentiality agreement and to exchange summarised business plans and financial statements for their respective companies. Notably, David was very interested in better understanding HFT's past performance, and what it would take to sustain future growth. Barry was interested in evaluating UG's ability to finance a transaction. Together, they laid out a timeline that would enable UG to perform a modest preliminary due diligence review. At the end of 30 days, UG would have to provide a formal letter of intent suggesting a specific purchase price.

David and his chief financial officer (CFO), Chang Lee, poured over HFT's historical financial statements for the last five years, as well as their five-year forecast. David expressed some disappointment that the cashflow numbers showed substantial annual variation. He was hoping that HFT could demonstrate a stable, predictable cashflow stream. Predictable cashflows, he reasoned, would enable UG to convince bankers that UG could assume significant leverage to purchase HFT for cash. Lee assured Duncan that if the historical numbers were restated to eliminate one-time occurrences, HFT's cashflow would show a smooth upward trend.

David designated Lee as the acquisition project leader with clear authority to draw on others with specialised skills throughout UG. Lee was quick to establish teams to address such areas as strategy and operations, financial review, and legal issues. Following several days of hectic number crunching by Lee's minions, Lee reported to Duncan that the assumptions looked reasonable, except for what appeared to be an overly optimistic improvement in the ratio of the cost of goods sold to net revenue built into the forecast period beginning in 2002.

Beecham was questioned about the realism of this assumption. He reflected:

'This reduction reflected the implementation of a modular software development system that HFT had been working on for several years. This system would enable HFT's developers to more readily reuse existing software code in new product introductions. The resulting reduction in coding time would substantially lower product introduction costs.'

David's experience led him to believe that these types of projects rarely provided the expected productivity improvements. Consequently, David told Lee to re-run the HFT projections with regard to more modest growth assumptions, and to assume that the cost of goods sold as a percentage of sales would be in line with HFT's historical performance. Based on these more conservative assumptions, the preliminary discounted cashflow stand-alone value for HFT was $102.7 million, which was about $6 million more than the market value (including debt) of UG.[4]

With the revised forecast, Duncan and Lee turned to identifying 'hidden' sources of value that UG could unlock to provide additional cash generated by the combination of HFT and UG. To identify these sources of value (measured in terms of incremental cashflow), Lee and his associates poured over HFT's financial statements and operations looking for assets not recorded in the books at fair value. They considered under-utilised borrowing capacity and the potential for cost savings

(e.g., shared overhead, duplicate facilities). Other potential sources of value included new customer relationships, opportunities for UG to use new technologies and processes, and intellectual property such as patents, trademarks, and royalty rights. They also looked for factors that would reduce future cashflow such as product quality problems, employee turnover, duplicate customer relationships, and so on.

Determining the initial offer price

Lee's approach to valuation involved a four-step procedure. First, initially UG and HFT were valued as stand-alone businesses, with all operating revenues and costs stated at market prices. Second, the present value of net synergy was determined by subtracting the sum of the stand-alone values of UG and HFT from the present value of consolidated UG and HFT, including the effects of estimated synergy.[5] Third, the initial offer price was determined as being equal to the minimum offer price (i.e., HFT's current share price times total shares outstanding) plus the percentage of estimated net synergy UG was willing to share with HFT shareholders. Fourth, Lee determined if UG could finance the transaction at the initial offer price determined during the third step. This initial offer price would be further validated by comparing the discounted cashflow valuations with purchase prices based on P/E, price-to-revenue, and price-to-book ratios for recent transactions involving comparable companies. These ratios confirmed that $150.6 million ($50.20 per share) was a fair price for HFT's outstanding equity. This price represented a 46 per cent premium over HFT's current share price of $34.50 (Table 1).

David reasoned that a substantial premium over HFT's current share price would pre-empt other potential bidders from making a 'run' for HFT. The last thing David wanted at this time was a protracted and contentious bidding war for HFT. David knew that UG did not have the financial resources to outbid companies the size of Megamedia. Nonetheless, even with this lofty premium, the HFT acquisition looked attractive. It promised to boost the market value of the combined companies to almost $300 million, including about

---

[4] A stand-alone business is one whose financial statements reflect all the costs of running the business and all revenue generated by the business.

[5] Net synergy represents the difference between sources of value less destroyers of value. Each is measured in terms of its impact on cashflows. Note that net synergy should be further reduced by expenses incurred to realise synergy such as severance and training expenses.

Table 1 Offer price determination

Financing metrics	Stand-alone value		Consolidated UG and HFT		Value of synergy
	UG (1)	HFT (2)	Without synergy (3) (1) + (2)	With synergy (4)	PV net synergy (4) − (3)
Valuation ($m)	72.8	99.6	172.4	290.2	117.9
Minimum offer price ($m)	103.5	HFT share price ($34.50) at close of business day before offer presented to HFT management × number of HFT shares outstanding			
Maximum offer price ($m)	221.4	Minimum offer price plus 100% of estimated net synergy			
Initial offer price ($m)	150.6	Minimum share price + 40% of estimated net synergy, where .4 is portion of synergy UG initially is willing to share with HFT shareholders			
Initial offer price per share ($)	50.20	Initial offer price/number of HFT's shares outstanding			
Purchase price premium per share (%)	.46	Initial offer price/current HFT share price			

$118 million in estimated synergy. The expected synergy consisted of a combination of revenue enhancements and cost savings. The additional revenue was expected to come from improved product quality, a broader product offering and cross-selling to each firm's customers. Production cost-related savings would result from economies of scale (i.e., better utilisation of existing facilities) and scope (i.e., the use of existing operations to support more products), as well as the elimination of duplicate jobs.

Deal structuring

David knew that a stock-for-stock purchase was problematic because of Wall Street's tendency to focus on earnings per share (EPS) as a proxy for stock returns (Dechow, 1994; Cheng et al., 1996; Sloan, 1996). Wall Street analysts increasingly viewed UG's above-average industry growth rate as suspect. With industry growth slowing, they reasoned that product pricing would become very competitive. Although UG had been able to maintain attractive margins in recent years, the lack of new products that had blockbuster potential made the analysts increasingly wary of the firm's ability to sustain both high growth and attractive margins.

An acquisition resulting in dilution was not likely to be acceptable to Wall Street. With long-term debt comprising about 60 per cent of total capital, an all-cash transaction did not seem possible. Consequently, it seemed increasingly obvious that UG would have to convince HFT that some combination of stock and cash

would be attractive. Duncan, Lee, and their investment banker knew that if an exciting 'story-line' could be created for the combined companies, it would be possible to convince HFT's shareholders to accept something other than an all-cash or all-stock offer. Indeed, a combination of stock and cash might appeal to a wider range of HFT shareholders. HFT shareholders could continue to hold UG stock to participate in the potential appreciation, while using the cash portion of the purchase price to diversify their investment portfolios, or to satisfy any short-term cash requirements they might have. Desirous of retaining key HFT managers, Duncan was also willing to offer selected employees employment contracts.

To determine the appropriate composition of the initial offer price, UG's management reviewed 15 alternative scenarios. UG's own analysis suggested that its stand-alone equity value could total about $73 million, even without the acquisition of HFT, if their assumptions underlying their current five-year projections turned out to be correct. UG's management and shareholders would have to be convinced that they could do markedly better to justify the risk associated with acquiring HFT.

The most acceptable scenario would be the one that resulted in the highest net present value and the least EPS dilution. This scenario could not jeopardise the combined companies' ability to satisfy loan covenants, or to maintain fixed payment coverage and debt-to-total capital ratios consistent with the average for other

Table 2 Determining the composition of the offer price

Cash per share ($)	12.55
Share exchange ratio[1]	1.14
New shares issued by UG[2]	3.42
Total shares outstanding (UG/HFT)[3]	4.42
Ownership distribution in combined firm	
HFT shareholders (%)[4]	.77
UG shareholders (%)	.23
Offer price composition per share	1.14 shares of UG stock + $12.55 for each HFT share outstanding
Offer price including assumed HFT debt[5] ($ m)	153.8

[1]Number of UG shares to be exchanged for each share of HFT stock.
[2]Share exchange ratio times the number of HFT shares outstanding (i.e., 3 million).
[3]UGS existing shares plus the new shares issued to acquire HFT.
[4]Number of UG shares held by HFT shareholders divided by total shares outstanding for the combined firms (i.e., 3.42/4.42).
[5]HFT's outstanding long-term debt at the time of the proposed acquisition totalled $3.2 million.

companies in the industry. All-cash and all-stock offers were included in the analysis (although it was felt that neither was a realistic option) as benchmarks, or baselines for comparing the other options. The most attractive scenario to UG consisted of 1.14 shares of its stock plus $12.55 in cash for each share of HFT's stock.

Negotiations heat up: Developing counter-offers

Although this offer had great appeal from HFT's perspective, the transaction would create a significant tax liability for HFT's shareholders. David learned very quickly from Beecham that this could be a stumbling block. Although he did not mention it to Beecham at this point, David was willing to increase the number of UG shares offered for each HFT share. David was also willing to share up to one-half of the expected synergy if he had to in order to complete the transaction. Beecham made it clear that although Duncan's proposal was 'in the ballpark' on a pre-tax basis, it was wholly inadequate on an after-tax basis. A high proportion of HFT's stock was held by a few shareholders that had a very low tax basis in the stock. Consequently, their tax liabilities from a taxable transaction would be substantial. Beecham indicated that UG would have to raise the total price on a basis to compensate for any tax liability, or increase the equity portion of the offer price, thereby softening the potential tax bite to HFT shareholders.[6]

David agreed to review his options and get back to Beecham.

Subsequent analysis indicated that it would be difficult for UG to increase significantly the share exchange ratio without savaging the EPS of the combined firms.[7] David and his board of directors did not find these results acceptable. However, UG was willing to 'sweeten' their initial offer by assuming all of HFT's long-term debt, which totalled $3.2 million. Although this proposal did not address specifically Beecham's concern about taxes, it did add to the overall purchase price being offered. Without UG's assumption of this debt, HFT would have to repay this amount to lenders from the cash portion of the purchase price (Table 2).

Although Barry Beecham initially expressed disappointment with the offer, he agreed to present it to his board of directors. HFT's board and shareholders found the improved offer acceptable, because it was substantially non-taxable. It offered a significant premium over the firm's current share price, and represented an increase (albeit small) of 2.1 per cent (i.e., $153.8/$150.6) above the initial offer price.

Due diligence: Looking for a needle in a haystack

Chang Lee organised three teams (i.e., financial, strategy and operations as well as legal) to conduct due diligence. The strategy and operations team's responsibilities were to review past business and operating plans

---

[6]If certain criteria are satisfied, HFT shareholders could defer paying taxes on the equity portion of the purchase price until they actually sell the UG shares.

[7]Share exchange ratios represent the number of acquirer shares to be exchanged for each share of outstanding target stock.

in order to evaluate actual performance to plan, to evaluate the effectiveness of sales and marketing plans, and to assess customer relationships.[8] In addition, the team was to evaluate the integrity of operations in terms of facility design and layout, software design and development capabilities, and project management skills. This was to be accomplished through a series of personal interviews with mid-level and senior management. The financial team would concern itself with the integrity of HFT's books. They would conduct an inventory of assets to substantiate their existence, and to evaluate their quality. The legal team would review corporate records, material contracts and obligations of the seller, and current and pending litigation and claims.

Following an extensive review of HFT's operations and books, several areas of concern, as well as opportunities, emerged. Revenue recognition appeared as an issue. UG accountants noted that HFT might have been booking revenue too quickly. When disks were sent to retailers, allowance for the return of unsold disks from the retailers should have been taken into account. Areas that provided an opportunity for UG included in-process research and development (R&D) charges. These could be taken by UG at the time of the acquisition. These charges represented the estimated value of R&D at the target company. Because it is still 'in process', the research is not yet commercially viable. Further, because it may prove worthless it can all be written off. By separating the expenses from revenues that might be gained in the future from the R&D, however, future earnings can get a big boost.

Obtaining financing

To raise money, Duncan and Lee had to go on the typical road show to make presentations to banks, insurance companies and pension funds. They would need to borrow about $40 million to finance the cash portion of the purchase price. Their challenge was to convince bankers that the cashflow of the combined companies could meet debt service requirements. The combined companies' total debt was expected to reach $70.5 million, including transaction-related debt totalling $40 million. Loan covenants on existing debt required that the new firm's debt-to-total capital be less than one, fixed payment coverage charges be greater than one, and current

assets be at least twice current liabilities. At the end of 2001, the new firm's financial ratios complied with the covenants. After extended negotiations, a bank provided an unsecured loan to UG for $40 million amortized in equal payments over 15 years at an annual interest rate of 11 per cent. The loan was subject to normal covenants, which restricted the amount UG could borrow in the future, and the types of spending it could undertake without the bank's approval. Furthermore, UG would have to ensure that certain other financial ratios such as earnings before interest and taxes as a multiple of interest expense did not fall below a contractually determined multiple.

Integrating the organisations: Consistent communication is key

Duncan knew from experience that combining the firms would lead to inevitable concerns, particularly among HFT employees, about job security and compensation, and about how the new firm would be managed. Although he expected to lose some key employees to competitors following the acquisition, Duncan felt that the situation was manageable if proper planning was undertaken. He had to start by clearly communicating his own priorities to his subordinates. Also, he established an appropriate integration team infrastructure.

Before the acquisition deal closing, he appointed Amy Pettibone, one of his best operating and project managers, to oversee the operational combination of the two firms once the transaction had been completed. Amy had a demonstrated ability to set and communicate priorities, to size up people accurately, to make tough but fair decisions, to establish a timeline, and to stick to even the most ambitious schedule. Based on the information collected during due diligence, Amy Pettibone and Chang Lee worked closely to determine what near-term expenditures might be required to ensure that HFT's operations would continue without interruption during the next 12 to 24 months. This included the identification of key managers that were to be retained, key technologies, and a review of vendors and customers. The pair also reviewed industry-wide operating norms in order to determine other adjustments that might have to be made in the immediate future. These norms included executive compensation, billing procedures, product delivery times, quality metrics, and employee benefit and compensation packages. Retention bonuses were offered to employees, who were to be terminated within the first full year following the

---

[8]Comparing the actual historical performance of a firm to plan is a proxy for the competence of management in delivering its commitments.

closing, to stay with the firm during that period to ease the integration of the two firms.

UG's management knew that the time to address integration issues was before the closing. Issues such as severance expenditures, pension plan buyouts, employment contracts, capital expenditures that should have been made by HFT as part of the normal course of business, non-compete agreements, and so on, should be addressed as part of the negotiation process. When appropriate, UG would seek a reduction in the purchase price as a possible offset to expenses that were not apparent when the preliminary indication of value for HFT was given in the letter of intent.

Key managers at HFT were offered one-year employment contracts with UG. Retaining key HFT managers was considered important enough that Duncan instructed his attorneys to make the acceptance of employment contracts by designated employees a condition of closing.[9] Barry Beecham also signed an agreement that he would not work for a competitor or start a business that could compete with the combined firms for a period not to exceed three years from the deal closing date. Further, a detailed communications plan was devised for use immediately following closing. The plan included press releases and announcements to employees (addressing questions about job security, compensation, and benefits), customers (providing assurances of an uninterrupted service), and vendors. Duncan would speak to HFT employees at their headquarters to answer questions, and provide reasonable assurances of continuity of pay and benefits. In addition, 'talk tracks' were written for the sales force, who were instructed to contact all major customers directly on the day of the announcement of the acquisition of HFT.

The dream comes true

The stress level rose sharply during the days just before the closing of the acquisition deal. Heated negotiations were conducted surrounding a number of issues that surfaced during the due diligence. Several potential lawsuits against HFT disclosed during due diligence involving disgruntled customers and employees could cost the new company millions of dollars over the next three to five years. Although it was not clear if they actually would go to trial, UG estimated that the future value of their potential impact to be $7 million to $10 million.

In addition, the new company would have to spend $1 million to $3 million in normal maintenance and repair of HFT operations during the next several years.

The combination of potential or pending expenses had an estimated present value of $10 million, consisting of $8 million in potential jury awards, and $2 million in deferred maintenance. Because they had been identified late in the due diligence process, their impact had not been included in the projected operating cashflows used in HFT's initial valuation. Moreover, Duncan was concerned enough about what was uncovered during due diligence that he wanted Beecham to agree to put 5 per cent of the purchase in escrow for at least one year until all the 'surprises' were known.

Despite several days of aggressive negotiating, Duncan capitulated and agreed to absorb these additional costs without any reduction in the purchase price. Duncan believed that the $10 million would be more than offset by certain non-operating assets that were identified during the due diligence process. These included HFT's holdings of cash and marketable securities in excess of normal working capital requirements of $1.5 million, and a series of process patents, software copyrights, and content licences that were owned by HFT, but were not being used in the operation of the company. Duncan believed that by using these assets, the new company could save at least $12 million to $15 million in future expenses, which would have been incurred to develop these processes and patents, or to gain access to certain types of content. Moreover, HFT owned a piece of undeveloped commercial property that UG believed could be sold during the next 12 to 18 months for approximately $3 million. The estimated present value of these non-operating assets was $14 million. Further, the equity value for HFT adjusted to include the estimated value of these non-operating assets and liabilities totalled $103.6 million, which was $4 million more than the initial estimate made before completing due diligence (Table 3).

After the respective companies' boards of directors and shareholder approvals had been received, the customer and vendor contracts had been assigned, the financing was in place, and other closing conditions had been satisfied, the acquisition closing finally took place. For the first time in six months both parties could relax. Whereas Lee's stress level eased, Pettibone's escalated as she faced the challenges of meeting the demanding integration schedule. Duncan's role changed from that of the dealmaker to that of the chief executive charged with meeting the expectations of his shareholders and

---

[9]Closing conditions are requirements made by both the buyer and seller that must be satisfied before ownership can be transferred.

Table 3 Adjusted HFT stand-alone valuation ($ m)

PV (2001–2005) @ 15%	6.7
PV of terminal value @ 10%	96.0
Total PV (market value of firm—equity + debt)	102.7
Less market value of debt	3.1
Equity value	99.6
Plus non-operating assets	
Excess operating cash and short-term marketable securities	1.5
PV of undeveloped commercial property	2.5
PV of unused process patents, software copyrights, and content licenses	10.0
Total non-operating assets	14.0
Less non-operating liabilities	
PV of potential jury awards	8.0
PV of deferred maintenance	2.0
Total non-operating liabilities	10.0
Adjusted equity value	103.6

Wall Street analysts. As the CEO of one of the major firms in his industry niche, Duncan was trading one set of challenges for another. But he was happy because he was living his dream.

Questions and issues

1 Identify the range of reasonable options available to UG to grow its business. Discuss the key advantages and disadvantages of each option. Of the available options, which would you have selected and why?

2 What were UG's key acquisition plan objectives and tactics (i.e., management preferences)? What other key objectives and tactics might UG have included? Discuss the importance of these additional objectives and tactics.

3 What were the key assumptions made in the UG business plan used to justify the acquisition of HFT? Consider key assumptions, both explicit and implicit, with regard to the market, financial performance, acquisition tactics, valuation, and integration.

4 What factors did Duncan consider in structuring the initial purchase price offer to HFT? What other factors should he have considered?

5 Suppose that another CD-ROM company is sold during the negotiations between UG and HFT at a significantly higher P/E ratio than that implicit in the current terms of the UG and HFT transaction. How would this informa-

tion affect negotiations? What would HFT's likely position be? How would Duncan counter HFT's arguments? Assuming Duncan still wanted to complete the transaction, how might he have restructured the purchase price to make it acceptable to HFT while still making the transaction attractive to UG shareholders?

References and additional reading

Cheng, C. S., Chao-Shin, L. and Schaefer, T. F. (1996). Earnings Performance and the Incremental Information Content of Cash Flow from Operations. *Journal of Accounting Research*, 173–181.

DePamphilis, D. (2008). *Mergers, Acquisitions, and other Restructuring Activities: An Integrated Approach to Process, Tools, Cases, and Solutions*, 4th edition. San Diego, California: Elsevier/Academic Press, pp. 388–427.

Deschow, P. M. (1994). Accounting Earnings and Cash Flows as Measures of Firm Performance: The Role of Accounting Accruals. *Journal of Accounting and Economics*, 3–42.

Porter, M. (1987). From Competitive Advantage to Corporate Strategy. *Harvard Business Review*, 43–59.

Sloan, R. G. (1996). Do Stock Prices Fully Reflect Information in Accruals and Cash Flows about Future Earnings. *Accounting Review*, 289–315.

Private family health practice: Limits to growth

Suzanne Hetzel Campbell and Christopher L. Huntley

Summary

This case study describes a unique medical practice that experienced significant growth. The practice faces several growth related challenges relating to process capacity, demand management, staffing, planning, financial risk management, information technology, and competition from similar service providers in the region.

Introduction

A mother walks into the office with a tear-stained face, dishevelled hair, exhausted eyes, and a crying, ill-content child in her arms. She says:

'You are my last hope, I've been to La Leche League, the hospital lactation consultant, my paediatrician . . . if you cannot help me I'll be forced to quit! No one ever told me it would be this hard!'

This scene is not at all unusual at Dr Thompson's Breastfeeding Practice. Dr Thompson has been able to help increasing numbers of families after establishing her specialty practice five years ago. While the growth of her practice has been very gratifying, it has left her with numerous challenges to deal with.

Background

Breastfeeding is a natural part of mothering. The health and social benefits of breastfeeding are clear. Besides its role in the prevention of infectious disease, it also provides ideal nutrition for infants, contributes to women's health, provides social and economic benefits to families and nations, and empowers women, providing them with a sense of satisfaction when carried out successfully (UNICEF, 1990). The World Health Organization recommends breastfeeding for at least two years, whilst the American Academy of Pediatrics recommends at least 12 months (AAP, 1997). Despite the benefits, the percentage of cases that meet these guidelines is very small. Only 64 per cent of mothers in the United States breastfeed early after birth, and only 29 per cent still breastfeed their infants after six months. Worldwide, less than half of infants are exclusively breastfed at four months of age.

After ten years as a primary care physician, Dr Elizabeth Thompson left general paediatric practice to specialise in breastfeeding medicine. She was motivated by her desire to help women and their children become competent at breastfeeding. Dr Thompson was supported by a practice where breastfeeding was recognised as a normal physiological process, and where there was time enough to learn from each other. Her experience suggested that traditional paediatric practice could not provide this kind of support. She decided to start her own practice. Dr Thompson opened an office in Marin County, California in the United States. Her rented office space included a small reception area, an office, one exam room, and a small conference room. Notably, her business plan was to 'build it and they will come.'

Despite her experience and credentials, when Dr Thompson set out to establish a private solo practice limited to breastfeeding medicine, she was unsure about its feasibility, and her knowledge base. Prior to opening the practice she spent time preparing herself in the following ways: reading, going to conferences, doing independent study; attending monthly La Leche League meetings; joining the International Lactation Consultant Association (ILCA); and attending quarterly meetings of LacCA, ILCA's California affiliate. In July 1995, Dr Thompson sat the International Board Certified

Lactation Consultant (IBCLC) exam, and she became certified as a lactation consultant. The office opened several months later in November 1995.

Treatment of breastfeeding patients

When Dr Thompson opened her practice she knew what had not worked when attempting to assist breastfeeding women in a general paediatric practice. Visit times were too short – 15 to 30 minutes was not long enough to adequately assess the situation or to help. The tension surrounding the hectic pace of a general practitioner's office was not conducive to breastfeeding, which requires a relaxed mood, particularly for new mothers and children. Further, the lack of medical knowledge surrounding the problems and solutions relating to the breastfeeding dyad (i.e., mother and child pair) added to the inability to provide adequate care.

By specialising, Dr Thompson was able to tailor care to the needs of breastfeeding patients. In her practice, an average initial visit takes between 1½ to 2 hours minimum, and repeat visits seldom last less than 40 minutes. Comfortable exam rooms, with lovely seats and pillows galore, provide a safe environment. Most mothers, relieved to be receiving help from understanding professionals, relax and leave the office with increased self-confidence and problems solved.

Dr Thompson's method is to diagnose and treat the physical problem in mother and child. More importantly, she supports, encourages, and provides accurate information so that the mother is renewed in her capabilities to parent, and to continue breastfeeding. Dr Thompson has gained her expertise through plenty of time, effort, and energy spent one-on-one with breastfeeding dyads. In many hospital settings, every staff member presents a different 'method' of breastfeeding, and often mother and child feel incompetent. Dr Thompson's practice, on the other hand, focuses on mother–child competence and capabilities. Staff members strive to be consistent in the advice and assistance they provide. Buying into the paradigm of 'mother–child competence' is a prerequisite to working for Dr Thompson.

The first contact with a patient is usually by telephone. When patients receive a referral to Dr Thompson, they usually call to identify themselves, the age of their child, and their perceived problem. Whenever possible, the call is answered by a registered nurse, and counselling begins immediately. All staff are trained in telephone consultation. They quickly identify the issues and seriousness of the situation. A registered nurse determines if further consultation with Dr Thompson is required. Moreover, they determine whether a nurse practitioner, or one of the lactation consultants, is necessary prior to scheduling an appointment.

Appointments are made as quickly as possible, but telephone advice is given regarding the patient's specific situation, handouts are e-mailed, faxed or mailed, and support for immediate action is provided. Upon arrival at the office, the patient completes an insurance form with background information. They are shown into an exam room and, depending on the situation and child's condition (i.e., sleeping, ready to eat, crying), child weights are measured, and child and maternal physical exams are conducted in the midst of gathering an extensive history. The office visit is on 'baby time', meaning that Dr Thompson and her staff wait for mother and child to be ready for feeding, sharing, and relaxing. Pressure to perform on either the mother or child is avoided. This calm approach provides the opportunity for healing and problem solution. Although a 'care plan' is developed individually for each mother–child dyad, nothing is written in stone, with adjustments made through telephone contact and follow-up as needed. Mother and child intuition are paramount in recovery, and often just getting the mother to trust her instincts with regard to her own child is the major obstacle to be overcome.

All health care staff are involved in direct patient contact. They each provide counselling, education, demonstration, and support in the pathophysiology and management of lactation, and the art of breastfeeding. In addition to telephone counselling, office visits and home visits, Dr Thompson provides classes for parents-to-be and back-to-work classes. The services provided by the clinic are summarised in Table 1. Monitoring of each type of visit over a 12-month period is summarised in Table 2.

Health care personnel

Dr Thompson is a board-certified paediatrician who graduated from the University of California School Of Medicine in Davis, California. Dr Thompson is a fellow of the American Academy of Pediatrics, certified by the International Board of Lactation Consultant Examiners (IBLCE), and a member of the Academy of Breastfeeding Medicine. Like all her staff, she has personal

Table 1 Services provided by Dr Thompson's practice

Counselling
• Providing help with initiation of breastfeeding and lactation
• Providing advice on problems as they arise
• Dealing with colicky infants
• Assisting with cases of refusal of the breast
• Breastfeeding adopted children, twins, triplets, etc.

Medical services
• Treating complications in labour, delivery, or postpartum
• Advising on the effects of medications on lactation
• Dealing with complications due to health problems of the mother or infant
• Helping with relactation
• Resolving conflicting medical advice
• Treating plugged ducts, mastitis, sore nipples and sore breasts

Education
• Offering classes for prenatal mothers
• Offering classes for mothers returning to work

Table 2 Summary of patient visits over a 12-month period

Type code	Description	Time (minutes)	Quantity	Cost/visit ($)
41010	Frenulotomy	Procedure	5	115.00
99079	Lactation consult	Procedure	5	194.00
99201	New patient, focused	10	2	55.00
99202	New patient, expanded	20	4	85.00
99203	New patient, detailed	30	14	115.00
99204	New patient, comprehensive (NPC)	45	8	175.00
99205	NPC	60	23	210.00
99212	Return office visit (ROV)	10	5	45.00
99213	ROV	15	435	65.00
99214	ROV	25	326	100.00
99215	ROV	40	279	150.00
99241	New patient, consult (NP,C)	15	46	75.00
99242	NP,C	30	189	120.00
99243	NP,C	40	136	155.00
99244	NP,C	60	209	215.00
99245	NP,C	80	208	290.00
99252	Hospital consult (HC)	40	3	120.00
99253	HC	55	6	155.00
99254	HC	80	4	215.00
99341	Home visit new (HVN)	20	1	85.00
99343	HVN	45	3	170.00
99344	HVN	60	4	210.00
99345	HVN	75	7	275.00
99347	Home visit returning patient (HVRP)	15	1	75.00
99348	HVRP	25	4	100.00
99349	HVRP	40	6	150.00
99350	HVRP	60	6	210.00

Table 3 Current employees

Employee	Hours worked	Responsibilities
Dr Elizabeth Thompson, MD	40 to 60 +	Patient care: diagnosis/treatment, on call prescription, referral, telephone/e-mail consultation
Women's health nurse practitioner; IBCLC × 10 years	32 to 40	Patient care including all above with MD consultation
Women's health nurse practitioner; LLL leader × 11 years, PhD; sitting for IBCLC exam	6 to 8 (20+ in summer)	Same as above; research and writing
IBCLC (LLL clinical assistant consultation to Dr Thompson × 1 year +)	24	Patient care, assessment, phone
IBCLC, LLL Leader × 6 years	15	Patient care, assessment, phone
RN with Dr Thompson × 1 year; LLL leader; sitting for IBCLC exam	30	Telephone triaging, appointments, insurance data, e-mail information, pharmacy calls
Receptionist	20	Filing, telephone, office management, insurance claims
Billing/bookkeeping: accountant, claims/payroll	10 to 15	Patient accounting/insurance
Billing/bookkeeping	8 to 10	Accounts receivable/accounts payable

breastfeeding experience, having nursed her two children, now 16 and 20 years old.

Dr Thompson's staff is composed of lactation consultants, nurse practitioners, and administrative personnel (Table 3). While any of these personnel may be involved with a particular office visit, each plays a particular role in the organisation.

Lactation consultants (LCs) and consultants in training comprise the bulk of the staff. LCs provide support and education, but not diagnosis or treatment of medical problems. Some LCs are registered nurses (RNs). LCs are trained and certified through a separate educational process that culminates with the International Board Certified Lactation Consultant (IBCLC) exam. Further, some LCs have been group leaders in La Leche League International (LLLI), which is a volunteer organisation offering 'mother-to-mother' support to breastfeeding women. These employees are well-versed in telephone counselling, have the knowledge and skills background to offer initial breastfeeding assistance, and quickly pick up the skills to manage the more highly complex patients. However, lactation consultation is generally not covered under medical insurance plans in the United States. Time with an LC is not billable and must be considered a financial loss for the practice.

The most independent and versatile members of the support staff are the nurse practitioners (NPs). In the state of California, NPs have prescription privileges, work in collaboration with physicians and their services (including home visits) are billable through health insurance. All NPs in the practice are certified LCs, allowing them to fill in for other LCs. Skilled NPs are quite scarce and they receive higher salaries than other staff members.

Organisational growth

Breastfeeding medicine is time-intensive and requires a continuous source of new referrals. When she started the practice, Dr Thompson perceived she had incomplete knowledge relating to patients, providers, payers, and breastfeeding itself. She managed these challenges by starting a specialty practice. Her low initial overhead (herself as the only employee) allowed more time with each patient, and kept start-up costs low. Not providing primary care meant Dr Thompson could immerse herself in a specialist's education, and referrals for her services would be easier because physicians were not afraid of 'stolen' patients. Finally, she decided to evaluate and manage the mother–child dyad as a single unit.

A self-financed Dr Thompson rented and furnished her office space. Dr Thompson had hospital privileges at four hospitals, and she introduced her new specialty practice at paediatric grand rounds at local hospitals. She sent announcements to local paediatricians' and obstetricians' offices and letters to area health maintenance organisations (HMOs). In her letter to HMOs, she described the health advantages of breastfeeding and the cost savings to HMOs. She provided a description with examples of her care, and how it was distinct from lactation counselling. The provision of medical care, diagnosing and treating medical problems, as well as prescribing medications for treatment made her practice distinct from lactation counselling. Dr Thompson also developed the charting system, forms, handouts, and accounts for her practice. The charting system and forms have periodically changed as the practice has grown.

Starting from this minimalist base, Dr Thompson had gradually increased the number of staff employed in the practice (Table 3). In 1997, she hired a receptionist and billing employee for 15 hours per week, and in 1998 their hours increased to 20 per week. In 1999, she had the same receptionist and billing employee for 20 hours per week, plus a paediatric nurse practitioner (PNP) for 6 hours per week. In 2000 there were 4 employees who were employed for 15 hours per week (i.e., an administrative assistant, a registered nurse IBCLC, a La Leche League Leader (LLLL) clinical assistant, and an RN). In 2001, two NPs were added to the practice, as were two new certified LCs. Also added were two individuals managing office billing and insurance claims, and an RN who began in 2000. A receptionist was hired for 20 hours per week in 2002.

Demand for breastfeeding services

Dr Thompson serves a small but enthusiastic market for her breastfeeding services. The office currently sees between six and nine patients per day. The patients seen in Dr Thompson's office are often in need of acute care, and have exhausted the community resources for assistance with breastfeeding. Active La Leche League groups in the area provide support and encouragement. Patients are generally drawn from the northern San Francisco Bay area. The practice also attracts patients from northern California. Some telephone counselling with e-mail contact has been made to patients outside the state, but this is not common.

The number of patients has grown steadily over time (Table 4). Despite this steady growth, demand is erratic and subject to seasonality effects. In November and December, related to the stressful holiday preparations, many new mothers develop plugged ducts and mastitis

Table 4 New dyads over time

Year	Number of dyads
1996	60
1997	135
1998	198
1999	314
2000	276 (8/12 months)
2001	427

and seek treatment and care. In the summer, related to family vacations and the hot temperatures, yeast infections seem to proliferate.

Co-operative competition

Dr Thompson receives patient referrals from paediatricians, nurse midwives and nurse practitioners, obstetricians, lactation consultants, and La Leche League leaders. She maintains these referrals by providing presentations at hospitals and conferences. Her membership in groups related to breastfeeding within the state and nationally also provides access to practitioners who may be interested in her services.

Besides providing a supply of referrals, these outreach efforts help her to acquire the resources needed to sustain the practice. Many of her employees are registered nurses who learn of Dr Thompson from the La Leche League, or her hospital visits. Her status as a licensed IBCLC makes her ideally qualified to train prospective lactation consultants. The conference presentations allow her to share information gained from research and clinical practice with possible collaborators.

Despite the benefits associated with co-operating with these other organisations, Dr Thompson recognises that some are potential competitors. Many practitioners seek to meet their clients' needs within their own practice (for example, many paediatricians, obstetricians, and hospitals now employ lactation consultants) as a way to retain revenues. Similarly, La Leche League also provides lactation consulting as part of its mother-to-mother counselling community. To keep these relationships friendly, Dr Thompson is careful to direct her services primarily to patients with specialised needs, which are not easily served by her competitors. Once these needs are met, the patient returns to her original service provider.

Facilities

The practice began with one exam room, a reception area and a conference area. There are now three exam rooms, a conference area for prenatal and back-to-work group meetings, and a staff area, with kitchen, washer and dryer, computer for e-mailing and other services, and tables and telephones to chart and return patient calls. This expansion has taken time but has enhanced the productivity and efficiency of the office space. However, it is quite costly, particularly for a practice where many of the staff do not produce any direct revenue. Any further expansion of the practice would require opening a second office, or moving to a larger facility.

Finance

Given current health care priorities in the United States, it is unlikely that Dr Thompson's practice will ever be a major financial success. Failure to breastfeed is not considered a medical problem, and consultations are not covered by medical insurance. Unless a mother has developed a treatable medical condition, all expenses must be paid out-of-pocket by the patient, which limits the practice's ability to rapidly increase income.

Fortunately for Dr Thompson, there are just enough affluent mothers in the northern San Francisco Bay area to sustain the practice at its current size. The per capita income of Marin County, where her office is located, is among the highest in the United States. However, it has been a struggle to remain financially viable. Out of $280,000 billed in 2001, only $180,000 was covered by insurance, leaving the remaining $100,000 to be paid out-of-pocket by the patients themselves. Often Dr Thompson finds she must absorb these costs herself. While some of these costs could potentially be covered through grants or subsidies, Dr Thompson finds that she has little time to pursue them.

Information technology

The practice uses PC-based software for most of its administrative needs. QuickBooks is used for office accounting and payroll. Medi-Soft is used for insurance claims and patient billing. Medical charting is performed by hand using paper forms. While the current paper-based system is cheap, portable and familiar, it is ill-suited for the statistical analyses required by Dr Thompson's research. Data gathering and analysis to demonstrate the growth of the practice and identify patterns in diagnosis occurrence and treatment results is time-consuming.

Recent events

The early years of her practice allowed time for the practical application of her theories, but with the subsequent rapid growth the practice has experienced, Dr Thompson is consumed with providing care. The physical and mental stress of meeting the needs of this 'high need' patient population is compounded by worries regarding her financial stability. Dr Thompson never intended the practice to be a business enterprise per se, but rather as a means of meeting her professional goals, which have always been altruistic and educational rather than financial.

Dr Thompson has begun to explore her options. She has approached some medical doctors who may be interested in part-time employment positions. Like herself almost 20 years ago, they are breastfeeding mothers who seek the time and flexibility to raise their children without giving up their medical careers. The spiral continues, with Dr Thompson's practice growing even as she becomes ever more ambivalent about her business.

Questions and issues

1 What does Dr Thompson perceive as the 'problem' here? Is she meeting her goals?

2 What are Dr Thompson's alternatives within a strategic timeframe? More specifically, what options should she consider for restructuring her business?

3 What limits the growth of Dr Thompson's practice? In other words, what factors stand in the way of growing the practice beyond its current size?

References

AAP. (1997). Work Group on Breastfeeding, American Academy of Pediatrics. Breastfeeding and the Use of Human Milk. *Pediatrics*, 100 (6): 1035–1039.

List, B. A., Ballard, J. L., Langworthy, K. S., Vincent, A. M., Riddle, S. W., Tamayo, O. W. and Geraghty, S. R. (2008). Electronic Health Records in an Outpatient Breastfeeding Medicine Clinic. *Journal of Human Lactation*, 24 (1): 58–68.

UNICEF. (1990). *Innocenti Declaration on the Protection, Promotion, and Support of 1990 Breastfeeding*. Florence, Italy: UNICEF and World Health Organization.

References

Abetti, P. (2002). From Science to Technology to Products and Profits, Superconductivity at General Electric and Intermagnetics General. *Journal of Business Venturing*, 17: 83–98.

Acharya, V. and Kehoe, C. (2008). *Corporate Governance and Value Creation Evidence from Private Equity*. London: London Business School Working Paper.

Achleiner, A-K., Nathusius, E., Herman, K. and Lerner, J. (2008). Impact of Private Equity on Corporate Governance, Employment and Empowerment of a Family in a Divisional Buyout: The Case of Messer Griesheim (January 2008). *The Global Economic Impact of Private Equity Report*, pp. 91–102, 2008. Available at SSRN: http://ssrn.com/abstract=1120222.

Acs, Z. J. (1996). *Small Firms and Economic Growth. The International Library of Critical Writings in Economics 61*. Cheltenham: Edward Elgar.

Acs, Z. J. (2006). Start-Up and Entry Barriers: Small and Medium-Sized Firms Population Dynamics. In M. Casson, B. Yeung, A. Basu and N. Wadeson (eds). *The Oxford Handbook of Entrepreneurship*. Oxford: Oxford University Press, pp. 194–224.

Acs, Z. J., Audretsch, D. B. and Feldman, M. P. (1992). Real Effects of Academic Research: Comment. *American Economic Review*, 82: 363–367.

Acs, Z. J., Morck, R., Shaver, J. M. and Yeung, B. (1997). The Internationalization of Small and Medium-Sized Enterprises: A Policy Perspective. *Small Business Economics*, 9 (1): 7–20.

Acs, Z. J. and Storey, D. J. (2004). Introduction, Entrepreneurship and Economic Development. *Regional Studies*, 38: 871–877.

Aernoudt, R. (2004). Incubators: Tool for Entrepreneurship. *Small Business Economics*, 23 (2): 127–135.

Agarwal, R., Echambadi, R., Franco, A. and Sarkar, M. (2004). Knowledge Transfer Through Inheritance: Spin-out Generation, Development and Survival. *Academy of Management Journal*, 47: 501–522.

Ajzen, I. (2002). Perceived Behavioral Control, Self-Efficacy, Locus of Control and the Theory of Planned Behavior. *Journal of Applied Social Psychology*, 32 (4): 665–683.

Alcacer, J. and Chung, W. (2007). Location Strategies and Knowledge Spillovers. *Management Science*, 53 (5): 760–776.

Aldrich, H. and Zimmer, C. (1986). Entrepreneurship Through Social Networks. In D. Sexton and R. Smilo (eds). *The Art and Science of Entrepreneurship*. Cambridge, MA: Ballinger, pp. 3–23.

Alemany, L. and Marti, J. (2005). *Unbiased Estimation of Economic Impact of Venture Capital Backed Firms*. Working Paper.

Alsos, G. A. and Carter, S. (2006). Multiple Business Ownership in the Norwegian Farm Sector: Resource Transfer and Performance Consequences. *Journal of Rural Studies*, 22 (3): 313–322.

Alsos, G. A. and Kolvereid, L. (1998). The Business Gestation Process of Novice, Serial and Parallel Business Founders. *Entrepreneurship Theory and Practice*, 22 (4): 101–114.

Alsos, G. A., Kolvereid, L. and Isaksen, E. J. (2006). New Business Early Performance: Differences Between Firms Started by Novice, Serial and Portfolio Entrepreneurs. In P. R. Christensen and F. Poulfeldt (eds). *Managing Complexity and Change in SMEs, Frontiers in European Research*. Cheltenham, UK: Edward Elgar, pp. 35–49.

Alsos, G. A., Ljunggren, E. and Pettersen, L. T. (2003). Farm-Based Entrepreneurs, What Triggers the Start-Up of New Business Activities? *Journal of Small Business and Enterprise Development*, 10 (4), 435–443.

Alvarez, S. and Busenitz, L. (2001). The Entrepreneurship of Resource-Based Theory. *Journal of Management*, 27: 755–775.

Amabile, T. M., Hill, K. G., Hennesey, B. A. and Tighe, E. M. (1994). The Work Preference Inventory: Assessing Intrinsic and Extrinsic Motivational Orientations. *Journal of Personality and Social Psychology*, 66 (5): 950–967.

Amess, K. (2003). The Effect of Management Buyouts on Firm-Level Technical Efficiency: Evidence from a Panel of UK Machinery and Equipment Manufacturers. *Journal of Industrial Economics*, 51: 35–44.

Amess, K., Girma, S. and Wright, M. (2008). *What are the Wage and Employment Consequences of Leveraged Buy-outs, Private Equity and Acquisitions in the UK?* Nottingham: Nottingham University Business, Centre for Management Buyout Research, CMBOR Working Paper.

Amess, K. and Wright, M. (2007). The Wage and Employment Effects of Leveraged Buy-outs in the UK. *International Journal of Economics and Business*, 14 (2): 179–195.

Amess, K. and Wright, M. (2010). Barbarians at the Gate: Do LBOs and Private Equity Destroy Jobs? *Small Business Economics*, forthcoming.

Amit, R. and Shoemaker, P. J. H. (1993). Strategic Assets and Organizational Rent. *Strategic Management Journal*, 14: 33–46.

Anderson, O. (1993). On the Internationalization Process of Firms: A Critical Analysis. *Journal of International Business Studies*, 24: 209–231.

Andrade, G. and Kaplan, S. (1998). How Costly is Financial (Not Economic) Distress? Evidence from Highly Leveraged Transactions that Became Distressed. *Journal of Finance*, 53: 1443–1493.

Anselin, L, Varga, A. and Acs, Z. (1997). Local Geographic Spillovers Between University Research and High Technology Innovations. *Journal of Urban Economics*, 42: 422–448.

Ardichvili, A., Cardozo, R. and Ray, S. (2003). A Theory of Entrepreneurial Opportunity Identification and Development. *Journal of Business Venturing*, 18: 105–123.

Armington, C. and Acs, Z. J. (2002). The Determinants of Regional Variations in New Firm Formation. *Regional Studies*, 36 (1): 33–45.

Aspelund, A. and Moen, Ø. (2005). Small International Firms: Typology, Performance and Implications. *Management International Review*, 45 (3): 37–57.

Astrachan, J. H. and Shanker, M. C. (2003). Family Businesses' Contribution to the US Economy: A Closer Look. *Family Business Review*, 16 (3): 211–219.

Atkinson, J. and Hurstfield, J. (2004). *Small Business Service. Annual Survey of Small Businesses UK 2003*. London: Institute for Employment Studies, Small Business Service.

Audretsch, D. B. (1995). *Innovation and Industry*. Cambridge, MA: MIT Press.

Audretsch, D. B. and Keilbach, M. (2004a). Does Entrepreneurship Capital Matter? *Entrepreneurship Theory and Practice*, 28 (5): 419–429.

Audretsch, D. B. and Keilbach, M. (2004b). Entrepreneurship Capital and Economic Performance. *Regional Studies*, 38 (8): 949–960.

Audretsch, D. B. and Keilbach, M. (2006). Entrepreneurship, Growth and Restructuring. In M. Casson, B. Yeung,

A. Basu and N. Wadeson (eds). *The Oxford Handbook of Entrepreneurship*. Oxford: Oxford University Press, pp. 281–310.

Audretsch, D. B., Keilbach, M. and Lehmann, E. (2006). *Entrepreneurship and Economic Growth*. Oxford: Oxford University Press.

Audretsch, D. and Lehmann, E. (2004). Financing High Tech Growth: The Role of Banks and Venture Capitalists. *Schmalenbach Economic Review*, 56: 340–357.

Austin, J. E., Stevenson, H. and Wei-Skillern, J. (2006). Social and Commercial Entrepreneurship: Same, Different, or Both? *Entrepreneurship Theory and Practice*, 30 (1): 1–22.

Autio, E. (2005). Creative Tension: The Significance of Ben Oviatt's and Patricia McDougall's Article 'Toward a Theory of International New Ventures'. *Journal of International Business Studies*, 36 (1): 9–19.

Autio, E. and Kauranen, I. (1994). Technologist-Entrepreneurs versus Non-Entrepreneurial Technologists: Analysis of Motivational Trigger Factors. *Entrepreneurship and Regional Development*, 6: 315–328.

Autio, E., Sapienza, H. J. and Almeida, J. G. (2000). Effects of Age at Entry, Knowledge Intensity, and Imitability on International Growth. *Academy of Management Journal*, 43: 909–924.

Bain, J. (1956). *Barriers to New Competition*. Cambridge, MA: Harvard University Press.

Baker, T. and Nelson, R. E. (2005). Creating Something from Nothing: Resource Construction Through Entrepreneurial Bricolage. *Administrative Science Quarterly*, 50: 329–366.

Bandura, A. (1995). Perceived Self-Efficacy. In A. S. R. Manstead and M. Hawstone (eds). *The Blackwell Encyclopaedia of Social Psychology*. Oxford: Blackwell Publishers Ltd, pp. 434–436.

Bandura, A. (1997). *Social Learning Theory*. Englewood Cliffs, NJ: Prentice Hall.

Barney, J. B. (1991). Firm Resources and Sustained Competitive Advantage. *Journal of Management*, 17: 99–120.

Barney, J. B. (2001). Is the Resource-Based 'View' a Useful Perspective for Strategic Management Research? Yes. *Academy of Management Review*, 26: 41–56.

Barney, J., Wright, M. and Ketchen, D. (2001). The Resource-Based View of the Firm: Ten Years after 1991. *Journal of Management*, 27 (6): 625–641.

Baron, R. A. (1998). Cognitive Mechanisms in Entrepreneurship, Why and When Entrepreneurs Think Differently Than Other People. *Journal of Business Venturing*, 13 (4): 275–294.

Baron, R. A. (2004). The Cognitive Perspective, A Valuable Tool for Answering Entrepreneurship's Basic 'Why' Questions. *Journal of Business Venturing*, 19 (2): 221–239.

Baron, R. A. and Ensley, M. D. (2006). Opportunity Recognition as the Detection of Meaningful Patterns, Evidence from Comparison and Novice and Experienced Entrepreneurs. *Management Science*, 52: 1331–1344.

Baruch, Y. and Gebbie, D. (1998). Cultures of Success – the Leading UK MBOs. *Journal of Business Venturing*, 13: 423–430.

Batstone, S. and Pheby, J. (1996). Entrepreneurship and Decision Making: The Contribution of G. L. S. Shackle. *International Journal of Entrepreneurial Behaviour & Research*, 2 (2): 34–51.

Baum, J. R. and Locke, E. A. (2004). The Relationship of Entrepreneurial Traits, Skill, and Motivation to Subsequent Venture Growth. *Journal of Applied Psychology*, 89: 587–598.

Baum, J. A. C. and Silverman, B. S. (2004). Picking Winners or Building Them? Alliance, Intellectual, and Human Capital as Selection Criteria in Venture Financing and Performance of Biotechnology Startups. *Journal of Business Venturing*, 19: 411–436.

Baumol, W. J. (1968). Entrepreneurship in Economic Theory. *American Economic Review*, 58 (2): 64–71.

Baumol, W. J. (1990). Entrepreneurship: Productive, Unproductive and Destructive. *Journal of Political Economy*, 98 (5): 893–921.

Becker, G. S. (1975). *Human Capital*. New York, National Bureau of Economic Research.

Becker, G. S. (1993). Nobel Lecture, The Economic Way of Looking at Behavior. *The Journal of Political Economy*, 101: 385–409.

Bell, J., Crick, D. and Young, S. (2004). Small Firm Internationalization and Business Strategy: An Exploratory Study of 'Knowledge-Intensive' and 'Traditional' Manufacturing Firms in the UK. *International Small Business Journal*, 22: 23–56.

Bell, J., McNaughton, R. and Young, S. (2001). 'Born-Again Global' Firms. An Extension to the 'Born Global' Phenomenon. *Journal of International Management*, 7: 173–189.

Bell, J., McNaughton, R., Young, S. and Crick, D. (2003). Towards an Integrative Model of Small Firm Internationalization. *Journal of International Entrepreneurship*, 1: 339–362.

Bengtsson, O. (2007). *Repeated Relationships Between Venture Capitalists and Entrepreneurs*. Chicago: University of Chicago Working Paper.

Bennett, R. (2008). SME Policy Support in Britain Since the 1990s: What Have We Learnt? *Environment and Planning C: Government and Policy*, 26: 375–397.

Bennett, R. J. and Robson, P. J. A. (2003). Changing Use of External Business Advice and Government Support During the 1990s. *Regional Studies*, 37: 795–811.

Bertoni, F., Colombo, M. and Grilli, L. (2008). *Venture Capital Financing and the Growth of New Technology Based Firms*. Milan: WP Politechnico di Milano.

Binks, M. (2000). *Entrepreneurship*. Nottingham: Nottingham University Business School, Institute for Enterprise and Innovation.

Binks, M. and Jennings, A. (1986). New Firms as a Source of Industrial Regeneration. In M. Scott, A. Gibbs, J. Lewis and T. Faulkner (eds). *Small Firms' Growth and Development*. Aldershot: Gower, pp. 3–11.

Birch, D. (1979). *The Job Generation Process*. Cambridge, MA: MIT Program on Neighborhood and Regional Change.

Birley, S. (1985). The Role of Networks in the Entrepreneurial Process. *Journal of Business Venturing*, 1(1): 107–117.

Birley, S. (1998). *Entrepreneurship*. Ashgate: Dartmouth.

Birley, S., Ng, D. and Godfrey, A. (1999). The Family and the Business. *Long Range Planning*, 32 (6): 598–608.

Birley, S. and Westhead, P. (1990a). Growth and Performance Contrasts Between 'Types' of Small Firms. *Strategic Management Journal*, 11 (7): 535–557.

Birley, S. and Westhead, P. (1990b). Private Business Sales Environments in the United Kingdom. *Journal of Business Venturing*, 5 (2): 349–373.

Birley, S. and Westhead, P. (1992). A Comparison of New Firms in 'Assisted' and 'Non-Assisted' Areas in Great Britain. *Entrepreneurship and Regional Development*, 4 (3): 299–338.

Birley, S. and Westhead, P. (1993a). A Comparison of New Businesses Established by 'Novice' and 'Habitual' Founders in Great Britain'. *International Small Business Journal*, 12 (1): 38–60.

Birley, S. and Westhead, P. (1993b). The Owner–Managers Exit Route. In H. Klandt (ed.) *Entrepreneurship and Business Development*. Avebury: Gower, pp. 123–140.

Birley, S. and Westhead, P. (1994). A Taxonomy of Business Start-Up Reasons and their Impact on Firm Growth and Size. *Journal of Business Venturing*, 9 (1): 7–31.

Bjuggren, P-O. and Sund, L-G. (2001). Strategic Decision-Making in Intergenerational Successions of Small- and Medium-size Family-owned Businesses. *Family Business Review*, 14 (1): 11–23.

Block. Z. and MacMillan, I. C. (1993). *Corporate Venturing: Creating New Businesses Within the Firm*. Boston: Harvard Business School Press.

Bloodgood, J. M., Sapienza, H. J. and Almeida, J. G. (1996). The Internationalization of New High-Potential U.S. Ventures: Antecedents and Outcomes. *Entrepreneurship Theory and Practice*, 20: 61–76.

Bodas Freitas, I. M. and von Tunzelmann, N. (2008). Mapping Public Support for Innovation: A Comparison of Policy Alignment in the UK and France. *Research Policy*, 37 (9): 1446–1464.

Bøllingtoft, A. and Uhløi, J. (2005). The Networked Business Incubator: Leveraging Entrepreneurial Agency? *Journal of Business Venturing*, 20 (2): 265–290.

Bolton, B. and Thompson, J. (2000). *Entrepreneurs: Talent, Temperament, Technique*. Oxford: Butterworth Heinemann.

Bosma, N., van Praag, M., Thurik, R. and de Wit, G. (2004). The Value of Human and Social Capital Investments for the Business Performance of Startups. *Small Business Economics*, 23: 227–236.

Botazzi, L. and Da Rin, M. (2002). Venture Capital in Europe and the Financing of Innovative Companies. *Economic Policy*, 17: 229–269.

Bottazzi, L., Da Rin, M. and Hellmann, T. (2008). Who are the Active Investors? Evidence from Venture Capital. *Journal of Financial Economics*, 89 (3), 488–512.

Boyd, N. G. and Vozkis, G. S. (1994). The Influence of Self-Efficacy on the Development of Entrepreneurial Intentions and Actions. *Entrepreneurship Theory and Practice*, 18 (4): 63–77.

Brandstätter, H. (1997). Becoming an Entrepreneur – A Question of Personality Structure? *Journal of Economic Psychology*, 18: 157–177.

Braunerhjelm, P. and Boargman, B. (2004). Geographic Concentration, Entrepreneurship and Regional Growth: Evidence from Regional Data in Sweden, 1975–99. *Regional Studies*, 38 (8): 929–948.

Bridge, S., O'Neill, K. and Cromie, S. (2003). *Understanding Enterprise, Entrepreneurship and Small Business, 2nd edition*. Basingstoke: Macmillan Press Ltd.

Brüderl, J., Preisendorfer, P. and Ziegler, R. (1992). Survival Chances of Newly Founded Business Organizations. *American Sociological Review*, 57: 227–242.

Bruining, H. and Wright, M. (2002). Entrepreneurial Orientation in Management Buy-outs and the Contribution of Venture Capital. *Venture Capital*, 4: 147–168.

Bruining, H., Bonnet, M. and Wright, M. (2004). Management Control Systems and Strategy Change in Buy-outs. *Management Accounting Research*, 15: 155–177.

Brush, C. (1992). Research on Women Business Owners: Past Trends, A New Perspective and Future Directions. *Entrepreneurship Theory and Practice*, 16: 5–30.

Brush, C. G., Carter, N. M., Gatewood, E. J., Greene, P. G. and Hart, M. M. (2006). *Women and Entrepreneurship: Contemporary Classics*. Cheltenham: Edward Elgar Publishing Ltd, pp. 563–572.

Brush, C. G., Edelman, L. F. and Manolova, T. S. (2002). The Impact of Resources on Small Firm Internationalization. *Journal of Small Business Strategy*, 13: 1–17.

Bruton, G. D., Ahlstrom, D. and Obloj, K. (2008). Entrepreneurship in Emerging Economies: Where are We Today and Where Should the Research Go in the Future. *Entrepreneurship Theory and Practice*, 32 (1): 1–14.

Buckley, P. and Casson, M. (1976). *The Future of the Multinational Enterprise*. London: MacMillan.

Bull, I. (1989). Management Performance in Leveraged Buy-outs: An Empirical Analysis. *Journal of Business Venturing*, 3: 263–278.

Burgel, O., Fier, A., Licht, G. and Murray, G. (2000). *Internationalisation of High Tech Start-Ups and Fast Growth: Evidence from Germany and UK*. Centre for European Economic Research, Mannheim: DP 00–35.

Burgel, O., Fier, A., Licht, G. and Murray, G. (2001). *The Rapid Internationalisation of High-Tech Young Firms in Germany and the United Kingdom*. London: Anglo-German Foundation.

Burke, A., Fraser, S. and Greene, F. J. (2010). Multiple Effects of Business Plans on New Ventures. *Journal of Management Studies*, 47 (3): 391–415.

Burns, P. (2007). *Entrepreneurship and Small Business*. Basingstoke: Palgrave Macmillan.

Busenitz, L. W. and Barney, J. B. (1997). Differences Between Entrepreneurs and Managers in Large Organizations: Biases and Heuristics in Strategic Decision-Making. *Journal of Business Venturing*, 12: 9–30.

Busenitz, L. W., West, P., Shepherd, D., Nelson, T., Zacharakis, A. and Chandler, G. (2003). Entrepreneurship in Emergence: Past Trends and Future Directions. *Journal of Management*, 29 (3): 285–308.

Butchart, R. I. (1987). A New UK Definition of the High Technology Industries. *Economic Trends*, February: 82–88.

Bygrave, W. D. and Hofer, C. W. (1991). Theorizing About Entrepreneurship. *Entrepreneurship Theory and Practice*, 16 (2): 13–22.

Cambridge Small Business Research Centre. (1992). *The State of British Enterprise: Growth, Innovation and Competitive Advantage in Small and Medium-Sized Firms*. Cambridge: University of Cambridge.

Cantillon, R. (1755). *Essai sur la Nature du Commerce en General*. Translated by H. Higgs (1931). London: Macmillan.

Carree, M., van Stel, A., Thurik, R. and Wennekers, S. (2007). The Relationship Between Economic Development and Business Ownership Revisited. *Entrepreneurship and Regional Development*, 19 (3): 281–291.

Carsrud, A. L. and Johnson, R. W. (1989). Entrepreneurship: A Social Psychological Perspective. *Entrepreneurship and Regional Development*, 1 (1): 21–31.

Carter, N., Williams, M. and Reynolds, P. D. (1997). Discontinuance Among New Firms in Retail: The Influence of Initial Resources, Strategy, and Gender. *Journal of Business Venturing*, 12, pp. 125–145.

Carter, S. (1999). Multiple Business Ownership in the Farm Sector, Assessing the Enterprise and Employment

Contributions of Farmers in Cambridgeshire. *Journal of Rural Studies*, 15 (4): 417–429.

Carter, S. and Jones-Evans, D. (2006). *Enterprise and Small Business: Principles, Practice and Policy, 2nd edition.* Harlow: Financial Times, Prentice Hall.

Carter, S. and Ram, M. (2003). Reassessing Portfolio Entrepreneurship, Towards a Multidisciplinary Approach. *Small Business Economics*, 21 (4): 371–380.

Carter, S., Tagg, S. and Dimitratos, P. (2004). Beyond Portfolio Entrepreneurship, Multiple Income Sources in Small Firms. *Entrepreneurship and Regional Development*, 16: 481–499.

Carter, S. and Rosa, P. (1998). The Financing of Male- and Female-Owned Businesses. *Entrepreneurship and Regional Development*, 10: 225–241.

Casson, M. (1982). *The Entrepreneur: An Economic Theory.* Oxford: Martin Robertson.

Casson, M. (1990). Introduction. In M. Casson (ed.) *Entrepreneurship.* Aldershot: Edward Elgar, pp. xiii–xxvi.

Casson, M. Yeung, B., Basu, A. and Wadeson, N. (2006). *The Oxford Handbook of Entrepreneurship.* Oxford: Oxford University Press.

Castanias, R. and Helfat, C. (2001). The Managerial Rents Model: Theory and Empirical Analysis. *Journal of Management*, 6: 661–678.

Castells, M. and Hall, P. (1994). *Technopoles of the World: The Making of 21st Century Industrial Complexes.* London: Routledge.

Cefis, E. and Marsili, O. (2006). Survivor: The Role of Innovation in Firms' Survival. *Research Policy*, 35: 626–641.

Centre for Management Buyout Research (CMBOR). (2008). *Trends in Management Buy-outs. Management Buy-outs: Quarterly Review from the Centre for Management Buy-out Research.* Nottingham: Nottingham University Business, Centre for Management Buyout Research, Autumn.

CMBOR (2009). *Management Buyouts. Quarterly Review from CMBOR, Autumn.* Nottingham: Nottingham University Business School, Centre for Management Buyout Research.

Chaganti, R. and Schneer, J. A. (1994). A Study of the Impact of Owner's Mode of Entry on Venture Performance and Management Patterns. *Journal of Business Venturing*, 9: 243–61.

Chancellor of the Exchequer. (2004). Speech by the Chancellor of the Exchequer of the Launch of the Enterprise Insight Campaign. 28 June, available at http://www.hm-treasury.gov.uk/newsroom_and_speeches/press/2004/press_60_04.cfm.

Chandler, G. N. (1996). Business Similarity as a Moderator of the Relationship Between Pre-Ownership Experience and Venture Performance. *Entrepreneurship Theory and Practice*, 20: 51–65.

Chandler, G. and Hanks, S. (1993). Measuring the Performance of Emerging Businesses: A Validation Study. *Journal of Business Venturing*, 8: 391–408.

Chandler, G. N. and Hanks, S. H. (1998). An Examination of the Substitutability of Founders Human and Financial Capital in Emerging Business Ventures. *Journal of Business Venturing*, 13 (5): 353–369.

Chandler, G. N. and Jansen, E. (1992). The Founder's Self-Assessed Competence and Venture Performance. *Journal of Business Venturing*, 7 (3): 223–236.

Chang, E. P. C., Chrisman, J. J., Chua, J. H. and Kellermans, F. W. (2008). Regional Economy as a Determinant of the Prevalence of Family Firms in the United States: A Preliminary Report. *Entrepreneurship Theory and Practice*, 32 (3): 559–573.

Cheah, H-B. (1990). Schumpeterian and Austrian Entrepreneurship: Unity Within Duality. *Journal of Business Venturing*, 5 (6): 341–347.

Checkland, S. G. (1981). *The Upas Tree: Glasgow, 1875–1975 . . . and After, 2nd edition.* Glasgow: University of Glasgow.

Chen, C. C., Gene Greene, P. and Crick, A. (1998). Does Entrepreneurial Self-Efficacy Distinguish Entrepreneurs from Managers? *Journal of Business Venturing*, 13 (4): 295–316.

Chittoor, R. and Das, R. (2007). Professionalization of Management and Succession Performance – A Vital Linkage. *Family Business Review*, 20: 65–79.

Chrisman, J. J., Chua, J. H. and Sharma, P. (2005). Trends and Directions in the Development of a Strategic Management Theory of the Family Firm. *Entrepreneurship Theory and Practice*, 29 (3): 555–575.

Chrisman, J. J., Chua, J. H. and Steier, L. P. (2003a). An Introduction to the Theories of Family Business. *Journal of Business Venturing*, 18 (4): 441–448.

Chrisman, J. J., Chua, J. H. and Zahra, S. (2003b). Creating Wealth in Family Firms through Managing Resources: Comments and Extensions. *Entrepreneurship Theory and Practice*, 27 (4): 359–366.

Churchill, N. and Lewis, V. (1983). The Five Stages of Small Business Growth. *Harvard Business Review*, 61: 30–50.

Citron, D., Robbie, K. and Wright, M. (1997). Loan Covenants and Relationship Banking in MBOs. *Accounting and Business Research*, 27: 277–296.

Citron, D., Wright, M., Rippington, F. and Ball, R. (2003). Secured Creditor Recovery Rates from Management Buy-Outs in Distress. *European Financial Management*, 9: 141–162.

Clarysse, B., Bruneel, J. and Wright, M. (2007). *Growth Strategies of Young, Technology-Based Firms.* Paper presented at the Babson Entrepreneurship Conference, Madrid.

Clarysse, B., Bruneel, J. and Wright, M. (2011). *Growth, Value Creation and Resources in Young High Growth Technology Based Firms: the Impact of Environmental Contingencies*. Strategic Entrepreneurship Journal (forthcoming).

Clarysse, B., Wright, M., Lockett, A., van de Elde, E. and Vohora, A. (2005). Spinning Out New Ventures: A Typology of Incubation Strategies from European Research Institutions. *Journal of Business Venturing*, 20 (2): 183–216.

Clarysse, B., Wright, M. and VandeVelde, E. (2010). Entrepreneurial Origin, Technological Knowledge and the Growth of Spin-off Companies. *Journal of Management Studies*, forthcoming.

Clarysse, B., Wright, M. and Mustar, P. (2009). Behavioural Additionality of R&D Subsidies: A Learning Perspective, *Research Policy*, 38 (10): 1517–1533.

Colombo, M. G. and Grilli, L. (2005). Founders' Human Capital and the Growth of New Technology-Based Firms: A Competence-Based View. *Research Policy*, 34: 795–816.

Colombo, M. and Grilli, L. (2008). *On Growth Drivers of High Tech Start-Ups: Exploring the Role of Founders' Human Capital and Venture Capital*. Milan: WP Politechnico di Milano.

Cooper, A. C. (1993). Challenges in Predicting New Firm Performance. *Journal of Business Venturing*, 8: 241–253.

Cooper, A. C., Folta, T. B. and Woo, C. (1995). Entrepreneurial Information Search. *Journal of Business Venturing*, 10 (2): 107–120.

Cooper, A. C., Gimeno-Gascon, F. J. and Woo, C. Y. (1994). Initial Human and Financial Capital as Predictors of New Venture Performance. *Journal of Business Venturing*, 9 (5): 371–395.

Cornelius, B., Landstöm. H. and Persson, O. (2006). Entrepreneurial Studies: The Dynamic Research Front of a Developing Social Science. *Entrepreneurship Theory and Practice*, 30 (3): 375–398.

Cornelli, F. and Karakas, O. (2008). Private Equity and Corporate Governance: Do LBOs Have More Effective Boards? In J. Lerner and A. Gurung (eds). *The Global Impact of Private Equity Report 2008, Globalization of Alternative Investments, Working Papers Volume 1*. World Economic Forum, pp. 65–84.

Cosh, A., Duncan, J. and Hughes, A. (1998). *Investing in Training and Small Firm Growth and Survival: An Empirical Analysis for the UK 1987–97*. Norwich: HMSO: DfEE Research Report RR36.

Cosh, A. and Hughes, A. (2000). *British Enterprise in Transition*. Cambridge: ESRC Centre for Business Research, Cambridge University.

Cosh, A. and Wood, E. (1998). Innovation: Scale, Objectives and Constraints. In A. Cosh and A. Hughes (eds). *Enterprise Britain: Growth, Innovation and Public Policy in the Small and Medium Sized Enterprise Sector 1994–1997*. Cambridge: Cambridge University, ESRC Centre for Business Research, pp. 38–48.

Covin, J. and Miles, M. (1999). Corporate Entrepreneurship and the Pursuit of Competitive Advantage. *Entrepreneurship Theory and Practice*, 23 (3): 47–63.

Covin, J. G. and Slevin, D. P. (1989). Strategic Management of Small Firms in Hostile and Benign Environments. *Strategic Management Journal*, 10 (1): 75–89.

Covin, J. G. and Slevin, D. P. (1991). A Conceptual Model of Entrepreneurship as Firm Behaviour. *Entrepreneurship Theory and Practice*, 16: 7–26.

Cressy, R. (1996). Are Business Start-Ups Debt Rationed? *Economic Journal*, 1061: 1253–1270.

Cressy, R., Malipiero, A. and Munari, F. (2007). Playing to Their Strengths? Evidence that Specialization in the Private Equity Industry Confers Competitive Advantage. *Journal of Corporate Finance*, 13: 647–669.

Cressy, R. C. and Storey, D. J. (1994). *New Firms and their Bank*. London: National Westminster Bank.

Crick, D. (2004). The Internationalisation Process of Firms in the United Kingdom. In L.P. Dana (ed.) *Handbook of Research on International Entrepreneurship*. Cheltenham, Edward Elgar, pp. 580–595.

Cromie, S., Stephenson, B. and Montieth, D. (1995). The Management of Family Firms: An Empirical Investigation. *International Small Business Journal*, 13 (4): 11–34.

Cross, M. (1981). *New Firm Formation and Regional Development*. Farnborough: Gower.

Cuervo, A., Domingo, R. and Salvador R. (2007). *Entrepreneurship: Concepts, Theory and Perspectives*. Springer: Berlin.

Cuevas, J. G. (1994). Towards a Taxonomy of Entrepreneurial Theories. *International Small Business Journal*, 12 (4): 77–88.

Cumming, D., Sapienza, H., Siegel, D. and Wright, M. (2009). International Entrepreneurship: Managerial and Policy Implications. *Strategic Entrepreneurship Journal*, 3 (4): 283–296.

Cumming, D., Siegel, D. S. and Wright, M. (2007). Private Equity, Leveraged Buy-outs and Governance. *Journal of Corporate Finance*, 13: 439–460.

Dahlqvist, J. and Davidsson, P. (2000). Business Start-up Reasons and Firm Performance. In P. D. Reynolds, E. Autio, C. G. Brush, W. D. Bygrave, S. Manigart, H. J. Sapienza and K. G. Shaver (eds). *Frontiers of Entrepreneurship Research 2000*. Wellesley, MA, Babson College, pp. 46–54.

Dahlqvist, J., Davidsson, P. and Wiklund, J. (2000). Initial Conditions as Predictors of New Venture Performance: A Replication and Extension of the Cooper et al. Study. *Enterprise and Innovation Management Studies*, 1: 1–18.

Daily, C. M. and Dollinger, M. J. (1992). An Empirical Examination of Ownership Structure and Family and Professionally Managed Firms. *Family Business Review*, 5: 117–136.

Daily, C. M. and Dollinger, M. J. (1993). Alternative Methodologies for Identifying Family-Versus Non-family-Managed Businesses. *Journal of Small Business Management*, 31: 79–90.

Dana, L-P. (2004). *Handbook of Research on International Entrepreneurship*. Cheltenham, UK: Edward Elgar.

Dana, L-P. and Wright, R. W. (2004). Emerging Paradigms of International Entrepreneurship. In L-P. Dana (ed.). *Handbook of Research on International Entrepreneurship*. Cheltenham: Edward Elgar, pp. 3–15.

Davidsson, P. (2006a). *New Firm Start-Ups: The International Library of Entrepreneurship 7*. Cheltenham: Edward Elgar Publishing Ltd.

Davidsson, P. (2006b). The Entrepreneurial Process. In S. Carter and D. Jones-Evans (eds). *Enterprise and Small Business: Principles, Practice and Policy, 2nd edition*. Harlow: Financial Times, Prentice Hall, pp. 129–151.

Davidsson, P., Delmar, F. and Wiklund, J. (2006). *Entrepreneurship and the Growth of Firms*. Cheltenham, UK: Edward Elgar.

Davidsson, P. and Honig, B. (2003). The Role of Social and Human Capital among Nascent Entrepreneurs. *Journal of Business Venturing*, 18: 301–331.

Davidsson, P., Steffens, P. and Fitzsimmons, J. (2009). Growing Profitable or Growing from Profits: Putting the Horse in Front of the Cart? *Journal of Business Venturing*, 24: 388–406.

Davidsson, P. and Wiklund, J. (2001). Levels of Analysis in Entrepreneurship Research: Current Research Practice and Suggestions for the Future. *Entrepreneurship Theory and Practice*, 25 (4): 81–99.

Davis, S., Lerner, J., Haltiwanger, J., Miranda, J. and Jarmin, R. (2008). Private Equity and Employment. In J. Lerner and A. Gurung (eds). *The Global Impact of Private Equity Report 2008, Globalization of Alternative Investments, Working Papers Volume 1*. World Economic Forum, pp. 43–64.

Davis, S., Lerner, J., Haltiwanger, J., Miranda, J. and Jarmin, R. (2009). Private Equity, Jobs and Productivity. In A. Gurung and J. Lerner (eds). *The Global Economic Impact of Private Equity Report 2009, Globalization of Alternative Investments, Working Papers Volume 2*, World Economic Forum, pp. 25–46.

Day, D. L. (1994). Raising Radicals: Different Processes for Championing Innovative Corporate Ventures. *Organization Science*. 5: 148–172.

Deakins, D. and Freel, M. (2006). *Entrepreneurship and Small Firms*. Maidenhead: McGraw-Hill Education.

De Clerq, D. and Dimov, D. (2008). Internal Knowledge Development and External Knowledge Access in Venture Capital Investment Performance. *Journal of Management Studies*, 45 (3): 585–612.

De Clerq, D., Sapienza, H. and Crijns, H. (2005). The Internationalization of Small and Medium-Sized Firms. *Small Business Economics*, 24: 409–419.

Degroof, J. J. and Roberts, E. B. (2004). Overcoming Weak Entrepreneurial Infrastructure for Academic Spin-off Ventures. *Journal of Technology Transfer*, 29 (3–4): 327–357.

Della-Gusta, M. and King, Z. (2006). Enterprise Culture. In M. Casson, B. Yeung, A. Basu and N. Wadeson (eds). *The Oxford Handbook of Entrepreneurship*. Oxford: Oxford University Press, pp. 629–647.

Delmar, F. (2000). The Psychology of the Entrepreneur. In S. Carter and D. Jones-Evans (eds). *Enterprise and Small Business: Principles, Practice and Policy, 1st edition*. Harlow: Financial Times, Prentice Hall, pp. 132–154.

Delmar, F., Davidsson, P. and Gartner, W. (2003). Arriving at the High Growth Firm. *Journal of Business Venturing*, 18: 189–216.

Delmar, F. and Shane, S. (2004). Legitimating First, Organizing Activities and the Survival of New Ventures. *Journal of Business Venturing*, 19 (3): 385–410.

De Meza, D. and Southey, C. (1996). The Borrower's Curse: Optimism, Finance and Entrepreneurship. *Economic Journal*, 106: 375–386.

de Meza, D. and Webb, D. (1987). Too Much Investment: A Problem of Asymmetric Information. *The Quarterly Journal of Economics*, 102: 281–292.

Department for Culture, Media and Sport. (2006). *Developing Entrepreneurship for the Creative Industries: The Role of Higher and Further Education*. London: Department for Culture, Media and Sport, Creative Industries Division.

Department of Trade and Industry (DTI). (2004). *A Government Action Plan for Small Business. Making the UK the Best Place in the World to Start and Grow a Business: The Evidence Base*. London: DTI, Small Business Service.

Desrochers, P. and Sautet, F. (2008). Entrepreneurial Policy: The Case of Regional Specialization vs. Spontaneous Industrial Diversity. *Entrepreneurship Theory and Practice*, 32 (5): 813–832.

Dess, G. G., Ireland, R. D., Zahra, S. A., Floyd, S. W., Janney, J. J. and Lane, P. J. (2003). Emerging Issues in Corporate Entrepreneurship. *Journal of Management*, 29 (3): 351–378.

DeTienne, D. and Cardon, M. S. (2006). *Entrepreneurial Exit Strategies: The Impact of Human Capital*. URL (consulted 16.4.2008): http://www.babson.edu/entrep/fer/2006FER/chapter_v/paperfr_v_1.html.

Di Gregorio, D. and Shane, S. (2003). Why Do Some Universities Generate More Start-ups than Others? *Research Policy*, 32: 209–227.

Dimitratos, P., Plakoyiannaki, E., Pitsoulaki, A. and Tüselmann, H. J. (2010). The Global Smaller Firm in International Entrepreneurship. *International Business Review*, forthcoming.

Dimitratos, P., Lioukas, S. and Carter, S. (2004). The Relationship Between Entrepreneurship and International Performance: The Importance of Domestic Environment. *International Business Review*, 13: 19–41.

Dimov, D. and Shepherd, D. (2005). Human Capital Theory and Venture Capital Firms: Exploring Home Runs and Strike Outs. *Journal of Business Venturing*, 20: 1–22.

Donaldson, L. (1990). The Ethereal Hand: Organizational Economics and Management Theory. *Academy of Management Review*, 15: 369–381.

Donckels, R., Dupont, B. and Michel, P. (1987). Multiple Business Starters: Who? Why? What? *Journal of Small Business and Entrepreneurship*, 5 (1): 48–63.

Donckels, R. and Fröhlich, E. (1991). Are Family Businesses Really Different? European Experiences from STRATOS. *Family Business Review*, 4 (2): 149–160.

Dorado, S. (2006). Social Entrepreneurial Ventures: Different Values so Different Process of Creations, No? *Journal of Developmental Entrepreneurship*, 319–343.

Downie, J. (1958). *The Competitive Process*. London: Gerald Duckworth.

Druilhe, C. and Garnsey, E. (2004). Do Academic Spin-Outs Differ and Does it Matter? *Journal of Technology Transfer*, 29 (3–4): 269–285.

Dyer, W. G. (1994). Toward a Theory of Entrepreneurial Careers. *Entrepreneurship Theory and Practice*, 19 (2): 7–21.

Easterwood, J. C. (1998). Divestments and Financial Distress in Leveraged Buy-outs. *Journal of Banking and Finance*, 22: 129–159.

Ehrlich, S, DeNoble, A, Moore, T. and Weaver, R (1994). After the Cash Arrives: A Comparative Study of Venture Capital and Private Investor Involvement in Entrepreneurial Firms, *Journal of Business Venturing*, 9: 67–82.

EIM. (2005). *Internationalization in the Netherlands*. Zoetemeer: Netherlands, EIM.

Eisenhardt, K. M. and Martin, J. A. (2000). Dynamic Capabilities: What Are They? *Strategic Management Journal*, 21: 1105–1121.

Engel, D. and Keilbach, M. (2007). Firm Level Implications of Early Stage Venture Capital Investment: An Empirical Investigation. *Journal of Empirical Finance*, 14: 150–167.

Eriksson, K., Johnson, J., Majkård, A. and Sharma, D. (1997). Experimental Knowledge and Cost in the Internationalization Process. *Journal of International Business Studies*, 28: 337–360.

Estrin, S., Meyer, K. and Bytchkova, M. (2006). Entrepreneurship in Transition Economies. In Casson, M., Yeung, B., Basu, A. and Wadeson, N. (eds). *The Oxford Handbook of Entrepreneurship*. Oxford: OUP, pp. 693–725.

Etemad, H. (2004). A Typology. In L-P. Dana (ed.) *Handbook of Research on International Entrepreneurship*. Cheltenham: Edward Elgar, pp. 94–125.

European Union. (2000). *European Charter for Small Enterprises*. Feira European Council, June.

Fama, E. and Jensen, M. (1983). Separation of Ownership and Control. *Journal of Law and Economics*, 26: 301–325.

Fiegener, M. K. (2010). Locus of Ownership and Family Involvement in Small Private Firms. *Journal of Management Studies*, 47 (2): 296–321.

Fiegener, M. K., Brown, B. M., Dreux IV, D. R. and Dennis W. J. Jr (2000). The Adoption of Outside Boards by Small Private US Firms. *Entrepreneurship and Regional Development*, 12 (4): 291–309.

Fiet, J. (1995). Reliance Upon Informants in the Venture Capital Industry. *Journal of Business Venturing*, 10: 195–223.

Fiet, J. O. (1996). The Informational Basis for Entrepreneurial Discovery. *Small Business Economics*, 8: 419–430.

Fiet, J. O. (2000). The Theoretical Side of Teaching Entrepreneurship. *Journal of Business Venturing*, 16: 1–24.

Filatotchev, I., Wright, M., Buck, T. and Zhukov, V. (1999). Corporate Entrepreneurship and Privatized Firms in Russia, Ukraine and Belarus. *Journal of Business Venturing*, 14: 475–492.

Flores-Romero, M. G. and Blackburn, R. (2006). *Is Entrepreneurship More About Sticking with a Firm or About Running Several of Them?* Paper Presented at Exit and Serial Entrepreneurship Workshop, Jena, Germany, Max Plank Institute, January.

Flynn, D. M. (1993). A Critical Exploration of Sponsorship, Infrastructure and New Organizations. *Small Business Economics*, 5: 129–156.

Folta, T. B., Cooper, A. C. and Baik, Y. (2006). Geographic Cluster Size and Firm Performance. *Journal of Business Venturing*, 21: 217–242.

Forbes, D. (2005). Are Some Entrepreneurs More Overconfident than Others? *Journal of Business Venturing*, 20: 623–640.

Frank, H., Lueger, M. and Korunka, C. (2007). The Significance of Personality in Business Start-Up Intentions, Start-Up Realization and Business Success. *Entrepreneurship and Regional Development*, 19 (3): 227–251.

Franklin, S., Wright, M. and Lockett, A. (2001). Academic and Surrogate Entrepreneurs in University Spin-out Companies. *Journal of Technology Transfer*, 26 (1–2): 127–141.

Freel, M. (1999). Entrepreneurial and Growth Firms. In D. Deakins *Entrepreneurship and Small Firms, Second edition.* London: McGraw-Hill, pp. 201–222.

Gabrielsson, M., Kirpalani, V. H. M., Dimitratos, P., Solberg, C. A. and Zucchella, A. (2008). Conceptualizations to Advance Born Global Definition: A Research Note. *Global Business Review*, 9 (1): 45–50.

Galbraith, C., Rodriquez, C. L. and DeNoble, A. F. (2008). SME Competitive Strategy and Location Behavior: An Exploratory Study of High-Technology Manufacturing. *Journal of Small Business Management*, 46 (2): 183–202.

Gallagher, C. C. and Miller, P. (1991). New Fast-Growing Companies Create Jobs. *Long Range Planning*, 24: 96–101.

Gartner, W. B. (1985). A Conceptual Framework for Describing the Phenomenon of New Venture Creation. *Academy of Management Review*, 10 (4): 696–706.

Gartner, W. B. (1989). 'Who is an Entrepreneur?' Is the Wrong Question. *Entrepreneurship Theory and Practice*, 13 (4): 47–68.

Gartner, W. B. (2001). Is There an Elephant in Entrepreneurship? Blind Assumptions in Theory Development. *Entrepreneurship Theory and Practice*, 25 (4): 27–39.

Gartner, W. B., Davidsson, P. and Zahra, S. A. (2006). Are You Talking to Me? The Nature of Community in Entrepreneurship Scholarship. *Entrepreneurship Theory and Practice*, 30 (3): 321–331.

Gartner, W. B. and Gatewood, E. (1992). Thus the Theory of Description Matters Most. *Entrepreneurship Theory and Practice*, 17 (1): 5–10.

Gavetti, G. and Levinthal, D. A. (2000). Looking Forward and Looking Backward: Cognitive and Experiental Search. *Administrative Science Quarterly*, 45: 113–137.

George, G., Wiklund, J. and Zahra, S. (2005). Ownership and the Internationalization of Small Firms. *Journal of Management*, 31: 210–233.

Gibrat, R. (1931). *Les Inégalités Économiques.* Paris: Librairie de Recueil Sirez.

Gilbert, B. A., McDougall, P. P. and Audretsch, D. B. (2008). Clusters, Knowledge Spillovers and New Venture Performance: An Empirical Examination. *Journal of Business Venturing*, 23 (4): 405–422.

Gilligan, J. and Wright, M. (2010). *Private Equity Demystified. 2nd edition.* London: ICAEW.

Gimeno, J., Folta, T. B., Cooper, A. C. and Woo, C. Y. (1997). Survival of the Fittest? Entrepreneurial Human Capital and the Persistence of Underperforming Firms. *Administrative Science Quarterly*, 42 (4): 750–783.

Global Entrepreneurship Monitor (GEM) (2004). *Global Entrepreneurship Monitor: 2003 Summary Report.* Babson Park, MA: Babson College.

Gnyawali, D. R. and Fogel, D. S. (1994). Environments for Entrepreneurship Development: Key Dimensions and Research Implications. *Entrepreneurship Theory and Practice*, 18 (4): 43–62.

Golder, P. N. and Tellis, G. J. (1993). Pioneer Advantage: Marketing Logic or Marketing Legend. *Journal of Marketing Research*, 30: 158–170.

Gomez-Mejia, L.R., Haynes, K., Nunez-Nickel, M., Jacobson, K. and Moyano-Fuentes, J. (2007). Socioemotional Wealth and Business Risks in Family Controlled Firms: Evidence from Spanish Olive Oil Mills. *Administrative Science Quarterly*, 52: 106–137.

Gompers, P. (1996). Grandstanding in the Venture Capital Industry. *Journal of Financial Economics*, 42: 133–156.

Gormon, G., Hanlon, D. and King, W. (1997). Some Research Perspectives on Entrepreneurship Education, Enterprise Education and Education for Small Business Management: A Ten-Year Literature Review. *International Small Business Journal*, 15: 56–77.

Gould, A. and Keeble, D. (1984). New Firms and Regional Industrialization in East Anglia. *Regional Studies*, 18: 189–201.

Grayson, L. (1993). *Science Parks: An Experiment in High Technology Transfer.* London: The British Library.

Grégoire, D. A., Noël, M. X., Déry, R. and Béchard, J-P. (2006). Is There Conceptual Convergence in Entrepreneurship Research: A Co-Citation Analysis of Frontiers of Entrepreneurship Research, 1981–2004. *Entrepreneurship Theory and Practice*, 30 (3): 333–373.

Greiner, L. (1972). Evolution and Revolution as Organisations Grow. *Harvard Business Review*, 50: 37–46.

Guo, S., Hotchkiss, E. and Song, W. (2007). Do Buy-outs (Still) Create Value? SSRN Working Paper.

Gustafsson, V. (2006). *Entrepreneurial Decision-Making: Individuals, Tasks and Cognitions.* Northampton, MA and Cheltenham: Edward Elgar Publishing Ltd.

Guth, W. D. and Ginsberg, A. (1990). Guest Editors' Introduction: Corporate Entrepreneurship. *Strategic Management Journal*, 11 (special issue): 5–15.

Hall, G. (1992). Reasons for Insolvency Amongst Small Firms – A Review and Fresh Evidence. *Small Business Economics*, 4 (3): 237–250.

Handler, W. (1994). Succession in Family Business: A Review of the Research. *Family Business Review*, 7: 133–157.

Hannan, M. T. and Carroll, G. R. (1992). *Dynamics of Organizational Populations: Density, Legitimation and Competition.* New York: Oxford University Press.

Hannon, P. (2007). Enterprise for All? The Fragility of Enterprise Provision Across England's HEIs. *Journal of Small Business and Enterprise Development*, 14: 183–210.

Hansemark, O. C. (2003). Need for Achievement, Locus of Control and the Prediction of Business Start-Ups: A Longitudinal Study. *Journal of Business Economic Psychology*, 24: 301–319.

Harper, D. (2003). *Foundations of Entrepreneurship and Economic Development*. New York: Routledge.

Harris, R., Siegel, D. S. and Wright, M. (2005). Assessing the Impact of Management Buy-outs on Economic Efficiency: Plant-Level Evidence from the United Kingdom. *The Review of Economics and Statistics*, 87: 148–153.

Harris, R. and Trainor, M. (1995). Innovations and R&D in Northern Ireland Manufacturing: A Schumpeterian Approach. *Regional Studies*, 29: 593–604.

Harvey, M. and Lusch, R. (1995). Expanding the Nature and Scope of Due Diligence. *Journal of Business Venturing*, 10: 5–21.

Haugh, H. (2007). Community-Led Social Venture Creation. *Entrepreneurship Theory and Practice*, 31 (2): 161–182.

Hayek, F. (1945). The Use of Knowledge in Society. *American Economic Review*, 35 (4): 519–530.

Hayek, F. A. (1949). The Meaning of Competition. In F. A. Hayek *Individualism and Economic Order*. London: Routledge and Kegan Paul (1959), pp. 92–106.

Haynes, P. J. (2003). Differences among Entrepreneurs. 'Are you Experienced?' May be the Wrong Question. *International Journal of Entrepreneurial Behaviour and Research*, 9 (3): 111–128.

Hayward, M. L. A., Shepherd, D. A. and Griffin, D. (2006). A Hubris Theory of Entrepreneurship. *Management Science*, 52: 160–172.

Heath, C. and Tversky, A. (1991). Preference and Belief: Ambiguity and Competence in Choice Under Uncertainty. *Journal of Risk and Uncertainty*, 47: 5–28.

Hébert, R. and Link, A. (1988). *The Entrepreneur, 2nd edition*. New York: Praeger.

Hébert, R. and Link, A. A. (2006). Historical Perspectives on the Entrepreneur. *Foundations and Trends® in Entrepreneurship*, 2 (4): 261–408.

Heirman, A. and Clarysse, B. (2005). *The Imprinting Effect of Initial Resources and Market Strategy on the Early Growth Path of Start-Ups*. Ghent: Ghent University Working Paper Series.

Heirman, A. and Clarysse, B. (2007). Do Intangible Assets and Pre-Founding R&D Matter for Innovation Speed in Start-Ups? *Journal of Product Innovation Management*, 24: 303–315.

Hellmann, T. and Puri, M. (2000). The Interaction Between Product Market and Financing Strategy: The Role of Venture Capital. *Review of Financial Studies*, 13: 959–984.

Helweg-Larsen, M. and Shepperd, J. (2001). Do Moderators of the Optimistic Bias Affect Personal or Target Risk Estimates? *Personality and Social Psychology Review*, 5: 74–95.

Hewitt-Dundas, N., Andréosso-O'Callaghan, B., Crone, M., Murray, J. and Roper, S. (2005). Selling Global, Buying Local? What Determines the Sourcing Patterns of Multinational Plants in Ireland? *Regional Studies*, 39: 225–239.

Hitt, M. A. and Ireland, R. D. (2005). *The Blackwell Encyclopedia of Management, Second edition. Entrepreneurship*. Oxford: Blackwell Publishing.

Hitt, M. A., Ireland, R. D., Camp, M. and Sexton, D. L. (2001). Guest Editors' Introduction to the Special Issue Strategic Entrepreneurship: Entrepreneurial Strategies for Wealth Creation. *Strategic Management Journal*, 22 (6–7): 479–491.

Hmieleski, K. M. and Baron, R. A. (2009). Entrepreneurs' Optimism and New Venture Performance: A Social Cognitive Perspective. *Academy of Management Journal*, 52 (3): 473–488.

Holmlund, M., Kock, S. and Vanyushyn, V. (2007). Small and Medium-Sized Enterprises' Internationalization and the Influence of Importing on Exporting. *International Small Business Journal*, 25 (5): 459–477.

Holtz-Eakin, D. (2000). Public Policy Toward Entrepreneurship. *Small Business Economics*, 15 (4): 283–291.

Honig, B. and Karlsson, T. (2010). *Institutional Forces and the Written Business Plan*. Chicago: University of Illinois at Urbana-Champaign's Academy for Entrepreneurial Leadership Historical Research Reference in Entrepreneurship. Available at SSRN: http://ssrn.com/abstract=1501585.

Hornsby, J. S., Kuratko, D. F., Shepherd, D. A. and Bott, J. P. (2009). Managers' Corporate Entrepreneurial Actions: Examining Perception and Position. *Journal of Business Venturing*, 24 (3): 236–247.

Howorth, C., Westhead, P. and Wright, M. (2004). Buyouts, Information Asymmetry and the Family Management Dyad. *Journal of Business Venturing*, 19 (4): 509–534.

Hoy, F. and Verser, T. G. (1994). Emerging Business, Emerging Field: Entrepreneurship and the Family Firm. *Entrepreneurship Theory and Practice*, 19 (1): 9–23.

Hsu, D. (2007). Experienced Entrepreneurial Founders, Organizational Capital and Venture Capital Funding. *Research Policy*, 36: 722–741.

Iacobucci, D. (2002). Explaining Business Groups Started by Habitual Entrepreneurs in the Italian Manufacturing Sector. *Entrepreneurship and Regional Development*, 14 (1): 31–47.

Iacobucci, D. and Rosa, P. (2005). Growth, Diversification, and Business Group Formation in Entrepreneurial Firms. *Small Business Economics*, 25 (1): 65–82.

Ireland, R. D., Hitt, M. A. and Sirmon, D. G. (2003). A Model of Strategic Entrepreneurship: The Construct and its Dimensions. *Journal of Management*, 29 (6): 963–989.

Isaksen, E. J. (2006). *Early Business Performance – Initial Factors Effecting New Business Outcomes*. Unpublished Dr Oecon Dissertation, Bodø Graduate School of Business, Norway.

Jack, S. L. and Anderson, A. R. (2001). Entrepreneurship Education Within the Enterprise Culture: Producing Reflective Practitioners. In A. R. Anderson and S. L. Jack (eds) *Enterprise and Learning*. Aberdeen, Centre for Entrepreneurship, Department of Management Studies, University of Aberdeen, pp. 331–358.

Jain, B. and Kini, O. (1995). Venture Capitalists' Participation and the Post-Issue Operating Performance of IPO Firms. *Managerial and Decision Economics*, 6: 593–606.

Jensen, M. C. (1989). Eclipse of the Public Corporation. *Harvard Business Review*, 67: 61–74.

Johannisson, B., Alexanderson, O., Nowicki, K. and Senneseth, K. (1994). Beyond Anarchy and Organization: Entrepreneurs in Contextual Networks. *Entrepreneurship and Regional Development*, 6: 329–356.

Johannisson, B. and Huse, M. (2000). Recruiting Outside Board Members in the Small Family Business: An Ideological Challenge. *Entrepreneurship and Regional Development*, 12 (4): 353–378.

Johannisson, B., Ramirez-Pasillas, M. and Karlsson, G. (2002). The Institutional Embeddedness of Local Inter-Firm Networks: A Leverage for Business Creation. *Entrepreneurship and Regional Development*, 14: 297–315.

Johanson, J. and Vahlne, J. (1977). The Internationalization Process of the Firm – A Model of Knowledge Development and Increasing Foreign Market Commitment. *Journal of International Business Studies*, 8 (1): 23–32.

Johnson, B. R. (1990). Toward a Multidimensional Model of Entrepreneurship: The Case of Achievement Motivation and the Entrepreneur. *Entrepreneurship Theory and Practice*, 14 (3): 39–54.

Johnson, P. (1986). *New Firms: An Economic Perspective*. London: Allen & Unwin.

Johnson, P. (2004). Differences in Regional Firm Formation Rates: A Decomposition Analysis. *Entrepreneurship Theory and Practice*, 28 (5): 431–445.

Johnson, P. (2007). *The Economics of Small Firms*. London: Routledge.

Jones, C. and Spicer, A. (2005). The Sublime Object of Entrepreneurship. *Organization*, 12: 223–246.

Jones, C. S. (1992). Accounting and Organizational Change: An Empirical Study of Management Buy-outs. *Accounting, Organizations and Society*, 17: 151–168.

Jones, M. and Coviello, N. (2005). Internationalization: Conceptualising An Entrepreneurial Process of Behaviour in Time. *Journal of International Business Studies*, 36 (3): 284–303.

Kahneman, D. and Tversky, A. (1979). Prospect Theory: An Analysis of Decision under Risk. *Econometrica*, 47 (2): 263–291.

Kaish, S. and Gilad, B. (1991). Characteristics of Opportunities Search of Entrepreneurs Versus Executives: Sources, Interests, General Alertness. *Journal of Business Venturing*, 6 (1): 45–61.

Kanter, R. M., Richardson, L., North, J. and Morgan, E. (1991). Engines of Progress: Designing and Running Vehicles in Established Companies; The New Venture Process at Eastman Kodak, 1983–1989. *Journal of Business Venturing*, 6: 63–82.

Kaplan, S. N. (1991). The Staying Power of Leveraged Buyouts. *Journal of Financial Economics*, 29: 287–313.

Kaplan, S. (2009). The Future of Private Equity. *Journal of Applied Corporate Finance*, 21 (3): 8–20.

Kaplan, S. and Strömberg, P. (2003). Financing Contracting Theory Meets the Real World: Evidence from Venture Capital Contracts. *Review of Economic Studies*, 70: 281–315.

Kaplan, S. N. and Strömberg, P. (2009). Leveraged Buyouts and Private Equity. *Journal of Economic Perspectives*, 23 (1): 121–146.

Katsikeas, C. S., Leonidou, L. C. and Morgan, N. A. (2000). Firm Level Export Performance Assessment: Review, Evaluation and Development. *Journal of Academy of Marketing Science*, 28: 493–511.

Keasey, K. and Watson, R. (1991). The State of the Art of Small Firm Failure Prediction: Achievements and Prognosis. *International Small Business Journal*, 9 (4): 11–29.

Keasey, K. and Watson, R. (1992). *Investment and Financing Decisions and the Performance of Small Firms*. London: National Westminster Bank.

Keeble, D. and Walker, S. (1994). New Firms, Small Firms and Dead Firms: Spatial Patterns and Determinants in the United Kingdom. *Regional Studies*, 28 (4): 411–427.

Keeble, D. and Wever, E. (1986). Introduction. In D. Keeble and E. Wever (eds). *New Firms and Regional Development in Europe*. London: Croom Helm, pp. 1–34.

Kelly, P. and Hay, M. (1996). Serial Investors and Early Stage Finance, Entrepreneurial and Small Business. *Finance*, 5 (2): 159–174.

Kets de Vries, M. F. R. (1977). The Entrepreneurial Personality: A Person at the Crossroads. *Journal of Management Studies*, 14 (1): 34–57.

Keupp, M. M. and Gassmann, O. (2009). The Past and the Future of International Entrepreneurship: A Review and Suggestions for Developing the Field. *Journal of Management*, 35 (3): 600–633.

Kirby, D. (2003). *Entrepreneurship*. Maidenhead: McGraw-Hill Education.

Kirzner, I. M. (1973). *Competition and Entrepreneurship*. Chicago: University of Chicago Press.

Kirzner, I. (1997). Entrepreneurial Discovery and the Competitive Market Process: An Austrian Approach. *Journal of Economic Literature*, 35 (1): 60–85.

Klein, S. B., Astrachan, J. H. and Smyrnios, K. X. (2005). The F-PEC Scale of Family Influence: Construction, Validation and Further Implication for Theory. *Entrepreneurship Theory and Practice*, 29: 321–339.

Klepper, S. and Sleeper, S. (2005). Entry by Spinoffs. *Management Science*, 51 (8): 1291–1306.

Knight, F. H. (1921). *Risk, Uncertainty and Profit*. (ed. G. J. Stigler). Chicago: University of Chicago (1971).

Knight, F. H. (1942). Profit and Entrepreneurial Functions. *The Tasks of Economic History: Supplement to Journal of Economic History*, 2: 126–132.

Koellinger, P., Minniti, M. and Schade, C. (2007). 'I Think I Can, I Think I Can': Overconfidence and Entrepreneurial Behavior. *Journal of Economic Psychology*, 28: 502–527.

Kolvereid, L. and Bullvåg, E. (1993). Novices Versus Experienced Founders: An Exploratory Investigation. In S. Birley, I. MacMillan and S. Subramony (eds). *Entrepreneurship Research, Global Perspectives*. Amsterdam: Elsevier Science Publishers, pp. 275–285.

Kolvereid, L. and Isaksen, E. (2006). New Business Start-Up and Subsequent Entry into Self-Employment. *Journal of Business Venturing*, 21 (6): 866–885.

Kor, Y. Y. and Mahoney, J. T. (2000). Penrose's Resource-Based Approach: The Process and Product of Research Creativity. *Journal of Management Studies*, 37: 109–139.

Korunka, C., Frank, H., Lueger, M. and Mugler, J. (2003). The Entrepreneurial Personality in the Context of Resources, Environment, and the Startup Process – A Configurational Approach. *Entrepreneurship Theory and Practice*, 28 (1): 23–42.

Krueger, N. F. J. and Dickson, P. R. (1994). How Believing in Ourselves Increases Risk Taking: Perceived Self-Efficacy and Opportunity Recognition. *Decision Sciences*, 25 (3): 385–400.

Krueger, N. F., Reilly, M. D. and Carsrud, A. L. (2000). Competing Models of Entrepreneurial Intentions. *Journal of Business Venturing*, 15 (5–6): 411–432.

Kunda, S. K. and Katz, J. A. (2003). Born International SMEs: BI-Level Impacts of Resources and Intentions. *Small Business Economics*, 20: 25–47.

Kuratko, D. and Audretsch, D. (2009). Strategic Entrepreneurship: Exploring Different Perspectives of an Emerging Concept. *Entrepreneurship Theory and Practice*, 33: 1–19.

Kuratko, D. F. and Hodgetts, R. M. (2004). *Entrepreneurship Theory, Process and Practice*, 6th edition. Mason, OH, Thomson South-Western.

Lafuente, A. and Salas, V. (1989). Types of Entrepreneurs and Firms: The Case of New Spanish Firms. *Strategic Management Journal*, 10 (10): 17–30.

Lambert, R. (2003). *Lambert Review of Business – University Collaboration*. London: HM Treasury.

Lansberg, I. (1999). *Succeeding Generations: Realizing the Dream of Families in Business*. Boston, MA: Harvard Business School Press.

Lee, D. Y. and Tsang, E. W. K. (2001). The Effects of Entrepreneurial Personality, Background and Network Activities on Venture Growth. *Journal of Management Studies*, 38: 583–602.

Lee, S. S. and Osteryoung, J. S. (2004). A Comparison of Critical Success Factors for Effective Operations of University Business Incubators in the United States and Korea. *Journal of Small Business Management*, 42 (4): 418–426.

Le Galès, P., Trigilia, C., Voelzkow, H. and Crouch, C. (2001). *Local Production Systems in Europe*. Oxford: Oxford University Press.

Le Galès, P., Trigilia, C., Voelzkow, H. and Crouch, C. (2004). *Changing Governance of Local Economies: Responses of European Local Production Systems*. Oxford: Oxford University Press.

Leibenstein, H. (1966). Allocative Efficiency vs 'X-efficiency'. *American Economic Review*, 56: 392–415.

Leibenstein, H. (1978). *General X-Efficiency Theory and Economic Development*. New York: Oxford University Press.

Lerner, J. (1995). Venture Capitalists and the Oversight of Private Firms. *Journal of Finance*, 50 (1): 301–318.

Lerner, J., Strömberg, P. and Sørensen, M. (2008). Private Equity and Long-run Investment: The Case of Innovation. In J. Lerner and A. Gurung (eds). *The Global Impact of Private Equity Report 2008, Globalization of Alternative Investments, Working Papers Volume* 1. World Economic Forum, pp. 27–42.

Licht, A. N. and Siegel, J. I. (2006). The Social Dimensions of Entrepreneurship. In M. Casson, B. Yeung, A. Basu and N. Wadeson (eds). *The Oxford Handbook of Entrepreneurship*. Oxford: Oxford University Press, pp. 511–539.

Lichtenberg, F. R. and Siegel, D. S. (1990). The Effect of Leveraged Buy-outs on Productivity and Related Aspects of Firm Behaviour. *Journal of Financial Economics*, 27: 165–194.

Liebeskind, J., Wiersema, M. and Hansen, G. (1992). LBOs, Corporate Restructuring and the Incentive-Intensity Hypothesis. *Financial Management*, Spring: 73–86.

Lindelöf, P. and Löfsten, H. (2004). Proximity as a Resource Base for Competitive Advantage: University–Industry Links for Technology Transfer. *Journal of Technology Transfer*, 29 (3–4): 311–326.

Ling, Y. and Kellermans, F. (2010). The Effects of Family Firm Specific Sources of TMT Diversity: The Moderating Role of Information Exchange Frequency. *Journal of Management Studies*, 47 (2): 322–344.

Link, A. N. and Rees, J. (1990). Firm Size, University-Based Research, and the Returns to R&D. *Small Business Economics*, 2: 25–32.

Link, A. N. and Scott, J. T. (2003). U.S. Science Parks: The Diffusion of an Innovation and its Effects on the Academic Missions of Universities. *International Journal of Industrial Organization*, 21 (9): 1323–1356.

Link, A. N. and Scott, J. T. (2004). Opening the Ivory Tower's Door: An Analysis of the Determinants of the Formation of US University Spin-off Companies. Paper presented at the Technology Transfer Society Meetings, Albany, N.Y., 30 September 2004.

Loasby, B. J. (1991). *Equilibrium and Evolution: An Exploration of Connecting Principles in Economics*. Manchester: Manchester University Press.

Lockett, A., Murray, G. and Wright, M. (2002). Do UK Venture Capitalists Still Have a Bias Against Investment in New Technology Firms? *Research Policy*, 31: 1009–1030.

Lockett, A. and Wright, M. (2005). Resources, Capabilities, Risk Capital and the Creation of University Spin-Out Companies. *Research Policy*, 34 (7): 1043–1057.

Lockett, A., Wright, M., Burrows, A., Scholes, L. and Paton, D. (2008). The Export Intensity of Venture Capital Backed Companies. *Small Business Economics*, 31: 39–58.

Löfsten, H. and Lindelöf, P. (2003). Determinants for an Entrepreneurial Milieu – Science Parks and Business Policy in Growing Firms. *Technovation*, 23 (1): 51–64.

Long, W. F. and Ravenscraft, D. (1993). LBOs, Debt and R and D Intensity. *Strategic Management Journal*, 14: 119–135.

Louis, K., Blumenthal, D., Gluck, M. E. and Stoto, M. A. (1989). Entrepreneurs in Academe: An Exploration of Behaviors Among Life Scientists. *Administrative Science Quarterly*, 34: 110–131.

Low, M. B. and MacMillan, I. C. (1988). Entrepreneurship: Past Research and Future Challenges. *Journal of Management*, 14: 139–161.

Lowe, R. A. and Gonzalez-Brambila, C. (2007). Faculty Entrepreneurs and Research Productivity. *Journal of Technology Transfer*, 32: 173–194.

Lu, J. and Beamish, P. (2001). The Internationalization and Performance of SMEs. *Strategic Management Journal*, 22, Special Issue: 565–586.

Lumsdaine, E. and Binks, M. (2003). *Keep on Moving! Entrepreneurial Creativity and Effective Problem Solving*. McGraw-Hill.

Luostarinen, R. and Gabrielsson, M. (2004). Finnish Perspectives of International Entrepreneurship. In L-P. Dana (ed.). *Handbook of Research on International Entrepreneurship*. Cheltenham: Edward Elgar, pp. 383–403.

MacMillan, I. C. and Katz, J. A. (1992). Idiosyncratic Milieus of Entrepreneurial Research: The Need for Comprehensive Theories. *Journal of Business Venturing*, 7: 1–8.

Madsen, E. L. (2007). The Significance of Sustained Entrepreneurial Orientation on Performance of Firms – A Longitudinal Study. *Entrepreneurship and Regional Development*, 19 (2): 185–204.

Malecki, E. J. (1991). *Technology and Economic Development: The Dynamics of Local, Regional and National Change*. London: Longman.

Malone, S. (1989). Characteristics of Smaller Company Leveraged Buy-outs. *Journal of Business Venturing*, 4: 345–359.

Manigart, S., DeWaele, K., Wright, M., Robbie, K., Desbrieres, P., Sapienza, H. and Beekman A. (2002). Determinants of Required Returns in Venture Capital Investments: A Five-Country Study. *Journal of Business Venturing*, 17: 291–312.

Manigart, S. and Van Hyfte, W. (1999). Post Investment Evolution of VC-backed Companies. In Reynolds, P., et al. (eds). *Frontiers of Entrepreneurship Research*. Wellesley: Babson College.

Manigart, S, Wright, M., Robbie, K., Desbrieres, P. and De Waele, K. (1997). Venture Capitalists' Appraisal of Investment Projects: An Empirical European Study. *Entrepreneurship Theory and Practice*, 21: 29–44.

Manimala, M. J. (1992). Entrepreneurial Heuristics: A Comparison Between High PI (Pioneering-Innovative) and Low PI Ventures. *Journal of Business Venturing*, 7: 477–504.

Markman, G., Phan, P., Balkin, D. and Gianiodis, P. (2005). Entrepreneurship and University-Based Technology Transfer. *Journal of Business Venturing*, 20 (2): 241–263.

Marshall, A. (1890). *Principles of Economics* (ed. G. W. Guilleband). 2 volumes, 9th edition. London: Macmillan (1961).

Marshall, A. (1920). *Principles of Economics. 8th edition*, reset 1949. London: Macmillan.

Marvel, M. R. and Lumpkin, G. T. (2007). Technology Entrepreneurs' Human Capital and its Effects on Innovation Radicalness. *Entrepreneurship Theory and Practice*, 31: 807–828.

Mason, C. and Harrison, R. (1994). The Informal Venture Capital Market in the UK. In A. Hughes and D. J. Storey (eds). *Financing Small Firms*. London: Routledge, pp. 64–111.

Mason, C. and Harrison, R. T. (2002). Is it Worth it? The Rates of Return from Informal Venture Capital Investments. *Journal of Business Venturing*, 17: 211–236.

Mason, C. and Harrison, R. (2004). Does Investing in Technology-Based Firms Involve Higher Risk? An Exploratory Study of the Performance of Technology and Non-Technology Investments by Business Angels. *Venture Capital*, 6 (4): 313–332.

Massey, D., Quintas, P. and Wield, D. (1992). *High Tech Fantasies: Science Parks in Society, Science and Space*. London: Routledge.

Matlay, H. and Westhead, P. (2005). Virtual Teams and the Rise of e-Entrepreneurship in Europe. *International Small Business Journal*, 23 (3): 279–302.

McClelland, D. C. (1965). Achievement Motivation Can Be Developed. *Harvard Business Review*, November–December: 6–24.

McDougall, P. P. and Oviatt, B. M. (1996). New Venture Internationalization, Strategic Change, and Performance: A Follow-Up Study. *Journal of Business Venturing*, 11: 34–40.

McDougall, P. P. and Oviatt, B. M. (2000). International Entrepreneurship: The Intersection of Two Research Paths, Special Research Forum. *Academy of Management Journal*, 43 (5): 902–906.

McDougall, P. P., Shane, S. and Oviatt, B. M. (1994). Explaining the Formation of International New Ventures: The Limits of Theories from International Business Research. *Journal of Business Venturing*, 9: 469–487.

McGrath, R. G. (1999). Falling Forward: Real Options Reasoning and Entrepreneurial Failure. *Academy of Management Review*, 24: 13–30.

McGrath, R. G. and MacMillan, I. C. (2000). *The Entrepreneurial Mindset*. Boston, MA: Harvard Business School Press.

McMullen, J. S. and Shepherd, D. A. (2006). Entrepreneurial Action and the Role of Uncertainty in the Theory of the Entrepreneur. *Academy of Management Review*, 31 (1): 132–152.

McNally, K. (1994). Sources of Finance for UK Venture Capital Funds: The Role of Corporate Investors. *Entrepreneurship and Regional Development*, 6: 275–297.

McNaughton, R. B. and Brown, P. (2004). The Case of Canadian Computer Software Firms. In L-P. Dana (ed.) *Handbook of Research on International Entrepreneurship*. Cheltenham: Edward Elgar, pp. 338–351.

Meuleman, M., Amess, K., Wright, M. and Scholes, L. (2009). Agency, Strategic Entrepreneurship and the Performance of Private Equity Backed Buyouts. *Entrepreneurship Theory and Practice*, 33 (1): 213–239.

Milne, T. and Thompson, M. (1982). *The Infant Business Development Process*. Glasgow: University of Glasgow, Management Studies Working Paper 1.

Miner, J. B., Smith, N. R. and Bracker, J. S. (1992). Predicting Firm Survival from a Knowledge of Entrepreneur Task Motivation. *Entrepreneurship and Regional Development*, 4 (2): 145–153.

Miner, J. B. (2000). Testing a Psychological Typology of Entrepreneurship Using Business Founders. *Journal of Applied Behavioral Science*, 36: 43–70.

Minichilli, A., Corbetta, G. and MacMillan, I. C. (2009). Top Management Teams in Family Controlled Companies: 'Familiness', 'Faultines' and their Impact on Financial Performance. *Journal of Management Studies*, 47 (2): 205–222.

Mitchell, R. K., Busenitz, L., Lant, T., McDougall, P. P., Morse, E. A. and Smith, B. (2002). Entrepreneurial Cognition Theory: Rethinking the People Side of Entrepreneurship Research. *Entrepreneurship Theory and Practice*, 27 (2): 93–104.

Mitchell, R. K., Busenitz, L. W., Bird, B., Gaglio, C. G., McMullen, J. S., Morse, E. A. and Smith, J. B. (2007). The Central Question in Entrepreneurial Cognition Research 2007. *Entrepreneurship Theory and Practice*, 31 (1): 1–27.

Mitchell, F., Reid, G. and Terry, N. (1995). Post Investment Demand for Accounting Information by Venture Capitalists. *Accounting and Business Research*, 25 (99): 186–196.

Moen, Ø. (1999). The Relationship Between Firm Size, Competitive Advantages and Export Performance Revisited. *International Small Business Journal*, 18: 53–72.

Mole, K., Hart, M., Roper, S. and Seal, D. (2008). Differential Gains from Business Link Support and Advice: A Treatment Effects Approach. *Environment and Planning C: Government and Policy*, 26: 315–334.

Morris, M., Kuratko, D. and Covin, J. (2008). *Corporate Entrepreneurship and Innovation*. Mason, OH: Thomson/South-Western Publishers.

Mosey, S., Lockett, A. and Westhead, P. (2006). Creating Network Bridges for University Technology Transfer: The Medici Fellowships Programme. *Technology Analysis & Strategic Management*, 18 (1): 71–91.

Mosey, S. and Wright, M. (2007). From Human Capital to Social Capital, A Longitudinal Study of Technology-based Academic Entrepreneurs. *Entrepreneurship Theory and Practice*, 31: 909–936.

Mueller, C. M. F. (2010). *Resources and Signalling to Attract Venture Capital: University Spin-Outs in the UK*. Durham: Durham Business School, Durham University, Unpublished PhD dissertation.

Mueller, S. L. and Thomas, A. S. (2000). Culture and Entrepreneurial Potential: A Nine Country Study of Locus of Control and Innovativeness. *Journal of Business Venturing*, 16: 51–75.

Murray, G. C. (1994). The Second Equity Gap: Exit Problems for Seed and Early Stage Venture Capitalists and their Investee Companies. *International Small Business Journal*, 12 (4): 59–76.

Murray, G. C. and Lott, J. (1995). Do Venture Capitalists Have a Bias Against Investment in New Technology Firms? *Research Policy*, 24: 283–299.

Mustar, P. (1997). Spin-off Enterprises: How French Academies Create Hi-tech Companies: The Condition for Success or Failure. *Science and Public Policy*, 24 (1): 37–43.

Mustar, P. and Wright, M. (2009). Convergence or Path Dependency in Policies to Foster the Creation of University Spin-Off Firms? A Comparison of France and the United Kingdom. *Journal of Technology Transfer*, 35 (1): 42–65.

Muzyka, D., Birley, S. and Leleux, B. (1996). Trade-Offs in the Investment Decisions of European Venture Capitalists. *Journal of Business Venturing*, 11 (4): 273–287.

Naman, J. L. and Slevin, D. P. (1993). Entrepreneurship and the Concept of Fit: A Model and Empirical Tests. *Strategic Management Journal*, 14 (2): 137–153.

Narayanan, V., Yang, Y. and Zahra, S. (2009). Corporate Venturing and Value Creation: A Review and Proposed Framework. *Research Policy*, 38 (1): 58–76.

Nicolaou, N. and Birley, S. (2003). Social Networks in Organizational Emergence: The University Spinout Phenomenon. *Management Science*, 49 (12): 1702–1725.

Nikoskelainen, E. and Wright, M. (2007). The Impact of Corporate Governance Mechanisms on Value Increase in Leveraged Buy-outs. *Journal of Corporate Finance*, 13 (4): 511–537.

Nyssens, M. (2006). *Social Enterprise*. London: Routledge.

Obrecht, J-J. (2004). Entrepreneurial Capabilities: A Resource-Based Systematic Approach to International Entrepreneurship. In L-P. Dana (ed.). *Handbook of Research on International Entrepreneurship*. Cheltenham: Edward Elgar, Cheltenham, pp. 248–264.

O'Farrell, P. N. and Hitchens, D. M. W. N. (1988). Alternative Theories of Small-Firm Growth: A Critical Review. *Environment and Planning A*, 20: 1365–1382.

O'Farrell, P. N., Wood, P. A. and Zheng, J. (1996). Internationalization of Business Services: An Interregional Analysis. *Regional Studies*, 30: 101–118.

O'Farrell, P. N., Wood, P. A. and Zheng, J. (1998). Regional Influences on Foreign Market Development by Business Service Companies: Elements of a Strategic Context Explanation. *Regional Studies*, 32: 31–48.

One NorthEast. (1999). Regional Economic Strategy for the North East. Unlocking the Potential. Newcastle: One NorthEast.

Organisation for Economic Co-Operation and Development (OECD). (1998). *Fostering Entrepreneurship*. Paris: Organisation for Economic Co-Operation and Development.

OECD. (2006). *Government R&D Funding and Company Behaviour – Measuring Behavioural Additionality*. Paris, OECD, Directorate for Science, Technology and Industry, Committee for Scientific and Technological Policy.

O'Shea, R., Allen, T. and Chevalier, A. (2005). Entrepreneurial Orientation, Technology Transfer, and Spin-off Performance of US Universities. *Research Policy*, 34 (7): 994–1009.

Oviatt, B. and McDougall, P. (1994). Toward a Theory of International New Ventures. *Journal of International Business Studies*, 25 (1): 45–62.

Oviatt, B. and McDougall, P. (2005). The Internationalization of Entrepreneurship. *Journal of International Business Studies*, 36: 2–8.

Parhankangas, A. and Arenius, P. (2003). From a Corporate Venture to an Independent Company: A Base for a Taxonomy for Corporate Spin-Off Firms. *Research Policy*, 32: 463–481.

Parker, S. C. (2004). *The Economics of Self-Employment and Entrepreneurship*. Cambridge: Cambridge University Press.

Parker, S. C. (2005). Economics of Entrepreneurship: What We Know and What We Don't. *Foundations and Trends® in Entrepreneurship*, 1 (1): 1–54.

Parker, S. C. (2006). Entrepreneurship, Self-Employment and the Labour Market. In M. Casson, B. Yeung, A. Basu and N. Wadeson (eds). *The Oxford Handbook of Entrepreneurship*. Oxford: Oxford University Press, pp. 435–460.

Parker, S. C. and Robson, M. T. (2004). 'Explaining' International Variations in Self-Employment: Evidence From a Panel of OECD Countries. *Southern Economic Journal*, 71: 287–301.

Parr, J. B. (2002). Agglomeration Economies: Ambiguities and Confusion. *Environment and Planning, A*, 34 (4): 717–731.

Pasanen, M. (2003). Multiple Entrepreneurship among Successful SMEs in Peripheral Locations. *Journal of Small Business and Enterprise Development*, 10 (4): 418–425.

Penrose, E. (1959). *The Theory of the Growth of the Firm*. Oxford: Blackwell Scientific Publications.

Peredo, A. M. and Chrisman, J. J. (2006). Toward a Theory of Community-Based Enterprise. *Academy of Management Review*, 31 (2): 309–328.

Pfeffer, J. and Salancik, G. R. (1978). *The External Control of Organizations: A Resource Dependence Perspective*. New York: Harper & Row.

Phan, P. and Hill, C. (1995). Organizational Restructuring and Economic Performance in Leveraged Buy-outs: An Ex Post Study. *Academy of Management Journal*, 38: 704–739.

Phan, P. H., Siegel, D. S. and Wright, M. (2005). Science Parks and Incubators: Observations, Synthesis and Future Research. *Journal of Business Venturing*, 20 (2): 165–182.

Phan, P., Wright, M., Ucbasaran, D. and Wee, L. (2009). Corporate Entrepreneurship: Current Research and Future Directions. *Journal of Business Venturing*, 24: 197–205.

Phelps, N. A., Fallon, R. J. and Williams, C. L. (2001). Small Firms, Borrowed Size and the Urban–Rural Shift. *Regional Studies*, 35 (7): 613–624

Piore, M. and Sabel, C. (1984). *The Second Industrial Divide: Possibilities for Prosperity*. New York: Basic Books.

Pisano, V., Ireland, R. D., Hitt, M. A. and Webb, J. W. (2007). International Entrepreneurship in Emerging Economies: The Role of Social Capital, Knowledge Development and Entrepreneurial Actions. *International Journal of Technology Management*, 38 (1–2): 11–28.

Politis, D. (2005). *Entrepreneurship, Career Experience and Learning. Developing our Understanding of Entrepreneurship as an Experimental Learning Process*. PhD dissertation. Lund, Lund University.

Porter, M. E. (1980). *Competitive Strategy: Techniques for Analyzing Industries and Competitors*. New York: Free Press.

Porter, M. E. (1985). *Competitive Advantage: Creating and Sustaining Superior Performance*. New York: Free Press.

Porter, M. E. (1990). *The Competitive Advantage of Nations*. New York: Macmillan.

Porter, M. (1991). Towards a Dynamic Theory of Strategy. *Strategic Management Journal*, 12 (Winter Special Issue): 95–117.

Porter, M. E. (1998). *On Competition*. Boston, MA: Harvard Business Review Press.

Poutziouris, P. and Chittenden, F. (1996). *Family Businesses or Business Families*. Leeds: Institute for Small Business Affairs.

Poutziouris, P. Z., Smyrnois, K. X. and Klein, S. B. (2006). *Handbook of Research on Family Business*. Cheltenham: Edward Elgar.

Préfontaine, L. and Bourgault, M. (2002). Strategic Analysis and Export Behaviour of SMEs. *International Small Business Journal*, 20: 123–138.

President and Fellows of Harvard College. (1999). *Harvard Business Review on Entrepreneurship*. Boston, Mass: Harvard Business Review.

Putnam, R. (1993). *Making Democracy Work. Civic Traditions in Modern Italy*. Princeton: Princeton University Press.

Rabin, M. (1998). Psychology and Economics. *Journal of Economic Literature*, 36: 11–46.

Ram, M. and Hillin, G. (1994). Achieving 'Break-out': Developing Mainstream Ethnic Minority Businesses. *Small Business and Enterprise Development*, 1: 15–21.

Rasmussen, E. (2006). *Facilitating University Spin-Off Ventures – An Entrepreneurship Process Perspective*. Bodø: Bodø Graduate School of Business, Nordland University, Unpublished PhD dissertation.

Reader, D. and Watkins, D. (2006). The Social and Collaborative Nature of Entrepreneurship Scholarship: A Co-Citation and Perceptual Analysis. *Entrepreneurship Theory and Practice*, 30 (3): 417–441.

Requena-Silvente, F. (2005). The Decision to Enter and Exit Foreign Markets: Evidence from UK SMEs. *Small Business Economics*, 25: 237–253.

Rerup, C. (2005). Learning from Past Experience: Footnotes on Mindfulness and Habitual Entrepreneurship. *Scandinavian Journal of Management*, 21 (4): 451–472.

Reuber, A. R. and Fischer, E. (1994). Entrepreneurs' Experience, Expertise, and the Performance of Technology-Based Firms. *IEEE Transactions on Engineering Management*, 41 (4): 365–374.

Reuber, A. R. and Fischer, E. (1997). The Influence of the Management Team's International Experience on the Internationalization Behaviours of SMEs. *Journal of International Business Studies*, 28: 807–825.

Reuber, A. R. and Fischer, E. (1999). Understanding the Consequences of Founders Experience. *Journal of Small Business Management*, 37 (2): 30–45.

Reynolds, P. D. (1991). Sociology and Entrepreneurship: Concepts and Contributions. *Entrepreneurship Theory and Practice*, 16 (2): 47–70.

Reynolds, P. D. (1995). Family Firms in the Start-Up Process: Preliminary Explorations. *Paper Presented at the 1995 Annual Meeting of the International Family Business Program Association*. Nashville, Tennessee, 20–22 July.

Reynolds, P. D. and Maki, W. (1990). *Business Volatility and Economic Growth*. Final Project Report Submitted to the Office of Advocacy, Contract SBA 3067-OA-88, US Small Business Administration.

Reynolds, P., Storey, D. J. and Westhead, P. (1994). Cross-National Comparisons of the Variation in New Firm Formation Rates. *Regional Studies*, 28 (4): 443–456.

Robbie, K. and Wright, M. (1995). Managerial and Ownership Succession and Corporate Restructuring: The Case of Management Buy-ins. *Journal of Management Studies*, 32: 527–550.

Roberts, E. (1991), *Entrepreneurs in High Technology, Lessons from MIT and Beyond*. Oxford: Oxford University Press.

Robson, P. J. A., Akuetteh, C. K., Westhead, P. and Wright, M. (2010). Export Intensity, Human Capital and Business Ownership Experience. *International Small Business Journal*, 29, forthcoming.

Robson, P. J. A., Akuetteh, C. K., Westhead, P. and Wright, M. (2011). Innovative Opportunity Pursuit, Human Capital and Business Ownership Experience in an Emerging Region: Evidence from Ghana. *Regional Studies*, 45, forthcoming.

Robson, P. J. A. and Bennett, R. J. (2000). SME Growth: The Relationship with Business Advice and External Collaboration. *Small Business Economics*, 15: 193–208.

Rocha, H. O. (2004). Entrepreneurship and Development: The Role of Clusters. *Small Business Economics*, 23: 363–400.

Rocha, H. O. and Sternberg, R. (2005). Entrepreneurship: The Role of Clusters. Theoretical Perspectives and Empirical Evidence from Germany. *Small Business Economics*, 24 (3): 267–292.

Rogoff, E. G. and Heck, R. K. Z. (2003). Evolving Research in Entrepreneurship and Family Business: Recognizing Family as the Oxygen that Feeds the Fire of Entrepreneurship. *Journal of Business Venturing*, 18 (5): 559–566.

Romanelli, E. (1989). Environments and Strategies of Organizational Start-Up: Effects on Early Survival. *Administrative Science Quarterly*, 34: 369–387.

Rønning, L. and Kolvereid, L. (2006). Income Diversification in Norwegian Farm Households, Reassessing Pluriactivity. *International Small Business Journal*, 24 (4): 405–420.

Ronstadt, R. (1986). Exit, Stage Left: Why Entrepreneurs End Their Entrepreneurial Careers Before Retirement. *Journal of Business Venturing*, 1 (3): 323–338.

Ronstadt, R. (1988). The Corridor Principle. *Journal of Business Venturing*, 3 (1): 31–40.

Rosa, P. (1998). Entrepreneurial Processes of Business Cluster Formation and Growth by 'Habitual' Entrepreneurs. *Entrepreneurship Theory and Practice*, 22 (4): 43–61.

Rosa, P. and Scott, M. (1999a). Entrepreneurial Diversification, Business-Cluster Formation, and Growth. *Environment and Planning C*, 17 (5): 527–548.

Rosa, P. and Scott, M. (1999b). The Prevalence of Multiple Owners and Directors in the Same Sector: Implications for Our Understanding of Start-up and Growth. *Entrepreneurship and Regional Development*, 11 (1): 21–37.

Rotter, J. (1966). Generalised Expectancies for Internal Versus External Control of Reinforcement. *Psychological Monographs*, 80: 1–27.

Sapienza, H. J. and Korsgaard, A. (1996). The Role of Procedural Justice in Entrepreneur–Venture Capital Relations. *Academy of Management Journal*, 39: 544–574.

Sapienza, H. J., Korsgaard, M. A., Goulet, P. K. and Hoogendam, J. P. (2000). Effects of Agency Risks and Procedural Justice on Board Processes in Venture Capital-Backed Firms. *Entrepreneurship and Regional Development*, 12: 331–351.

Sapienza, H. J., Parhankangas, A. and Autio, E. (2004). Knowledge Relatedness and Post-Spin-Off Growth. *Journal of Business Venturing*, 19 (6): 809–829.

Sarasvathy, S. D. (2001). Causation and Effectuation: Toward a Theoretical Shift from Economic Inevitability to Entrepreneurial Contingency. *Academy of Management Review*, 26 (6): 246–263.

Sarasvathy, S. D. (2004). Making it Happen: Beyond Theories of the Firm to Theories of Firm Design. *Entrepreneurship Theory and Practice*, 28 (6): 519–531.

Sarasvathy, S. (2008). *Effectuation: Elements of Entrepreneurial Expertise*. Cheltenham, UK: Edward Elgar.

Saxenian, A. (1994). *Regional Advantage: Culture Competition in Silicon Valley and Route 128*. Cambridge, MA: Harvard University Press.

Say, J. B. (1821). *A Treatise on Political Economy: Or, the Production, Distribution and Consumption of Wealth*. Translation of 4th edition of the French, with additional notes by C. C. Biddle, 1880. Reprinted by Augustus M. Kelley, New York (1964).

Scheré, J. (1982). Tolerance of Ambiguity as a Discriminating Variable Between Entrepreneurs and Managers. *Academy of Management Best Papers Proceedings*, Academy of Management, pp. 404–408.

Scherr, F. C., Sugrue, T. F. and Ward, J. B. (1993). Financing the Small Firm Start-Up: Determinants of Debt Use. *Journal of Small Business Finance*, 3 (1): 17–36.

Schildt, H. A., Zahra, S. A. and Sillanpää, A. (2006). Scholarly Communities in Entrepreneurship Research: A Co-Citation Analysis. *Entrepreneurship Theory and Practice*, 30 (3): 399–415.

Scholes, M. L., Wright, M., Westhead, P., Burrows, A. and Bruining, H. (2007). Information Sharing, Price Negotiation and Management Buy-outs of Private-owned Firms. *Small Business Economics*, 29 (3): 329–349.

Scholes, M. L., Wright, M., Westhead, P., Bruining, H. and Klockner, O. (2010). Strategic Orientation of Family Firms: Before and After a Management Buy-Out. *International Small Business Journal*, 28, forthcoming.

Schollhammer, H. (1991). Incidence and determinants of multiple entrepreneurship. In N. C. Churchill, W. D. Bygrave, J. G. Covin, D. L. Sexton, D. P. Slevin, K. H. Vesper and W. E. Wetzel (eds). *Frontiers of Entrepreneurship Research 1991*. Wellesley, MA: Babson College, pp. 11–24.

Schulze, W. S., Lubatkin, M. H. and Dino, R. N (2003). Toward a Theory of Agency and Altruism in Family Firms. *Journal of Business Venturing*, 18 (4): 473–490.

Schumpeter, J. A. (1934). *The Theory of Economic Development*. Cambridge, MA: Harvard University Press.

Schumpeter, J. A. (1943). *Capitalism, Socialism and Democracy*. London: Allen and Unwin.

Scott, M. and Bruce, R. (1987). Five Stages of Growth in Small Business. *Long Range Planning*, 20 (3): 45–62.

Scottish Enterprise. (1993). *Improving the Business Birth Rate: A Strategy for Scotland*. Glasgow: Scottish Enterprise.

Shackle, G. (1962). Concluding Comment. In C. Carter, G. Meredith and G. Shackle (eds). *Uncertainty and Business Decisions*. Liverpool: Liverpool University Press.

Shackle, G. (1966). *The Nature of Economic Thought*. Cambridge: Cambridge University Press.

Shackle, G. (1979). *Imagination and the Nature of Choice*. Edinburgh: Edinburgh University Press.

Shane, S. (2000). Prior Knowledge and the Discovery of Entrepreneurial Opportunities. *Organization Science*, 11 (4): 448–469.

Shane, S. (2002). Introduction. In S. Shane (ed.). *Foundations of Entrepreneurship (Volume I)*. Cheltenham, UK: Edward Elgar Publishing Ltd, pp. xi–xix.

Shane, S. (2003). *A General Theory of Entrepreneurship: The Individual–Opportunity Nexus*. Cheltenham, UK: Edward Elgar Publishing Ltd.

Shane, S. and Khurana, K. (2003). Career Experience and Firm Founding. *Industrial and Corporate Change*, 12 (3): 519–544.

Shane, S. and Venkataraman, S. (2000). The Promise of Entrepreneurship as a Field of Research. *Academy of Management Review*, 25 (1): 217–226.

Shanker, M. C. and Astrachan, J. H. (1996). Myths and Realities: Family Businesses Contribution to the US Economy – A Framework for Assessing Family Business Statistics. *Family Business Review*, 9 (2): 107–124.

Sharma, P. (2004). An Overview of the Field of Family Business Studies: Current Status and Directions for Future Research. *Family Business Review*, 17 (1): 1–36.

Sharma, P., Chua, J. H. and Chrisman, J. J. (2000). Perceptions About the Extent of Succession Planning in Canadian Family Firms. *Canadian Journal of Administrative Sciences*, 17 (3), 233–244.

Sharma, P. and Chrisman, J. J. (1999). Toward a Reconciliation of the Definitional Issues in the Field of Corporate Entrepreneurship. *Entrepreneurship Theory and Practice*, 23 (3): 11–27.

Sharma, P., Chrisman, J. and Chua, J. (2003). Predictors of Satisfaction with the Succession Process in Family Firms. *Journal of Business Venturing*, 18: 667–687.

Sharma, P. and Irving, P. G. (2005). Four Bases of Family Business Successor Commitment: Antecedents and Consequences. *Entrepreneurship Theory and Practice*, 29: 13–33.

Shaver, K. G. (2003). The Social Psychology of Entrepreneurial Behaviour. In Z. J. Acs and D. B. Audretsch (eds). *Handbook of Entrepreneurship Research. An Interdisciplinary Survey and Introduction*. Dordrecht, The Netherlands: Kluwer Academic Publishers, pp. 331–357.

Shaver, K. and Scott, L. R. (1991). Person, Process, Choice: The Psychology of New Venture Creation. *Entrepreneurship Theory and Practice*, 16 (2): 23–45.

Shepherd, D. A. (2003). Learning from Business Failure: Propositions of Grief Recovery for the Self-Employed. *Academy of Management Review*, 28: 318–329.

Shepherd, D. A. and DeTienne, D. R. (2005). Prior Knowledge, Potential Financial Reward and Opportunity Identification. *Entrepreneurship, Theory and Practice*, 29: 91–112.

Shook, C. L., Priem, R. L. and McGee, J. E. (2003). Venture Creation and the Enterprising Individual: A Review and Synthesis. *Journal of Management*, 29 (3): 379–399.

Shutt, J. and Whittington, R. (1987). Fragmentation Strategies and the Rise of Small Units: Cases from the North West. *Regional Studies*, 21: 13–23.

Siegel, D. S. (2006). *Technological Entrepreneurship*. Cheltenham, UK: Edward Elgar Publishing Ltd.

Siegel, D., Westhead, P. and Wright, M. (2003a). Science Parks and the Performance of New Technology-Based Firms: A Review of Recent UK Evidence and An Agenda for Future Research. *Small Business Economics*, 20 (2): 177–184.

Siegel, D. S., Westhead, P. and Wright, M. (2003b). Assessing the Impact of University Science Parks on Research Productivity: Exploratory Firm-Level Evidence from the United Kingdom. *International Journal of Industrial Organization*, 21 (9): 1357–1369.

Simon, M., Houghton, S. M. and Aquino, K. (2000). Cognitive Biases, Risk Perception, and Venture Formation: How Individuals Decide to Start Companies. *Journal of Business Venturing*, 15 (2): 113–134.

Singh, R. P., Hills, G. E., Hybels, R. C. and Lumpkin, G. T. (1999). Opportunity Recognition Through Social Network Characteristics of Entrepreneurs. In P. D. Reynolds, W. D. Bygrave, S. Manigart, C. Mason, G. D. Meyer, H. J. Sapienza and K. G. Shaver (eds). *Frontiers of Entrepreneurship Research 1999*. Wellesley, MA: Babson College, pp. 228–241.

Sitkin, S. B. (1992). Learning Through Failure: The Strategy of Small Losses. In B. M. Staw and L. L. Cummings (eds). *Research in Organizational Behaviour, 14*. Greenwich, CT: JAI Press, pp. 231–266.

Slevin, D. P. and Covin, J. G. (1992). Creating and Maintaining High-Performance Teams. In D. L. Sexton and J. D. Kasarda (eds). *The State of the Art of Entrepreneurship*. Boston, MA: PWS-Kent Publishing Company, pp. 358–386.

Smart, S. B. and Waldfogel, J. (1994). Measuring the Effect of Restructuring on Corporate Performance: The Case of Management Buy-outs. *Review of Economics and Statistics*, 76: 503–511.

Smillie, I. (2009). *Freedom from Want*. Sterling, VA: Kumarian Press.

Smith, D. M. (1981). *Industrial Location: An Economic Geographical Analysis. Second edition*. New York: John Wiley.

Smith, N. R. (1967). *The Entrepreneur and His Firm: The Relationship Between Type of Man and Type of Company*. East Lansing, Michigan: Michigan State University Press.

Smyrnios, K. and Romano, C. (1994). *The Price Waterhouse/ Commonwealth Bank Family Business Survey 1994*. Sydney: Department of Accounting, Monash University.

Snyder, M. and Cantor, N. (1998). Understanding Personality and Social Behavior: A Functional Strategy. In D. T. Gilbert, S. T. Fiske and G. Lindsey (eds). *The Handbook of Social Psychology, 4th edition.* Boston, MA: The McGraw-Hill Companies, Inc., pp. 635–679.

Solesvik, M. Z. and Westhead, P. (2010). Partner Selection for Strategic Alliances: Case Study Insights from the Maritime Industry. *Industrial Management & Data Systems,* 110(6): 841–860.

Solomon, G. (2007). An Examination of Entrepreneurship Education in the United States. *Journal of Small Business and Enterprise Development,* 14: 168–182.

Somerville, P. (2007). Co-operative Identity. *Journal of Co-operative Studies,* 40 (1): 5–17.

Somerville, P. and McElwee, G. (2010). Situating Community Enterprise: A Theoretical Exploration. *Entrepreneurship and Regional Development,* forthcoming.

Spanos, Y. E. and Lioukas, S. (2001). An Examination into the Causal Logic of Rent Generation: Contrasting Porter's Competitive Strategy Framework and the Resource-Based Perspective. *Strategic Management Journal,* 22: 907–934.

Starr, J. and Bygrave, W. (1991). The Assets and Liabilities of Prior Start-Up Experience: An Exploratory Study of Multiple Venture Entrepreneurs. In N. C. Churchill, W. D. Bygrave, J. G. Covin, D. L. Sexton, D. P. Slevin, K. H. Vesper and W. E. Wetzel (eds). *Frontiers of Entrepreneurship Research 1991.* Wellesley, Massachusetts, Babson College, pp. 213–227.

Sternberg, R. (1990). The Impact of Innovation Centres on Small Technology-Based Firms: The Example of the Federal Republic of Germany. *Small Business Economics,* 2: 105–118.

Stevenson, H. and Coveney, P. (1994). *Survey of Business Angels.* Henley on Thames: Venture Capital Report Ltd.

Stiglitz, J. and Weiss, A. (1981). Credit Rationing in Markets with Imperfect Information. *American Economic Review,* 71: 303–410.

Stokes, D. and Blackburn, R. (2001). *Opening Up Business Closures, A Study of Businesses that Close and Owners' Exit Routes.* Kingston: Kingston University, Small Business Research Centre.

Stopford, J. M. and Baden-Fuller, C. W. F. (1994). Creating Corporate Entrepreneurship. *Strategic Management Journal,* 15 (1): 521–536.

Storey, D. J. (1982). *Entrepreneurship and the New Firm.* London: Routledge.

Storey, D. J. (1994). *Understanding the Small Business Sector.* London, Thomson Learning.

Storey, D. J. (2000). *Small Business: Critical Perspectives on Business and Management.* London: Routledge.

Storey, D. J. (2006). Evaluating SME Policies and Programmes: Technical and Political Dimensions. In M. Casson, B. Yeung, A. Basu and N. Wadeson (eds). *The Oxford Handbook of Entrepreneurship.* Oxford: Oxford University Press, pp. 248–278.

Storey, D. J. and Greene, F. (2010). *Small Business and Entrepreneurship.* Harlow: Financial Times, Prentice Hall.

Storey, D. J., Keasey, K., Watson, R. and Wynarczyk, P. (1987). *The Performance of Small Firms: Profits, Jobs and Failures.* London: Croom Helm.

Storey, D. J. and Tether, B. (1998). Public Policy Measures to Support New Technology-Based Firms in the European Union. *Research Policy,* 26: 1037–1057.

Storey, D. J. and Westhead, P. (1997). Management Training in Small Firms: A Case of Market Failure? *Human Resource Management Journal,* 7: 61–71.

Strömberg, P. (2008). The New Demography of Private Equity. In J. Lerner and A. Gurung (eds). *The Global Impact of Private Equity Report 2008, Globalization of Alternative Investments, Working Papers, Volume* 1. World Economic Forum, pp. 3–26.

Tan, J. (1996). Regulatory Environment and Strategic Orientations: A Study of Chinese Private Entrepreneurs. *Entrepreneurship Theory and Practice,* 21: 31–44.

Tan, J. (2006). Growth of Industry Clusters and Innovation: Lessons from Bejing Zhongguancum Science Park. *Journal of Business Venturing,* 21 (6): 827–850.

Taylor, M. (1999). The Small Firm as a Temporary Coalition. *Entrepreneurship and Regional Development,* 11: 1–19.

Technology Strategy Board. (2008). *Connect and Catalyse: A Strategy for Business Innovation 2008–2011.* London: Stationery Office.

Thompson, J. and Doherty, B. (2006). The Diverse World of Social Enterprise: A Collection of Social Enterprise Stories. *International Journal of Social Economics,* 33 (5/6): 399–410.

Thompson, S. and Wright, M. (1995). Corporate Governance: The Role of Restructuring Transactions. *Economic Journal,* 105: 690–703.

Thrift, N. (1996). *Spatial Formations.* London: Sage Publications.

Thursby, J. G. and Thursby, M. C. (2002). Who is Selling the Ivory Tower? Sources of Growth in University Licensing. *Management Science,* 48: 90–104.

Tkachev, A. and Kolvereid. L. (1999). Self-Employment Intentions among Russian Students. *Entrepreneurship and Regional Development,* 11: 269–280.

Tötterman, H. and Sten, J. (2005). Business Incubation and Social Capital. *International Small Business Journal,* 23 (5): 487–511.

Townsend, D. M. and Hart, T. A. (2008). Perceived Institutional Ambiguity and the Choice of Organizational Form in Social Entrepreneurial Ventures. *Entrepreneurship Theory and Practice,* 32 (4): 685–700.

Tversky, A. and Kahneman, D. (1974). Judgement Under Uncertainty: Heuristics and Biases. *Science*, 185: 1124–1131.

Ucbasaran, D., Alsos, G. A., Westhead, P. and Wright, M. (2008a). Habitual Entrepreneurs. *Foundations and Trends® in Entrepreneurship*, 4 (4): 309–449.

Ucbasaran, D., Lockett, A., Wright, M. and Westhead, P. (2003). Entrepreneurial Founder Teams: Factors Associated with Team Member Entry and Exit. *Entrepreneurship Theory and Practice*, 28 (2): 107–128.

Ucbasaran, D., Westhead, P. and Wright, M. (2001). The Focus of Entrepreneurial Research: Contextual and Process Issues. *Entrepreneurship Theory and Practice*, 25 (4): 57–80.

Ucbasaran, D., Westhead, P. and Wright, M. (2006a). *Habitual Entrepreneurs.* Aldershot, UK: Edward Elgar.

Ucbasaran, D., Westhead, P. and Wright, M. (2006b). *Entrepreneurial Entry, Exit and Re-Entry: The Extent and Nature of Opportunity Identification.* Max Planck Institute Discussion Paper, No. 0906.

Ucbasaran, D., Westhead, P. and Wright, M. (2008b). Opportunity Identification and Pursuit: Does an Entrepreneur's Human Capital Matter? *Small Business Economics*, 30 (2): 153–173.

Ucbasaran, D., Westhead, P. and Wright, M. (2009). The Extent and Nature of Opportunity Identification by Experienced Entrepreneurs. *Journal of Business Venturing*, 24 (2): 99–115.

Ucbasaran, D., Westhead, P., Wright, M. and Flores, M. (2010). The Nature of Entrepreneurial Experience, Business Failure and Comparative Optimism. *Journal of Business Venturing*, 25 (6): 541–555.

United Kingdom Science Park Association (UKSPA). (1999). *15th Anniversary 1984–1999.* Birmingham: The United Kingdom Science Park Association.

Vaessen, P. and Keeble, D. (1995). Growth-orientated SMEs in Unfavourable Regional Environments. *Regional Studies*, 29 (6): 489–505.

Vanaelst, I., Clarysse, B., Wright, M., Lockett, A., Moray, N. and S'Jegers, R. (2006). Entrepreneurial Team Development in Academic Spin-Outs: An Examination of Team Heterogeneity. *Entrepreneurship Theory and Practice*, 30: 249–272.

Van de Ven, A. H. (1993). The Development of an Infrastructure for Entrepreneurship. *Journal of Business Venturing*, 8 (3): 211–230.

Van Looy, B., Ranga, L.M., Callaert, J., Debackere, K. and Zimmermann, E. (2004). Combining Entrepreneurial and Scientific Performance in Academia: Towards a Compounded and Reciprocal Matthew Effect? *Research Policy*, 33 (3): 425–441.

Van Osnabrugge, M. (1998). Do Serial Investors and Non-Serial Investors Behave Differently? *Entrepreneurship Theory and Practice*, 22 (4): 23–42.

van Stel, A. J. and Storey, D. J. (2004). The Link Between Firm Births and Job Creation: Is There an Upas Tree Effect? *Regional Studies*, 38 (8): 893–910.

Venkataraman, S. (1997). The Distinctive Domain of Entrepreneurship Research. In J. A. Katz (ed.). *Advances in Entrepreneurship, Firm Emergence and Growth.* Connecticut: JAI Press, 3, 139–202.

Vohora, A., Wright, M. and Lockett, A. (2004). Critical Junctures in the Growth in University High-Tech Spinout Companies. *Research Policy*, 33: 147–175.

Wadeson, N. S. (2006). Cognitive Aspects of Entrepreneurship: Decision-Making and Attitudes to Risk. In M. Casson, B. Yeung, A. Basu and N. Wadeson (eds). *The Oxford Handbook of Entrepreneurship.* Oxford: Oxford University Press, pp. 91–113.

Wang, C. K. and Ang, B. L. (2004). Determinants of Venture Performance in Singapore. *Journal of Small Business Management*, 42 (4): 347–363.

Ward, J. L. (1987). *Keeping the Family Business Healthy: How to Plan for Continued Growth, Profitability and Family Leadership.* San Fransisco: Jossey-Bass Publishers.

Watson, R. and Wilson, N. (2002). Small and Medium Size Enterprise Financing: A Note on Some of the Empirical Implications of a Pecking Order. *Journal of Business Finance & Accounting*, 29 (3 & 4): 557–578.

Weick, K. E. (1979). *The Social Psychology of Organizing. 2nd edition.* Reading, MA: Addison-Wesley.

Weick, K. E. (1995). *Sensemaking in Organizations.* Thousand Oaks, CA: Sage.

Weir, C, Wright, M. and Jones, P. (2008). Public to Private Transactions, Private Equity and Performance in the UK: An Empirical Analysis of the Impact of Going Private. *SSRN working paper.*

Wennberg, K., Wiklund, J., DeTienne, D. R. and Cardon, M. S. (2010). Reconceptualizing Entrepreneurial Exit: Divergent Exit Routes and their Drivers. *Journal of Business Venturing*, 25 (4): 361–375.

Westhead, P. (1995). Survival and Employment Growth Contrasts Between Types of Owner-Managed High-Technology Firms. *Entrepreneurship Theory and Practice*, 20 (1): 5–27.

Westhead, P. (1997a). R & D 'Inputs' and 'Outputs' of Technology-Based Firms Located On and Off Science Parks. *R&D Management*, 27 (1): 45–62.

Westhead, P. (1997b). Ambitions, 'External' Environment and Strategic Factor Differences between Family and Non-Family Companies. *Entrepreneurship and Regional Development*, 9 (2): 127–157.

Westhead, P. (2003). Succession Decision-Making Outcomes Reported by Unquoted Family Companies. *International Small Business Journal*, 21 (4): 369–399.

Westhead, P. (2008). International Opportunity Exploitation Behaviour Reported by 'Types' of Firms Relating to

Exporting Experience. *Journal of Small Business and Enterprise Development*, 15 (3): 431–456.

Westhead, P. and Batstone, S. (1998). Independent Technology-Based Firms: The Perceived Added Value of a Science Park Location. *Urban Studies*, 35 (12): 2197–2219.

Westhead, P. and Batstone, S. (1999). Perceived Benefits of a Managed Science Park Location for Independent Technology-Based Firms. *Entrepreneurship and Regional Development*, 11 (2): 129–154.

Westhead, P. and Birley, S. (1995). Employment Growth in New Independent Owner-Managed Firms in Great Britain. *International Small Business Journal*, 13 (3): 11–34.

Westhead, P. and Cowling, M. (1995). Employment Change in Independent Owner-Managed High-Technology Firms in Great Britain. *Small Business Economics*, 7 (2): 111–140.

Westhead, P. and Cowling, M. (1997). Performance Contrasts Between Family and Non-Family Unquoted Companies in the UK. *International Journal of Entrepreneurial Behaviour & Research*, 3 (1): 30–52.

Westhead, P. and Cowling, M. (1998). Family Firm Research: The Need for a Methodological Rethink. *Entrepreneurship Theory and Practice*, 23 (1): 31–56.

Westhead, P., Cowling, M. and Howorth, C. (2001). The Development of Family Companies: Management and Ownership Issues. *Family Business Review*, 14 (4): 369–385.

Westhead, P., Cowling, M. and Storey, D. J. (1997). *The Management and Performance of Unquoted Family Companies in the United Kingdom*. Coventry: The University of Warwick, Centre for Small and Medium-Sized Enterprises.

Westhead, P. and Howorth, C. (2006). Ownership and Management Issues Associated with Family Firm Performance and Company Objectives. *Family Business Review*, 19 (4): 301–316.

Westhead, P. and Howorth, C. (2007). 'Types' of Private Family Firms: An Exploratory Conceptual and Empirical Analysis. *Entrepreneurship and Regional Development*, 19 (5): 405–431.

Westhead, P. and Matlay, H. (2006). Skills Associated with Employment Positions in SMEs and Favourable Attitudes toward Self-Employment: Longitudinal Evidence from Students who Participated in the Shell Technology Enterprise Programme. *Technology Analysis & Strategic Management*, 18 (1): 93–124.

Westhead, P. and Moyes, A. (1992). Reflections on Thatcher's Britain: Evidence from New Production Firm Registrations 1980–88. *Entrepreneurship and Regional Development*, 4 (1): 21–56.

Westhead, P. and Storey, D. J. (1995). Links Between Higher Education Institutions and High Technology Firms.

Omega, International Journal of Management Science, 23 (4): 345–360.

Westhead, P. and Storey, D. (1997). Financial Constraints on the Growth of High Technology Small Firms in the UK. *Applied Financial Economics*, 7 (2): 197–201.

Westhead, P., Storey, D. J. and Cowling, M. (1995). An Exploratory Analysis of the Factors Associated with the Survival of Independent High-Technology Firms in Great Britain. In F. Chittenden, M. Robertson and I. Marshall (eds). *Small Firms: Partnerships for Growth*. London: Paul Chapman, pp. 63–99.

Westhead, P., Ucbasaran, D. and Binks, M. (2004c). Internationalization Strategies Selected by Rural and Urban SMEs. *Journal of Small Business and Enterprise Development*, 11 (1): 8–22.

Westhead, P., Ucbasaran, D. and Wright, M. (2003a). Differences Between Private Firms Owned by Novice, Serial and Portfolio Entrepreneurs: Implications for Policy-Makers and Practitioners. *Regional Studies*, 37 (2): 187–200.

Westhead, P., Ucbasaran, D. and Wright, M. (2004a). Policy Toward Novice, Serial and Portfolio Entrepreneurs. *Environment and Planning C*, 22 (6): 779–798.

Westhead, P., Ucbasaran, D., Wright, M. and Binks, M. (2005a). Novice, Serial and Portfolio Entrepreneur Behaviour and Contributions. *Small Business Economics*, 25 (2): 109–132.

Westhead, P., Ucbasaran, D. and Wright, M. (2005b). Decisions, Actions and Performance: Do Novice, Serial and Portfolio Entrepreneurs Differ? *Journal of Small Business Management*, 43 (4): 393–417.

Westhead, P., Ucbasaran, D. and Wright, M. (2005c). Experience and Cognition: Do Novice, Serial and Portfolio Entrepreneurs Differ? *International Small Business Journal*, 23 (1): 72–98.

Westhead, P., Ucbasaran, D., Wright, M. and Binks, M. (2005d). Policy Toward Novice, Serial and Portfolio Entrepreneurs. *Small Business Economics*, 25 (2): 109–132.

Westhead, P., Ucbasaran, D., Wright, M. and Martin, F. (2003b). *Habitual Entrepreneurs in Scotland, Characteristics, Search Processes, Learning and Performance – Summary Report*. Glasgow, Scottish Enterprise. A copy of the full report can be downloaded from www.scottish-enterprise.com in the Research and Publications section.

Westhead, P. and Wright, M. (1998a). Novice, Portfolio and Serial Founders: Are They Different? *Journal of Business Venturing*, 13 (3): 173–204.

Westhead, P. and Wright, M. (1998b). *Habitual Entrepreneurs and Business Angels*. Leeds: Institute of Small Business Affairs.

Westhead, P. and Wright, M. (1998c). Novice, Portfolio and Serial Founders in Rural and Urban Areas. *Entrepreneurship Theory and Practice*, 22 (4): 63–100.

Westhead, P. and Wright, M. (1999). Contributions of Novice, Portfolio and Serial Founders Located in Rural and Urban Areas. *Regional Studies*, 33 (2): 157–173.

Westhead, P. and Wright, M. (2000). *Advances in Entrepreneurship*. Aldershot: Edward Elgar Publishing Ltd.

Westhead, P., Wright, M. and Ucbasaran, D. (2001a). The Internationalization of New and Small Firms: A Resource-Based View. *Journal of Business Venturing*, 16 (4): 333–358.

Westhead, P., Wright, M. and Ucbasaran, D. (2002). International Market Selection Strategies Selected by 'Micro' and 'Small' Firms. *Omega, International Journal of Management Science*, 30 (1): 51–68.

Westhead, P., Wright, M. and Ucbasaran, D. (2004b). Internationalization of Private Firms: Environmental Turbulence and Organizational Strategies and Resources. *Entrepreneurship and Regional Development*, 16 (6): 501–522.

Westhead, P., Wright, M., Ucbasaran, D. and Martin, F. (2001b). International Market Selection Strategies by Manufacturing and Services Firms. *Entrepreneurship and Regional Development*, 13 (1): 17–46.

Wickham, P. A. (2006). *Strategic Entrepreneurship, 4th edition*. London: Prentice-Hall.

Wiedersheim-Paul, F., Olson, H. C. and Welch, L. S. (1978). Pre-Export Activity: The First Step in Internationalization. *Journal of International Business Studies*, 9: 47–58.

Wiersema, M. and Liebeskind, J. (1995). The Effects of Leveraged Buy-outs on Corporate Growth and Diversification in Large Firms. *Strategic Management Journal*, 16 (6): 447–460.

Wiklund, J. and Shepherd, D. (2008). Portfolio Entrepreneurship, Habitual and Novice Founders, New Entry and Mode of Organizing. *Entrepreneurship Theory and Practice*, 32 (4): 701–725.

Wilson, N., Wright, M. and Altanlar, A. (2010a). Private Equity, Buyouts, Leverage and Failure. Nottingham: Nottingham University Business, Centre for Management Buyout Research, Working Paper.

Wilson, N., Wright, M. and Cressy, R. (2010b). *Private Equity and Insolvency*. London: BVCA.

Woo, C. Y., Cooper, A. C. and Dunkelberg, W. C. (1991). The Development and Interpretation of Entrepreneurial Typologies. *Journal of Business Venturing*, 6 (2): 93–114.

Woo, C. Y., Folta, T. and Cooper, A. C. (1992). Entrepreneurial Search: Alternative Theories of Behavior. In N. C. Churchill, S. Birley, W. D. Bygrave,. D. F. Muzyka, C. Wahlbin and W. E. Wetzel (eds). *Frontiers of Entrepreneurship Research 1992*. Wellesley, MA: Babson College, pp. 31–41.

Wright, M. (1986). The Make Buy Decision and Managing Markets: The Case of Management Buy-outs. *Journal of Management Studies*, 23: 443–464.

Wright, M. and Bruining, H. (eds) (2008). *Private Equity and Management Buy-outs*. Cheltenham, UK: Edward Elgar Publishing Ltd.

Wright, M., Burrows, A., Ball, R., Scholes, L., Meuleman, M. and Amess, K. (2007). *The Implications of Alternative Investment Vehicles for Corporate Governance: A Survey of Empirical Research*. Paris, OECD, Report prepared for the Steering Group on Corporate Governance.

Wright, M., Chiplin, B., Thompson, S. and Robbie, K. (1990). Management Buy-outs and Large-Small Firm Relationships. *Management International Review*, 30: 55–72.

Wright, M., Clarysse, B., Lockett, A. and Binks, M. (2006). University Spin-Out Companies and Venture Capital. *Research Policy*, 35 (4): 481–501.

Wright, M., Clarysse, B., Mustar, P. and Lockett, A. (2008a) *Academic Entrepreneurship in Europe*. Cheltenham, UK: Edward Elgar.

Wright, M., Filatotchev, I., Hoskisson, R. and Peng, M. W. (2005). Strategy Research in Emerging Economies: Challenging the Conventional Wisdom. *Journal of Management Studies*, 42 (1): 1–34.

Wright, M., Hoskisson, R., Busenitz, L. and Dial, J. (2000a). Entrepreneurial Growth through Privatization: The Upside of Management Buy-outs. *Academy of Management Review*, 25 (3): 591–601.

Wright, M., Hoskisson, R. and Busenitz, L. (2001a). Firm Rebirth: Buyouts as Facilitators of Strategic Growth and Entrepreneurship. *Academy of Management Executive*, 15 (1): 111–125.

Wright, M., Hoskisson, R., Busenitz, L. and Dial, J. (2001b). Finance and Management Buyouts: Agency versus Entrepreneurship Perspectives. *Venture Capital*, 3 (3): 239–261.

Wright, M., Liu, X., Buck, T. and Filatotchev, I. (2008b). Returnee Entrepreneurs, Science Park Location Choice and Performance: An Analysis of High-Technology SMEs in China. *Entrepreneurship Theory and Practice*, 32 (1): 131–155.

Wright, M. and Lockett, A. (2003). The Structure and Management of Alliances: Syndication in the Venture Capital Industry. *Journal of Management Studies*, 40: 2073–2104.

Wright, M. and Robbie, K. (1996). Venture Capitalists, Unquoted Investment Appraisal and the Role of Accounting Information. *Accounting and Business Research*, 26: 153–170.

Wright, M. and Robbie, K. (1998). Venture Capital and Private Equity: A Review and Synthesis. *Journal of Business Finance and Accounting*, 25 (5 & 6): 521–570.

Wright, M., Robbie, K., Chiplin, B. and Albrighton, M. (2000b). The Development of an Organisational Innovation: Management Buy-outs in the UK, 1980–97. *Business History*, 42 (4): 137–184.

Wright, M., Robbie, K. and Ennew, C. (1997a). Serial Entrepreneurs. *British Journal of Management*, 8 (3): 251–268.

Wright, M., Robbie, K. and Ennew, C. (1997b). Venture Capitalists and Serial Entrepreneurs. *Journal of Business Venturing*, 12 (3): 227–249.

Wright M, Robbie, K., Thompson, S. and Starkey, K. (1994). Longevity and the Life Cycle of MBOs. *Strategic Management Journal*, 15: 215–227.

Wright, M., Sapienza, H. and Busenitz, L. (2003). *Venture Capital Volumes I to III*. Cheltenham: Edward Elgar.

Wright, M., Thompson, S., Chiplin, B. and Robbie, K. (1991). *Management Buy-ins and Buy-outs: New Strategies in Corporate Management*. London: Graham & Trotman.

Wright M., Thompson, S. and Robbie, K. (1992). Venture Capital and Management-led Leveraged Buy-outs: A European Perspective. *Journal of Business Venturing*, 7: 47–71.

Wright, M., Thompson, S., Robbie, K. and Wong, P. (1995). Management Buy-outs in the Short and Long Term. *Journal of Business Finance and Accounting*, 22: 461–482.

Wright, M., Westhead, P. and Ucbasaran, D. (2007). The Internationalization of Small and Medium-sized Enterprises (SMEs) and International Entrepreneurship: A Critique and Policy Implications. *Regional Studies*, 41 (7): 1013–1029.

Wright, M., Wilson, N. and Robbie, K. (1996). The Longer Term Effects of Management-led Buy-outs. *Journal of Entrepreneurial and Small Business Finance*, 5: 213–234.

Yamakawa, Y., Peng, M. W. and Deeds, D. L. (2008). What Drives New Ventures to Internationalize from Emerging to Developed Economies? *Entrepreneurship Theory and Practice*, 32 (1): 59–82.

Yli-Renko, H., Autio, E. and Tontti, V. (2002). Social Capital, Knowledge and the International Growth of Technology-Based New Firms. *International Business Review*, 11: 279–304.

Young, S., Dimitratos, P. and Dana, L-P. (2003). International Entrepreneurship Research: What Scope for International Business Theories? *Journal of International Entrepreneurship*, 1: 31–42.

Zacharakis, A. L., Meyer, G. D. and DeCastro, J. O. (1999). Differing Perceptions of New Venture Failure: A Matched Exploratory Study of Venture Capitalists and Entrepreneurs. *Journal of Small Business Management*, 37 (3): 1–14.

Zafirovski, M. (1999). Probing into the Social Layers of Entrepreneurship: Outlines of the Sociology of Enterprise. *Entrepreneurship and Regional Development*, 11: 351–371.

Zahra, S. A. (1991). Predictors and Outcomes of Corporate Entrepreneurship: An Exploratory Study. *Journal of Business Venturing*, 6 (4): 259–285.

Zahra, S. A. (1993a). A Conceptual Model of Entrepreneurship as Firm Behavior: A Critique and Extension. *Entrepreneurship Theory and Practice*, 17 (4): 5–21.

Zahra, S. A. (1993b). Environment, Corporate Entrepreneurship and Financial Performance: A Taxonomic Approach. *Journal of Business Venturing*, 8: 319–340.

Zahra, S. A. (1995). Corporate Entrepreneurship and Financial Performance: The Case of Management Leveraged Buy-outs. *Journal of Business Venturing*, 10: 225–247.

Zahra, S. (2005). A Theory of International New Ventures: A Decade of Research. *Journal of International Business Studies*, 36: 20–28.

Zahra, S. A. and Covin, J. G. (1995). Contextual Influences on the Corporate Entrepreneurship – Performance Relationship: A Longitudinal Analysis. *Journal of Business Venturing*, 10 (1): 43–58.

Zahra, S., Filatotchev, I. and Wright, M. (2009). How do Threshold Firms Sustain Corporate Entrepreneurship? The Role of Boards and Absorptive Capacity. *Journal of Business Venturing*, 24 (3): 248–260.

Zahra, S., Gedajlovic, E., Neubaum, D. O. and Shulman, J. M. (2009). A Typology of Social Entrepreneurs: Motives, Search Processes and Ethical Challenges. *Journal of Business Venturing*, 24 (5): 519–532.

Zahra, S. A. and George, G. (2002). International Entrepreneurship: Research Contributions and Future Directions. In M. A. Hitt, R. D. Ireland, S. M. Camp and D. L. Sexton (eds) *Strategic Entrepreneurship: Creating a New Mindset*. Oxford: Blackwell, Oxford, pp. 255–288.

Zahra, S. A., Hayton, J. C. and Salvato, C. (2004). Entrepreneurship in Family vs Non-Family Firms: A Resource-Based Analysis of the Effect of Organizational Culture. *Entrepreneurship Theory and Practice*, 28 (4): 363–381.

Zahra, S., Ireland, D. and Hitt, M. (2000). International Expansion by New Venture Firms: International Diversity, Mode of Market Entry, Technological Learning, and Firm Performance, *Academy of Management Journal*, 43: 925–950.

Zahra, S., Neubaum, D. and Naldi, L. (2007). The Effects of Ownership and Governance on SMEs' International Knowledge-Based Resources. *Small Business Economics*, 29: 309–327.

Zellweger, T., Sieger, P. and Halter, F. (2010). Should I Stay or Should I Go? Career Choice Intentions of Students with Family Business Background. *Journal of Business Venturing*, forthcoming.

Zucker, L. G. and Darby, M. R. (2001). Capturing Technological Opportunity Via Japan's Star Scientists: Evidence from Japanese Firms' Biotech Patents and Products. *Journal of Technology Transfer*, 26 (1–2): 37–58.

Index